THE
ANNUAL REGISTER
Vol. 234

Rex Features (top), *Popperfoto* (bottom)

Two Faces of America

Los Angeles/New Jersey, April-May/November 1992: After the people of Los Angeles had taken stock of unprecedented civil disorder following the Rodney King verdict (*top*), the Democratic challengers, Governor Bill Clinton (*bottom, second from right*) and Senator Al Gore, cruised easily to victory in the US presidential elections of 3 November, supported by their respective wives, Hillary and Tipper.

Ethnic Cleansing in Former Yugoslavia

Bosnia-Hercegovina, June 1992: As the civil conflict in former Yugoslavia intensified, Western reporters uncovered evidence of Serbian atrocities against Muslims and others in prison camps redolent of the worst excesses of World War II.

THE
ANNUAL REGISTER

A Record of World Events
1992

Edited by
ALAN J. DAY

assisted by
VERENA HOFFMAN

FIRST EDITED IN 1758
BY EDMUND BURKE

THE ANNUAL REGISTER 1992
Published by Longman Group UK Limited, Longman House,
Burnt Mill, Harlow, Essex, CM20 2JE, United Kingdom

Distributed exclusively in the United States and Canada by Gale Research Company, Book Tower,
Detroit, Michigan 48226, USA

ISBN 0-582-21787-3 (Longman)

Library of Congress Catalog Card Number: 4-17979

© Longman Group UK Limited 1993
All rights reserved; no part of this publication may be reproduced,
stored in a retrieval system, or transmitted in any form or by any
means, electronic, mechanical, photocopying, recording or otherwise
without either the prior written permission of the Publishers or a licence permitting restricted
copying issued by the Copyright Licensing Agency Ltd.
90 Tottenham Court Road, London, W1P 9HE

British Library Cataloguing in Publication Data
The Annual Register—1992
  1. History—Periodicals
  909.82'8'05   D410

ISBN 0-582-21787-3

Set in Times Roman by
THE MIDLANDS BOOK TYPESETTING COMPANY LIMITED, LOUGHBOROUGH

PRINTED IN GREAT BRITAIN BY BPCC WHEATONS LTD, EXETER

011759282

CONTENTS

Sensational stories continued to be published, however, together with growing criticism of royal finances and especially Civil List payments to minor members of the royal family.

On 6 July, a year after the closure of the Bank of Credit and Commerce International (see AR 1991, pp. 24–5), the Basle Committee on Banking Supervision reached agreement on new measures to try to prevent a repetition of fraud on that scale.

The Trades Union Congress (TUC) met in Blackpool from 7 September, still in a partial state of shock after Labour's election defeat and under threat from the government's intention to reintroduce an employment bill seen by the TUC as further eroding trade union powers. The bill's provisions effectively outlawed the TUC's Bridlington rules, under which affiliated unions undertook not to poach one another's members.

Self-criticism was the order of the day. General secretary Norman Willis set the tone with his statement that the TUC must learn to live within its means, and concentrate on a number of 'key priorities backed by the will to deliver them'. Delegates were much preoccupied with unemployment and the latest government bill to regulate union conduct. But much emphasis was also placed on services to members and connections with the European Commission. The TUC was said to be facing the biggest shake-up in its 124-year history. Membership was still falling, and barely half had voted Labour in April. For the first time an employers' representative, the director-general of the Confederation of British Industry (CBI), addressed the conference. The way was also opened for the readmission of the electricians' union under the umbrella of the Amalgamated Electrical and Engineering Union (see AR 1988, p. 31).

The Green Party was in trouble despite considerable public interest in environmental issues, and at a time when the Treasury was holding back promised payments on parts of its conservation programme. Internal divisions and fears of extremism had already cost the party some supporters. Sara˙ Parkin decided not to stand for re-election to the party leadership. Several members of the executive resigned in sympathy.

The Liberal Democrat conference in Harrogate (14–17 September) found the party in some disarray over a policy document which, it was said, gave too little weight to communal values as opposed to the free market. Much more serious was the controversy which had followed a speech by the party leader in Chard four months earlier. This had advocated cooperation between all the anti-Conservative parties. Mr Ashdown now agreed that this was not an option so long as Labour was 'unelectable'. Fears of a hung parliament during the election, he said, had swung many electors away from proportional representation, and this issue should now take second place to the creation of a 'climate

CONTRIBUTORS

HUNGARY	**George Schöpflin,** Joint Lecturer in East European Political Institutions, London School of Economics and School of Slavonic and East European Studies, University of London
ROMANIA	**Gabriel Partos,** Senior Talks Writer, BBC World Service
BULGARIA	**Stephen Ashley,** MA, DPhil, Senior Talks Writer, BBC World Service
FORMER YUGOSLAVIA	**J. B. Allcock,** MA, PhD, Head of Research Unit in South-East European Studies, University of Bradford
ALBANIA	**Richard Crampton,** PhD, Fellow of St Edmund Hall, Oxford; formerly Professor of East European History, University of Kent
RUSSIA, BELORUSSIA, UKRAINE, MOLDAVIA AND CAUCASIA	**Stephen White,** PhD, Professor of Politics, University of Glasgow
BALTIC REPUBLICS	**John Hiden,** Professor of Modern European History and Director, Baltic Research Unit, University of Bradford

PART IV

USA	**Neil A. Wynn,** MA, PhD, Principal Lecturer and Head of History, University of Glamorgan
CANADA	**David M. L. Farr,** Professor Emeritus of History, Carleton University, Ottawa
LATIN AMERICA	**Peter Calvert,** AM, MA, PhD, Professor of Comparative and International Politics, University of Southampton
THE CARIBBEAN	**Julian C. J. Saurin,** PhD, Lecturer in International Relations, School of African and Asian Studies, University of Sussex

PART V

ISRAEL	**Noah Lucas,** PhD, Fellow in Israeli Studies, The Oxford Centre for Postgraduate Hebrew Studies
ARAB WORLD, EGYPT, JORDAN, SYRIA, LEBANON, IRAQ	**Christopher Gandy,** Formerly UK Diplomatic Service; writer on Middle Eastern affairs
SAUDI ARABIA, YEMEN	**R. M. Burrell,** Lecturer in the Contemporary History of the Near and Middle East, School of Oriental and African Studies, University of London
ARAB STATES OF THE GULF	**George Joffe,** Consultant Editor, Economist Intelligence Unit; Deputy Director, Geopolitics and International Boundaries Research Centre, School of Oriental and African Studies, University of London
SUDAN	**Ahmed al-Shahi,** DPhil, Lecturer in Social Anthropology, Department of Social Policy, University of Newcastle-upon-Tyne
LIBYA, TUNISIA, ALGERIA, MOROCCO, WESTERN SAHARA	**R. I. Lawless,** PhD, Reader in Modern Middle Eastern Studies, Centre for Middle Eastern and Islamic Studies, University of Durham

PART VI

ETHIOPIA, SOMALIA, DJIBOUTI	**Christopher Clapham,** MA, DPhil, Professor of Politics and International Relations, University of Lancaster
KENYA, TANZANIA, UGANDA	**William Tordoff,** MA, PhD, Emeritus Professor of Government, University of Manchester
GHANA	**D. G. Austin** (see Pt. III, Malta)
NIGERIA	**Robin Theobald,** PhD, Principal Lecturer in Sociology, University of Westminster
SIERRA LEONE, THE GAMBIA, LIBERIA	**Arnold Hughes,** BA, Director, Centre of West African Studies, University of Birmingham
CHAPTER 3 (SENEGAL to EQUATORIAL GUINEA)	**Kaye Whiteman,** Editor-in-Chief, *West Africa*

PART VII

CHAPTER 1 (ZAIRE TO ANGOLA)	**Robin Hallett,** MA, Writer and lecturer on African affairs
ZAMBIA, MALAWI	**Robin Hallett** (see above)
ZIMBABWE	**R. W. Baldock,** BA, PhD, Senior Editor, Yale University Press; writer on African affairs
NAMIBIA, BOTSWANA, LESOTHO, SWAZILAND, SOUTH AFRICA	**Gerald Shaw,** MA, Associate Editor, *The Cape Times*, Cape Town

PART VIII

IRAN	**Keith McLachlan,** BA, PhD, Professor of Geography, Director, Geopolitics and International Boundaries Research Centre, School of Oriental and African Studies, University of London
AFGHANISTAN, INDIA, BANGLADESH, NEPAL, BHUTAN	**Peter Lyon,** BSc(Econ), PhD, Reader in International Relations and Academic Secretary, Institute of Commonwealth Studies, University of London; Editor, *The Round Table*
CENTRAL ASIAN REPUBLICS	**Shirin Akiner,** PhD, Director, Central Asia Research Forum, School of Oriental and African Studies, University of London
PAKISTAN	**David Taylor,** Senior Lecturer in Politics with reference to South Asia, School of Oriental and African Studies, University of London
SRI LANKA	**James Jupp,** MSc(Econ), PhD, FASSA, Director, Centre for Immigration and Multicultural Studies, Australian National University, Canberra
SEYCHELLES, MAURITIUS, MALDIVES	**George Bennett,** MA, Former Head, BBC African Service; freelance writer and broadcaster
MADAGASCAR AND COMOROS	**Kaye Whiteman** (see Pt. VI, Ch., 3)

PART IX

MYANMAR (BURMA), INDONESIA, PHILIPPINES	**Robert H. Taylor,** PhD, Professor of Politics, School of Oriental and African Studies, University of London
THAILAND, VIETNAM, CAMBODIA, LAOS	**Jonathan Rigg,** PhD, Lecturer in South-East Asian Geography, School of Oriental and African Studies, University of London

MALAYSIA, BRUNEI, SINGAPORE	**Michael Leifer,** BA, PhD, Professor of International Relations, London School of Economics and Political Science
CHINA, TAIWAN, HONG KONG	**Robert F. Ash,** MSc(Econ), PhD, Director, Contemporary China Institute and Senior Lecturer in Economics, School of Oriental and African Studies, University of London
JAPAN	**I. H. Nish,** Emeritus Professor of International History, London School of Economics and Political Science
SOUTH AND NORTH KOREA	**James H. Grayson,** PhD, Director, Centre for Korean Studies, University of Sheffield
MONGOLIA	**Alan Sanders,** FIL, Lecturer in Mongolian Studies, School of Oriental and African Studies, University of London

PART X

AUSTRALIA	**James Jupp** (see Pt. VIII, Sri Lanka)
PAPUA NEW GUINEA	**Norman MacQueen,** Reader in International Relations, University of Sunderland
NEW ZEALAND, PACIFIC ISLAND STATES	**Roderic Alley,** PhD, School of Political Science and Public Administration, Victoria University of Wellington

PART XI

UNITED NATIONS	**Sam Daws,** United Nations Association, London.
COMMONWEALTH	**Derek Ingram,** Editor of *Gemini News Service* and author and writer on the Commonwealth
EUROPEAN COMMUNITY	**Michael Berendt,** Expert on affairs of the European Communities
OECD, EFTA	**Roger East,** Editor of *Keesing's Record of World Events*; founder and director of CIRCA Research and Reference Information
NON–ALIGNED MOVEMENT	**Peter Willetts,** PhD, Senior Lecturer in International Relations, The City University, London
CONFERENCE ON SECURITY AND COOPERATION IN EUROPE	**Adrian G. V. Hyde-Price,** BSc(Econ), PhD, Lecturer, Department of Politics, University of Southampton
EUROPEAN BANK FOR RECONSTRUCTION AND DEVELOPMENT	**Michael Kaser,** MA, Reader in Economics, Oxford University and Professional Fellow of St Antony's College, Oxford
COUNCIL OF EUROPE	**Richard Lambert,** Secretary to the UK delegation to the Parliamentary Assembly of the Council of Europe
NORDIC AND BALTIC COUNCILS	**Hilary Allen** (see Pt. II, Nordic Countries)
AFRICAN CONFERENCES AND ORGANIZATIONS	**Kaye Whiteman** (see Pt. VI, Ch. 3)
S. ASIAN ASSOCIATION FOR REGIONAL COOPERATION	**Peter Lyon** (see Pt. VIII, Afghanistan, etc.)
S.E. ASIAN ORGANIZATIONS	**D. J. Sagar,** Regional Editor, *Keesing's Record of World Events;* director, CIRCA Research and Reference Information
PACIFIC ORGANIZATIONS	**Roderic Alley** (see Pt. X, New Zealand, etc.)
LATIN AMERICAN ORGANIZATIONS	**Peter Calvert** (see Pt. IV, Latin America)

CARIBBEAN ORGANIZATIONS

Ciarán Ó Maoláin, BA, Research Fellow, Centre for the Study of Conflict, University of Ulster; writer on Caribbean, Latin American and Pacific affairs

PART XII
SECURITY, ARMS CONTROL AND DISARMAMENT

Phil Williams, PhD, Professor of Security Studies, Graduate School of Public and International Affairs, University of Pittsburgh

PART XIII
RELIGION

Geoffrey Parrinder, MA, PhD, DD, Emeritus Professor of the Comparative Study of Religions, University of London

PART XIV
MEDICAL, SCIENTIFIC AND INDUSTRIAL RESEARCH

John Newell, Science writer and broadcaster

INFORMATION TECHNOLOGY

David Powell, A director of Electronic Publishing Services Ltd; editor, *EP Journal*

ENVIRONMENT

Lloyd Timberlake, Director for External Affairs, International Institute for Environment and Development (IIED)

PART XV
INTERNATIONAL LAW

Christine Gray, MA, PhD, Fellow in Law, St Hilda's College, Oxford

EUROPEAN COMMUNITY LAW

N. March Hunnings, LLM, PhD, Editor, *Common Market Law Reports*

LAW IN THE UK

David Ibbetson, MA, PhD, Fellow and Tutor in Law, Magdalen College, Oxford

LAW IN THE USA

Robert J. Spjut, ID, LLM, Member of the State Bars of California and Florida

PART XVI
OPERA, THEATRE

Charles Osborne, Author; opera critic, *The Jewish Chronicle*

MUSIC

Francis Routh, Composer and author; founder director of the Redcliffe Concerts

BALLET/DANCE

Jane Pritchard, Archivist, Rambert Dance Company and English National Ballet

CINEMA

Derek Malcolm, Film critic, *The Guardian*

TV & RADIO

Raymond Snoddy, Media correspondent, *The Financial Times*

ART

Marina Vaizey, MA, Editor, National Art Collections Fund publications; critic and author

ARCHITECTURE

Paul Finch, Editor, *Building Design*

LITERATURE

Alastair Niven, Literature director of the Arts Council

PART XVII
SPORT

Tony Pawson, OBE, Sports writer, *The Observer*; cricket, football and fly-fishing international

PART XVIII
THE INTERNATIONAL ECONOMY
STATISTICS

Victor Keegan, Assistant Editor, *The Guardian*
Sue Cockerill, Former member of the Statistical Department, *Financial Times*

PART XX
OBITUARY

H. V. Hodson, Former editor of *The Annual Register*; editor, *The Sunday Times*, 1950–61

MAPS

MJL **Graphics,** N. Yorks, YO14 9BE

ACKNOWLEDGEMENTS

THE Advisory Board again gratefully acknowledges its debt to a number of institutions for their help with sources, references and documents, notably the UN Information Centre and the European Commission Office in London. Acknowledgement is also due to the principal sources for the national data sections (showing the situation as at end-1992 unless otherwise stated), namely *Keesing's Record of World Events* (Longman), *People in Power* (CIRCA) and *World Development Report* (OUP for the World Bank). The Board and the bodies which nominate its members disclaim responsibility for any opinions expressed or the accuracy of facts recorded in this volume.

ABBREVIATIONS

ACC	Arab Cooperation Council
ACP	African, Caribbean and Pacific states associated with EEC
AfDB	African Development Bank
AID	Agency for International Development
AIDS	Acquired Immune Deficiency Syndrome
AMU	Arab Maghreb Union
ANC	African National Congress
ANZUS	Australia-New Zealand-USA Security Treaty
AR	Annual Register
ASEAN	Association of South-East Asian Nations
CAP	Common Agricultural Policy
CARICOM	Caribbean Common Market
CEEAC	Economic Community of Central African States
CFE	Conventional Force Reductions in Europe
CSCE	Conference on Security and Cooperation in Europe
Cwth.	Commonwealth
EBRD	European Bank for Reconstruction and Development
EC	European Community
ECO	Economic Cooperation Organization
ECOWAS	Economic Community of West African States
EEC	European Economic Community (Common Market)
EFTA	European Free Trade Association
EMS	European Monetary System
ESCAP	Economic and Social Commission for Asia and the Pacific (UN)
FAO	Food and Agriculture Organization
GATT	General Agreement on Tariffs and Trade
GCC	Gulf Cooperation Council
GDP/GNP	Gross Domestic/National Product
IAEA	International Atomic Energy Agency
IBRD	International Bank for Reconstruction and Development
ICO	Islamic Conference Organization
IDA	International Development Association
ILO	International Labour Organization
IMF	International Monetary Fund
INF	Intermediate-range Nuclear Forces
IRA	Irish Republican Army
MBFR	Mutual and Balanced Force Reductions
NAFTA	North American Free Trade Agreement
NAM	Non-Aligned Movement
NATO	North Atlantic Treaty Organization
OAS	Organization of American States
OAU	Oganization of African Unity
OECD	Organization for Economic Cooperation and Development
OPEC (OAPEC)	Organization of (Arab) Petroleum Exporting Countries
PLO	Palestine Liberation Organization
SAARC	South Asian Association for Regional Cooperation
SADCC	Southern African Development Coordination Conference
SDI	Strategic Defence Initiative
START	Strategic Arms Reduction Treaty
SWAPO	South-West Africa People's Organization
UN	United Nations
UNCTAD	United National Conference on Trade and Development
UNDP	United Nations Development Programme
UNESCO	United Nations Educational, Scientific and Cultural Organization
UNHCR	United Nations High Commission for Refugees
UNRWA	United National Relief and Works Agency
WEU	Western European Union
WHO	World Health Organization

PREFACE

THE year may have been an '*annus horribilis*' for Queen Elizabeth and the British royal family. For many lesser mortals, in Britain and elsewhere, it was certainly one of increasing gloom about economic and political prospects. Western euphoria over the post-1989 collapse of communism in Europe and the consequential end of the Cold War disappeared almost entirely in 1992. Indeed, deepening economic recession, spreading national/ethnic conflict in Eastern Europe and political/social disintegration in black Africa gave pause for thought as to whether the world really had been changed for the better by the ending of East-West global rivalry. Some commentators even opined that future historians would look back on the four-and-a-half post-war decades as a halcyon age of relative stability, growth and optimism, and identify 1992 as the year in which things clearly changed for the worse.

As this volume chronicles, what had been federal Yugoslavia experienced the most violent reversion, descending into a bloody civil war in which ethnic identity counted for everything. One consequence of this and other conflicts in Eastern Europe, and of the harsh post-communist economic realities, was increasing immigration pressure on relatively prosperous Western Europe. This in turn stoked up simmering anti-foreigner feeling in Germany and other countries, some of which were already finding it difficult to cope with Third World immigration.

On the plus side, the United Nations continued its belated flowering into being an active arbiter and policeman of international disputes. It also, in the case of Somalia, for the first time took responsibility in the face of the disappearance of any recognizable state structure in a supposedly sovereign country. There were, however, limits to what the UN and other international bodies could achieve, given the Western world's preoccupation with its own problems. Especially remarked was the failure of the European Community (EC) to exert collective influence in ex-Yugoslavia. At year's end, moreover, the countries of the rich industrialized world had still not found an agreed escape route from a looming three-cornered EC-US-Japanese trade war.

Away from politics and economics, vitality and inventiveness continued to be abundant in the fields of the arts and the sciences. This volume records such achievements, as well as a notable year for sport, crowned by a glorious Olympic Games in Barcelona and a riveting European Nations football championship in Sweden. But even in the non-political world there was a sense of deterioration and threat, exemplified by the inexorable progress of death-dealing AIDS in many parts of the world.

The editor and Advisory Board welcome several new contributors to the AR circle, some covering countries which did not exist as sovereign entities in 1991. They also express gratitude to John Newell, whose contribution in this volume is the last in a 30-year sequence.

THE ANNUAL REGISTER

200 years ago

1792. *Suspension of Regal Functions*. [10 August, Paris] The firing of cannon and musquetry continued: the Assembly remained for some time silent. A motion was then made and agreed to, that all property and persons should be under the safeguard of the law and of the people: and another for an act or proclamation to all the citizens, who had sworn to save the country. While the contest was yet doubtful [a mob was attacking the Tuileries], the Assembly kept terms, and were respectful to the King and constitution. When that was decided, the Assembly, just like the national guards, joined the prevailing party. Elated by the victory, they resumed their former arrogance, and basely insulted the unfortunate prince by the most injurious motions. A decree was passed, by which his regal functions were suspended, and he himself and his family retained as prisoners, in the name of hostages.

150 years ago

1842. *Lord Ashley Describes Mines to the Commons*. [7 June] 'I have a belt round my waist,' says Betty Harris, 'and a chain passing between my legs, and I go on my hands and feet. The road is very steep; and we have to hold by a rope, and, where there is no rope, by any thing we can catch hold of. It is very hard work for a woman. The pit is very wet. I have seen water up to my thighs. My clothes are wet through almost all day long. I have drawn till I have had the skin off me. The belt and chain is worse when we are in the family way.'

100 years ago

1892. *Columbus and Other Anniversaries*. The year just past will be remembered as the 400th anniversary of the discovery of the New World by Columbus. It was also a hundred years ago since William Murdoch lighted his office at Redruth with the illuminating gas he obtained by the distillation of coal. To railway engineers it will be noted as the year in which the seven-foot railway gauge adopted by Brunel was finally abandoned in favour of its rival, and in which, by the opening of the railway line from Jaffa to Jerusalem, Palestine was for the first time invaded by the locomotive.

50 years ago

1942. *Fall of Tobruk*. [21 June] The loss of the rest of Cyrenaica had already shaken the British public out of the complacency which had been induced by the first successes of the Eighth Army and the optimistic official comments on the situation. But the surrender of Tobruk, with the loss of thousands of men and much valuable material, stung it to the quick and filled it with both anger and despondency, much as the loss of Singapore had done four months before. From a military point of view, it was true, the loss of Libya with Tobruk was not nearly so serious as that of Malaya with Singapore. . . . But the blow was felt more keenly because it was unexpected; it gave an even greater shock to the confidence of the public in the direction of military affairs both at home and on the spot. If this could happen, anything could happen; the enemy seemed suddenly to have developed a marked and decisive superiority over the British forces opposing him, and there was no telling how far he would be able to exploit it.

ANNUAL REGISTER

FOR THE YEAR 1992

EDITORIAL
EUROPE AFTER 1992

AMONG the less spectacular events of 1992 was one having a certain symbolic aura: the rehabilitation of Galileo Galilei. Condemned as a heretic in 1633 for pronouncing that the Earth was in orbit round the Sun, contrary to Holy Scripture's opposite belief, he was at last acquitted: the Vatican thus formally endorsed the heliocentric theory, four and a half centuries after Copernicus had first propounded it. The incident illustrates more than the peculiar conservatism of the Catholic Church. It recalls the gradual but decisive victory of material science over religious sentiment and certitude to the point where it has become the dominant ideology of the age. And it reminds us all of our persistent error in adopting a Ptolomaic view of contemporary history, whereby everything revolves round our own place, perceptions and prejudices, and neglecting the Copernican truth that we ourselves revolve round foci of action elsewhere on the globe. Thus Europeans, 500 years after Columbus's discovery of the western continent—celebrated in 1992—still tend to think of the Americas as offspring of Europe, while Americans picture themselves as the hub of Western civilization.

For most citizens of the United States, the key event of the past year was undoubtedly the presidential election, entangled as it was with the nation's material problems, which mostly stemmed from the economic depression. For people in southern Africa, the most dynamic developments took place in the Republic of South Africa, Namibia, Angola and Mozambique, shaking the kaleidoscope of races, tribes and factions into a new, more hopeful but still menacing pattern. One could describe in like fashion the view of the evolving world scene from Moscow, Beijing, Colombia, Israel or anywhere else.

For us in Europe, 1992 was, above all, Europe's year of trouble and discontent. And surely, for the nations of every continent, the European experience was central in the flow of political and economic events. Two world wars began in Europe, and the fear of igniting another was still alive. Of all international constructions since World War II, after the United Nations, the European Community was the most novel, the most dynamic, and the most expressive of a new international order. Together, the countries of Europe are the greatest market, the greatest source of capital, the greatest exporter of goods in the world. People of every European nation, race, language and religion have peopled the New World, keeping their ties of family, sentiment and residual loyalty with the lands of their forebears. The fate of Europe carries with it the fate of the civilized world.

Europe's travails in 1992 were suffered on two opposite planes, those of dangerous internal rupture and unsteady progress towards closer unity. Although the Treaty of Maastricht ran into ratification pot-holes, it remained the chosen vehicle of Community advance into the area of foreign affairs and defence, and towards a common European currency, with the ultimate ideal of political and economic union; the single European market moved to its inauguration in 1993; and the queue of nations wanting to join the Community lengthened. On the other hand, the fission of Czechoslovakia and above all the cruel warfare in former Yugoslavia exposed a Europe of rival nationalities no longer willing to live under one governmental roof. And the Maastricht hitches, along with other phenomena such as the Swiss referendum vote against joining the European Economic Area, signalled a wave of popular resentment towards handing national power to supranational authority.

Taken together, those experiences displayed the perennial conflict between international aspiration and national emotion. Since World War II, international organization had scored great achievements: the United Nations and its agencies, GATT, the World Bank, NATO, the European Community, regional free trade areas, OAU, OAS and many other instruments, all qualifying the exercise of national sovereignty. It was only to be expected that at some time there would be a reaction, an ebb in the tide of hope for a less fragmented, more organized world.

That time arrived, it seems, when deep economic depression overtook a Western world confused and dislocated by the collapse of the Soviet empire and the communist system. When trade and industry shrink, and unemployment swells, governments and their electors begin to assume defensive national postures. Sectional domestic causes take priority over wider aims, as did the interests of France's farmers in the last stages of the Uruguay Round of GATT. Atavistic nationalism strikes a popular chord. Maastricht was a high-water mark in European integration: the popular reaction to it, in more Community countries than Denmark and Britain, showed that the tide of international zeal was on the ebb.

Tides rise and fall, and that one will flood again. But the shorescape will have changed. As 1992 closed, the omens were that ratification of the Maastricht treaty could be completed by mid-1993. The Community could then settle down to working out its future conduct under the new order, giving content to the precious principle of 'subsidiarity', finding a better route than the discredited ERM to exchange stability (the prerequisite of monetary union), and opening its portals to wider membership. But the chastening experience of the previous two years cannot be forgotten, and the need for constitutional reform will soon become apparent. Maastricht can be regarded only as a holding measure. A review of the Community's progress is indeed scheduled for 1996, but the problems will begin at once, and three years is not too long a time for ideas on reform to mature and weather debate.

The complications of the task are formidable. The aspirants to membership or at least 'association'—which must involve some form of participation in the Community's institutions—include countries which have enjoyed continuous experience of independence and democracy; former Warsaw Pact members, which have yet to establish their credentials as stable democracies with market economies; and, more distantly, others in the Balkans and on the European fringe of the CIS. The prospect is that the Community of 12 will soon become one of 16, then, within a measurable length of time, one of more than 20, and eventually, if it is to encompass all Europe, twice as many. A structure designed for half-a-dozen countries, alike in culture, law, economy and national purpose, cannot be apt for so large and so various a set of nations.

The difficulties are compounded by the widening of the sphere of Community authority. For many countries of an expanded Community, foreign policy and its partner, defence, will mainly concern relations with their immediate neighbours. From a Community point of view, this is internal, not external, policy. Reaction to the strife in former Yugoslavia, from the hasty recognition of the independence of Croatia to the argument about armed intervention in Bosnia and the tension with Greece over Macedonia, shows how difficult are the problems thus raised. The Brussels structure is inadequate to deal with them. It has yet to prove itself capable of handling such issues as the flood of refugees and economic migrants following the collapse of communist hegemony, the reunification of Germany and the civil war and horrible 'ethnic cleansing' in what was Yugoslavia.

Let us pause, and listen to two German voices. In his memorable Ditchley Foundation Lecture 1992, Dr Kurt Biedenkopf, minister-president of Saxony, advanced the idea of a Europe organized in regions, 'comparable in size and importance'. The central authority would be concerned with 'those functions that are vital to the common endeavour of a political Europe, namely, the basics of the economy, common security, at least the basics of common foreign policy, and the basics of a common legal system.' Dr Biedenkopf did not specify how the regions would be composed; the gist of his thought was that, having cultural and historical cohesion, they would form themselves. This is an attractive idea for academic debate, but in the real world of international politics it is an imaginative sketch rather than an architect's drawing or an engineer's blueprint. It raises many difficult questions. Where, for instance, do the 'basics' of economic life, of security, foreign policy and law begin and end?

A much more conventional approach to Community reform was expressed in another prestigious political sermon, the 1992 Gresham Special Lecture delivered by Baron Hermann von Richthofen, German ambassador to London, which, for all his personal distinction, must be taken as reflecting the philosophy of his government. History, he said, never stands still: either the members of the Community continue its development, internally by 'deepening' and externally by 'enlarging' it, or it will gradually break down. Enlargement must look beyond the EFTA countries to others in Eastern and Central Europe, and to new forms of treaties between the Community and the ex-Soviet independent states. 'Integration and enlargement', said the ambassador, 'are not policy choices that are alternatives. They are first parallel and ultimately converging'—a proposition by no means self-evident. He presented no ideas on how they could be brought to converge, nor did he offer any way of reconciling 'the increasing global "Europeanization" on one side and the growing weight of regional or nationalistic movements on the other.' That is the heart of the matter. Until a path towards that double reconciliation is mapped, both the conventional Europhile view of the Community's future and the more romantic ideas of such thinkers as Dr Biedenkopf will remain day-dreams.

A constitutional effort and innovation are needed, comparable with the original construction of the European Economic Community. A federal structure of the classical kind is out of the question: too strong adverse opinion in too many member countries makes it unviable, and it will never be the right solution for so numerous, so variant and so often discordant a bunch of nations. Any reform must start from the Community structure as it is, after Maastricht and Edinburgh.

It does not follow, however, that thought about reforming the Community must consider in turn each of the three structural elements—Council of Ministers, Commission, Parliament—seeking to improve its separate working in the new conditions. Nothing commensurate with the problem of simultaneous deepening and enlarging would emerge, only small modifications of a machine already defective and inept for the future. Rather should ideas follow the *functions* of the Community, which concern all three constitutional organs. A functional (or, perhaps better, operational) structure would have to be so designed as to accord with the overall executive responsibility of the whole Commission, and with the direction of policy by the supreme Council of Ministers. Those two bodies should be regarded not as rival centres of authority but—within the range of Community powers—as forming together a composite government of Europe, under the constant scrutiny of the European Parliament, its true function.

It is not the *Annual Register's* business to propose in any detail the structural changes that could fit the Community for its deeper and wider role in a new phase of its maturing life. But it can assert a chain of propositions which can hardly be denied. The peace and prosperity of the whole world are tied to peace and prosperity in Europe. Although geographical Europe is a tangle of cultures, languages, religions, economies, historical perceptions, hitherto patterned in nation states jealous of their independence, it shows a growing recognition of interdependence and a growing sense of its identity and common destiny. The principal organ through which its corporate identity and common interests are expressed is the European Community. Waxing in membership and in depth of authority, the Community needs imaginative reform, or it will groan and stumble under the weight it must bear. Needs are pressing, and time is short.

(*London, January 1993*)

I UNITED KINGDOM

CAPITAL: London   AREA: 244,100 sq km   POPULATION: 57,000,000 ('91)
OFFICIAL LANGUAGE: English (also Welsh in Wales)
POLITICAL SYSTEM: parliamentary democracy
HEAD OF STATE: Queen Elizabeth II (since Feb '52)
RULING PARTY: Conservative Party (since May '79)
HEAD OF GOVERNMENT: John Major, Prime Minister (since Nov '90)
PRINCIPAL MINISTERS: Douglas Hurd (foreign & Commonwealth affairs), Norman
    Lamont (Exchequer), Kenneth Clarke (home affairs), Lord Mackay of Clashfern
    (Lord Chancellor), Malcolm Rifkind (defence), Michael Heseltine (trade &
    industry), Michael Howard (environment) (*for full list see* XIX.4)
INTERNATIONAL ALIGNMENT: NATO, OECD, EC, Cwth.
CURRENCY: pound sterling (end-'92 £1=US$1.51)   GNP PER CAPITA: US$16,100 ('90)
MAIN EXPORT EARNERS: machinery & transport equipment, mineral fuels and
    lubricants, manufactured goods, chemicals, financial services, tourism

1. PRE-ELECTION MANOEUVRES

THE inevitability of a general election in 1992 (one had to be held not
later than July) dominated politics from the outset. Ministers faced the
daunting prospect of having to fight it with the country in the depths of
a recession. They did their best to encourage the belief that an economic
recovery was on the way. But business confidence remained low. A
record number of firms (40,000) had failed in 1991. Car sales were the
poorest since 1982. Retailers were counting the cost of a disappointing
Christmas, despite exceptionally early and throat-cutting 'sales'. More
than 74,000 families in England and Wales had had their homes
repossessed in 1991. In January unemployment rose to 9.2 per cent
of the workforce, the largest percentage increases occurring in southern England—and not least in London. The Prime Minister himself
conceded that economic recovery might be delayed. The recession had
been longer and deeper than expected.

It was soon evident that the election campaign would be stronger on
insults and generalities than detailed debate, especially since the two
main parties were no longer so sharply divided as they had been for
much of the previous decade. It often seemed as if they were more
intent on frightening the electorate with the bleak prospects of rule
by the other side rather than on painting a confident picture of the
future. Labour, for instance, set out to highlight the rise in job losses
and mortgage repossessions in Tory marginal seats. It promised an
emergency programme which would include tax incentives to help
manufacturers, but problems of funding were only vaguely addressed.

As the phoney election campaign warmed up, so the narrowness of
Labour's lead in the opinion polls (some 5 or 6 per cent) encouraged
speculation over the implications of a hung parliament. Paddy Ashdown,
the Liberal Democrat leader, insisted that there would be no pre-election

pact with Labour to meet such an eventuality and to ensure the exclusion of the Tories from office. If neither of the two main parties should win an overall majority, the price of Liberal Democrat support, he said, would be a commitment to electoral reform and an agreed legislative programme for a minimum of four years.

The Tories were quick to attack Labour's plans to increase income tax and national insurance at the expense of the better-off. There followed fierce exchanges as to how many people would be affected, and by how much. Tories also claimed that key Labour measures, including a minimum wage and a training levy on employers, would increase unemployment. In any case, rises in the public sector borrowing requirement (PSBR) were threatening to limit a hypothetical Labour government's ability to fund increases in public expenditure. This simultaneously underlined the importance of the tax issue and raised doubts concerning Labour's ability to fulfil its promises except over a long period of time and on the basis of the most optimistic projections concerning the speed of recovery when it finally occurred.

Labour appreciated the need to appear responsible and respectable, especially as the polls were not giving the party the eight-point lead it needed for an outright majority. Some polls were even putting the Tories narrowly ahead. This was galling at a time when so many people had reason to feel aggrieved over their present plight or future prospects.

In the first week of February stories appeared in the press relating to mysterious break-ins at the offices of Labour MPs, to earlier contacts between Labour leaders and the Kremlin, and to a relationship between Mr Ashdown and a woman member of his staff in 1987. In fact, Mr Ashdown's popular rating rose sharply in the days immediately following his admission and explanation. Meanwhile, Gerald Kaufman, for Labour, had little success with his charge that John Major was approving the start of the 'dirtiest general election campaign of the century'.

The government recognized that it would have to fight the election with little or no hope of an economic recovery, and with the recession biting hard in many of its own constituencies. The nation was in the grip of the longest recession since the 1930s. Statistics published on 13 February were so bad that it was dubbed 'Black Thursday'. Shortly afterwards, George Simpson, the chairman of the Rover Group, condemned government reliance upon untrammelled market forces as 'fundamentally flawed' and as out of step with the world's most successful economies.

Ministers, with the support of the Bank of England and the CBI, did their best to argue that the conditions for recovery were already in place. They continued to claim credit for the fall in inflation, which stood at only 4.1 per cent at the end of January. But for the time being they had only limited room for manoeuvre on interest rates—the most sensitive issue for numerous businesses, home-owners and consumers. The Treasury admitted in February that British prosperity had declined since 1988 in comparison with much of Europe. Nevertheless, polls continued to suggest that only three voters in ten felt comfortable with the thought of Labour control of the economy. Here was one albatross which the Labour Party was unable to remove from around its neck.

In March the nation had the novel experience of being presented with two budgets—an official one from the Chancellor of the Exchequer, Norman Lamont, and an unofficial one from shadow chancellor John Smith. Mr Lamont inserted an innovation of his own with his announcement on 10 March that there would be only one more spring budget (in 1993). Thereafter, it would be merged with the autumn statement on government spending plans, with the Finance Bill being presented in January rather than the spring.

The Chancellor also resisted the temptation to offer many 'goodies' to the electorate. He did, however, cut the rate of income tax to 20p in the pound on the first £2,000 of taxable income for everyone. In time he hoped that this would become the basic rate, but for the time being the latter would remain at 25p. The new 20p band would cost £1,800 million in 1992/93, about three-quarters of which would go to tax-payers earning less than the average male wage. There were also rises for pensioners on income support. The tax on new cars was halved as a gesture to the hard-hit motor industry.

Britain's gross domestic product (GDP) in the current year (1991/92) had fallen by nearly 2.5 per cent (or half a per cent more than had been forecast). Mr Lamont put special stress on success in the fight against inflation—'the scourge of our economy for decades'. This was now close to the German level. He stressed that half of American and Japanese direct investment in the European Community (EC) was centred on the United Kingdom, and claimed that this was a reward for low taxes, good industrial relations and a stable currency. However, Mrs Thatcher's former economic adviser, Sir Alan Walters, declared that the Chancellor was performing the last rites in the burial of Thatcherism, and argued that membership of the EC's exchange rate mechanism (ERM) had left the Treasury with almost no room for manoeuvre. (For further details on economic developments, see I.7 below.)

Labour's 'budget for the ordinary family', as set out by Mr Smith on 16 March, promised tax cuts for everyone with earnings of less than £22,000 a year. The new 20 per cent income tax band would be cancelled, and there was to be a new 50 per cent top rate for those earning over £36,375. The ceiling on national insurance contributions was to be lifted, thus in effect adding 9 per cent to the tax bill of all those whose earnings exceeded £21,000. Labour proposed to borrow £26,000 million to invest, whereas an imprudent government, in its view, was borrowing to spend. The Liberal Democrats for their part promised to increase income tax by 1p to provide £2,000 million for educational improvements.

On 11 March Mr Major put an end to speculation by announcing that the general election would be held on 9 April. He also claimed that economic recovery was being held back by the political uncertainty. His election announcement, however, brought the biggest fall on the stock market since the Soviet coup attempt on 19 August 1991. Dealers feared a Labour victory or a hung parliament.

At a time of growing concern over the soundness of the judicial system (see AR 1991, p. 16, for instance, for the case of the Birmingham Six), the choice in February of a new Lord Chief Justice in succession to Lord Lane attracted more than usual attention. On being appointed to the post, Lord Justice (Sir Peter) Taylor immediately promised a more accessible and open judiciary, adding: 'We all have a job to do in restoring public confidence', particularly with respect to criminal justice. He wanted a judiciary that was both independent and 'more user-friendly'. His appointment was welcomed by those who believed that the system had been 'going wrong for a long time' in the hands of people who believed in its virtual perfection. In June the Appeal Court ordered the release of Judith Ward after 18 years in prison for alleged IRA activities.

On 15 January, in response to the disastrous insurance market losses suffered by several thousand investors (or 'names') in Lloyd's of London, a report was published which proposed far-reaching reforms. But complaints persisted, and Lloyd's chairman, David Coleridge, found himself involved in a six-hour confrontation with angry critics on 24 June. He denied that any illegalities had taken place, but admitted that this was one of the 'darkest chapters' in the market's 304-year history. A 'wave' of court actions was threatened by the losers. Two reports, both highly critical of Lloyd's, appeared on 2 July. These spoke of outdated management practices and attacked widespread incompetence among market professionals. From 1993 the Lloyd's council was to be replaced by two new bodies to run and regulate the institution.

The IRA set off a large bomb near government offices in Whitehall on 10 January. A warning enabled the area to be cleared. On 28 February another bomb, this time at London Bridge station, injured 29 people and caused widespread transport disruption. Immediately after the election, on 10 April, the two biggest IRA bombs so far planted on the British mainland exploded in the City of London (killing three people) and at the M1 motorway junction in north London; damage from the bombs was estimated at some £1,000 million. An army sergeant died in Derby a few days later after being shot by the Irish National Liberation Army. The police, however, were able to prevent the launch of another London bombing campaign in August. Further explosions at the beginning of October caused disruption but no fatalities.

A White Paper proposing the establishment of a national lottery to raise money for good causes was published on 6 March. One-third of the proceeds would be used to assist projects of lasting benefit to the nation; these would include sport, the arts and charities. The scheme was to operate under the aegis of the new Department of National Heritage.

2.   THE GENERAL ELECTION

THE main parties published their election manifestos between 16 and 26 March. The Tories' (*The Best Future for Britain*) was easily the longest. It claimed that everywhere 'socialism is in retreat and democracy, human rights and market economies are advancing'. Further privatization would include British Coal, but the manifesto spoke guardedly only of 'ending British Rail's monopoly'. There was much emphasis on opportunity for all and freedom of choice, while the Citizen's Charter was described as 'the most far-reaching programme ever devised to improve quality in the public services'.

Labour in its manifesto (*It's Time To Get Britain Working Again*) stressed the need to strengthen the economy, the National Health Service (NHS) and education. It also promised a charter of rights and an elected Scottish parliament. The Liberal Democrats (*Changing Britain For Good*) underlined the interdependence of the economy, the governmental system and education. Proportional representation and decentralization were essential for political and economic progress.

The election turned out to be the closest since 1974. A plenitude of opinion polls detected a fairly consistent but usually narrow lead for Labour, with the Liberal Democrats apparently gaining in popularity to around the 20 per cent mark. At one point *The Guardian* began to dream of a watershed comparable with 1945, 1964 and 1979, although this newspaper conceded, three weeks into the campaign, that despite the frantic efforts of parties and media the campaign had still to excite the public.

Labour was anxious to cultivate its image as a party prepared for government, with sober and responsible leaders ready to step into the great offices of state. 'Populist' electioneering by Neil Kinnock was thought unbecoming in a prime minister in-waiting. But such restraint could not be preserved indefinitely. Belief that the party would be the largest in the next parliament brought a display of what Dennis Skinner (a Labour MP) later described as 'triumphalism gone mad' at a large rally in Sheffield on 1 April. A number of other people similarly agreed that this event had frightened some floating voters at a critical moment. A Labour Party political broadcast on 24 March also proved controversial. Both its accuracy and its handling of the sensitive case of a young girl in need of specialist hospital treatment were furiously debated. In general, however, Labour was credited with running a more coherent campaign than the Tories.

The Liberal Democrats depended heavily on the popularity of Mr Ashdown. But they continued to be excited by the possibility of a hung parliament—even if they as a party should fail to garner many extra seats. Mr Ashdown repeated that Liberal Democrat support for a minority government would require concessions on proportional representation. But while some in the Labour Party had shown at least theoretical interest in electoral reform, both main party leaderships declined to make any commitments. Mr Kinnock finally promised a commission of inquiry (which did not go far enough for Mr Ashdown), while Mr Major declared that in no circumstances would he countenance change.

Mrs Thatcher gave her public blessing to Mr Major as her successor on 23 March. In what was widely regarded as a lacklustre Tory campaign, her own performance and that of Michael Heseltine were among the few to reassure the faithful. The Tories soon found that the tax cuts in the budget had made little impact. Voters gave the government low ratings on the NHS, education and other public services. Its record on law and order also troubled many of its own supporters—there had been a 16 per cent increase in reported crime in the last year. But the Conservatives retained one important asset whatever the deficiencies in their campaign and despite the policy errors and failures attributed to them. Despite the recession, they continued to be trusted by more people (around 40 per cent) than Labour (less than 30 per cent) over the management of the economy.

Nevertheless, the Conservatives remained very much on the defensive throughout the campaign. Their counter-attacks chiefly took the form of attempts—backed by the largely pro-Tory tabloid press—to frighten voters with images of Labour as the party of high taxation. But Tory critics were soon remarking that it was not enough for people to 'like nice Mr Major' if they did not go on to vote Conservative; by the end of March they were demanding a harder-hitting campaign from ministers. Mrs Thatcher herself intervened on 28 March to complain of the lack of 'oomph' and 'steam' in the Tory campaign, causing the *Daily Mail* to assert that she had 'thrown a typically well-directed bucket of cold water over this yapping, squealing, political dogfight'. *The Times* weighed in by accusing Mr Major of sounding too much like a cautious Treasury apologist, and criticizing 'the leaden spokesmanship' of most of the cabinet. The *Sunday Times* on 29 March opined that the Prime Minister's progress around the country was as directionless as the *Marie Celeste*.

It was in Luton on 28 March that Mr Major first mounted a soap box to make himself heard against hecklers. This gained him useful television coverage, and injected some spontaneity into what was mostly a highly-orchestrated campaign by both the main parties. On 1 April the Prime Minister turned his fire on the Liberal Democrats (who seemed to be making inroads into the Tory vote), describing them as the 'Trojan horse to a Labour Britain'. On the same day there were renewed signs of nervousness on the stock market at the possibility of a Conservative defeat. Mr Ashdown intervened to promise that his party would veto Labour's top tax plans if the latter were to form a minority government. On 5 April he demanded four cabinet seats if Labour opted for a coalition.

Interest rates were reduced by half a point to 10 per cent (the lowest for nearly four years) shortly before election day. The Tories intensified their warnings of the dangers of a Labour government. Mr Major urged the country not to don the 'tatty red vest of socialism'. The polls continued to show greater personal support for Mr Major than for Mr Kinnock. But they also indicated that more voters than usual were having difficulty in making up their minds. Some estimates during the last weekend in March put this group as high as 32 per cent. The polls themselves fuelled expectations (and fears) of a hung parliament, while Labour's position might have been further weakened when Mr Kinnock seemed to hint at future cross-party talks on proportional representation.

In the end the indecision among voters did not prevent a high turnout of 77.7 per cent of registered voters (against 73.2 per cent in 1987). Above all, it seemed that fears of higher taxes and a deeper economic crisis under Labour did much to persuade waverers that it was one thing to consider voting Labour and quite another to put a cross on a ballot paper to that effect. There was the fear, too, that a vote for the Liberal Democrats might mean a Labour government.

Even the exit-polls left the TV election programmes floundering and unprepared for the Tory victory. The government was returned with an overall majority of 21 seats. Labour's net gain of 42 seats compared with the election of 1987 still left them with 65 MPs fewer than the Tories. Indeed, the latter had secured only a fractionally smaller share of the votes (41.93 against 42.22 per cent) than in 1987, and had even gained a couple of seats in Scotland to raise their total to 11 (out of 72). For the first time since the 1820s a government had been returned for a fourth successive term. The results are given in the table below (comparable 1987 figures in brackets):

	Seats	% of votes
Conservatives	336 (375)	41.93 (42.22)
Labour	271 (229)	34.39 (30.83)
Liberal Democrats	20 (22*)	17.85 (22.57*)
Scottish National Party	3 (3)	1.87 (1.28)
Plaid Cymru	4 (3)	0.47 (0.38)
Official Ulster Unionists	9 (9)	0.81 (0.85)
Democratic Unionists	3 (3)	0.31 (0.26)
Ulster Popular Unionist	1 (1)	0.06 (0.06)
Social Democratic and Labour Party	4 (3)	0.55 (0.47)

Total 651 (650)

* Liberal/Social Democratic (SDP) Alliance

Labour emerged from the contest with an extra one and a half million votes compared with 1987, an advance of about 3.5 per cent. But this still left them about 7.5 points behind the Tories, whose vote total was the highest by a single party in British parliamentary history. The Liberal Democrats won two seats fewer (and 5 per cent fewer votes) than the Liberal/SDP Alliance tally in 1987, while the last two Social Democrats were eliminated.

Among those to lose their seats was the Conservative Party chairman, Chris Patten. Several major figures had not stood for re-election. These included Mrs Thatcher, Norman Tebbit and Sir Geoffrey Howe (Conservative), Denis Healey and Michael Foot (Labour), and David Owen (SDP). Apart from Mr Foot, who declined to accept a peerage, all these ex-MPs were subsequently elevated to the Lords. Labour, having been out of office since 1979, was left with only two ex-cabinet ministers on its front bench, namely Mr Smith and the party's deputy leader, Roy Hattersley—the number being reduced to one by Mr Hattersley's subsequent move to the back benches (see I.3 below).

3.   RELATIVE QUIET ON THE HOME FRONT

IN the new cabinet Michael Heseltine became President of the Board of Trade and Secretary of State for Trade and Industry. If this seemed to point to a more interventionist industrial policy, Michael Portillo, the new Chief Secretary to the Treasury, was reckoned to rank among the 'dryest of the dries'. Others entering the cabinet for the first time were John Patten, who succeeded Kenneth Clarke (the new Home Secretary) at education; Sir Patrick Mayhew, as Secretary of State for Northern Ireland; and two women, namely Virginia Bottomley (health) and Gillian Shephard (employment). In other job changes, Malcolm Rifkind took over defence and John MacGregor was moved from education to transport. The party chairmanship was entrusted to Sir Norman Fowler, while his predecessor, Chris Patten, became Governor of Hong Kong. Kenneth Baker left the cabinet, having declined an offer of the Welsh Office. In general it was felt that the Prime Minister had been careful to strike a balance between the main groups within the party (for full cabinet list, see XIX.4).

When the new House of Commons assembled, Betty Boothroyd (Labour) became the first woman ever to be elected Speaker. This was also the first time since the war that a Speaker had been chosen from the opposition benches. The election was presided over by Sir Edward Heath, now 'father of the House' and a Knight Companion of the Order of the Garter.

The general election was followed by two post mortems: a search for the reasons behind Labour's latest defeat, and a debate over the accuracy of the opinion polls during the campaign. Pollsters pointed to a number of exceptional circumstances, but some agreed that they would have to become 'a bit more humble' and look critically at their methods. In particular, it seemed that many potential Tory voters were becoming more difficult to identify and pin down.

Labour, meanwhile, was trying to recover from the shock of defeat. Having led the party to two election defeats, Mr Kinnock announced his resignation on 13 April (as did his deputy, Mr Hattersley). It later emerged (in June) that twice in the previous year, when Mr Kinnock's standing in the country had been at a particularly low ebb, attempts had been made to replace him as leader with Mr Smith. The latter, however, had refused to cooperate with Mr Kinnock's critics. Mr Kinnock was widely praised for his contributions to the reorganization and revitalization of his party. It was agreed that he had taken many difficult and brave decisions. But while Labour had begun to seem electable as a result of his leadership, it had not necessarily followed that it was electable under him.

Labour research into the reasons for the defeat reached the dismal conclusion early in May that fundamental voter perceptions of the two main parties had heavily influenced the outcome, even though at the start of the campaign up to one-third of the voters had not made up their minds how or whether to vote. The Tories were seen by many as standing for personal investment and 'self-improvement', whereas Labour stood for 'clawing-back and altruism'. These factors mattered far more than any of the controversial incidents, or the possible influence in some key marginal seats of the Tory tabloids such as *The Sun* with its 'Nightmare on Kinnock Street' portrayal of Britain under Labour.

Mr Kinnock, appearing on TV-AM's *Frost on Sunday* on 28 June, said that he had begun to have doubts from the Sunday before the election. He stressed that the Labour campaign had failed to expose Tory 'lies' that Mr Smith's 'budget' would hurt all taxpayers. Furthermore,

Mr Major had given electors the impression that they were dealing with a new government whereas they would have rejected the Tories had Mrs Thatcher still been Prime Minister. Post-election reflection also prompted some observers to upgrade Mr Major's performance. Both in office and during the election, he was seen as having developed into a credible leader.

Other leading Labour figures thought the party had still not taken sufficient account of the changes in British society resulting from the Thatcher years. Middle-class voters had increased as a proportion of the electorate from 33 to 42 per cent between 1979 and 1992, while trade union members had fallen from 30 to 21 per cent. Despite the recession, there were enough contented voters to put the Tories back. If prosperity had doomed Labour to defeat in 1987, recession had not given it enough votes in 1992. Mr Kinnock himself, on 1 July, described the election as a contest between hope and fear—'and it was fear that won'. He also insisted that the next party leader had to be given the opportunity to put Labour's message to the people and not, as he personally had been forced to do, to spend so much time on party reorganization.

The local elections on 7 May were most directly comparable with those held in 1988. On this basis the Tories gained 308 seats, the Liberal Democrats 61 and the Scottish National Party 30. Labour lost 365 seats and independents and others 37. The Tories themselves were surprised by the extent of their successes (including some in Scotland). The results also gave them control of five additional local authorities at the expense of Labour. Labour, however, remained the largest party in local government. Interest in the elections was low after the long-drawn-out general election.

Campaigning for the Labour leadership had begun in the middle of April. This election was regarded as unnecessarily precipitate by some. Labour was battle-weary from the campaign and shell-shocked by the result. Mr Smith and Bryan Gould were the two candidates. The former accepted the need to broaden the party's appeal, but continued to stress wealth redistribution. The left-leaning Mr Gould favoured a more radical shake-up of party thinking in a bid to increase public support—especially in the south and among the more ambitious young people—by taking more account of 'pocketbook issues'. Labour could not be sure of winning in four or five years' time merely by reiterating its 1992 programme more effectively, asserted Mr Gould, who also challenged many parts of the Maastricht treaty, warning that the financial orthodoxy involved in ERM membership could bring about a permanent slump in Britain. Mr Gould also stood for the deputy leadership against Margaret Beckett and John Prescott.

Labour's national executive committee (NEC) voted on 27 May in favour of one member, one vote in the selection of parliamentary candidates (at the expense of the unions' current 40 per cent share).

But a later meeting effectively and controversially decided to post-pone any changes in the selection process until after the 1993 party conference. Labour with a deficit of £2.5 million had to tread with some circumspection when dealing with its traditional paymasters, the unions. But the unions, too, had problems, membership having fallen by one-third to 8 million since 1979.

Mr Smith won the Labour leadership on 18 July by an overwhelming margin of the party's electoral college (91 per cent)—the most emphatic mandate given in the party's history..Mrs Beckett (57 per cent) became deputy leader, comfortably defeating Mr Prescott (28 per cent) and Mr Gould (14.5 per cent). The new leader immediately committed himself to 'a fair society and a strong economy'. He promised to abolish the union block vote in 1993. He emphasized electoral reform, regional assemblies, a rethink of welfare benefits, and hoped to woo women voters back to Labour (58 per cent had voted Conservative in April). Gordon Brown became shadow chancellor, while Jack Cunningham and Tony Blair took charge of foreign and home affairs respectively in a reshaped shadow cabinet.

The Queen's Speech on 6 May outlined a programme of 16 bills, including coal privatization and a scheme whereby various British Rail services would be offered as franchises to private companies. There would be more trade union legislation and measures to boost opting-out by schools and to make further extensions to home own-ership. Mr Major also stressed his desire to 'sweep away the cobwebs of secrecy which needlessly' veiled too much government activity. The secret intelligence services, for instance, were to be placed on a statutory footing. Mr Kinnock, still speaking for Labour, complained that the government had no programme for economic recovery, and dismissed its commitment to a classless society as a pretence, just as its promise of choice and opportunity was fraudulent.

It was not long before the government ran into trouble, though with some of its own supporters rather than with the opposition. Indeed the battle between the two main parties was surprisingly muted until September. Euro-sceptics were soon taking the offensive against ratification of the Maastricht treaty, with Lady Thatcher at their head. She set out to disprove Disraeli's description of the Lords as 'the Elysian Fields of the politically dead', and broke with tradition by making an unusually combative maiden speech. Earlier she had insisted that there was no such thing as 'Majorism'. His government, she asserted, was following her principles.

On 25 June the government announced a £144 million scheme to widen a seven-mile south-western stretch of the M25 to fourteen lanes between the M4 and M3—the busiest section of any motorway in Britain. The plan evoked strong protests from environmentalists. Other critics complained of the neglect of the railways, which received only about 4 per cent of public investment in transport compared with 93 per cent on the roads. Government support for British Rail (BR) had fallen by one-third in real terms since 1979.

The government provided a guide to its thinking on BR in a White Paper issued on 14 July shortly before parliament rose for the summer recess. This postponed wholesale privatization for the time being, but a new infrastructure authority, Railtrack, was proposed, and a franchising authority would sell or rent specific BR operations to private operators wherever possible. The authority would also supervise the new operators. Subsidies would continue for loss-making services.

The Transport Secretary stressed that the new scheme to improve rail efficiency would be practical and flexible, while admitting that BR could not be sold off as a single entity when losses were of the order of £145 million a year despite a government subsidy of £900 million. For Labour Mr Prescott argued that the new plan would not produce modernization. Doubtless with the history of railways since the late 1940s in mind, he added: 'It will mean new paint on old trains.' The Railway Development Society dismissed the White Paper as 'a dog's dinner of random ideas'. Free-marketeers were equally critical because the scheme was so tentative.

Worries continued over education standards. Her Majesty's Inspectorate had reported on 30 January that nearly one-third of schools in England were failing their pupils. Some blamed the confusion and uncertainty caused by the removal of so many codes and guidelines in the name of individual freedom. This was a question in which Mr Major himself showed much interest. He held left-wing local councils to be the cause of many of the problems. The question of standards resurfaced on 1 September when it was reported that the Inspectorate had only 'limited confidence' in the results of the latest GCSE examination. Critics argued that there were bound to be difficulties with an examination designed to be passed in some degree by no less than 90 per cent of all pupils.

On 28 July a White Paper, *Choice and Diversity*, was offered as a blueprint for the state education system over the next generation. This placed great emphasis on education as the bedrock of civilized society. Under it, local authorities would lose many of their powers to new central bodies. Schools would be encouraged to opt out, and to specialize in subjects such as technology, languages or business studies. Inadequate schools would, if necessary, be taken under the wing of a Whitehall-appointed team and steered to grant-maintained status. Overall, it was hoped that the number of grant-maintained schools over the next three years would rise from less than 300 to 4,000 (or roughly one-sixth of the schools in England and Wales). The White Paper promised action against truancy, with more thought being given to religious and moral teaching. Meanwhile, the government's youth training initiative was failing to meet its promise of a place for all those under 18 who were not in full-time education. More than 100,000 16/17-year-olds had no jobs or income.

Rioting or serious incidents occurred in several cities in June and July involving youths and the police. Among the worst affected were housing estates in Bristol (16–18 July), Burnley (19 July) and Blackburn (22 July). Police action against joy-riders and drug-dealing provided the spark. Orchestration by trouble-makers and high levels of unemployment among teenagers were held responsible. The Chief Constable of the West Midlands and the retiring Metropolitan Police Commissioner, Sir Peter Imbert, both urged study of the problems posed by a disadvantaged underclass. Recorded crimes in the United Kingdom had more than doubled since 1979, despite the recruitment of an extra 1,600 police officers and an annual budget which now stood at £5,000 million. Kenneth Clarke began his tenure of the Home Office with a drive for greater efficiency. Also in July, the Policy Studies Institute reported that inner cities were still deteriorating 15 years after the first government initiative to reverse the decline.

In June the government offered £2.5 million by way of temporary relief to victims of the pension fund crisis which had followed the death of Robert Maxwell (see AR 1991, pp. 35, 577), while efforts were made to track down the missing millions. On 9 March the House of Commons social security select committee had recommended a drastic overhaul of pensions legislation. Further demands followed for increased protection for pension funds, reinforced by complaints against some other companies. The chairman of the Investment Management Regulatory Organization (IMRO) resigned on 29 June, admitting that IMRO was open to a share of the criticism in the Maxwell case, but adding that they were not the only people at fault. Kevin Maxwell, son of the newspaper magnate, became Britain's biggest-ever bankrupt on 3 September, with debts in excess of £400 million.

One part of the Maxwell newspaper empire, *The European*, was bought by David and Frederick Barclay on 6 January and continued weekly publication. The last issue of the famous humorous magazine *Punch*, founded in 1841, appeared on 8 April. In contrast, Rupert Murdoch's News Corporation was reporting increased profits a year after fears of its collapse. BSkyB, its satellite television arm, had become almost profitable (see XVI.1.vi).

Controversy over media relations with royalty reached new heights. Speculation mounted over the future of the marriage of the Prince and Princess of Wales, while negotiations for a separation of the Duke and Duchess of York were announced in March. The appearance of extracts from Andrew Morton's book *Diana: Her True Story* in the *Sunday Times* on 7 June caused a brief sensation, while the conduct of some journalists led the Press Complaints Commission to issue a warning later in the month that 'prurient' reporting could lead to statutory press controls.

of pluralism' in politics from which a 'post-socialist' alternative might emerge. After a passionate debate on 16 September, the Liberal Democrats firmly rejected formal pacts, but agreed to 'develop and debate ideas with people of all parties and none, and at all levels'. Mr Ashdown asked if Labour was prepared to become part of a 'coalition for change' or remain 'the road-block which guards the Tories from defeat'.

4.   FROM THE 'CENTRE' OF EUROPE TO THE 'SIDELINES'

ON 12 May the Queen delivered her first address to the European Parliament at Strasbourg. This set out the principles which the UK government hoped could be kept to the fore during Britain's presidency of the Community in the second half of the year. The Queen emphasized the 'diverse personalities' of the European family and their need for 'tolerance and mutual support'. Without its diversity Europe would be weakened, not strengthened, she said. At Maastricht the right balance had been struck between Europe and its components. But it was also essential that a dynamic entity should open its doors to new members and 'enrich' its relations with 'the wider world'.

The warm reception given to this speech in Europe, however, only added to the alarm of the Euro-sceptics at home. Although the EC had scarcely figured in the general election, it was evident that Lady Thatcher and some other Tories were determined that it should remain an issue no matter how much Mr Major might argue that the sovereignty of the Commons was 'not up for grabs'. Lady Thatcher was soon warning of the power of Germany and the European Commission. In the two-day Commons debate on Maastricht (20–21 May), the Foreign Secretary, Douglas Hurd, claimed that Britain had saved the EC from becoming 'increasingly centralized and arthritic'. But he was unable to dissuade 22 Tory Euro-sceptics from voting against the Maastricht ratification bill (as did some Labour MPs). The government still emerged with a majority of 244.

On 21 May ministers claimed that a new agreement to begin the reform of the EC's common agricultural policy was a vindication of government policy on Europe. The reform was expected to take some 1.5 million acres of land out of production within two years. The Agriculture Minister promised plans to promote a 'greener' countryside, so that the former farmland would not become neglected waste.

Government hopes of retaining the initiative over Europe were rudely shaken by the Danish referendum on 2 June, when ratification of Maastricht was rejected by a narrow majority (see II.2.i). No less than 82 Tories proceeded to sign a motion calling for a 'fresh start' in Britain's relations with the EC. Such was the tension and speculation that on 10 June the government was forced to issue denials of any split within its ranks. An opinion poll in the middle of June revealed that the British were the least pro-European of the peoples who made up the EC (53 per cent took a positive view, while 32 per cent wished to leave). The 'yes' in the Irish referendum of 19 June (see II.1.vii) failed to discourage the Euro-critics. The government accepted that legislation to ratify the treaty would have to be delayed.

Before his departure for the EC summit in Lisbon at the end of June, Mr Major offered a forthright defence of government policy. He reminded critical Tory MPs that they had been returned on an election manifesto commitment to the Maastricht treaty and that the Commons had passed the second reading of the ratification bill by a large majority. But Tory divisions made it all the more important for him to be seen to standing up to the 'federalists' and centralizers in Lisbon. His government, in any case, had differences of its own with the EC Commission—over the budget, on subsidiarity, the 48-hour week and the question of border controls when the single European market came into operation at the start of 1993. It agreed with some reluctance to another term for Jacques Delors as the Commission's president (see XI.3). The British also hoped to persuade other member states that the current difficulty with Denmark over Maastricht might be lessened if entry talks were opened with its neighbours, Sweden and Finland. Mr Major was anxious to make enlargement of the EC a high priority during his six-month presidency of the Community, which began with such high hopes in July.

On 26 June, at the start of the Lisbon summit, *The Times* described the occasion as 'one of the most difficult challenges [to British diplomacy] since entry into the European Community in 1973'. It was suspicious of some government policies, and was fearful of creeping federalism. Indeed, Mr Major himself lost no time in warning fellow EC leaders that many in Europe now feared that the Community had become a 'voracious super-state monster' which was running out of control. The time had come to return many powers to national governments and to ensure that decisions were taken at the lowest practical level. He was able to exclude any reference in the concluding conference statement to a proposed doubling of money for the EC's poorest regions. But he made no progress towards an accelerated build-up of a wider Community to include the comparatively wealthy members of the European Free Trade Association, despite the view that this would increase the resources at the disposal of the EC to help its poorer members. Admission of new members remained dependent on agreement over the budget and ratification of Maastricht.

The Prime Minister had more success on the delicate issue of the respective powers of EC institutions and national governments. It was agreed that all present Community legislation should be examined in the light of the principle of subsidiarity, though not immediately. Mr Major also called for the Commission to give up obsolete directives and to justify future plans against the appropriate criteria of subsidiarity. There was even talk of a 'subsidiarity filter' to ensure that decisions and actions were taken at the lowest suitable level.

But if Mr Major felt that he had emerged from Lisbon with at least some ammunition with which to deal with critics and sceptics in his party, he was immediately exposed to a broadside from Lady Thatcher in a television interview on 28 June. She stated that she intended to vote against the Maastricht treaty in the Lords, arguing that it transferred excessive powers to the European Commission. Indeed, she seemed determined to disagree with the Prime Minister on many European issues. She repeated her demand for a referendum on Maastricht, criticized the reappointment of M. Delors, and praised the Danish voters for saving parliamentary democracy from what she described as 'a treaty too far'. As for Maastricht's attempt to define subsidiarity, this was mere 'gobbledegook'.

The Prime Minister responded in the Commons on 29 June with a reminder of his predecessor's previous hostility to referendums. He robustly defended his policy on Maastricht, arguing that Britain had to be at the centre of Europe if it was to exert influence and that those who were looking for an alternative should spell out the economic implications. There were other signs of ministerial exasperation with Lady Thatcher.

The EC reached agreement on 28 July on a minimum VAT rate of 15 per cent for all member states until 1996, though with the retention of some differential duties and zero-rated items. Mr Lamont argued that the agreement was necessary for the completion of the single European market. Euro-critics such as Lord Tebbit denounced it as 'contrary to 1,000 years of British sovereignty'.

Meanwhile, the government was insisting that sterling's position within the ERM would be defended by all means necessary, including a rise in interest rates. The defeat of inflation was the key to future economic success, and it was an illusion, claimed ministers, to think that Britain would be better off outside the ERM or through a devaluation of the pound. However, Lady Thatcher, a number of Tory backbenchers and some leading economists continued to call for policy changes, including a cut in interest rates, a devaluation or realignment of sterling and withdrawal (if only temporarily) from the ERM. Lord Tebbit protested that the German Bundesbank and the ERM authorities were being allowed to dictate the running of the British economy.

The threats to the pound from the second half of August had both longer-term internal and immediate external causes. The latter arose from a dollar crisis, high German interest rates in response to the problems generated by reunification and growing fears of a 'no' vote in the French referendum on Maastricht due on 20 September.

Consequential uncertainty in the currency markets was encouraging a flight to the mark. On 21 August sterling was trading dangerously close to its permitted ERM floor of DM 2.778. The pound was not alone in its troubles, but longer-term domestic weaknesses in the economy were underlined by the continuing trade gap. The current-account deficit worsened sharply in the middle of the year.

On 26 August the Chancellor put his political future at risk by reiterating his absolute commitment to the ERM and no devaluation. There was also intervention on behalf of sterling by the Bank of England. On 2 September the British joined in a European move to support President Mitterrand in his campaign for a 'yes' vote in the French referendum. But Mr Major also said that a 'no' vote would render British ratification of the Maastricht treaty out of the question. Ministers were clearly hoping they could have the best of both worlds.

Meanwhile, August was witnessing the sharpest fall (more than £600 million) in the UK foreign exchange and gold reserves for three years. EC finance ministers, meeting in Bath on 5–6 September, ruled out currency realignments, but promised only low European growth in 1992–93. Mr Major, speaking to the Scottish CBI in Glasgow on 10 September, made his most emphatic commitment yet to the established exchange-rate and anti-inflation policies. Britain, he said, had won no competitive advantages despite the halving of the external value of the pound since the 1960s. He cited the current problems in Scandinavia to support his claim that there was 'a cold world outside the ERM'. Britain would be condemned to lasting 'second-rate status in Europe'. *The Times* of 11 September was unimpressed. No more than his predecessors could the Prime Minister defy the market's perceptions of the British economy. Mr Major, it was suggested by some, was beginning to appear more dogmatic than his predecessor.

The situation rapidly worsened over the weekend of 12–13 September, as the Bundesbank was increasingly persuaded that some currency realignments were inevitable. This was confirmed by the collapse of the Italian lira. There were later claims to the effect that sterling realignment had been discussed within the EC as early as July, but that Mr Lamont had preferred to wait until the outcome of the French referendum was known and then to participate in a general downward realignment only if it included the French franc. The Germans might have been more helpful had Britain agreed to a general realignment as early as 5 September, or at the time of the devaluation of the lira on 13 September. Even so, it was estimated that the Bundesbank spent DM 44,000 million in one week to support the lira and sterling (with most going in support of the latter). But relations between the British and Germans were far too strained by the middle of September for any concerted rescue action to be agreed or to have a hope of success.

'Black Wednesday', 16 September, began with a 2 per cent rise to 12 per cent, in British interest rates. When this failed to steady the pound, a further 3 per cent increase with effect from 17 September was announced. Finally, on the evening of 16 September, the Chancellor announced the temporary suspension of British membership of the ERM. For the time being sterling was being left to find its own level. The Chancellor also revoked the second interest rate rise. Parliament was recalled to discuss the crisis on 24 September. Meanwhile, in New York the pound was trading at nearly eight pfennigs below its ERM floor. The market, as matters then stood, could no longer be 'bucked'.

In the wake of 'Black Wednesday', insulting Germanophobic headlines appeared in sections of the British press. Relations between the Treasury and the Bundesbank were particularly strained. But the British could find little sympathy in Europe. The Italian Prime Minister, as well as Chancellor Kohl, dismissed any complaints as childish. Meanwhile, the government was also being fiercely attacked from many sides at home. Critics complained of long-term mismanagement of the economy, of medium-term illusions concerning the viability of the fixed exchange policy within the ERM, of exaggeration of the resources which could be used to defend the pound, and of inept handling of day-to-day policy once the lira had been devalued, especially in view of the Bundesbank's doubts concerning the defensibility of the current rate. Ministers, it was said, had become extraordinarily credulous and inflexible.

Estimates of the proportion of the foreign reserves expended in the abortive defence of the pound varied between one-third and a half. It was later claimed that the Bank of England had spent £11,000 million on 16 September alone, on the instruction of the Treasury but against the advice of two officials. Whatever the figures, Treasury actions were likened to pouring funds into a currency 'black hole'. Many called for Mr Lamont's resignation. The government had also suffered a political defeat, given its determination to be at the heart of the EC to prevent a federal Europe and to enhance its own influence.

The Prime Minister and the cabinet continued to support Mr Lamont, and the latter was able to announce a return to a 10 per cent interest rate on 17 September. Meanwhile, the government held its breath while awaiting the outcome of the French referendum on 20 September. Once a 'yes' vote (albeit by a whisker) became apparent that same evening (see II.1.i), John Major sent his congratulations to President Mitterrand. But he added, in looking to the future, that it was necessary to await the result of the Danish review of its policy on Maastricht, deal with the shortcomings (or 'fault-lines') in the ERM, and take account of the many concerns relating to the future of the EC which had emerged in recent public debates in Britain and abroad.

The Chancellor said that Britain could not return to the ERM until the British and German economies were more in line with each other.

Monetary policy had been too tight, but modifications could not be made at the expense of the fight against inflation. The government would return to using the money supply, among a range of indicators, to guide economic policy. On 21 September Mr Lamont insisted that 'sound finance, low inflation and good growth' were the fundamentals of British policy. 'That has nothing to do with ERMs and currency targets', he now claimed.

The narrow 'yes' vote in France greatly encouraged and strengthened the Euro-critics, especially among the Tories. On 19 September Lady Thatcher congratulated the government on leaving the ERM 'straitjacket', and called for a similar change of policy on Maastricht. Mr Major responded on 21 September to threats of a Tory revolt with the promise of 'a profound look' at the future of the EC at an emergency summit (held in Birmingham on 16 October). Lord Tebbit, however, demanded a referendum on economic and political union (an increasingly popular view according to the opinion polls), while other Euro-critics threatened 'trench warfare' if the Maastricht bill were reintroduced. More than 70 Tory MPs demanded a fresh start on economic and EC policies.

Labour, too, had its problems following the economic upset. Official policy on the exchange rate, Maastricht and a referendum had been close to that of the government, with Mr Smith expressing tentative interest in a general and controlled realignment against the mark to encourage economic growth. But there were also Euro-sceptics in the Labour Party, with Mr Gould as a particularly articulate spokesman.

On 22 September interest rates were cut by 1 per cent, and the building societies quickly followed suit with reductions of around 0.75 per cent. Mr Lamont, however, added his warnings to those from others (including the Prime Minister) against undue optimism concerning the supposed benefits from a floating pound. There would be no 'free lunch' outside the ERM. Interest rates would be raised to counter any threat from inflation. Business welcomed the move, but only as the first of many steps which were seen as necessary to reactivate the economy.

5.   A BELEAGUERED GOVERNMENT

THE Commons debate of 24 September on the ERM crisis gave Mr Smith an excellent opportunity to make his debut as Labour leader. Any divisions in his own party on Europe were submerged for the time being, as he accused Mr Major of being the 'devalued Prime Minister of a devalued government'. With others, he assailed the government for mismanagement of the economy and for its U-turn on policy. Although Labour's amendment was defeated by 42 votes, eight Tories abstained rather than support the government's motion on its economic policy. On the same day the Prime Minister reluctantly accepted the resignation of David Mellor, the National Heritage Secretary. Since July Mr Mellor's private life had been exposed to ruthless scrutiny by sections of the press, which had disclosed, among other things, that he had recently had an affair with an aspiring actress. Peter Brooke (the former Northern Ireland Secretary) was appointed to replace him.

The Labour leadership again vigorously played the European card at the party conference in Blackpool. The NEC had earlier heavily defeated a proposal for a referendum on Maastricht, and adopted a paper called *Europe: Our Future*, which argued that national interests could not be properly defended if Britain were pushed to the periphery of the continent. An eventual return to a reformed ERM was essential, but only after the British economy had been restored to health. These proposals were overwhelmingly endorsed in Blackpool on 28 September. Mr Gould, having already resigned from the shadow cabinet on the ground that he could no longer support current policy on the economy and Europe, was voted off the NEC—a setback he shared with left-winger Dennis Skinner. Gordon Brown and Tony Blair, both strong supporters of Mr Smith, were elected in their stead. Nevertheless, Euro-scepticism could not be dismissed as a spent force in the party.

In his first conference speech as leader, Mr Smith called for 'active' government to lift Britain out of 'this downward spiral of decline'. Labour would be guided by the values of both individual opportunity and social justice. The Labour leadership, however, saw no need to adopt detailed policy positions so soon after an election. There were some protests from the Labour left over the watering-down of socialist principles and the takeover of the party by middle-class graduate image-makers. But the conference broke up on 2 October in a mood of relief, pleasure and confidence. Relative dullness and lack of controversy were deemed sure proof of success.

Anglo-German relations continued to be soured by the dispute over responsibility for the recent sterling crisis. A leading Tory backbench Euro-critic accused the Germans of 'getting too big for their jackboots'. A German scholar retorted that the British tabloid press was continuing to project an image of Germany based on 'all those films of Nazis without real German accents'. An opinion poll suggested that 68 per cent of Britons would vote against Maastricht in the event of a referendum. Ministers, however, needed an end to the 'war of words' and as many friends in Europe as possible if Britain's presidency of the EC was not to end in humiliation. Yet even Mr Hurd, in a revealing comment, conceded that Britain's return to the ERM would have to be determined by economic rather than foreign policy goals.

The Prime Minister staunchly defended Mr Lamont against the latter's many critics, and on 1 October boldly stated his intention to complete the passage of the Maastricht bill during the current parliamentary session. But the government's already weak position was further damaged by the sharp increase in job losses and business closures at this time. The dismay over industrial decline extended to the tabloid press, with *The Sun* plaintively asking 'Why isn't it made in Britain any more?' Against such a bleak backcloth the party chairman, Sir Norman Fowler, opened the Conservative's annual conference in Brighton on 6 October with a stark warning of the dangers of disunity: did the Tories want to tear themselves apart like Labour in the 1980s? He was also careful to stress the continuance of the radical revolution begun by Lady Thatcher.

Europe cast a dark shadow over the conference, Lord Tebbit won enthusiastic applause from Euro-sceptics and Euro-phobes (estimates ranged from perhaps one-third of the delegates to a 'sizeable minority') with a belligerent speech in which he demanded a 'Maastricht II' treaty with 'no mention of economic, monetary and political union'. Lady Thatcher briefly stole the headlines with her condemnation of Maastricht as 'yesterday's vision' in *The European* of 8 October. Yet many felt that her reception at the conference was stronger on noise than substance, and that her reputation had been damaged by her conduct.

The ministerial counter-offensive took several forms. Mr Hurd argued that Maastricht enshrined the principle of minimum interference, and reminded the party of the damage it had suffered in earlier times from internecine strife over the Corn Laws and tariff reform. Despite the efforts of some highly vocal critics, a motion to 'continue to build an open and outward-looking Community'—coupled with amendments to end unnecessary interference from Brussels—won strong support. On 7 October Mr Heseltine launched a vigorous assault on the Euro-sceptics—first goading and then silencing the hecklers. Kenneth Clarke became involved in even blunter exchanges with Lord Tebbit outside the conference hall.

Mr Major's aim in his speech on 9 October was to maximize party unity. 'I will never', he promised, 'come hell or high water, let our distinctive British identity be lost in a federal Europe'. Yet he still insisted that this meant putting Britain at the heart of Europe. Although this was considered a reasonably successful performance, the party seemed more divided than at any time since the battle over tariffs in the early 1900s.

Nor were ministers able to offer much reassurance concerning the nation's economic prospects. Brighton itself was a painful reminder to ministers of a south coast town hard-hit by the recession. The Chancellor's speech on 8 October gave most attention to the battle against inflation (the target was 2 per cent a year, or less) and the strict control of public spending. He outlined terms for re-entry to the ERM, but doubted if these could be satisfied in the near future.

His speech disappointed those who were looking for positive action on the economy, and who feared that the recession might slide into a slump. *The Observer* argued on 11 October that it was time to think of an 'old-fashioned Keynesian stimulus to the economy'. Inventiveness and imagination were essential. Mr Lamont was also roughly handled by the Commons Treasury committee on 12 October.

Yet another crisis erupted on 13 October when it was announced that the coal-mining workforce was to be cut by 60 per cent over the next six months—a decision which (it was later revealed) had been formally approved by only an inner group of ministers. Some 30,000 jobs and 31 out of 50 pits were to go. This decision provoked an immediate and an increasingly bitter national outcry. Critics disputed the government's claim that there was no market for much of the coal being produced. There existed, it was said, no truly competitive energy market. The government, through its privatization of the electricity industry, had not only given special and costly protection to the nuclear sector, but had opened the door to large increases in the use of gas and imported cheap coal at the expense of longer-term considerations, including Britain's balance of payments. Sir John Harvey-Jones, former chairman of ICI, thought it 'somewhat perverse' that Britain, with its abundant fossil fuel in and around its islands, should have the 'highest energy costs in Europe'.

Mr Heseltine agreed that the nation was living in a 'very uncomfortable world'. But he ruled out subsidies for ailing industries, from coal to defence. The decision on the coal industry was, in his view, both 'dreadful' and 'right'. A £1,000 million government redundancy package was promised. But this did nothing to allay fears concerning the future of whole communities and the spin-off effects on other industries. Tory critics began to sound more vehement than the miners' own leaders.

On the same day there was more bad news on the economy. The underlying rate of growth was put at 0.5 per cent at best (a figure confirmed later). Tories were among those to demand a new economic strategy, and to accuse the government of 'drift and weakness'. Unemployment topped 10 per cent of the workforce in September (a post-war record for people out of work). Lord Ridley accused the government of overkill in its battle against inflation. A 1 per cent interest rate cut (to 8 per cent) on 16 October did, however, bring mortgages to their lowest (nominal) level since June 1978. But the pound fell below DM 2.50. Opposition leaders dismissed the interest cut as 'a panic move'.

Denunciation of the government's coal policy reached a climax on Sunday 18 September. This owed much to the feeling that the cabinet had lost its way on economic policy as a whole. The most vociferous and important critics came from sections of the Conservative Party. The staunchest Tory newspapers attacked the Prime Minister with extraordinary ferocity. Questions were being asked about his political future as well as those of Mr Heseltine and Mr Lamont. Mr Major's ratings in the polls slipped to the lowest recorded for a British prime minister. Euro-sceptics were hoping for a ministerial reshuffle which would increase their representation in the cabinet (currently standing at three or four).

Ministers were particularly impressed by dire warnings from the whips that they lacked a Commons majority to push through their current policy on the mines. A number of concessions followed over the next three days. On 21 October Mr Heseltine promised the Commons a full and open review of the future of 21 pits, the other ten under threat being placed on a care and maintenance basis for the time being. The enquiries might extend to the privatized electricity industry. All aspects of Britain's energy policy were to be examined. By the end of a fighting speech, and helped by an extraordinarily rowdy debate, Mr Heseltine appeared to have recovered the support and confidence of much of his party. The government prevailed by 320 votes to 307, only six Tories voting with the opposition and six more abstaining.

Mr Heseltine spoke later (on 27 October) of his frustration with present legislation, which prevented him from getting all the key units in the electricity industry together to discuss future coal contracts. Even so, he doubted if there was a market for more than 40 million tonnes of British coal a year. There was a further twist to the story when, on 21 December, the High Court ruled the closure decisions illegal because of lack of consultation with the mining unions. Mr Heseltine stated that production would not be renewed in the ten pits scheduled for immediate closure.

Meanwhile, the government had been confronted by another crisis of confidence at the end of October. Mr Major responded with promises of a new 'strategy for growth'. But the new signals were still equivocal, and suggested a measured acceleration rather a sudden change of gear. The weekend of 24–25 October brought no respite for ministers, as some 200,000 rain-soaked demonstrators paraded in Hyde Park in protest against job losses. 'Kamikaze Tories' ran the headline of a leader in *The Observer*. In addition, Tory rebels continued to threaten the government over the Maastricht bill despite warnings that the Prime Minister was prepared to risk his own future, and perhaps that of his government, on this issue. Mr Major and Mr Heseltine themselves confronted individual backbench dissidents at a time when up to 40 Tory MPs were threatening to vote against any substantive motion on Maastricht in the Commons 'paving debate' planned for 4 November. Many thought Mr Major had provoked an unnecessary trial of strength, since the bill's second reading had already paved the way for the committee stage.

On 28 October Labour decided to make the debate an issue of confidence. Ministers responded by drafting a motion designed to minimize any backbench revolt without at the same time forfeiting the promise of Liberal Democrat support. The Tory rebels themselves were made up of a mixture of outright opponents of the EC, of those who feared an erosion of British sovereignty and of dedicated free-marketeers.

The actual debate on 4 November was as fierce and as much of a cliff-hanger as expected. Apart from the Tory civil war and the battle between the two main front benches, a clash also developed between Labour and the Liberal Democrats, with the latter being accused of naïvely protecting the government. Mr Ashdown in reply charged Labour with political opportunism by opposing a motion on Britain's future relations with Europe. Mr Major claimed that a defeat would reduce the government's ability to protect Britain's interests at the Edinburgh summit, as well as in the longer run. Ratification of Maastricht was a matter of 'national self-interest'. In the end, direct pressure on potential Tory rebels had to be exerted by ministers as well as whips to ensure that enough reluctant voters were propelled into the correct division lobby.

Thus Labour's amendment to delay further debate on the Maastricht bill was defeated by 319 votes to 313. The government motion that the UK should play a leading role in the development of the EC was carried by a mere three votes. The majority was made up of 300 Tories and 19 Liberal Democrats, while 26 Tories voted against their leaders. After the debate ministers again found themselves caught in the cross-fire within their own party. Rebels protested angrily that a promise to lengthen the timetable for the Maastricht ratification process had proved less generous than they had been led to believe. On the other hand, pro-Marketeers were critical of ministers for making any concessions to the rebels. Outsiders suggested that ministers had added the S-turn to the U-turn in their tactical repertoire. There was violent criticism too from some of Britain's EC partners.

Another pitfall awaited the cabinet on 9 November. This was the Matrix Churchill affair—soon to be dubbed Iraqgate—which began with the collapse of a trial involving three engineering company executives who were accused of breaching an arms embargo against Iraq. It was alleged that the government had secretly promoted defence-related exports to Baghdad during and after the later stages of the Iran–Iraq war in defiance of guidelines laid down by the Foreign Office in December 1984. In addition, ministers were accused of a cover-up. Indeed, it was said that some had been prepared to let the businessmen go to prison rather than reveal what they knew to the court.

In the face of bitter opposition attacks, the Prime Minister promised an independent judicial inquiry under Lord Justice Scott. Its terms of reference were later extended in the light of more charges and under political pressure. Lady Thatcher and Mr Major were among the former and present ministers under suspicion. A Labour motion of censure on 23 November was defeated by 310 votes to 265, Mr Heseltine arguing that the ministers had had to weigh conflicting interests in changing circumstances, including the need to protect British sales in a highly competitive market. Robin Cook, for Labour, claimed that Britain had not only armed Saddam Husain but had paid part of the bill with export credits. It was also alleged that British equipment had been used in the Iraqi nuclear programme.

The economy continued to haunt the government. An offer was made to the TUC to discuss ideas for recovery. But although Mrs Shephard, the Employment Secretary, on 5 November promised an end to the 'war' with the trade unions, and added that there was likely to be only one further bill to curb union powers; this was to include the abolition of the wage councils—a move which would affect 2.5 million low-paid workers. An opinion poll taken on 7–8 November suggested a 23 per cent Labour lead over the Tories, half the population having felt a drop in their standard of living in the past year.

The Chancellor delivered his autumn statement on 12 November. Some had already described his Mansion House speech on 29 October as the biggest change in Tory economic philosophy since the adoption of monetarism. On that occasion he had also announced reforms to make the Treasury and Bank of England more open and therefore more accountable in their policy-making. His Commons statement on 12 November was well received by Tory backbenchers. Yet it was still widely regarded as a 'nudge' rather than a 'kickstart' to the economy. There was another one-point base rate cut to 7 per cent, plus special measures to stimulate the housing market, the construction and car industries. Other measures were designed to encourage company investment, and to facilitate private participation in public projects such as the Jubilee Line rail extension to London's Docklands.

Nearly £1,750 million of local council capital receipts were unfrozen for construction purposes. A 1.5 per cent ceiling was imposed on pay increases for five million public sector workers. Despite a rise in the 1992–93 borrowing requirement to £37,000 million (at 6 per cent of GDP this was double the Maastricht criterion), the government hoped to keep within its £244,500 million spending target for 1992–93. Ministers issued repeated warnings against large pay increases in the private sector. The Treasury expected the economy to grow by 1 per cent in 1993 (in contrast with a fall of 0.5 per cent in 1992).

Mr Lamont later conceded that unemployment would continue to rise for some time and that an increase in taxes might be necessary in the next budget. His attempt at an up-beat speech in the Commons on 18 November was challenged by Labour's shadow spokesman, Gordon Brown. The latter claimed that the government still lacked a long-term strategy, while its new investment incentives were an admission that the free-market economics of the 1980s had failed. No less than 10,000 job losses were announced on 19 November, half of them by British Rail due to the recesssion and to the limited government funding promised in the autumn statement.

Mr Major was in great need of success at the EC summit in Edinburgh on 11–12 December. Quite apart from controversy at home, the setbacks to his presidency of the EC and delays over the ratification of the Maastricht treaty were provoking much hostile criticism in Europe. The conference was widely viewed as crucial to the future of the Community. Mr Major himself likened the various interlocking problems to a Rubik's Cube. But after much hard bargaining he claimed that the Community had been put 'back together' (see also XI.3). It was hoped that the concessions to the Danes would produce a 'yes' vote in a second referendum, while Mr Major and Mr Hurd were both confident that the bill to ratify Maastricht would be pushed through parliament at home. But Mr Hurd also insisted that Britain would not agree to negotiate a new treaty in the event of a second Danish 'no'.

The British won some concessions on the subject of subsidiarity, although environmentalists were disturbed by the reduction in the Commission's powers over environmental regulations. It was agreed that talks should start on the enlargement of the EC, while the British were broadly successful with their compromise plan over increased funds for the four poorest members. (For details of the Edinburgh decision, see XIX.3.) After months of criticism from EC partners, Mr Major had emerged from the summit with some credit, although how much was a matter of debate in Britain and Europe. Success in any case would not have been possible without the formidable backing of Chancellor Kohl. At home Tory Euro-sceptics remained unrepentant, while Labour's qualified its support for the outcome by criticizing the inadequacy of the economic growth package. Labour would also pursue its own objectives during the rest of the debate on Maastricht.

On 11 November the General Synod of the Church of England voted narrowly in favour of the ordination of women (see XIII). This historic vote also brought with it the danger of a split in the Church.

On 20 November a serious fire at Windsor Castle did not prove to be the national heritage disaster that was at first feared. Damage to the structure was serious, but the works of art escaped lightly. A government announcement that it would meet the full cost of restoration added to current demands for reductions in royal privileges. The Queen herself, when describing the 40th year of her reign as 'tumultuous' and an '*annus horribilis*', accepted that the monarchy was not above reproach. On 26 November it was announced that she would end a 55-year-old exemption by paying income tax on her private fortune. She would also in future pay the Civil List allowances of the lesser members of the royal family. Even these concessions did not satisfy all

MPs, but Tories generally welcomed the move, not least because of fears that controversy over royalty might implicate the government.

What had long been suspected was confirmed on 9 December when the Prime Minister announced that the Prince and Princess of Wales were to separate. He assured the House of Commons that the decision carried no constitutional implications. This was greeted with much scepticism in many quarters. On 12 December the Princess Royal, following her divorce earlier in the year, married Commander Timothy Laurence at Balmoral.

Renewed mainland bombing by the IRA caused one death in October. The government finally responded to extensive lobbying from commerce and the insurance companies by agreeing on 21 December to underwrite much of the cost of terrorism-related claims.

6.   INTERNATIONAL AFFAIRS

TWO visits to London by President Yeltsin (in January and November) resulted in the signature of the first bilateral treaty between Britain and Russia since 1766, as well as of agreements on security and some economic matters. But there were no promises of British aid until Russian inflation was brought under control. Mr Major was equally cautious during his visit to Prague on 27 May when he formally apologized for the 'shame' of the 1938 Munich agreement. In a message to Eastern Europe on 28 October he said that no precise timetable for EC membership was yet possible.

The Defence White Paper published on 7 July described Britain as a middle-ranking European power with no global pretensions. But its £24,000 million budget (as a percentage of national income still well above the NATO average) reflected how little British strategic thinking had changed despite the end of the Cold War. A fourth Trident submarine was ordered. In Lisbon Mr Major did his best to persuade Chancellor Kohl to persist with the joint development of the European fighter aircraft (EFA) project. The Germans argued that it was unnecessarily sophisticated, and seemed determined to pull out from the programme. On 10 December, however, they agreed to continue on the basis of the promise of a 30 per cent saving in the cost of the cheapest version of the plane. Although some delays were likely, the British were confident that the plane (renamed the Eurofighter 2000) would come into service with the RAF in the year 2000. Up to 40,000 jobs had also been saved.

Questions continued to be asked as to the sort of defence industry Britain needed and could afford, as well as the character and scale of operations for which it should prepare in a post-Cold War era. The armed forces, however, found themselves being drawn into a number of international crises. The situation in Bosnia-Hercegovina was worsening (see III.1.vi), and the RAF commenced relief flights to Sarajevo on 2 July. The Royal Navy assisted in the monitoring of trade to Serbia through the Montenegrin port of Bar. But criticism of government caution increased in response to horrific reports of ethnic cleansing, concentration camps and other atrocities. Lord Owen and Mr Ashdown pressed for more positive action, and they were joined on 5 August by Lady Thatcher, who insisted that the Bosnians needed military help within days in their fight against 'a communist war of aggression' and that what was happening in Bosnia 'is reminiscent of the worst crimes of the Nazis'.

The government stepped up its consultations with France and the United States. It was one of the co-sponsors of UN Security Council resolutions on 13 August enjoining the ending of all military action in Bosnia, the safe passage of humanitarian aid convoys, and unimpeded access to prison and detention camps. A cabinet committee agreed on 18 August to dispatch up to 1,800 troops (later increased to 2,400) to escort relief convoys as 'part of a UN operation'. But troops were definitely not being sent 'to fight their way to Armageddon and back'. Tougher options had been considered and rejected in favour of continuing sanctions and diplomacy.

On 26–27 August Mr Major co-chaired a conference in London which tried to bring international influence to bear on the belligerents in Bosnia. But no more resulted than the creation of a framework within which further talks might develop. Lord Owen succeeded Lord Carrington as the head of the EC peace delegation to work in tandem with Cyrus Vance, the UN envoy. British troops came under fire for the first time in Bosnia on 7 November, and more incidents soon followed.

By the first weeks in December the British government was coming under increasing pressure from the United States, Labour, the Liberal Democrats and some Tories for more action. The Defence Secretary agreed that some extension of the UN mandate might be required, but he ruled out active intervention by ground forces, claiming that this would require some 100,000 troops. A meeting of Mr Major and President Bush on 20 December resulted in agreement to work for a UN resolution on the enforcement of the 'no-fly zone' in Bosnia, but the Prime Minister continued to insist that the safety of the British troops engaged in relief work was paramount.

A decision had been taken in August to send some British aircraft to assist the United States and France in the maintenance of a round-the-clock air exclusion zone over southern Iraq. Mr Major accused Saddam Husain of engaging in 'systematic murder and genocide' against the Shia Muslims and marsh Arabs in Iraq. Mr Hurd added that, while the air exclusion zone was not as yet covered by a UN resolution, action in cases of extreme humanitarian need was permitted under international law. In December two British aircraft joined in relief operations in Somalia.

Memories of allied bombing of Dresden at the end of World War II clouded the Queen's state visit to Germany in October. The five-day tour was marked by several outbursts of ill-feeling and criticism on both sides. *Die Welt*, however, welcomed the visit as an important sign of European solidarity.

On 23 November the Beijing government, in response to efforts by the new governor of Hong Kong to win Chinese acceptance of moves towards greater democracy in the colony by 1995, ruled out further talks until the reform plans were dropped (see also IX.2.iii). China subsequently stepped up the pressure with a warning that it would not honour leases or contracts signed before 1997 without its approval. There were also hints that China might cease to uphold the joint Anglo-Chinese declaration of 1984 under which the island's way of life was to be protected for 50 years after the handover of sovereignty in 1997.

The GATT global trade talks reached a crisis in the autumn, with the British anxiously searching for a compromise between the EC and the United States on farm subsidies and other issues. Following an apparent breakthrough, on 18 December the UK and US governments announced their determination to complete a substantive agreement within a month. However, French opposition to the proposed terms meant that progress to a final accord remained uncertain.

7.   THE ECONOMY

'AFTER hubris, nemesis', commented *The Guardian* on government economic policy shortly before sterling's mid-September collapse and the consequential suspension of membership of the ERM (see I.4). For almost nine months ministers had insisted that there was no alternative to the pursuit of low (or even zero) inflation through membership of the ERM, despite the cripplingly high interest rates attached to the privilege. The September crisis and its outcome represented a major humiliation for the government and brought renewed criticism of the Treasury's judgment and skills. Evidence later in the year suggested that the Bank of England had been giving some thought to the merits of devaluation as early as June, and that it had become increasingly pessimistic in the days immediately before 'Black Wednesday'.

Finally the government itself seemed willing to concede that it might have been too dogmatic and too reliant on its own officials in the Treasury. Among the seven experts selected in December to serve on a new advisory panel on economic policy were three economists who had been described by Mr Major before the September crisis as 'quack doctors' and peddlers of miracle cures. The choice included Professor Wynne Godley of Cambridge, who had incurred particular displeasure during the Thatcher years. In the interval the government itself had been struggling to put together a new policy. It now stressed the importance of low interest rates and a more competitive pound. But given heavy government borrowing, the fears of higher interest rates and inflation if there were too sharp a fall in sterling, ministers had only limited room for manoeuvre.

The Treasury conceded early in the year that Britain was suffering the biggest one-year fall in output since the Great Depression of the early 1930s. Estimates of growth for 1992 were revised downwards. The governor of the Bank of England highlighted the uncontrolled credit boom of the late 1980s as a major cause of the present troubles. Others were more pointed in their criticism of market deregulation in the 1980s, tax cuts at the peak of the boom and neglect of manufacturing industry.

In his budget speech on 10 March the Chancellor was moderately hopeful concerning the current account deficit, and anticipated a PSBR of £28,000 million for 1992–93. These estimates were soon being revised upwards, with £40,000 million emerging as the possible PSBR level in 1993–94. The Treasury Chief Secretary, facing departmental bids for an extra £14,000 million, issued a mid-summer reminder that government spending had already reached 42 per cent of national output.

In July ministers scrapped the National Economic Development Council (NEDC or 'Neddy'), a relic of a Conservative bid in 1962 to improve the nation's economic performance. At the same time there were hints that the Department of Trade and Industry under Mr Heseltine was disposed to question some aspects of the hands-off, market-based approach to manufacturing industry of the 1980s. Although it was stressed that any changes would have to be implemented without extra money, the DTI professed interest in the methods used with great success by the Japanese Ministry of Trade and Industry (MITI). Particular emphasis was laid on helping to improve the competitiveness of British industry—mainly by assisting in the acquisition and use of relevant information.

On 22 July the cabinet reached agreement on a far-reaching overhaul of public expenditure. The old system of bargaining between the Treasury and individual departments was to be replaced by a cabinet committee chaired by the Chancellor of the Exchequer. There would be strict spending limits for every year up to and including 1995–96 (a possible election year), and gains by any departments would be balanced by cuts elsewhere. Small increases in public spending in real terms were envisaged.

A number of small cuts in interest rates in the months before the September crisis supplied no lasting stimulus to the economy. Given the fall in inflation, real interest rates remained relatively high, thus having a deterrent effect on borrowers. The collapse of the housing market had left many people with mortgages in excess of the current value of their homes. By November more than a million were reckoned to be in the position of having what was called 'negative equity value' in their homes. This was particularly true of first-time buyers in the south-east of England on homes bought since 1988. Property prices fell by an average of 10 per cent between April 1991 and the end of 1992.

An alarming acceleration occurred in company, and still more so in individual, insolvencies in the third quarter. Rises of 20 and 37 per cent were recorded compared with the same period in 1991. Fewer than one in five companies were reported to be working at full capacity. There was a widespread fall in confidence at this time.

The decline in Britain's manufacturing base over the years since 1979 was again attracting attention. Employment in this sector had fallen from 39 per cent of the national total in 1979 to less than 28 per cent in 1991, leaving Britain with one of the smallest manufacturing bases among leading industrial states. Manufactures accounted for some 62 per cent of foreign trade but only a quarter of GDP. Imports met some 30 per cent of the national demand for such goods. The financial sector and other 'invisible' earners, it was argued, could not hope to fill all the gaps left by this industrial decline.

After the September ERM crisis, the Chancellor outlined a 'British' economic policy based on 'a range of indicators'—including the money supply, inflation and the exchange rate. But jobs cuts were accelerating as employers lost hope of an early upswing. At the end of October British Steel announced a 20 per cent cut in production due to a worldwide slump in demand, and put much of its workforce on short time. It had already declared a loss of £55 million in the year to 31 March, with serious job cuts planned for 1993. Other industries and services to announce job losses were British Aerospace, British Telecom, the Post Office, several banks, Ford, Vickers and Swan Hunters, as well as British Coal (see I.5 above). The building industry was also facing a bleak future, and begged for prompt government action. A CBI spokesman called for 'a clear and coherent explanation' of government economic strategy, together with public spending on capital programmes. Hopeful signs in October were confined to low inflation and a cheaper pound.

In the eyes of foreign investors in the context of the EC, Britain lay somewhere between the high cost and high productivity levels of Northern Europe and the low cost and less productive South. Energy prices were noted as a disincentive together with the current uncertainties as to Britain's future in the Community. Although one-third of all Japanese and American investment in the EC was concentrated in the UK, new Japanese investment in 1991 had fallen to only 20 per cent of the European total. On 16 December, however, Toyota's chairman (as his company began car production in a large new factory in Derbyshire) expressed great confidence in Britain's future in the EC and as a car producer.

A CBI report, called *Making it in Britain* was published on 8 November. This identified a performance gap of 20–40 per cent between the UK and its main competitors. Some of the economic achievements of the 1980s were being put at risk. The CBI was looking for a partnership with the government and the financial community to develop a long-term strategy for greater competitiveness to raise Britain from a position of 13th among 22 leading countries. Although Britain had some first-rate companies, it needed many more with comparable levels of investment, research and development. Productivity rises of 5 per cent a year were required and an increase in the share of world manufacturing exports from 4.6 to 5.6 per cent to erase the seemingly intractable trade gap. This implied a £10,000 million increase in exports.

Leading businessmen complained that they had been held at arm's length by the government since the 1980s, and of too much short-term thinking (the 'dogma of the day') in political and financial circles. Some hoped that current government vulnerability and problems would give industry greater influence over future policy-making. Many harsh words were uttered at a CBI conference in November. 'Vacuity', insisted one critic of government policy, had replaced 'vanity' after the ERM disaster.

Sections of industry derived some comfort from the Chancellor's autumn statement on 12 November (see I.5), though many economists thought even the Treasury's modest prediction of 1 per cent growth in 1993 too optimistic. There was also the worry that recovery, when it came, would soon run into difficulties through shortages of skilled workers arising from the inadequacies of British training schemes.

The five top UK export performers were aircraft, oil, machine tools, financial services and Scotch whisky. Commercial vehicle manufacturers, sections of the car industry and car components manufacturers were also showing themselves to be increasingly competitive if and when market conditions permitted.

The main economic indicators for 1992 were mostly disappointing, and even the hints of an upturn were not easy to interpret. Retail sales in the last quarter rose by 0.3 per cent compared with the previous one, despite a seasonally adjusted fall of 0.7 per cent in December. This was a 1.3 per cent increase over the same quarter in 1991. The service sector as a whole fell by 0.3 per cent during the year to October, and was 2.6 per cent below its peak at the beginning of 1991. Manufacturers found the cost of imported raw materials rising at a time when they could not increase their prices on the domestic market. Factory gate prices rose by only 3.3 per cent in the twelve months to August (the lowest rise since February 1968). Productivity was growing at around 3.2 per cent in the middle of the year.

Manufacturing output in November was virtually unchanged compared with the same month in 1991. Even with the buoyant North Sea oil and gas production, industrial output had risen by only 0.2 per cent. Manufacturing output actually fell by 0.5 per cent in the three months to November. The recession had now sliced 4 per cent off the GDP since the 1990 peak. There were, however, some renewed signs of confidence in the car industry, with the exception of Ford, which was reducing its workforce.

In December the PSBR reached £25,700 million for the first nine months of the financial year, more than double the figure at the same point in 1991. Progress in the reduction of the current account deficit in 1991 was reversed. Indeed, record imports caused the trade gap to widen to £1,740 million in December, the largest monthly gap since July 1990. Given the addition of invisible earnings, the current account deficit for the year as a whole stood at £11,820 million, or nearly twice that recorded for 1991. Devaluation was adding to the cost of imports, while there was little evidence as yet of consistent export growth. The figures confirmed fears of deep underlying structural problems in the British economy. Export penetration on this scale was unprecedented at this stage in the economic cycle. The CBI did, however, report a rise in business optimism in the last quarter, though many more job losses were expected in 1993. The reserves, which had been reasonably steady, fell by £1,284 million in August even before the autumn crisis. Losses in September-October totalled around £7,500 million.

By December inflation had dropped to 2.6 per cent. Manufacturing pay settlements averaged only 3.1 per cent in the three months to November, with one manufacturer in three imposing a pay freeze. Unemployment rose from 9.2 per cent in January to 10.4 per cent (2,970,000) in December, an increase of 1.4 million since April 1990. It topped 10 per cent in the south-east of England (London 11.3 per cent) for the first time, with job losses rising by no less than a quarter during the year.

With devaluation, Britain seemed by some calculations to be in danger of slipping into the ranks of the poorer states within the EC. This definition applied to states with a per capita income of less than 90 per cent of the European average (the British figure having stood at 103 per cent in 1985). The Low Pay Unit reported on 27 September that nearly 10 million (or almost four in ten) of the workforce were earning less than the European 'decency' threshold of £207 per week.

8. SCOTLAND

THE recession, which had hitherto affected Scotland less severely than many regions, deepened in 1992, causing a fall of some 1.7 per cent in GDP. Unemployment reached almost a quarter of a million. One estimate put the loss of manufacturing jobs in Scotland at four out of ten since 1979. In June British Steel's works at Ravenscraig closed, with the loss of 2,000 jobs, two years ahead of the original plan. Defence cutbacks included the American withdrawal from the Holy Loch submarine base. An order for three Type 23 frigates provided some relief for the Yarrow shipyard (on the Clyde), but despite this and two orders from Malaysia the workforce was cut by 510. A big question-mark also hung over the future of the Rosyth dockyard. The biggest private sector employer in the Highlands, McDermott-Scotland, announced major job cutbacks. A fall of 27 per cent in Scottish farm incomes was reported for 1991.

While exports from the chemical industry had increased by almost 28 per cent in the year to October, computer and related products fell by 7.3 per cent. Nevertheless, this sector (with whisky) continued to head the list of exporters. The electronics industry received further boosts in November with new investment by the American company, Jabil Circuits, at Livingstone, and from a new defence contract for GEC Ferranti in Edinburgh.

The future of the Union was the focus of much debate in Scotland, especially during the general election. But the polls gave contradictory signals. Estimates of support for independence continued to run ahead of actual votes for the SNP. Overall it appeared that political change was given less weight than economic and social issues.

Both Labour and Liberal Democrats promised Scots their own parliament. Even Scottish Tories were not in entire agreement on the Union as it stood. But Mr Major insisted on 24 February that the United Kingdom would be 'infinitely diminished' without Scotland. Independence, he claimed, would cause bitterness and chaos. Although he later conceded that 'no nation can be held irrevocably in a union against its will', he implied that Westminster would not easily be persuaded to let Scotland go its own way. He did offer a vague promise not to close his mind to ideas to improve the quality of government for Scots.

The Conservatives were relieved by the outcome of the general election. A small increase in their share of the Scottish vote (it rose by 1.6 per cent to 25 per cent) gave them 11 seats (instead of nine). In contrast, the SNP, though increasing its vote by 50 per cent to 630,000 (21.5 per cent), had to be content with three MPs. Both the Tories and SNP claimed successes in the subsequent local elections on 7 May, with the latter squeezing into second place in votes gained. *The Times* on 18 April warned the Tories not to be complacent. It thought some devolution appropriate and not incompatible with the Union. The Scottish TUC on 21 April joined the call for a referendum. The SNP went further and declared that Scots should hold their own multi-option referendum unless the government assented.

This was ruled out by Mr Major on 11 September. At most he promised to preserve Scotland's culture and traditions in genuine partnership within the UK as a whole, but he offered no clues as to the likely outcome of the stocktaking exercise which he had ordered after the election. Meanwhile, plans to privatize Scottish water threatened to be almost as unpopular as the community charge (poll tax).

The SNP at its annual conference in September promised all-out war on this issue. It also outlined a four-year plan to secure victory at the next general election. Faced by left-right divisions in the party, its leader, Alex Salmond, expressed his determination to 'anchor [the SNP] . . . on the left of centre of Scottish politics' and in the traditions of European social democracy.

Ian Lang, the Scottish Secretary, announced a £13,450 million programme for 1993–94, hailing it as a package for jobs and growth. He challenged earlier claims that Scotland would be less generously treated than in the past when figures were revised in the light of a fall in population. Spending per head, he claimed, would be 30 per cent higher than in England. But opposition spokesmen remained sceptical, and argued that the programme did not begin to address the nation's social and economic problems.

On 11 December (the first day of the EC summit in Edinburgh) 4,000 Scottish fishermen and their families demonstrated against government plans which threatened to keep fishing fleets in port for more than half of 1993. On 20 December the outcome of talks between the EC and Norway entrusted conservation to national governments, and greatly increased haddock quotas in 1993.

At least 20,000 people on 12 December took part in a 'Scotland Demands Democracy' march through Edinburgh. Representatives from all the opposition parties (which had polled an aggregate of 75 per cent of the votes in the general election) signed a three-page declaration calling for 'our own parliament'. The speeches from SNP, Labour and Liberal Democrat spokesmen, however, revealed important differences of emphasis once they departed from attacks on the government.

The Centennial Mod was held in Oban in October and demonstrated the continuing vitality of the Gaelic culture.

9. WALES

ONCE again, despite voting overwhelmingly for parties other than the Conservatives in the general election on 9 April, the Welsh people found themselves ruled by a Conservative government. This was a particular disappointment to the Labour Party, which polled 49.5 per cent of the vote in Wales and which had hoped to see a Welsh MP, Neil Kinnock, become Prime Minister. The Conservative share of the vote in Wales fell to 28.6 per cent. Although Brecon and Radnor, Monmouth and the Vale of Glamorgan, previously lost at by-elections, were regained by the Conservatives with narrow majorities, three seats were lost to Labour. These included Pembroke, the seat of the under-secretary at the Welsh Office, Nicholas Bennett, as well as that of his predecessor, Ian Grist, at Cardiff Central. The Liberal Democrats lost two seats, leaving Alex Carlile at Montgomery as the only Liberal Democrat MP in Wales. The surprise result was that in Ceredigion and Pembroke North, where the long-serving Liberal Democrat, Geraint Howells, was defeated by Plaid Cymru's Cynog Dafis. Supported by the Green Party, he won on a swing of 13.3 per cent, by far the highest in Wales. Party representation in Wales after the election was Labour 27, Conservative 6, Plaid Cymru 4 and Liberal Democrat 1.

David Hunt remained Secretary of State for Wales after the election, despite reports that the post had been offered to Kenneth Baker. He was supported at the Welsh Office by Sir Wyn Roberts, the long-serving minister of state, and a new parliamentary under-secretary, Gwilym Jones. Ann Clwyd succeeded Barry Jones as shadow Secretary of State, but in October she was moved to shadow the Heritage Secretary and was replaced by the ambitious MP for Caerphilly, Ron Davies.

The Secretary of State came under criticism on a number of matters during the autumn. His ignorance of the announcement to close the Point of Ayr colliery in Clwyd led to accusations that decisions of importance to Wales were taken without consulting him. Critics also pointed to Mr Hunt's powers of patronage which, it was alleged, led to a high proportion of Conservative Party supporters being nominated to Welsh quangos. It was reported that there were over 80 operating in Wales, the Welsh Office being directly responsible for 55 of them. With local government powers being diminished, critics claimed that Wales was now governed by quangos, and this appeared to strengthen the argument of those campaigning for greater democratic control of the Welsh Office through a Welsh Assembly. In December one quango, the Welsh Development Agency, was heavily criticized by the Commons public accounts committee for its ineffective financial control, following a damning National Audit Office report.

Although the Welsh Office continued to be optimistic in its assessment of the Welsh economy, in general economists were more circumspect. They pointed to a weak infrastructure ill-equipped to compete in Europe and to the uneven development of the Welsh economy whereby the south-east and north-east of Wales prospered while the north-west and the south Wales valleys remained depressed. Government figures revealed that aid to industry in assisted areas in Wales fell from £197 million in 1981 to £134 million in 1991 and that during the same period average earnings in Wales plunged to 11 per cent below the average for Britain. By the end of the year the unemployment figure for Wales was over 10 per cent.

Unease over police methods in south Wales was highlighted by two cases brought before the Court of Appeal. Two brothers gaoled in 1985 for the murder of a Swansea sex-shop manageress were released in July, while the so-called Cardiff Three, imprisoned for the brutal killing of a prostitute, were freed in December. Meanwhile, police in north Wales were investigating disturbing allegations of the sexual and physical abuse of up to 200 children in council care in Clwyd and Gwynedd. In Gwent evidence of cruelty led to the closure of the Tŷ Mawr children's home near Abergavenny.

The results of the 1991 census, published during the year, showed a small decrease in the number of Welsh speakers but there was a substantial increase among children able to speak Welsh, suggesting that years of decline in the language were coming to an end. The long-awaited Welsh Language Bill was published in December but it was immediately criticized for not going far enough in establishing equal rights for Welsh speakers. The bill proposed that a new Welsh Language Board should be set up to administer schemes which public bodies would be required to provide when giving services in Welsh. It would also investigate complaints and award grants to assist Welsh language groups.

10.   NORTHERN IRELAND

THE year was one of political talks, sometimes historic, struggling in the context of a serious security situation. The public weariness with violence impelled the four main religious leaders to carry the message to prime ministers in London and Dublin; it also provoked individual churchmen to engage the paramilitaries in private discussions. The economy suffered in the recession, unemployment reaching 15 per cent. There were other local historic events, including the acceptance of 100 per cent state finance by Catholic schools, the provision of wind-powered electricity on Rathlin Island and the province's most expensive libel case, in which Barry McGuigan lost to his former boxing manager, Barney Eastwood. Two other legal cases provoked interest: in July three of the 'UDR Four' (former members of the Ulster Defence Regiment convicted of murder in 1986) were released by the Court of Appeal; and in October the first parliamentary election petition in the province since 1955 was heard into claims that Dr Joe Hendron's victory for the Social Democratic and Labour Party (SDLP) over Gerry Adams of Sinn Féin (SF) in West Belfast was the result of over-spending.

The high level of violence, including 33 deaths and regular car bombs in Belfast in January and February, required additional security resources. The extra troops remained after a review in July and the total deployed was 18,000 at one time. The official total of 84 deaths in 1992 was 10 fewer than in 1991 but the impression was of an even bloodier year. In part, this was because the 3,000 deaths milestone was passed in August, in part because of the number of multiple killings. Moreover seven deaths related to the Northern Ireland problem—six in England and one in the Republic of Ireland—were not counted in the total. Nine members of the security forces were killed, including three Royal Ulster Constabulary (RUC) personnel (one a woman) and six soldiers, three from the Royal Irish Regiment formed only in July. There were 75 civilian deaths, including paramilitaries. The security forces were responsible for ten deaths; the other 74 victims were fairly evenly divided between alleged republican and loyalist paramilitaries, with the latter slightly ahead. In August the UK government proscribed the Ulster Defence Association (UDA) because it was 'actively and primarily engaged in the commission of criminal, terrorist acts'.

After a very destructive year with respect to property, payment for criminal damage was expected to be nearer £75 million than the estimated £55 million. The IRA continued to attack a wide range of targets but the car and van bomb in the centre of towns and cities was the main device. Belfast was a frequent target but provincial towns, such as Lurgan, Bangor and Coleraine were also hit. Incendiaries were used in shops and stores. Similar tactics were also used in England, where a huge bomb at the Baltic Exchange in London in April (see also I.1) cost three lives and an estimated £750 million repair bill (exceeding all criminal damage claims in Northern Ireland since 1969). Bombs were again placed in Whitehall, and in May MI5 was given responsibility for anti-terrorist intelligence in Britain. Loyalist terrorists placed incendiaries in Dublin, Dundalk and Donegal.

Whereas the talks process had been suspended in the summer of 1991 (see AR 1991, p. 40), the intervention of the Prime Minister in the security situation in January, and an invitation to party leaders to Number 10, broke the logjam. The party leaders agreed on 28 February to renew political talks and the first plenary session took place at Stormont on 9 March. The general election (on 9 April) stalled proceedings, but the new Secretary of State, Sir Patrick Mayhew, resumed the three-strand approach on 29 April after Anglo-Irish Conference meetings were suspended for three months. In the elections, the Unionist parties again took 13 of the 17 Northern Ireland seats, while the SDLP, by dint of its gain in West Belfast, increased from three seats to four.

A plenary session on 5 May revealed that the parties disagreed on the future agenda and timetable of the process. Although no agreement was reached on strand one, it was decided to proceed to a strand two meeting on 19 June in London, under the chairmanship of Sir Ninian Stephen. Moreover, the first meeting of strand three took place in London on 30 June, after which strands two and three began work concurrently on 1 July. The talks were the first formal discussions between Unionist politicians and Irish government ministers since Sunningdale in 1973. After a summer break, the strand two talks resumed on 2 September with smaller delegations and a new business committee, but unresolved problems reappeared. An agenda dispute led to the withdrawal of the main Democratic Unionist (DUP) delegates, Rev Ian Paisley and Peter Robinson, and a warning three days later, on 12 September, that the Ulster Unionists (UUP) might also leave. Despite the secrecy of the talks, the leaking of separate British and Irish documents on North-South links revealed differences over consultative and executive institutions. When the talks reconvened in Dublin on 21–23 September, the Ulster Unionists attended but the DUP did not. On the Dublin side the problems of the then coalition government were evident when Progressive Democrats were refused participation by the Taoiseach. The talks reached an impasse on the territorial question and moved on to North-South economic co-operation. Further disagreement over the Anglo-Irish Conference due that month was resolved in London on 25 September, when Prime Ministers Major and Reynolds agreed a final postponement until 16 November.

In view of this deadline, the DUP leaders returned to the Stormont talks on 30 September. After a further six days of discussion, Sir Patrick presented a summary paper on 12 October and a lengthy strand three meeting between the two governments took place two days later. Another ten days of bilateral meetings between Sir Ninian Stephen and the parties occurred before Sir Patrick told the Commons on 29 October that it was still possible to reach some agreement before the deadline. However, the volume of inter-party criticism increased by the day. Early in November Sir Ninian began another round of bilaterals, but the calling of a general election on 5 November in the Republic (see II.1.vii) effectively ended the strand two and three talks, the final meeting of which occurred at Stormont on 10 November. The Irish government regarded the break as 'an intermission', and Sir Patrick told the Commons on 11 November that 'a comprehensive settlement' could still be achieved and that the parties could still meet informally. Unionists were less optimistic, DUP in particular regarding the talks as 'dead'. However, the Anglo-Irish Conference in Dublin on 16 November reaffirmed that the objectives of the talks were valid and achievable.

In December Sir Patrick Mayhew caused something of a stir by making a speech of the 'what if' variety at the University of Ulster at Coleraine, in which he seemed to be setting out a vision of life after an IRA ceasefire. For the third successive year, a ceasefire was called by the IRA at Christmas, but it lasted only 72 hours.

It was a difficult year for the economy. Business failures—2 per cent up on 1991 at 578—were the worst ever. Bankruptcies were also up 10 per cent, the service, retail and building sectors being particularly affected. A survey published at the end of July showed that the industrial base was the smallest for 40 years. Unemployment continued to rise from its already high level of 14.5 per cent in January to a peak of 15.2 per cent in August. By November it had fallen for three successive months, but only to 14.3 per cent.

In further privatization steps, Northern Ireland's power stations were sold in March for £353 million, despite the unanimous opposition of local parties. At the end of the year discussion of the imminence and costs of water privatization increased. Harland and Wolff declared a pre-tax profit of £2.1 million but suffered cancelled orders. On the other hand, Bombardier Shorts continued to find new work, receiving orders from Boeing worth £80 million and a new missile order from Malaysia. The agricultural sector lived with difficult times after a fall of 10 per cent in farm incomes in 1991. The focus of the GATT world trade talks on food subsidies and the effect of EC agricultural policy reform meant that local producers expected pressure on several sectors.

After two months of dire warnings about coming stringency, the public expenditure figures, published in November, showed a 5.3 per cent increase to £7,460 million. The Secretary of State announced that he had negotiated a safety net for the Compensation Agency, which was expected to need £75–80 million in 1992/93. Despite the safety net, the costs of compensation for the continuing destruction in Northern Ireland could not but affect the general range of expenditure on health, housing, education and social services.

II WESTERN, CENTRAL AND SOUTHERN EUROPE

1. FRANCE—GERMANY—ITALY—BELGIUM—THE NETHERLANDS— LUXEMBOURG—IRELAND

i. FRANCE

CAPITAL: Paris   AREA: 544,000 sq km   POPULATION: 56,400,000 ('90)
OFFICIAL LANGUAGE: French   POLITICAL SYSTEM: presidential parliamentary
democracy
HEAD OF STATE AND GOVERNMENT: President François Mitterrand (since May '81)
RULING PARTIES: Socialist Party (PS) holds presidency; government is centre-left
coalition of the PS, Left Radicals (MRG), Union for French Democracy (UDF) and
independents
PRINCIPAL MINISTERS: Pierre Bérégovoy (PS/prime minister), Roland Dumas
(PS/foreign affairs), Michel Sapin (PS/economy, finance), Michel Charasse
(PS/budget) Pierre Joxe (PS/defence), Paul Quilès (PS/interior, public security),
Michel Vauzelle (PS/justice)
INTERNATIONAL ALIGNMENT: NATO (outside command structure), OECD, EC,
Francophonie
CURRENCY: franc (end-'92 £1=F8.36, US$1=F5.52)   GNP PER CAPITA: US$19,490 ('90)
MAIN EXPORT EARNERS: machinery & transport equipment, manufactures, chemicals,
food & beverages, tourism

THERE was an air of *fin de règne* to 1992 as the political shadows
gathered around President François Mitterrand and his ministers, and
a seemingly endless succession of *affaires* fed the traditional national
cynicism about the political class in general.

At the start of the year Edith Cresson's deeply unpopular government, appointed in May 1991 (see AR 1991, p. 97), struggled for
survival. In January the ruling Socialists (PS) found themselves snubbed
and barracked at an anti-racist demonstration in Paris by groups who
were formerly strong supporters. Pierre Mauroy resigned as PS first
secretary in frustration at his inability to end the party's endemic
factional warfare. He was succeeded by the former prime minister,
Laurent Fabius. In February the government ran into a storm for
allowing the Palestinian leader, George Habash, to come to Paris for
medical treatment. The incident led to five senior officials, but no
politicians, losing their posts and enhanced the impression of muddle or
worse at the top. The final nail in Mme Cresson's coffin came when the
Socialists polled only 16.4 per cent of the vote in the regional elections
in March, by far their worst result since the party's renaissance in the
early 1970s. The moderate right-wing opposition parties, the Rally for
the Republic (RPR) and Union for French Democracy (UDF), took
33.2 per cent, the two Green parties 14.4 per cent, the National Front
13.9 per cent and the Communists 8.7 per cent. The result was seen not

only as reflecting the electorate's boredom and frustration but also as implying that several decades in which stable government had rested on one or two large parties might be coming to an end.

Sacked in the wake of her party's regional defeat, Mme Cresson complained bitterly that the President had never been prepared to let her choose her own team. Jacques Delors declined the poisoned chalice, so the premiership passed to the Finance Minister, Pierre Bérégovoy. He worked hard to restore the government's fortunes, but was dogged by ill luck. Within weeks the new Minister for Urban Affairs, Bernard Tapie, a flamboyant self-made millionaire business-man, stepped down after being accused of swindling a business partner (who was also an opposition politician). But this was only one of a series of scandals mostly relating to the murky waters of party finance. Although almost all parties were affected, the Socialists were the most cruelly spotlighted.

The gravest affair of all was the trial of senior medical administrators for supplying contaminated blood to haemophiliacs in the mid-1980s, resulting already in 250 deaths from AIDS and a further 1,200 HIV-positive cases. The extent of the tragedy and evidence about the administrators' behaviour and attitudes deeply shocked the public. There were demands that the prime minister of the time, M. Fabius, and two other ministers should also face trial. Just before Christmas, amid great acrimony, parliament set the appropriate procedures in motion, but not before M. Fabius (whom few seriously believed to be culpable) had defended himself so maladroitly as to jeopardize his not inconsiderable political ambitions.

M. Bérégovoy was also unfortunate enough to inherit a dispute over the implementation of a new system of penalty points for driving convictions that led to thousands of road hauliers blocking major roads for a fortnight in the holiday season. The readiness of the Communists to vote with the conservative parties in a censure debate in June (which the government survived by only three votes) was a further sign of its fragility at the parliamentary level. M. Bérégovoy also had to contend with the farmers. Though reduced in numbers, their electoral influence and capacity for disruptive protest pushed his government into intransigence towards further compromises over agriculture in the GATT negotiations.

However, the most substantial issue of the year was Europe. The Maastricht treaty met unexpectedly strong opposition in parliament, where an RPR deputy, Philippe Séguin, broke party ranks to fight the ratification bill, which passed by 398 votes to 77 with 99 abstentions. With Maastricht apparently enjoying substantial public support and the moderate right in deep disarray, President Mitterrand must have expected to strengthen his position by calling a referendum on the constitutional changes required by Maastricht in the immediate wake of the Danish rejection (see II.2.i). However, energetic campaigning by M. Séguin and Charles Pasqua, and the opportunity the referendum gave to voters to voice their wider discontents, meant that the proposal soon appeared in danger of defeat. It was saved, but only just, as much by the rallying of Jacques Chirac and Valéry Giscard d'Estaing from the conservative opposition as by the government's own efforts. On a turnout of 69.78 per cent, 13,162,992 voted 'yes' (51.04 per cent) on 20 September and 12,623,582 'No' (48.95 per cent), a margin of only 539,410 votes.

So precarious a victory added nothing to the government's strength. A few days before the vote, President Mitterrand underwent surgery for a prostate condition which was subsequently diagnosed as cancerous. He was soon active again, especially in a busy autumn of international contacts. In December he proposed a substantial programme of constitutional reform, which he presented as giving parliament a greater role than it had hitherto had in the Fifth Republic. Denounced by M. Chirac as 'a fresh attempt at diversion and division', the proposals were referred to a special committee of experts who were to report before the March 1993 parliamentary elections. Nevertheless, though the President was determined to show that he was in charge, there were inevitably doubts about whether he would complete his term, which ran to 1995. His political survival was no less in question as the Socialists increasingly despaired at the apparently inevitable prospect of a devastating defeat, even though their opponents remained deeply divided. Short of a miracle, President Mitterrand would have to find some *modus vivendi* with a hostile coalition. The return of M. Tapie to the Urban Affairs Ministry in December, after charges against him had been withdrawn, did little to raise PS morale.

Yet despite the country's morose political mood, the French economy was in better shape than many others. The franc withstood speculative pressure in September, at the time of Britain's exit from the European exchange rate mechanism (see I.4). Subsequent uncertainty whether its parity could be maintained reflected political uncertainties rather than compelling weaknesses in the economy. While economic activity slowed during the year, GDP rose some 1.4 per cent, more than in most neighbouring countries, and retail prices increased by only 2.0 per cent. Earnings rose 3.8 per cent and the trade balance was modestly healthy. The main black spot was unemployment, which went over 10 per cent during the autumn—another bleak omen for the approaching election. The 1993 budget envisaged a 3.4 per cent increase in expenditure and a 2.8 per cent fall in receipts; no new taxes were imposed, so the deficit was projected, optimistically, to rise to the equivalent of £19,000 million. However, at the end of the year sharp rises in tobacco taxes were announced, following on the heels of widely-flouted restrictions on smoking in public places and more successful bans on tobacco advertising.

DEFENCE AND FOREIGN AFFAIRS. The government's defence restructuring plan, Project 1997, launched the armed forces into a period of unprecedented change. Although M. Bérégovoy insisted that the nuclear deterrent remained the keystone of defence policy, weapons tests in the Pacific were suspended, several nuclear defence projects were cut or deferred in favour of conventional arms, and France at last signed the Non-Proliferation Treaty (NPT). The new 'restructured' army would be essentially denuclearized, falling from 260,000 men to 224,000 over five years. It would be reduced from 11 divisions to seven, one of them having a dual role as part of the Franco-German corps that President Mitterrand and Chancellor Kohl agreed in May should become operational by 1995. The army's main tasks would be overseas intervention by the Rapid Action Force and home defence by the Mechanized Armour Corps.

The 1992–94 weapons programme embodied a reduction in armaments expenditure in real terms. Fiercely criticized by the opposition, for the first time it was not presented to parliament. The air force would have 375 combat aircraft rather than 450. The Mirage 2000 programme was cut and delivery of the new Rafale fighter spread over a longer period. Development of the M5 nuclear missile for the new generation of Triumphant-class submarines would continue, but for only four vessels, to be delivered between 1995 and 2005. The number of Atlantic 2 patrol aircraft would be 28 in place of 42, while the army would now receive 800 rather than 1,100 of the new Leclerc tanks. The Hadès missile programme, frozen earlier, was now halted. The one notable area of expansion was in satellite intelligence systems. This 'deceleration' of expenditure was a combination of peace dividend and recognition that earlier plans had been financially over-optimistic. It produced anguished cries from areas losing military installations and anxiety among commanders, who saw involvement in humanitarian operations in Bosnia and Somalia as stretching even their present resources.

Diplomatically, a quietly active year had few high points. A visit by President Yeltsin of Russia in February was the occasion for mending fences after his chilly reception on the previous occasion. January had seen the withdrawal of additional troops sent to Chad, once it was clear that the offensive by supporters of ex-President Hissène Habré had failed (see VI.3.xi), but in March there were bitter protests in Niger at the French refusal to help the government of Amadou Cheiffou in the face of an apparent attempted coup (see VI.3.vii). To the French this reflected a reluctance to be Africa's gendarme; to critics it seemed at odds with President Mitterrand's pressure for democratic reforms in the continent.

In July the President's surprise visit to Sarajevo caught the headlines as a demonstration of French determination to be at the centre of any joint European action (see III.1.vi). French political opinion was mainly critical of the inertia of the Western allies in former Yugoslavia, seen as further proof that 'Europe' did not as yet exist politically. In all, some 2,800 troops were dispatched to the country to support humanitarian efforts. France also sent a sizeable contingent to the United Nations operations in Somalia (see VI.1.ii). The year ended with a clash with China over the sale of 60 Mirage 2000 aircraft to Taiwan. The Chinese closed the French consulate-general in Canton and barred France from tendering for Canton's new metro.

OVERSEAS DEPARTMENTS AND TERRITORIES. Overseas France in many respects had a troubled year, with anxieties about the impact of the single European market, notably among the banana growers of Martinique and Guadeloupe (partly relieved at the Edinburgh EC summit in December). There were also serious allegations of corruption by local politicians in Guadeloupe, French Guiana, New Caledonia, Réunion and Polynesia.

The situation was most serious in Polynesia, where alleged wrongdoing by the territory's three leading indigenous politicians combined with interminable quarrels between them. The head of the territorial government, Gaston Flosse, was sentenced to six months, suspended, for corruption but continued in office. The territorial assembly was occupied and paralysed for six weeks by supporters of its president, Emile Vernaudon. The opposition called for 'emancipation' of the colony on the New Caledonia model. An attempt by the Minister for Overseas Departments and Territories, Louis Le Pensec, to bring the colony's warring factions together in a 'pact of progress' in May was only partly successful. After being evicted from the presidency, at the end of 1992 M. Vernaudon was forced from his seat, having boycotted sittings for over six months. The territory was also affected by a prolonged strike of port workers at Papeete in the early months of the year, while the suspension of French nuclear tests threatened the mainstay of its economy (see also X.2.ii).

In New Caledonia the nationalist FLNKS movement became increasingly critical of the slow pace of progress towards the 'Melanesianization' of public sector posts. Réunion experienced a renewed bout of rioting at the end of the year despite an earlier visit by M. Le Pensec with a pledge of a £15 million aid programme to create 5,000 jobs on the island. The long-running dispute with Canada over fishing rights in the Gulf of St Lawrence continued after a New York arbitration court awarded St Pierre and Miquelon a disappointingly small exclusive fishing zone. The islanders condemned the 'intransigence' of the Canadians in ensuing negotiations.

ii. GERMANY

CAPITAL: Berlin   AREA: 357,000 sq km   POPULATION: 79,500,000 ('90)
OFFICIAL LANGUAGE: German   POLITICAL SYSTEM: federal parliamentary democracy
HEAD OF STATE: President Richard von Weizsäcker (since July '84)
RULING PARTIES: Christian Democratic Union (CDU), Christian Social Union (CSU) &
    Free Democratic Party (FDP)
HEAD OF GOVERNMENT: Helmut Kohl (CDU), Federal Chancellor (since Oct '82)
PRINCIPAL MINISTERS: Friedrich Böhl (CDU/head of chancery), Klaus Kinkel
    (FDP/foreign affairs), Rudolf Seiters (CDU/interior), Sabine Leutheusser-
    Schnarrenberger (FDP/justice), Theo Waigel (CSU/finance), Jürgen Möllemann
    (FDP/economy), Volker Rühe (CDU/defence)
INTERNATIONAL ALIGNMENT: NATO, OECD, EC
CURRENCY: Deutschmark (end-'92 £1=DM2.45, US$1=DM1.62)
GNP PER CAPITA: US$22,320 ('90, West German figure)
MAIN EXPORT EARNERS: machinery and transport equipment, manufactures, chemicals

A period of relative normality for Germany after the country became
unified in 1990 was clouded by increasing economic difficulties, social
and political problems, and by disappointments for the federal government in the international sphere. For the most part, the reverses could
be traced to the largely unforeseen consequences of German unification
and the way in which it was implemented.

Despite all the evidence that had accumulated during the previous
year of the mounting costs of German unification and the economic
disaster in eastern Germany (the former German Democratic Republic), it was not until June that Chancellor Kohl was prepared to admit to
the Bundestag that there had been 'setbacks' in the unification process.
The effects of the boom which initially had benefited industry and
commerce in western Germany petered out during the year, and the
Federal Republic was also affected by the worldwide recession. Nonetheless, because of the high costs of subsidizing the bankrupt east
German economy and the consequent escalation of public borrowing,
inflationary pressures were a cause of concern, especially as the trade
unions were determined not to lose out. In February the public service
sector was hit by the first strikes since 1974; although the unions settled
for a wage rise of around 5.4 per cent, the Bundesbank, following its
own independent monetary policy, pushed interest rates higher. The
key discount rate reached a post-war high of 8.75 per cent in July.

The recession deepened towards the end of the year, amid some
forecasts of nil growth in the succeeding 12 months. In December the
rate of unemployment increased sharply. Official figures gave a total of
3,130,000 for Germany as a whole: around 2 million (6.6 per cent) in
the west and over 1 million (13.5 per cent) in the east. In an attempt
to remedy the situation, the government proposed a 'solidarity pact',
to be concluded between the government, the opposition, business
organizations and the trade unions. However, by the end of the year
little progress had been made, since the government ruled out any

general income tax increases before 1995, while the opposition was firmly against making cuts in social benefits.

With a major recession in prospect, the outlook for east Germany was serious, since it was dependent on the strength of the west German economy for subsidies and transfer payments. The official unemployment figure understated the true position, because 'disguised' unemployment (short-time working, enforced early retirement, work-creation schemes, retraining) effectively added a further 2 million, to give a rate in excess of 30 per cent. The problem was exacerbated by the policy of rapid privatization of former state concerns, implemented by the state holding company, the Treuhandanstalt. Originally it had 12,500 firms in its charge; by the end of the year there were still about 3,000, employing 500,000 people, a fifth of whom were on short-time working. German and foreign investment was held back mainly because of the low productivity and relatively high labour costs in east Germany.

The economic plight in the east was a major cause of social disaffection there, especially among young people. One result was an outbreak of anti-foreigner violence which led to international condemnation. In all, there were some 2,200 attacks in the course of the year, mainly, but not entirely, in eastern Germany. In August a hostel for foreign workers and political asylum seekers in Rostock was besieged and set on fire by a mob, virtually unhindered by the police, and applauded by local residents. These attacks continued throughout the rest of the year. Majority public opinion was incensed by these outrages and the damage they caused to Germany's standing abroad. In November a mass demonstration in protest was attended by 350,000 people in Berlin, and during November and December candle-lit processions were held in several west German cities. The federal government took some measures to counter the growth of right-wing extremism, since it was clear that neo-nazi groups were behind much of the violence. Four extremist organizations were banned.

One of the underlying problems, affecting both parts of Germany, was the continuing high level of immigration. In addition to 240,000 ethnic Germans from eastern Europe, no fewer than 430,000 people claimed political asylum in Germany in the course of the year. Despite the general recognition that an influx of this order could not be tolerated, the political parties were unable to agree on how the constitutional right to political asylum should be redefined in order to keep out those entering Germany purely on economic grounds. Negotiations between the ruling coalition of Christian Democrats (CDU/CSU) and Free Democrats (FDP) and the opposition Social Democratic Party (SPD) dragged on for the whole year without result and amid growing public concern.

An indication of this disquiet was shown in the results of elections, since both the CDU and the SPD lost ground, and right-wing parties benefited. In the Berlin municipal elections in May the right-wing Republicans scored 8.3 per cent of the vote and won seats on 23 of 25 local councils. In April elections in two west German states right-wing parties had notable successes: in Baden-Württemberg the previously unrepresented Republicans won 11 per cent of the vote, and in Schleswig-Holstein the right-wing German People's Union (DVU) came ahead of both the FDP and the Greens. These results shook the political establishment and were interpreted as a protest against the major parties for their failure to resolve the issue of political asylum.

Chancellor Kohl's hopes of speeding European unification in accordance with the EC's Maastricht treaty (ratified by the Bundestag in December) were dashed by its rejection by Danish voters in June (see II.2.i), and by the partial breakdown of the European Monetary System in September, when both Britain and Italy were forced to float their currencies. At the time, British official opinion put the blame on the Bundesbank for sticking to its high interest-rate policy and its failure to give sufficient support to sterling (see also I.4). Another event to sour Anglo-German relations was the decision to erect a statue in London to honour the memory of 'Bomber' Harris, who was responsible for the destruction of Dresden and other German cities during World War II. As a result, the subsequent state visit to Germany made by Queen Elizabeth in October, which included Dresden in the itinerary, was adversely affected. In Germany a celebration in October to mark the 50th anniversary of the start of space travel (i.e. the construction at Peenemünde of the V2 rocket used against Britain during the war) was scaled down after hostile publicity.

The retirement of Hans-Dietrich Genscher (FDP) in May, after 18 years as the country's Foreign Minister, marked the end of an era. His successor was Klaus Kinkel, relatively a political unknown (he had joined the FDP less than two years previously), who was appointed only after the FDP parliamentary group had rejected the choice made by the party leaders. The Defence Minister, Gerhard Stoltenberg (CDU), who had served in Herr Kohl's government since 1982, was forced to resign in March following the disclosure of illegal arms shipments to Turkey. The new Defence Minister, Volker Rühe (CDU), took the decision in June to withdraw from participation in the European fighter aircraft (EFA) project on the grounds that the plane was too costly; instead, a cheaper and more appropriate development plan was agreed in December.

Another departure from government was the federal Minister of Posts, Christian Schwarz-Schilling (CDU), who resigned in protest against Germany's lack of involvement in the international effort to bring peace to Bosnia (see III.1.vi). The issue underlined the government's political and constitutional difficulties in winning agreement for Germany to assume its share of international responsibilities, as had already been made evident during the course of the Gulf War. The main opposition party, the SPD, argued that a constitutional change was needed for German armed forces to be deployed out of the NATO area, and to make such a change the government depended on SPD agreement. In December the government announced plans to send 1,500 troops to Somalia in support of the UN relief efforts, but had to back-track when the FDP insisted that prior agreement with the SPD was necessary.

Germany's policies towards Eastern Europe met with some success. A friendship treaty with Czechoslovakia was signed in June, although no agreement was reached about compensation for Sudeten Germans who had been expelled from Czechoslovakia at the end of World War II. The Constitutional Court upheld the validity of the Oder-Neisse line (the present border with Poland) in a ruling made in July; in effect, this judgment recognized the irrevocable loss of Germany's former eastern territories. Agreement was reached with Romania in September that the latter would accept back all Romanian nationals whose applications for political asylum in Germany had been rejected (a high proportion of so-called 'economic migrants' to Germany being from Romania). At the same time, the federal government, and Germans generally, showed greater willingness than other European countries to accept refugee Croats and Muslims from the former Yugoslavia—some 200,000 all told reached Germany in 1992.

East Germany was still dogged by the political legacy of communist rule. Several leading politicians were found to have cooperated with the Stasi state security police in the past. The most notable person under investigation for this kind of involvement was Manfred Stolpe (SPD), the popular minister-president of Brandenburg. However, Herr Stolpe maintained that his contacts with the Stasi had been inevitable in the course of his official church duties at the time. In July Erich Honecker, the former East German communist leader, was returned from Moscow to stand trial. The case against him and five other prominent communists, including Erich Mielke (former head of the Stasi), began in November, but it was likely that proceedings against Herr Honecker would be dropped in view of his apparently terminal illness. One surprise was the support the communists, renamed the Party for Democratic Socialism (PDS), still mustered. In the May Berlin municipal elections the PDS won no less than 29.7 per cent of the votes in the eastern districts of the city. It was surprising, too, that whereas an opinion poll showed that only 34 per cent of west Germans took an optimistic view of the future, the figure for east Germans was 47 per cent.

Efforts to harmonize the regulations governing abortion in the two parts of Germany were successful in June when the Bundestag approved measures which had the effect of liberalizing conditions in west Germany, legalizing abortions performed within the first 12 weeks of conception. The new provisions were opposed by the Catholic Church and by many Christian Democrats, so that the law was referred to the Constitutional Court for a ruling, to be given in 1993.

In September the official opening took place of the Rhine-Main-Danube canal—a spectacular project finally linking the Black Sea to the North Sea. Opponents, especially in Bavaria, had for years protested at the alleged damage to the environment caused by the canalization of rivers. It was widely doubted whether the new canal system could ever be made financially viable.

Willy Brandt, SPD Chancellor in 1969–1974 and for many years the party's leader, died in October. He had become a symbol of post-war German democracy as well as of reconciliation with Eastern Europe and for this contribution was awarded the Nobel Peace Prize in 1971. The death also occurred in May of Karl Carstens (CDU), West German President in 1974–84. In tragic circumstances, two leading Green politicians of the 1980s, Petra Kelly and Gerd Bastian, were found dead in October in their Bonn flat; it was concluded that General Bastian had shot Ms Kelly before killing himself. The actress Marlene Dietrich died in Paris in May, and her wish to be buried in her native city, Berlin, was respected. However, it was a sad reflection on contemporary Germany that her grave was later vandalized, presumably by neo-nazis. (For obituaries of Brandt, Carstens, Kelly and Dietrich, see XX:OBITUARY.)

iii.   ITALY

CAPITAL: Rome   AREA: 301,000 sq km   POPULATION: 57,700,000 ('90)
OFFICIAL LANGUAGE: Italian   POLITICAL SYSTEM: parliamentary democracy
HEAD OF STATE: President Oscar Luigi Scalfaro (since May '92)
RULING PARTIES: Christian Democratic (DC), Socialist (PSI), Democratic Socialist
   (PSDI) & Liberal (PLI) parties
HEAD OF GOVERNMENT: Giuliano Amato (PSI), Prime Minister (since June '92)
PRINCIPAL MINISTERS: Claudio Martelli (PSI/justice), Vincenzo Scotti (DC/foreign
   affairs), Nicola Mancino (DC/interior), Piero Barruci (non-party/treasury),
   Franco Reviglio (PSI/budget, planning, Mezzogiorno), Giovanni Goria
   (DC/finance), Salvo Ando (PSI/defence)
INTERNATIONAL ALIGNMENT: NATO, OECD, EC
CURRENCY: lira (end-'92 £1=Lit2,230.75, US$1=Lit1,473.41)
GNP PER CAPITA: US$16,830 ('90)
MAIN EXPORT EARNERS: machinery and transport equipment, manufactures, chemicals,
   agricultural products, tourism

THE year began with the veteran Christian Democrat, Giulio Andreotti (73), still presiding over the four-party coalition government he had formed in April 1991 (see AR 1991, p. 108). However, with elections due to be held sometime before June 1992, the coalition proved fragile and in early February parliament was dissolved and elections called for 5 April.

The parties approached the campaign by appealing to their regular supporters and attempting to prevent defections. Their caution was understandable, for the June 1991 referendum which resulted in the abolition of a system of preference voting had revealed that public opinion was moving against the parties. Moreover, a new political movement composed of right-wing leagues had done well in the north in regional elections in 1990. To compound the novelties, the elections were to be the first since World War II in which the Communist Party would not be a factor, having completed its transformation into the Democratic Party of the Left (PDS) in February 1991.

The main choice offered the electorate was between continuity and change. The two principal parties of government, the Christian Democrats (DC) and the Socialists (PSI), warned that a fragmentation of the vote would render the country ungovernable. For their part, the parties of opposition pointed to the long-overdue need for institutional reform, action on the public sector deficit, measures to reduce the power of the parties and a strategy to deal with organized crime. The corruption issue was lent weight by the arrest in Milan on 17 February of a leading Socialist, Mario Chiesa. The importance of the crime issue was highlighted by the murder in Palermo on 11 March of an MEP and former mayor, Salvatore Lima, who had long been suspected of collusion with the Mafia.

The election produced some significant shifts in the party system. The DC scored 29.7 per cent (down 4.6 per cent on its 1987 share), falling below 30 per cent for the first time. It retained its share of the vote in the south but lost support in the north, including its strongholds in the Veneto region. Reacting to the result, the party secretary, Arnaldo Forlani, offered to tender his resignation. The biggest losers were the ex-Communists. Whereas the PCI had taken 26.6 per cent in 1987, the PDS won just 16.1 per cent. A party of hardliners who had refused to join the PDS, called the Communist Refoundation Party (PRC), took 5.6 per cent. The Socialists slipped slightly to 13.6 per cent (down 0.7 per cent), losing votes in the north and especially in Milan.

The Republicans, who left the government in April 1991, improved their position by a small margin (up 0.9 per cent). The real beneficiaries were the Northern League, which became the largest party in Milan and the second-largest in Lombardy. Overall it won 8.7 per cent. The recently founded anti-Mafia party, La Rete ('Network') did especially well in Palermo and Turin, where its lists were headed by popular former mayors. The neo-fascist MSI, which fielded Mussolini's 28-year-old grand-daughter among its candidates, held its ground at 5.4 per cent.

The results were described in the Italian press as an 'earthquake'. This was an exaggeration. There was a shift to the right of proportions not dissimilar to that occurring elsewhere in Europe. There were also signs of dissatisfaction with the established parties in an increased protest vote. As a result, several prominent Christian Democrats and some leading members of the PDS failed to win re-election. However, on paper at least, the four government parties still commanded a narrow 16-seat majority in the Chamber of Deputies, even though in aggregate they fell slightly below 50 per cent of the popular vote. Moreover, the disparate nature of the opposition meant that no alternative coalition was possible.

On 25 April President Francesco Cossiga resigned one month before the end of his seven-year mandate. In his last two years in office President Cossiga had behaved erratically, making ample use of the media to defend the past role of the Christian Democrats in the nation's affairs while attacking violently the present DC, as well as the PDS. Latterly he had urged the creation of a presidential-style republic. However, commentators agreed that his resignation was a judicious decision that would allow his successor to take responsibility for the appointment of a new prime minister.

An electoral college consisting of all members of parliament and representatives of the regions met to elect a new head of state. Repeated rounds of voting produced deadlock, as each candidate presented by one or more of the four parties of government proved unacceptable to some members of the coalition. An attempt by all the parties of the left to elect a candidate also failed. The process might have continued at length had not a car bomb in Palermo killed Giovanni Falcone, his wife and three members of his escort on 24 May. The murder of Italy's top anti-Mafia investigator sent a shock wave through the country. Almost immediately the politicians broke their deadlock and elected the president of the Chamber of Deputies, Oscar Luigi Scalfaro, aged 73, to the office of President. A fervent Catholic and former DC interior minister, Signor Scalfaro won wide support on account of his unblemished character, his independence of the factions within his party and his long record of loyalty to parliament. In his inaugural address the new President urged that a bicameral commission be established to revise the constitution, whose drafting he had personally contributed to as a member of the Constituent Assembly elected in 1946.

It had been expected that President Scalfaro would offer the post of prime minister to the PSI leader, Bettino Craxi. But in April and May the Milan bribery scandal developed into a major political affair—the most significant such case since a similar scandal broke in Turin in 1983. With the collaboration of Signor Chiesa, magistrates arrested current and former assessors in the city belonging to the DC, PSI and PDS. All were accused of taking bribes on public works contracts. The reasons why the corruption came to light were complex. Party 'kickbacks' were more widespread in Italy than in other West European countries because of the lack of alternation in government, the clientelist practices of the main parties and the lack of controls on the administration of their finances. Probably the reduced willingness of businesses to pay bribes in a recession and the diminished standing of the parties in public estimation helped blow the cover on practices which by all accounts became routine in the 1980s. In any event, the party to suffer most damage was the PSI. When magistrates asked parliament's permission to start proceedings against two Socialist former mayors of Milan, Signor Craxi was forced to remove his own son from his post as PSI secretary in the city. These events fatally damaged the Socialist leader's prospects of becoming prime minister.

The impact of the burgeoning scandal on public opinion was underscored in local elections in Trieste and Naples on 7 June. While the traditional parties held their ground in the southern city, the League and the MSI made substantial gains in the north.

In the middle of June Giuliano Amato, a 54-year-old law professor, was given the task of forming a government. A Socialist first elected to parliament in 1983, Signor Amato was a technocrat who had worked closely with Signor Craxi. Aided by President Scalfaro, he assembled a slim-line administration that excluded several controversial former ministers, including Giulio Andreotti and Gianni De Michelis. A number of technicians were given portfolios. Among these were the banker Piero Barucci (finance), the EC commissioner Carlo Ripa Di Meana (environment) and the journalist Alberto Ronchey (culture). Signor Amato presented his government to parliament on a platform that he hoped would win votes beyond the four-party coalition. He listed his priorities as institutional reform, the public sector deficit, anti-corruption legislation and organized crime.

It was the last of these that presented the Prime Minister with his first test. On 19 July the Mafia struck again in Palermo, killing a close associate of Signor Falcone's, the judge Paolo Borsellino, who had been tipped to take the former's place. In response, the government issued an anti-Mafia decree that was rapidly turned into law with the backing of the PDS and the Republicans. Some 7,000 regular troops were deployed in Sicily and gaoled *mafiosi* were transferred to a remote prison island, where they were denied visitors or use of telephones.

The issue which chiefly preoccupied Signor Amato was the impending financial crisis. Throughout the 1980s Italian governments had allowed the national debt to rise, until it reached 10.5 per cent of GDP in 1992, nearly three times the European Community average. Interest charges alone for the year amounted to the equivalent of the entire budget deficit, which by October was projected at Lit160,000,000 million. In order to meet an imminent shortfall in the second half of the year, Signor Amato announced an emergency package in July involving a one-off tax on property and savings. He also proposed reducing the public sector, partly through privatization, and removing it from the effects of political patronage. These proposals, which left many fundamental problems untouched, provoked considerable opposition. However, the Prime Minister was able to secure parliamentary backing, as the measures were recognised to be unavoidable.

In the first half of September a lira widely perceived to be over-valued fell victim to speculation on the foreign exchange markets. Despite the desperate attempt of the Bank of Italy to shore up the currency, a devaluation of 15 per cent was forced on the government. When this failed to halt the downward spiral the government was compelled to withdraw the lira from the exchange rate mechanism (ERM) of the European Monetary System (see also XI.3). These events were described by Italian commentators as a 'new Caporetto' (after Italy's humiliating World War I defeat), as the authorities had presented ERM membership and the discipline it provided as a cornerstone of their strategy for imposing financial rectitude.

Galvanized by the crisis, Signor Amato exploited the situation to demand new powers and force through sweeping cuts in public spending. By the end of the year he had forced through an emergency budget for 1992 and a rigorous austerity package for 1993 requiring reform to the health service, pensions, the civil service, local administration and the system of revenue collection. He had also initiated steps towards privatization of state holdings in banking, foods, engineering, insurance and energy. The result was a restoration of international confidence that permitted the Bank of Italy to lower the discount rate by steps to 12 per cent, easing the high interest rates charged by the banks to industry. For a government that had not been expected to survive, it was a considerable accomplishment. In a bad year for heads of government worldwide, Signor Amato was singled out by the *Financial Times* (of 31 December) for his particular success in 'turning political dross into gold'.

Political reform proceeded much more slowly than economic reform. A 60-member bicameral commission was established by parliament to work on proposals for electoral reform, but by the end of the year it had not come to any specific conclusions. It was obliged to do so by April 1993 if a series of referenda on electoral reforms (subject to their approval by the Constitutional Court) was to be avoided.

Although Signor Amato enjoyed personal popularity, the loss of legitimation by the political elite continued unabated in the second half of the year. Magistrates in Milan continued their inquiries and ordered the arrest of numerous businessmen as well as politicians. The systematic nature of corruption and illegal funding of political parties was confirmed by the blossoming of similar inquiries in Rome, Naples, Varese and Reggio Calabria. By the end of 1992 nearly 100 members of parliament were under investigation for corruption or taking kickbacks. Local elections in Mantua in September and in Varese, Monza and Reggio Calabria in December supplied barometers of the decline in support for the mainstream parties. While the Christian Democrats dropped markedly and the Socialists crumbled to half the share of the vote they had won in April, the League advanced dramatically. In northern communes it captured an average 35 per cent of the vote. Even the south, traditionally slower to change, accorded important if smaller successes to the MSI and La Rete.

The responses of the parties were mixed. They allowed Signor Amato to govern with relatively little interference but they proved slow to start putting their own houses in order. In October Signor Forlani was finally replaced as DC secretary by Mino Martinazzoli, a member of the party's left wing, who pledged renewal but found it difficult to override the powerful Christian Democratic factions. Mario Segni, the DC deputy who had been the chief force in the referendum movement, made more of the running by forming a pre-splinter group, Popolari per la Riforma, which supported some non-DC candidates in the December elections. In the PSI Signor Craxi's long-time deputy, Claudio Martelli, openly challenged the former's leadership. However, he managed to muster only 37 per cent support at a meeting of the party's national assembly, and Signor Craxi refused to resign even when, on 15 December, he was officially warned that he could face charges of corruption by Milan magistrates. For its part, the PDS maintained the support it won in April and completed its transformation by gaining admission to the Socialist International in September. However, continuing internal strife and its own implication in corruption prevented it from fully exploiting the opportunities of the situation. In consequence, the future shape of the political map in Italy remained highly uncertain at the end of the year.

iv. BELGIUM

CAPITAL: Brussels   AREA: 30,500 sq km   POPULATION: 10,000,000 ('90)
OFFICIAL LANGUAGES: French & Flemish
POLITICAL SYSTEM: parliamentary democracy, devolved structure based on language
   communities
HEAD OF STATE: King Baudouin (since July '51)
RULING PARTIES: Christian People's Party (CVP/Flemish), Christian Social Party
   (PSC/Walloon), Socialist Party (SP/Flemish), Socialist Party (PS/Walloon), People's
   Union (VU/Flemish nationalist)
HEAD OF GOVERNMENT: Jean-Luc Dehaene (CVP) Prime Minister (since March '92)
PRINCIPAL MINISTERS: Willy Claes (SP/deputy premier, foreign affairs), Melchior
   Wathelet (PSC/deputy premier, justice, economic affairs), Mieke Offeciers-
   Van De Weile (CVP/budget), Philippe Maystadt (PSC/finance), Guy Coëme
   (PS/deputy premier, communications, public enterprises), Robert Urbain
   (PS/foreign trade, European affairs)
INTERNATIONAL ALIGNMENT: NATO, OECD, EC, Benelux, Francophonie
CURRENCY: franc (end-'92 £1=BF50.30, US$1=BF33.22)
GNP PER CAPITA: US$15,540 ('90)
MAIN EXPORT EARNERS: machinery & transport equipment, manufactures, chemicals,
   agricultural products

As the year opened the country was still without a government following the November 1991 general election (see AR 1991, p. 112). The main political parties, which had all lost seats to fringe parties and were in any case increasingly becoming polarized along regional lines, found it ever-more problematic to establish the basis for a new coalition government. After an earlier failure, a leading French-speaking Christian Social sought to recreate the coalition with the Socialists, but in the face of regional antagonisms had to admit failure on 1 February. Next, Jean-Luc Dehaene, also a Christian Social but, importantly, a Flemish-speaker, sought to form a government. Given that the Flemish Christian Socials (CVP) remained the single largest party even after their poor electoral performance, Mr Dehaene's task was relatively straightforward. His new version of the Christian Social/Socialist coalition took office in early March. However, it lacked the two-thirds majority needed to pass the constitutional changes required for further regional devolution of government functions and thus had severely limited authority on this key issue.

Nevertheless, devolution, together with preparing Belgium for European economic and monetary union and reform of social and environmental policies, were the main declared political aims of Mr Dehaene's new administration. The focus of economic policy continued to be on reducing the massive budget deficit. Increases in the main rate of VAT and new spending cuts were also agreed.

The EC's Maastricht treaty was easily ratified on 17 July. But the reassessment of social and environmental policies was effectively submerged by more pressing issues of devolution and the budget deficit, neither lending themselves to ready solutions.

Beginning in April, discussions involving most of the political parties attempted to establish common ground for the next stage of devolution to the regions. Typically, lesser issues caused the biggest problems: i.e., whether French-speaking residents of Flanders should have the right to vote in Wallonia; and whether each region should run its own separate social security system (Flanders wanted to reduce, if not eliminate, its transfers to poorer Wallonia). By July there was an impasse, the talks were suspended and the government looked more and more threatened. It was widely considered that only the low opinion poll ratings of the individual coalition parties, and their fear of further losses in a new general election, caused them to put together a devolution compromise agreement late in the year. This took the form of further moves towards a federal state, with the regions taking new responsibilities for foreign trade and agriculture, and the existing regional executives becoming directly-elected regional governments. Flanders agreed to a continuing transfer of resources via central government to underfunded Wallonia. However, as 1992 ended the proposals still needed to be approved by a two-thirds majority in both houses of parliament.

By mid-summer agreement had been reached by the coalition partners on the 1993 budget, an important element in the plan to enable Belgium to achieve the convergence objectives set in the Maastricht treaty. The agreed aim was to cut the budget deficit to 5.2 per cent of GDP by 1993 with a view to attaining the 3 per cent Maastricht target by 1996. The essential means of achieving the objectives were to be a nil real increase in spending, revenue growth to match the rise in GDP and (a difficult target) a balanced social security budget through increases in contributions and by lower unemployment benefits and healthcare expenditure. Problems quickly arose in the shape of parliamentary objections that the spending cuts were insufficient and the revenue growth assumptions too optimistic. Under pressure, the government agreed to tougher reductions in expenditure. These difficulties were increased when it emerged that the 1992 budget deficit target would be greatly exceeded.

Notwithstanding these problems, the economy was relatively strong. Personal consumption grew faster and business investment recovered. Against this, exports were weak, while imports were sucked in by the strengthening of consumer and investment demand.

v.   THE NETHERLANDS

CAPITAL: Amsterdam   AREA: 37,000 sq km   POPULATION: 14,900,000 ('90)
OFFICIAL LANGUAGE: Dutch   POLITICAL SYSTEM: parliamentary democracy
HEAD OF STATE: Queen Beatrix (since April '80)
RULING PARTIES: Christian Democratic Appeal (CDA) & Labour Party (PvdA)
HEAD OF GOVERNMENT: Ruud Lubbers (CDA), Prime Minister (since Nov '82)
PRINCIPAL MINISTERS: Wim Kok (PvdA/deputy premier, finance), Ien Dales
   (PvdA/home affairs), Hans van den Broek (CDA/foreign affairs), Relus ter Beek
   (PvdA/defence), Koos Andriessen (CDA/economic affairs), Ernst Hirsch Ballin
   (CDA/justice)
INTERNATIONAL ALIGNMENT: NATO, OECD, EC, Benelux
CURRENCY: guilder (end-'92 £1=f2.75, US$1=f1.82)
GNP PER CAPITA: US$17,320 ('90)
MAIN EXPORT EARNERS: oil & gas, machinery & transport equipment, chemicals,
   agricultural products

THE stability of the Christian Democrat/Labour coalition government seemed to be threatened early in the year when the Labour Party, experiencing a sharp drop in its opinion poll ratings, appeared to be coalescing into divergent left and right wings and experiencing great difficulty in speaking with a single voice. The commitment of the leaders of the coalition parties proved sufficient to prevent intra-party squabbles from undermining the government, which survived the various crises that occurred during the year. Nevertheless, in May Ruud Lubbers, leader of the Christian Democrats and the country's longest-serving Prime Minister, indicated his intention to resign in 1994.

Among the areas of contention were proposals to cut back the armed forces and possibly end conscription. Also controversial was a national identity card scheme with provision for identity checks. The surge of immigrants and asylum seekers from eastern Europe and from developing countries increasingly became a major political issue, leading to counter-measures in the shape of tightened regulations, fines for employers of illegal immigrants, speedier processing of asylum applications and the opening of a detention centre for those deemed unlikely to secure permanent admittance to the Netherlands.

In February an ultimatum to the metals industry, that it should meet the anti-pollution targets in the national environment plan or else face the introduction of tight legislation, quickly produced compliance. Moreover, energy levies were introduced to secure improved fuel use efficiency in Dutch industry, which also faced the possible introduction of a carbon dioxide emission levy in 1993. The anguished claims by industry that resulting cost increases would harm Dutch international competitiveness caused some tensions within the coalition. Nevertheless, the responsible minister, Hans Alders (Labour), pressed ahead unrepentant, making proposals for new taxes on use of pesticides, artificial fertilizers, cattle feed containing phosphorus and nitrogen, and on waste incineration and dumping.

Pollution and related problems caused by heavy traffic congestion in the Randstad conurbation of the central Netherlands impelled both the central government and the local authorities to introduce counter-measures. In April the government accepted the Minister for Transport's outline proposal for a levy on all traffic entering the Randstad during the morning rush hour. It was in Amsterdam, however, that the most radical and immediate move was made, following a majority vote in a local referendum, to curb traffic. The city council accepted the referendum decision to ban cars and vans from the city centre, and authorized extensive enabling measures for new car parks on Amsterdam's outskirts, new subsidized public transport facilities and more cargo barges on the canal network.

The Amsterdam suburb of Bijlmermeer was the scene of a major disaster on 4 October, when an Israeli Boeing 747 cargo plane, laden with fuel, crashed into an apartment block complex. The death toll, initially put at over 250, was later officially revised to about 70, although officials admitted that the exact number and identities of all those killed would never be known. Many of the dead were believed to be illegal immigrants.

On the economic front, the Government presented a budget in September which proposed to sever the linkage between private sector pay increases and social security payments. Welfare payments were to be increased by only 2.5 per cent in the year ahead, while private sector pay was projected to rise by 4 per cent. The objective was to encourage a shift of welfare recipients into paid employment. However, the likelihood that those living on social security would suffer a 1 per cent fall in their real purchasing power split the government, with many Labour Party members indicating that they would not vote for the budget unless this problem were remedied. In the event, a more generous increase in welfare payments restored the consensus between the coalition members.

Developments in the economy as a whole were largely positive during the year, with strong investment and exports producing a 3 per cent surge in real gross domestic product. However, consumer demand was feeble and industrial production showed no real sign of recovery.

vi. LUXEMBOURG

CAPITAL: Luxembourg   AREA: 3,000 sq km   POPULATION: 379,000 ('90)
OFFICIAL LANGUAGE: Letzeburgish   POLITICAL SYSTEM: parliamentary democracy
HEAD OF STATE: Grand Duke Jean (since Nov '64)
RULING PARTIES: Christian Social People's Party (PCS) & Luxembourg Socialist
    Workers' Party (LSAP)
HEAD OF GOVERNMENT: Jacques Santer (PCS), Prime Minister (since July '84)
PRINCIPAL MINISTERS: Jacques Poos (LSAP/deputy premier, foreign affairs),
    Jean Spautz (PCS/interior), Jean-Claude Juncker (PCS/finance, labour, budget),
    Robert Goebbels (LSAP/economy)
INTERNATIONAL ALIGNMENT: NATO, OECD, EC, Benelux, Francophonie
CURRENCY: Luxembourg franc (end-'92 £1=LF50.30, US$1=LF33.22)
GNP PER CAPITA: US$28,730 ('90)
MAIN EXPORT EARNERS: basic manufactures, machinery & transport equipment,
    tourism, financial services

IN a surprise move on 1 January the government took advantage of the low rate of inflation and anticipated by a full year its planned timetable to increase VAT rates in preparation for harmonization in the single EC market. The standard rate was increased from 12 to 15 per cent.

Shaken by the realization that for the first time in many years there had been a deficit on the 1991 budget outturn, the authorities announced cuts in current spending for 1992 but emphasized that the public investment programme would not be affected. Similarly, the 1993 budget announced in September confirmed that capital spending to support economic and social development would be maintained.

In July Luxembourg became the first EC member state to ratify the Maastricht treaty. Remarkably, voting rights were agreed for the 28.5 per cent of the population consisting of other EC nationals, though the European Council was asked to agree that, in order to stand in Luxembourg elections, other EC nationals would need to demonstrate ten years of residence in Luxembourg and an ability to speak Letzeburgish.

The steel industry, which still accounted for nearly a third of total industrial output, saw a short-lived rise in production during the first quarter. However, production declined from mid-year in the face of weak demand from the European motor vehicle and construction industries.

Notwithstanding its record of compliance with EC commitments, Luxembourg resisted a ruling that it must withdraw its widespread subsidies to industry, asking for exemptions to permit continued support for smaller companies throughout the country.

vii. REPUBLIC OF IRELAND

CAPITAL: Dublin   AREA: 70,280 sq km   POPULATION: 3,500,000 ('90)
OFFICIAL LANGUAGES: Irish and English   POLITICAL SYSTEM: parliamentary democracy
HEAD OF STATE: President Mary Robinson (since Dec '90)
HEAD OF GOVERNMENT: Albert Reynolds (FF), Prime Minister/Taoiseach (since Feb
    '92, in caretaker capacity at year's end)
INTERNATIONAL ALIGNMENT: neutral, OECD, EC
CURRENCY: punt (end-'92 £1=IR£0.93, US$1=IR£0.62)
GNP PER CAPITA: US$9,550 ('90)
MAIN EXPORT EARNERS: tourism, machinery and electronic equipment, agricultural
    products, tourism

WHEN allegations were made in January associating the Taoiseach (Prime Minister), Charles Haughey, with phone-tapping incidents ten years earlier, the Progressive Democrats, the junior partners with Mr Haughey's Fianna Fáil party in the ruling coalition, insisted that his resignation was needed to preserve the government's credibility. Although Mr Haughey denied the allegations, he agreed to go. On 11 February Albert Reynolds, who had been dismissed as Finance Minister for his part in an attempt to unseat Mr Haughey the previous November (see AR 1991, p. 117), was elected Taoiseach in his place. While continuing the coalition with the Progressive Democrats, Mr Reynolds dropped eight of the 12 Fianna Fáil ministers whom he inherited, replacing most of them with prominent party critics of the Haughey regime.

The new government had no sooner been installed than a major crisis arose over the law on abortion. In a case involving a 14-year-old girl, pregnant following an alleged rape, the Supreme Court decided that the phrasing of the ban on abortion voted into the Republic's constitution in 1983 (see AR 1983, p. 147) permitted the termination of a pregnancy which constituted a risk to the mother's life, and that a threat by the mother to kill herself could amount to such a risk. On another aspect of the case, the Court refused to prohibit the Attorney-General from seeking injunctions to prevent women leaving the country to have abortions.

The immediate implications of this judgment concerned European Community (EC) law regarding freedom to travel and to avail oneself of services lawfully provided in another EC member country. The issue was complicated by the Maastricht treaty on European Union, which would be the subject of a referendum within a matter of months and which incorporated a protocol allowing the local law on abortion to prevail in Ireland over EC regulations. Through skilful consultation with the opposition parties and the EC council of ministers, Mr Reynolds succeeded in holding the question in abeyance so that it did not become a serious factor in the referendum debate. This was despite efforts by conservative and liberal pressure groups alike to secure rejection of the treaty because it copper-fastened the Supreme Court's interpretation of the law with which, for opposing reasons, neither side agreed.

The Maastricht referendum took place on 18 June, only two weeks after the Danish rejection of the treaty (see II.2.i). It was widely feared that the Irish might follow this example, not least because the pro-Maastricht political parties, including the government, had devoted little energy to promoting the treaty's positive aspects. Instead, they took it for granted that the strong support for the EC among Irish agricultural, industrial and labour interests would again be reflected in the popular vote. In the event, this calculation proved correct and the treaty was approved by almost 70 per cent of those who voted. The low poll of 59 per cent, however, indicated the degree to which the political establishment had failed to stimulate public interest.

The favourable vote could be attributed, like similar votes in the past, to the substantial net benefit of EC membership for the Republic, which had been annually receiving back from Community funds six times its contribution to the EC budget. This the Taoiseach underscored by claiming that the Maastricht proposals would result in payments of IR£6,000 million to the Republic, an assertion greeted with scepticism at the time but largely vindicated at the Edinburgh EC summit in December (see XI.3 & XIX.3). Criticism of the supposed domination of national policies by Brussels bureaucrats, much heard in Denmark, France and the United Kingdom during the year, made little impact in Ireland. The Irish argued, as they had consistently done for 20 years, that the international forum assured them a voice in decision-making which the small size and relative poverty of the Republic would prevent them from ever acquiring on their own.

A dramatic demonstration of Irish commitment to European union came in September when the United Kingdom withdrew from the exchange rate mechanism (ERM) of the European Monetary System and sterling was effectively devalued (see I.4). It was assumed on the money markets that the Irish would have to follow suit and the punt quickly came under heavy pressure. However, the government, with almost total support from the opposition parties, Irish business and the trade unions, refused to countenance devaluation or withdrawal from the ERM. By a variety of stratagems, and with a heavy commitment of the country's limited foreign reserves by the central bank, this determination was sustained to the year's end. The punt, which before the crisis had an exchange rate of IR£1=£0.93 sterling, soared to £1.10 before settling at a level of about £1.07. Irish firms exporting to Britain, which accounted for 30 per cent of total exports, were severely disadvantaged and had to be given immediate tax and other concessions to enable them to continue to compete. Notwithstanding this costly support, serious job losses were being envisaged, especially when the New Year would bring into force the single European market, within which some of the Irish support mechanisms would no longer be permissible. Although a demand for some degree of devaluation was beginning to harden before Christmas, it was still very much a minority attitude. Most financial and other institutions saw the country's long-term advantage as lying in attracting foreign investment and securing the full value of EC membership by maintaining a strong currency impervious to speculative manipulation.

The autumn was marked by mounting political tension. The three-strand talks on Northern Ireland, initiated the previous year by the then UK Secretary for Northern Ireland, Peter Brooke, had been suspended *sine die* and Unionist participants were blaming the Republic for intransigence on the constitutional claim to jurisdiction over the area (see also I.10). Unemployment had reached a record total of nearly 20 per cent of the workforce. A tribunal investigating allegations of malpractices in the beef industry ensured that the kind of business scandals which had so undermined public confidence in Fianna Fáil (see AR 1991, pp. 116–17) were not forgotten. In evidence to the tribunal the leader of the Progressive Democrats and Minister for Industry, Desmond O'Malley, strongly criticized decisions made by Fianna Fáil ministers prior to the formation of the coalition government. In October, also as a witness before the tribunal, the Taoiseach described Mr O'Malley's evidence as 'dishonest'. The Progressive Democrats then resigned from the government and a general election was called for 25 November.

Unemployment dominated the campaign and Mr Reynolds himself was blamed for creating the circumstances in which an unwanted election had become inevitable. The main opposition party, Fine Gael, failed to enthuse the electorate with a policy that looked insufficiently different from that of Fianna Fáil. The promise of a radical change of emphasis, with priority for tackling social needs and opposition to the inclination of Fianna Fáil and Fine Gael to raise money by privatizing state enterprises, came from the small Labour Party. This met with considerable public approval, not least because of the dynamic and hyper-intelligent image of the Labour leader, Dick Spring. The election resulted in a loss of nine seats by Fianna Fáil (down to 68), of ten by Fine Gael (down to 45) and a doubling of Labour's representation (up to 33).

In an assembly of 166 members elected by proportional representation, this was a quite phenomenal change even if the relative position of the parties remained unaltered. Labour showed little interest in the idea of a 'rainbow coalition' put forward by Fine Gael, which would have meant a government of Fine Gael, Labour and the Progressive Democrats (who had also gained extra seats). Although he made contact with the other party leaders, Mr Spring fastened on Fianna Fáil as the partner most likely to agree to extensive implementation of Labour policies in return for Labour's agreement to an alliance in government. The year ended with Mr Reynolds still in office on a caretaker basis, while his party and Labour were negotiating the programme for a coalition.

Almost as incidentals to the election, referenda were held on the same day on various aspects of the abortion question. The voters agreed to new constitutional guarantees of the right to travel and to receive information about services legitimately available abroad, but rejected a proposal which, except in the case of a suicide threat, would have permitted abortion if the mother's life were at risk. The latter proposal was considered too liberal by conservatives, too conservative by liberals, and simply dangerous by people who felt that the whole problem had arisen in the first place from the attempt to deal with abortion in the inappropriate context of the constitution.

A happy feature of a difficult year was the continuing success of President Mary Robinson in highlighting matters of national and international concern by carefully chosen gestures. She hosted a reception for 100 unemployed persons at her official residence, and similarly received representatives of gay and lesbian groups despite the fact that Irish law still criminalized homosexual behaviour. Above all, she paid a three-day visit to the famine-stricken areas of Somalia—the first head of state to do so and in circumstances of no small danger. It was also cause for some satisfaction that, with so many difficulties at home, the Irish could still maintain a major part of the famine relief effort through their voluntary agencies, Concern, Goal and Trocaire.

A major publishing event was the appearance of *The Great Melody* by Dr Conor Cruise O'Brien, a magisterial 'thematic biography' of Edmund Burke, first editor of the *Annual Register*.

2. DENMARK—ICELAND—NORWAY—SWEDEN—FINLAND—
AUSTRIA—SWITZERLAND—EUROPEAN MINI-STATES

i. DENMARK

CAPITAL: Copenhagen   AREA: 43,000 sq km   POPULATION: 5,100,000 ('90)
OFFICIAL LANGUAGE: Danish   POLITICAL SYSTEM: parliamentary democracy
HEAD OF STATE: Queen Margrethe II (since Jan '72)
RULING PARTIES: Conservative People's Party (KF) & Venstre Liberals (V)
HEAD OF GOVERNMENT: Poul Schlüter (KF), Prime Minister (since Sept '82)
PRINCIPAL MINISTERS: Uffe Ellemann-Jensen (V/foreign affairs), Henning Dyremose
   (KF/finance), Anders Fogh Rasmussen (V/economic affairs), Hans Engell
   (KF/justice), Knud Enggard (V/defence), Thor Pedersen (V/interior, Nordic affairs)
INTERNATIONAL ALIGNMENT: NATO, OECD, EC, Nordic Council
CURRENCY: Krone (end-'92 £1=DKr9.50, US$1=DKr6.27)
GNP PER CAPITA: US$22,080 ('90)
MAIN EXPORT EARNERS: agricultural produce, machinery and transport equipment,
   manufactures

IN January the Conservative-Liberal minority government agreed with the Social Democrats, the largest opposition party, that the referendum on the EC's Maastricht treaty would be held on 2 June. The result would be binding. The treaty was supported by most political and economic leaders and by six of the eight parties represented in parliament. It was opposed by the left-wing Socialist People's Party (SFP) and by the right-wing Progress Party. In May parliament ratified the treaty by 130 votes to 25.

A major problem for supporters was that during the spring the Social Democrats were diverted from campaigning strongly for the treaty by an internal leadership struggle. There was strong dissatisfaction with the style of the party chairman, Svend Auken, who also incurred the hostility of the small centre parties as regards his suitability for the premiership. This led the vice-chairman, Poul Nyrup Rasmussen, to challenge Mr Auken for the chairmanship. On 11 April, at an extraordinary party congress, Mr Rasmussen was elected leader.

Also in April, judicial hearings ended in the so-called 'Tamilgate' affair, having sought to establish responsibility for the attempt in 1987 to prevent Tamils from joining their relatives in Denmark. The judicial report was expected to influence the government's survival, including that of the Prime Minister, Poul Schlüter. In the event, the report was delayed until 1993. On 10 September Mr Schlüter celebrated the 10th anniversary of his accession to the premiership. During that decade a persistent balance-of-payments deficit had been transformed into a trade surplus equivalent to 6 per cent of GDP and a current-account surplus of 1 per cent of GDP. Denmark belonged to the few EC countries which already met the Maastricht treaty's convergence criteria for economic and monetary union.

Nevertheless, on 2 June Denmark's voters narrowly rejected the treaty, by 50.7 per cent to 49.3 per cent on an 82.9 per cent turnout.

Fears of loss of sovereignty, participation in a European army and a dilution of Denmark's advanced social welfare system were cited as key factors. A key factor in assuring the treaty's rejection was that 60 per cent of Social Democratic voters ignored their leaders' recommendation and voted against it. The vote was widely interpreted as revealing a worrying gulf between Denmark's voters and politicians, although Foreign Minister Ellemann-Jensen drew some comfort from Denmark's unexpected victory over Germany a few days later in the European football championship (see XVII). In one of the quotes of 1992, he linked the two events by saying: 'If you can't join them, beat them.'

The other 11 EC countries reacted to the Danish vote by refusing to renegotiate the treaty and by continuing the process of national ratifications. The Danish government called for a period of reflection followed by the search for a national consensus on the terms on which Denmark would negotiate its future relationship with its EC partners. Several factors strengthened Denmark's position. Denmark's 'No' vote had released the latent opposition to the Maastricht treaty in other EC member countries. The general demand grew for less centralization and more openness in EC decision-making. In November the British government made British ratification dependent on Denmark's.

On 28 October Denmark published its negotiating position. It was supported by seven of the eight parties in parliament, including now the SFP. Denmark wanted legally-binding, unlimited opt-out clauses from the third stage of economic and monetary union, a future European army, common citizenship, and community policies on justice and immigration. At the Edinburgh summit on 11-12 December Denmark obtained the substance of these demands (see XI.3 & XIX.3). In addition, the EC leaders issued a declaration on subsidiarity and greater openness in EC decision-making. The Danish government promised in return to hold a second referendum in the spring of 1993.

ii. ICELAND

CAPITAL: Reykjavik   AREA: 103,000 sq km   POPULATION: 255,000 ('90)
OFFICIAL LANGUAGE: Icelandic   POLITICAL SYSTEM: parliamentary democracy
HEAD OF STATE: President Vigdis Finnbogadóttir (since Aug '80)
RULING PARTIES: Independence Party (IP) & Social Democratic Party (SDP)
HEAD OF GOVERNMENT: David Oddsson (IP), Prime Minister (since April '91)
PRINCIPAL MINISTERS: Jón Baldvin Hannibalsson (SDP/foreign affairs), Fridrik Sophuson
   (IP/finance), Thorsteinn Pálsson (IP/fisheries, justice, ecclesiastical affairs),
   Jón Sigurdsson (SDP/industry & commerce)
INTERNATIONAL ALIGNMENT: NATO, OECD, EFTA, Nordic Council
CURRENCY: króna (end-'92 £1=ISK96.93, US$1=ISK64.03)
GNP PER CAPITA: US$21,400 ('90)
MAIN EXPORT EARNERS: fish and fish products, tourism

IN late January negotiations began to renew the historic national incomes agreement of February 1990 which had led to the virtual elimination of Iceland's high inflation (see AR 1990, p. 169). Against a background of falling GDP, rising unemployment and government spending cuts, the objectives were to preserve low inflation while protecting purchasing power and employment. The unions wanted an end to welfare cuts; employers and unions both wanted lower interest rates. On 27 April agreement was reached on a second national incomes agreement for the period 1 May 1992 to 1 March 1993. The government promised to pursue policies designed to reduce interest rates and unemployment, maintain the external value of the króna and moderate welfare cuts.

The Foreign Minister, Jón Baldvin Hannibalsson, signed the European Economic Area treaty on 2 May. On 19 May the government presented the treaty to the Allting (parliament) for ratification, rejecting opposition calls for a referendum as being contrary to Iceland's tradition of parliamentary democracy. Representatives of the two coalition parties, the Independence Party and Social Democrats, were expected to vote for the treaty, while the Women's League and People's Alliance broadly opposed it and the Progress Party was split. Ratification was subsequently delayed until January 1993, following Switzerland's rejection of the treaty (see II.2.vii; XI.5.iv).

The government responded positively to the WEU's offer of associate member status to non-EC NATO states such as Iceland. It regarded this as a means of safeguarding NATO, and Iceland's position within it. On 20 November, with Norway and Turkey, Iceland signed an agreement providing for this status. In the spring Iceland had also begun negotiations with the USA on post-Cold War defence cooperation aimed at preserving existing close relations.

On 16 June Iceland's Ocean Research Institute recommended a three-year reduction of one-third in cod catch quotas in order to rebuild stock levels. The consequence would have been an estimated 4–5 per cent reduction in GDP and higher unemployment in coastal areas. After prolonged debate, the government on 28 July announced a smaller cod catch quota cut, along with higher quotas for other, non-threatened species, involving an estimated loss of only 1 per cent of GDP.

By the autumn the economic outlook had further deteriorated. Unemployment, bankruptcies and the forecast budget deficit had risen alarmingly. In October Prime Minister David Oddsson rejected the idea of direct government intervention to help industry. Employers, unions and opposition political parties then began negotiations to establish a national consensus on cost-cutting measures to help industry, and in particular the hard-hit fishing industry. By November the government had joined them. On 23 November, in response to international currency turmoil and industry's severe problems, the government announced a package of emergency measures. The króna was devalued by 6 per cent. This was accompanied by the abolition of the business expenditure tax on industry, increases in income tax and VAT, and further cuts in welfare benefits.

In May the President since 1980, Vigdis Finnbogadóttir, was automatically re-elected unopposed. She thus began a fourth four-year term in office.

iii. NORWAY

CAPITAL: Oslo   AREA: 324,000 sq km   POPULATION: 4,200,000 ('90)
OFFICIAL LANGUAGE: Norwegian   POLITICAL SYSTEM: parliamentary democracy
HEAD OF STATE: King Harald V (since Jan '91)
RULING PARTY: Labour Party (minority government)
HEAD OF GOVERNMENT: Gro Harlem Brundtland, Prime Minister (since Nov '90)
PRINCIPAL MINISTERS: Gunnar Berge (local government & labour), Thorvald Stoltenberg (foreign affairs), Sigbjørn Johnsen (finance), Finn Kristensen (petroleum, energy & industry), Johan J. Holst (defence), Kari Gjesteby (justice), Odrunn Pettersen (fisheries)
INTERNATIONAL ALIGNMENT: NATO, OECD, EFTA, Nordic Council
CURRENCY: krone (end-'92 £1=NKr10.47, US$1=NKr6.92)
GNP PER CAPITA: US$23,120 ('90)
MAIN EXPORT EARNERS: oil and gas, machinery and transport equipment, manufactures, chemicals, fish

POLITICAL debate was dominated by Norway's relations with the EC. There were two separate but closely related issues: ratification of the European Economic Area (EEA) treaty and whether Norway should join Sweden and Finland in applying for EC membership. Finland's decision, taken in February, had a greater impact on the Norwegian debate than Sweden's. Preserving Nordic solidarity now became an argument in support of membership, in contrast to 1972, when Norway had in the end opted against membership. On 4 April the Prime Minister, Gro Harlem Brundtland, declared for membership. She was backed by the minority Labour government and Labour regional organizations, but there was opposition from the northern party organizations and a significant body of Labour activists and voters. A majority for membership was assured at the party's national conference in November. Less clear was whether in the autumn the EEA treaty would gain the three-quarters parliamentary majority required to transfer sovereign powers to an international organization.

Public opinion was moving against EC membership. During the spring a majority for membership was transformed into a majority against. The 'No' campaign received a boost from the Danish voters' rejection of the Maastrict treaty on 2 June (see II.2.i). Public opinion polls showed growing support for the Centre and Socialist Left parties, both opposed to any closer integration into the EC, including the EEA.

Support for the Labour Party was declining, to below 30 per cent by mid-summer. Although officially the party's position on EC membership would not be decided until the national conference, the EC issue was already losing it support. So was rising unemployment, which had reached a post-war high of 7 per cent. The government identified reducing unemployment as its most important objective, but argued that new jobs must come from the private sector through increased competitiveness and economic growth. Renewed growth was forecast for 1993. Real incomes were rising as a result of tax reforms and lower inflation. But high personal and corporate debt levels and interest rates kept domestic demand weak, while recession in Norway's main international markets had hit exports. The banking sector was still in severe crisis. In August confidence was further undermined by the bankruptcy of UNI Storebrand, Norway's largest insurance company. The forecast 1993 budget deficit announced in October was a record NKr 50,000 million, including petroleum revenues.

On 16 October parliament ratified the EEA treaty by 130 votes to 35. At the Labour national conference on 6–8 November the party delegates voted by 183 to 106 to apply for EC membership. By then Labour's support in the public opinion polls had sunk to under 25 per cent, while 55 per cent of voters opposed EC membership and only 35 per cent supported it. At the conference Mrs Brundtland, for family reasons, resigned as party chairman (after 12 years in the position), although she remained Prime Minister. She was succeeded as chairman by Thorbjoern Jagland. On 19 November parliament voted by 104 to 55 to apply for EC membership. On 25 November in London Mrs Brundtland formally submitted Norway's application.

On 10 December Norway's central bank floated the krone by cutting its link to the EC's ecu, to which it had been pegged since 19 October 1990. The move followed heavy speculation against the Norwegian currency after Sweden's devaluation on 19 November (see II.2.iv). It brought Norway into line with its main trading partners, Britain, Sweden and Finland, which during the autumn had all devalued after abandoning fixed exchange rates.

iv. SWEDEN

CAPITAL: Stockholm   AREA: 450,000 sq km   POPULATION: 8,600,000 ('90)
OFFICIAL LANGUAGE: Swedish   POLITICAL SYSTEM: parliamentary democracy
HEAD OF STATE: King Carl XVI Gustav (since Sept '73)
RULING PARTIES: Moderate Unity Party (MSP), Liberal Party (FP), Centre Party (CP),
    Christian Democratic Community Party (KDS)
HEAD OF GOVERNMENT: Carl Bildt (MSP), Prime Minister (since Oct '91)
PRINCIPAL MINISTERS: Bengt Westerberg (FP/deputy premier, health and social
    affairs), Gun Hellsvik (MSP/justice), Margaretha af Ugglas (MSP/foreign affairs),
    Anders Björck (MSP/defence), Anne Wibble (FP/finance)
INTERNATIONAL ALIGNMENT: neutral, OECD, EFTA, Nordic Council
CURRENCY: krona (end-'92 £1=SKr10.71, US$1=SKr7.07)
GNP PER CAPITA: US$23,660 ('90)
MAIN EXPORT EARNERS: machinery and transport equipment, timber and wood
    products, iron and steel, tourism

CARL Bildt's minority non-socialist coalition government presented its first budget on 10 January, against a background of deep recession. The priorities were low inflation, improved industrial competitiveness and maintaining the value of the krona, linked to the EC's ecu since June 1991. Despite planned public spending cuts of SKr 14,000 million the deficit was forecast at SKr 70,000 million. The government pledged to maintain its medium-term strategy of liberalization, privatization and tax cuts. It later announced that restrictions on foreign ownership of shares in Swedish companies would be removed on 1 January 1993 and that 35 wholly or partly state-owned companies would be privatized, starting in the summer. In April the government announced plans to help industry by abolishing taxes on energy and commercial property and lowering VAT. Inflation was down to 2.5 per cent, but unemployment was rising and the budget deficit forecast had been revised upwards to SKr 111,000 million. The coalition's legislation depended on the support of New Democracy, which in the spring voted with the Social Democrats against the abolition of part-time pensions, throwing into doubt its continued support for government policies.

The government's timetable for completing Sweden's negotiations for EC membership by December 1993 was likewise cast into doubt by Denmark's rejection of the Maastricht treaty on 2 June (see II.2.i). Public opinion was moving against membership. On 16 June, however, the Centre Party reaffirmed its support for the negotiations.

By summer the seriousness of Sweden's banking crisis, and its potential drain on government finances, were apparent. In the autumn the government was forced to rescue a third large bank. In November it announced impending legislation to guarantee state support for the country's banks and credit institutions. This was considered necessary to maintain domestic and international confidence in Sweden's financial system.

In August tensions in the EC's exchange rate mechanism (ERM) and a further upward revision of the forecast budget deficit led to heavy selling of the krona. There followed three months of ultimately unsuccessful measures to avoid devaluation. Interest rates were raised to unprecedented levels in September following Finland's devaluation and the UK's withdrawal from the ERM. In two historic compromises, on 20 and 30 September, the government and Social Democrats agreed to emergency packages which together would cut public expenditure by SKr 70,000 million over five years. The Social Democrats agreed to further cuts in welfare benefits, while the government postponed contentious parts of its programme, including privatization and abolition of the wealth tax. It was also agreed to transfer the burden of health insurance from the state to employers and employees. The second agreement, aimed at lowering industry's costs, cut employers' social security contributions by 4.5 per cent. It also reduced the length of guaranteed national holidays, income tax allowances and housing subsidies.

In November an even larger outflow of capital threatened to wipe out Sweden's reserves. Higher interest rates failed to stem the flow. Efforts to strengthen the krona by obtaining associate membership of the European Monetary System (EMS) had failed. The Social Democrats refused to support another crisis package, and New Democracy argued for floating the krona. On 19 November the krona's link to the ecu was abandoned. Mr Bildt argued that this would not solve Sweden's problems and the medium-term objective remained membership of the EMS. Interest rates remained high to prevent a renewal of the inflationary price-wage spiral.

On 18 November parliament ratified the treaty creating the European Economic Area (EEA), widely regarded as the first step to Sweden's eventual membership of the EC. In the same month public opinion polls showed that opposition to EC membership had risen to over 50 per cent.

v. FINLAND

CAPITAL: Helsinki   AREA: 338,000 sq km   POPULATION: 5,000,000 ('90)
OFFICIAL LANGUAGES: Finnish & Swedish   POLITICAL SYSTEM: presidential democracy
HEAD OF STATE: President Mauno Koivisto (since Sept '81)
RULING PARTIES: Centre Party (KESK), National Coalition Party (KOK), Swedish
    People's Party (SFP), Finnish Christian Union (SKL)
HEAD OF GOVERNMENT: Esko Aho (KESK), Prime Minister (since April '91)
PRINCIPAL MINISTERS: Paavo Väyrynen (KESK/foreign affairs), Mauri Pekkarinen
    (KESK/interior), Hannele Pokka (KESK/justice), Elisabeth Rehn (SFP/defence),
    Iiro Viinanen (KOK/finance)
INTERNATIONAL ALIGNMENT: neutral, OECD, EFTA, Nordic Council
CURRENCY: markka (end-'92 £1=Fmk7.94, US$1=Fmk5.24)
GNP PER CAPITA: US$26,040 ('90)
MAIN EXPORT EARNERS: timber and wood products, manufactures, machinery and
    transport equipment, tourism

ON 20 January Finland and Russia signed three treaties replacing the 1948 Treaty of Friendship, Cooperation and Mutual Assistance between Finland and the Soviet Union. The political treaty omitted any reference to the character of Finland's foreign policy or to military consultations, specifying instead that relations would be based on the principles of the United Nations and the Final Act of the CSCE. The two countries committed themselves to respect their existing frontier. In a separate statement, Russia said it would not oppose Finland's eventual membership of the EC.

On 7 February President Koivisto spoke in favour of applying for EC membership, which on 27 February was backed by the four-party coalition government, despite opposition within the Centre Party. With the opposition Social Democrats also in favour, broad support was assured when parliament voted on 18 March. Immediately after the vote Finland lodged its formal membership application.

Thus, only months after the disintegration of the Soviet Union, Finland's foreign policy had turned decisively towards Western Europe. Events in the former Soviet Union had profoundly affected Finland. Freed from the constraints of the 1948 treaty, Finland could now participate fully in the process of Western European integration. The pressure to do so was both economic and political: the need to replace lost East European markets and to avoid isolation between an expanding European Community in the west and a disintegrating, unstable Eastern Europe. Finland also faced the prospect of Swedish EC membership, and once the European Economic Area (EEA) came into being on 1 January 1993, economic integration with the EC without equal participation in its decision-making processes. EC membership, argued President Koivisto, would enable Finland to regain the sovereignty lost through EEA membership.

Finland remained in the worst recession this century following a 6 per cent fall in GDP in 1991. Unemployment was 10 per cent and the banking sector in crisis. Lack of international confidence in the markka's link to the EC's ecu following its devaluation in November 1991 kept interest rates high and pressure on the government to satisfy the international financial markets. The dangers were illustrated in early April. On 2 April the governor of the Bank of Finland abruptly resigned following a public dispute with the Prime Minister, Esko Aho, over responsibility for economic policy mistakes. This led to an outflow of capital and higher interest rates, and the government was forced to announce public spending cuts of Fmk 10,000 million. A further Fmk 7,000 million of cuts were announced in June.

In early August heavy capital outflows began again. Publicly-expressed differences over economic policy, this time within the coalition, again undermined investor confidence. Budget deficit forecasts had risen with the unemployment rate and banking sector losses. On 6 August the government reaffirmed its policy of no devaluation and spending cuts. Real interest rates reached record heights. On 20 August it announced further budget cuts for 1993. Support for the broad thrust of government policy came from both the IMF and OECD. On 8 September, faced with seriously-depleted reserves, the Bank of Finland was forced to devalue the markka.

On 14 October the government announced an austerity programme to cut public spending by another Fmk 54,200 over three years. In the local elections four days later the two major ruling parties, the Conservatives (National Coalition) and Centre, suffered heavy losses. The Social Democrats and Greens made large gains. On 25 November the unions accepted an agreement containing no wage increases in 1993. There would, however, be index-linked pay compensation if living standards dropped by more than 4.3 per cent.

On 4 November the EC Commission recommended opening negotiations on Finland's membership application. On 11-12 December the EC's Edinburgh summit (see XI.3) opened the way for negotiations to begin in 1993.

vi.   AUSTRIA

CAPITAL: Vienna   AREA: 84,000 sq km   POPULATION: 7,700,000 ('90)
OFFICIAL LANGUAGE: German   POLITICAL SYSTEM: federal parliamentary democracy
HEAD OF STATE: Federal President Thomas Klestil (since Aug '92)
RULING PARTIES: Social Democratic (SPÖ) & People's (ÖVP) parties
HEAD OF GOVERNMENT: Franz Vranitzky (SPÖ) Federal Chancellor (since June '86)
PRINCIPAL MINISTERS: Erhard Busek (ÖVP/vice-chancellor), Aloïs Mock (ÖVP/foreign
    affairs), Ferdinand Lacina (SPÖ/finance), Franz Löschnack (SPÖ/interior),
    Werner Fasslabend (ÖVP/defence), Nikolaus Michalek (non-party/justice)
INTERNATIONAL ALIGNMENT: neutral, OECD, EFTA
CURRENCY: schilling (end-'92 £1=Sch17.25, US$1=Sch11.39)
GNP PER CAPITA: US$19,060 ('90)
MAIN EXPORT EARNERS: basic manufactures, machinery and transport equipment,
    chemicals, tourism

THE most important event of 1992 was probably the election as Federal President of the distinguished diplomat Dr Thomas Klestil, candidate of the People's Party (ÖVP). In the second round of voting on 24 May Dr Klestil won an unexpectedly decisive 56.9 per cent of the vote, with a majority in every federal province over his Social Democratic Party (SPÖ) opponent, Dr Rudolf Streicher. Dr Klestil took office, in succession to Dr Kurt Waldheim, on 8 July, so opening the way for a more normal pattern of exchanges with the outside world. A particularly noteworthy visitor, in early December, was the Israeli Foreign Minister, Shimon Peres, who invited Dr Klestil to visit Israel. He also extended invitations to the Federal Chancellor, Dr Franz Vranitzky, and the Foreign Minister, Dr Aloïs Mock. Another landmark event in the field of foreign policy had occurred on 19 June, when Italy and Austria formally notified the United Nations that the longstanding dispute between them over the South Tyrol was closed. Austria had previously acknowledged the implementation of the autonomy package for the German-speaking inhabitants of South Tyrol, in a note handed by Dr Mock to the Italian ambassador on 11 June.

Satisfaction at these events was tempered by uncase at the potential security threats posed by instability in eastern Europe and turmoil in the former Yugoslavia (see II.1.vi), of which the steady influx of refugees from the fighting in Bosnia was a continual reminder. On 15 January Austria recognized Slovenia and Croatia, and also the 11 former Soviet republics affiliated to the Commonwealth of Independent States (CIS). By mid-February Dr Mock, Vice-Chancellor Busek and the Minister for Economic Affairs, Dr Schlüssel, had all visited Slovenia and Croatia. Moreover, parliament had agreed to make Sch 25 million immediately available to alleviate hardship and to aid reconstruction in Croatia. By the end of October the total Austrian contribution to humanitarian aid for the former Yugoslavia, excluding food aid, was in excess of Sch 716 million, while an estimated 70,000 refugees were resident in Austria.

In the wake of Danish and British difficulties over ratification of the Maastricht treaty, the prospects for Austria's application for EC membership also caused concern, as did the problems of reconciling EC membership with permanent neutrality. Vigorous debate continued inside and outside the SPÖ/ÖVP grand coalition on the form of Austria's future relationship with European security institutions. The requirement for WEU membership was increasingly, if grudgingly, accepted by SPÖ politicians, but strong emotional attachment to neutrality was still evident among the public, in spite of the concern aroused by the fighting in Bosnia. On 22 September parliament ratified the European Economic Area (EEA) treaty, and continued work on the mass of legislative amendments required by the terms of the treaty. The EC's European Council in Edinburgh on 11–12 December decided that formal accession negotiations with Austria, Sweden, Norway and Finland could begin in 1993, although their conclusion would have to await ratification of the EC's Maastricht treaty.

There were few ministerial changes during 1992. Dr Streicher's resignation as Minister of Transport, to fight the presidential election, prompted a minor reshuffle among SPÖ members of the cabinet on 30 March. His successor was Viktor Klima, with Michael Ausserwinkler taking over from Harald Ettl as Minister of Health. At the same time, Brigitte Ederer succeeded Dr Peter Jankowitsch as state secretary in the Federal Chancellery with responsibility for Austrian integration into the EC. On 25 November Maria Rauch-Kallat was sworn in as Minister for the Environment, Youth and Family Affairs. The economy continued to perform moderately well, but persistent economic stagnation in Germany caused forecasts to be revised sharply downwards at the end of the year. Real increase in GDP for 1992 was estimated as unlikely to exceed 2 per cent, in that inflation rose slightly to 4 per cent and the estimated unemployment rate to about 6 per cent. Forecasters warned that falling tax receipts would increase the budget deficit in 1993.

Immigration and refugees (legal and illegal) were the main domestic issues in 1992, with the Freedom Party (FPÖ) under its controversial leader, Dr Jörg Haider, continuing to play upon public fears and prejudices. After several incidents in January, including a petrol bomb attack on a refugee home, the government tightened up its anti-nazi legislation on 26 February, by amending the 1945 constitutional ban on the Nazi party to penalize those seeking to contest or to justify nazi crimes. Although the FPÖ sedulously disassociated itself from violent incidents, in a series of dramatic moves at the beginning of March Dr Haider effectively purged his party's leading liberals, so moving the FPÖ much further towards the extreme nationalist and xenophobic right. He also announced his intention of returning from Carinthia to national politics in Vienna as FPÖ parliamentary leader, but failed during 1992 to achieve his stated objective of breaking up the grand coalition and bringing about fresh elections before the due date of 1994. Indeed, the FPÖ's rightward lurch effectively strengthened the coalition by making it harder for the ÖVP to regard Dr Haider as an acceptable coalition partner. Nonetheless, the FPÖ leader kept up the pressure, presenting a package of demands on immigration on 21 October and, on 21 November, launching a petition for a referendum on the issue, as provided for by the constitution.

Confronted with this delicate and emotive political issue, the government took a tougher line on immigration policy during 1992. A new asylum law distinguishing between political and economic refugees came into force on 1 June, and further restrictive legislation was in the pipeline. On 1 July a visa regime was introduced for former Yugoslav nationals, and on 14 September, after the provinces of Vienna, Salzburg and Carinthia had declared that they could accept no more Bosnian refugees, tighter border controls were imposed to admit only those coming directly from the war zones. The Minister for Internal Affairs, Franz Löschnak, appealed for a pan-European solution to the problem and for a more equitable distribution of refugees among West European countries. In such troubled times, the disastrous fire which destroyed part of the historic Hofburg Palace in Vienna on 27 November was an apt symbol of loss and change.

vii. SWITZERLAND

CAPITAL: Berne   AREA: 41,300 sq km   POPULATION: 6,850,000 ('90)
OFFICIAL LANGUAGES: German, French, Italian & Rhaeto-Romanic
POLITICAL SYSTEM: federal canton-based democracy
RULING PARTIES: Christian Democratic People's (CVP), Radical Democratic (FDP),
    Social Democratic (SPS) & Swiss People's (SVP) parties
HEAD OF STATE & GOVERNMENT: René Felber (SPS), 1992 President of Federal
    Council, Foreign Minister
OTHER MINISTERS: Adolf Ogi (SVP/vice-pesident, communications & energy),
    Otto Stich (SPS/finance), Jean-Pascal Delamuraz (FDP/economy), Arnold Koller
    (CVP/justice), Kaspar Villiger (FDP/defence), Flavio Cotti (CVP/interior)
INTERNATIONAL ALIGNMENT: neutral, OECD, EFTA
CURRENCY: Swiss franc (end-'92 £1=SwF2.22, US$1=SwF1.46)
GNP PER CAPITA: US$34,064 ('91)
MAIN EXPORT EARNERS: financial services, machinery, chemicals, tourism

THE process of European integration and definition of the part Switzerland would play in it was the dominating topic of Swiss politics
throughout the year. On 2 May the heads of government of the seven
EFTA members and the 12 EC members signed the treaty for the creation
of the European Economic Area (EEA). Shortly after this, the Federal
Council submitted an application for talks about full membership of
Switzerland in the EC. Two main reasons were given for this rather
unexpected step. The first was the government's judgment that the
Community was now willing to admit new members and therefore
could evolve within a few years from a West European alliance to
an all-European organization, from which Switzerland could no longer
stay apart. The second reason was the fear that negotiations between
the EC and Austria, Sweden and Finland (which had all already applied
for membership) would define the role of neutral countries within the
Community regardless of Swiss interests.

Under the Swiss constitution, ratification of the EEA treaty required
not only the consent of parliament but also a popular vote. Both
chambers of parliament accepted the treaty by a large majority (128
votes to 58 in the National Council and 38 votes to 2 in the Council of
States). Parliament also agreed on the approximately 60 amendments
to federal law which were necessary to ensure conformity with EC
internal market regulations and the *acquis communautaire*. The three
big governmental parties (FDP, SPS and CVP), as well as the Liberal
Party and the small centrist parties, voted in favour of the treaty. The
opposition was formed by the smallest governmental formation (SVP),
the Green Party and the three right-wing parties (Automobile Party,
Lega dei Ticinesi and Swiss Democrats).

The supporters of the EEA included the unions, the associations of
business and banking and, by a narrow vote, the Union of Small
Traders. According to the treaty's supporters, it was absolutely necessary for Switzerland to join the EEA in order to prevent political

marginalization and costly discrimination against Swiss exporters inside the internal market. In addition, they said that the EEA would bring many advantages to Swiss citizens, such as lower prices for goods and services and better possibilities for working and studying abroad.

The opponents mainly criticized three aspects of the EEA. Right-wingers in particular opposed the liberalization of immigration laws, stressing the fact that Switzerland already had the highest proportion of foreign population in Europe (almost one-fifth of the population and a quarter of the workforce, most of them from southern EC countries). The Green Party criticized the EEA for its underlying concept of fostering unlimited economic growth. It was also opposed to the obligation to adapt Swiss environmental law to EC regulations, which were in most fields less strict. Not only the opponents but also many supporters of the EEA agreed that the institutional regulations for the further evolution of law governing the EEA were its weakest part. Even if the Community was willing to concede a right of consultation to the EFTA states, the right of co-decision was simply denied. So the citizens had to decide not only on integration of Switzerland into the single European market but also on transferring a part of their own legislative rights to the bodies of the EC.

Both sides conducted intense and also very emotional and rather polemical campaigns for the referendum, which was held on 6 December. The voter turnout was almost 80 per cent, the highest in a referendum since 1947. By a very small margin of only 20,000 votes (50.3 per cent to 49.7 per cent), the citizens rejected the EEA treaty. Entry into a supranational organization like the EEA also required acceptance by the voters of a majority of the cantons. This aim was clearly missed: in only seven of the 23 cantons did the vote go in favour.

The result showed a clear split between the French-speaking part of Switzerland, where an overwhelming majority voted in favour, and the rest of the country, where the treaty was rejected by 54 per cent (German-speaking regions) and 61 per cent (Italian-speaking Ticino canton). But the cleavage was not only along language lines: most urban areas in the German-speaking part also voted in favour, whereas opposition was almost unanimous in remote Alpine areas. While very disappointed by the outcome of the vote, the Federal Council did not withdraw the EC membership application. It nevertheless agreed with the EC authorities that the necessary preparatory work should be postponed (see XI.3; XI.5.iv).

Even opponents of the EEA mostly declared that they were not advocating isolationist politics for the future (and polls showed that 90 per cent of the population would not support such a strategy). The citizens had confirmed this attitude in two earlier popular votes. First, they agreed on 17 May that Switzerland should join the International

Monetary Fund and the World Bank as a full member. Later, on 27 September, they voted by a large majority in favour of a SwF 15,000 million project for the construction of two new railway tunnels through the Alps, mainly for the transit of goods between Italy and the northern EC countries.

Only three years after the popular vote on the proposal to abolish the Swiss army (see AR 1989, p. 177), a new fundamental controversy on this matter broke out in 1992. The starting-point was a parliamentary decision to order 34 F/A-18 fighter planes at a cost of SwF 3,500 million. The Group for Switzerland Without an Army seized the opportunity to launch another popular initiative, which if accepted (in a referendum due in summer 1993) would not only cancel this decision but also introduce a new constitutional amendment prohibiting the acquisition of any new fighters till the year 2000. The high cost of the F/A-18 and widespread hostility to new armaments made the task of collecting the required 100,000 signatures for this initiative rather easy: in less than one month more than 500,000 citizens (10 per cent of the electorate) had backed the proposal.

The economic situation further deteriorated. The number of unemployed increased from 60,000 to 130,000 by the end of the year (4.2 per cent of the workforce). Late in the year, and without much emphasis, the Social Democrats and the unions called, unsuccessfully, for a government programme to stimulate economic growth. The National Bank maintained its tight monetary policy and succeeded in reducing the inflation rate from 5.9 to 3.4 per cent.

After a steady increase during the past decade, the number of persons seeking asylum in Switzerland dropped to approximately 20,000 new applications in 1992 (compared with 42,000 in 1991). This number did not include 8,500 released prisoners of the Bosnian war and their families who were granted temporary asylum by the Federal Council nor the 70,000 displaced persons from former Yugoslavia who took refuge with relatives already living in Switzerland.

As usual in Switzerland, not even the defeat of the Federal Council in the popular vote on the EEA treaty produced any changes in government. Adolf Ogi, who supported the treaty in spite of his party's opposition to it, was elected to the annually-rotating post of President of the Federal Council for 1993.

viii. EUROPEAN MINI-STATES

Andorra
CAPITAL: Andorra la Vella   AREA: 460 sq km   POPULATION: 51,500 ('90)
OFFICIAL LANGUAGE: Catalan   POLITICAL SYSTEM: qualified democracy
HEADS OF STATE: President Mitterrand of France & Bishop Joan Marti Alanis of
    Urgel (co-princes)
HEAD OF GOVERNMENT: Oscar Ribas Reig, President of Executive Council (since '90)
CURRENCY: French franc & Spanish peseta
MAIN EXPORT EARNERS: tourism, banking, smuggling

Holy See (Vatican)
CAPITAL: Vatican City   AREA: 0.44 sq km   POPULATION: 760 ('90)
OFFICIAL LANGUAGES: Italian & Latin   POLITICAL SYSTEM: theocracy
HEAD OF STATE: Pope John Paul II (since '78)
HEAD OF GOVERNMENT: Most Rev Angelo Sodano, Secretary of State (since Dec '90)
CURRENCY: Vatican lira (pegged to Italian lira)

Liechtenstein
CAPITAL: Vaduz   AREA: 160 sq km   POPULATION: 29,000 ('90)
OFFICIAL LANGUAGE: German   POLITICAL SYSTEM: parliamentary democracy
HEAD OF STATE: Prince Hans Adam II (since Nov '89)
RULING PARTIES: Patriotic Union (VU) & Progressive Citizens' Party (FBP)
HEAD OF GOVERNMENT: Hans Brunhart (VU), Prime Minister (since '78)
CURRENCY: Swiss franc   GNP PER CAPITA: US$15,000 ('89)
MAIN EXPORT EARNERS: manufactured goods, tourism, financial services

Monaco
CAPITAL: Monaco-Ville   AREA: 1.95 sq km   POPULATION: 28,000 ('90)
OFFICIAL LANGUAGE: French   POLITICAL SYSTEM: constitutional monarchy
HEAD OF STATE: Prince Rainier III (since '49)
HEAD OF GOVERNMENT: Jacques Dupont, Minister of State (since April '91)
CURRENCY: French franc
MAIN EXPORT EARNERS: tourism, financial services

San Marino
CAPITAL: San Marino   AREA: 60.5 sq km   POPULATION: 23,000 ('90)
OFFICIAL LANGUAGE: Italian   POLITICAL SYSTEM: parliamentary democracy
HEADS OF STATE AND GOVERNMENT: Captains-Regent Romeo Morri & Marino Zanotti
RULING PARTIES: Christian Democratic & Socialist parties
CURRENCY: Italian lira
MAIN EXPORT EARNERS: tourism, agricultural products, postage stamps

THE year 1992 saw Andorra, Liechtenstein and San Marino take further steps towards greater integration in the diplomatic community.

In a general election in ANDORRA, held in two rounds on 5 and 12 April, supporters of Oscar Ribas Reig, the outgoing President of the Executive Council (head of government), won an absolute majority of the 28 seats in the General Council of the Valleys. Of the electorate of just over 8,500, 82 per cent went to the polls and Sr Ribas Reig was confirmed in office on 4 May. The result was seen as a vote of confidence in his plans for a constitution which would legalize political parties and trade unions and protect civil rights, thus bringing Andorra into line with the majority of other European states. On 19 December a commission comprising representatives of Andorrans and of the two Andorran co-princes or heads of state (i.e. of the French President and the Bishop of the Spanish diocese of Urgel) approved a draft constitution drawn up on this basis. This draft then required approval by parliament and by the electorate in a referendum, which was scheduled for March 1993.

By contrast, in MONACO, Monegasques appeared content to continue existing arrangements whereby, under Prince Rainier III as head of state, the head of government (Jacques Dupont during 1992) was appointed on the recommendation of the French government. Early in the year, on 6 January, Monaco's National Council approved legislation tightening the principality's citizenship law under which foreign women (though not foreign men) marrying a Monegasque citizen had hitherto been automatically granted citizenship and thus benefited from tax-free living and other privileges. In future, the woman would have to stay with her husband for at least five years before becoming a citizen. On 18 December the National Council further decided that female citizens of Monaco should be able to hand on their nationality to their children, a right hitherto enjoyed only by Monegasque men.

In LIECHTENSTEIN 55.8 per cent of the electorate voted in a referendum on 13 December in favour of joining the European Economic Area (EEA) as set out in an agreement signed in May 1992 by the EFTA and EC member states. The vote was greeted with considerable surprise, since it followed a Swiss referendum the previous week which had opposed ratification of the agreement (see II.2.vii). Yet it confirmed the policy of greater integration in Europe as passionately advocated by Prince Hans Adam II, despite the principality's customs union and other traditionally close links with neighbouring Switzerland.

Earlier in the year there were difficulties in relations between Liechtenstein and Czechoslovakia, where the Grand Duke had owned territory in Bohemia and Moravia ten times the area of Liechtenstein itself. (Indeed, it was only in 1719 that his forbears had formally acquired the fiefs of Vaduz and Schellenburg which comprise present-day Liechtenstein.) These lands were, however, confiscated in 1919 by the newly-established Czechoslovak republic. Under pressure on all sides in 1938, the Czechoslovak government eventually recognized Liechtenstein, promised to return half the territory and to pay compensation for the remainder. However, World War II intervened and the lands were again seized after 1945. Although compensation agreements were subsequently reached by Czechoslovakia with most countries with citizens whose property had been seized, Liechtenstein was excluded, along with West Germany and Argentina.

In SAN MARINO the Christian Democrats switched coalition partners on 19 March from the Progressive Democratic Party (PDP), which had until March 1990 been called the Communist Party, to the Socialists (PSS). The Christian Democrats maintained that their alliance with the PDP had become outdated following the demise of communism elsewhere in Europe. On 2 March San Marino, which had previously had only observer status at the United Nations, became a UN member and on 23 September it joined the International Monetary Fund.

During 1992 the HOLY SEE sought to establish contact with the new states which replaced the former Soviet Union and Yugoslavia. Diplomatic relations were established on 2 February with Croatia and Slovenia, both of which were predominantly Roman Catholic, while diplomatic relations with ethnically and religiously diverse Bosnia were established on 20 August. As regards the former Soviet Union, diplomatic relations were established with the Russian Federation on 28 December 1991 and during 1992 with the republics as follows: Ukraine (10 February), Armenia, Azerbaijan, Georgia, Moldavia (all 23 May), Kirghizia (27 August), Uzbekistan, Kazakhstan (both 19 October) and Belorussia (11 November). The other significant diplomatic initiative of the year was towards Mexico, which had the second-largest Roman Catholic population in Latin America. Having been broken off in 1861, relations between the Holy See and Mexico were restored on 20 September after changes to the anti-clerical 1917 constitution had been approved in late 1991. As a result, churches were allowed to own property and run schools, while priests and nuns were given the right to vote and wear their religious attire in public.

In the Vatican City itself, Secretary of State Angelo Sodano sought to reduce the Holy See's budget deficit. In 1991 it had increased by only 2.1 per cent which, given inflation in Italy of over 6 per cent, represented a decrease in real terms.

3. SPAIN—PORTUGAL—GIBRALTAR—MALTA—GREECE—CYPRUS—TURKEY

i. SPAIN

CAPITAL: Madrid   AREA: 505,000 sq km   POPULATION: 39,000,000 ('90)
OFFICIAL LANGUAGE: Spanish   POLITICAL SYSTEM: parliamentary democracy
HEAD OF STATE: King Juan Carlos (since Nov '75)
RULING PARTY: Spanish Socialist Workers' Party (PSOE)
HEAD OF GOVERNMENT: Felipe González, Prime Minister (since Nov '82)
PRINCIPAL MINISTERS: Narcís Serra Serra (deputy premier), Julian García Vargas (defence), José Luis Corcuero (interior), Javier Solana Madariaga (foreign affairs), Carlos Solchaga (economy, finance), Tomás de la Quadra Salcedo (justice)
INTERNATIONAL ALIGNMENT: NATO, OECD, EC
CURRENCY: peseta (end-'92 £1=Ptas173.75, US$1=Ptas114.762)
GNP PER CAPITA: US$11,020 ('90)
MAIN EXPORT EARNERS: tourism, transport equipment, agricultural products, minerals and base metals

SPAIN was in 1992 the cynosure of millions of visitors and, it was reckoned, of 1,000 million television viewers. It had three great successes:

the organization and conduct of some 1,800 special events in Madrid
as that year's cultural capital, a World Fair in Seville at which over
100 nations had pavilions, and the XXV Olympic Games in Barcelona,
in which sportsmen from a similar number of countries took part (see
also XVII).

Seville was chosen for the Fair because of its links with Christopher
Columbus and the New World, which he discovered for Spain in 1492.
A new international air terminal, a new high-speed railway track, a new
motorway from Madrid and a network of dual-carriage roads from elsewhere all made rapid access to Seville possible. As late as mid-February
foreign observers doubted whether the Fair's infrastructure, planned to
cope with 300,000 visitors a day, would be ready for its inauguration on
20 April. It was ready, however, and successfully withstood the pressure
of a record 629,000 visitors on 3 October, nine days before its closure.
The Fair left Andalucia with modern and efficient communications
likely to attract foreign investment, and Seville with a high-technology
research centre, buildings with substantial industrial and commercial
potential, and new housing in what had long been a run-down area
of the city. The Fair's success had given proof that Spain had a skilled
workforce and organizers.

The Olympic Games were equally meticulously planned and successfully executed. Here too there was much investment in roads and
buildings of lasting value to the city of Barcelona and the surrounding
area. During the preparations there were risks of clashes between
Spanish and Catalan nationalists, between the central government
and the Generalitat (the autonomous government of Catalonia), and
even between the politically right-of-centre president of the Generalitat,
Jordi Pujol Soley, and the Socialist mayor of Barcelona. The two
Catalans, normally at odds with each other, decided to cooperate for
once, and the central government conceded that the nomination of
Catalan as one of the official languages of the Games was not prejudicial
to Spanish sovereignty. In March, at the election for the autonomous
parliament, Sr Pujol's party, Convergencia i Unió, had won 71 of the
135 seats, an increase of two over the 1988 election, but the militant
and vociferous Catalan Republican Left (Esquerra Republicana) had
won 11, an increase of five.

King Juan Carlos astonished his audience when, at the inauguration
ceremony—on 25 July, the feast of St James and traditionally Spain's
national day—he addressed them firstly in Catalan and then in Spanish.
Throughout the Games he went among the public, the 30,000 voluntary
helpers and especially the Spanish competitors, chatting with everyone
as an equal. He embraced enthusiastically the 22 Spanish medallists, as
did Queen Sofia, and the pair won the affection even of Socialists and
Communists, and the respect at least of some republican leftists.

Within Spain and abroad fears had been expressed early in the year

that the Basque separatist ETA would attempt a spectacular act of terrorism at the World Fair or the Games. The fears had been well enough
founded for the Prime Minister, Felipe González, publicly to declare in
February that such was indeed ETA's intention. At a secret meeting in
France in December, its leaders had vehemently rejected arguments by
subordinates that the 'armed struggle' had proved useless and damaging
to its aim of an independent Basque state, and should therefore be
abandoned. Accordingly, during January ETA had exploded bombs in
Bilbao, Valencia and Barcelona, causing the deaths of three soldiers,
a policeman and a former government minister.

Basques had then marched through Bilbao demanding an end to
terrorism. ETA's response was, first, a public reaffirmation of its
intention to persist with similar actions, as long as central government
continued 'to deny the Basque nation its political, social and cultural
rights'. Second, on 6 February, a bomb explosion in central Madrid
killed four soldiers and a civilian and wounded several others, while
four days later there was another in Murcia. The government thereupon
filed criminal charges against three leading members of Herri Batasuna,
ETA's political wing, who had a record of statements which could be
construed as incitements to terrorism. The principal of the three,
however, being a member of the Cortes, was immune from arrest.
Undeterred, ETA had claimed responsibility for the deaths of another
nine persons by the last week of March. The only arrest was that of a
priest who was accused of giving temporary sanctuary to two suspects.

On 29 March ETA suffered a severe setback. The French police caught
Francisco Mugica Garmendia (ETA director of operations), his deputy
and its chief explosives expert together in a house in Bidart (near
Biarritz). Moreover, in April they arrested the man expected to be
Sr Mugica's successor, the suspected ETA treasurer, as he boarded a
flight from Paris to Mexico. Captured documents revealed to them
the secret addresses in St Jean de Luz, Bordeaux, Paris and Brittany
of some 30 ETA activists, who were rounded up on 4 May. In June
in Paris they detained ETA's coordinator of purchases of arms and
explosives, and also found a 15-page type-written letter which they
and the Spanish police attributed to ETA's erstwhile leader, Eugenio
Etxebeste (see AR 1987, p. 175 and AR 1988, p. 182), now in exile in
the Dominican Republic. This letter advised the organization that it
lacked the strength to fight both France and Spain simultaneously.
The 'armed struggle' was doomed, it continued, and should therefore
be abandoned in favour of political action. The Basque revolutionary
left should seek better relations with other Basque parties, and espouse
popular causes such as 'women's lib, the fight against drug addiction,
the green movement, etc.'.

Disclosure of the letter had some effect. Herri Batasuna tempered
its enmity towards other parties, and on 10 July ETA issued a pledge to

abstain from violence for two months, provided the Spanish government made a gesture, such as the release of some ETA activists from prison. On 3 August another possible successor ETA leader was arrested in France. As there was no sign of the required gesture from the Spanish government, two weeks later ETA declared the truce over, and its men killed two more policemen. Nevertheless, it was evident that ETA had been weakened by the loss of France as a safe haven, and perturbed by the letter. Over the rest of the year there were only minor and infrequent terrorist incidents. In October Herri Batasuna persuaded the small Basque Solidarity party (EA) to join in a demonstration demanding the independence of Euskadi (the Basque region), but the other Basque parties remained suspicious of its new friendliness.

At the beginning of the year there were strikes in Asturias in protest against the speed at which the government planned to adapt the coal and steel industry to compete in the EC single market. The government agreed to slow down the process, and promised investment to create alternative employment in the region. Unemployment also rose with the collapse of numerous firms through a fall in the demand for their products or services. The government proposed to cut unemployment benefits; the unions called a one-day general strike on 28 May. But generally the unions showed moderation, which was rewarded in the government's 1993 budget. While reducing allocations for defence and administration, the budget increased those for unemployment benefits, pensions and health. Cordial relations between the ruling PSOE and the UGT trade union confederation, broken in 1988 (see AR 1988, pp. 180–2), were re-established at the end of September.

The Bank of Spain was unable to defend the peseta when, in succession to the pound and the lira, it came under speculative attack in September. A 5 per cent devaluation on 23 September was followed by a 6 per cent downward adjustment on 23 November. This realignment, coupled with exchange-rate controls, enabled the peseta to remain in the exchange rate mechanism of the European Monetary System (EMS). A statement by the Minister of Economy and Finance, Carlos Solchaga, that the devaluation would make Spain more competitive and strengthen its position in the EMS, met with almost unanimous assent from opposition parties, unions and employers. The only fear expressed was that it would now be more difficult to lower the prevailing high rates of interest. At the December EC summit in Edinburgh Prime Minister González fought hard for the retention of the cohesion fund agreed upon at Maastricht, winning the battle, although not for as large an amount as he had hoped (see XI.3). Earlier, the Cortes had completed its ratification of the Maastricht treaty on 25 November.

In October the PSOE celebrated the completion of its tenth year in government under Sr González. In a long press interview he considered the present and the future rather than the past. He recognized that he and the PSOE had lost popularity: unemployment was still high, the ETA remained untamed, cases of corruption existed among officials, and there was frustration over the time taken by bureaucrats in resolving the problems of individuals. He was confident, however, that at the next election, due no later than the following October, the PSOE would gain more votes than any other party, although if it did not have an overall majority he would not be averse to a coalition. On 25 October Sr González confirmed that he would seek a fourth term in the premiership.

ii.   PORTUGAL

CAPITAL: Lisbon   AREA: 92,000 sq km   POPULATION: 10,400,000 ('90)
OFFICIAL LANGUAGE: Portuguese
POLITICAL SYSTEM: presidential/parliamentary democracy
HEAD OF STATE: President Mário Soares (since March '86)
RULING PARTY: Social Democratic Party (PSD)
HEAD OF GOVERNMENT: Anibal Cavaco Silva, Prime Minister (since Nov '85)
PRINCIPAL MINISTERS: Joaquim Fernando Nogueira (presidency, defence),
   Jorge Braga de Macedo (finance), Manuel Dias Loureiro (home affairs),
   José M. Durão Barroso (foreign affairs), Alvaro Laborinho Lucío (justice)
INTERNATIONAL ALIGNMENT: NATO, OECD, EC
CURRENCY: escudo (end-'92 £1=Esc222.25, US$1=Esc146.79)
GNP PER CAPITA: US$7,600 ('92)
MAIN EXPORT EARNERS: tourism, basic manufactures, textiles, agricultural products

THE dominant event of the year was Portugal's six-month tenure of the rotating EC presidency from January to June—the first since Portugal's admission in 1986. With the impending controversy over the proposed Maastricht treaty in view, the government deflected suggestions for a referendum on grounds of cost and time. It adopted a low-profile, conciliatory style in its handling of EC issues and meetings, leaving its successor, the United Kingdom, to deal with the crisis caused by the negative Danish vote (see II.2.i). Discreetly, and with varying degrees of success, Portugal tried to focus other members' attention on matters of Portuguese interest, including preferential concessions for the African Portuguese-speaking countries. It also raised the forgotten but unsettled issue of East Timor, the unhappy remaining postscript to the end of Portuguese empire in 1975, over which Indonesia claimed sovereignty (see IX.1.vi). The only major success of the Portuguese EC presidency was the approval for much-needed alterations to the common agricultural policy (CAP), which came in June. This vindicated the efforts of Agriculture Minister Arlindo Cunha, who had campaigned for what was regarded as the most significant reform in the CAP since its creation 30 years previously. All in all, this policy of circumspection, plus conciliatory diplomacy towards other members directly involved in objections and disputes, resulted in a positive contribution to the EC's future at a time of controversy.

Later in the year Foreign Minister Deus Pinheiro was rewarded with the post of Portugal's new commissioner in Brussels, replacing Cardoso e Cunha. The latter became the head of the commission in charge of Expo 98, to be held in Lisbon in commemoration of the fifth centenary of the opening of the maritime route from Europe to India by Vasco da Gama. Deus Pinheiro was replaced as Foreign Minister by his deputy, José M. Durão Barroso, who as secretary of state in charge of African affairs had played an important role in achieving a ceasefire in the civil war in Angola (see VII.1.vi).

The relative success of Portugal's EC presidency and other diplomatic factors benefited Prime Minister Cavaco Silva to the extent that *Publico*, one of Portugal's best modern newspapers, hailed 1992 as the '*annus Cavacus*'. Significantly, the year saw the replacement of the leaders of all the other major left- and right-wing parties: Jorge Sampaio of the Socialist Party (PS) was replaced by Antonio Guterres; Professor Freitas do Amaral of the Social Democrat Centre (CDS) was succeeded by the much younger lawyer Antonio Monteiro; and even the octogenarian Alvaro Cunhal, for over 30 years secretary-general of the Communist Party (PC), finally gave way to Carlos Carvalhas. But for Sr Cavaco Silva 1992 was also the year when many began to voice the possibility that he might be a strong candidate for the presidency of the republic when Dr Mário Soares ended his current, and constitutionally last, term as head of state.

Internally, like the British Conservatives and other European ruling parties, the PSD government owed its electoral success and durability to its reputation for being better than its rivals at keeping inflation down and economic expansion up. There was considerable capital movement, as a result of privatizations and investment by multinational concerns in insurance and luxury hotels. The Portuguese Grupo Entreposto took over a chain of Brazilian-owned supermarkets in Portugal, and there were further Portuguese investments in Spain, where the Caixa Geral dos Depositos took over two banks and another Portuguese group, Cimpor, acquired the Galician cement group, Corporación Noroeste. The inflation rate remained at 9 per cent in both 1991 and 1992, which although high compared with the EC average was seen as one of the achievements of Finance Minister Braga de Macedo. With these and other indicators showing an encouraging degree of stability and expansion, Sr Cavaco Silva somewhat over-confidently announced in April the adherence of the escudo to the EC's exchange rate mechanism (ERM). Within six months disarray in the system, brought about by the weakness of the lira and the pound, necessitated improvised measures to maintain the escudo's ERM parity.

The chronic negative trade gap remained for most of 1992, while earnings from tourism and immigrants' remittances continued to decrease, in reflection of the international recession. Stringent cuts and redundancies were imposed on public services in anticipation of an announced cut of 5 per cent in the proposed budget for 1993.

The year was marked by other reminders that modern economic and financial expansion was not without its shortcomings and side-effects. Portugal saw an unprecedented number of speculative practices and scandals, including the flight to South America of a stock exchange dealer widely regarded in business circles as a paradigm of the Portuguese 'yuppie'. In mid December, following an FAO-sponsored international conference on nutrition in Rome, the Portuguese press carried several critical reports showing that most social indicators still placed Portugal, with Greece and Ireland, at the bottom of the EC scale—by a long margin when compared with the average per capita incomes of the bigger industrial states. According to the reports, Portugal contained pockets of extreme poverty, even hunger, comparable to those of the so-called Third World. Unemployment rose to over 4.2 per cent of the workforce in 1991, and there were renewed international accusations that industries such as textiles and shoe manufacturing still owed their relative export success to exploitation of child labour.

From the Cavaco government's point of view, however, the year ended on a positive note. After avoiding being too eager on the question of the EC cohesion fund during its EC presidency, and leaving it to Spain to exercise the necessary pressures at the December Edinburgh summit, the Portuguese were gratified by the decision to allocate the equivalent of 2,660 million escudos in EC subsidies, to be shared over the next seven years with Spain, Greece and Ireland. Apart from the tangible economic significance, the political and psychological benefit was of crucial importance for a small country that only two decades previously feared that it could not survive, let alone prosper, without its centuries-old overseas empire.

iii.   GIBRALTAR

CAPITAL: Gibraltar   AREA: 6.5 sq km   POPULATION: 31,000 ('90)
OFFICIAL LANGUAGE: English   POLITICAL SYSTEM: UK dependency, democracy
HEAD OF STATE: Queen Elizabeth II   GOVERNOR: Adml. Sir Derek Reffell
RULING PARTY: Socialist Labour Party (SLP)
HEAD OF GOVERNMENT: Joe Bossano, Chief Minister (since March '88)

FOR Chief Minister Joe Bossano the year could not have begun better. At the election in January for the house of assembly his Socialist Labour Party (GSLP) polled 73.3 per cent of the votes, the Social Democrats (GSDP) under Peter Caruana 20.2 per cent and the recently-founded National Party (GNP) 4.7 per cent. Under the constitution, no party could take more than eight seats in the 15-member Assembly; so the GSLP got eight and the GSDP the remainder. The winners were pledged to wrest from the United Kingdom a new constitution giving Gibraltar greater autonomy and recognition of the Gibraltarians' right to self-determination.

During his previous four years as Chief Minister, Mr Bossano had concentrated on the development of the colony as an off-shore financial centre. His objective was to make Gibraltar economically self-sufficient as a first step to greater political autonomy and even independence. Land had been reclaimed, and on it and elsewhere there had risen extensive new buildings for the hoped-for throng of foreign financial houses and their staffs. It had been expected that all this development would provide employment for Gibraltarians no longer required by the British Ministry of Defence as it reduced its forces. However, by mid-1992 it had become evident that these expectations were not being fulfilled. UK, Danish and Dutch contractors and business houses had brought their own nationals even for middle management and clerical staff, and these preferred to commute from Spain, where housing and food were cheaper and more to their liking. During the summer, in the face of a considerable drop in the number of tourists visiting Gibraltar, shops and banks reduced their staffs, and the number of Gibraltarians out of work increased substantially.

In August Gibraltarians were shocked by the news that the Danish insurance company Baltica, which had invested well over £100 million in the construction of a vast complex called Europort to provide the infrastructure of the Rock as an important international financial centre, had suffered severe monetary losses. Europort was virtually empty, with only seven firms having taken up offices in it. The Gibraltar government decided to transfer to it some of the civil service departments. Suspicions in Denmark that Baltica had been involved in fraud, and the arrival in Gibraltar of investigators looking into its business affairs, did not encourage other firms to move into Europort.

At the end of the year Mr Bossano conceded publicly that he had neglected economic affairs. He had in fact spent much time in London discussing with the British government Gibraltar's position in the EC as well as the concession by Britain of greater autonomy. He had been assured that Britain was prepared to give Gibraltar 'the widest autonomy possible consistent with meeting the EC obligations for which Britain was responsible before the European Court of Justice'.

iv.   MALTA

CAPITAL: Valletta   AREA: 316 sq km   POPULATION: 354,000 ('90)
OFFICIAL LANGUAGES: Maltese, English   POLITICAL SYSTEM: parliamentary democracy
HEAD OF STATE: President Vincent Tabone (since April '89)
RULING PARTY: Nationalist Party (NP)
HEAD OF GOVERNMENT: Edward Fenech Adami, Prime Minister (since May '87)
PRINCIPAL MINISTERS: Guido De Marco (deputy premier, foreign affairs), John Dalli
    (finance), Ugo Mifsud Bonnici (education, interior), Joseph Fenech (justice)
INTERNATIONAL ALIGNMENT: NAM, Cwth.
CURRENCY: lira (end-'92 £1=Lm0.56, US$1=Lm0.37)
GNP PER CAPITA: US$6,610 ('90)
MAIN EXPORT EARNERS: tourism, manufactured goods, machinery

TWO events stood out in the year: the general election on 22 February and the three-day visit of Queen Elizabeth and the Duke of Edinburgh on 28–30 May.

The last election had been in 1987, when the ruling Labour Party lost narrowly to the Nationalist Party (see AR 1987, p. 182). The margin of victory was wider in the 1992 election, which returned Edward Fenech Adami to office as Prime Minister. A third party, the Democratic Alternative, made little headway. The distribution of votes and seats was as follows (1987 figures in brackets):

	% of votes	Seats
Nationalists	51.8 (50.9)	34 (35*)
Labour Party	46.5 (48.9)	31 (34)
Democratic Alternative	1.7 (-)	0 (5)

*Included 4 'bonus' seats.

The new government took office on 27 February. There was little change in the distribution of portfolios. On 6 March, however, Karmen Mifsud Bonnici, the former prime minister, announced his resignation as leader of the Labour Party and was succeeded by Alfred Sant. One happy feature of the election was the absence of any inter-party thuggery and electoral violence, continuing the trend of the previous election. As always, voter turnout was very high, at 95 per cent of the registered electorate.

In May politics gave way to ceremony and remembrance. Queen Elizabeth and Prince Philip came to mark the 50th anniversary of the award to Malta of the George Cross (on 15 April 1942) 'for a heroism and devotion that will long be famous in history'. According to one local account, the royal visit was 'nothing short of a triumphal progress', the high point being the dedication by the Queen of the Siege Bell of Malta, designed by Michael Sandle and situated high above the entrance to the Grand Harbour of Valletta. The affection with which the Queen and the Prince were greeted, in both Malta and Gozo, reflected not only the long association between Britain and Malta but, more personally, the time spent by the Queen (before her accession) as a naval officer's wife in Valletta. In welcoming the Queen, President Tabone referred to Malta's application for membership of the European Community (on which no progress was made in 1992). Debate on the merits of full or associate membership continued throughout the year, as did arguments over the government's continued programme of economic liberalization. The long years of Labour rule were still evident in the high proportion (44 per cent) of state to private employment. In the election the Nationalist government renewed its pledge to reduce the state's role in the economy.

v. GREECE

CAPITAL: Athens   AREA: 132,000 sq km   POPULATION: 10,100,000 ('90)
OFFICIAL LANGUAGE: Greek   POLITICAL SYSTEM: parliamentary democracy
HEAD OF STATE: President Konstantinos Karamanlis (since May '90)
RULING PARTY: New Democracy (ND)
HEAD OF GOVERNMENT: Konstantinos Mitsotakis, Prime Minister (since April '90)
PRINCIPAL MINISTERS: Tzannis Tzannetakis (deputy premier), Michalis Papakonstantinou (foreign affairs), Yannis Varvitsiotis (defence, justice), Nikolaos Kleitos (interior), Stefanos Manos (economy & finance) Yannis Paleokrassas (commerce)
INTERNATIONAL ALIGNMENT: NATO, OECD, EC
CURRENCY: drachma (end-'92 £1=Dr325.18, US$1=Dr214.78)
GNP PER CAPITA: US$5,990 ('90)
MAIN EXPORT EARNERS: tourism, merchant marine, textiles, agricultural products

GREEK politics in 1992 were dominated by a single issue: the unremitting campaign to prevent the recognition by Greece's EC partners of the independence of the former Yugoslav republic of Macedonia for as long as it insisted on using the word 'Macedonia' in its title. Athens maintained that it had an exclusive claim to this name for its northernmost province and that its use by a neighbouring state implied territorial ambitions at Greece's expense (see also III.1.vi).

Despite the fact that the ex-Yugoslav republic amended its constitution so as to disclaim any irredentist ambitions, and despite the finding of the EC's own Badinter commission that Macedonia met with the necessary criteria for recognition, the EC on 15 January deferred any decision. At the Lisbon summit in June the EC bowed to Greek pressure by insisting that the name adopted by an independent Macedonian state must be acceptable to Greece. The Greek Prime Minister, Konstantinos Mitsotakis, was apparently able to convince his European colleagues that his government's wafer-thin majority in parliament would be threatened by the rejection of Greece's veto, opening up the prospect of a return to power by Andreas Papandreou and his populist PASOK party, which had occasioned problems for the Community during the 1980s. Verisimilitude was given to this threat by the fact that in April Mr Mitsotakis had been obliged to dismiss his militantly nationalist Foreign Minister, Antonis Samaras (who in

October resigned his seat in parliament), although at the price of toughening his own stance over the issue. He survived a subsequent vote of confidence in parliament when he secured the support of all 152 New Democracy deputies in the 300-seat parliament.

The domestic constraints under which Mr Mitsotakis was operating were considerable. Mr Papandreou claimed that for the new Foreign Minister, Michalis Papakonstantinou, even to meet with the Macedonian leader, Kiro Gligorov, could result in de facto recognition. In February a short-lived Greek boycott of Dutch and Italian products was launched in protest against what was seen as the unhelpful attitude of the Dutch and Italian governments. When, in April, four students distributed leaflets accusing the government of cultivating a climate of nationalist hysteria, they were arrested and sentenced to 19 months in gaol for undermining the country's foreign relations. When 169 intellectuals subsequently protested at the infringement of the students' constitutional rights, they were in turn censured by 600 employees of the University of Thessaloniki.

Despite its victory at Lisbon, the Greek government kept up pressure over the Macedonian issue in the run-up to the Edinburgh EC summit in December. This included a massive officially-inspired demonstration in Athens in December, which followed an equally large demonstration in Thessalonika in February. Once again the EC shirked the issue of recognition but promised humanitarian and technical aid to Macedonia and refused Greece's demand for a pledge that the EC members of the Security Council (Britain, France and Belgium) would veto a Macedonian application for membership of the UN, to which forum the issue now moved. In November Macedonia rejected a Greek initiative which proposed that its borders be guaranteed by its four neighbouring states. Turkey's speedy recognition of Macedonia further soured relations with Greece, reinforcing fears of the establishment of an 'Islamic crescent' to its north. Bulgarian recognition of Macedonia likewise contributed to tension with Greece.

Greek apprehensions were heightened by the possibility that the Bosnian conflict might spill over into Kosovo and Macedonia, leading at best to refugees flooding in northern Greece, at worst to Greece being sucked into armed conflict. Relations with Albania were strained by allegations of discrimination against the Greek minority (and, specifically, of a ban on parties representing ethnic minorities in the Albanian elections of March) and by the presence of over 100,000 illegal Albanian immigrants in Greece (see also III.1.vii). Groups of these were periodically rounded up and sent back to Albania, but there were no concerted moves to tackle the presence of as many as 400,000 illegal immigrants of various nationalities. Such people were prepared to work in the least desirable jobs for much lower wages (and without social security benefits) than their Greek counterparts.

In November Greece was made a full member of the Western
European Union but with the proviso that Athens could not invoke
Article 5 of the pact (providing for mutual assistance if attacked) in
its dispute with Turkey.

There was little improvement in the economic situation. The EC
reported in March that GDP per capita fell between 1983–85 and
1988–90 from 52 per cent of the Community average to 48 per cent,
despite large-scale Community aid. Attempts were made to curb the
inflated bureaucracy, to privatize the substantial state-owned sector
in industry and transport, to reform Byzantine pension provisions
and to crack down on widespread tax evasion. Coupled as they
were with increased taxes and public utility prices, such initiatives
prompted numerous strikes. Moreover, the government's economic
policies attracted criticism from influential figures within the New
Democracy party itself, notably from Athanasios Kanellopoulos (who
resigned in February as Deputy Prime Minister) and Antonis Samaras.
The government was twice reshuffled, in August and December. In
the latter changes Mr Mitsotakis' daughter Dora became Minister
of Culture. More than one in three New Democracy deputies now
held ministerial office. This was largely dictated by the government's
precarious majority in parliament, which was reduced to one in October
following the decision of Mikis Theodorakis, the maverick musician,
former communist and ND deputy, to sit as an independent.

There was near-unanimity in parliament, however, over the ratification of the Maastricht treaty in July. A total of 286 out of 300 deputies,
one of the largest parliamentary majorities in modern times, voted for
a treaty which was expected to bring Greece an additional 2,000 million
ecus over a five-year period.

The repercussions of the Koskotas scandal, which had contributed
to the downfall of the PASOK government in 1989 (see AR 1989,
pp. 186–7), continued to be felt. In January a special tribunal appointed
by parliament acquitted Mr Papandreou (who had boycotted the proceedings throughout) of corruption charges, but two former cabinet
ministers, Dimitris Tsovolas and Georgios Petsos, were sentenced
respectively to two-and-a-half years and ten months (the latter sentence
suspended). Mr Tsovolas was obliged to resign his parliamentary seat.
In the ensuing by-election in the Athens-B constituency in April,
which was boycotted by New Democracy and the Communist Party,
PASOK secured a resounding victory in a 70 per cent turnout. The
trial of George Koskotas, on charges involving the embezzlement of
US$230 million from the Bank of Crete, began on 19 October. He had
already been sentenced in January to five years in prison for forging a
document which had been used in evidence against Mr Papandreou.

February saw the death of Markos Vafiades ('General Markos'), one
of the last surviving major communist leaders of the period of the

wartime occupation and the subsequent civil war. Purged as leader of the communist Democratic Army in 1948, and expelled from the party, he returned from a prolonged exile in the Soviet Union to Greece in 1983, aligning himself with the PASOK party, on whose ticket he was elected to parliament in 1989.

Terrorism continued to be a major problem. On 14 July the then Minister of Finance, Yannis Paleokrassas, had a narrow escape in a rocket attack aimed at his car; this killed one bystander and injured six others. Responsibility for this attack, and for the December shooting in the legs of a New Democracy deputy, Eleftherios Papadimitriou, on the eve of a critical vote in parliament on an austerity budget, was claimed by the '17 November' group. In the course of the year rocket attacks were also launched against tax offices.

In June Amnesty International published a report alleging serious mistreatment of prisoners in police stations and prisons. The Minister of Public Order, Theodoros Anagnostopoulos, while rejecting most of the allegations, conceded that some abuses had taken place.

vi.   CYPRUS

CAPITAL: Nicosia   AREA: 9,250 sq km   POPULATION: 710,000 ('92 est.)
POLITICAL SYSTEM: separate presidential democracies in Greek area and in Turkish
    Republic of Northern Cyprus (recognized only by Turkey)
HEAD OF STATE AND GOVERNMENT: President Georgios Vassiliou (since Feb '88);
    Rauf Denktash has been President of Turkish area since Feb '75
PRINCIPAL MINISTERS: (Greek Cyprus) Georgios Iacovou (foreign affairs), Georgios
    Syrimis (finance), Christodoulos Veniamin (interior), Andreas Aloneftis (defence),
    Nikolaos Papaioannou (justice)
INTERNATIONAL ALIGNMENT: (Greek Cyprus) NAM, Cwth.
CURRENCY: Cyprus pound (end-'92 £1=£0.73, US$1=£0.48
GNP PER CAPITA: Republic US$11,695, TRNC c.US$3,500 ('92)
MAIN EXPORT EARNERS: tourism, textiles, agricultural products

THE US-sponsored initiative for a settlement summit between the Greek and Turkish Cypriot communities and the governments of Greece and Turkey ran into the sand in 1992. It had been side-lined in autumn 1991 because of the Turkish elections. Two months of shuttle diplomacy during January and February 1992 by US State Department special coordinator Nelson Ledsky and the UN Secretary-General's special representatives led by Oscar Camilion failed to resurrect it.

The new Secretary-General, Dr Boutros Boutros-Ghali, arguing that the UN effort 'cannot be expected to continue indefinitely' and noting that there were mounting claims on peace-keeping resources, adopted a more active policy, attempting to lead rather than guide the negotiations. In April he codified all the elements of agreement achieved over long years of negotiation into a 100-paragraph 'set of ideas' designed to form the basis for an overall framework agreement.

The Secretary-General's ideas were accompanied by a 'non-map' tentatively delineating a boundary between the two federated states. It envisaged the return to Greek Cypriot control of the Varosha district of the east coast port of Famagusta, as well as the north-western citrus-growing centre of Morphou and 34 other villages. In terms of control, the 'non-map' implied that the Turkish Cypriot area would be reduced from just under 37 per cent of the island to just over 28 per cent.

Dr Boutros-Ghali proposed proximity talks, in which the Greek Cypriot President, Georgios Vassiliou, and the Turkish Cypriot leader, Rauf Denktash, would meet separately with him. This would be followed by joint talks which, if successful, would be followed by a high-level meeting of all the parties to arrive at the overall framework agreement. This would be put to the two communities in separate referenda; subject to approval, a constitution would be drafted within 18 months.

Three rounds of talks (on 18–23 June, 15 July–14 August and 28 October–11 November) did more to identify differences between the two communities than to create the basis for compromise. They did, however, elicit negotiating positions on the issues of territory and displaced persons which had never before been publicly aired.

The Greek Cypriots accepted the ideas as the basis of negotiation but with provisos. The Turkish Cypriots agreed to 91 of the 100 paragraphs but registered objections to the remainder which the Secretary-General described as fundamentally at odds with basic concepts.

The ideas were predicated on the notion of a federal republic with a single international personality and sovereignty as well as a single citizenship. The Turkish Cypriots argued that there already existed 'sovereign states from which the sovereignty of the federation will emanate' and that the federated states should have the right to enter into international agreements in their areas of competence and to retain influence in federal fields including citizenship and immigration, trade, patents and trademarks, environment and health.

The ideas provided for the President and the Vice-President of Cyprus to be elected from different communities, with each having the right of veto, and for a 7:3 distribution of posts in the Council of Ministers, in which one of the key posts of foreign affairs, defence or finance would be reserved for the Turkish Cypriots. The Turkish Cypriots demanded that there should be a rotating presidency with separate Community elections, a 50–50 allocation of ministerial posts and cabinet decision by consensus.

The 'non-map' would have allowed about half of the 160,000 Greek Cypriot refugees to return to their homes and remain under Greek Cypriot administration. Mr Denktash described it as 'ludicrous and inhumane' and claimed that it would lead to the dislocation of 37,433 of the 45,000 Turkish Cypriot refugees in the north. He said that no map could be drawn until the issue of power-sharing in government had been resolved.

The UN ideas foresaw programmes for displaced persons allowing them to choose to remain in, or relocate from, the areas of territorial adjustment. The rights of movement, settlement and ownership of property—key concerns of the Greek Cypriots—were to be implemented gradually. The Turkish Cypriots, while recognizing Greek Cypriot rights of residence and ownership in the north, demanded that any person dislocated by eventual boundary changes should be compensated for loss of property regardless of whether they owned it prior to the division of the island. This, it was argued, could be achieved by a global swap of Greek and Turkish Cypriot properties and their sale. The Greek Cypriots declared the Turkish Cypriot 'misappropriation' of lands to be 'null and void' and claimed that the Greek Cypriots had an entitlement to have the benefit of their former properties.

In his November report to the Security Council, the UN Secretary-General called upon both parties to reflect on their positions and to resume negotiations in March 1993 after the Greek Cypriot presidential elections due in February. Dr Boutros-Ghali called for more 'direct' involvement of the five permanent members of the Security Council but stopped short of recommending measures such as sanctions. In the intervening period he called for a programme of goodwill measures, including reduction of Turkish forces on the island and a suspension of the Greek Cypriots' weapons acquisitions programme. The measures also envisaged the transfer of the Varosha district from Turkish Cypriot to UN control.

The countries contributing troops to the UN Force in Cyprus (UNFICYP), namely Austria, Canada, Denmark, Finland, Ireland, Sweden and the United Kingdom, increasingly lost patience, not least because of arrears in payments towards the cost of the upkeep of the Force. Finland, Ireland and Sweden had already reduced their commitments to token levels. During 1992 Denmark announced that it would withdraw all but its headquarters staff, while Austria and Canada announced cuts which reduced UNFICYP from 2,078 to 1,488, prompting the Secretary-General to report to the Security Council that its viability was 'in doubt'. In December Canada announced that it would withdraw its remaining force of just over 500 personnel at the end of the current mandate period in June 1993.

In February the Republic of Cyprus played host to the Non-Aligned Movement conference and the government was among those urging a new role for the organization in the post-Cold War era (see XI.4.ii).

The European Commission's opinion on the Republic's application for EC membership was delayed because of the continuing division of the island. The question of whether Cyprus might become an EC member before Turkey (which had also applied) was one of the contentious issues in the inter-communal negotiations.

vii. TURKEY

CAPITAL: Ankara AREA: 779,000 sq km POPULATION: 56,500,000 ('90)
OFFICIAL LANGUAGE: Turkish POLITICAL SYSTEM: parliamentary democracy
HEAD OF STATE: President Turgut Özal (since Nov '89)
RULING PARTIES: True Path Party (DYP) and Social Democratic Populists (SHP)
HEAD OF GOVERNMENT: Süleyman Demirel (DYP), Prime Minister (since Nov '91)
PRINCIPAL MINISTERS: Erdal İnönü (SHP/deputy premier), Hikmet Çetin (foreign
 affairs), Seyfi Oktay (justice), Nevzat Ayaz (defence), Ismat Sezgin (interior),
 Sümer Oral (finance)
INTERNATIONAL ALIGNMENT: NATO, OECD, ICO, ECO
CURRENCY: lira (end-'92 £1=LT13,161.35, US$1=LT8,693.10)
GNP PER CAPITA: US$1,630 ('90)
MAIN EXPORT EARNERS: textiles, iron and steel, agricultural products, tourism

PRIME Minister Süleyman Demirel's coalition of his own centre-right
True Path Party (DYP) and Professor Erdal İnönü's centre-left Social
Democratic Populist Party (SHP), which was formed after the general
elections of October 1991, survived, but its majority was reduced to
eight seats in an increasingly fragmented parliament. At home, the
coalition government presided over a resumption of economic growth
(which exceeded 5 per cent in 1992), but failed to meet its election
promise of reducing inflation from the level of 60–70 per cent inherited
from the previous administration. The government gave its full support
to the security forces in the battle against Kurdish ethnic terrorism, while
taking some cautious steps to widen democratic freedoms. Abroad, it
pursued an active diplomacy in pursuit of cooperative action to meet
challenges to regional stability.

While Mr Demirel increased his block of deputies from 178 to 182 in
the 450-member parliament, his junior coalition partner could not avert
two successive splits, which reduced the parliamentary strength of the
SHP from 88 to 52. In March and April 18 radical Kurdish deputies, who
had left the Toiling People's Party (HEP) to secure election in the ranks
of the SHP, reverted to their old allegiance. One of their number, Ahmet
Türk, later became leader of HEP. Then, in September, Deniz Baykal,
Professor İnönü's rival within the SHP, was elected leader of the revived
Republican People's Party (CHP), which had represented the centre-left
constituency until it was dissolved by the military in 1980. Mr Baykal
and 17 of his supporters thereupon resigned from SHP.

The main opposition Motherland Party (ANAP) was also weakened.
President Turgut Özal, who had founded the party in 1983, tried to oust
its current leader, Mesut Yilmaz, by supporting a more conservative
figure, Mehmet Keçeciler, at an extraordinary convention in November.
When Mr Keçeciler was defeated, he and his allies left ANAP, which was
reduced from 115 seats to 95.

Disillusion with both the government and the official opposition
was reflected in the local government by-elections on 1 November.
An Islamist formation, the Welfare Party (RP), emerged in first place

with nearly a quarter of the 580,000 valid votes cast, and won four out of the six vacant borough mayoralties in Istanbul.

A law permitting the revival of political parties closed down by the military was one of the measures of democratic reform introduced by the coalition government. Others included a new criminal justice law, reducing the period of detention before charge to 24 hours in individual cases and providing for the presence of lawyers during interrogation. However, this last provision did not apply to terrorist offences, in that suspects could be detained without charge for much longer periods.

The terrorist campaign waged by the secessionist and marxist Kurdish Workers' Party (PKK) intensified, causing more than 2,000 deaths. The most notable incidents occurred on 21 March, when security forces opened fire on violent demonstrators celebrating the Kurdish new year, and on 18 August, when much damage was done to the provincial capital Şirnak as the security forces responded massively to sniper fire. PKK terrorists, whose headquarters in the Syrian-controlled Bekaa valley in Lebanon were closed as a result of Turkish diplomatic pressure, transferred their forward bases to the Kurdish safe haven in northern Iraq, whence they launched assaults on Turkish frontier posts. Turkish security forces mounted a cross-border ground operation in October–November, which cleared the area of terrorists, at least temporarily. The move into Iraq was preceded by an agreement with Masud Barzani and Jalal Talabani, the elected leaders of Iraq's Kurds. Nevertheless, the Turkish government deplored the proclamation of a federated Iraqi Kurdish state, and sponsored a meeting in Ankara in November with the Foreign Ministers of Syria and Iran, at which support was expressed for the territorial integrity of Iraq.   The difficulty of preventing a renewed assault on Iraqi Kurds by Saddam Husain, while at the same time avoiding the emergence in northern Iraq of an embryonic Kurdish state, made Ankara hesitate before extending the permission given to the USA, Britain and France to station aircraft at the joint NATO base at Incirlik in southern Turkey as a guarantee of Kurdish safety. A six-month extension was finally approved by parliament on 24 December.

Prime Minister Demirel continued President Özal's policy of promoting his country as a centre of stability in a troubled region. The positive role which Turkey could play, with Western help, was stressed when Mr Demirel met President Bush in Washington on 11 February and when President Mitterrand of France visited Ankara on 13 April. Turkish diplomacy tried to develop two interlocking systems: the first, embracing the states bordering the Black Sea and their immediate neighbours, and the second, the Turkic-speaking republics of the former Soviet Union. The project, originally launched by President Özal, of an 11-nation Black Sea economic cooperation region was officially endorsed at a summit meeting in Istanbul on 25 June.

Turkey cooperated with the USA in trying to devise a solution of the dispute between Armenia and Azerbaijan over the status of Nagorno-Karabakh, whose Armenian inhabitants had risen against the central government of Azerbaijan. Turkey advanced to Armenia 100,000 tonnes of wheat on behalf of the European Community (EC), but a further decision to supply electricity to Armenia had to be rescinded in the face of protests by Azerbaijan, which continued to blockade Armenia.

A summit conference of the Turkic-speaking republics was held in Ankara at the end of October. President Abulfaz Elchibey of Azerbaijan, whose election in June caused much satisfaction in Ankara, then stayed on for an official visit. A Turkish International Cooperation Agency (TICA) was formed in Ankara largely to coordinate aid to the Turkic republics. Small telephone exchanges were donated to the republics to secure direct telecommunications with Turkey and, through Turkey, with the rest of the world. Turkey also agreed to take 10,000 students from the Turkic republics.

The Turkic republics joined the Economic Cooperation Organization (ECO), which had been founded by Turkey, Iran and Pakistan. Within this ineffective body, Turkey and Iran kept an eye on each other as they developed their links with the successor states of the former Soviet Union. Prime Minister Demirel visited both Iran and Pakistan, as well as Japan, whose involvement in the Turkish economy grew with the flotation of a US$560 million Turkish loan on the Tokyo exchange.

In the Balkans, Turkey successfully cultivated relations with Bulgaria and Albania, thereby causing unease in Greece, which refused to take part in a meeting of Balkan states and their immediate neighbours, convened in Istanbul on 25 November in order to discuss the Yugoslav crisis (see III.1.vi). The meeting endorsed Turkish demands (i) that measures be taken to prevent the spread of ethnic conflict to Kosovo and the former Yugoslav republic of Macedonia; (ii) that the latter should be recognized by the international community; and (iii) that the Serbs in Bosnia should be threatened with air strikes if they did not stop their attacks on Bosnian Muslims. These demands, which Turkey also advanced at the Geneva conference on Yugoslavia, in NATO, the UN, the CSCE, the Islamic Conference Organization and in bilateral contacts, produced scant results. In December, the Turkish parliament gave the government authority to send troops under international auspices both to Somalia and to Bosnia. A small contingent did go to Somalia to serve under US command, but there was no international call for Turkish troops to be deployed in Bosnia.

A meeting of the EC-Turkey association council in Brussels on 9 November resolved on a regular system of consultations and was followed by a visit by Mr Demirel to London and Brussels on 24–25 November. Turkey reaffirmed its determination to enter into a customs union with the Community by the end of 1995. Also in November, Turkey became an associate member of the Western European Union (WEU) and was promised full participation in its activities. Fears that Greece, as a full member, might be able to use the WEU against Turkey were dispelled by the statement that the organization's mutual aid obligation did not apply to conflicts between NATO members.

Discussions between Mr Demirel and the Greek Prime Minister, at the Black Sea cooperation meeting in Istanbul and elsewhere, did not produce an improvement in relations with Greece, in the absence of progress towards the settlement of the Cyprus problem (see II.3.vi). Turkey promised to contribute to such a settlement, but was critical of the approach adopted by the UN Secretary-General in a series of meetings with the Greek and Turkish Cypriot leaders in New York. Turkey believed that it was unrealistic, after nearly 30 years of separation, to recreate a mixed administration in Cyprus, as endorsed in UN Security Council resolutions.

The Atatürk dam, forming the core of the ambitious south-east Anatolia project (GAP), began generating electricity in July. On 14 March an earthquake devastated the provincial capital of Erzincan in eastern Turkey, causing some 400 deaths.

III EASTERN EUROPE

1. POLAND—CZECHOSLOVAKIA—HUNGARY—ROMANIA—BULGARIA—
YUGOSLAVIA—ALBANIA

i. POLAND

CAPITAL: Warsaw   AREA: 313,000 sq km ('90)   POPULATION: 38,200,000 ('90)
OFFICIAL LANGUAGE: Polish   POLITICAL SYSTEM: presidential democracy
HEAD OF STATE: President Lech Walesa (since Dec '90)
RULING PARTIES: Democratic Union heads coalition
PRINCIPAL MINISTERS: Hanna Suchocka (prime minister), Jerzy Osiatynski (finance),
    Krzystof Skubiszewski (foreign affairs), Janusz Onyszkiewicz (defence)
CURRENCY: zloty (end-'92 £1=Zl.23,846.00, US$1=Zl.15,750.30)
GNP PER CAPITA: US$1,690 ('90)
MAIN EXPORT EARNERS: engineering equipment, coal, metals, agricultural produce

THE political crisis which had paralysed Polish politics since late 1991
(see AR 1991, p. 154) was resolved on 10 July by the election of
Hanna Suchocka as Poland's fifth post-communist Prime Minister.
By re-establishing political authority at home and credibility abroad,
the new government removed the threat to earlier achievements of
'post-communism'. This ended nine months of political stalemate and
released the further IMF credits on which the country's economic future
depended.

The year began in disarray. The Olszewski government announced
a relaxation of the tight monetary controls of the previous two years.
Growth of the money supply was to exceed inflationary targets, subsidy
of state enterprises was to increase and the ensuing deficit was to
be covered by boosting exports. But this programme, under Finance
Minister Andrzej Olechowski, was rejected by the parliamentary right
as too rigorous and by the centre-left as not tough enough. A majority
of deputies still preferred to heed IMF warnings of a return to the
hyper-inflation of 1990–91. They voted instead for a budget deficit
within the 5 per cent of GNP which IMF conditionally prescribed.
Even so, the consequences were painful: doubling council house rents,
reducing state subsidies for transport and energy, and cutting old-age
and disability pensions.

In response to this setback, the Defence Minister, Jan Parys, accused
the government's opponents, including by implication the President,
of plotting a political-military coup. President Walesa called for his
resignation and was in turn accused by the main daily newspaper
(*Gazeta Wyborcza* of 22 April) of political incompetence. In response,
Mr Walesa demanded a French-style constitution under which the
President would have powers to appoint and dismiss ministers.

Political tension was heightened by the effort of the Interior Minister, Antoni Maceriewicz, to expose alleged 'agents' of the former authorities from 1945 to 1990 who still remained in high office.

This clumsy attempt to frame former government and police officials and their collaborators, supposedly including Mr Walesa, was condemned by the episcopate as 'slanderous' and by a parliamentary commission as 'capable of destabilizing the state'. Mr Maceriewicz and Mr Parys were both dismissed. But procedures for bringing past crimes within a proper legislative framework remained elusive and the highly controversial issue of justification for the imposition of martial law in 1981 remained unresolved.

On 4 June the Olszewski government resigned. President Walesa then turned, for the first time, to a non-Solidarity politician to form a government, but Waldemar Pawlak eventually gave up the attempt. Mr Walesa then hinted that the presidency might break the deadlock by ruling through decree. This prospect galvanized the post-Solidarity parties into forming a coalition government. On 10 July Hanna Suchocka (born 1946), a constitutional lawyer from Poznan, was elected Prime Minister by 233 votes to 61, with 113 abstentions. Her multi-party cabinet, containing several members of the first Solidarity government in 1989, was approved the next day.

The new team at once addressed the problem of workers' protests. Labour Minister Jacek Kuron told the Sejm (parliament) that 38 strikes (including 28 in mines) and 47 other serious work stoppages had taken place in July alone. In response, the government offered to negotiate with trade unions a draft 'social pact on state firms in the process of transformation'. This stated that methods of transfer from state control to forms of private or collective ownership should be agreed within five months. Although this deadline was not kept, the will to implement privatization was now firmly on the political agenda. In addition, the government remained adamant that 18 of the country's least profitable coal mines must close. On 30 September a comprehensive restructuring plan was announced for mining, underpinned by two loans of $200 million from the IMF.

The macro-economic record showed sustained improvement. Annual inflation fell to 43 per cent (from 60 per cent in 1991) and the rise in unemployment slowed. There was a growth in industrial sales after three years of decline. The World Bank concluded that this secured a basis for sustained recovery, including parts of the state sector where Western 'know-how' was being used to improve management practices and accountability. That in turn was expected to attract more substantial Western capital investment than had been forthcoming so far.

To promote this, Poland continued to evolve an independent foreign policy. The pre-war distrust of the two great neighbours, Germany and Russia, was being replaced by one of understanding, based on mutual recognition of sovereignty. Prime Minister Suchocka visited Bonn to discuss eventual full membership of the EC, which her hosts thought feasible within a decade. The issue of Russian troop withdrawals from Polish territory was resolved, although some concern was expressed about Russian forces remaining in Kaliningrad. At the same time, all former Soviet republics were recognized as independent states and diplomatic ties were established with them. The main anxiety continued to be the fear of mass emigration from the east: 10 million former Soviet citizens entered Poland through its eastern borders during 1992.

Multilateral ties were established with Hungary, the Czech Republic and Slovakia, through a Central European Free Trade Agreement signed in Krakow on 21 December. It aimed to reduce tariffs over the five years from March 1993, both to boost trade generally and to facilitate eventual EC membership. However, as Defence Minister Onyszkiewicz recognized on an official visit to the United States, NATO membership was possible 'much sooner'. A Polish-US working group on military cooperation was established, and the invitation renewed to the Americans to use Polish training areas for military exercises.

Despite government achievements, many social issues remained tense and unresolved. Workers feared for their jobs and peasant activists were vociferous—though unsuccessful—in demanding the continuation of state subsidies. The country was largely immune from the nationalist upsets of its neighbours, though the raising of memorials in Silesia to German soldiers killed in World War II gave rise to comment. The most explosive social question, the legality of abortion, was extensively debated, with the Catholic Church hierarchy and its parliamentary allies pressing for near-total prohibition. The year ended with the Sejm continuing to decriminalize (though not necessarily condone) abortion, amidst a general awareness that the deputies might be overridden by a majority in the Senate for total abolition.

An encouraging sign of stability was the approval of a 'small constitution' on 1 August. It provided for a greater balance between the 'round-table' presidency negotiated in 1989, which was given sweeping powers on paper without the means of exercising them in practice, and parliament which had great scope for obstructing administration or legislation. In future the President would not be obliged to accept a Prime Minister he did not want (such as Mr Olszewski) and parliament could not block his candidate (such as Mr Pawlak). On the other hand, the installation of an executive presidency, as earlier mooted, was averted. A charter of liberties and human rights was to be added to form a 'big' constitution during 1993. At the year's end, the excellent relations between the President and new Prime Minister were the best guarantee of political stability.

ii.   CZECHOSLOVAKIA

CAPITAL: Prague   AREA: 128,000 sq km   POPULATION: 15,700,000 ('90)
OFFICIAL LANGUAGES: Czech & Slovak
POLITICAL SYSTEM: federal parliamentary democracy
RULING PARTIES: (*federal from June '92*) coalition of (Czech) Civic Democratic Party
   (CDP) and Movement for a Democratic Slovakia (MDS); (*Czech Republic from
   June '92*) coalition of CDP, Christian and Democratic Union (CDU) and Civic
   Democratic Alliance (CDA); (*Slovakia from June '92*) coalition of MDS and Slovak
   National Party (SNP)
HEADS OF REPUBLICAN GOVERNMENTS: Václav Klaus (CDP), Czech Prime Minister;
   Vladimir Mečiar (MDS), Slovak Prime Minister
PRINCIPAL FEDERAL MINISTERS: Jan Strásky (CDP/prime minister, foreign trade),
   Rudolf Filkus (MDS/first deputy premier), Ján Klak (CDP/finance), Imrich
   Andrejcak (MDS/defence), Petr Cermak (CDP/interior), Jozef Moravcik
   (MDS/foreign affairs)
CURRENCY: koruna (end-'92 £1=K43.79, US$1=K28.92)
GNP PER CAPITA: US$2,980 ('90 est.)
MAIN EXPORT EARNERS: machinery, chemicals and fuels, manufactured goods

*In that the Czechoslovak federation continued to exist legally until the end of 1992,
its affairs are covered in a single section below.*

Seventy-four years after its foundation Czechoslovakia ceased to exist
at the end of 1992. On 25 November the Federal Assembly (the
tricameral parliament) adopted a constitutional law on the division of
the state into two fully sovereign and independent states, the Czech
Republic and the Slovak Republic. The process that culminated in
the dissolution of the country had begun shortly after the toppling
of the communist regime in November 1989. By late 1991 the federal
parliament had become deadlocked to such a degree that it proved
impossible to pass a number of crucial laws because Czech and Slovak
legislators were often blocking each other's initiatives. Hopes that the
parliamentary elections of June would break the deadlock were dashed.
While the elections produced clear majorities in both republics, the
political and economic programmes of the new republican leaders were
totally incompatible. Moreover, the distribution of seats in the Federal
Assembly made Czechoslovakia almost ungovernable.

   The elections in Slovakia were won by the Movement for a Democratic Slovakia (MDS) of Prime Minister Vladimir Mečiar, which gained
74 seats in the 150-member Slovak National Council. The MDS then
formed a coalition government with the Slovak National Party (15
seats), which openly supported the dissolution of Czechoslovakia.
Only three other parties gained seats in the Slovak parliament: the
ex-communist Party of the Democratic Left (29 seats), the Christian
Democratic Movement (18 seats) and a coalition of ethnic Hungarian
parties (14 seats). The opposition in the Slovak parliament was splin-
tered and at no point posed a serious challenge to Mr Mečiar's coalition
government.

   In the Czech Republic the clear winner was Václav Klaus and his Civic
Democratic Party (CDP), which took 76 seats in the 200-member Czech

National Council. The Communist Party of Bohemia and Moravia, with 35 seats in the Czech National Council, emerged as the second strongest party in the republic. Six other parties gained seats: the Czech Social Democrats (16 seats), the left-of-centre Liberal and Social Union (16 seats), the right-of-centre Christian and Democratic Union—(CDU) (15 seats), the extreme-right Republican party, the conservative Civic Democratic Alliance (CDA) and the Association for Moravia and Silesia (14 seats each). Mr Klaus formed a coalition government with the CDU, the CDA and the Christian Democratic Party (which ran on one ticket with the CDP) and was elected Czech Prime Minister.

With two exceptions, the same Czech and Slovak parties were represented in the Federal Assembly. Given the composition of the federal parliament, none of the larger parties was in a position to form a solid coalition government. The only arithmetical option, a coalition between the election winners in the two republics, the CDP and the MDS, was totally unrealistic at that stage: nationally, politically and personally, these parties were incompatible.

To overcome the deadlock at the federal level, the new republican Prime Ministers held several meetings throughout June, but these only confirmed that their positions were irreconcilable. While Mr Klaus insisted on the continuation of economic shock therapy and a 'strong federation', Mr Mečiar made it clear that Slovakia would declare its sovereignty, elect a president and adopt a new constitution giving the republic the attributes of an independent state. Instead of the federation, he proposed a confederation between the two republics, an option that was immediately ruled out by Mr Klaus. Mr Mečiar also stressed that the economic reform, which created considerably greater problems in Slovakia than in the Czech Lands, would be slowed down and adapted to Slovak conditions.

After efforts to find a common denominator had failed, Mr Klaus and Mr Mečiar decided at a meeting on 20 June to dissolve Czechoslovakia. They stressed that the process would be carried out exclusively by constitutional means. Based on this decision, the CDP and the MDS formed a coalition government at the federal level whose only task was to prepare and carry out the division of the country. The cabinet was headed by Ján Strasky (CDP) and had a total of five Czech and five Slovak members. At a further meeting held in August, the two republican Prime Ministers set the date for the eventual split at 1 January 1993 and began preparing a draft law that was to abolish all federal institutions and regulate the distribution of Czechoslovak property. Despite indications that a majority of Czechs and Slovaks favoured the continuation of a common state, both Mr Klaus and Mr Mečiar categorically rejected calls for a referendum, arguing that it could not halt the disintegration process and that an emotional debate on the issue could sour future relations.

After MDS deputies in the Federal Assembly had blocked the re-election of President Václav Havel, he stepped down on 20 July, announcing his decision only hours before the Slovak National Council passed a declaration of sovereignty for Slovakia. Several attempts to find a suitable successor failed. With the departure of Mr Havel, the leading personal and political symbol of the federation, the process of disintegration began to accelerate.

On 3 September the Slovak National Council adopted a new Slovak constitution which went into effect on 1 October. After the Federal Assembly failed to pass a draft law on the division of Czechoslovakia on 18 November, the Czech National Council reacted by approving a resolution in which it assumed 'full responsibility for the affairs of the Czech Republic'. By that time, the opposition's efforts to slow down the disintegration process had been reduced to a mere political game. Given the steps already taken by the republics, a law on the dissolution of the federation would have merely confirmed the state of affairs. The federation was crippled, a head of state could not be elected and real power was in the hands of the republican governments. The final verdict on the future of Czechoslovakia came on 25 November, when the Federal Assembly eventually adopted the law in a slightly modified version. What was probably more important than the fact that the disintegration was prescribed from above, rather than based on solid popular support, was that it was carried out in a remarkably civilized manner and thus contrasted with the disintegration of Yugoslavia and the former Soviet Union.

Indeed, more than 30 treaties and inter-governmental agreements defining the nature of bilateral relations between Prague and Bratislava were signed before the end of the year, ranging from the creation of a customs union to the free movement of people. While Czech representatives rejected proposals for monetary and defence unions, it was agreed that both republics would keep a common currency for the first months of 1993 and that the two new national armies would cooperate. The distribution of federal property was a major bone of contention between Mr Klaus and Mr Mečiar, and negotiations were time-consuming and complex. It was eventually agreed to apply two principles: all immobile federal property was granted to the republic on whose territory it was located; the remaining property, including military assets and diplomatic missions abroad was divided by a ratio of 2:1, reflecting the populations of the two republics.

The launching of the voucher privatization scheme was the most important economic development of the year. More than 8.5 million people purchased vouchers which could be exchanged for shares in more than 1,400 companies during the first wave of the scheme. But while the privatization process as a whole was seen as a success, Czechoslovakia's overall economic performance produced mixed results. Industrial production dropped by almost 20 per cent in comparison with 1991, but the private sector continued to expand, accounting for some 20 per cent of industrial production in the second half of 1992. There was an inflation rate of 12.5 per cent in 1992 as a whole. Unemployment continued to drop throughout 1992. In November the unemployment rate for all of Czechoslovakia was 5 per cent (2.5 per cent in the Czech Republic, 10.4 per cent in Slovakia), which represented a 2 per cent drop since January. Both republics registered a foreign trade surplus in 1992. Moreover, Czechoslovakia had a $1,000 million current account surplus, according to most estimates. Some analysts warned, however, that the surplus was a result of the lack of investment in Czechoslovakia, which had curtailed imports. Indeed, foreign investment in the country slowed down in 1992, because numerous foreign investors chose to wait for the outcome of the constitutional stalemate. In general, the Czech Republic benefited much more from foreign investment than Slovakia. Apart from protests by several thousand miners in the autumn, there was no labour unrest in either republic.

Although political developments in the republics were overshadowed by the dissolution of the federation, there were various challenges to both governments throughout the year. Unlike in Slovakia, the opposition in the Czech parliament was well-organized and relatively strong, so that Mr Klaus was forced on several occasions to make concessions. The difficult adoption of the new Czech constitution was just one example of the many quarrels between the governing coalition and the predominantly left opposition. The Czech parliament eventually adopted the new Czech constitution on 16 December. The adoption was made possible after compromises had been reached on the powers of the Czech president, the mechanism of the adoption of constitutional laws, and the inclusion of provisions concerning environmental protection and human rights.

Probably the greatest challenge to the Slovak government was the escalation of tensions with Hungary. Charges and counter-charges concerning Slovakia's treatment of its 600,000-strong Hungarian minority poisoned the atmosphere, and Hungarian deputies in the Slovak National Council frequently boycotted the parliament's sessions after Mr Mečiar had refused to meet them. The MDS charged Hungarian politicians with trying to undermine the territorial integrity of Slovakia. But the already-strained relations between Bratislava and Budapest worsened significantly in October when Slovakia began damming the Danube to divert it into an artificial channel leading to the Gabcikovo hydroelectric dam. Only in November, after the federal government's intervention, did Slovakia agree to stop work on the project to allow an EC commission to evaluate the project and mediate in the dispute. While the potential for conflict between the two countries remained, tensions decreased somewhat in November and December. The Slovak leadership obviously realized that its conflict with Hungary considerably harmed its image abroad.

In addition to the tensions with Hungary, the Slovak government also had to deal with growing domestic and international criticism concerning its treatment of the Slovak media. Mr Mečiar openly threatened to punish newspapers for 'slandering his government and himself' and replaced virtually all high-ranking radio and television managers with MDS loyalists. He also tried to close down the new university of Trnava, which was created under his predecessor Ján Čarnogurský, charging it with unprofessionalism. Critics warned that these were first indications of a drive aimed at weakening the basic principles of democracy.

iii. HUNGARY

CAPITAL: Budapest   AREA: 93,000 sq km   POPULATION: 10,600,000 ('90)
OFFICIAL LANGUAGE: Hungarian   POLITICAL SYSTEM: multi-party democracy
HEAD OF STATE: President Arpád Göncz (since Aug '90)
RULING PARTY: Hungarian Democratic Forum (HDF) heads coalition
HEAD OF GOVERNMENT: József Antall, Prime Minister (since May '90)
PRINCIPAL MINISTERS: Géza Jeszenszky (foreign affairs), Lajos Für (defence),
   Peter Boross (interior), Mihaly Kupa (finance), Istvan Balsai (justice)
CURRENCY: forint (end-'92 £1=Ft127.35, US$1=Ft84.11)
GNP PER CAPITA: US$2,780 ('90)
MAIN EXPORT EARNERS: machinery and transport equipment, agricultural products,
   basic manufactures

THE year 1992 was spent in marking time. The political decision-making machinery, instead of being employed in attempts to ease the increasingly serious economic burdens faced by the country, was employed in debates over issues of status, prestige and identity. In a sense, this was an unavoidable consequence of the devastation caused by 40 years of communist rule and the need to reconstruct society in a new image, but in the interim society was increasingly irritated as the standard of living dropped.

The party political system, while at first sight reasonably stable, in reality exhibited a good deal of fluidity. The level of underlying tension was shown by the election fever that came to dominate the minds of the elite by the third quarter of the year, although elections were not due until 1994. The parties of the government coalition, led by the Hungarian Democratic Forum, proved very unpopular with the electorate, which demonstrated its dislike of the government by voting for the opposition at by-elections. The Smallholders split into two factions, with the party outside parliament on the whole backing the minority, making them rather ineffectual coalition partners.

The Forum itself was split by a document produced by one of the party deputy presidents, the populist István Csurka, in August. Mr Csurka attacked his own party and the leadership of József Antall for having been too lenient with the opposition, for not having introduced radical changes to eliminate the remnants of communism and for not having established what he regarded as proper control over the media. As his critics, both inside and outside the Forum, pointed out, Mr Csurka's proposals, had they been accepted, would have amounted to an end to the democratic institutions that were set up after the collapse of communism.

In particular, his demand for eliminating the vestiges of communism was a disguised attack on liberal values, which Mr Csurka would have liked to replace by populist-nationalist practices, under which there would be no need for argument or debate, as a united nation would think as one. To this should be added Mr Csurka's barely-veiled anti-semitism. Mr Csurka's tract was widely assailed, but the party leadership distanced itself from its propositions only cautiously, fearful presumably that a direct attack might split the party.

The opposition was likewise in some disarray. The Alliance of Free Democrats remained divided between its formerly dissident wing and its pragmatists, and the two found it very difficult to sink their differences. In the autumn Iván Petö, a member of the former dissident wing, was elected as leader of the parliamentary faction, replacing the pragmatist Péter Tölgyessy. In terms of popular support, however, the Free Democrats were quite unable to capitalize on the government's difficulties and their showing in the polls and by-elections was unconvincing.

More surprisingly, the Alliance of Young Democrats (Fidesz) also found it hard to convert support in the opinion polls to support at by-elections. Although Fidesz led the popularity contest in the polls, it was the former communist party, now called the Hungarian Socialist Party (MSzP), that consistently outperformed all the others in terms of votes. This was attributable, at least in part, to the superiority of the MSzP's organizational abilities and experience gained under the old regime.

At the same time, the by-elections were also revealing in another respect—popular apathy or distaste for politics. Turnouts were low to very low, and several elections had to be repeated because they failed to reach the required level of participation, one or two up to six times. The explanation for this apathy was to be sought in the population's difficulties in understanding the function of politics in a democracy—a continuing debate about the distribution of power—coupled with the failure of the ruling elites (and their predecessors of course) to educate the public on this topic. From the popular standpoint, politics seemed to be about obscure discussions, often highly technical, and very public quarrels, at a time when economic standards were felt to be plummeting.

The fate of the electronic media was an acute case in point. The government took the view that the media should represent government views rather than those of the opposition; it launched a series of bitter attacks on the heads of radio and television because it felt it was treated unfairly. The government clearly rejected the argument that the function of the media was to criticize as much as it was to report and that direct government control would produce propaganda and apologetics. By the end of the year, the government seemed to be winning. The head of television was suspended on vague charges of incompetence, while the budgets of both television and radio were brought directly under the office of the Prime Minister, thereby effectively ensuring that their future independence was in question.

The most important counterbalancing institution, the Constitutional Court, issued a number of important decisions during the year. It threw out the bill on retroactive legislation aimed at highly-placed communists who had survived the advent of democracy. Equally, the court set a time-limit by which a new media bill, guaranteeing the independence of radio and television, should be passed. As the Media Bill contained entrenched law, requiring a two-thirds majority, the government could enact it only with the consent of the opposition. However, the antagonism between the two sides was such that this degree of agreement was inconceivable.

The economy continued to fare badly. Output declined and industrial production was in a particularly poor way in the first half of the year, although there was some improvement later. Unemployment was rising, but inflation seemed to have levelled off. The one positive sign was that foreign investment maintained its high level and Hungary continued to attract around half of all the Western funds going to central and eastern Europe. According to preliminary estimates, well over $1,000 million flowed into the country during the year. This was also explained by the appearance of stability that Hungary managed to project in a troubled region.

In foreign affairs there was no serious change in the broad direction of forging closer relations with the West and keeping out of trouble locally. The latter aim was increasingly difficult, given the war in former Yugoslavia and the coming independence of Slovakia (see III.1.vi and III.1.ii). As far as the former was concerned, Hungary gave shelter to perhaps 100,000 refugees, was anxious about the fate of the roughly 350,000 ethnic Hungarians in Serbia, was subjected to a vitriolic propaganda campaign by the Serbian press and was fearful of a possible Serbian attack. It was partly in this light that a new radar system was installed and that an arms deal was signed with Russia during President Yeltsin's visit to Hungary. A part of Russia's outstanding debt to Hungary, incurred by the Soviet Union, would be paid off by arms deliveries.

With Slovakia, problems were not as acute as those with Serbia, although the dispute over the Slovakian barrage project on the Danube (which the Hungarians argued would cause irremediable environmental damage to Hungary) and fears over the future of the Hungarian minority in southern Slovakia cast a pall over relations with the future state. Matters were not helped by the rather tactless way in which the Hungarian government handled matters. It tended to ignore Slovakia and Slovak interests until very late in the day and believed that the barrage question could be solved through negotiations with the Czechoslovak federal government. This proved to be a mistaken assessment.

Relations with Romania did not change significantly during the year; they remained uneasy, but no worse than that. Hungary took some comfort from the fact that the Democratic Convention performed quite respectably in the Romanian elections (see III.1.iv) and that the party representing the Hungarian minority in Romania was a member of the Convention. On the other hand, the rise in the vote for Romanian nationalist parties was a source of concern. There were no difficulties with Hungary's other neighbours, namely Austria, Croatia, Slovenia and Ukraine.

iv.   ROMANIA

CAPITAL: Bucharest   AREA: 237,500 sq km   POPULATION: 23,200,000 ('90)
OFFICIAL LANGUAGE: Romanian   POLITICAL SYSTEM: emerging democracy
HEAD OF STATE: President Ion Iliescu (since Dec '89)
RULING PARTY: Democratic National Salvation Front (NSF) heads coalition
HEAD OF GOVERNMENT: Nicolae Văcăroiu, Prime Minister (since Nov '92)
PRINCIPAL MINISTERS: Theodor Viorel Melescanu (foreign affairs), Gen. Nicolae
    Constantin Spiroiu (defence), Petre Ninosu (justice), Gheorghe Ion Danescu
    (interior), Florin Gheorghescu (finance), Dumitru Popescu (industry)
CURRENCY: leu (end-'92 £1=694.83 lei, US$1=458.94 lei)
GNP PER CAPITA: US$1,640 ('90)
MAIN EXPORT EARNERS: oil, raw materials and metals, machinery and transport
    equipment, chemicals, tourism

ROMANIA's year of elections and electioneering brought several new political figures to prominence but produced little change in direction at the top. The results confirmed Ion Iliescu in his post as President, while the fragmentation of the parties represented in parliament, including his own National Salvation Front (NSF), considerably strengthened his own personal authority. For the first time since 1988 there were no major riots in the country, indicating that, despite continuing economic decline, a degree of social stability—albeit perhaps temporary—had been achieved.

The year began with campaigning for the local elections scheduled for February, the first to be held since the overthrow of President Ceauşescu. The results were a disappointment for the NSF, the party led by former communists, which had dominated government at all levels since the December 1989 revolution. The NSF saw its nationwide vote halved compared with the parliamentary elections of May 1990. However, the NSF's 33.6 per cent share was still sufficient to make it the strongest party, particularly in the countryside. Its main challenger was the Democratic Convention (DC), an umbrella group of 14 opposition parties, which secured 24.3 per cent of the vote and took several cities, including Bucharest.

The NSF's time of troubles continued in March with an acrimonious party congress which led to a split within its ranks. The majority supported Petre Roman, an advocate of radical economic reforms, who had been forced out of the premiership in September 1991 (see AR 1991, p. 162) with the apparent connivance of President Iliescu. The minority conservative wing rallied behind Mr Iliescu's more cautious policy and formed a new party, the Democratic National Salvation Front (DNSF), to support his bid for re-election.

The divisions within the NSF, which led to its two-way split, were matched within the DC. In April the National Liberal Party (NLP) withdrew from the Convention, partly because Radu Câmpeanu, the NLP leader, failed to get the DC's nomination as its presidential candidate. The NLP's motives were also grounded in an espousal of populism. Since the DC included the Hungarian Democratic Union of Romania (HDUR), Mr Câmpeanu was hoping to gain some of the electoral support that was expected to go to the Romanian nationalist parties. The NLP's populism was also reflected in its nomination of ex-King Michael as its presidential candidate—an offer the former ruler turned down.

The long-awaited elections on 27 September confounded pollsters, who had predicted that the DC would come first, followed by Mr Roman's NSF. In fact, President Iliescu's DSNF gained the largest number of votes, followed by the DC, the NSF, the nationalist Romanian National Party (RNUP), the HDUR, the extreme nationalist Greater Romania Party (GRP) and the neo-communist Socialist Party of Labour (SPL). The NLP's pre-election manoeuvring proved to be a costly mistake; the party that in the 1990 elections had been the main challenger to the NSF failed to clear the 3 per cent threshold. The full results were as follows:

	Assembly of Deputies		Senate	
	% of votes	seats	% of votes	seats
DNSF	27.7	117	28.3	49
DC	20.0	82	20.2	34
NSF	10.2	43	10.4	18
RNUP	7.7	30	8.1	14
HDUR	7.5	27	7.6	12
GRP	3.9	16	3.9	6
SPL	3.0	13	3.2	5

President Iliescu failed to get an absolute majority in the first round of the presidential elections, in which his main rival was Emil Constantinescu, the rector of Bucharest University, a highly-respected academic but a comparative newcomer to politics. In the second round Mr Iliescu comfortably beat his rival, gaining 61.43 per cent against Mr Constantinescu's 38.57 per cent.

Mr Iliescu's electoral victory was attributed to his policy of gradualism, his caution towards radical economic reforms, his emphasis on social security and his strong dose of nationalism. With the earlier split in the ranks of the NSF now confirmed at the elections and with the failure of Mr Roman's challenge to Mr Iliescu's authority, the President's personal power and influence were substantially increased.

The selection of the new government confirmed this trend. Theodor Stolojan, the outgoing Prime Minister, who left for a job with the World Bank, was replaced by Nicolae Văcăroiu, an economist like his predecessor but with a much less prominent public image. Mr Văcăroiu had previously worked in the Finance Ministry on tax matters. His government, formed in November, consisted of technocrats with a strong presence of DSNF supporters. It was expected to pursue cautious economic reforms.

The reason for keeping the pace of reforms relatively slow was concern that the simmering social discontent, caused by severe economic problems, could once again rise to the surface. Hopes that Romania's economy would be stabilized in 1992 were dashed by preliminary reports of a further 16.5 per cent decline in GDP. Although it did not get out of control, the annual inflation rate remained far too high, at around 200 per cent. Unemployment trebled in the 12 months to December, surpassing the one million figure. According to estimates, one in six Romanian families lived below the subsistence level.

The results of privatization were, at best, mixed. Although much of the previously-collectivized land had been restored to its previous owners or been otherwise redistributed, the lack of capital among the peasantry to buy machinery and fertilizers contributed to the failure to boost food production. Only two out of a planned 30 privatization projects envisaged in a pilot scheme were actually carried out. The distribution to the population of vouchers, accounting for 30 per cent of the capital in state-owned companies, took place as planned but there were no indications during the year that the exercise would make any difference to economic efficiency.

In June the International Monetary Fund approved the government's stabilization programme and this cleared the way for a package of loans, worth nearly $1,000 million, to be granted to Romania by the IMF and the World Bank. Further good news came in November when Romania and the European Community (EC) signed an association agreement to forge closer links. However, external economic relations suffered a setback when the US Congress refused, once again, to extend most-favoured-nation trading status to Romania. The American decision followed allegations of irregularities in the Romanian elections in September.

Romania's trade also suffered from the imposition of UN sanctions on Serbia/Yugoslavia in May. Estimates of the damage to Romania varied but a figure of $500 million for the year was considered appropriate. However, Romania failed to enforce the sanctions in full, allowing barges on the Danube to continue taking large quantities of oil, coal, iron ore and other goods from ports in Ukraine to Yugoslavia. These shipments continued even after the deployment in the autumn of a few customs officers from EC countries. Bucharest argued that it had no powers to stop the deliveries because the Danube was an international waterway.

Romania's concern about the escalating war in former Yugoslavia (see III.1.vi) was coupled with apprehension about the situation in Moldova (Moldavia), where clashes between Russians and Romanians continued in the Dnestr region (see also III.2.i). In January Romania became the first country to open an embassy in Chişinău, the Moldovan capital. In general, Bucharest was pursuing a low-key, step-by-step approach towards possible unification with Moldova. Romania concluded a series of cooperation agreements with Greece, Turkey and Bulgaria in the hope of counteracting the growing insecurity in the Balkans. In June it became one of the signatories of the Istanbul declaration, which was designed to establish a zone of regional economic cooperation (see also II.3.vii).

Relations with Hungary, embittered for years by arguments over the position of Romania's Hungarian minority, remained at a low ebb (see also III.1.iii). The ethnic Hungarians found further cause for complaint with the election of Gheorghe Funar—later in the year the RNUP's presidential candidate—as mayor of Cluj. Mr Funar ordered the removal of bilingual signs and imposed severe restrictions on public meetings considered to be anti-Romanian. Meanwhile, the government also fuelled tension by replacing the ethnic Hungarian prefects (the local authority leaders) of Hargitha and Covasna counties with two ethnic Romanians. The ensuing row was only partially resolved by appointing two prefects for each county, one Romanian and one Hungarian. These moves further radicalized the Hungarian minority, prompting more explicit demands by their representatives for autonomy.

v. BULGARIA

CAPITAL: Sofia   AREA: 110,000 sq km   POPULATION: 8,600,000 ('92)
OFFICIAL LANGUAGE: Bulgarian   POLITICAL SYSTEM: parliamentary democracy
HEAD OF STATE: President Zhelyu Zhelev
RULING PARTIES: coalition sponsored by Movement for Rights and Freedoms (MRF)
HEAD OF GOVERNMENT: Lyuben Berov, Prime Minister (since Dec '92)
PRINCIPAL MINISTERS: Valentin Karabashev (deputy premier, trade), Evgeni Matinchcv
   (deputy premier, labour & social welfare), Neycho Neev (deputy premier,
   transport), Stoyan Aleksandrov (finance), Valentin Aleksandrov (defence),
   Viktor Mihaylov (interior), Rumen Bikov (industry)
CURRENCY: lev (end-'92) £1=L36.64, US$1=L24.198)
GNP PER CAPITA: US$2,250 ('90)
MAIN EXPORT EARNERS: machinery and equipment, agricultural produce, tourism

BULGARIA'S first entirely non-communist government since the war had been formed in November 1991 following a narrow election victory by the Union of Democratic Forces (UDF) led by Filip Dimitrov (see AR 1991, pp. 164–5). UDF hegemony in Bulgaria looked assured when, in January, its original leader, Zhelyu Zhelev, was re-elected for a five-year term in the first-ever popular presidential elections in the country's history.

Although Dr Zhelev failed to win outright in the first round on 12 January he secured a 6 per cent advantage (53 to 47 per cent) in the run-off one week later, beating the independent nationalist, Velko Vulkanov, who had backing from the ex-communist Bulgarian Socialist Party (BSP). During the campaign there was friction between Dr Zhelev and the fiercely anti-communist UDF. The UDF accused the President of back-sliding, hesitated about endorsing his candidature and finally imposed the poetess, Blaga Dimitrova, as vice-presidential running-mate, effectively to monitor his politics. The tension between President and government worsened during the year, as they disputed the distribution of powers, especially the right to shape foreign policy, supervise the security service and control the secret police files of the communist era.

In March Dr Zhelev denounced a de-communization bill, which the UDF had drafted but was never to legislate, as placing unwarranted restrictions on personal freedom and imperilling Bulgaria's admission into the Council of Europe. In fact, Bulgaria joined the Council without opposition in May; moreover, in December the Sofia government finalized an association agreement with the European Community after difficult negotiations over trade terms. The year's other main foreign policy achievements were the signing of friendship and cooperation treaties with Turkey and Russia. On 16 January Bulgaria became the first state to recognize the independence of Macedonia (see III.1.vi), a move demanded by President Zhelev although it caused strains with Greece.

The UDF government's relations with the trade unions soured as fast as those with the President. Following a one-day general strike by the Confederation of Independent Trade Unions on 8 January, the pro-UDF Podkrepa union federation withdrew from its 'social peace' agreement with the government and employers in February. Both union groups demanded higher wages to offset the 1992 inflation rate of 80 per cent and measures to combat unemployment, which reached 16 per cent by December. Government concessions, such as reimposing price controls on necessities, were too limited to offset a wave of strikes that lasted into the autumn and hit mines, ports, hospitals and city transport in Sofia.

The two labour federations also agitated for government changes and were instrumental in bringing about a reshuffle on 20 May, in which a new Industry Minister, Rumen Bikov, was appointed. Probably the main cabinet change was the sacking of President Zhelev's ally, Dimitur Ludzhev, as Defence Minister. He had allegedly offended the government's American advisers by insisting that Bulgaria must maintain its lucrative arms exports. Once outside the cabinet, Mr Ludzhev led an increasingly disaffected band of centrist UDF MPs, who broke ranks in December to vote in an alternative non-party government, which Mr Dimitrov castigated as a government of 'restoration' (i.e. communist-oriented).

Before its fall, however, the UDF cabinet secured the enactment of several major reforms. In February it sponsored a redrafted Foreign Investment Law which removed restrictions on the foreign ownership of Bulgarian companies and the repatriation of profits. There followed a Banking Act, two laws making restitution of land and properties nationalized between 1947 and 1962 and an amended version of the 1991 Land Law, which established a market in agricultural property. After criticism of its dilatoriness by the IMF and the World Bank, the government forced through a Privatization Law in April, creating a specialist agency; but its scheme, published in October, for selling off up to 92 companies within two months failed. Indeed, not one major enterprise had been privatized by the end of 1992.

Nonetheless, the international financial institutions were reassured by the performance of the Finance Minister Ivan Kostov. His annual budget in April set a deficit of just 4.2 per cent of GNP, a figure well within IMF norms. The Fund responded by advancing a stand-by credit of $212 million; but in November, dismayed by the resignation of the UDF cabinet, it suspended further instalments of its long-term $503 million loan (see AR 1991, p. 166). Mr Kostov achieved a rescheduling agreement covering the $1,000 million of national debt owed to the Paris Club of banks; but a comparable deal concerning the $10,000 million owed to private banks of the London Club was put back for at least half a year by the government's fall.

The removal of the UDF from power was a protracted, conspiratorial affair. A vital prelude was Mr Dimitrov's loss of his alliance with the party of Bulgaria's ethnic Turks, the MRF, which held the balance of power in the National Assembly. Unemployment rates of over 50 per cent in the south-east and a racial bias in the land reform triggered a fresh Muslim exodus to Turkey; so that by the time that Ankara had tightened entry rules at least 80,000 fresh immigrants had arrived. Dismayed by the potential electoral repercussions, the MRF demanded a special regional aid programme and new amendments to the Land Law. As a warning to the government, the MRF combined with the BSP in September to force Stefan Savov, a leader of the right-wing faction of the UDF, to resign as parliamentary chairman.

The BSP had already failed to unseat the government by tabling a no-confidence vote on 17 July. The pretext had been a parliamentary decision on 9 July, stripping the former BSP Prime Minister, Andrei Lukanov, of his immunity as an MP, so that he could be prosecuted for embezzlement. Mr Lukanov spent the next five months in prison until his release was ordered by a second parliamentary vote on 29 December. His immediate predecessor as Prime Minister, Georgi Atanasov, was sentenced to ten years in prison for a similar offence on 3 November. The much-adjourned trial of the octogenarian ex-President, Todor Zhivkov, reached a conclusion after 19 months on 4 September, when he was gaoled for seven years for corruption.

The demise of the government could be dated back to a press conference given by President Zhelev on 30 August, in which he berated Mr Dimitrov for seeking 'confrontation with everyone' and proposed a national consensus cabinet. The UDF responded by holding a nationwide conference and calling rallies against the President; but it could not recover its authority. Finally, the defection of the MRF ensured that Mr Dimitrov lost a confidence vote in the Assembly on 28 October. Resisting any personnel or policy changes, he tried to seek a new mandate but was defeated on 20 November.

The BSP squandered its opportunity to sponsor a government—a possibility guaranteed by the constitution—when it proposed an ineligible ex-dissident with dual nationality as prime minister. A parliamentary dissolution was only avoided because the MRF then persuaded the President's economic adviser, Lyuben Berov, to become premier. He formed a non-party cabinet of little-known experts, naming no Turks or women as ministers; surprisingly, it won parliamentary approval on 30 December. The success was due to splits in the UDF and BSP. However, few observers reckoned that, with an effective majority of just five, the new government would survive for more than a few weeks.

vi.   STATES EMERGING FROM THE FORMER
YUGOSLAV FEDERATION

Bosnia–Hercegovina
CAPITAL: Sarajevo   AREA: 51,129 sq km   POPULATION: 4,542,014
OFFICIAL LANGUAGE: Serbo-Croat   POLITICAL SYSTEM: republic, currently divided by
  civil war
HEAD OF STATE: President Alija Izetbegović
CURRENCY: dinar   GNP PER CAPITA: US$3,590 ('90 est.)

Croatia
CAPITAL: Zagreb   AREA: 56,538 sq km   POPULATION: 4,688,507 ('91)
OFFICIAL LANGUAGE: Croatian   POLITICAL SYSTEM: republic
HEAD OF STATE: President Franjo Tudjman
CURRENCY: Croatian dinar (end-'92 £1 = CD1,208.30, US$1 = CD798.08)
GNP PER CAPITA: US$7,110 ('90 est.)

Macedonia
CAPITAL: Skopje   AREA: 25,713 sq km   POPULATION:2,147,090 ('91)
OFFICIAL LANGUAGE: Macedonian   POLITICAL SYSTEM: republic
HEAD OF STATE: President Kiro Gligorov
CURRENCY: denar   GNP PER CAPITA: US$3,330 ('90 est.)

Montenegro
CAPITAL: Podgorica   AREA: 13,812 sq km   POPULATION: 648,483 ('91)
OFFICIAL LANGUAGE: Serbo-Croat   POLITICAL SYSTEM: republic
HEAD OF STATE: President Momir Bulatović
CURRENCY: dinar (end-'92 £1=Din1,137.35, US$1=Din751.22)
GNP PER CAPITA: US$3,970 ('90 est.)

Serbia
CAPITAL: Belgrade   AREA: 88,316 sq km   POPULATION: 9,916,068 ('91)
OFFICIAL LANGUAGE: Serbo-Croat   POLITICAL SYSTEM: republic
HEAD OF STATE: President Slobodan Milošević
CURRENCY: dinar (end-'92 £1=Din1,137.35, US$1=Din751.22)
GNP PER CAPITA: US$4,950 ('90 est.)

Slovenia
CAPITAL: Ljubljana   AREA: 20,251 sq km   POPULATION: 1,970,000 ('91)
OFFICIAL LANGUAGE: Slovene   POLITICAL SYSTEM: republic
HEAD OF STATE: President Milan Kučan
CURRENCY: tolar (end-'92 £1=T149.09, US$1=T98.48)
GNP PER CAPITA: US$12,520 ('90 est.)

Federal Republic of Yugoslavia
CONSTITUENTS: Montenegro, Serbia
CAPITAL: Belgrade   AREA: 102,128 sq km   POPULATION:10,564,551 ('91)
OFFICIAL LANGUAGE: Serbo-Croat   POLITICAL SYSTEM: federation of republics
HEAD OF STATE: President Dobrica Ćosić
CURRENCY: dinar (end-'92 £1=Din1,137.35, US$1=Din751.22)

ALTHOUGH the Socialist Federal Republic of Yugoslavia could be said
to have ended its existence on 27 April 1991 (see AR 1991, pp. 167–74),
the states which began to emerge from the debris remained intimately
involved with each other. A quarter of the 8.4 million Serbs lived outside
Serbia. Former communists remained in power, especially in Serbia
and Montenegro. On the economic plane, all of the Yugoslav republics
were faced with the effects of economic disintegration. Economic sanc-

tions against Serbia and Montenegro damaged all of their neighbours. There was a succession of devaluations of the dinar. Rampant inflation returned, with the National Bank in Belgrade printing money on demand. Although to some extent shielded from this by the issue of their own currencies, Croatia and to a lesser extent Slovenia also had their problems. Continuing instability in the area resulted in a slower growth of capital imports, even in Slovenia, although the Slovenes had some success in the reorientation of export markets. In Croatia the general economic crisis resulted in an almost complete failure to make progress with the promised privatization.

BOSNIA-HERCEGOVINA. The EC peace conference on Yugoslavia reconvened in Brussels on 9 January and on 15 January the Badinter commission (see AR 1991, p. 173) reported on the recognition of the former Yugoslav republics. In the case of Bosnia-Hercegovina recognition was deferred pending a referendum, which was held 29 February–1 March. A boycott by the Serb population (about 31 per cent of the total) resulted in a turnout of only 63 per cent, but of those voting there was virtual unanimity in favour of independence, which was proclaimed on 3 March. Talks continued between the leaders of the three Bosnia-Hercegovina communities (Muslims, Serbs and Croats), chaired by UN mediator Cyrus Vance, but tension grew and fighting broke out in several areas. An agreement negotiated under the auspices of the EC, signed on 18 March, provided for the division of Bosnia-Hercegovina into ten autonomous units (cantons). This was repudiated on 25 March by the Muslim Party of Democratic Action (SDA). Serb leaders also declared their reluctance to accept the withdrawal of the republic from Yugoslavia, and on 27 March proclaimed a 'Serbian Repubic of Bosnia-Hercegovina'.

A 7,000-strong demonstration for peace in Sarajevo on 6–7 April was fired upon by snipers concealed in a hotel, which was then stormed by demonstrators. President Alija Iztebegović declared a state of emergency. Serious armed clashes began in the north and east of the republic, as Serb forces initiated a plan to create territorial corridors linking the principal areas of Serb settlement. Sarajevo itself came under artillery fire on 22 April.

On 5 May Marrack Goulding, UN under-secretary-general, visited Yugoslavia to enquire into the possible need to extend UN intervention into Bosnia-Hercegovina. On 17 May, following his visit, as a result of the collapsing security situation, the headquarters of the United Nations Protection Force (UNPROFOR) were moved from Sarajevo to Belgrade, as were the missions of the UNHCR, the ICRC and the EC.

Negotiation between the three principal ethnic groups continued under EC auspices in Lisbon, leading to a succession of ceasefires, none of which had more than momentary effect. Further attempts were made during the year, within different negotiating contexts, to reach a solution on the basis of Bosnia-Hercegovina's division into ethnic cantons, but no plan secured the agreement of all parties.

By 20 June the situation in the republic had deteriorated to the point at which the Presidency declared a 'state of war'. The position of besieged Sarajevo was becoming increasingly difficult as attempts to negotiate humanitarian relief to the city repeatedly failed. On 28 June the French President, François Mitterrand, made a brief visit to the city, following which agreement was reached that control of the airport would be handed over to the UN. Some 1,000 Canadian troops of UNPROFOR were deployed to this purpose, but the movement of aid remained intermittent and dangerous throughout the rest of the year, whether through the airport or on equally vulnerable overland routes.

In spite of an agreement on 15 June between the Presidents of Croatia and Bosnia-Hercegovina regarding joint military cooperation, on 4 July the formation of a new Croatian state of 'Herceg-Bosna' (western Hercegovina) was declared, under the leadership of Mate Boban. Relations between the Croatian and Bosnian leaderships remained very insecure throughout the year. A joint defence committee was set up on 23 September, but there were reported allegations of duplicity, bad faith and lack of cooperation by both sides. By the year's end Croatian forces remained in effective control of western Hercegovina, and a substantial segment of central Bosnia (see maps in this section).

CROATIA. Upon receipt of the report of the Badinter commission, the Presidency of the EC recognized Croatia (and Slovenia) on 15 January (Germany having done so on 23 December 1991).

UN military liaison officers arrived on 8 January, heralding the installation of UNPROFOR. Deployment went ahead despite the collapse of the 15th negotiated ceasefire, and the shooting-down of an Italian/EC helicopter by the federal army (JNA) on 7 January. The main body of the force was deployed in late February, in spite of repeated violations of the ceasefires, especially in eastern Slavonia. UNPROFOR consisted of units from 30 countries, including for the first time Russia.

President Milošević accepted the UN's proposed conditions for the guarantee of autonomous area minority rights within the 'Krajina' (see AR 1991, pp. 169–70), against vigorous resistance from the local Serb leaderships. Their compliance was only secured after the president of 'Krajina' (Milan Babić) was ousted on 16 February, his minister of defence dismissed and local Serb militias placed under JNA control. Serb acceptance was influenced by rapid improvements in organization, weaponry and morale among Croatian troops. Croatian acceptance was also reluctant, because the arrangement was thought to institutionalize the loss of Croatian territory to the Serbs.

THE CONFLICT IN AND AROUND BOSNIA-HERCEGOVINA

CROATIA

⊙ Zagreb

Karlovac

Osijek

Pakrac

Vinkovci   Vukovar

Slav. Brod   Županja

Bihać

Bos. Brod   Orasje

Banja Luka   Doboj   Brčko

Gospić

Maglaj   Gradačac

Zadar   Knin

BOSNIA - HERCEGOVINA   SERBIA

Jajce   Zvornik

Skradin

Drniš   Kupres   Konjić   Sarajevo   Bratunac

Višegrad

Goražde

Mostar

Nevesinje

KEY

□ Risk zones

■ High-risk zones

//// UN-protected areas (UNPA) in Croatia

Trebinje   **MONTENEGRO**

0   50
Km

Prevlaka

THE UN/EC 10-PROVINCE PLAN FOR BOSNIA-HERCEGOVINA

KEY

⬚ **Serb provinces**

A BANJA LUKA
B NEVESINJE
C BIJELJINA

⬚ **Muslim provinces**

D ZENICA
E TUZLA

⬚ **Croat provinces**

F BIHAĆ
G ODŽAK
H TRAVNIK
I MOSTAR

☐ **Sarajevo - Open City**

Banja Luka

Brčko

Tuzla   SERBIA

CROATIA

Gornji
Vakuf

Sarajevo

Mostar

MONTENEGRO

0   50
Km

UNPROFOR became fully deployed during April; by mid-April, although serious fighting had broken out in Bosnia-Hercegovina, the ceasefire in Croatia was generally effective. Four UN-protected areas (UNPAs) were established, in eastern and western Slavonia and along the borders of north-western Bosnia.

A comprehensive Croatian government reshuffle in April was aimed at retaining international support. In response to the comments of the Badinter commission, legislation on human and minority rights was passed in May. The rudimentary character of its provisions alienated the Croatian People's Party, which withdrew from the government of national unity.

Following an acrimonious campaign, the first elections to the Sabor (parliament) since independence were held on 2 August. The legitimacy of the election was strongly challenged on several grounds. Nevertheless, Franjo Tudjman's Croatian Democratic Union (HDZ) was returned to power, although with a reduced majority (56 per cent of the vote for President and 85 of the 138 seats in the Sabor). Following the contest, President Tudjman announced a substantially restructured government.

Croatian concern that the UN involvement signified the de facto secession of Serb majority areas was reinforced in late September when their assemblies adopted resolutions in favour of union with the Federal Republic of Yugoslavia and took measures to harmonize their political systems and economies. By the end of the year there was still no significant progress in the disarming and withdrawal of Serb irregular and JNA units from the occupied areas of Croatia, as stipulated by the ceasefire agreements.

MACEDONIA. The EC's Badinter commission recommended without precondition the recognition of Macedonian independence. Nonetheless the EC Foreign Ministers, in order to meet the objections of Greece, requested that the republic first renounce 'the use of a denomination which implies territorial claims'. On 6 January the Macedonian constitution was amended to the effect that the country had no territorial claims on other countries; but the issue of the new republic's name remained unresolved in the eyes of Greece. At the same time Macedonia declared its independence from Yugoslavia. The JNA began pulling out of Macedonia on 2 February and this was completed by the end of March. Bulgaria recognized the republic on 16 January (the first state to do so).

In spite of several occasions on which international action was construed as de facto recognition (such as the visit of Russian Foreign Minister Kozyrev to Skopje on 27 May) Greek diplomacy sustained an effective veto on EC recognition of Macedonia for the remainder of the year. Talks between Macedonian Foreign Minister Denko Malevski and the Greek Prime Minister Konstantinos Mitsotakis on 16 June failed to resolve the issue. The Greeks were reluctant to countenance recognition of a state which bore the name 'Macedonia', and the Skopje regime refused to adopt any title which they regarded as compromising their right to use that name (see also II.3.v).

The failure to achieve general international recognition was one of the primary causes of the resignation of the republican government after a vote of no confidence in the Sobranie (parliament) on 16 July. A new government headed by Branko Crvenkovski, of the Social Democratic Alliance, took office on 13 August, in coalition with the Albanian Party of Democratic Prosperity.

The unstable position of the government was underlined from 6 November, when riots in Skopje developed into an armed clash between the police and the Albanian population. The events were alternatively blamed upon the growing radicalization of separatist Albanian youth groups and the action of agents of the Yugoslav intelligence organization KOS. Additional burdens weighing on Macedonia were the influx of 45,000 refugees, the effects of the trade embargo on Yugoslavia and the prevailing insecurity attending the expectation of Macedonia being drawn into war.

MONTENEGRO. Boycotted by the ethnic minorities, a referendum on the republic's continuing association with Yugoslavia on 1 March returned a massive majority in favour (96 per cent). The electorate of the capital, Titograd, also voted to restore the former name of Podgorica. These two events effectively symbolized the struggle within the republic throughout the year between the ruling Democratic Socialist (former Communist) Party (DSP), which supported the creation of the new Federal Republic and close alliance with Serbia, and the growing forces for cultural and economic independence. Montenegro was hit hard by the UN's economic sanctions, especially in that these undermined the important tourism industry. The negotiation of accords with Croatia over the control of the Prevlaka peninsula in October was greeted by rioting among Montenegrins who felt that their interests were being subordinated to the tactical needs of Serbia. Montenegrin representatives defended the Yugoslav Prime Minister, Milan Panić, when he faced a vote of confidence in the Federal Assembly in September (see below under FEDERAL REPUBLIC). Elections to the republican Assembly in December returned the DSP as the largest party, but with no overall majority. The presidency and the nature of a ruling coalition were left to be determined by a second round in the New Year.

SERBIA. The deteriorating situation elsewhere in former Yugoslavia drew fierce criticism against President Milošević from the Serb opposition; from 9–12 March a series of protest rallies was held in Belgrade, directed especially against state control of the media. A rally on 31 May passed off with little impact, although for the first time the Serbian Orthodox hierarchy dissociated itself from the regime. Demonstrations drawing a crowd of 100,000 on 'Vidovdan' (the Serbian national day, 28 June) were attended by Crown Prince Aleksandar Karadjordjević, on his first visit to Serbia.

Throughout the year the situation in Kosovo became steadily more tense. Following the declaration of the province as an independent republic (see AR 1991, p. 173), the Democratic Alliance of Kosovo led by Ibrahim Rugova held elections to a 130-seat assembly on 24 May, but these were dismissed as illegal by the authorities. The government responded by closing schools and other public institutions to Albanians, dismissing Albanians from public office and stepping up the colonization programme, involving the resettlement of Serb refugees from other areas of Yugoslavia. Both the official security forces and unofficial terrorist bands were accused of numerous acts of violence and intimidation.

Despite forceful declarations by Prime Minister Panić, following his inauguration, about the need for an amicable and just settlement in Kosovo, and his visits to Tirana and Priština, no visible progress was made in the amelioration of the conditions of the Albanian population. Accordingly, tension continued to rise in the province throughout the year, although without fulfilling predictions of the extension of civil war to the province.

On 20 December elections were held to the Serbian Assembly (Skupština). The result confirmed President Milošević's Socialist Party as the major force in the Assembly, with 100 of the 250 seats, but denied him a ruling majority, so that he was expected to rely on the 75 votes of the extreme nationalist Serbian Radical Party. The tactical alliance (known as DEPOS) between Vuk Drašković's Serbian Renewal Movement and Dragoljub Mićunović's Democratic Party failed to make significant headway against the Socialists, gaining only 50 seats.

SLOVENIA. Although Slovenia had extricated itself from the fighting, it was by no means free of political conflict in 1992. The ruling DEMOS coalition had been constructed principally around a platform of defeat of the Communists and the securing of independence. Both of these aims having been achieved, its lack of natural coherence came to the surface. On 22 April the Assembly passed a vote of no confidence in the government. Prime Minister Lojze Peterle resigned, to be replaced by a new coalition under the leadership of Janez Drnovšek, chair of the Liberal Democratic Party and a former head of the federal government.

Even relations with Croatia were not easy, especially as Croatia had a massive negative trade balance with Slovenia. An acrimonious dispute broke out over fishing rights in territorial waters in April. A summit meeting between Presidents Tudjman and Kučan on 13 October stated that principles for the future friendly resolution of problems had been agreed, but these remained to be tested. The lifting of UN economic sanctions with respect to Slovenia on 28 August relieved to some extent the economic situation of the republic.

The first presidential and parliamentary elections since independence were held on 6 December. Standing as an independent, Milan Kučan easily retained the presidency, with 63.8 per cent of the vote. The main parties of the existing coalition, the Christian Democrats and Liberal Democrats, headed the parliamentary returns with 22 and 15 seats respectively (out of 80). Seven other parties or alliances also won seats.

FEDERAL REPUBLIC. The Serbs, always keen to retain a Yugoslav federation, held a 'Convention on Yugoslavia' on 3 January, and the Federal Assembly later passed a law providing for a Constituent Assembly, hoping for support from Montenegro, Macedonia and Bosnia-Hercegovina. In the event, on 27 April only Serbia and Montenegro formally adopted the constitution of the new Yugoslav state, called the Federal Republic of Yugoslavia (FRY), thus in effect acknowledging the secession of the other republics. Yugoslavia as it had been known since 1945 could be said to have ceased to exist from that date. The proclamation ceremony was largely shunned by the EC diplomatic community, although relations with Greece became particularly cordial. The FRY was not accepted as the successor state to the former Yugoslavia by any major international organization.

The new Federal Republic chose as its President in June the eminent writer Dobrica Ćosić. The politics of the federation took a new turn when he chose as his Prime Minister an American businessman, Milan Panić, and a 'cabinet of experts'. Mr Panić immediately began an energetic round of diplomacy designed to improve the tarnished image of Yugoslavia abroad and to alleviate international sanctions, but with no significant success.

During July and August relations between the 'Yugoslav' government and President Milošević of Serbia worsened rapidly, as serious differences emerged over the conduct of the war. The Panić government survived a vote of no confidence in the Federal Assembly on 4 September, which was followed by a major government reshuffle. Relations appeared to reach their nadir on 19 October, when Serbian paramilitary forces seized control of the federal Interior Ministry building in Belgrade. The conflict came to a head in the elections to the Serbian Assembly and presidency on 20 December, in which President Milošević secured 56 per cent of the vote and Mr Panić only 34 per cent. The result terminated attempts to generate international legitimacy for the new federation.

INTERNATIONAL MEDIATION. A significant aspect of events during the year was a shift in the balance between the international organizations bearing responsibility in negotiating a settlement of the Yugoslav crisis. In August-September 1991 the CSCE had devolved responsibility to the EC (see AR 1991, pp. 172–3). Strains on the unanimity of the Community, the lack of success of the Carrington mission and the practical problems of providing effective military intervention steadily swung the balance toward the UN, which by May 1992 had effectively marginalized continuing EC endeavours. The UN emerged as offering the only effective vehicle for the legitimation and organization of economic sanctions (as decreed by UN Security Council resolution 757 of 30 May).

International efforts took a new direction in August, when active attention was given to the possibility of direct military intervention to impose a settlement in Yugoslavia. Urgency was added to these discussions by growing press reports of atrocities, the conditions in prisoner-of-war camps and the plight of those displaced by 'ethnic cleansing'. On 4 August the USA successfully proposed a resolution to the UN Security Council condemning detention camps and other violations of human rights. A week later an extraordinary session of the UN human rights commission in Geneva also voted a strongly-worded motion. Security Council resolution 770, passed on 13 August, authorized 'all measures necessary' and was widely interpreted as an implicit anticipatory legitimation of direct military intervention. A second resolution (771) authorized unimpeded access for the International Red Cross to all detention camps.

On 26–27 August the British government hosted a major international conference in London with the aim of reaching a negotiated solution. At the start of the conference Lord Carrington tendered his resignation as chairman of the EC peace process. He was replaced by Lord (David) Owen, who together with UN special envoy Cyrus Vance took on responsibility for the conduct of subsequent negotiations.

The London conference issued declarations on compulsory displacement of persons, human rights and the desirability of a negotiated solution, but made no concrete advances on substantive issues. Following the meeting, however, both the WEU and NATO issued declarations on the measures necessary to tighten sanctions in the Adriatic and the Danube, and on the provision of additional troops for the UN. The only substantial diplomatic achievement of the summer was the negotiation of accords between the Croatian and Montenegrin governments over the disputed Prevlaka peninsula, which controlled access to the important naval base at Kotor.

During September the UN discussed the possible implementation of a 'no-fly zone' over Bosnia-Hercegovina. However, although this proposal was later adopted and reiterated in December, air exclusion over the republic was not enforced. International military presence on the ground expanded steadily, principally in support of humanitarian aid convoys to Sarajevo and other besieged towns. By the end of the year UN military involvement amounted to 7,500 men in Bosnia-Hercegovina and 15,000 in Croatia. The increasing vigour of UN military intervention throughout the year went alongside a growing scepticism on all sides within ex-Yugoslavia about its moral value and practical effectiveness.

A significant factor behind the increase in UN activity was the growing concern of the Islamic nations about the possible genocide of Bosnia's Muslims, and the reciprocal concern of Western governments that they should not be seen to be indifferent to the fate of Muslims. A conference on the Yugoslav crisis was arranged by the Turkish government in Istanbul on 25 November. The event was indicative of the importance of Turkey's role in the Balkans and of the growing involvement of the Islamic states in Balkan problems. A plan for Turkish engagement with the UN effort, funded by countries of the Islamic Conference Organization (ICO), was approved by an ICO meeting in Jeddah 1–2 December.

The problem of displaced persons emerged upon the international agenda as early as 23 January, when the Yugoslav Red Cross claimed that there were already 170,000 registered refugees in Croatia and 158,000 in Serbia (while 20,000 had fled to Hungary). These numbers grew steadily during the year, when to those simply fleeing the fighting were added many thousands displaced by 'ethnic cleansing' of mixed areas. By July the UNHCR estimated that the Yugoslav conflict had created more than 2.5 million refugees.

Growing concern was expressed in several European countries about the burden which this was imposing. Germany had by then taken around 200,000, Austria and Hungary around 50,000 each. Croatia announced in mid-July that it was supporting so many refugees that only those in transit would be permitted to enter its territory. The UNHCR sponsored a conference in Geneva on 29 July to examine responses to the problem.

vii. ALBANIA

CAPITAL: Tirana AREA: 29,000 sq km POPULATION: 3,300,000 ('90)
OFFICIAL LANGUAGE: Albanian POLITICAL SYSTEM: emerging democracy
HEAD OF STATE: President Sali Berisha (since April '92)
RULING PARTIES: coalition of Democratic Party (DP), Republican Party (RP) and
   Social Democratic Party (SDP)
HEAD OF GOVERNMENT: Alexander Meksi (DP), Prime Minister (since April '92)
PRINCIPAL MINISTERS: Rexhep Uka (DP/deputy premier, agriculture), Bashkim Kopliku
   (DP/deputy premier, public order), Vullnet Ademi (SDP/general secretary),
   Genc Ruli (DP/finance), Alfred Sarreqi (DP/foreign affairs), Safet Xhulali
   (DP/defence), Artan Hoxha (DP/foreign trade)
CURRENCY: lek (end-'92 £1=AL166.80, US$1=AL110.17)
GNP PER CAPITA: US$600 ('90)
MAIN EXPORT EARNERS: crude oil, minerals, agricultural products

DOMESTIC political affairs were dominated by two elections. In March a
new National Assembly was elected according to electoral laws enacted
in February. The Assembly was to consist of 100 members chosen in
single-member constituencies and 40 deputies selected by proportional
representation. A party had to secure 4 per cent of the national vote
to achieve representation and no party was to be based on ethnic
affiliation. The latter regulation put the Greek-based Omonia party
under grievous restraint. In the single-member constituencies successful
candidates had to win an overall majority in the first round of voting or
a simple majority in the second.

The first round was held on 22 March and the second a week later.
The Democratic Party (DP) emerged victorious with 62 per cent of the
poll and 92 seats. The Socialist Party of Albania (SPA) won 25 per cent
and 38 seats, while the Social Democratic Party (SDP) took seven seats,
one of them in a single-member constituency. The Human Rights Union
(HRU), primarily a Greek party, elected two deputies, and there was
one from the right-wing Republican Party (RP). President Ramiz Alia
resigned after the vote and the new Assembly elected in his place
Sali Berisha, the leader of the DP. The new Prime Minister was
Alexander Meksi, a construction engineer with an interest in medieval
architecture. His cabinet was technically a coalition because it had two
nominal independents and the SDP and RP had one minister each; all
the others were from the DP.

A different picture emerged from local elections held on 26 July and
2 August. The DP again secured most votes, but at 43 per cent was only
a whisker in front of the SPA, with 41 per cent. Both the HRU and the
RP had less than 5 per cent of the total vote. The DP had control of most
large towns, including its bastion in Tirana, but the SPA made a strong
showing in the countryside as well as significant inroads in the north,
which was usually considered safe DP territory. The decline of the DP
was primarily the result of a lower turnout of 70.5 per cent, compared
with 95 per cent in the general election, but that in itself reflected some
disillusion with the performance of the DP administration. Furthermore,

the DP had shown signs of serious divisions at the top, leading in August to the expulsion from the DP parliamentary group of one of the party's co-founders, Gramoz Pashko. The local elections were of considerable importance because the collapse of the central government and the disappearance of local party secretaries meant that real power, especially in the distribution of the exiguous but desperately-needed social welfare payments, now lay with these local authorities whose number had been increased immediately before the elections.

The new rulers took some revenge on their former oppressors. Parties loyal to Enver Hoxha were amongst those banned in July; Mr Alia was placed under house arrest in September; and in December the legal profession was closed to graduates of the Communist Party school.

Social problems were much more pressing. In the first quarter of the year food shortages were so severe that attacks on shops and warehouses reduced the country to near anarchy. The then Prime Minister, Vilson Ahmeti, agreed to link wages to prices and to extend unemployment benefits, but this had little effect when there was almost no food to buy. Some easement came from foreign aid. In July a Group of 24 meeting in Tirana ended with the promise of food aid at least until the 1993 harvest had been taken in. The previous month Mr Berisha had come back from a visit to the USA with a promise of $60 million worth of aid in addition to the $35 million granted in April. Greece also promised $70 million for agricultural development.

Outside assistance could not prevent social unrest. Although the near-anarchy of the early months subsided, strikes continued. In July the government declared many of them illegal and insisted that they had been fomented by former Communists. The most serious outbreaks began in October when workers at the Bulqize chromium mines and the oil-processing plant at Ballsh went on strike. The miners did not go back to work until Christmas Day. At the end of the year the Ballsh plant was still strike-bound.

The Meksi government, prompted by Western statesmen and banks, introduced an economic reform package on 20 April which entailed privatization of land and industrial enterprises, banking reforms and the reduction of price controls. Legislation for decollectivization was introduced in November and considerable privatization was seen in the service sector. In an end-of-the-year review Prime Minister Meksi pointed to a decrease in the state budget deficit, real reforms in taxation and banking, the reduction of inflation and an increase in food supplies. Nevertheless, Albania remained in a parlous economic and social condition.

In external affairs Albania, in May, ended its long-standing dispute with Britain over the Corfu Channel incident of 1946. Other indications of closer ties with the West included the unveiling in November of a memorial to Allied servicemen killed in Albania in World War II and cooperation with NATO forces in enforcing the Adriatic blockade of Serbia and Montenegro. It was the crisis in former Yugoslavia, and above all in Kosovo, which dominated foreign affairs (see also III.1.vi). The realization that Albanian forces could do little that was effective, together with the restraining influences of the West, meant that official statements avoided the extremism seen in some of the media. Nevertheless, at the Independence Day ceremony on 28 November Mr Berisha said that, although Albania did not want any change in its borders by force, it would 'never tolerate the ethnic cleansing of Albanians from their centuries-old territories'.

Albania also drew closer to the Muslim world. In December it established diplomatic relations with Saudi Arabia and joined the Islamic Conference Organization. Access to the Islamic Bank for Development was not the only motive for such a move.

2.   WESTERN CIS REPUBLICS AND GEORGIA – BALTIC STATES

i.   RUSSIA—BELORUSSIA—UKRAINE—MOLDAVIA— CAUCASIAN REPUBLICS

Russia
CAPITAL: Moscow   AREA: 17,075,000 sq km   POPULATION: 148,000,000 ('91)
OFFICIAL LANGUAGE: Russian   POLITICAL SYSTEM: republic
HEAD OF STATE AND GOVERNMENT: President Boris Yeltsin
CURRENCY: rouble   GNP PER CAPITA: US$2,242 ('90 est.)

Belorussia (Belarus)
CAPITAL: Minsk   AREA: 208,000 sq km   POPULATION: 10,500,000 ('91)
OFFICIAL LANGUAGE: Russian   POLITICAL SYSTEM: republic
HEAD OF STATE AND GOVERNMENT: Stanislav Shushkevich, Chairman of Supreme Soviet
CURRENCY: rubel   GNP PER CAPITA: US$1,880 ('90 est.)

Ukraine
CAPITAL: Kiev   AREA: 604,000 sq km   POPULATION: 52,000,000 ('91)
OFFICIAL LANGUAGES: Ukrainian & Russian   POLITICAL SYSTEM: republic
HEAD OF STATE AND GOVERNMENT: President Leonid Kravchuk
CURRENCY: karbovanets coupon   GNP PER CAPITA: US$1,320 ('90 est.)

Moldavia (Moldova)
CAPITAL: Chisinau (Kishinev)   AREA: 34,000 sq km   POPULATION: 4,500,000 ('91)
OFFICIAL LANGUAGES: Romanian & Russian   POLITICAL SYSTEM: republic
HEAD OF STATE AND GOVERNMENT: President Mircea Snegur
CURRENCY: rouble   GNP PER CAPITA: US$1,519 ('90 est.)

Georgia
CAPITAL: Tbilisi   AREA: 70,000 sq km   POPULATION: 5,500,000 ('91)
OFFICIAL LANGUAGES: Georgian & Russian   POLITICAL SYSTEM: republic
HEAD OF STATE AND GOVERNMENT: Eduard Shevardnadze, Chairman of State Council
CURRENCY: rouble   GNP PER CAPITA: US$1,157 ('90 est.)

Armenia
CAPITAL: Yerevan AREA: 30,000 sq km POPULATION: 3,500,000 ('91)
OFFICIAL LANGUAGES: Armenian & Russian POLITICAL SYSTEM: republic
HEAD OF STATE AND GOVERNMENT: President Levon Ter-Petrosyan
CURRENCY: rouble GNP PER CAPITA: US$1,248 ('90 est.)

Azerbaijan
CAPITAL: Baku AREA: 87,000 sq km POPULATION: 7,100,000 ('91)
OFFICIAL LANGUAGES: Azeri & Russian POLITICAL SYSTEM: republic
HEAD OF STATE & GOVERNMENT: President Abulfaz Elchibey
CURRENCY: manat & rouble GNP PER CAPITA: US$832 ('90 est.)

IF 1991 saw the end of Communist rule throughout the republics which had formerly constituted the Soviet Union, 1992 saw the uncertain development of the political and economic forms that were to replace it. There was no longer, after the attempted coup of August 1991 (see AR 1991, pp. 177–80), a Communist Party exercising a leading role throughout the wider society. There was no longer an official ideology. The earlier commitment to public ownership and planning had steadily been dismantled. Relations with the outside world—already, in the case of the United States, based on 'partnership'—became very largely normal. And yet at year's end the overwhelming bulk of industry remained in the hands of the state; former members of the Communist Party occupied many of the dominant positions; and a series of minor incidents, from the expulsion of Russian diplomats in France to covert action in Swedish territorial waters, made it clear that there was still a wide gulf between the Soviet successor states and their former adversaries.

One change, however, was reasonably clear: the ending of a centralized system based in Moscow and its replacement by a diversity of independent states. Eleven of the original 15 republics had been allied, since December 1991, in a hastily-conceived Commonwealth of Independent States (see AR 1991, pp. 183–4, 557–61). All of them, whether associated or not, began to assert their distinctive identities; indeed, there were strongly centrifugal pressures within many of the former Soviet republics, as well as disputes between them. It was also clear that no formula of rule had developed to take the place of the 'command-administrative system' of the Soviet years. Party systems, outside the Baltic states (see III.2.ii), were weakly developed; the legal system found itself overwhelmed by a rising tide of official as well as popular lawlessness; and there was an enduring tension, particularly in Russia, between a strong executive presidency and representative democracy as expressed through the parliaments elected in the last years of Communist rule. All of these tensions were played out, during 1992, against a sharply deteriorating economic situation which made it difficult for politicians at any level to retain popular support.

The framework through which the former republics sought to address their common problems was, after December 1991, the Commonwealth of Independent States (CIS). A series of meetings throughout the year nonetheless made little progress in establishing closer relations within the CIS. There were continuing tensions between republics—such as Ukraine—that were suspicious of any form of supranational 'centre' and others—particularly in central Asia (see VIII.1.iii)—that favoured a greater degree of integration. Two issues proved particularly intractable: control over the unitary armed forces established in December 1991 and division of responsibility for the former Soviet debt to other nations. A dispute between Russia and Ukraine over control of the Black Sea fleet developed within weeks of the establishment of the Commonwealth. According to the Ukrainian Defence Ministry in early January, all troops in the republic, other than strategic nuclear forces, were subordinate to the Ukrainian President and were required to take an oath of allegiance. The Black Sea fleet, although it did have nuclear capability, was not regarded as a part of the CIS strategic forces in this sense. The fleet's commander, Admiral Kasatonov, insisted for his part that he was subordinate directly to the commander-in-chief of the CIS armed forces, while President Yeltsin insisted that the Black Sea fleet 'was, is and will continue to be Russian'. Negotiations between the two republics began in April. It was eventually decided, in May, that the fleet should not form part of CIS strategic forces, and Admiral Kasatonov was moved to other duties. A further, more formal, agreement in August provided that the fleet would be placed under the control of the two republics until 1995, when it was expected to be divided.

Despite these and other differences, the CIS did at least survive the year, and in several respects developed an institutional framework within which common purposes could be advanced. In January a common oath was agreed for servicemen in the CIS armed forces (in which Ukraine, Belorussia, Azerbaijan and Moldavia from the outset took no part). An inter-parliamentary conference held in Minsk in late January agreed to coordinate legislation among the states that were represented. A meeting of CIS heads of state in February established a framework for the joint armed forces, and appointed Yevgeny Shaposhikov as commander-in-chief. Other agreements covered the use of the rouble for inter-republican trade and the free transit of goods between member states. In March an agreement was reached on the repayment of the Soviet foreign debt; and later in the month seven CIS members agreed to establish an inter-parliamentary assembly (its first meeting being held in September). In May a five-year collective security agreement was signed by Russia, Armenia, Kazakhstan, Kirghizia, Tajikistan and Uzbekistan; and in June it was agreed to establish Commonwealth peace-keeping forces.

Most of these documents, however, were signed by only a majority of the states concerned, not by all of them. In the case of Azerbaijan and Moldavia, their affiliation to the CIS itself had not been formally ratified by the end of 1992. In October, following elections which confirmed the National Front in power, the Azerbaijani parliament announced that it would not be confirming its original decision to adhere. And there were new sources of tension as the year advanced, among them the question of national currencies. The agreement establishing the CIS had committed its members to a 'single economic space', but not necessarily to a common currency. Estonia, which was not a CIS member, became the first former Soviet republic to establish its own currency (in mid-1992). Parallel currencies based upon a coupon system were introduced by Ukraine and Belorussia; more formal national currencies were being planned by Kazakhstan, Ukraine, Azerbaijan and Armenia. In October, in Bishkek, six CIS states—Belorussia, Russia, Kirghizia, Uzbekistan, Kazakhstan and Armenia—agreed to establish an inter-state bank to coordinate fiscal policy in the rouble zone. This was, at least implicitly, an admission that the Commonwealth contained states that were pursuing entirely independent economic policies.

The Russian Federation was the largest and most important member of the new Commonwealth, even more so than in the former USSR. A new constitution was approved in principle during the year, but it was agreed in December that the formal endorsement of a new text should follow a popular referendum in 1993. There was some movement in relations between the various constituents of the Federation, particularly through a federation treaty signed on 31 March by 18 of the 20 autonomous republics that were located within Russian borders. The treaty gave central bodies jurisdiction over international relations, minority rights, transport and economic policy. The federal authorities and the republics were jointly to control natural resources, taxation within the republics and the principles of local self-administration. In all other respects the republics were given 'complete state power on their territory', and they were allowed to become 'autonomous participants in international and foreign economic relations'. Two of the autonomous republics, Tatarstan and Chechen-Ingushetia, refused to initial or sign the new treaty. A referendum in Tatarstan on 21 March—held to be illegal by the Russian courts—produced a majority of over 61 per cent in favour of the republic becoming a 'sovereign state'.

Political developments in Russia during 1992 centred around two sessions of the Congress of People's Deputies. Originally elected in 1990, the Congress was led by its increasingly influential Speaker, Ruslan Khasbulatov, and included a substantial representation of former Communists and directors of state industry. It showed little sympathy for the market-oriented reforms associated with the Yeltsin government. At the first Congress, in April, an attempt to debate a motion of no confidence in the government was narrowly defeated, although a resolution was adopted that criticized the reforms and called for higher levels of social spending. The government promptly resigned, warning that the adoption of a resolution of this kind would prejudice economic reform and jeopardize the assistance promised by the West. The government's resignation, however, was not accepted, and the Congress subsequently adopted a more moderate resolution which supported at least the principle of 'radical transformation' of the economy. The Congress did, nonetheless, require President Yeltsin to give up the prime ministership within three months. On 15 June Yegor Gaidar, chief architect of the reforms, was appointed to these duties by presidential decree.

The reformers were spared the opposition of the Soviet Communist Party and of its Russian counterpart, both of them suspended and then banned (in November 1991) by Russian presidential decision. The Russian Constitutional Court began to consider the legality of these decisions in May 1992, and also to consider the legality of the party itself. Counsel for the Russian government argued that the party had been, in effect, a state mechanism, not a party as such; its opponents argued that the ban was a violation of the law on political parties, and one that exceeded the powers of the President. The former Soviet President himself, Mikhail Gorbachev, was called upon to give evidence but refused to appear. The court's ruling, at the end of November, was hailed by both sides. It supported President Yeltsin's ban on the party's central institutions, but rejected his claim that the party was itself illegal and that its local activities could be prohibited. Political opposition, during the year, came in practice from rather different sources: not just from ex-Communists, but also from right-wing nationalists, who argued that the Yeltsin government was betraying Russia's national interests.

Demonstrations were organized in February by supporters as well as opponents of the Yeltsin government, and again in March, on the first anniversary of the all-union referendum which had produced a large majority in favour of a 'renewed' USSR (see AR 1991, pp. 180–1). An attempt to convene a sixth extraordinary session of the USSR Congress of People's Deputies was not successful, but an anti-government demonstration in central Moscow attracted about 70,000 participants. In June 'anti-fascist rallies' were held near the Ostankino television centre in Moscow, and in the city centre. A more broadly-based opposition began to form later in the year, following the publication in the conservative daily *Sovetskaya Rossiya* of a 'political declaration of the left-wing and right-wing opposition'. The declaration, which appeared on 21 September, insisted that Mr Yeltsin was 'ruining Russia' and called for 'national-state salvation'. Its sponsor, the National Salvation Front, was banned in October.

A less directly confrontational opposition began to develop in late 1992 based around the Civic Union, a grouping of centrist parties headed by Arkadii Volsky (a former Communist Party secretary and now the representative of an organization of state managers) and Vice-President Alexander Rutskoi. Mr Volsky, in a series of interviews, called for a closer look at the Chinese model, which combined economic reform with a strong state; Vice-President Rutskoi described current policies as 'economic genocide' and called for changes in the composition of the government.

Pressures of this kind made themselves apparent in December at the seventh session of the Russian Congress of People's Deputies. President Yeltsin, who addressed the Congress on 1 December, accepted that the economy was in crisis, but insisted that the strategy of reform was not itself responsible. Mr Khasbulatov, in a speech that was more warmly received, accepted the principle of market relations but attacked the 'tendency to privatize everything', calling instead for the mixed, socially-oriented economy that had been successful in many European and Asian countries. Several issues were involved, not only the direction of future reform but also the composition of the government and the respective powers of parliament and President. In the end, despite Mr Yeltsin's public support, Mr Gaidar was forced to step down as acting Prime Minister; his place was taken by Viktor Chernomyrdin, formerly a deputy prime minister in charge of energy and with a background in the gas industry. Mr Chernomyrdin (born April 1938) told the Congress that he was in favour of reforms, but 'without deepening the impoverishment of the people'. Among his first acts was the freezing of the prices of basic foodstuffs. The government announced on 23 December, however, included most of the members of the Gaidar team, including Foreign Minister Andrei Kozyrev (who had been fiercely criticized by hardliners) and Privatization Minister Anatolii Chubais. It was meanwhile agreed that there would be a referendum on 11 April 1993 on the principles of a new constitution, which would presumably be followed by fresh elections to a reconstituted Russian parliament.

The background to these developments, as in the other post-Soviet republics, was a sharply deteriorating economic situation. The report of the State Statistics Committee on economic performance in 1991 was published in February. It described the year as one of 'intensified decline in the economy and people's standard of living and an exacerbation of the social atmosphere'. Gross national product, which had fallen slightly in 1990, had slumped by 17 per cent over the year. Foreign trade had deteriorated sharply as exports of fuel and raw materials—the main sources of hard currency—had declined. Production levels of oil and coal in 1991 were 90 per cent of those of the previous year, mainly because of outdated equipment and low investment; a further 15 million tonnes of coal had been lost because of industrial action. Foreign trade turnover was just 39 per cent of the level attained in 1990. Control over the money supply, it was acknowledged, had been lost entirely: the volume of cash in circulation had increased 4.8 times over 1990, and the consumer price index by 196 per cent. The budgetary deficit, meanwhile, had reached 150,000 million roubles, or 12–14 per cent of GNP.

The solution proposed by the Yeltsin government was what had become known in other countries as à monetarist policy. First of all, prices were freed: in Russia on 2 January and in most of the other republics shortly afterwards. Prices in state shops rose immediately between three and 30 times, although many goods still had to be bought at private markets. A further and important stage of reform followed in June, when deputies approved privatization legislation under which vouchers worth up to 10,000 roubles would be distributed to all citizens to allow them to buy shares in state property. It was envisaged that about 25 per cent of state enterprises would be sold by the end of 1992; a number of sectors were, however, to remain in state hands, including natural resources and strategic enterprises. A further presidential decree of 14 June authorized the sale of land to private owners during the privatization of enterprises, and also permitted the sale of land for 'entrepreneurial activity'. Another decree allowed state enterprises which failed to pay their debts to be declared bankrupt and either liquidated or sold off to the highest bidder at auction. Privatization vouchers, as the legislation had provided, began to be distributed to all citizens on 1 October, with a face value of 10,000 roubles. 'We don't need a few millionaires', Mr Yeltsin had told a press conference in August; 'we need millions of private property-owners.'

Measures of this kind had in fact introduced only a modest degree of change into the Russian economy by the end of 1992. The larger picture, moreover, remained a gloomy one. Official figures for the first half of the year, published in July, showed that industrial production was 13 per cent down on 1991. The payment of salaries and pensions was in substantial arrears, and half the population was said to be on or below subsistence level. Mr Gaidar, speaking to the Congress in September, indicated that industrial production for the year as a whole was likely to be down by over 20 per cent, and capital investment by more than half, as compared with 1990. The monthly rate of inflation had reached 20 per cent, and the budgetary deficit had risen sharply. This, moreover, was only part of a much wider deterioration in the quality of Russian life. Births, by early 1992, were running behind the number of deaths. And a report presented to the Russian parliament in October indicated that about 15 per cent of the country's land area was 'ecologically unsafe'. Some 40 per cent of hospitals did not have hot water (12 per cent had no water at all), up to 2.7 million people were still living in areas affected by radiation from the Chernobyl explosion, and only about 25 per cent of all 16-year-olds were healthy.

The Russian President, like his predecessor, was able to make relatively more progress on the international arena. Mr Yeltsin started the year by making his first appearance, in January, at the United Nations.

Addressing a Security Council summit concerned with peace-making and peace-keeping, the Russian President unveiled proposals for a new global anti-missile system in cooperation with the United States. Emphasizing that 'we do not want to be mere partners, we want to be allies', Mr Yeltsin added that a new democratic Russia (which had succeeded to the USSR's membership of the Security Council and other UN bodies) would play a full part in the maintenance of collective security. On his way to New York, Mr Yeltsin stopped over briefly in London where a joint declaration, 'Partnership for the 1990s', was signed on 30 January. The declaration committed both parties to cooperation on nuclear weapons and materials; the United Kingdom agreed to lift the 18-month freeze on export credit insurance for business projects in the former Soviet Union, and would continue to advocate Russia's membership of the International Monetary Fund. Following the UN summit, Mr Yeltsin visited Canada, where on 2 February he signed a treaty of friendship and cooperation. This was followed by a visit to France, where a similar treaty was signed on 7 February.

The first summit between the Russian President and his US counterpart took place in June in Washington. On 17 June both leaders endorsed an unprecedented arms reduction agreement which would eventually cut the two powers' nuclear arsenals by two-thirds, going far beyond the START treaty signed by Presidents Bush and Gorbachev in July 1991 (see AR 1991, pp. 187–8, 555–7). The new package, to be formalized in a START II treaty, involved an initial reduction of strategic nuclear warheads to between 3,800 and 4,250 for each side, with further reductions by the year 2003, together with the elimination of all independently-targeted MIRV missiles (see also Pt. XII). Describing nuclear weapons as 'obsolete and unnecessary', the Russian President announced that he had ordered Russia's SS-18 missiles—the most important land-based weapons of their kind—to be taken off alert. The two Presidents also signed a charter on American-Russian partnership and friendship and more specific agreements on cooperation in space research, on an early warning system for nuclear missile launches, on the elimination of chemical weapons and on investment in Russia. The Bush administration, for its part, granted most-favoured-nation status to Russian exports. Mr Yeltsin, addressing the US Congress on 17 June, obtained an enthusiastic response to his message that 'communism is dead'; he coupled it with a warning that democracy in his own country might not survive without massive Western aid.

Assistance to the scale required appeared to have been pledged by the Group of Seven (G7) meeting in Munich on 6–8 July. There was some resistance to the idea that Russia should become a full member of the Group; but just as discussions had taken place in 1991 with President Gorbachev, his Russian successor was invited to join multilateral talks after the summit had formally concluded.

The summit itself recommended that most-favoured-nation treatment should be applied to all trade with the former Soviet republics, and called for a closer relationship between the Russian government and the IMF. On 8 July the G7 leaders met with President Yeltsin and formally endorsed the disbursement of the first tranche of an aid package worth US$24,000 million. The package had been approved in principle at a meeting of the World Bank and IMF in Washington on 26–28 April, which had approved massive financial backing for the former Soviet republics on condition that they took rigorous action to privatize and stabilize their economies. The funds earmarked included a $6,000 million rouble stabilization fund; the Fund's managing director explained that the former Soviet republics were likely to need more than $100,000 million in support over the next four years, including loans, investment and other funding from the IMF, World Bank, individual countries and private investors. Most of the former Soviet republics, including Russia, became IMF members at this time; Mr Gaidar, at this time First Deputy Prime Minister, was in Washington to represent his government at the talks.

The later part of the year saw several further initiatives in foreign policy, including a visit by the Russian President to South Korea in November and to China in December. Mr Yeltsin, on his arrival in Beijing, called for a 'new era' in Sino-Russian relations, but his visit was cut short by domestic differences associated with the formation of the new government. A planned visit to Japan did not take place because of continuing differences over the fate of the southern Kurile islands (see also IX.2.iv). A visit to Britain in November, however, produced a treaty of friendship and cooperation, the first of its kind to be concluded between the two countries since 1766. A still more spectacular development was the formal conclusion of the START II agreement with the United States, finalized at Geneva on 29 December.

Many Russian concerns were shared by the governments of other post-Soviet republics. All of them faced a sharp decline in national income, and many political instability. Three of the republics—Ukraine, Belorussia, and Kazakhstan—were also nuclear powers, and their relationship to the disarmament commitments of the USSR was unclear for some time. The three republics finally agreed a protocol to the START treaty on 23 May in which they pledged to eliminate nuclear weapons by the end of the decade; all three republics similarly agreed to eliminate all nuclear weapons either through transfer to Russia or destruction, and to formalize their non-nuclear status by signing the Non-Proliferation Treaty in due course. Most republics meanwhile established their own armed forces; many began to introduce their own currencies; and all of them (apart from Georgia) joined the United Nations and established a wide range of international contacts.

Several bitter disputes within or between the non-Russian republics continued during the year, among them the longstanding conflict between Armenia and Azerbaijan about the status of the predominantly Armenian enclave of Nagorno-Karabakh (for its origins, see AR 1988, pp. 109–10). A ceasefire, concluded in September 1991, broke down in January and the whole region was placed under direct Azerbaijani presidential rule. Fighting intensified in February around the Nagorno-Karabakh capital, Stepanakert, and Armenian troops took the village of Khodzhaly, amid accusations that more than a thousand of the town's fleeing Azeri inhabitants had been murdered. CIS troops were ordered out of the region on 28 February, and international mediation—by CSCE representatives, the Iranian Foreign Minister and others—proved of no avail. On 9 May Armenian forces took Shusha, the last remaining Azerbaijani stronghold within the enclave, while on 17 May they took Lachin. An Azeri counter-attack began in June, enjoying some success, and in August the Armenian President, Levon Ter-Petrosyan, appealed to other members of the CIS to come to his assistance. Ceasefires were negotiated by Kazakhstan, on 28 August, and by Russia, on 19 September, but had little effect. It was announced that 216 Azerbaijanis and 270 Armenians had died during 1991, and that more than 600 had been wounded; the toll during 1992 was expected to be considerably higher.

Another dispute became much graver during 1992, centred on the predominantly Russian Dnestr region of Moldavia. The region had declared itself a republic in September 1991, and the following December it held its own presidential elections, together with a referendum on independence which was overwhelmingly supported. The referendum was declared illegal by the Moldavian authorities, and fighting broke out in which the Russian army was accused of supporting the separatists. The Moldavian President, Mircea Snegur, introduced a state of emergency on 28 March and called on the population to support the 'motherland'. The Dnestr government, for its part, condemned the emergency and called upon the Russian 14th army to defend the region. Attempts at international mediation were unsuccessful, and skirmishes continued; the town of Bendery was taken by Moldavian forces on 20 June, but recaptured by Dnestr forces the following day. President Snegur, speaking to parliament, announced that 'we are at war with Russia'. The head of the 14th army, in early July, described Moldavian policies as 'genocide' and condemned the President as a 'fascist'. An agreement was nonetheless concluded between Mr Yeltsin and the Moldavian President in late July, providing for a special status for the Dnestr region and self-determination in the event of Moldavian reunification with Romania. Subsequent discussions dealt with the gradual withdrawal of Russian troops and the resettlement of substantial numbers of refugees.

There were even greater disturbances in Georgia, following an increasingly open confrontation between President Zviad Gamsakhurdia and other nationalist leaders. The tension erupted into full-scale conflict in late December and early January 1992, leaving 113 dead and 420 wounded. Mr Gamsakhurdia, who had refused to enter into negotiations with 'terrorists and bandits', was finally forced out of his headquarters on 6 January, and his supporters were gradually overcome throughout the country. A military council took power on 2 January, announcing a state of emergency and the suspension of parliament pending fresh elections. The former Soviet Foreign Minister, Eduard Shevardnadze, returned to Georgia on 6 March and became chairman of a newly-created State Council four days later. In October he was popularly elected to the chairmanship by over 95 per cent of those who voted, and began to form a coalition government from among the many parties that had obtained representation. Disputes with South Ossetia and Abkhazia continued throughout the year, despite these changes. South Ossetia had voted in a January referendum for reintegration into the Russian Federation, and the Abkhazian parliament had voted in favour of 'state sovereignty' in July. Armed conflict in August and September had left over 180 dead.

The Ukraine, like Russia, experienced a change in its Prime Minister during the year. The slow pace of economic reform had been criticized by President Kravchuk as well as by parliamentary deputies, and on 30 September it was announced that he had accepted the resignation of Premier Fokin. The Ukrainian parliament then passed a vote of no confidence in the government for its mishandling of the economy, leading to the resignation of the entire cabinet. Mr Fokin's successor, approved by parliament on 13 October by 316 votes to 23, was Leonid Kuchma (aged 54), head of the Yuzhmash missile factory in Dnepropetrovsk and a representative of the powerful military-industrial lobby. In his acceptance speech, Mr Kuchma promised 'evolutionary' change and progress towards the market through a 'sensible combination of administrative and economic measures'. The economy, he suggested, was not in crisis but in a state of 'catastrophe', and the measures that he proposed included a reduction in the budgetary deficit, a cut in corporate taxation and the devolution of greater power to the regions. Mr Kuchma's cabinet, presented to parliament on 27 October, included some members of the opposition parties, and he indicated his wish to govern through a broadly-based coalition as well as through ministers with practical experience.

Political changes of a still more far-reaching character took place in Azerbaijan, where Abulfaz Elchibey, leader of the Azerbaijani Popular Front, was elected President on 16 June after receiving 59 per cent of the vote in a five-sided presidential election. The elections had been called after the resignation in March of Ayaz Mutalibov, following a series of setbacks in the dispute with Armenia over Nagorno-Karabakh. The new President was expected to prosecute the war more vigorously, and also to take the republic out of the CIS. Azerbaijan's adhesion had not, in fact, been approved by its parliament. In October it formally decided not to do so, adding a further element of uncertainty to the confused world of post-Soviet politics.

ii. ESTONIA—LATVIA—LITHUANIA

Estonia
CAPITAL: Talinn   AREA: 45,000 sq km   POPULATION: 1,600,000 ('91)
OFFICIAL LANGUAGE: Estonian   POLITICAL SYSTEM: republic
HEAD OF STATE: President Lennart Meri (since Oct '92)
PRINCIPAL MINISTERS: Mart Laar (prime minister), Trivimi Velliste (foreign affairs), Kaido Kama (justice), Lagle Parek (interior), Hain Rebas (defence), Ain Saarmann (economy)
CURRENCY: kroon (end-'92 £1=K19,896, US$1=K13,1413)
GNP PER CAPITA: US$2,857 ('90 est.)

Latvia
CAPITAL: Riga   AREA: 64,000 sq km   POPULATION: 2,700,000 ('91)
OFFICIAL LANGUAGE: Latvian   POLITICAL SYSTEM: republic
HEAD OF STATE: President Anatolijs Gorbunovs (since March '90)
PRINCIPAL MINISTERS: Ivars Godmanis (prime minister), Georgs Andrejevs (foreign affairs), Elmars Silins (finance), Talavs Jundzis (defence)
CURRENCY: rublis
GNP PER CAPITA: US$2,440 ('90 est.)

Lithuania
CAPITAL: Vilnius   AREA: 65,000 sq km   POPULATION: 3,700,000 ('91)
OFFICIAL LANGUAGE: Lithuanian   POLITICAL SYSTEM: republic
HEAD OF STATE: Algirdas Brazauskas, acting President (since Nov '92)
PRINCIPAL MINISTERS: Aleksandras Abisala (prime minister), Algirdas Saudargas (foreign affairs), Albertas Simenas (economy), Audrius Butkevicius (defence)
CURRENCY: talonas
GNP PER CAPITA: US$2,585 ('90 est.)

THE Baltic states necessarily devoted 1992 to the awesome tasks of political and economic reconstruction following on from their recovery of full independence in the last quarter of 1991 (see AR 1991, pp. 188–90).

The end of the Soviet-originated parliaments came in Estonia and Lithuania through elections, whereas Latvia was not due to make the transition until 1993. The Estonian poll on 20 September, when voters were also asked to choose a President, brought the right-wing Fatherland Election Alliance (ISAMAA) to power as well as a new Prime Minister, Mart Laar. Lennart Meri, former Estonian Foreign Minister and also of ISAMAA, was elected President in a second round of voting. The Alliance had promised 'house cleaning' in Estonia to eradicate all traces of the Soviet past. In office, however, the new administration declared itself against the old system as such rather than individuals. As to the opposition, the elections revealed the divisions which had developed in the Popular Front, once in the vanguard of the independence movement.

Lithuania's equivalent to the Estonian Popular Front, Sajudis, was likewise defeated in elections held in October–November, having become too closely identified for voter comfort with President Vytautas Landsbergis. Admirable in leading Lithuania to independence, he was less decisive when it came to political and economic reform. Electoral victory went to the only other party with significant grassroots support, the former Communists, renamed the Lithuanian Democratic Labour Party (LDDP), under Algirdas Brazauskas. Even as Communist Party first secretary in Lithuania, Mr Brazauskas had enjoyed huge popularity for his advocacy of greater independence for the Baltic states. He clearly profited from his reputation for practicality and from Mr Landsbergis's entirely negative electoral campaign. As chairman of the Lithuanian parliament (*Seimas*), Mr Brazauskas also became in effect head of state, pending direct presidential elections. The cabinet he chose reflected his commitment to plurality by containing only four ministers from the LDDP.

Electioneering fanned controversies about citizenship, particularly in Estonia. Most of the Russians in Estonia could not vote because the Estonian citizenship law of 26 February 1992 ruled that the two years' residency required of non-Estonian applicants could begin only from March 1990. Even those who had already applied for citizenship were denied the vote in 1992. Citizenship applicants were also required to have a knowledge of Estonian and to swear loyalty to the republic. Latvia's citizenship legislation was not yet finalized, although the so-called zero option, conveying citizenship rights to all those living in Latvia when independence was first declared in 1990, met with too much popular resistance to become policy. Discussions of residency requirements ranged from five to 16 years. In Lithuania, where the ethnic balance was more favourable to the native population than in Estonia or Latvia, a liberal citizenship law of December 1991 generated less resentment from Russians.

Whilst Moscow accused Latvia and Estonia of violating human rights in their treatment of Russian minorities, the Baltic governments insisted that they were engaged in a process of decolonization. They made only slow headway in countering the Russian media machine. A UN report of 7 December observed that a sense of insecurity rather than any violation of human rights was characteristic in Latvia. In the same month Estonia indicated a softening of some aspects of its citizenship legislation for Russian pensioners, coupling this with hopes for a rapid withdrawal of former Soviet troops, legal responsibility for which fell to the Russian government. These relics of empire, lingering on in the Baltic states, played a major role in raising the temperature of the citizenship debate in 1992.

Piecemeal departure of the troops continued in 1992 but Russia insisted that troop relocation and housing costs were beyond its means and that full evacuation could take three years. Subsequently the Kremlin favoured Lithuania with a separate agreement. Although President Yeltsin briefly suspended withdrawal at the end of October, the agreed date for the final departure of the troops from Lithuania remained 31 August 1993. Latvia and Estonia awaited a firm date, notwithstanding a UN resolution of 25 November calling for early withdrawal of the former Soviet troops. Related measures by the Baltic states to defend their sovereignty included taking over border duties in early 1992 from the former Soviet guards and slowly building their own armed forces. Improving relations between the Baltic states and NATO was discussed in March during a visit to the Baltic by the Secretary-General of NATO Manfred Wörner. At that stage the Baltic states were only members of the NATO Cooperation Council, set up in 1991.

The presence of the former Soviet troops also deterred foreign investors in 1992, intensifying the economic challenges facing Baltic governments. They planned far-reaching economic reform but remained dependent on Russian and other CIS supplies. Existing markets in the East were also vital until the Baltic states were able to build up new openings in the West. In the event, trade between the Baltic and the CIS states declined sharply in the winter of 1991/92. The Baltic states resorted to bilateral supply agreements with Russia and other CIS members but trade remained unpredictable, increasingly financed by a chaotic mixture of rouble payments, barter and hard currency. Production slumped in all three Baltic republics, an official state of crisis being declared in Estonia between 16 January and 11 February following fuel and food shortages. It became imperative for the Baltic states to accelerate their reform programmes and to control their own money supplies.

Secure borders were an essential pre-condition for the Baltic states to issue their own currencies through their central banks. Estonia was the first to leave the rouble zone, on the weekend of 20–22 June, reinstating the kroon as its currency unit, pegged to within 3 per cent of the German mark. The independent Estonian currency increased pressures on Lithuania and Latvia to move in the same direction. For the latter, the Latvian rouble became the only legal currency from 20 July, whilst Lithuania declared that the rouble was no longer legal tender on 24 September. Both Latvia and Lithuania planned to complete their currency reform at a suitable moment, with the reinstatement of the lat and lit respectively. The financial bases of the Baltic central banks were further reinforced by the return of much of the pre-war Baltic gold to its rightful owners, including that held by the Bank of England since 1940. The commercial banking sector in the Baltic states continued to suffer from shortages of cash and often bad management.

The Baltic central banks received support and advice from the

International Monetary Fund (IMF), which body had also agreed tough economic reform programmes with the three governments by early autumn. In general, the IMF pushed for tight tax, revenue, emission and credit policies as conditions for funding. The programmes entailed ending price controls even on essentials and pushing on with the privatization of industry. This made some progress but was retarded partly by the predictable difficulty in shifting the old apparatchiks from state enterprises, partly by the fact that many of the large-scale concerns had been locked into the military-industrial base of the former Soviet Union and partly by insufficient foreign investment, urgently required to modernize industry. All three Baltic governments continued to try to make investment opportunities attractive but had yet to clarify the sort of property ownership foreigners could expect. Whereas Latvia and Lithuania deliberately involved their own citizens in privatization by issuing them with vouchers entitling them to shares, in Estonia a centralized body—the Estonian Privatization Company, modelled on German lines—elected to seek only foreign capital. It had attracted considerable interest from abroad by December.

If private foreign investment in the Baltic states fell below what was wanted, important foreign aid and loans went to Estonia, Latvia and Lithuania in 1992 to help offset shortages or to assist in restructuring the economy. Apart from World Bank loans in the autumn totalling US$135 million, dependent on continuing economic reform, the Baltic states were also offered aid packages by the Nordic countries and by the EC. The EC grants were conditional on the Baltic states following IMF guidelines and on corresponding credits from the Group of 24 countries, which were duly agreed in late November (600 million ecu in total).

The loans confirmed the rapid advances made by Estonia, Latvia and Lithuania in 1992 in building new foreign relations. Although there was only minimal progress in economic collaboration between the Baltic states themselves, they participated with seven other Baltic nations in setting up a new forum for political and economic cooperation, the Council of Baltic Sea States (see XI.5.v). The then German Foreign Minister, Herr Genscher, predicted that within ten years all the members of the Council would be either EC members or have close ties with the EC. Indeed, the Community declared its readiness in May to sign trade and cooperation agreements with the Baltic states, even though it was likely to be years before they had open access to European markets. This tantalizing mixture of promise and frustration exemplified the prevailing situation in the Baltic states in 1992, their first year of full independence since 1940.

IV THE AMERICAS AND THE CARIBBEAN

1. UNITED STATES OF AMERICA

CAPITAL: Washington, DC   AREA: 9,372 sq km   POPULATION: 250,000,000 ('90)
OFFICIAL LANGUAGE: English   POLITICAL SYSTEM: democratic federal republic
HEAD OF STATE: President George Bush, Republican (since Jan '89)
PRESIDENT-ELECT: Bill Clinton, Democrat (to be inaugurated Jan '93)
RULING PARTIES: From Nov '92 elections, Democrats control both presidency and
    Congress
PRINCIPAL CABINET MEMBERS: J. Danforth Quayle (vice-president), Lawrence
    Eagleburger (secretary of state), Nicholas Brady (treasury), Richard Cheney
    (defence), Manuel Lujan (interior), William P. Barr (attorney-general) (*outgoing
    Republican administration: for list see XIX.5*)
INTERNATIONAL ALIGNMENT: NATO, OECD, OAS, ANZUS
CURRENCY: dollar (end-'92 £1=US$1.51   GNP PER CAPITA: $21,790 ('90)
MAIN EXPORT EARNERS: machinery and transport equipment, agricultural products,
    chemicals, miscellaneous manufactures.

EVERY leap year America is dominated by the presidential election, and almost every other event is seen in relation to the political contest. A year before, in the afterglow of the Gulf War, the outcome had seemed a foregone conclusion, and few observers saw any threat to President Bush. However, during the 1992 campaign the President faced a strong challenge from within his own party, and eventually from the Democratic candidate, Governor Bill Clinton of Arkansas. Both major campaigns were affected by scandals, as well as the entry, withdrawal and re-entry into the race of an independent third-party candidate; but ultimately it was the state of the US economy which ensured the defeat of President Bush by his Democratic challenger.

President Bush acknowledged the economic issue in his third annual State of the Union message to Congress on 28 January, but concentrated first on what he called 'big changes' and 'big problems'. Firstly, he declared, 'communism died this year', leaving America the victor in the Cold War and the pre-eminent world power. As a consequence the President felt able to accelerate the cut-backs in military spending he had begun two years before. Savings totalling $50,000 million over the next five years would result in a 30 per cent cut in defence spending since the President took office. However, Mr Bush declared that the cut was 'this deep, and no deeper'. America would continue to protect itself and should also continue its world role 'in support of freedom everywhere'.

On the economic front President Bush reiterated his established policy. He declared his intention 'to set the economy free', to make investment and the development of new industries and jobs easier, by clearing away 'obstacles to growth—high taxes, high regulation, red tape and, yes, wasteful government spending'. The President announced an immediate 90-day moratorium on 'any new federal regulations that could hinder growth'. Cabinet departments and federal agencies were also directed 'to speed up pro-growth expenditures' to inject an additional $10,000 million into the economy. The Federal Reserve would continue to hold down interest and inflation rates.

Mr Bush called for cooperation from Congress in securing the passage of other elements of his package. He proposed reductions in certain forms of taxation, a new investment tax allowance and a tax credit for first-time home buyers. Saying he could not take no for an answer, the President said Congress 'must cut the capital gains tax' to increase jobs and must pass these measures by 20 March.

In a long-term plan, Mr Bush called for open markets and free trade everywhere, the improvement of American education through his New American Schools proposal, encouragement for research and development, and the passage by Congress of the comprehensive crime bill he had introduced previously. Further measures included legislation on enterprise zones, increased expenditures to help educationally-disadvantaged children, and reform of health care. Rejecting a national health system, Mr Bush urged measures to make basic health insurance available to all low-income people by provision of a tax credit. The President planned to control the federal deficit by freezing discretionary budget authority and federal government employment, and by removing 246 programmes from federal funding. He called for the rediscovery of the 'home truth' that 'this government is too big and spends too much'.

After calling for the passage of bills still awaiting congressional action, such as bank and civil justice reform, President Bush outlined measures aimed at strengthening the family. First was the establishment of a Commission on America's Urban Families to determine 'what we can do to keep families together, strong and sound'. In order to help immediately in easing the burden of child-care, the President asked Congress to raise child tax exemptions by $500 per child and to allow interest on student loans to be tax-deductible. In his final words the President denounced the rise in 'bitterness, racist comments, anti-semitism, an increased sense of division'. Rejecting 'talk of decline', Mr Bush told his listeners that America was still 'the freest, the kindest and the strongest' nation on earth.

Congress moved unusually quickly to put together a tax package which included six of the anti-recession proposals included in the President's speech. However, they also increased the top rate of income tax and introduced a 10 per cent surtax on millionaires to provide relief for lower income families. Passed by both houses on 20 March, the bill was vetoed within minutes by Mr Bush, who accused Congress of 'irresponsibility' and denounced the Democrats for their apparent 'natural impulse to raise taxes'. Attempts to override the veto failed when supporters of the bill fell short of the necessary two-thirds majority in the House of Representatives.

National attention switched to social issues on 29 April when rioting broke out in Los Angeles after the acquittal of four white police officers charged with having assaulted a black motorist, Rodney King, in March 1991 (see AR 1991, p. 48). The case had been the subject of massive publicity following the showing of an amateur videotape of the incident on national television. The trial had already been the subject of controversy because the judge had changed the venue to Ventura County, an almost entirely white area where many police officers lived. The jury included one Hispanic and one Asian American, but no blacks.

Violence broke out within hours of the verdict, and in six days over 58 people were killed. Passing white motorists were attacked, and many shops and businesses (especially those owned by Koreans) were looted, forcing Mayor Tom Bradley to ask Governor Pete Wilson to call out the National Guard. On 29 April Governor Wilson declared a state of emergency and imposed a curfew until 4 May. In a televised address the following night, President Bush appealed for 'calm and tolerance'. In the end 4,000 marines and infantrymen joined with the 6,000 National Guardsmen to bring an end to the disorder. Protests and violence also erupted briefly among black communities in a number of other towns and cities including San Francisco, Atlanta and Dallas.

During a visit to the riot area of Los Angeles on 7–8 May, President Bush announced a $19 million anti-drug and anti-gang programme for the city. On 28 June the controversial Los Angeles chief of police, Daryl F. Gates, finally retired, and the four police officers involved in the King case were indicted on federal charges of denial of civil rights on 4 August.

At least one person was killed when rioting broke out among the Hispanic community in New York city on 6 July following the shooting of a Dominican immigrant by police. Observers claimed that the victim was unarmed and was shot while being beaten; the police said he was armed. Until this incident the administration of Mayor David Dinkins had been successful in preventing racial outbursts in the wake of the Los Angeles rioting.

That Los Angeles was not an exception in its police methods became apparent on 5 November when Malice Wayne Green, a 35-year-old black man in Detroit, was dragged from his car by police officers and beaten so badly that he later died from his injuries. Seven officers, some black, were suspended for what the police chief described as 'a disgrace to the department'.

In addition to social and political conflict, the United States was also affected by major natural disasters in 1992. At least 35 people were killed when Hurricane Andrew swept across southern Florida and

Louisiana on 24–26 August. With hundreds of thousands of people left homeless, and damage in excess of $20,000 million in Florida alone, the hurricane was the most expensive natural disaster in US history. Some 7,000 federal and state troops were used to distribute assistance and prevent looting, but the tardy federal response led to criticism of President Bush. During a visit to the state (which had 25 key electoral college votes) on 1 September, the President promised that federal relief would continue 'until the job is done', and committed the government to 100 per cent reimbursement of local authorities for recovery operations.

On 28 June California was struck by two severe earthquakes which resulted in two deaths and around 170 injured. Both were centred east of Los Angeles, and the first measured 7.4 on the Richter scale, the third largest in the USA this century. On 11 September winds of up to 160 mph caused devastation as Hurricane Iniki hit Hawaii. Most of the damage was on the island of Kauai, a tourist resort with a population of about 50,000. At least two people were killed and thousands were left homeless. President Bush, mindful no doubt of the criticism levelled at him after Hurricane Andrew, declared the islands a disaster area and called for immediate federal aid.

More storms on the American mainland at the end of November produced tornados which affected 12 states, resulting in 25 deaths and a trail of devastation. On 11 December Governor Mario Cuomo had to declare New York and its surrounding region a disaster area after huge Atlantic storms hit the city, flooding parts of Manhattan, destroying property on Long Island and the New Jersey shoreline, and killing at least 16 people.

POLITICS AND THE ELECTION. The elections gave politics a particular edge. Early in the year the spotlight was turned on Congress when an inquiry by the House ethics committee revealed that more than 300 Representatives used the House bank to cash cheques which their accounts could not cover. The inquiry into 'Rubbergate', as it became known, began in 1991. On 13 March the House voted to make the names of the offenders public, but publication was delayed when it became apparent that the bank records might be faulty. A number of offenders came forward of their own volition, including the House's Republican whip, Newt Gingrich. On 17 April a full list of 303 members and former members who had written uncovered cheques in a three-year period up to 3 October 1991 was released. It included the current Speaker, Tom Foley, his predecessor, Jim Wright, and majority leader Dick Gephardt. These revelations encouraged the widespread anti-incumbent feeling in the run-up to the elections.

Some political issues related directly to the elections. On 30 April the Senate approved a campaign finance bill passed earlier by the House, which offered federal subsidies to those who voluntarily limited their spending on political campaigns. However, on 9 May President Bush vetoed the measure, which he described as a 'taxpayer-financed incumbent protection plan' because it did not eliminate donations from political action committees or indicate how it would be funded. The Senate failed to obtain the necessary two-thirds majority to override the veto on 13 May.

In May a constitutional amendment first introduced in 1789, intended to prevent Congress from voting pay rises for its members while in session, finally secured majority support when it was approved by the legislatures of four states. There was some doubt, however, whether the amendment was still valid, and House Speaker Tom Foley suggested that it violated the principle of 'contemporaneous consideration by the states'. On 13 May, however, the head of the National Archives, Don W. Wilson, indicated that he recognized the amendment as valid and was prepared to certify its adoption as the 27th amendment.

Another proposed amendment to the constitution, which would have required an annually-balanced budget, failed by nine votes to get the necessary two-thirds majority in the House on 11 June. The measure, scheduled to come into effect in 1997, had been championed by President Bush. It was supported by all but two of the 160 Republican congressmen, and by 115 Democrats.

President and Congress were at loggerheads over extending benefits for the unemployed. Following the announcement of an increase in unemployment, the House voted on 9 June to extend benefits by up to 26 weeks. On 19 June the Senate voted in favour of benefit for an additional 33 weeks. Mr Bush, who favoured a maximum of 20 weeks of extra payments, threatened to veto the compromise text likely to appear, but in the light of further increases in unemployment he signed the bill providing benefits for a further 26 weeks on 3 July.

Compromise was achieved on emergency urban aid. After much intensive negotiation a package of $1,100 million was passed by Congress on 18 June and signed by Mr Bush on 22 June. It provided funds for disaster relief and established a programme to employ 414,000 teenagers in jobs administered by the Department of Labour. Further agreement was reached on 1 July approving urban aid totalling $2,500 million over five years and the creation of enterprise zones.

The House adjourned on 6 October and the Senate on 9 October. The partisan conflict continued right to the end. Major bills, including the crime bill and a bill to upgrade schools, were dropped in the face of Republican opposition. However, the sequence of 35 presidential vetos ended on 5 October when the Senate and House both achieved sufficient votes to approve a bill to re-regulate the cable television industry, thus overturning Mr Bush's earlier veto. The first significant energy measure since the 1970s, to promote the development of alternative fuels and encourage energy conservation, was approved on 8 October.

President Bush launched his re-election campaign in New Hampshire on 15 January, promising that the recession would be overcome and announcing his intention to initiate comprehensive health care reform. Having once seemed invincible, he now faced an uphill task as his popularity fell to a new low. His apparent inability to resolve economic difficulties was compounded by a generally lacklustre performance, poor speeches and press conferences, which even led to suggestions that he might be suffering from the brain disorder aphasia, causing jumbled speech patterns.

Early polls suggested that the President's lead over his right-wing challenger for the Republican nomination, Pat Buchanan, was decreasing. The threat that David Duke, the former Ku Klux Klansman who almost won the governorship of Louisiana in 1991 (see AR 1991, p. 56), might run as an independent was also seen as potentially damaging. When the votes in the New Hampshire primary on 18 February were counted, Mr Bush's position looked weaker than ever. He gained only 53 per cent of the vote compared with Mr Buchanan's 37 per cent. Precedents since 1952 suggested that, faced with such strong opposition, it was unlikely that Mr Bush would be re-elected.

The race for the Democratic nomination did not offer any clear early indications as to who would contest the election against the Republicans. The only black candidate, Governor Douglas Wilder of Virginia, withdrew in January, having lagged behind the other five contenders, namely Governor Clinton of Arkansas, Senator Paul Tsongas of Massachusetts, the former governor of California, Jerry Brown, Senator Bob Kerrey of Nebraska and Senator Tom Harkin of Iowa. The principal beneficiary of Governor Wilder's withdrawal among black voters was thought to be Governor Clinton, who emerged from the second nationally-televised debate between the Democratic candidates on 19 January as the front-runner. However, a disgruntled former state employee from Arkansas, Larry Nichols, raised doubts about Mr Clinton's personal life when he issued a lawsuit claiming that the Governor had used state funds to entertain women with whom he was conducting extra-marital affairs.

Mr Clinton strenuously denied such charges, and his wife, Hillary, was brought into the campaign. The charges were revitalized when Gennifer Flowers, one of the women named by Mr Nichols, stated that she had been sexually involved with Governor Clinton between 1977 and 1989. Tapes of alleged telephone conversations between Ms Flowers and Mr Clinton seemed to support her claims. On 27 January Mr and Mrs Clinton appeared together on a television programme to contest these accusations. While he denied Ms Flowers's charges, Mr Clinton refused to say that he had not committed adultery in the past, but insisted that his marriage was now stable and strong.

On 12 February another scandal involving Mr Clinton began when it became known that he had avoided the draft during the Vietnam War, possibly by manipulating his student status while he was a Rhodes scholar at Oxford Univerisity. His equivocal answers on this and other issues led his opponents to label him 'Slick Willy', but Mr Clinton managed a creditable second place to Senator Tsongas (26 per cent to 35 per cent of the vote) in the New Hampshire primary.

Mr Buchanan continued to win sufficient votes in primary elections in early March to point to Mr Bush's unpopularity. To keep his momentum going, however, he needed to win at least one primary. On 'super Tuesday', 10 March, Mr Bush won all eight primaries, and then went on to win in Illinois and Michigan on 17 March, Connecticut on 24 March, and Vermont on 31 March. Mr Buchanan's support slipped well below 30 per cent in subsequent primaries. Mr Duke was overwhelmingly defeated in all the primaries he entered, including his home state. He withdrew on 22 April.

Meanwhile, after winning little support beyond their own states, both Mr Kerrey and Mr Harkin withdrew from the Democratic race early in March. Mr Clinton described himself as the 'Comeback Kid' after he won contests in southern and border states. His overwhelming victories in Illinois and Michigan forced Senator Tsongas to concede defeat, and he withdrew on 19 March. Only Mr Brown continued his increasingly quixotic campaign. His victory in Connecticut on 24 March, following a fierce personal attack on Mr Clinton's character, enabled him to fight on until defeated in Pennsylvania and New York. Mr Clinton won the primaries in New York, Wisconsin and Kansas on 7 April, the caucus in Virginia on 11–13 April and the primary in Pennsylvania on 28 April.

By now Mr Bush and Mr Clinton were clearly the two contenders for the presidency, both winning their remaining primaries by convincing margins. In the end Mr Bush won all 38 Republican primaries, a record equal to that of Richard Nixon in 1972 and Ronald Reagan in 1984. Mr Clinton won 28 of the 36 Democratic contests. However, exit polls indicated that an undeclared independent candidate, the Texan billionaire businessman Ross Perot, would be preferred to either. Charges that Mr Perot had employed investigators to examine the private lives of the President and members of his family forced him onto the defensive. On 24 June he claimed that the controversy was the result of a 'Republican dirty tricks committee'.

Speculation about Mr Clinton's choice of running mate ended on 9 July when he named Senator Albert Gore of Tennessee as his choice. Mr Gore, aged 44, had become known nationally during his own unsuccessful bid for the nomination in 1988. Although also a southerner, he was seen as balancing the ticket with his expertise on arms control, foreign affairs and environmental issues. Some critics, like Rev Jesse Jackson, said the ticket was too narrow, but he gave his endorsement on 11 July, joining Senator Tsongas, who had done so three days earlier.

The Clinton camp was largely able to side-line Rev Jackson's followers, as well as those of Mr Brown, at the Democratic convention which took place at Madison Square Gardens, New York, on 14–18 July. In a carefully stage-managed and controlled show of party unity, which adopted the moderate tone of its candidate, the convention formally endorsed Mr Clinton by 3,372 votes to 596 for Mr Brown and 209 for Senator Tsongas. In his acceptance speech, Mr Clinton stressed both his own relatively humble and unprivileged upbringing in Hope, Arkansas, and the 'new covenant' between government and governed in which the middle class would 'be forgotten no more'.

After the convention Mr Clinton's lead in popularity polls rose to 30 per cent. This was attributed in part to Mr Perot's withdrawal from the race on 16 June, when he conceded that the Democratic Party had done 'a brilliant job' in reviving itself. Mr Perot's support in the polls had declined as details of his autocratic style and conservative business practices became better known. He alienated many blacks when, in an address to the National Association for the Advancement of Colored People on 12 July, he referred to the largely African-American audience as 'you people'.

Prior to the Republican convention in Houston, Mr Bush had to answer allegations about his personal life when the press for the first time published allegations that he had had an affair with a former personal assistant. Mr Bush refused to answer what he called 'sleazy questions' on the subject, 'other than to say it is a lie'. To revitalize his campaign, Mr Bush appointed Secretary of State James Baker as White House Chief of Staff on 13 August. Lawrence Eagleburger took over at the State Department.

The Republican convention, which opened on 17 August, saw an emphasis on 'family values' in attacks on Mr Clinton made by Mr Buchanan, and in the milder speeches by Barbara Bush and Marilyn Quayle (wife of the Vice-President). Following his nomination by the 2,210 delegates on 19 August, Mr Bush promised that his second term would be a 'crusade to bring peace and prosperity'. The President declared that his decision to raise taxes in 1990 had been a mistake, and promised tax cuts if re-elected.

When campaigning began in earnest on Labour Day, 7 September, a change was immediately apparent in the Republican strategy. Moving away from the right-wing agenda of 'family values' (including opposition to abortion and to gay rights), Mr Bush presented new economic proposals in a speech in Detroit on 10 September promising that he would not raise taxes 'ever, ever' again. On 11 September he announced that he would proceed with the sale of fighter aircraft to Saudi Arabia, which would maintain thousands of jobs. He also offered $1,000 million in new subsidies to boost grain exports.

Both political parties were thrown into some confusion when Mr Perot announced his return to the presidential contest as leader of the United We Stand America party in Dallas on 1 October. Admiral James Stockdale, a former navy fighter pilot and a prisoner-of-war in Vietnam, remained his vice-presidential candidate. Having pronounced government a mess, Mr Perot claimed that neither party had addressed the problems, and that popular demand had brought him back into the race.

Despite some concern that Mr Perot could affect the election in key states such as Texas and California, public opinion polls showed Mr Clinton still clearly in the lead. However, the gap between the two main contenders narrowed, as the President fought back. Television advertising targeted the Democrats' 'tax and spend' policies which, it was claimed, would adversely affect the middle classes.

After much negotiation, a series of three presidential debates (and one vice-presidential encounter) took place. In the first, on 11 October at Washington University, St Louis, in front of a panel of journalists, Mr Perot presented himself as the people's candidate; Mr Clinton claimed that he offered 'hope for change' and emphasized the need for economic recovery; and Mr Bush said that he represented experience and pointed to his positive achievements. Mr Bush singled out Governor Clinton's character as an issue for concern; Mr Clinton compared Mr Bush to Senator Joseph McCarthy in questioning his patriotism, and reminded the President that his own father, Prescott Bush, had spoken against Senator McCarthy. Asked about his lack of experience, Mr Perot replied, 'I don't have any experience in running up a $4 trillion debt', but claimed a lot of experience in getting things done. On the matter of tax increases, Mr Clinton insisted that under his proposals only families with an income of $200,000 or above would pay more taxes, and he promised a programme of tax credits to encourage growth.

Most observers felt that the standings of Mr Bush and Mr Clinton had not been changed by the first debate, but that Mr Perot had come across well with his folksy humour and down-to-earth attitudes. The Republicans made some gains after the vice-presidential debate, which took place on 13 October in Atlanta, Georgia. It was a generally more direct and lively affair, with Mr Gore and Vice-President Quayle freely swapping insults in an exchange which neither side won. Admiral Stockdale began his opening remarks by asking 'Who am I? Why am I here?', and responded to one question by saying that he was 'all out of ammunition' on the subject.

In the second presidential debate, held in Richmond, Virginia, on 15 October before an audience of 209 politically-uncommitted questioners in a format chosen by Governor Clinton, the Democratic candidate was generally judged to have performed well. President Bush never appeared very comfortable, and at one point was observed looking at his watch. When he again raised the character issue, one of the audience asked the candidates to 'focus on the issues and not the personalities or the mud'. While Mr Bush laid stress on his experience, Mr Clinton continued to emphasize the economy and the need for change.

President Bush was judged to have performed better in the final debate in East Lansing, Michigan, on 19 October. However, Mr Clinton maintained his lead after a competent performance. Mr Perot again attracted support with his lively style. He declined to comment on Mr Clinton's position during the Vietnam War, but Mr Bush criticized the Democratic candidate for wanting to have things both ways on a number of issues. Governor Clinton responded by attacking the President for changing policies on issues such as taxation and trickle-down economics. Mr Perot raised the subject of US support for Saddam Husain before the invasion of Kuwait, and Mr Clinton too was critical of US policy in the Middle East.

Opinion polls immediately following the last debate continued to show Mr Clinton in the lead, and there was even talk of President Bush facing a landslide defeat. While rumours suggested that some members of the Bush administration were already looking for new posts, Mr Clinton boasted of his endorsement by some 400 business executives and 21 former senior military officers, including General Cal Waller, who had been deputy commander of US forces in the Gulf War. Even some of the attempts to smear Mr Clinton now bounced back on his critics when it was revealed that stories about alleged gaps in his passport records were false, but that investigations had also been made of his mother's records. Mr Perot revealed that 'dirty tricks' involving his daughter on the eve of her wedding in August had been the cause of his withdrawal from the campaign. The Bush camp denied the charges, but a State Department official subsequently resigned over the affair of Mr Clinton's records.

Mr Perot concentrated on using television advertising to get his message across, spending over $23 million in the first two weeks of October alone. Some of his programmes, known as 'info-commercials', lasted a half-hour or more, and his last broadcast, titled 'Deep Voodoo, Chicken Feathers and the American Dream', summed up his idiosyncratic campaign. Both Mr Clinton and Mr Bush embarked on extensive, physically punishing campaign tours across the country.

Mr Clinton's lead narrowed as Mr Bush experienced a late surge in the opinion polls following some aggressive campaigning. In a speech in Michigan on 29 October the President described Mr Clinton and Mr Gore as 'crazy bozos', and Mr Gore as 'Ozone Man'. Only days before the election, polls showed Mr Clinton just one or two points ahead of Mr Bush, and some observers began to draw comparisons with the British election result. The swing to Mr Perot seemed to halt after an intemperate outburst against supposed Republican 'dirty tricks' on 25 October, which led White House spokesman Marlin Fitzwater to describe him as a 'paranoid person'.

As the polls opened on 3 November, the outcome of the election was still uncertain. In the event, Mr Clinton scored a considerable victory, to end 12 years of Republican presidencies, becoming the 42nd President with 43 per cent of the popular vote to 38 per cent for Mr Bush and 19 per cent for Mr Perot. The Democrats won back many of the states lost to the Republicans in the 1970s and 1980s, carrying a total of 32 of the 50 plus the District of Columbia (see map in this section). This translated into 370 electoral college votes (270 were needed to ensure victory), to Mr Bush's 168. Mr Perot's support was the highest achieved by a third-party candidate since Theodore Roosevelt in 1912, and may have been significant in certain marginal states. In some states more than 20 per cent of the voters supported him; in Utah he obtained 25 per cent to come second to Mr Bush.

Mr Clinton was particularly successful among certain groups, appealing to those between the ages of 18 and 30 (44 per cent) and those over 60 (52 per cent), women (47 per cent), blacks (83 per cent) and Hispanics (62 per cent). While Bush held on to the mid-American states, from North Dakota to Texas, and the southern states from Virginia to Florida, Mr Clinton won everywhere else except Alaska, splitting the Republican hold over the south and west. The excitement generated by the election produced a relatively high turnout of over 55 per cent (100 million voters), which also favoured the Democratic candidate.

At 46, Mr Clinton became the youngest President-elect since John F. Kennedy and the first born after World War II, being a member of the 'baby-boomer' generation which had come of age in the 1960s. His childhood, of a broken family and domestic violence, suggested an individual who had triumphed over disadvantages in life. Being governor of a small state with a population of only 2.4 million might not have been a qualification to run the country, but Mr Clinton had demonstrated sufficient ability to serve as governor for 12 years, and could point to a record of growth. He had also successfully chaired the National Governors' Association in 1987–88.

Mr Bush conceded defeat shortly after polling in the western states had ended, and congratulated Mr Clinton on running 'a strong campaign'. He called upon everyone to stand behind the new President and promised all necessary help in the transitional period. Vice-President Quayle was also magnanimous in defeat, suggesting that the country would have nothing to fear if Mr Clinton ran the country as well as he had run his campaign. In an almost celebratory post-election rally, Mr Perot congratulated the winner and urged his supporters to 'forget

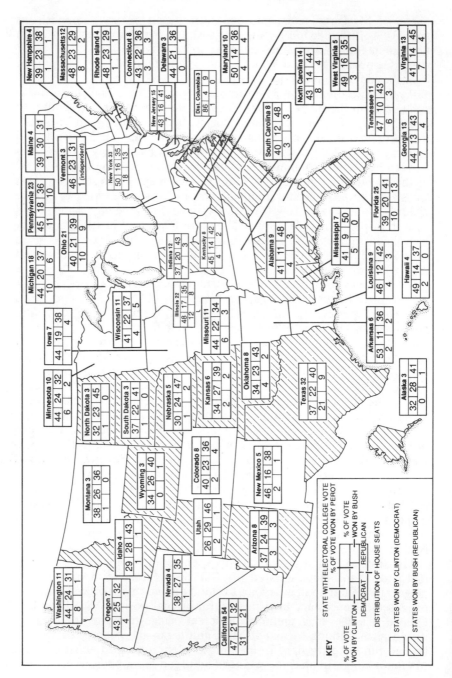

the election' and work together to help 'rebuild our great country'. Before dancing to his campaign theme tune, 'Crazy', Mr Perot hinted that he might run again in 1996, saying 'we'll keep going as long as you want to keep going'.

There were some changes, too, as a consequence of the congressional and gubernatorial elections which also took place on 3 November, although the anti-incumbent mood among voters did not produce as many upsets as predicted. Some 89 per cent of sitting candidates were returned, compared with 95 per cent four years earlier, and the overall political balance in the Senate did not change. With 35 seats up for election, the Senate remained composed of 57 Democrats and 43 Republicans (taking account of subsequent run-off and special elections). The Democrats were thus denied the two-thirds majority which would have given them virtual total control.

In the House of Representatives, the Republicans gained ten seats, to bring their total to 175 against the Democrats' 259 and one independent. Of the 12 gubernatorial contests, the Democrats won eight to the Republicans' four. This brought the overall number of Democratic governors to 30—an increase of two—compared with 18 Republicans and two independents. Democrats also continued to dominate the state legislatures.

Among those newly-elected to the Senate were four women, making a total of six in all. California returned Dianne Feinstein, the former mayor of San Francisco, and former congresswoman Barbara Boxer, both Democrats. The voters of Illinois returned the first-ever black woman senator (and the first black senator since 1976) when they chose Carol Mosely Braun (Democrat). Female representation in the House of Representatives also increased, from 28 to 47, and Nydia Velazquez from New York became the first Puerto Rican female congresswoman. In Colorado Ben Nighthorse Campbell (Democrat), a Cheyenne, became the first native American senator for 60 years.

Mr Clinton made his first visit to the White House on 18 November, when he had a private meeting with Mr Bush. In a symbolic gesture of the change in approach, the President-elect then went into a nearby neighbourhood to meet people on the streets. The next day he called into a McDonald's eating-house before meeting with congressional leaders on Capitol Hill. In his subsequent appearance before the cameras with congressional leaders, Mr Clinton announced the beginning of the end of 'grid-lock government'.

Mr Clinton's choices for cabinet positions were keenly awaited, given his promise to create an administration 'that looks like America'. His first appointments—of Lloyd Bentsen, the 71-year-old senator from Texas famous for his savaging of Mr Quayle in the 1988 election, as Treasury Secretary, and of the Californian congressman and chairman of the House budget committee, Leon Panetta, as Budget Director—were seen as conservative. The Harvard economist, Robert Reich, was named as Secretary of Labour. The chairman of the House armed services committee, Les Aspin, was to become Secretary of Defence, and Warren Christopher, aged 67, deputy secretary of state in the Carter administration, was to be Secretary of State.

Mr Clinton quickly named women to key posts, including Donna Shalala, chancellor of the University of Wisconsin, as head of the Health and Human Services Department; Carol Browner, a former Florida environmental official, as head of the Environmental Protection Agency; and Laura D'Andrea Tyson, professor in economics at the University of California, to chair the Council of Economic Advisers. Moreover, Joycelyn Elders, director of the Arkansas health department, was later named as head of the US Public Health Service, and Zoe Bair, a legal counsel in the Carter administration, was nominated as Attorney-General. Nevertheless, there was still some criticism of the President-elect for failing to appoint more women to senior posts.

The first black cabinet appointment was that of Ron Brown, the Democratic Party chairman, as Secretary of Commerce. The Hispanic leader and former mayor of San Antonio, Henry Cisneros, was to become Secretary of Housing and Urban Development, and Frederico Pena, former mayor of Denver, was named Secretary of Transport. A personal friend of Mr Clinton's, and complete political outsider, the Arkansas businessman Thomas McLarty was named as White House Chief of Staff.

SOCIAL AND LEGAL DEVELOPMENTS. The Iran-Contra affair, involving the illegal sale of arms to Iran and diversion of profits to Contra rebels in Nicaragua (see AR 1991, pp. 50–1), dogged the Bush administration through the year. Former Defence Secretary Caspar Weinberger, who had claimed to be unaware of the sales, was indicted on 16 June on charges of perjury and making false statements, after some of his personal notes found in the Library of Congress revealed that he, and other senior officials, had been aware of shipments to Iran. In August Mr Weinberger's trial was postponed until January 1993, but just before the elections new indictments were added against him, after a memorandum of his record of discussions on 7 January 1986 came to light. Mr Weinberger had always denied making such a record.

In the case of Clair George, a former CIA deputy director, a mistrial was declared on 26 August, but in October he was found guilty on two charges of lying to Congress. On 17 September Lawrence Walsh, the independent counsel investigating the affair, announced that he did not expect any further indictments and was winding down his investigation. However, further life was given to the subject when, in an interview on 24 September, a participant in the Iran-Contra affair, former air force major-general Richard V. Secord, claimed that Mr Bush, as the then

Vice-President, not only knew of the arrangements but was a powerful supporter of them. The President always maintained that he was 'out of the loop' and knew nothing of the affair until it became public in November 1986.

Suspicions of the President's involvement seemed justified when he used the power of 'executive clemency' on Christmas Eve to pardon Mr Weinberger, Mr George and four other individuals who had pleaded guilty to, or were still facing, charges arising from the alleged 'cover-up' of the Iran-Contra affair. Mr Walsh angrily accused the President of acting to save himself, and of having completed the cover-up, 'which has continued for more than six years'. Mr Clinton expressed concern about 'any action which sends a signal that if you work for government you're above the law'. In contrast, former President Ronald Reagan applauded Mr Bush, saying: 'These men have served their country for many years with honour and distinction.'

The preliminary findings of the congressional investigation into the 'October Surprise' allegations—that the Reagan campaign team delayed the release of American hostages in Iran in order to influence the 1980 election—were released on 1 July. While investigation was to continue into the broad charge, 'all credible evidence' suggested that the then vice-presidential candidate, Mr Bush, had not been involved. At the end of November the Senate foreign relations committee ended its investigation, finding that 'the weight of evidence is that there was no such deal'. It did, however, find that the Republican campaign chairman and later CIA director, William Casey, acted 'on the outer limits of propriety' in secretly gathering information on the hostage negotiations.

Mr Bush also came under pressure on 10 July when the House judiciary committee called for the appointment of a special prosecutor to investigate 'Saddamgate'—the possibility that senior members of the Bush administration had illegally allowed the use of funds to enable Iraq to build up its military strength prior to the invasion of Kuwait in 1990. Preliminary investigations indicated that government members had tampered with records and impeded inquiries into the $4,000 million fraud at the Atlanta branch of the Banco Nazionale de Lavoro (BNL), used by Iraq to arrange loans. On 8 October CIA director Robert Gates indicated that a formal investigation of the agency's evidence to Congress about the possible use of food credits to Iraq to buy armaments would be initiated. By then it was clear that the agency did know about diverted funds, contrary to the President's claims.

Further pressure on the administration came on 5 October when Judge Marvin H. Shoob of the federal court in Atlanta, hearing the case against BNL manager Christopher Drogoul, made an outspoken attack on the government. He said that decisions made 'at the top levels of the US Justice Department, Agriculture Department and within the intelligence community to shape this case' had enabled Mr Drogoul to change his plea from guilty to innocent. The judge called for the trial to be postponed to allow a special prosecutor to be appointed. The CIA subsequently admitted failing to provide accurate information to the federal prosecutors. However, during hearings before the Senate select committee on intelligence, officials claimed to have been pressurized by the Justice Department. On 16 October Attorney-General William Barr acceded to pressure by appointing Judge Frederick Lacey to investigate the charges against the administration and the Justice Department.

Abortion was a significant issue in the election campaign and in the courts. The Supreme Court agreed on 21 January to rule on Pennsylvania's restrictive abortion law before July. The following day the 'annual march for life' held in Washington DC was addressed via telephone by President Bush, who reaffirmed his opposition to abortion. A staunch opponent of abortion, Senator Don Nickles of Oklahoma, was named as chairman of the 1992 Republican platform committee.

On 4 March the House judiciary sub-committee on civil and constitutional rights opened hearings on an abortion rights measure called the Freedom of Choice Bill, intended to prevent individual states from restricting the right to abortion. While its defenders, mostly Democrats, suggested that this would merely write into law the principles of the Supreme Court's 1973 decision in *Roe* v. *Wade*, its opponents, mostly Republicans, suggested that it would lead to abortion on demand. Mr Bush made it clear that the bill would not pass while he was President.

Mr Bush reaffirmed his opposition to abortion when he vetoed legislation to lift the ban on federally-funded medical research using foetal tissue from abortions. He described the bill as unacceptable 'on almost every ground: ethical, fiscal, administrative, philosophical and legal', and criticized its 'potential for promoting and legitimizing abortion'. On 24 June Congress failed to achieve the two-thirds majority needed to override the veto.

On 29 June in *Planned Parenthood of South-Eastern Pennsylvania* v. *Casey*, the Supreme Court surprisingly upheld the right to abortion, but accepted a state's right to restrict access as long as it did not place an 'undue burden' on those seeking a termination. The decision was generally seen as a defeat for the opponents of abortion. Moreover, on 22 September the US Court of Appeals for the 5th Circuit struck down as 'clearly unconstitutional' a Louisiana statute which criminalized abortion in most cases other than those where the mother's life was at risk or pregnancy had resulted from rape.

Vice-President Quayle created a furore in May when he raised the subject of family values in a speech to the Commonwealth Club in San Francisco. Linking 'lawless social anarchy' with the 'breakdown in family structure', he attacked a weekly television series called

Murphy Brown for showing a single woman 'bearing a child alone and calling it another "lifestyle choice"'. Hillary Clinton suggested that his remarks showed how out of touch the administration was with America.

Family values were also raised in a court case in which a 12-year-old boy in Orlando, Florida, was granted a 'divorce' from his natural mother. Lawyers for the boy began the case in June in order to enable his adoption by his foster parents and argued that his mother had neglected and abandoned him. The circuit court judge accepted the argument when he ruled in the boy's favour on 25 September.

Political capital was made out of the much-publicized break-up of the relationship between actor/director Woody Allen and actress Mia Farrow, and the subsequent court battles for custody of their children. When it was revealed that Mr Allen was having an affair with Ms Farrow's adopted 21-year old daughter and that Ms Farrow was also claiming that Mr Allen had sexually abused a younger child, Republican Newt Gingrich described the situation as typical of the Democratic Party. Mr Allen's latest movie, starring Ms Farrow, was entitled *Husbands and Wives* (see also XVI.1.v).

A number of major trials were concluded during the year. On 17 February the serial killer Jeffrey Dahmer was sentenced to life in prison without parole in Milwaukee, for the killing of 15 young men and boys. In Indianapolis on 26 March, the heavyweight boxing world champion, Mike Tyson, began a six-year jail sentence after having been found guilty of raping Desiree Washington, a Miss America contestant, in July 1991. On 23 June John Gotti, head of the powerful Gambino Mafia family, was sentenced to life imprisonment following his conviction for murder, extortion, illegal gambling and obstruction of justice. Three previous attempts to obtain convictions against the so-called 'Dapper Don' had failed, but taped evidence and the testimony of one of Gotti's lieutenants provided an irrefutable case against the Mafia leader.

On 10 July General Manuel Noriega, the former Panamanian dictator, who had been found guilty of eight out of ten counts of drug-trafficking and racketeering by a federal jury in Miami in April, was sentenced to 40 years' imprisonment. General Noriega claimed that he was the victim of a vendetta by the Bush administration, but was unable to present evidence that he had been working with US military and intelligence agencies in dealing with the Colombian Medellín drug cartel. He faced additional charges, including murder, in Florida and Panama. However, at the beginning of December a federal judge in Miami ruled that General Noriega was a prisoner-of-war, and so raised questions about the legitimacy of his imprisonment.

THE ECONOMY. On 29 January President Bush presented his budget for fiscal year 1993 to Congress. The $1,520,000 million package, intended to stimulate the economy with the tax and spending cuts promised in his State of the Union address, provided for a budget deficit of $351,000 million. The President proposed increased spending on education, energy and veterans' affairs, and in the Justice, State and Treasury Departments. Cuts were to be borne by the Departments of Agriculture, Commerce, Defence, Housing and Urban Development, Interior and Transportation. Increased spending in some programmes was offset by the termination or reduction of spending in 330 others. The biggest single item of expenditure, totalling $299,700 million, was on social security.

The changes in taxation included a proposed cut in the amount of personal income tax withheld by employers, increased exemption for each child per family for those with an income of less than $157,000 per annum, a temporary tax-credit of 10 per cent of the purchase price for first-time home buyers, and short-term compensation for those selling their homes at a loss. Longer-term changes included reductions in capital gains taxes, the repeal of the luxury tax on boats and aircraft, and a tax credit of up to $3,750 to help poor families meet health insurance costs.

Shortly before the Republican convention, on 12 August, Mr Bush announced the completion of negotiations on the North American Free Trade Agreement (NAFTA) with Canada and Mexico, as part of his 'long-term economic growth plan'. The administration predicted that with the removal of tariffs the number of US jobs dependent on exports to Mexico would increase by 400,000 by 1995. However, critics argued that the agreement would destroy jobs by opening up the cheap Mexican labour market, while environmentalists said the treaty lacked substance.

During the second week of September Mr Bush announced a 13-point 'agenda for American renewal' to reinvigorate the economy. Essentially a restatement of previous policy, the President's proposals included a $132,000 million cut in federal spending and federal pay-cuts to finance a further 1 per cent tax reduction. The plan also included the creation of a 'strategic network' of free trade agreements in Asia and eastern Europe to combine with the NAFTA. He reaffirmed his faith in the free market economy, and declared: 'We know that the clumsy hand of government is no match for the uplifting hand of the market place.' The President pledged to double the US gross domestic product to $10,000,000 million by early in the next century, an echo of the promise in his acceptance speech of 1988 to create 30 million jobs over eight years.

The recession continued to affect the economy, and in February the three largest carmakers, General Motors, Ford and Chrysler, announced total losses of $7,600 million in 1991. On 1 July the government announced that unemployment had reached 7.8 per cent, the highest level in eight years. At that stage there was no sign of improvement, despite low rates of interest and inflation. The dollar fell to a record low against the Deutschmark and sterling at the beginning of September. However, figures for the third quarter, released on 25 November, suggested that the economic upturn, long forecast by President Bush, had finally begun—too late to save him from electoral defeat. Gross domestic product increased by the equivalent of 3.9 per cent per annum, and increases in consumer spending, business investment and home sales were also recorded. Unemployment decreased slightly, to 7.4 per cent.

President-elect Clinton began to prepare his economic strategy by holding a televised two-day conference in Little Rock on 14–15 December. The conference involved economists, corporation leaders, trade unionists, small business representatives and others, and provided the opportunity for viewers to phone in with questions and comments. Mr Clinton described the conference as an attempt 'to reconnect the American people to their government and to ask their help in making economic progress'. The conference was judged a great media success, although Mr Clinton warned against undue optimism.

DEFENCE AND INTERNATIONAL AFFAIRS. On 1 January President Bush began a 12-day tour of the Far East postponed from November 1991, starting in Australia and including Singapore, South Korea and Japan. In order to combat charges that he had neglected domestic matters in favour of foreign affairs, Mr Bush linked his visit with the American economic situation, and promised to open up markets to US goods. He was accompanied on the visit by 21 American businessmen.

Whilst in Australia Mr Bush gave a commitment that the US presence in Asia would remain until 'the end of eternity'. During his visit to South Korea on 5–7 January, Mr Bush said the 39,000 US troops stationed there would remain 'so long as there is a need and we're welcome'; however, joint South Korean–US military exercises, which were a cause of friction with North Korea, were cancelled.

In the course of his visit to Japan from 7 to 10 January, Mr Bush and Prime Minister Miyazawa issued the Tokyo Declaration committing the two countries to work together to uphold the new world order. The Japanese also made a number of trade concessions, including an agreement to increase the import of American-made components and automobiles. However, the President's visit was marred when he was taken ill during a state banquet on 8 January, and vomited into the lap of the Japanese Prime Minister before collapsing. Although this was subsequently diagnosed as an attack of gastric influenza, and the President quickly recovered, it caused great embarrassment. It also raised fears once more about the President's health—and the suitability of Vice-President Quayle to be his successor.

Mr Bush was host to the Russian President, Boris Yeltsin, at Camp David on 1 February. After three hours of talks a general statement of trust and friendship was signed, and plans were made for two more summit meetings. Secretary of State Baker subsequently paid a 10-day visit to the former Soviet Union, and on 17 February he and Mr Yeltsin announced the creation of a new institute of science and technology to employ the scientists from the former Soviet nuclear programme.

A further US-Russian summit meeting took place when President Yeltsin visited Washington on 16–17 June. President Bush and the Russian leader signed an arms reduction agreement on 17 June which went even further than the 1991 START treaty 1991 (see AR 1991, pp. 555–7); due to be formalized in a START II treaty, the agreement envisaged that the two sides would cut their nuclear arsenals by two-thirds (see also Pt XII). Mr Yeltsin was given an enthusiastic welcome when he addressed a joint session of Congress on 17 June, and he went on to meet Mr Clinton on 18 June. Most media attention focused on the possibility that American servicemen missing in action in Vietnam were still alive in the former Soviet Union. Mr Yeltsin promised to make all available information on the matter public.

On 2 September President Bush effectively ended a 10-year ban on US arms sales to Taiwan when he approved the sale of up to 150 F-16 fighter aircraft. While this action provoked an angry response from the Chinese government and became part of the growing trade dispute between the two countries, Mr Bush still vetoed a bill which sought to link China's most-favoured-nation status with human rights progress on the grounds that it was too broad.

The Bush administration ended as it had begun, concerned with foreign affairs and America's world role. In a television address on 4 December announcing the commitment of US forces to help the UN relief effort in Somalia in 'Operation Restore Hope' (see also VI.1.ii & XI.1), Mr Bush said: 'The US alone cannot right the world's wrongs, but some crises in the world cannot be resolved without American involvement.' Mr Bush said that the 28,000 US military personnel would use whatever force necessary 'to safeguard the lives of our troops and the lives of the Somali people'. He declared that America would 'not tolerate armed gangs ripping off their own people'.

Relations with Iraq again became strained when a US airforce plane shot down an Iraqi fighter in the no-fly zone in southern Iraq on 27 December. Mr Clinton supported the administration's response to such incursions as necessary to bring Iraq into compliance with UN resolutions (see also V.2.vi & XI.1).

Mr Bush spent New Year's Eve in Somalia before travelling to Russia to sign the START-II treaty agreed by Secretary of State Lawrence Eagleburger and Mr Yeltsin on 29 December in Geneva (see XII). Drastically reducing the number of land- and submarine-based nuclear missiles held by each side, the treaty was the culmination of a disarmament process which had begun under the Reagan administration.

2. CANADA

CAPITAL: Ottawa AREA: 9,9970,610 sq km POPULATION: 26,500,000 ('90)
OFFICIAL LANGUAGES: English & French
POLITICAL SYSTEM: federal parliamentary democracy
HEAD OF STATE: Queen Elizabeth II (since Feb '52)
GOVERNOR-GENERAL: Ramon John Hnatyshyn (since Jan '90)
RULING PARTY: Progressive Conservative Party (since Sept '84)
HEAD OF GOVERNMENT: Brian Mulroney, Prime Minister (since Sept '84)
PRINCIPAL MINISTERS: Donald Mazankowski (deputy premier, finance), Joe Clark
    (constitutional affairs, privy council), Barbara McDougall (external affairs),
    Marcel Masse (defence), Michael Wilson (industry, science & trade), Jake Epp
    (energy, mines & resources), Kim Campbell (justice)
INTERNATIONAL ALIGNMENT: NATO, OECD, OAS, Francophonie, Cwth.
CURRENCY: Canadian dollar (end-'92 £1=Can$1.93, US$1=Can$1.28)
GNP PER CAPITA: US$20,470 ('90)
MAIN EXPORT EARNERS: manufactured goods, fabricated & and crude materials,
    agricultural products, tourism

FOR the second time in two years Canadians attempted to reform their constitution in 1992. Again the effort was unsuccessful. In a referendum held on 26 October the country rejected a new set of arrangements, the Charlottetown Accord, by a vote of 55–45 per cent. The result surprised many observers, for the accord had been hammered out, over months of negotiations, by representatives of the federal, the ten provincial and the two territorial governments as well as by the leaders of four major aboriginal associations. In addition, the document was supported by all three national political parties and their leaders.

The Charlottetown Accord attempted to incorporate several historic principles in a new frame of government. These included representation by population, favoured by the two large provinces of central Canada, Ontario and Quebec, and the federal principle of the equality of the provinces, appealing to the western provinces. It also acknowledged Quebec's demand for a special status which would allow it to protect its language and culture. To meet western opinion, the accord proposed that the Senate be elected, rather than appointed by the government in office. It would be reduced from its current membership of 104 to 62 members: six from each of the ten provinces and one from each of the territories. Its legislative powers would be reduced. It would not be a 'chamber of confidence', i.e. a chamber to which the government would be responsible. Complementing the changes to the upper house was a plan to increase the size of the House of Commons from 295 to 337 members, 18 additional members going to each of Ontario and Quebec, four to British Columbia and two to Alberta. Quebec would be guaranteed representation in the Commons equal to its current proportion of the Canadian population: 25 per cent.

The accord promised a limited transfer of powers from the federal to the provincial governments. The most important jurisdiction transferred would be labour-market training. In the section dealing with aborigines, native people were recognized as having an inherent right of self-government within Canada, with authority to promote their customs, institutions and economies. Problems arising from the definition of native self-government would be turned over to the courts but only after it had been established that there had been five years of serious negotiations between the aborigines and governments. Native ordinances would have to be compatible with federal law assuring 'peace, order and good government' in Canada.

The Charlottetown Accord began as a scheme of constitutional change put forward by the Progressive Conservative administration of Prime Minister Brian Mulroney in September 1991 (see AR 1991, pp. 62–4). Submitted to a joint committee drawn from the Senate and the Commons, it was also examined in five three-day policy conferences attended by governmental and non-governmental participants held in scattered Canadian cities in January and February 1992. The policy conferences were followed by another series of meetings, this time limited to representatives of the federal, provincial and territorial governments as well as the leaders of major native groups. These meetings, which went on over 27 days, were patiently chaired by Joe Clark, the Minister for Constitutional Affairs. Their objective was to reach a 'multilateral consensus', one the provinces could support, on constitutional reform. This goal was obtained by 7 July.

Premier Robert Bourassa of Quebec did not attend these meetings, having made the decision not to participate in further federal-provincial negotiations at the time of the failure of the Meech Lake Accord in June 1990 (see AR 1990, pp. 70–1). Within Quebec M. Bourassa's Liberal Party, traditionally federalist, was moving towards a more nationalist position. A report adopted by the party in March advocated a sweeping transfer of powers from the Ottawa government to a semi-autonomous Quebec existing within a loose Canadian federation. M. Bourassa distanced himself from this report, arguing for a renewed federalism with meaningful powers for Quebec. He pointed out the serious economic costs of Quebec's separation. Later he stated that he would transform a referendum on Quebec's sovereignty, which he was obliged by law to hold by 26 October 1992, into a vote on Quebec's role in a renewed Canadian federal system.

With the 'multilateral consensus' achieved, Mr Mulroney believed that the time was ripe for a formal meeting of first ministers. The Prime Minister and the ten premiers were joined by leaders of the two territorial governments and by the country's principal aboriginal spokesmen. This series of meetings began at the Prime Minister's summer residence in the Gatineau Hills, north of Ottawa, on 4 August. M. Bourassa agreed to attend the sessions. The first ministers and their advisers moved forward steadily through a list of contentious issues, reaching approval on a final package of changes on the evening of 22 August. After a short recess the meeting adjourned to Charlottetown, Prince Edward Island, where the initial undertaking on terms for the union of the British North American colonies had been reached in 1864. The final text of the results of the deliberations was approved on 28 August and the group decided to hold a national plebiscite on the text. The Canadian electorate would be asked a simple question: 'Do you agree that the constitution of Canada should be renewed on the basis of the agreement reached on 28 August?' Quebec consented to submit the same question to its people but in a separate referendum. The date of 26 October was fixed for both referenda, the first to be held on a national basis since a question on conscription was put to the people during World War II.

The opponents of the accord in the referendum campaign were a mixed group but they expressed potent concerns about the proposed arrangements. The critics included the Quebec separatists: the Parti Québécois under Jacques Parizeau, hoping to form an independent government in Quebec, and the Bloc Québécois under former federal cabinet minister Lucien Bouchard, using membership in the House of Commons to advance the cause of Quebec sovereignty. Another element was the Reform Party, a western populist movement headed by Preston Manning of Alberta, which believed the proposals failed to redress the region's lack of weight in the Canadian federal system. Special interest groups, such as the women's movement, also criticized the accord for not protecting their interests. Finally, former Prime Minister Pierre Trudeau castigated the accord, which he denounced as going against the vision of Canada as a country of ten equal provinces with no special status for Quebec. Although Mr Trudeau's influence had waned in his native province, his opinions still carried considerable weight in the rest of the country.

The rejection of the accord on 26 October derived from many reasons. In Quebec it was branded as unacceptable because it did not transfer sufficient authority to the province. In the west the proposed Senate was criticized as ineffective and there were complaints about the guaranteed representation in the Commons for Quebec. Even Indians living on reserves voted against the accord, fearing that it jeopardized their historic treaty rights. Four of the ten provinces supported the proposals, but Quebec and the four western provinces turned it down. Some 75 per cent of registered voters participated in the referendum.

To many Canadians it seemed an opportunity had been lost with the defeat of the Charlottetown Accord. However, the consequences were not as serious as many had predicted. The accord had been turned down across the country, not just in Quebec. In that province the 'no' vote did not mean approval of sovereignty, because many federalists, unhappy with aspects of the accord, had voted against it. In fact, M. Parizeau had deliberately refrained from mentioning sovereignty in his campaign, and polls showed that public support for an independent Quebec was declining. Within the province Premier Bourassa was regarded as a more credible leader than either M. Parizeau or M. Bouchard. It was clear that another referendum would be required to clarify Quebec's position. This might occur in a provincial election, not required before 1994. In the meantime, there was a general disposition across Canada (except in sovereigntist circles) to put constitution-making aside for the immediate future. Prime Minister Mulroney announced that he intended to give highest priority to the improvement of the economy as he prepared to lead his party into the federal election, required in 1993.

The economy was in the doldrums during 1992, with industrial activity well below capacity and disturbingly-high unemployment rates (11.6 per cent of the labour force during the summer). The gross domestic product, on a seasonally-adjusted annual basis, stood at Can$684,300 million at the end of June, a figure about the same as recorded 12 months earlier. Inflation was down to its lowest level in years, the consumer price index in August standing at only 1.2 per cent above the year before. Interest rates were also down, at about 5 per cent, although the low rate for borrowing seemed to have little effect on the sluggish economy.

Finance Minister Donald Mazankowski, appointed in April 1991, delivered his first budget on 25 February. Seen as a prelude to a general election in 1993, the budget slightly reduced personal income tax rates and allowed prospective home-owners to withdraw funds from retirement savings plans without tax to buy or build a home. No less than 46 crown agencies and boards were eliminated to save money, and restraint was applied to many areas of government operations. Total federal spending for 1992/93 was projected at Can$159,600 million, with revenues at Can$132,100 million.

Canada experienced a busy year as a UN peace-keeper in 1992. In March 1,200 Canadian troops were sent to Yugoslavia to maintain truce lines in Croatia. Half the number spent July in Sarajevo (Bosnia–Hercegovina), where they tried to open the airfield to relief flights. Another 1,200 Canadians were dispatched to the war-torn Balkan state in October, while transport aircraft and troops were provided for the relief effort in Somalia.

A longstanding dispute on fishing zones around the tiny French islands of St Pierre and Miquelon (lying in the Gulf of St Lawrence off the south shore of Newfoundland) was decided by an international panel on June 10. France was awarded a zone of fisheries jurisdiction

24 nautical miles wide south and west of the islands, together with a strip 200 miles long and 10.5 miles wide leading from the islands to the open sea (see also II.1.i).

A North American Free Trade Agreement (NAFTA) was approved on 11 August after 14 months of difficult negotiations between Canada, the United States and Mexico (see also IV.1 and IV.3.xiv). The new free trade zone would contain 364 million people, making it the largest in the world. The new treaty was based on the Canada-US trade agreement of 1989. It differed from the earlier agreement in raising the North American content for duty-free automobiles from a 50 per cent level to 62.5 per cent for cars and light trucks and to 60 per cent for parts. The treaty required ratification in the three countries, where strong opposition was expected from labour unions and the environmental movement in both Canada and the United States.

3. LATIN AMERICA

ARGENTINA—BOLIVIA—BRAZIL—CHILE—COLOMBIA—ECUADOR—
PARAGUAY—PERU—URUGUAY—VENEZUELA—CUBA—
DOMINICAN REPUBLIC AND HAITI—CENTRAL AMERICA
AND PANAMA—MEXICO

i. ARGENTINA

CAPITAL: Buenos Aires   AREA: 2,766,890 sq km   POPULATION: 32,300,000 ('90)
OFFICIAL LANGUAGE: Spanish   POLITICAL SYSTEM: federal presidential democracy
HEAD OF STATE & GOVERNMENT: President Carlos Saúl Menem (since July '89)
RULING PARTY: Justicialist (Peronist) Party (since Dec '89)
PRINCIPAL MINISTERS: Guido di Tella (foreign relations), Antonio Ermán González (defence), Domingo Cavallo (economy), Gustavo Béliz (interior), Jorge Maiorano (justice)
INTERNATIONAL ALIGNMENT: OAS
CURRENCY: peso (end-'92 £1=AP1.51, US$1=AP0.99)
GNP PER CAPITA: US$2,370 ('90)
MAIN EXPORT EARNERS: wheat, other agricultural produce, manufactures

ON 1 January a new currency, the peso, equal to one US dollar, replaced 10,000 of the australes introduced by President Alfonsín's government in June 1985 (see AR 1985, p. 73). President Carlos Menem called for arbitration of his country's dispute with Britain over the sovereignty of the Falkland Islands/Islas Malvinas, but this fell on deaf ears. Accusations of corruption against some of his closest advisers, though denounced as opposition smears, did not. A week later, on 15 January, one of the President's private secretaries resigned after accusations in *Página/12* that he was a shareholder in a company that had sold excessively dear milk to the Ministry of Social Action. At the same time the deputy minister of the interior was dismissed after it became known he had served a prison sentence for fraud in 1981. However, following the severe defeat of Saúl Ubaldini in the September 1991 elections (see AR 1991, p. 67), at the end of March his Azopardo faction was formally reunited with the San Martín faction of the Peronist General Confederation of Labour (CGT), behind the President's programme of 'transformation' of society. Moreover, the defeat of the Peronist candidate for senator in the federal capital on 28 June by the Radical (UCR) candidate, Fernando de la Rua, was hardly the surprise foreign press reports suggested. Hence the decision of the UCR to end cooperation with the government, when on 8 September the Minister of Justice, León Carlos Arslanian, was dismissed for objecting to certain of the President's nominations for appeal judges, had little effect other than to facilitate the passage of the law privatizing the state oil company, Yacimientos Petrolíferos Fiscales (YPF).

On 27 February health ministers from 10 Latin American countries met in Buenos Aires to concert measures against the cholera epidemic (see AR 1991, pp. 426–7), which earlier in the month had spread to Salta. Ten had died and President Menem proclaimed a state of emergency. Meanwhile, between 12 and 22 February, the President visited Paris and Brussels. In an address to the European Parliament he alluded to his country's withdrawal from the Non-Aligned Movement in September 1991, while making an appeal for lower tariff barriers and more economic cooperation. On 7 April the Economy Minister, Domingo Cavallo, secured a refinancing agreement with the country's 400 creditor banks, which would reduce the overall debt by some $10,000 million. The detailed accord was announced on 24 June and ratification followed. Against this background, the decision of the government in December that compensation to the victims of the 1976–83 military government or their relatives would be paid only in bonds struck a sour note.

ii. BOLIVIA

CAPITAL: La Paz and Sucre AREA: 1,099,000 sq km POPULATION: 7,200,000 ('90)
OFFICIAL LANGUAGES: Spanish, Quechua, Aymará
POLITICAL SYSTEM: presidential democracy
HEAD OF STATE & GOVERNMENT: President Jaime Paz Zamora (since Aug '89)
RULING PARTIES: Revolutionary Left Movement (MIR) holds presidency, supported by
    Nationalist Democratic Action (ADN) in Patriotic Accord (AP)
PRINCIPAL MINISTERS: Luis Ossio Sanjinés (MIR/vice-president), Ronald Maclean
    Abaroa (ADN/foreign affairs), Carlos Armando Saavedra Bruno (MIR/interior
    & justice), Rear-Adml. Alberto Saínz Klinsky (ADN/defence), Jorge Quiroga
    Ramirez (ADN/finance)
INTERNATIONAL ALIGNMENT: NAM, OAS
CURRENCY: boliviano (end-'92 £1=Bs6.21, US$1=Bs4.11)
GNP PER CAPITA: US$630 ('90)
MAIN EXPORT EARNERS: natural gas, tin

CONTINUED unrest at government austerity plans led to a one-day general strike on 2 January. At a congress of the Bolivian Workers Confederation (COB) held in Sucre in May, delegates adopted a militant programme of resistance both to austerity and to US anti-drug plans, so distancing themselves from the ruling Patriotic Accord (AP). However, on 9 July, three days after the country had officially applied for membership of the South American Common Market (Mercosur), leaders of eight of the country's nine political formations, including the AP, agreed on a series of measures designed to strengthen democratic government and formally signed an agreement in the presence of Vice-President Luis Ossio Sanjinés.

When 130 US troops arrived unannounced for anti-drug duties in the department of Beni on 26 June strong anti-American feeling became manifest, almost for the first time in the country's history. An investigation of the numbers already present was ordered and there were demonstrations in Trinidad, the departmental capital. After the Congress threatened to censure the Ministers of Defence, Interior and Foreign Affairs, the Foreign Ministry announced that no new contingents would arrive for the time being. On 21 August the United States formally agreed to provide some $190 million in aid for alternative development projects and other matters related to drug elimination. Complaints in September by opposition politicians that there had been irregularities in the tender process held up the privatization of 100 state-run enterprises, and the bid by Iberia of Spain for Lloyd Aéreo Boliviano (LAB) was rejected as 'inadequate'. On 27 October Gonzálo Sánchez de Lozada resigned both as leader of the Revolutionary Nationalist Movement (MNR) and as its presidential candidate.

iii. BRAZIL

CAPITAL: Brasília   AREA: 8,512,000 sq km   POPULATION: 150,400,000 ('90)
OFFICIAL LANGUAGE: Portuguese   POLITICAL SYSTEM: federal presidential democracy
HEAD OF STATE & GOVERNMENT: President Itamar Franco (since Dec '92)
RULING PARTY: National Reconstruction Party (PRN) heads coalition
PRINCIPAL MINISTERS: Celso Lafer (independent/foreign affairs), Marcilio Marques
    Moreira (economy), Celio Borja (justice), João Melão Neto (labour, federal
    administration), Gustavo Kraus (finance)
INTERNATIONAL ALIGNMENT: OAS
CURRENCY: cruzeiro (end-'92 £1=Cz$18,534, US$1=Cz$12,241)
GNP PER CAPITA: US$2,680 ('90)
MAIN EXPORT EARNERS: coffee, iron ore, soyabeans, tourism

FOLLOWING a dispute with Congress over his attempt to limit the 1992 pension increase to 54 per cent, President Fernando Collor de Mello replaced four of his ministers in January. Between 30 March and 13 April he carried out a further major cabinet reshuffle to remove ministers accused of corruption, but failed to persuade the opposition Social Democratic Party (PSDB) to join a coalition with his National Reconstruction party (PRN). The PRN therefore continued to govern with the support of the Democratic Social party (PDS), the Liberal Front (PFL), the Christian Democrats (PDC) and some independents, including Hélio Jaguaribe, who resigned from the PSDB to accept the post of Science and Technology Minister, and Celso Lafer, who became Foreign Minister. Together they lacked a majority in Congress for the austerity programme of Marcilio Marques Moreira, who retained his post as Minister of Economy. However, amid evidence of growing unrest among the armed forces, the military portfolios were untouched and a substantial emergency pay increase was conceded. Agreement was reached with representatives of the Paris Club on 9 July for the rescheduling of $44,000 million of medium- and long-term commercial bank debt.

    For President Collor the highlight of the year was to have been the UN Conference on Environment and Development (UNCED) held in Rio de Janeiro on 3–14 June (see XIV.3). An early problem was the dismissal of José Lutzemberger as Environment Minister in April; not until after the Rio conference was a new minister, Flavio Perri, in place. More seriously, in an article in the news magazine *Veja* on 24 May, the President was accused of corruption by his brother Pedro. On 27 May the Chamber approved the establishment of a special commission of inquiry into the charges, from which it appeared that the President's campaign treasurer, Paulo Cesar ('P.C.') Farias, had diverted some $6.5 million from commission on government contracts into 'phantom' bank accounts controlled by the President and that some $2.5 million had been spent on a tropical garden for the President's home. On receiving the report, deputies voted by 434 votes to 34 for impeachment (29 September). On 2 October the Vice-President,

61-year-old Itamar Franco, took the oath of office as acting President, and successfully appointed a coalition cabinet of all the parties except the Party of the Brazilian Democratic Movement (PMDB) and the Workers Party (PT). Ten days later the former leader of the PMDB, 75-year-old Ulysses Guimarães, whose last major role had been to secure the impeachment vote, was killed in a helicopter crash at Paraty. Finally, when the Senate met on 29 December, Sr Collor presented his resignation. It was immediately accepted and Sr Franco took the oath of office as President in a 12-minute ceremony.

iv. CHILE

CAPITAL: Santiago   AREA: 756,000 sq km   POPULATION: 13,200,000 ('90)
OFFICIAL LANGUAGE: Spanish   POLITICAL SYSTEM: presidential democracy
HEAD OF STATE & GOVERNMENT: Patricio Aylwin Azócar (since March '90)
RULING PARTY: Christian Democratic Party heads 17-party Coalition of Parties for
    Democracy (CPD)
PRINCIPAL MINISTERS: Enrique Silva Cimma (foreign affairs), Enrique Krauss Rusque
    (interior), Carlos Ominami Pascual (economy), Alejandro Foxley Rioseco
    (finance), Francisco Cumplido Cereceda (justice), Patricio Rojas Saavedra
    (defence)
INTERNATIONAL ALIGNMENT: OAS, NAM
CURRENCY: peso (end-92 £1=Ch$579.80, US$1=Ch$382.96)
GNP PER CAPITA: US$1,940 ('90)
MAIN EXPORT EARNERS: copper, agricultural products

THE Bryan Commission, established in October 1991, ruled on 11 January that the Chilean government should pay some $2.6 million to the families of former foreign minister Orlando Letelier and his US associate Ronni Moffit, assassinated by car bomb in Washington in 1976 (see AR 1976, p. 83). A number of questions about the status of Michael Townley, the US-born Chilean secret police (DINA) agent convicted in the United States for the bombing, were to be forwarded to President George Bush who had been head of the US Central Intelligence Agency (CIA) in 1976. On 2 April General César Mendoza Durán, former head of the Carabineros, was arrested in connection with the kidnapping of eight people in 1985. Later in the month, after Ecuador had officially complained of his presence at an Ecuadorian military social centre, the commander of the army, General Augusto Pinochet, was told by President Patricio Aylwin that he must in future give advance notice of intended visits abroad.

In the municipal elections on 28 June the ruling Coalition of Parties for Democracy (CPD) won decisively, with 53.3 per cent of the vote. This was widely seen as an endorsement for the CPD plan to reform the authoritarian 1980 constitution, which the combined right-wing opposition, with only 29.8 per cent, had pledged to uphold. On 17 August the Finance Minister, Alejandro Foxley Rioseco, announced that Standard and Poor's had accorded the country a BBB investment grade rating. The Senate again refused to abolish the celebration of 11 September as the anniversary of the 1973 military coup which overthrew the Allende government. On 24 September the acting army commander-in-chief placed his forces on full alert after demonstrators had identified the headquarters of army intelligence.

v.   COLOMBIA

CAPITAL: Bogotá   AREA: 1,141,750 sq km   POPULATION: 32,300,000 ('90)
OFFICIAL LANGUAGE: Spanish   POLITICAL SYSTEM: presidential democracy
HEAD OF STATE & GOVERNMENT: President César Gaviria Trujillo (since Aug '90)
RULING PARTIES: Liberal Party (PL) heads coalition with Social Conservative Party
    (PSC), National Salvation Movement (MSN), New Democratic Force (NFD) & April
    19 Movement Democratic Alliance (ADM-19)
PRINCIPAL MINISTERS: Nohemí Sanin Posada (PSC/foreign affairs), Humberto
    de la Calle Lombana (PL/interior), Rudolf Hommes Rodríguez (PL/finance),
    Andrés González (PL/justice), Rafael Pardo Rueda (PL/defence), Luis Alberto
    Moreno (PSC-NFD/economic development)
INTERNATIONAL ALIGNMENT: NAM, OAS
CURRENCY: peso (end-'92 £1=Col$1,231.05, US$1=Col$813.11)
GNP PER CAPITA: US$1,260 ('90)
MAIN EXPORT EARNERS: coffee, oil & oil derivatives

REPORTS that Pablo Escobar Gaviria, the head of the Medellín cartel, was still running his drugs empire from the safety of his 'prison' at Envigado (see AR 1991, p. 72) prompted the government to order a review of security on 22 January. On 23 April the whole country was placed under a state of emergency following the admission by the power-generating companies in March that they could no longer cope with the prolonged drought, said to be caused by the El Niño current but believed to be at least partly the result of the accelerated destruction of tropical rain-forest. At the beginning of July President César Gaviria Trujillo reconstructed his coalition cabinet to bring in senior members of the left-wing April-19 Movement Democratic Alliance (ADM-19), thus protecting them from legal action in connection with the guerrilla attack on the Palace of Justice in November 1985 (see AR 1985, p. 78).

On 10 July the President proclaimed a state of emergency to pre-empt the release from prison of certain suspected members of the Medellín cartel. However, on 22 July, when the deputy minister of justice, Eduardo Mendoza, ordered the transfer of Escobar to an army barracks, Sr Mendoza was held hostage with the connivance of the guards, while Escobar and eight of his colleagues made good their escape. Four later surrendered (including Escobar's brother Roberto), and Brance Muñoz Mósquera, the cartel's 'military commander', was shot dead in Medellín on 28 October; but Escobar himself remained at liberty while negotiating fresh conditions for his own surrender.

Meanwhile, peace talks with the armed opposition, which broke down in March, were suspended in May. A new series of terrorist attacks followed, escalating in October. At the end of October Congress voted a massive increase in spending on counter-insurgency, and the President proclaimed a new 90-day state of emergency.

vi. ECUADOR

CAPITAL: Quito   AREA: 270,500 sq km   POPULATION: 10,300,000 ('90)
OFFICIAL LANGUAGE: Spanish   POLITICAL SYSTEM: presidential democracy
HEAD OF STATE & GOVERNMENT: President Sixto Durán Bailén (since Aug '92)
RULING PARTIES: Republican Unity Party (PUR) heads coalition
PRINCIPAL MINISTERS: Alberto Dahik (vice-president), Diego Paredes (foreign affairs), Roberto Dunn Barreiro (interior), Gen. José Gallardo (defence), Mario Rivadeneira (finance), Mauricio Pinto (industry), Andrés Barreiro (energy & mines)
INTERNATIONAL ALIGNMENT: NAM, OAS
CURRENCY: sucre (end-'92 £1=S/.2,805.50, US$1=S/.1,853.04)
GNP PER CAPITA: US$980 ('90)
MAIN EXPORT EARNERS: oil & oil derivatives, coffee, bananas

ON 11 and 12 January President Alberto Keinya Fujimori of Peru visited Quito and held talks with President Rodrigo Borja Cevallos on their boundary dispute in the Condor mountains, which had led to a brief war in 1981 (see AR 1981, p. 82). Whereas President Fujimori had proposed in November 1991 that the dispute should be settled on the basis of the 1942 protocol of Rio de Janeiro, Peru now indicated acceptance of President Borja's proposal that the Vatican, not the four protocol guarantor powers, should act as arbitrator. Peru was also prepared to offer Ecuador navigation rights on the Peruvian Amazon, without which Peru's potential territorial gains would be of little value. Ominously in an election year, the two main Ecuadorian opposition leaders were absent from the official banquet. A further historic step by the outgoing President was the grant on 13 May to over 20,000 indigenous people of legal title to some 3 million acres in the province of Pastaza.

In the first round of the presidential elections on 17 May, Sixto Durán Bailén, former mayor of Quito, leader of the recently-formed Republican Unity Party (PUR) and an advocate of free market and pro-business principles, led with 36.1 per cent of the votes cast. Jaime Nebot Saadi of the Social Christian Party (PSC) came second with 26.2 per cent; the former mayor of Guayaquil, Abdalá Bucaram Ortiz of the Ecuadorean Roldosista Party (PRE), who had been second in 1988 and was again the beneficiary of a congressional amnesty for alleged embezzlement, took third place (20.7 per cent); and the candidate of the ruling Democratic Left (ID), Raúl Baca Carbo, was fourth (8.4 per cent) in a field of 12.

The results of the congressional elections on 17 May were: PSC 21 seats, PRE 13, PUR 12, ID 7, Conservative Party (PCE) 6, Popular Democratic Movement (MPD) 4, Ecuadorian Socialist Party (PSE) 3, Liberal Radicals (PLR) 3 and four other small parties one each. This outcome meant that the winner in the second presidential round on 5 July, Sr Durán, lacked an overall congressional majority, even though he obtained 2,174,860 votes (57.9 per cent) to 1,584,482 (42.1 per cent) for Sr Nebot.

Sr Durán was sworn in on 10 August. On 3 September he announced a comprehensive package of austerity measures, touching off a series of violent street demonstrations in Quito and Guayaquil. Though the army was mobilized on 7 September, the violence continued and the Confederation of Indian Nationalities of Ecuador (Conaie) began a campaign of civil disobedience.

vii. PARAGUAY

CAPITAL: Asunción   AREA: 406,752 sq km   POPULATION: 4,300,000 ('90)
OFFICIAL LANGUAGE: Spanish   POLITICAL SYSTEM: republic
HEAD OF STATE & GOVERNMENT: President (Gen.) Andrés Rodríguez (since '89)
RULING PARTY: Colorado Party
PRINCIPAL MINISTERS: Alexis Frutos Vaesken (foreign affairs), Gen. Orlando
    Machuca Vargas (interior), Juan José Díaz Perez (finance), Gen. Angel Juan
    Souto Hernandez (defence), Hugo Estigarribia Elizache (justice & labour),
    Ualdo Scavone (industry & trade)
INTERNATIONAL ALIGNMENT: OAS
CURRENCY: guarani (end-'92 £1=G2,449.25, US$1=G1,617.73)
GNP PER CAPITA: US$1,110 ('90)
MAIN EXPORT EARNERS: cotton, soyabeans, meat

THE work of the National Constituent Assembly came to an end on 18 June, when President Andrés Rodríguez refused to attend its final session. The President had taken offence at a transitional provision of the new constitution, passed by a substantial majority with the aid of dissident Colorado votes, which debarred him formally from seeking re-election at the presidential elections due in August 1993; it was, he suggested, a slur on his honour in that he had already given 'the word of a soldier' that he would not be a candidate. However, after some concern at the possibility of a 'presidential coup', President Rodríguez swore allegiance on 22 June to the new constitution, which thereupon replaced that of 1940.

viii.   PERU

CAPITAL: Lima   AREA: 1,285,000 sq km   POPULATION: 21,700,000 ('90)
OFFICIAL LANGUAGES: Spanish, Quechua, Aymará
POLITICAL SYSTEM: presidential democracy
HEAD OF STATE & GOVERNMENT: President Alberto Keinya Fujimori (since July '90)
RULING PARTY: New Majority-Change 90 heads government coalition
PRINCIPAL MINISTERS: Maximo San Román Cáceres (1st vice-president), Carlos Garcia
   Garcia (2nd vice-president), Oscar de la Puente Raygada (prime minister, foreign
   affairs), Carlos Boloña Bohr (economy & finance), Gen. E.P. Victor Malca
   (defence), Fernando Santa Gadea (justice), Gen. Juan Briones (interior),
   Jorge Camet (induustry & commerce)
INTERNATIONAL ALIGNMENT: NAM, OAS
CURRENCY: new sol (end-'92 £1=NS2.43, US$1=NS1.61)
GNP PER CAPITA: US$1,160 ('90)
MAIN EXPORT EARNERS: copper, petroleum products

ON 5 April President Alberto Keinya Fujimori, with the aid of a well-executed military coup, suspended the constitution and dissolved Congress and the judiciary. The Prime Minister, Alfonso de los Heros Pérez Alba, and the Attorney-General, Pedro Méndez Jurado, immediately resigned, and were replaced by Oscar de la Puente Raygada and Hugo Ernesto Denegri Cornejo respectively. Although First Vice-President Maximo San Román Cáceres was formally sworn in as President before 200 members of Congress on 21 April (following his return from the United States), he received little support. President Fujimori refused to negotiate with the legal opposition and instead threatened them by decree with between four and seven years' imprisonment. Meanwhile, a series of 'basic decrees' had authorized a purge of the judiciary, which was widely regarded as corrupt and had been increasingly reluctant to act against terrorist suspects because of personal threats.

Only after pressure from the Organization of American States (see XI.6.v) did President Fujimori agree, without consultation, to allow a Democratic Constituent Congress (CCD) to be chosen in free elections. On 25 June, moreover, the government offered all legal opposition parties a dialogue on the country's future, and most accepted. Subsequently, the OAS decision to send observers to the elections was hailed by President Fujimori as an endorsement. The opposition American Popular Revolutionary Alliance (APRA), however, refused to take part as long as former President Alan García Pérez (who had been granted diplomatic asylum in Colombia on 1 June) was subject to legal investigation. Like the conservative Acción Popular (AP), which also boycotted the elections, it saw them as merely an excuse for dictatorship. In consequence, New Majority-Change 90 won 44 of the 80 seats in the CCD elections on 20 November, though with only 38 per cent of the vote.

In the first part of the year well-organized terrorist incidents had continued to inflict many casualties in Lima, despite a split in the Tupac Armarú Revolutionary Movement (MRTA). In response to the coup, fresh attacks by Sendero Luminoso (SL) on targets in Lima and Callao killed 10 and caused numerous other casualties. On 28 April, acting on its new powers, the government sent troops into the shanty-town of Raucana on the edge of Lima. On 5 May a decree increased penalties for terrorist offences and eliminated restraints on 'disappearances'. The following day paramilitary police led a four-day assault on the top-security Miguel Castro Castro prison in Lima, parts of which were said to be controlled by SL. After fierce resistance, it was reported that, at the cost of 35 prisoners and two police killed and 20 wounded, 451 prisoners had been forced to surrender. On the night of 4–5 June a bomb attack, apparently by SL, on the studios of TV Channel 2 in Lima killed five people. Four days later the leader of the MRTA, Víctor Polay Campos ('Comandante Rolando'), who had escaped from custody in July 1990, was arrested in San Borja, while on 3 July security forces captured Luis Arana Franco, SL's logistics chief.

On 16 July a new 'urban militia' was instituted. The same night a large car bomb killed 20 and injured over 250 people in the Miraflores district, and there were widespread attacks on police posts. A few days later President Fujimori decreed (25 July) that in future 'terrorist criminals' would be tried by military courts. Hence when, to general surprise, the 57-year-old leader of SL, Professor Abimael Guzmán Renoso, was captured in Lima on 12 September, together with his alleged 'number two', Elena Reboredo Iparaguirre, and 19 other members of the central committee, the President claimed that this justified his dictatorial measures. In a series of searches on 17 October more SL leaders were reportedly captured.

After Professor Guzmán had been exhibited to the press in a steel cage on 24 September, he was returned to custody at La Punta naval base at Callao. At his ten-day trial, which was held in secret and allowed no defence witnesses, he was sentenced to life imprisonment, the highest available penalty. SL attacks continued, 44 people being killed in a single action at Huayo, in the department of La Mar, on 11 October, though without disrupting the elections. Although a coup led by General Jaime Salinas on 13 November was a complete failure, unrest in the armed forces was known to be serious and the situation at year-end was still unstable.

ix. URUGUAY

CAPITAL: Montevideo   AREA: 176,200 sq km   POPULATION: 3,100,000 ('90)
OFFICIAL LANGUAGE: Spanish   POLITICAL SYSTEM: presidential democracy
HEAD OF STATE & GOVERNMENT: President Luis Alberto Lacalle Herrera (since '90)
RULING PARTY: National (Blanco) Party heading coalition with Colorados
PRINCIPAL MINISTERS: Gonzala Aguirre Ramirez (vice-president), Hector Gros Espiell
    (foreign relations), Juan Andres Ramirez (interior), Ignacio de Posadas (economy
    & finance), Mariano Brito (defence), Eduardo Ache (industry & energy)
INTERNATIONAL ALIGNMENT: OAS
CURRENCY: new peso (end-'92 £1=NUr$5,266.85, US$1=NUr3,478.76)
GNP PER CAPITA: US$2,560 ('90)
MAIN EXPORT EARNERS: wool, meat

DISSATISFACTION with President Luis Alberto Lacalle Herrera's policy of pay restraint for public sector workers led to a 24-hour general strike on 17 January. However, despite pressure within the governing National (Blanco) Party which led on 7 February to the dismissal of the Minister of Economy and Finance, Enrique Braga Silva, his successor, Ignacio de Posadas, announced on 27 February the third stage of the restructuring programme. Opponents of the government's plans to privatize major public utilities, such as the state airline, the electricity company, the state railways and the ports, failed to win sufficient support in a special poll on 5 July to force a referendum on the proposals.

x.   VENEZUELA

CAPITAL: Caracas   AREA: 912,000 sq km   POPULATION: 19,700,000 ('90)
OFFICIAL LANGUAGE: Spanish   POLITICAL SYSTEM: presidential democracy
HEAD OF STATE & GOVERNMENT: President Carlos Ándrés Pérez (since Feb '89)
RULING PARTY: Democratic Action (since Jan '84)
PRINCIPAL MINISTERS: Gen. Fernando Ochoa Antich (foreign affairs), Luis Pinerua
    Ordaz (interior), Pedro Rosas Bravo (finance), Gen. Ivan Jimenez Sanchez
    (defence), Alirio Parra (energy & mines), Jose Mendoza Angulo (justice)
INTERNATIONAL ALIGNMENT: OAS, NAM
CURRENCY: bolivar (end-'92 £1=Bs120.40, US$1=Bs79.52)
GNP PER CAPITA: US$2,560 ('90)
MAIN EXPORT EARNERS: oil, aluminium

THE growing tension of the previous two years was fractured when President Carlos Andrés Pérez narrowly escaped capture and probable assassination when on the night of 3–4 February rebel army units seized the Miraflores palace and key strong points in the capital. Simultaneous risings took place at Maracay, Valencia and Maracaibo. The attempt—the most serious challenge to the legitimacy of the democratic order since 1959—killed 14 and wounded 57. It was led by Colonel Hugo Chávez Frías, who ordered his followers—officers and men of the ultra-nationalist Revolutionary Bolivarist Movement

(MBR)—to surrender when, after more than 12 hours, the bulk of the army remained loyal under the command of the Minister of Defence, General Fernando Ochoa Antich.

Dissatisfaction with the country's steep economic decline and the tough measures planned to combat it, which had been accompanied by a soaring crime rate and a growing gap between rich and poor, had led to a demand for a 'junta of national reconstruction'. Though unemployment at 9 per cent was far below that for many other Latin American states, inflation for the year was expected to be 30 per cent, living standards had fallen well below those of the oil-rich 1970s and more than half the population were living below the poverty line. On 22 June, for the first time since nationalization in 1976, the government offered 20-year contracts to open up previously-unexplored oilfields to six overseas companies, with the proviso that all oil produced must be processed and sold through Petróleos de Venezuela (PDVSA).

Meanwhile, the President himself was under investigation for alleged speculation in currency, and a cabinet reshuffle on 9 January had been dismissed by the opposition as 'cosmetic'. However, in the aftermath of the attempted coup, President Pérez quickly lifted temporary restrictions on freedom of speech and the press, announced a substantial four-year social welfare programme and formed a 'cabinet of national unity' on 10 March. Full constitutional guarantees were restored on 9 April, this move pre-empting moves by some deputies to cut short the presidential term. Nevertheless, the government remained so unpopular that amid continuing unrest, in which at least four students died, the main opposition Social Christian Party (COPEI) withdrew again from the government on 11 June.

This time the President turned to the armed forces, replacing the Foreign Minister, Humberto Calderón Berti, by the Defence Minister, General Fernando Ochoa, who in turn was followed at defence by General Iván Jiménez Sánchez of the air force. On 29 June six more ministers were removed as part of a long-term strategy to reduce the size of the cabinet. However, the MBR warned that trouble would follow the alleged failure of the country's leadership to address social grievances, symbolized by a new austerity package announced on 23 August. Rumours of a second military coup spread in September as two clandestine radio stations called for the assassination of several public figures. A plot was said to have been foiled and on 12 October there was an unsuccessful attempt to ambush the presidential motorcade at Paraguaipoa in the state of Zulia. Eventually, on 27 November, a further major rebellion in the capital left some 230 dead and inflicted widespread damage.

xi. CUBA

CAPITAL: Havana AREA: 115,000 sq km POPULATION: 11,000,000 ('90)
OFFICIAL LANGUAGE: Spanish POLITICAL SYSTEM: republic, one-party communist state
HEAD OF STATE & GOVERNMENT: President Fidel Castro Ruz (since Jan '59)
RULING PARTY: Cuban Communist Party (PCC)
PRINCIPAL MINISTERS: Gen. Raúl Castro Ruz (1st vice-president, defence),
    Alarcon de Quesada (foreign relations), Gen Abelardo Colomé Ibarra (interior),
    Rodrigo García Leon (finance), Antonio Rodriques Maurell (planning)
INTERNATIONAL ALIGNMENT: NAM
CURRENCY: peso (end-'92 £1=Cub$1.15, US$1=Cub$0.76)
GNP PER CAPITA: n.a.
MAIN EXPORT EARNERS: sugar & sugar products

THREE members of a small anti-Castro organization, who had been arrested on 29 December 1991 at El Júcaro on the north coast, were executed by firing squad on 20 January. In a year of serious economic crisis following the end of oil supplies from the former Soviet Union, many sought to take refuge abroad. Despite a sharp increase in exile radio and TV broadcasts, little dissension was reported in Cuba itself. Instead, a determined effort was made to maintain a low-energy emergency economy, with the assistance of large consignments of bicycles from China. On 18 April President Bush closed all US ports to ships trading with Cuba. However, on 12 May a new barter agreement was concluded in Moscow by which Cuba would receive 1.8 million tonnes of oil in 1992. On 5 September, the 35th anniversary of the Cienfuegos uprising, President Fidel Castro Ruz gave further evidence of 'extraordinary damage' caused to Cuba's economy by the loss of its trading link with the former USSR. Only 7 million tonnes of sugar had been harvested, and each tonne sold abroad would only buy 1.5 tonnes of oil compared with 7.5 tonnes under the old agreement. On 16 September agreement was announced on the withdrawal of Russian forces from the island, to be completed by June 1993. However, the passage of the US Cuban Democracy Act in October was strongly opposed by other Latin American states on account of the extra-territorial application of US jurisdiction. On 24 November the UN General Assembly supported a Cuban resolution demanding its repeal by 59 votes to three with 71 abstentions. President Castro made a dramatic appearance at the Rio Earth Summit in June (see XIV.3), where he used only four of his allotted seven minutes to punch home two simple points: that it was the rich countries which had destroyed the world environment, and that it was for them to pay to clean it up again.

At the ordinary meeting of the National People's Power Assembly on 11–12 July the 1976 constitution was amended to allow the President to declare a state of emergency and to appoint himself leader of the National Defence Council, which was already the case in practice. Though in his closing speech the President congratulated delegates on not having made any concessions to the opponents of the revolution, other amendments limited ownership by the state to 'basic' means of production, allowed the transfer of state property to private ownership for economic or social development, and ended the state monopoly of foreign trade. On 29 October the Assembly passed a new electoral law to allow for its own replacement by direct and secret ballot in 1993. At the same time, the voting age was lowered to 16. The subsequent demotion and expulsion from the Cuban Communist Party (PCC) of Carlos Aldana, whose responsibilities for ideology and foreign policy were transferred to José Ramón Balaguer Cabrera, confirmed the ascendancy of the Castro brothers.

xii. HAITI AND THE DOMINICAN REPUBLIC

Haiti
CAPITAL: Port-au-Prince AREA: 27,750 sq km POPULATION: 6,500,000 ('90)
OFFICIAL LANGUAGE: French POLITICAL SYSTEM: military/presidential
HEAD OF STATE & GOVERNMENT: Joseph Nerette (since Oct '91)
CURRENCY: gourde (end-'92 £1=G17.45, US$1=G11.53)
GNP PER CAPITA: US$370 ('90)
MAIN EXPORT EARNERS: light manufactures, coffee, tourism

Dominican Republic
CAPITAL: Santo Domingo AREA: 48,400 sq km POPULATION: 7,100,000 ('90)
OFFICIAL LANGUAGE: Spanish POLITICAL SYSTEM: presidential democracy
HEAD OF STATE & GOVERNMENT: President Joaquín Balaguer (since Aug '86)
CURRENCY: peso (end-'92 £1=RD$19.71, US$1=RD$13.02)
GNP PER CAPITA: US$830 ('90)
MAIN EXPORT EARNERS: sugar, metals, tourism

FOLLOWING the breakdown on 8 January of an agreement which would have allowed the return of the elected President of HAITI, Fr Jean-Bertrand Aristide, the secretary-general of the Unified Party of Haitian Communists (PUCH), René Théodore, was installed as Prime Minister and the term of provisional President, Joseph Nerette, was extended indefinitely. Further talks foundered on Fr Aristide's unrealistic insistence that the commander in chief of the armed forces, General Raoul Cédras, the effective head of government, should be dismissed and prosecuted. Instead, General Cédras was promoted and a new agreement, acceptable to the armed forces and ratified by Congress on 25 May, provided only for unspecified future elections. Although Amnesty International reported in January that over 1,500 civilians had been killed and some 300 detained since 30 September 1991, demonstrations against the government continued, leading to the closing of all schools 'indefinitely' on 25 May.

Pope John Paul II visited the DOMINICAN REPUBLIC on 9–14 October but declined to switch on the massive lighthouse, the Faro a Colón, constructed on the orders of President Joaquín Balaguer at a cost of $25 million to commemorate the 500th anniversary of the voyage of Christopher Columbus. Instead, the Pope held a public mass there on 11 October and subsequently presided over the opening of the fourth General Latin American Episcopal Conference (CELAM), reemphasizing the Church's spiritual mission. Two demonstrators had been killed in September while protesting at the proposed celebration of the Spanish conquest.

xiii. CENTRAL AMERICA AND PANAMA

Guatemala
CAPITAL: Guatemala City   AREA: 109,000 sq km   POPULATION: 9,200,000 ('90)
OFFICIAL LANGUAGE: Spanish   POLITICAL SYSTEM: presidential democracy
HEAD OF STATE & GOVERNMENT: President Jorge Serrano Elias (since Jan '91)
RULING PARTY: Social Action Movement (MAS)
CURRENCY: quetzal (end-'92 £1=Q8.16, US$1=Q5.39)
GNP PER CAPITA: US$900 ('90)
MAIN EXPORT EARNERS: coffee, sugar, cotton, petroleum, cardamom, bananas

El Salvador
CAPITAL: San Salvador   AREA: 21,400 sq km   POPULATION: 5,200,000 ('90)
OFFICIAL LANGUAGE: Spanish   POLITICAL SYSTEM: presidential democracy
HEAD OF STATE & GOVERNMENT: President Alfredo Cristiani (since June '89)
RULING PARTY: National Republican Alliance (Arena)
CURRENCY: colón (end-'92 £1=C13.01, US$1=C8.59)
GNP PER CAPITA: US$1,110 ('90)
MAIN EXPORT EARNERS: coffee, cotton, sugar

Honduras
CAPITAL: Tegucigalpa   AREA: 112,000 sq km   POPULATION: 5,100,000 ('90)
OFFICIAL LANGUAGE: Spanish   POLITICAL SYSTEM: presidential democracy
HEAD OF STATE & GOVERNMENT: President Rafael Leonard Callejas (since Jan '90)
RULING PARTY: National Party (PN)
CURRENCY: lempira (end-'92 £1=L8.93, US$1=L5.89)
GNP PER CAPITA: US$590 ('90)
MAIN EXPORT EARNERS: bananas, coffee, tourism

Nicaragua
CAPITAL: Managua   AREA: 120,000 sq km   POPULATION: 3,900,000 ('90)
OFFICIAL LANGUAGE: Spanish   POLITICAL SYSTEM: presidential democracy
HEAD OF STATE & GOVERNMENT: President Violeta Chamorro (since April '90)
RULING PARTY: National Opposition Union (UNO)
CURRENCY: córdoba (end-'92 £1=C$7.583, US$1=C$5.008)
GNP PER CAPITA: US$830 ('87)
MAIN EXPORT EARNERS: coffee, cotton, sugar, bananas

Costa Rica
CAPITAL: San José   AREA: 51,000 sq km   POPULATION: 2,800,000 ('90)
OFFICIAL LANGUAGE: Spanish   POLITICAL SYSTEM: presidential democracy
HEAD OF STATE & GOVERNMENT: President Rafael Ángel Calderón Fournier (since '90)
RULING PARTY: Social Christian Unity Party (PUSC)
CURRENCY: colón (end-'92 £1=C208.35, US$1=C137.62)
GNP PER CAPITA: US$1,900 ('90)
MAIN EXPORT EARNERS: coffee, bananas, tourism

Panama
CAPITAL: Panama City   AREA: 77,000 sq km   POPULATION: 2,400,000 ('90)
OFFICIAL LANGUAGE: Spanish   POLITICAL SYSTEM: presidential
HEAD OF STATE & GOVERNMENT: President Guillermo Endara (since Dec '89)
RULING PARTY: Authentic Liberal Party (within Democratic Alliance)
CURRENCY: balboa (end-'92 £1=B1.51, US£1=B1.00)
GNP PER CAPITA: US$1,830 ('90)
MAIN EXPORT EARNERS: bananas, prawns, sugar, canal dues

IN GUATEMALA, where official human rights sources reported 228 'extra-judicial executions' and 45 'disappearances' in 1991 at the hands, according to the US State Department, of 'the military, the civil patrols, and the police', the government of President Jorge Serrano Elias announced fresh initiatives to end abuses. However, the armed forces still failed to cooperate to prosecute offenders and the latest round of talks between the government and the Guatemalan National Revolutionary Unity (URNG) ended on 23 February without result, following which a wave of bombings and bomb threats in the capital were taken to be the work of dissident officers planning a possible coup. In a concession to the right, the President dismissed four ministers of his Social Action Movement (MAS) on 27 April and replaced them by non-partisan appointees. However, on 23 July the Minister of the Interior, Fernando Hurtado Prem, whose term of office had been marked by an increase in human-rights abuses, was forced to resign after a group of 500 *campesinos* was forcibly evicted from the Central Plaza. He was replaced by Francisco Perdomo Scandoval, and on 7 August agreement was reached between the government and the URNG on the future of the Civil Defence Patrols. The award on 17 October of the Nobel Peace Prize to the 33-year-old human rights activist Rigoberta Menchú, whose parents and brother had been murdered by a former military government, received belated congratulations from President Serrano but no official reception.

A formal peace agreement between the government of EL SALVADOR and the Farabundo Martí National Liberation Front (FMLN) was finally signed in Mexico City on 16 January. Following the arrival several days later of a 290-member UN Observer Mission (ONUSAL), a ceasefire on 1 February effectively ended 11 years of civil war that had cost some 75,000 lives. On 20 February Roberto d'Aubuisson, founder of the governing National Republican Alliance (Arena) and the man who as leader of the right-wing 'death squads' was believed to have organized the assassination of Archbishop Oscar Romero in 1980, died of cancer aged 48. Arrangements for the disbanding both of some military units and of the former guerrillas (who officially became a political party on 23 May) started erratically owing to mutual suspicions, but in August the government demobilized the first of five US-trained counter-insurgency batallions. The FMLN responded in kind and the last stage was formally concluded on 15 December, after strong resistance within the officer corps. Meanwhile, in October an international team began the exhumation at El Mozote, department of Morazán, of hundreds of bodies believed to be the victims of a massacre by the US-trained Atlacatl Batallion in 1981.

The ruling of the International Court of Justice (ICJ) on 11 September on the longstanding border dispute between El Salvador and HONDURAS, which had led to war in 1969 (see AR 1969, p. 191), was accepted by both sides. Under its terms Honduras was to receive approximately two-thirds of the mainland territory under dispute as well as the island of El Tigre in the Gulf of Fonseca. The Gulf itself had now to be shared with Nicaragua.

In NICARAGUA the peace was disturbed by sporadic clashes between 'Recontras' (former Contras) and 'Recompas' (former Sandinista *compañeros*), some 4,000 of whom, following the demobilization of their high commands in February, banded together to launch a series of armed protests at the failure of government to honour their pledges of land and credits. However, although the third stage of the disarmament process had to be extended into May, it went ahead nevertheless. Meanwhile, on 9 January President Violeta Barrios de Chamorro appointed Ernesto Leal to the Foreign Ministry and replaced Silvio de Franco as Minister of Economy and Development by Julio Cárdenas. Within the ruling National Opposition Union (UNO) there was, however, growing right-wing dissension, led by Vice-President Virgilio Godoy Reyes, over the President's unofficial alliance with the opposition Sandinista National Liberation Front (FSLN), and on 2 April the Interior Minister, Carlos Hurtado, resigned and was replaced by Alfredo Mendieta *ad interim*. In May the US Congress blocked $100 million in aid in protest at what it considered was the undue influence of the Sandinistas over the new government. From the right wing of the UNO itself came accusations of corruption against a former deputy minister, implicating the Minister for the Presidency, Antonio Lacayo Oyanguren, and renewed demands for the dismissal of the commander in chief of the armed forces, General Humberto Ortega Saavedra, whom the Supreme Court ruled on 12 July might face court martial for allegedly concealing the murder of a youth by one of his bodyguards. Despite this pressure, on 5 September a Sandinista was appointed director-general of the National Police. Four days later the President signed three decrees for the restitution of land expropriated by the Sandinista government, but they safeguarded the position of peasants who had received title to expropriated lands, while lands seized from the Somoza family were not covered. On 1 September more than 200 died and thousands were left homeless when a tidal wave swept the Pacific coast south-west of Managua.

The calm of COSTA RICA was broken abruptly on 23 September when Luis Fishman Zonzinski, the Interior and Security Minister, who was mediating between the Honduran Cinchonero Popular Liberation

Movement (MPLC) and the Honduran government, was held hostage for 24 hours with three other dignitaries by Orlando Ordoñez Betancourt, who was subsequently given safe conduct to Mexico.

The government of President Guillermo Endara Gallimany of PANAMA, imposed by the US intervention in 1989 (see AR 1989,pp. 58–9, 78–9), continued to be widely unpopular. Between 5 and 11 May at least 30 people were seriously injured in riots in the port of Colón, after which passions were further inflamed when the President's wife, Aña Mae Díaz de Endara, publicly stated that the police should have fired directly into the crowds. As a result, when President Bush made his ill-advised decision to visit Panama on his way to the Rio Earth Summit, he was greeted by massive anti-American demonstrations. On 28 August Delia Cárdenas replaced the Second Vice-President, Guillermo Ford Boyd, as Minister for Planning and Economic Policy.

xiv. MEXICO

CAPITAL: Mexico City   AREA: 1,958,000 sq km   POPULATION: 86,200,000 ('90)
OFFICIAL LANGUAGE: Spanish   POLITICAL SYSTEM: federal presidential democracy
HEAD OF STATE & GOVERNMENT: President Carlos Salinas de Gortari (since Dec '88)
RULING PARTY: Party of the Institutionalized Revolution (since 1929)
PRINCIPAL MINISTERS: Fernando Solana Morales (foreign relations), Fernando
    Gutiérrez Barrios (government), Gen. Antonio Riviello Bazán (defence),
    Pedro Aspe Armella (finance, planning, budget), Fernando Hiriart Balderrama
    (energy, mines & public industries), Enrique Alvárez del Castillo (attorney-
    general)
INTERNATIONAL ALIGNMENT: OAS
CURRENCY: peso (end-'92 £1=Mex$4,728.38, US$1=Mex$3,123.10)
GNP PER CAPITA: US$2,490 ('90)
MAIN EXPORT EARNERS: oil, motor machinery, coffee, tourism

A further dramatic step was taken away from Mexico's revolutionary past in late January, when articles 27 and 130 of the constitution were amended, respectively to permit the alienation of *ejidal* (communal) land and to recognize the legal personality of the Church and lift the restrictions on the clergy imposed in 1857. Earlier in the month, following the resignation from the Department of Education of his former rival, Manuel Bartlett Díaz, President Carlos Salinas de Gortari had transferred the Secretary of Planning and Budget, Ernesto Cedillo Ponce de León, to education and consolidated planning with finance and public credit in a single 'super-ministry' under Pedro Aspe Armella. Five days later, for the third time in a year, the President annulled the results of local elections, this time November's local elections in the state of Tabasco, where following strong protests the city government of Cárdenas was awarded to the opposition Democratic Revolutionary Party (PRD). In state elections on 12 July further violence erupted when the PRI's candidate for governor, Eduardo Villaseñor, claimed victory over Cristóbal Arias of the PRD, in Michoacán, home state of the PRD's national leader, Cuauhtémoc Cárdenas Solórzano. Months of demonstrations followed, including a picket of the governor's palace after his inauguration on 15 September. On 6 October he asked for leave of absence and was replaced by Ausencio Chávez, also of the PRI. The right-wing National Action Party (PAN) won control of Chihuahua, Francisco Barrio Terrazas becoming governor. On 2 August the PRI claimed victory in all six states contested (Aguascalientes, Baja California, Durango, Oaxaca, Veracruz and Zacatecas) and bitter recriminations broke out between the PRI and the PRD, culminating in a mass rally led by Sr Cárdenas in the capital on 29 August. On 10 September Joaquín Hernández Galicia ('La Quina'), who had been president of the Union of Oil Workers (STPRM) for 25 years before breaking with the PRI in 1988, was sentenced to 35 years' imprisonment for the alleged murder of a union official in 1983.

Meanwhile, negotiations for a North American Free Trade Agreement (NAFTA) continued with the United States, which on 25 February announced an 'integrated border plan' by which the two governments would work to clean up environmental damage along their common frontier. A savage reminder of how serious this might be came on 22 April, when a series of underground explosions levelled 30 blocks of central Guadalajara, killing at least 200 people and injuring some 1,500. When investigation showed the cause to have been a leak from a PEMEX pipeline of petrol and other volatile substances, which had been ignored by the civic authorities, the mayor, four PEMEX executives, three directors of the sewage company and the State Secretary for State and Rural Development were all arrested. On 30 May the governor of the state of Jalisco, Guillermo Cosío Vidaurri, was forced to resign after he had tried to exonerate them. Having failed to get satisfaction from President Bush at his meeting with President Salinas at San Diego, on 14 July, Mexico formally announced on 27 July that, following the US Supreme Court ruling authorizing US personnel to kidnap foreign nationals, it would accept no further US aid in the war against drugs—which, however, it proposed to continue. Diplomatic relations with the Holy See were restored on 20 September (see also II.2.viii).

4. THE CARIBBEAN

JAMAICA—GUYANA—TRINIDAD & TOBAGO—BARBADOS—BELIZE—
GRENADA—THE BAHAMAS—WINDWARD AND LEEWARD ISLANDS—
SURINAME—NETHERLANDS ANTILLES
AND ARUBA

i. JAMAICA

CAPITAL: Kingston   AREA: 11,000 sq km   POPULATION: 2,400,000 ('90)
OFFICIAL LANGUAGE: English   POLITICAL SYSTEM: parliamentary democracy
HEAD OF STATE: Queen Elizabeth II   GOVERNOR-GENERAL: Howard Cooke
RULING PARTY: People's National Party (PNP)
HEAD OF GOVERNMENT: Percival J. Patterson, Prime Minister (since March '92)
PRINCIPAL MINISTERS: David Coore (foreign affairs), Hugh Small (finance &
  planning), K. D. Knight (national security & justice)
INTERNATIONAL ALIGNMENT: NAM, ACP, OAS, Caricom, Cwth.
CURRENCY: Jamaican dollar (end-'92 £1=J$36.169, US$1=J$23.889)
GNP PER CAPITA: US$1,500 ('90)
MAIN EXPORT EARNERS: bauxite/alumina, bananas, sugar, tourism

THE resignation of Michael Manley on 28 March, prompted by deteriorating personal health, as Prime Minister of Jamaica and leader
of the ruling People's National Party (PNP) ended the 40-year active
political career of a world statesman. As a champion of the right
to development of Third World societies, a constant advocate of a
new international economic order and major architect of South-North
cooperation, particularly through the Socialist International and United
Nations, Mr Manley had enjoyed a career reflecting the tensions and
vagaries of Jamaican development in particular and Third World
societies in general. Paradoxically, Mr Manley's last term in office
(since 1988) was marked by a dramatic departure from the democratic
socialism and 'Third Worldism' with which he made his international
reputation in the 1970s, to a liberal capitalist development strategy. This
had involved the privatization of 90 per cent of state-owned companies
since the mid-1980s, and rapid and widespread market deregulation
more recently.

On 28 May Percival J. Patterson, who had been out of the cabinet since a reshuffle on 1 January, was elected as Mr Manley's
successor by 2,322 PNP delegate votes to 756 for Portia Simpson.
Mr Patterson immediately confirmed his intention to continue the
policies of deregulation, public sector budget cutting and divestment
of state assets. Furthermore, following encouraging public opinion polls,
the new Prime Minister made clear at the PNP conference in September
that the government would see out its full term of office and would not
opt for an early election (on which there had been much speculation).

Public dissatisfaction with the PNP government focused on economic and social problems. Inflation topped 100 per cent in 1991; a series of major public sector redundancy notices included the announcement in May of civil service job cuts of 8,000, or 20 per cent of service staff; the privatization of many services tended to penalize the poor; the failure to meet IMF targets had delayed the release of further loan tranches; and there were rising levels of both political and social violence. Nevertheless, Mr Patterson's early record was encouraging, insofar as stated objectives were closely met. Inflation was contained in 1992 to around 15 per cent; income tax was reduced from 33 to 25 per cent and public expenditure, although it appeared to have risen following the May budget from J$18,000 million to J$26,000 million, was cut by some 40 per cent in real US dollar terms.

The government began negotiations for the tenth successive IMF extended fund facility since 1977. Declining terms of trade and the prospective impact of the single European market (see XI.3) depressed the bauxite and sugar industries, both critical to Jamaica's economy. Despite increases in violence, including well-publicized murders of tourists, visits were up by 8 per cent overall, while cruise ship visitors increased by 48 per cent. Growth in GDP was expected to be about 2–3 per cent in 1992.

Continued faction fighting within the opposition Jamaica Labour Party (JLP) throughout the year meant that the JLP was unable to exploit the latent unease with the PNP government, nor exploit the politics of Mr Manley's succession. By year's end Mr Patterson had largely restored a modicum of popular confidence in the PNP.

ii. GUYANA

CAPITAL: Georgetown   AREA: 215,000 sq km   POPULATION: 798,000 ('90)
OFFICIAL LANGUAGE: English   POLITICAL SYSTEM: cooperative presidential democracy
HEAD OF STATE AND GOVERNMENT: President Cheddi Jagan (since Oct '92)
RULING PARTY: People's Progressive Party (PPP)
PRINCIPAL MINISTERS: Sam Hinds (prime minister), Feroze Mohamed (home affairs),
   Bernard de Santos (justice)
INTERNATIONAL ALIGNMENT: NAM, ACP, Caricom, Cwth.
CURRENCY: Guyana dollar (end-'92 £1=G$191.05, US$1=G$126.19)
GNP PER CAPITA: US$330 ('90)
MAIN EXPORT EARNERS: bauxite, sugar, rice

THE question of the constantly-postponed general elections and the integrity of the electoral process dominated Guyanese political life throughout the year. Elections which should have been held by 1990 were finally held on 5 October, resulting in a narrow majority for the opposition People's Progressive Party (PPP) led by Dr Cheddi Jagan. The PPP won 52.2 per cent of the votes, while the ruling People's National Congress (PNC), led by Desmond Hoyte, took 43.7 per cent.

Of the other formations, the Working People's Alliance (WPA), led by Professor Clive Thomas, received 1.7 per cent and the United Force 1.2 per cent of the votes cast. Under the somewhat peculiar electoral system, 53 of the 65 seats in the National Assembly were distributed proportionally, ten were elected by regional democratic councils and two by the National Congress of Local Democratic Organizations. The final distribution was PPP 34 seats, PNC 27, WPA 2 and UF 1.

Although the WPA offered pragmatic support to the PPP, Dr Jagan's party commanded sufficient seats in its own right for a narrow overall majority. Nevertheless, the new President was keen to stress his desire to work with other parties rather than continue the exclusivist traditions of the PNC years or risk a repeat of the ethnicism of earlier administrations. Dr Jagan appeared to have the good fortune of returning to office (he was previously Prime Minister in 1957–64) as the economy grew for the first time since 1984. A 6.1 per cent increase in GDP was recorded in 1991, reflecting substantial increases in rice, sugar and gold production, which continued through 1992. A further boost was given to the economy, though not to Guyana's ecology, by the announcement of a contract under which Demerara Timber would export 6.7 million board feet of tropical hardwood timber in 1992 and 12 million board feet in 1993. The 1992 figure alone matched total current exports.

Whilst there were distinct signs of recovery, huge problems still confronted the economy. Government debt-servicing alone absorbed 55 per cent of current revenue, and total external debt was equivalent to a staggering 900 per cent annual export earnings. It was estimated that the balance-of-payments position would further deteriorate in 1992, and the unemployment rate was at least at 14 per cent, with 75 per cent of the population living below the poverty line.

Despite the refusal of opposition parties to participate in any budgetary debate before the election, Finance Minister Carl Greenidge presented a budget in March which limited public sector wage increases to well below the current inflation rate of 75 per cent. Even taking into account income from privatization programmes, the overall budget deficit for 1992 was expected to be G$12,800 million, or 35 per cent of GDP.

Although the Jagan government was likely to be more circumspect in the state divestment and deregulation programmes, radical departures from PNC policies were not expected, given international constraints and obligations. In the wake of his election defeat, ex-President Hoyte took the opportunity finally to remove the rump of the Burnhamite faction of the PNC from the parliamentary party. In conceding defeat, he expressed his intention to work as closely and cooperatively as possible with the new government. To some this looked like the proffer of a poisoned chalice, since for most of the 1980s the Hoyte government had kept no audited accounts of expenditure from which the PPP could now work.

iii.   TRINIDAD AND TOBAGO

CAPITAL: Port of Spain   AREA: 5,128 sq km   POPULATION: 1,200,000 ('90)
OFFICIAL LANGUAGE: English   POLITICAL SYSTEM: parliamentary republic
HEAD OF STATE: President Noor Mohammed Hassanali (since March '87)
RULING PARTY: People's National Movement (PNM)
HEAD OF GOVERNMENT: Patrick Manning, Prime Minister (since Dec '91)
PRINCIPAL MINISTERS: Ralph Maraj (foreign affairs), Wendell Mottley (finance),
    Keith Sobion (attorney-general), Brian Quei Tung (trade, industry & tourism),
    Barry Barnes (energy)
INTERNATIONAL ALIGNMENT: NAM, ACP, OAS, Caricom, Cwth.
CURRENCY: Trinidad & Tobago dollar (end-'92 £1=TT$6.43, US$1=TT$4.25)
GNP PER CAPITA: US$3,610 ('90)
MAIN EXPORT EARNERS: oil, chemicals, tourism

FOLLOWING a high court ruling that the pardon given during the failed coup attempt of August 1990 (see AR 1990, p. 95) was valid, 113 detained Jamaat al-Muslimeen members led by Yasin Abu Bakr were freed. During the attempted coup, acting president Emmanuel Carter had granted the plotters a pardon as a means of ending the siege and hostage crisis. The high court decision came after the case had been referred to the Privy Council in London, which ruled that the validity of the pardon should be established before the accused were formally tried. In the light of the release, not only did the plotters claim compensation from the state but also several of the hostages taken during the siege, including ministers and members of parliament, issued private writs against the plotters. The government appealed against the ruling.

Following his election victory of December 1991 (see AR 1991, p. 87), Prime Minister Patrick Manning of the People's National Movement (PNM) invited Basdeo Panday's United National Congress (UNC) to work with the government. The 1992 budget approved on 17 January aimed to increase revenue but provided for a fiscal deficit of about TT$314 million, in order that the state could mitigate some of the effects of recession. The government sought to reschedule some US$100 million in external debt through negotiations with its principal multilateral creditors. Despite the aim to invest TT$1,400 million in public sector programmes, the commitment to a broad state divestment programme was evident in that 13 of 18 state enterprises were targeted for immediate privatization.

As in other Caribbean states, extensive deregulation policies were being pursued in Trinidad and Tobago under World Bank 'guidance'. Not surprisingly, further deregulation of the currency markets provoked substantial capital flight, thereby undermining the domestic savings regime. The 1993 budget tabled on 20 November envisaged balanced revenue and expenditure, whereas the fiscal deficit for 1992 stood at 1.7 per cent of GDP or TT$382 million. External debt-servicing was expected to take 28 per cent of 1993 export earnings.

The general election defeat of A. N. R. Robinson prompted the

National Alliance for Reconstruction (NAR) to replace him as leader by Carson Charles. In the new parliament, Occah Seepaul became the first woman Speaker of the House of Representatives.

iv. BARBADOS

CAPITAL: Bridgetown   AREA: 430 sq km   POPULATION: 257,000 ('90)
OFFICIAL LANGUAGE: English   POLITICAL SYSTEM: parliamentary democracy
HEAD OF STATE: Queen Elizabeth II   GOVERNOR-GENERAL: Dame Nita Barrow
RULING PARTY: Democratic Labour Party (DLP)
HEAD OF GOVERNMENT: Erskine Sandiford, Prime Minister (since June '87)
PRINCIPAL MINISTERS: Philip Greaves (deputy premier, communications & public
   works), Maurice King (foreign affairs, attorney-general), Keith Simmons (justice
   & public safety), Warwick Franklin (trade & industry)
INTERNATIONAL ALIGNMENT: NAM, ACP, OAS, Cwth.
CURRENCY: Barbados dollar (end-'92 £1=BDS$3.05, US$1=BDS$2.021)
GNP PER CAPITA: US$6,540 ('90)
MAIN EXPORT EARNERS: sugar, tourism, light manufactures, chemicals

BARBADOS was one of several Caribbean economies, heavily dependent upon tourism, which suffered adverse publicity as a consequence of increasing incidences of violent attacks against tourists. Both the US and the UK governments issued formal travel warnings to tourists during 1992. In common with other Caribbean states, the government of Barbados provided joint army-police patrols in key tourist areas, seeking to contain a downturn in tourist arrivals attributed in part to the world recession.

Major reforms, though of doubtful impact, were implemented by the Democratic Labour Party (DLP) government of Prime Minister Erskine Sandiford. A standby arrangement and compensatory and contingency financing facilities were being negotiated with the International Monetary Fund (IMF) to cushion falls in tourist earnings. The negative growth of 1991 would, it was hoped, be turned into 2 per cent growth in 1992, combined with a halving of inflation to 3 per cent. However, Mr Sandiford's repeated claims that the government was on the right track were called into question when the junior finance minister, Harold Blackmann, resigned on the eve of the budget and denounced prevailing economic policy, along with Richie Haynes of the opposition National Democratic Party (NDP).

Unemployment was set to increase beyond 20 per cent by year's end. The state-owned Barbados Sugar Industry Limited (BSIL), now subject to Booker Tate management, was cut back throughout the year and finally went into receivership in October. Only if Booker Tate management plans were accepted would BSIL continue operations in future. The issue of this major part of the Barbados economy provoked cabinet splits during the year, finally causing a ministerial reshuffle in November.

Major revisions of the taxation system approved in July were condemned by opposition and civic groups as being too hastily prepared.
Popular confidence in Mr Sandiford's government remained at a low
ebb, and his competence to manage the economy in difficult times came
under serious challenge.

v. BELIZE

CAPITAL: Belmopan   AREA: 23,000 sq km   POPULATION: 188,000 ('90)
OFFICIAL LANGUAGE: English   POLITICAL SYSTEM: parliamentary democracy
HEAD OF STATE: Queen Elizabeth II
GOVERNOR-GENERAL: Dame Minita Elvira Gordon
RULING PARTY: People's United Party (PUP)
HEAD OF GOVERNMENT: George Price, Prime Minister (since Sept '89)
PRINCIPAL MINISTERS: Florencio Marin (deputy premier, industry & natural resources),
    Said Musa (foreign affairs & development), Glenn Godfrey (attorney-general)
INTERNATIONAL ALIGNMENT: NAM, ACP, Caricom, Cwth.
CURRENCY: Belize dollar (end-'92 £1=BZ$3.03, US$1=BZ$2.00)
GNP PER CAPITA: US$1,990 ('90)
MAIN EXPORT EARNERS: sugar, citrus products, fish, tourism

SIGNIFICANT political realignments arose out of consideration of the
detail of the Maritime Areas Bill, which was approved by parliament
on 17 January. The bill was an important step in smoothing relations
with Guatemala, (see AR 1991, p. 89–90), but the opposition United
Democratic Party (UDP) split over whether Belizean claims of territorial waters should be to three miles plus an exclusive economic
zone extending to the median line with Honduras, or whether the
territorial waters should be all those within the median line. Whilst the
UDP broadly backed the bill UDP dissidents advocated the latter position,
which would have deprived Guatemala of access to open waters. Five
leading UDP members resigned or were expelled on the issue. They
later formed the National Alliance for Belizean Rights (NABR), with
two parliamentary seats.
    The Belizean economy continued to be weakened through its agri-
cultural export dependency. Diseases on banana plantations and bad
weather damage to the major citrus crops, combined with low world
prices, harmed foreign exchange earnings. The major growth areas of
the economy were now construction, transport, communications and
utilities—all sectors relying on imported inputs, to the detriment of
the balance of trade. Attempts to encourage inward business investment through 'economic citizenship' were finally abandoned. However,
Belize's first export-processing zone was opened on the Mexican border,
while further links with the Mexican electricity grid confirmed the
gradual integration of Belize into the Central American economy. In
January Belize was invited to join the Central American Community.

vi.   GRENADA

CAPITAL: St. George's   AREA: 344 sq km   POPULATION: 91,000 ('90)
OFFICIAL LANGUAGE: English   POLITICAL SYSTEM: parliamentary democracy
HEAD OF STATE: Queen Elizabeth II   GOVERNOR-GENERAL: Sir Paul Scoon
RULING PARTY: National Democratic Congress (NDC)
HEAD OF GOVERNMENT: Nicholas Brathwaite, Prime Minister (since March '90)
PRINCIPAL MINISTERS: George Brizan (agriculture, trade & industry), Francis Alexis
   (attorney-general), Tillman Thomas (state, finance)
INTERNATIONAL ALIGNMENT: NAM, ACP, OAS, Caricom, Cwth.
CURRENCY: East Caribbean dollar (end-'92 £1=EC$4.09, US$1=EC$2.70)
GNP PER CAPITA: US$2,190 ('90)
MAIN EXPORT EARNERS: agricultural products, tourism

THE deep malaise affecting the Grenadian economy provoked a bizarre initiative by the National Democratic Congress (NDC) government, which launched its own structural adjustment programme without International Monetary Fund (IMF) or World Bank prompting. A government delegation dispatched to Washington in January sought IMF approval, not to secure IMF funds but to facilitate other multilateral and bilateral aid. In August a World Bank report criticized the Grenadian tax system following the February budget, asserting that the fiscal deficit was too high. The implementation of privatization measures gathered pace, including both the Genlec electricity company and the National Commercial Bank. The continued fall in revenue from Grenada's principal exports of bananas, cocoa, nutmeg and mace further weakened the economy. Throughout the year strikes in both the public and the private sector reflected deep dissatisfaction with the government, as also shown in opinion polls. Later in the year Prime Minister Nicholas Brathwaite indicated that he would not stand for re-election at the next general election.

vii.   THE BAHAMAS

CAPITAL: Nassau   AREA: 14,000 sq km   POPULATION: 255,000 ('90)
OFFICIAL LANGUAGE: English   POLITICAL SYSTEM: parliamentary democracy
HEAD OF STATE: Queen Elizabeth II   GOVERNOR-GENERAL: Sir Henry Taylor
RULING PARTY: Free National Movement (FNM)
HEAD OF GOVERNMENT: Hubert Ingraham, Prime Minister (since Aug '92)
PRINCIPAL MINISTERS: Orville Alton Turnquest (justice)
INTERNATIONAL ALIGNMENT: NAM, ACP, OAS, Cwth.
CURRENCY: Bahamas dollar (end-'92 £1=B$1.51, US$1=B$1.00)
GNP PER CAPITA: US$11,420 ('90)
MAIN EXPORT EARNERS: tourism, petroleum products

IN a dramatic shift of political fortune, Sir Lynden D. Pindling and his Progressive Liberal Party (PLP) were defeated in the August general election, after being in power since 1967. The Free National Movement (FNM) won 33 seats and the PLP only 16, this being a reversal of the previous distribution. The new Prime Minister, Hubert Ingraham, immediately launched an energetic shake-up of government and promised what were, by Bahamian standards, radical measures.

Declarations of a new era of open government were followed by the immediate proposal to overhaul the tax system to tighten up and streamline its operation. MP's and ministerial salaries were cut, and the long-debated sell-off and closure of, respectively, the Hotel Corporation and Bahamasair were finalized. The increasing meanderings and indecisiveness of the Pindling government seemed to have given way to a considered and open development strategy.

In an attempt to end the dominance of the old order, Mr Ingraham moved to break up the state television and radio monopoly, appointed three women to cabinet positions and sought to rationalize the range of tourist developments. Violence against tourists became a major problem, as was the increasing number of public figures involved in allegations of fraud or other financial crimes.

viii.   WINDWARD AND LEEWARD ISLANDS

St Kitts & Nevis
CAPITAL: Basseterre   AREA: 260 sq km   POPULATION: 40,000 ('90)
OFFICIAL LANGUAGE: English   POLITICAL SYSTEM: parliamentary democracy
HEAD OF STATE: Queen Elizabeth II
GOVERNOR-GENERAL: Clement Athelston Arrindell
RULING PARTY: People's Action Movement (PAM)
HEAD OF GOVERNMENT: Kennedy A. Simmonds, Prime Minister (since Feb '80)
CURRENCY: East Caribbean dollar (end-'92 £1=EC$4.09, US$1=EC$2.70)
GNP PER CAPITA: US$3,330 ('90)
MAIN EXPORT EARNERS: sugar, agricultural produce, tourism

Antigua & Barbuda
CAPITAL: St. John's   AREA: 440 sq km   POPULATION: 79,000 ('90)
OFFICIAL LANGUAGE: English   POLITICAL SYSTEM: parliamentary democracy
HEAD OF STATE: Queen Elizabeth II
GOVERNOR-GENERAL: Sir Wilfred Ebenezer Jacobs
RULING PARTY: Antigua Labour Party (ALP)
HEAD OF GOVERNMENT: C. Vere Bird Sr, Prime Minister (since Feb '76)
CURRENCY: East Caribbean dollar (end-'92 £1=EC$4.09, US$1=EC$2.70)
GNP PER CAPITA: US$4,600 ('88)
MAIN EXPORT EARNERS: tourism, miscellaneous manufactures

Dominica
CAPITAL: Roseau   AREA: 750 sq km   POPULATION: 72,000 ('90)
OFFICIAL LANGUAGE: English   POLITICAL SYSTEM: parliamentary republic
HEAD OF STATE: President Sir Clarence Augustus Seignoret
RULING PARTY: Dominica Freedom Party (DFP)
HEAD OF GOVERNMENT: Mary Eugenia Charles, Prime Minister (since July '80)
CURRENCY: East Caribbean dollar (end-'92 £1=EC$4.09, US$1=EC$2.70)
GNP PER CAPITA: US$2,210 ('90)
MAIN EXPORT EARNERS: bananas, tourism

St Lucia

CAPITAL: Castries   AREA: 616 sq km   POPULATION: 150,000 ('90)
OFFICIAL LANGUAGE: English   POLITICAL SYSTEM: parliamentary democracy
HEAD OF STATE: Queen Elizabeth II
GOVERNOR-GENERAL: Stanislaus A. James (acting)
RULING PARTY: United Workers' Party (UWP)
HEAD OF GOVERNMENT: John Compton, Prime Minister (since '64)
CURRENCY: East Caribbean dollar (end-'92 £1=EC$4.09, US$1=EC$2.70)
GNP PER CAPITA: US$1,900 ('90)
MAIN EXPORT EARNERS: agricultural products, tourism

St Vincent & the Grenadines

CAPITAL: Kingstown   AREA: 390 sq km   POPULATION: 107,000 ('90)
OFFICIAL LANGUAGE: English   POLITICAL SYSTEM: parliamentary democracy
HEAD OF STATE: Queen Elizabeth II   GOVERNOR-GENERAL: David Jack
RULING PARTY: New Democratic Party (NDP)
HEAD OF GOVERNMENT: James F. Mitchell, Prime Minister (since '72)
CURRENCY: East Caribbean dollar (end-'92 £1=EC$4.09, US$1=EC$2.70)
GNP PER CAPITA: US$1,720 ('90)
MAIN EXPORT EARNERS: bananas, tourism, agricultural produce

Montserrat

CAPITAL: Plymouth   AREA: 102 sq km   POPULATION:12,200 ('90)
OFFICIAL LANGUAGE: English   POLITICAL SYSTEM: democracy under UK rule
GOVERNOR-GENERAL: David G. P. Taylor
RULING PARTY: Nationl Progressive Party (NPP)
HEAD OF GOVERNMENT: Reuben Meade, Chief Minister (since Oct '91)
CURRENCY: East Caribbean dollar (end-'92 £1=EC$4.09, US$1=EC$2.70)
MAIN EXPORT EARNERS: banking, tourism

RELATIVELY buoyant economic activity in ST KITTS & NEVIS, manifested through a steady increase in tourism receipts and sugar production, allowed Prime Minister Kennedy Simmons to announce a range of tax increases in the June budget. Increases were necessary, in part to deal with the EC$30 million public deficit. Relative political security allowed Mr Simmonds to dismiss his increasingly dissenting but popular deputy, Michael Powell, in April, provoking street demonstrations. Elections for the Nevis Assembly in June resulted in the Concerned Citizens' Movement winning three of the five seats, the remaining two going to the Nevis Reformation Party.

ANTIGUA & BARBUDA continued to be rocked by scandal and riddled with intrigue, as Prime Minister Vere Bird was subject to constant and increasing charges of theft and corruption. Despite a series of large demonstrations calling for his resignation, including one on 27 February during which 200 demonstrators were shot at by police using teargas and rubber bullets and 30 arrests were made, Mr Bird clung tenaciously to power. Society-wide condemnation, from Archbishop Orland Lindsay to cricketer Viv Richards as well as from the three main opposition parties, failed to move him. Almost casually, he announced his intention to retire in 1994 after demonstrations by 10,000 people had failed to provoke a more precipitate departure.

Following a special meeting on 26 March, the three opposition formations merged to form a single party called the United Progressive

Party (UPP). The Chamber of Commerce threatened a campaign of non-payment of taxes if the Prime Minister did not give a full account of himself. High-handed manipulation of procedure ensured an effective end to parliamentary scrutiny. Elections were not due until 1994.

Attempts in DOMINICA to encourage inward foreign investment through the offer of 'economic citizenship' to investors from the Pacific Rim (almost exclusively from Taiwan) not only failed to live up to expectations but also generated considerable popular hostility. By year's end Prime Minister Eugenia Charles was obliged to tighten up the conditions of citizenship (though extending its geographical catchment area). Whilst the GDP growth rate decreased, and inflation and unemployment increased, the government was faced with external debt repayments equivalent to more than 11 per cent of government revenue.

In the wake of bitter allegations by the opposition Labour Party (SLP) that constituency boundaries in ST LUCIA were being gerrymandered in preparation for the April general election, the ruling United Workers' Party (UWP) was returned to office. Prime Minister John Compton's UWP won 11 seats and the SLP 6 seats. Mr Compton's new cabinet included the first woman Attorney-General, Lorraine Williams.

In ST VINCENT & THE GRENADINES, the New Democratic Party (NDP) government of James Mitchell remained firmly in charge. In a major reshuffle in January, Mr Mitchell appointed Herbert Young as Foreign Minister and also created new ministries for trade and consumer affairs and for Grenadines affairs.

Recovery from the 1989–90 banking turmoil in MONTSERRAT was further confirmed as the Legislative Council approved new and stricter measures controlling offshore financial companies. Since the scandal, 319 offshore banks had been closed, with only 21 offshore banks and three commercial banks were still permitted to operate. Inquiries into a stolen car racket implicated Chief Minister Reuben Meade, but a motion of no confidence in him was defeated on 10 November.

ix. SURINAME

CAPITAL: Paramaribo   AREA: 163,000 sq km   POPULATION: 447,000 ('90)
OFFICIAL LANGUAGE: Dutch   POLITICAL SYSTEM: republic, under military tutelage
HEAD OF STATE: President Ronald Venetiaan (since Sept '91)
RULING PARTIES: New Front for Democracy and Development, consisting of the
    Suriname National (NPS), Progressive Reform (VHP) and Unity and Harmony
    (KTPI) parties, plus the Suriname Labour Party (SPA)
PRINCIPAL MINISTERS: Jules Ajodhia (vice-president, head of government),
    Subhaas Mungra (VHP/foreign affairs), Siegfried Gilds (SPA/defence), Eddy Sedoc
    (NPS/finance), Soecil Girvasing (justice & police)
INTERNATIONAL ALIGNMENT: NAM, ACP, OAS
CURRENCY: Suriname guilder (end-'92 £1=Sf2.71, US$1=Sf1.79)
GNP PER CAPITA: US$3,050 ('90)
MAIN EXPORT EARNERS: bauxite/alumina, aluminium, rice

THE return to civilian and democratic rule was consolidated when constitutional amendments were approved on 25 March limiting army functions to national defence, banning serving army officers from representative public offices and transforming the State Council into an advisory body only (thereby removing its legislative veto power). Further amendments were under consideration.

A peace agreement between the two largest guerrilla groups and the government was finally signed on 8 August. Under its terms the Jungle Commando and Tucayana Amazonas agreed to suspend hostilities and, under the supervision of Organization of American States (OAS) officials, to hand over their weapons. An amnesty covering the period from 1985 was also agreed.

With the transition well on course, the Dutch government agreed to release US$720 million in aid, frozen since 1982. This would be of considerable help to the government, which inherited a budget deficit of some 650 million guilders. Former military leader Lt.-Colonel Desi Bouterse, now believed to be the richest man in Suriname, resigned as commander-in-chief of the army on 20 November. Over 1,600 Surinamese refugees remained in French Guiana, reluctant to return to Suriname because they were principally from the Moiwana area, site of an army massacre in 1987.

x. NETHERLANDS ANTILLES AND ARUBA

Netherlands Antilles
CAPITAL: Willemstad (Curaçao)   AREA: 800 sq km   POPULATION: 189,000 ('90)
OFFICIAL LANGUAGES: Dutch Papiamento, English
POLITICAL SYSTEM: parliamentary democracy under Dutch crown
GOVERNOR: Jaime Saleh
RULING PARTIES: National People's Party (PNP) heads coalition
HEAD OF GOVERNMENT: Maria Liberia Peters, Prime Minister (since May '88)
CURRENCY: Neth. Antilles guilder (end-'92 £1=NAf2.71, US$1=NAf1.79)
GNP PER CAPITA: US$5,300 ('88)
MAIN EXPORT EARNERS: oil, tourism

Aruba
CAPITAL: Oranjestad   AREA: 193 sq km   POPULATION: 61,000 ('90)
OFFICIAL LANGUAGE: Dutch
POLITICAL SYSTEM: parliamentary democracy under Dutch crown
GOVERNOR: Felipe B. Trompe
RULING PARTIES: People's Electoral Movement (MEP) heads coalition
HEAD OF GOVERNMENT: Nelson Oduber, Prime Minister (since Feb '89)
CURRENCY: Aruba guilder (end-'92 £1=Af2.71, US$1=Af1.79)
GNP PER CAPITA: US$12,000 ('88)
MAIN EXPORT EARNERS: oil, tourism

ST Maarten island in the NETHERLANDS ANTILLES was placed under Dutch 'curatorship' following the arrest of the former deputy prime minister, Louis Crastell Gumbs. Investigations into the integrity of the administration of St Maarten were initiated. Future official Dutch aid of 275 million guilders was to be carefully targeted and monitored to ensure appropriate use. The general economic and administrative crisis put the National People's Party (PNP) government of Maria Liberia Peters under considerable pressure. Employers and trade unions, as well as the government's Bonaire coalition partner, the Patriotic Union (UPB), were unhappy with policy and began to demand a general election. The constitutional and administrative status of St Maartens remained unresolved at year's end. There was a major expansion of Brazilian investment and trade with Curaçao, which now conducted 40 per cent of its trade with Brazil.

V MIDDLE EAST AND NORTH AFRICA

1. ISRAEL

CAPITAL: Jerusalem   AREA: 22,000 sq km   POPULATION: 5,200,000 ('92)
OFFICIAL LANGUAGE: Hebrew   POLITICAL SYSTEM: parliamentary democracy
HEAD OF STATE: President Chaim Herzog (since May '83)
RULING PARTIES: Labour Party (ILP) heads coalition with Meretz and Shas parties
HEAD OF GOVERNMENT: Yitzhak Rabin (ILP), Prime Minister (since July '92)
PRINCIPAL MINISTERS: Shimon Peres (ILP/foreign affairs), Michael Harish (ILP/trade &
   industry), Avraham Shohat (ILP/finance), David Libai (ILP/justice), Aryeh Der'i
   (Shas/interior), Shimon Shitrit (ILP/economy & social development)
CURRENCY: new shekel (end-'92 £1=NIS4.18, US$1=NIS2.76)
GNP PER CAPITA: US$10,920 ('90)
MAIN EXPORT EARNERS: diamonds, machinery, agricultural produce, tourism

THE year began with a brewing political crisis that brought down
Yitzhak Shamir's government prematurely. The process of collapse,
culminating in mid-January in the defection of the Moledet and Tehiya
Parties from the ruling coalition, was triggered by the withdrawal of
General Rafael Eitan's Tsomet party from the government in December
1991, on account of Mr Shamir's failure to honour a pledge that he
would allow a free vote in the Knesset on electoral reform (see AR
1991, p. 203). The general election was set for 23 June, some five
months before its due time.

The last act of the outgoing Knesset in March was to pass a diluted
electoral reform measure providing for the direct election of the Prime
Minister in a simultaneous but separate ballot from the Knesset poll.
This first major reform of the electoral system since the state was
established in 1948 was passed only when the bill was amended to
delay its effect until the election after that of 1992, which relieved
Prime Minister Shamir himself of the necessity to run under the new
system. Mr Shamir called off the party whips and allowed a free vote.
The new law was intended to strengthen the Prime Minister's personal
position, in order to reduce the leverage of small parties in the process
of forming a new government.

In the run-up to the election the Labour Party switched leaders,
dropping Shimon Peres in favour of Yitzhak Rabin under a new
primary election process involving the entire rank and file membership,
which earned Labour public credit for its successful democratization.
Mr Shamir's Likud, in the meantime, presented the electorate with a
dismal spectacle of rivalry and acrimony among its leaders, as well as
a ramshackle organization.

The general election swept the Labour Party back to power. However,
although the Labour trounced Likud, the Labour camp as a whole only
narrowly headed the right-wing nationalist camp, which retained the

support of the majority of religious Israelis. Labour itself obtained 44 seats in the Knesset compared with Likud's 32. Expectations of rapid change failed to take into account that Labour and its natural allies mustered only 61 seats in the 120-seat Knesset, including five Arab votes on which no Jewish Prime Minister would wish to depend for the survival of a government. By persuading Shas, the Sephardic religious party (six seats), to join Labour and the radical Meretz alliance (12 seats) in a left-of-centre coalition, Mr Rabin was able to form a government commanding 62 votes.

That this coalition was fragile became evident in early November, when the government narrowly survived a battery of no-confidence votes. The opposition mounted its challenge on the diplomacy of the peace process, but the government almost came unstuck on the unrelated issue of religious secular relations. Shas, responding to the constant impugning of its religious credentials by opposition religious parties, put on a show of displeasure at criticisms of religious values and practices uttered by Education Minister Shulamit Aloni, leader of Meretz. In return for a contrite apology from Mrs Aloni to the religious community, Shas absented itself from the confidence votes, thus enabling the government to survive.

Under Israel's system of precise proportional representation, the composition of the newly-elected 13th Knesset reflected the deadlock within the Israeli public on the issues of peace with the Arabs. Those favouring a return of occupied territory to Arab sovereignty were more or less evenly matched in public opinion against those who would not yield an inch for peace. The media focused their attention on the improved prospects under Mr Rabin's leadership for a revival of the desultory peace process, but the decision of the voters more probably reflected dissatisfaction with the lacklustre performance of the Shamir government than any significant swing in favour of a new policy towards the Arabs.

Apart from Labour's own strong showing under its old-new leader, the election yielded gains to Meretz, the civil rights-plus-peace alignment, and to Tsomet on the far right, which achieved eight seats in the Knesset. Notable changes included the failure of Tehiya on the far right to gain any representation, and the partial recovery of the mainstream nationalist/religious group Mafdal, at the expense of the ultra-orthodox Agudah alignment.

Mr Rabin formed his new government with record speed, within three weeks of the election. The most surprising of his appointments was that of Mrs Aloni to the Ministry of Education, which in recent years had been headed by a member of the National Religious Party. The appointment of Mrs Aloni, who was regarded as the most uncompromising opponent of religious influence, seemed to signal that Mr Rabin intended to put a stop to the tendency of secularist governments in recent years to submit to religious demands. At the same time, Mr Rabin tried to widen the coalition to include both the secularist Tsomet and the opposition religious parties. In the hope of inducing additional party participation, he kept three portfolios open until December, when he finally admitted failure and allocated them to his coalition partners. These appointments gave the radical Yossi Sarid of Meretz a seat in the government as Minister for Environment.

One effect of Mr Rabin's convincing victory over Mr Peres in the Labour leadership battle earlier in the year, and of the former's strong personal performance in the election campaign, was to enhance the Prime Minister's position in government. This effect was reinforced by the electoral reform providing for a separate election for the premiership next time. In the event of an early general election, before Likud could put its house in order and choose a new generation of leaders, Mr Rabin personally could expect to be elected easily and to carry his party on his coat-tails. This scenario perhaps accounted in part for Mr Rabin's novel presidential style of government, which enabled him to act without due consultation, and possibly too hastily, in responding in mid-December to terrorist acts by Hamas, the rejectionist Islamic fundamentalist movement active among the Palestinians under Israeli occupation.

In fact, Israel's year both began and ended under a cloud of international opprobrium. Following the deportation in January of 11 Palestinians, on 17 December the government ordered the temporary expulsion of 415 more. The latter deportees were considered to be leaders of Hamas, which Israel held responsible for terrorist strikes against Israelis and for the killing of scores of Palestinians thought to be collaborators. The immediate impulse for the December expulsions was the kidnap and murder of an Israeli policeman by Hamas activists. (For casualty figures over the five years of the Palestinian *intifada*, see V.2.i.)

Mr Rabin's two-year banishment of the entire intellectual leadership of Hamas, following a plan favoured by Chief of Staff Ehud Barak, was intended to contain at a stroke the spread of this terrorist movement among the disaffected Palestinian population. It was widely reported in the Israeli press that the Prime Minister took the decision alone, after hearing advice only from his small circle of military advisers, without good intelligence about the likely reaction of Lebanon to having over 400 Islamic radicals dumped in its territory. Many members of the government were said afterwards not to have realized the scale of the intended expulsion to which they were being asked to agree.

The Prime Minister had calculated, wrongly, that the PLO would applaud Israel's blow to its rival and challenger, Hamas, whose organization was believed in Israel to have been funded by Saudi Arabia in retaliation for the PLO's support for Iraq during the Gulf War. The

Lebanese refusal to accept the 415 exiles or to allow relief to be brought to them through Lebanese territory ensured maximum media attention to their plight, stranded as they were on a wintry hillside without basic provisions or shelter. Mr Rabin appeared willing to ride out the resultant chorus of condemnation, remaining convinced that the peace process would continue as scheduled soon after the installation of the new American President. There was no doubt that Mr Rabin's intention was to seek peace with the Palestinians and Syria, his reputation having been staked on achieving this within a short time. In that the act of banishment might indeed prove to be fatal to the peace process, it was a blunder rather than a calculated act of bad faith.

Immediately after his election victory, Mr Rabin managed to establish more cordial relations between Israel and the United States. By October he had secured a US promise of loan guarantees for up to $10,000 million in loans, which had been denied to Mr Shamir on account of his continued building of Jewish settlements, regarded as illegal, on the West Bank. The new government immediately terminated new building contracts on the West Bank and stopped work on any construction regarded as political rather than strategic in nature. Although Russian immigration decreased, to some 60,000 arrivals in the year, unemployment remained at a high of over 11 per cent. Nevertheless, the economy remained relatively stable and year-on-year inflation was under 10 per cent for the first time since the late 1960s.

In diplomatic breakthroughs in January and February respectively, China and India established formal diplomatic relations with Israel for the first time. On 9 March Menachem Begin, the Prime Minister who made peace with Egypt and then made war on the Palestinians in Lebanon, died aged 78 (see XX: OBITUARY).

2. ARAB WORLD—EGYPT—JORDAN—SYRIA—LEBANON–IRAQ

i. THE ARAB WORLD

SADDAM Husain's survival in Iraq, a still important Arab state, encouraged the Arab opponents of peace and distracted its Western champions. Islamic fundamentalism, though repressed in Algeria, remained potent in Tunisia and menacing in Egypt, with Sudan serving as its conduit from Iran; the latter also used its age-old links with south Lebanon to maintain instability. Among the Israeli-occupied Palestinians fundamentalism became stronger than traditional secular nationalism. Hopes of peace there, based on the advent of a more pragmatic Israeli Prime Minister (see V.1), were largely disappointed; the mounting tendency on both sides to reach for their guns did not help. In fact, the chances of peace seemed little if at all better in

December than in January, despite sincere efforts by the outgoing US administration and some of the Arab leaders.

Those efforts included round after round (six in 1992) of talks between the five parties to the dispute, besides sundry other meetings concerning subsidiary issues. At times the Jordanian and the Palestinian—even sometimes the Syrian and Israeli—representatives seemed to be moving towards businesslike compromises. The Palestinian-Jordanians appeared ready to accept that an independent Palestinian state could only be achieved, if at all, after years of limited but genuine autonomy. The new Israeli government would surrender some at least of the spoils of 1967, Syria recognizing that its basic national interest was simply to recover the Golan.

Hopes were brightest after the change of government in Jerusalem. Before that the Israelis had offered only 'autonomy of persons, not of territory', giving the Palestinians no control over defence, foreign affairs or settlement in the occupied territories (OT). Moreover, the Shamir government had not only refused to negotiate with the PLO or with any Palestinians other than those resident in the OT (from which Israel insisted on excluding East Jerusalem) but had also tried to debar those who had had contact with the PLO (e.g. in Jordan) by arresting them or preventing them from leaving for Washington. For their part, the Palestinian representatives sometimes boycotted the talks because of high-handed Israeli behaviour in the OT.

When the talks reconvened after the Israeli elections, this being their sixth round, Yitzhak Rabin's government made an apparently serious effort to improve the atmosphere. It announced the impending release of 800 of the 7,429 Palestinians imprisoned as a result of the *intifada* (another 300 were held without trial), cancelled 12 deportation orders against alleged PLO supporters and promised an amendment to existing legislation banning contacts between Israelis and the PLO.

These mitigations of the regime in the OT followed an important change in US policy. The Shamir government had busied itself, despite US objections, in settling Jews in the OT. On becoming Prime Minister, Mr Rabin said that his government would freeze Jewish settlement in the OT, except in areas 'vital to security' or to so-called strategic settlements. Although the US government did not accept this distinction, in August President Bush withdrew his objections to the $10,000 million loan guarantee sought by Israel (see AR 1991, p. 206). The ensuing legislation made no explicit link between the loan guarantee and settlements. Talks in Washington between Israelis and Arabs continued throughout the autumn, with a break for the US elections, but had recorded few positive results as the year ended.

A different scenario was often playing in the territories whose future the negotiators in Washington were supposed to be discussing. In February the Israeli army eased restrictions on soldiers opening fire on civilians and in April an Israeli human rights group alleged that each year 5,000 Palestinians were tortured by security forces. Meanwhile, Palestinians were regularly killing compatriots accused of collaboration. Even after the change of government, Israeli security forces and Palestinian activists went on killing each other; the less well-armed Palestinians died more often. In November it was reported that during the five years of the *intifada* Israeli forces had killed 959 Palestinians, while Palestinians had killed 103 Israelis, along with no less than 543 Palestinian 'collaborators'. Israeli deaths inspired, strengthened and multiplied hard-line Israeli right-wingers and weakened the doves; Palestinian deaths raised the fervour and influence of the Islamic organization Hamas. The latter began to rival the PLO, marking the spread among Palestinians of the fundamentalist wave in other Arab lands and threatening the previous non-confessionalism of the national movement, in which Christians were often prominent.

This reciprocal barbarization reached its peak in December, when several Israeli deaths, especially the murder of a kidnapped policeman, led the government to placate public opinion by arresting Hamas members en masse and expelling over 400 of them, without trial, into the no-man's-land between Israel and Lebanon (see also V.1). In Lebanon the new and more resolute government refused to admit the deportees as refugees, since that would have allowed the Israelis an escape from their responsibilities and intensified Lebanon's existing problems with Hizbullah (see V.2.v). The Israeli action was immediately condemned by the UN Security Council.

The marginalization of the PLO continued in 1992. This was partly a reflection of the rise of Hamas, partly because the PLO could not now, after its pro-Iraqi attitude in the Gulf War, count on largesse from the Arab oil states. In May the PLO in Tunis approved Palestinian participation in the peace process but in so doing distanced itself further from the two hard-line (but not fundamentalist) organizations, the Popular Front for the Liberation of Palestine (PFLP) and the Democratic Front for the Liberation of Palestine (DFLP). In July the PLO demanded a freeze on Jewish settlements in the OT and advocated early elections there to choose a legislative council for a five-year transitional period. The PLO central committee met in Tunis in October and by a narrow margin—the PFLP and DFLP voting against—again approved participation in the peace process.

Yassir Arafat, the PLO chairman, had personal as well as political difficulties. He was embarrassed by the leaking of the news of his secret marriage in February to a much younger Greek Orthodox lady while in April he survived an aircraft crash-landing in Libya, and had to be treated in an Amman hospital. However, this experience seemed to seal his reconciliation with King Husain of Jordan, who visited him in hospital and conferred a high decoration on him.

ii.   EGYPT

CAPITAL: Cairo   AREA: 1,000,000 sq km   POPULATION: 55,000,000 ('92 est.)
OFFICIAL LANGUAGE: Arabic   POLITICAL SYSTEM: presidential democracy
HEAD OF STATE AND GOVERNMENT: President Mohammed Husni Mubarak (since '81)
RULING PARTY: National Democratic Party (NDP)
PRINCIPAL MINISTERS: Atif Sidqi (prime minister), Kamal Ahmed Ganzouri
    (deputy premier, finance, economy & planning), Yusuf Amin Wali (deputy
    premier, agriculture), Gen. Mohammed Hussein Tantawi Sulayman (defence),
    Amr Mohammed Moussa (foreign affairs), Mohammed Abdel-Halim Moussa
    (interior), Mohammed al-Razaz (finance), Farouk Seif al-Nasr (justice)
INTERNATIONAL ALIGNMENT: NAM, Arab League, OAPEC, ACC, OAU, ICO, Francophonie
CURRENCY: Egyptian pound (end-'92 £1=LE5.03, US$1=LE3.32)
GNP PER CAPITA: US$600 ('90)
MAIN EXPORT EARNERS: oil and gas, cotton, tourism, agricultural produce

THE government's main preoccupations were fundamentalist trouble-making and a shaky economy, which tended to intensify each other. Foreign affairs were less important. President Husni Mubarak had less to fear than Arab leaders further east from the influence of Saddam Husain of Iraq, with whom Egyptians were disinclined to sympathize. Nor had Egypt, whose relations with Israel had been decided in the 1970s, to face such ticklish problems as other Arabs from the vicissitudes of the Middle East peace process (see V.2.i). On 12 October a severe earthquake hit Cairo.

Ever since the end of Nasser and his unambiguous hostility to the Muslim Brotherhood, Egyptian governments had tended to invoke Islamic sentiment, or to buy it off, only to find that they had released a genie from its bottle. This year, just as Algeria was demonstrating how threatening this could be (see V.4.iv), the authorities appeared unwilling to resist several fundamentalist encroachments on intellectual freedom.

In February the government discovered a subversive fundamentalist plot among computer staff and other intellectuals; this and other similar manifestations were reportedly linked to intrigues from Sudan, Iran and other countries. Early in March a policeman in the Fayyum was killed in a confrontation with fundamentalists, who, besides their presence in some poorer districts of Cairo, were particularly active in Upper Egypt. Some anti-Coptic outrages (in and around Asyut, for example, 11 Copts were murdered in May, and six more in June by a mob of looters) were perhaps connected with traditional feuds rather than with fundamentalism, whose leaders condemned them; but others were clearly fundamentalist in origin.

Upper Egypt was the centre of another fundamentalist activity—attacks on foreign tourists, which continued throughout the year; several tourists, including one Briton, were killed. In November an anti-tourist campaign was reported in Alexandria. Shaikh Umar Abdurrahman, leader of the Jama'at al Islamiyya, publicly attacked the very concept of tourism and threatened to destroy the Pharoanic sites which attracted it. By year's end tourist numbers had reportedly fallen by 40 per cent and foreign currency earnings by $1,500 million.

Copts and tourists were not the only victims. On 31 May an intellectual, Faraj Fudah, publicly advocated the complete separation of church and state. A week later he was murdered by adherents of Jihad, which had reportedly been responsible for the deaths of President Sadat and of Rifa'at al Mahjub (see AR 1981, p. 192; 1990, p. 205). The Muslim Brotherhood declared that blame lay with government for not forbidding provocations against Muslims.

The government prepared to confront the danger. On 30 March President Mubarak declared that Egypt's progress was being impeded by, inter alia, doctrinal divisions and fundamentalism. In June he promised new legislation against terrorism, which was approved by parliament on 16 July with only 23 deputies voting against. This legislation imposed the death sentence for some terrorist crimes. By 1 August nearly 400 people had been arrested, mostly in Upper Egypt. Terrorism continued, however, and in October it was reported that those accused of it would be tried in military courts. The Jama'at, doubtless using a Koranic definition of legitimacy, threatened to defend itself 'by all legitimate means'. In November privately-run mosques, suspected centres of fundamentalism, were put under the Ministry of Waqfs.

Religious opposition to the government was not confined to the lunatic fringes of terrorism. The now seemingly respectable Muslim Brotherhood, though again refused acknowledgement as a legal political party, was gaining influence among, for example, lawyers, doctors and engineers. Other professionals had long found 'Islamic' finance profitable (see AR 1988, p. 208); the government prepared to sell the assets of 'Islamic' banks (most, said the Chamber of Commerce, had been fraudulent) to pay off their depositors. To these operators, said President Mubarak in his 30 March speech, 'religion becomes a trade'.

The earthquake of 12 October reached 5.9 on the Richter scale, killed over 500 and wrecked many buildings, especially ill-built apartment blocks in poorer neighbourhoods. This gave the disaster political fall-out. Many of the collapsed blocks had been jerry-built by profiteers defying government regulation, and the state's help to victims of the disaster was slower than that afforded by fundamentalist organizations.

The Islamic surge went hand in hand with economic deterioration. The Gulf War had returned to Egypt many thousands of emigrants whom Egypt had difficulty in absorbing. Unemployment would soon reach 20 per cent, the population was climbing inexorably faster than resources and the country had reportedly spent, in six short months, $600 million on importing food. In the 1992/93 budget the government raised public sector pay by 20 per cent. There were mass demonstrations against price rises, especially when the railways increased fares by 25 per cent.

In these circumstances, as in 1977 (see AR 1977, p. 182), the remedies prescribed by orthodox finance seemed unrealistic, namely cuts in public expenditure, reduced subsidies, increased energy prices, privatization, trade liberalization and unified exchange rates. In the end, although the IMF thought Egypt had not done enough in these directions to deserve a new stand-by arrangement, it was agreed that the existing one would have to be prolonged into 1993.

Against this background run-of-the-mill foreign affairs attracted little attention, except insofar as they might be connected with Egypt's internal problems. Thus relations with the Sudan, seldom good, were impaired by suspicions that the Islamist-inspired government there had helped Iranian fundamentalist influence into Egypt. This aggravated friction over a frontier district where Egypt believed that the Sudanese were encroaching. President Mubarak welcomed the change of government in Israel, and Mr Rabin visited Cairo in July, the first Israeli Prime Minister to do so since 1986. President Mubarak said he would now visit Israel for the first time.

iii.   JORDAN

CAPITAL: Amman   AREA: 97,000 sq km   POPULATION: 3,200,000 ('90)
OFFICIAL LANGUAGE: Arabic
POLITICAL SYSTEM: monarchy
HEAD OF STATE AND GOVERNMENT: King Husain ibn Talal (since Aug '52)
PRINCIPAL MINISTERS: Field Marshal Sharif Zaid ibn Shaker (prime minister, defence),
    Dhuqan al-Hindawi (deputy premier, education), Ali al-Suhaymat (deputy
    premier, transport), Kamil Abu Jabir (foreign affairs), Basil Jardana (finance),
    Yusuf al-Mubayyidin (justice), Jawdat al-Subul (interior)
INTERNATIONAL ALIGNMENT: NAM, Arab League, ACC, ICO
CURRENCY: dinar (end-'92 £1=JD1.02, US$1=JD0.67)
GNP PER CAPITA: US$1,240 ('90)
MAIN EXPORT EARNERS: phosphates, chemicals, cement

KING Husain began to recover from his mistake in supporting Saddam Husain in the Gulf War and to repair relations with the West and its Arab allies. But there were still clouds on the horizon. The aftermath of the war aggravated Jordan's perennial economic hardships. The Saudis, resentful of Jordan's former support of Saddam Husain, added to them, besides being suspected of encouraging the fundamentalist opposition. The stalling of Middle East peace negotiations (see V.2.i) was a serious embarrassment. And the discovery that the King had cancer, while gaining him public sympathy, suggested that he might not long live to enjoy it.

The year began with a severe winter. Most crops in the north and some further south were reportedly destroyed; damage to infrastructure was severe. Total indebtedness was put by the central bank at $7,200 million, with large arrears of interest. Relations with the international financial community were uneasy. The IMF agreed to a stand-by loan; but creditors demanded terms which Jordan found unacceptable, while the IMF standby involved unpopular policies, especially a 35–40 per cent rise in oil prices, and consequent hardship. About 30 per cent of the workforce were unemployed and refugees formed a quarter of total population.

Many economic difficulties stemmed from the Gulf War, including the costs of a refugee influx (see AR 1991, p. 212) and the cessation of expatriates' remittances (somewhat mitigated by the surprisingly large funds they brought with them). The Saudis, irritated by Jordan's non-recognition of their primacy in organizing repairs to the Muslim shrines in Jerusalem, began to bar Jordanian produce from their markets. Further, Jordan's continuing trade with Iraq could be classified as 'sanctions-busting'. Iraq had continued to send oil to Jordan in part-payment of its debts; an American proposal to replace it from elsewhere was rejected as costlier. Another irritant was the Americans' naval anti-smuggling patrols; Jordan rejected the alternative of inspectors on Jordanian soil. The Jordanians attributed US action to mischief-making by the Saudis and Kuwaitis, the latter incensed by King Husain's criticism of their treatment of Palestinians. Relations with Egypt improved when he visited Cairo to offer condolences on the October earthquake (see V.2.ii).

A change was perceptible in Jordan's, and especially King Husain's, attitude to Iraq. True, he twice received Deputy Premier Tariq Aziz in Amman; but while in the United States in August he said, clearly referring to Saddam Husain, that he could not understand why some people were clinging to power. Later he spoke publicly of the need for change in Iraq, mentioning also the danger posed by tyrants and ambitious renegades. Jordan was indignant at executions of its merchants in Iraq for alleged economic crimes and Saddam's secret service harassment of Iraqi refugees in Jordan, one of whom was murdered in December. When the director of the US Central Intelligence Agency (CIA) visited Amman, the King denied that they had discussed how to topple the Iraqi leader. However, the CIA director embarrassingly commented later that King Husain had been far more helpful than the Saudi and Kuwaiti rulers. In November King Husain made a forthright attack on the latter, though not by name.

Jordan welcomed the apparent change in Israeli policy towards the Palestinians when Mr Rabin replaced Mr Shamir in June (see V.1). In late October Jordanian and Israeli officials gave the US government a joint draft agenda for talks about a settlement; however, it was later published, denounced in the Jordanian parliament and dropped. Yassir Arafat, the PLO leader, was honoured by the King and at least one

Jordanian spokesman appeared to advocate a confederal link between Jordan and a future Palestinian state. In broad terms, the Jordanian government demanded that Israel should establish a framework for its withdrawal from the occupied territories before entering peace negotiations with the Arab states.

Martial law was formally abolished on 3 March, while in July parliament legalized the formation of political parties. These relaxations told in favour of the fundamentalists, whose candidates were successful in various elections. In August police raids discovered arms caches linked to Hamas, the Islamic resistance movement in the occupied territories, and to another Islamic group, the Shabab al Nafir al Islami (Youths of the Islamic Vanguard), reportedly inspired from Iran and opposed to the Middle East peace process. Two deputies connected with Shabab (one being the most popular man in parliament) were arrested, tried and in November condemned for plotting to overthrow the monarchy. Less than a week later both were released on King Husain's birthday, the verdict having been found legally unsound.

The latter part of 1992 was clouded by news that King Husain had cancer. In August he had a kidney removed in the United States. On his return a month later reportedly over a million people came to greet him at the airport. He left for more tests in America in November, after saying on television that the life of a nation must not be measured by that of an individual.

iv. SYRIA

CAPITAL: Damascus   AREA: 185,000 sq km   POPULATION: 12,400,000 ('90)
OFFICIAL LANGUAGE: Arabic   POLITICAL SYSTEM: presidential
HEAD OF STATE AND GOVERNMENT: President Hafiz al-Asad (since March '71)
RULING PARTY: Baath Arab Socialist Party
VICE-PRESIDENTS: Abdul Halim Khaddam & Zuheir Masharqa
PRINCIPAL MINISTERS: Mahmud Zuabi (prime minister), Gen. Mustafa Tlas (deputy premier, defence), Salim Yassin (deputy premier, economic affairs), Faruq al-Shara (foreign affairs), Khalid Ansari (justice), Mohammad Harbah (interior)
INTERNATIONAL ALIGNMENT: NAM, Arab League, OAPEC, ICO
CURRENCY: Syrian pound (end-'92 £1=LS31.85, US$1=LS21.03)
GNP PER CAPITA: US$1,000 ('90)
MAIN EXPORT EARNERS: oil, cotton, textiles

As usual President Hafiz al-Asad seemed less attentive to internal than to external affairs such as Lebanon and the Israeli-occupied Golan Heights. Beirut's new government (see V.2.v) looked better able to control the troublesome factions there but perhaps less ready to accept Syrian tutelage. Israel seemed more flexible than before over the Golan; but President Asad's public vocabulary excluded the word compromise and Israel's new Prime Minister, Yitzhak Rabin, often used the word without following the principle. Syria remained in Lebanon and Israel in Golan. Relations with the West cooled as the common confrontation with Iraq receded.

Relations with Lebanon were dominated by the elections in that country. The government which emerged was less dependent on Christian militias, who had vainly demanded Syria's departure before the elections. But the Syrians wanted a stable and friendly government in place before they withdrew. The Lebanese elections had begun but no new government had been formed when President Asad met the Lebanese President at Lattakia in mid-September. They agreed to meet again after the elections to devise a timetable for withdrawal. In the event, the new Lebanese leadership agreed that the Syrian pull-out should be further delayed.

Before the Likud defeat in the Israeli elections in June, Damascus censured Israel's treatment of Hizbullah in Lebanon and accused Israel of sabotaging the peace process. Even when the incoming Israeli Prime Minister, Yitzhak Rabin, admitted that any settlement with Syria would need some Israeli compromise, such accommodating statements were usually followed by frosty Syrian comments. President Asad demanded a total Israeli withdrawal from the Golan; for him this issue clearly came first. Bur Mr Rabin, harried by Israeli settlers, insisted during the Washington talks (see V.2.i) that Syria must commit itself to a peace treaty before the return of the Golan could be discussed.

Relations with the United States were prickly. In February Washington refused Syria's request to be taken off the list of states deemed to be involved in terrorism and in June deprived it of preferential treatment under GATT rules because it allegedly refused workers their rights. For its part, Syria criticized Washington's unblocking the $10,000 million loan guarantee for Israel after Mr Rabin had replaced Mr Shamir (se V.1).

President Asad, traditionally Saddam Husain's most determined Arab enemy, was reported in March to have ended Syria's press campaign against Baghdad, opposed further military action against Iraq and to have generally modified its hostility. At the time, Syria was violently attacking the US government for its support of Israel. While touring the Gulf in April, President Asad tried, apparently unsuccessfully, to revive the concept of an Arab peace-keeping force in that region (see AR 1991, p. 212). The Gulf rulers were suspicious of a plan which they would be expected to finance, not to mention the possible drawbacks of the presence of Syrian (and Egyptian) troops in the Gulf. Kuwait's Foreign Minister visited Damascus in August to discuss the matter.

There was again tension with Turkey (see AR 1990, p. 210), which in April complained about the presence of Kurdish dissidents on Syrian or Syrian-controlled territory. However, in November Syria joined Turkey and Iran in expressing concern about Kurdish ambitions. In July the Turkish Prime Minister remarked that Euphrates river water was no more a Syrian or Iraqi concern than Syrian oil was of Turkey's. This gaffe provoked a lightning visit to Damascus by Turkey's Foreign Minister; it was agreed that Turkey would release more water for Syria and Iraq. The matter did not end there, however, and a Syrian-Turkish-Iraqi meeting in Damascus in October ended without agreement.

In the defence field there were other difficulties, mostly concerning Syrian attempts to acquire unusual weapons. In February German and Danish ships intercepted a cargo from North Korea containing missiles for Syria, over which the US government expressed concern. By October Washington was pressing India not to allow shipment to Syria of chemicals suitable for manufacturing nerve gas.

At home President Asad inaugurated his fourth term with a speech in parliament. He spoke vaguely of possible political and economic liberalizations—saying, according to one account, that Syria was too poor to afford Western-style democracy—and toughly about Israel and the United States. A new cabinet appointed in July contained few fresh faces, the most interesting being that of a senior oil company executive as Oil Minister. The inauguration was also marked by the release of 600, mostly political, prisoners. Later came news that Jews who so wished would be allowed to leave. In April the US government expressed alarm at arrests of human rights activists in Syria. In July Amnesty reported that thousands of political prisoners were still held; later on Jews were again being refused permission to leave Syria.

Syria's economic difficulties seemed undiminished. Total foreign debts were over $15,000 million, of which $400 million was owed to the World Bank. Russia's economic difficulties precluded further help from that quarter; indeed, the Russians began asking for their money back (perhaps about $15,000 million), although President Asad refused to see a delegation which came in November to discuss the issue. The Russians appeared to be still ready to deliver arms. China won a large contract for generating equipment and also offered arms. On 25 March Syria signed an agreement on nuclear safeguards with the IAEA.

The 1992 budget, approved on 11 May, showed expenditure slightly down in real terms, with 43 per cent being allocated to defence against 50 per cent in 1991. Inflation was believed to be about 10 per cent and growth in GNP 5–8 per cent.

The President's brother Rifa'at returned in July for their mother's funeral, but his chances of reinstatement suffered when he published a book in Paris attacking his brother's record. One chapter, devoted to Rifa'at's former boss, Defence Minister General Mustafa Tlas, was entitled '*La vache qui rit*'.

Dr Nureddin Atassi, President in 1965–70, was released in September after 22 years in gaol; he died in Paris on 3 December (see XX: OBITUARY).

v. LEBANON

CAPITAL: Beirut   AREA: 10,000 sq km   POPULATION: 2,670,000 ('85)
OFFICIAL LANGUAGE: Arabic   POLITICAL SYSTEM: presidential, based on power-sharing
HEAD OF STATE AND GOVERNMENT: President Elias Hrawi (since Nov '89)
RULING PARTIES: government of national unity
PRINCIPAL MINISTERS: Rafiq Hariri (prime minister), Michel al-Murr (deputy premier),
    Muhsin Dallul (defence), Faris Buwayz (foreign affairs), Bisharah Mirhij
    (interior), Bahij Tabbarah (justice), Hagob Yarman Dermerdjian (economy &
    trade)
INTERNATIONAL ALIGNMENT: NAM, Arab League, ICO, Francophonie
CURRENCY: Lebanese pound (end-'92 £1=LL2778.5, US$1=LL1835.2)
MAIN EXPORT EARNERS: agricultural products, precious metals and jewels

LEBANON underwent major changes in 1992. Militiamen were disarmed
and cleared from Beirut and the Lebanese army began returning to
the south. There, the deadly serious Hizbullah were different: facing
the Israelis and ready for martyrdom in the millennial Shia tradition,
they would not be disarmed, bought or frightened off. Their leaders,
devotees rather than gangsters, were backed financially from Iran.
Israeli attacks only intensified their zeal.

Beirut was in an economic crisis which foreign subsidies and the
smoke of gunfire had previously obscured. The central bank ceased trying to moderate currency fluctuations, the Lebanese pound plummeted
and inflation soared. The weakening of Maronite factions increased
Syrian power and made it more obvious. One well-born Prime Minister
followed another until a self-made multi-millionaire, Rafiq Hariri, left
his assured position in Saudi Arabia for a daunting premiership in
Lebanon. By mid-December, though hardly two months in office, he
had already made his mark by committing himself to the overriding task
of rescuing the economy and by robustly facing a moral and political
dilemma posed by Israel.

In January tension was already high around the 'security zone' in
south Lebanon nominally policed by Israel's surrogates, the South
Lebanon Army (SLA). They were besieging a village outside the
zone, claiming the right to extend the zone for security reasons.
Israel's forces, the SLA and the Hizbullah constantly exchanged fire.
In February Israel made retaliatory attacks, one directed personally at
the Hizbullah leader, Abbas Musawi; on 16 February he, his wife and
child died in an attack by an Israeli helicopter. Hizbullah retaliation
followed; it blew up an Israeli tank and killed four Israelis. In recurrent
and bloody exchanges throughout the year, Israel's reprisals did not
achieve the deterrence claimed for them, nor did Hizbullah's modify
Israel's ruthlessness.

The fighting militated against the reduction of the Syrian influence
which many, especially Maronite Christians, longed for. Maronite
politicians were already alarmed by government and Syrian plans to
hold parliamentary elections (the first since 1972) before Syrian forces

withdrew to the Beqaa valley, in accordance with the Taif Agreement of 1989.

Meanwhile, dissatisfaction with the economy and distrust of government were increasing. In mid-April the Lebanese pound fell below 1,500 to the US dollar, and a month later below 2,000. Government debt was in default and reportedly swelling by half a million dollars a day. Protest demonstrations in Beirut lasted three days and in Tyre the mob burned the house of the Economy Minister. On 6 May Prime Minister Omar Karami resigned; a week later Rashid al Solh formed an interim cabinet which key Maronite and Druze figures refused to support.

The Maronite politicians, with their patriarch's weighty support, denounced the plan to hold elections before Syria had withdrawn and refugees returned to their home constituencies; so did Amin Gemayel and other 'yesterday's men' from their Paris exile. But the Syrians were unwilling to withdraw until the establishment of a stable government not inimical to their interests.

The elections went ahead and lasted from August to October, being protracted by Maronite boycotts and, supposedly, by the inability of Lebanon's security forces to police them. Turnout seemed low; in some constituencies no Maronite candidates presented themselves. The Hizbullah did well. On 14 October the urgency of decisive action by a new government was underlined by an effective general strike.

In the new parliament, which met on 20 October, Muslims and Christians were evenly balanced. The moderate Shia leader, Nabih Berri, was elected Speaker and his followers formed the largest single group. On 22 October President Hrawi invited Rafiq Hariri to form a government—this news immediately increasing confidence and the value of the Lebanese pound.

The new Prime Minister, though mentioned earlier as a possibility, was fresh to Lebanese politics. He chose his cabinet (formed on 31 October) less for the customary inter-confessional balance than for administrative and technical competence. Some were new to politics, many of them Mr Hariri's personal friends and less accessible than their predecessors to Syrian influence. The new cabinet was supported by 104 of 119 deputies present, Hizbullah voting against.

Annual inflation had by now reached 170 per cent and Mr Hariri's declared priorities were economic, above all a reduction in the budget deficit, which he planned to limit to 41 per cent of expenditure. The new Prime Minister would reportedly apply a ruthless new broom to government, having concluded that the deficit stemmed largely from corruption and idleness in government offices, whose payroll could be drastically reduced.

The Lebanese and Syrian Presidents had announced in September that their coordinating body, the Lebanese-Syrian Council, would meet after the elections to formulate a plan for Syrian withdrawal. The problem was that, despite Christian eagerness for the withdrawal, Lebanon's own security forces were not yet able to replace Syria's in keeping order. When the Lebanese triumvirate—President, Prime Minister and Speaker—visited Damascus on 27 November, it was agreed that action on Syrian withdrawal and on the related 'deconfessionalization' of the political system could wait, since economic problems had precedence.

Now came an Israeli challenge to Lebanon which made an early Syrian withdrawal even less likely. Jerusalem's decision in December illegally to expel over 400 Palestinians and to rely on Lebanon to take them in (see V.1; V.2.i) faced the Beirut government with the cruel alternative of leaving the deportees to freeze and starve in no-man's-land or to infuriate Syria and irritate other Arabs by helping Israel to evade its moral and legal responsibilities. There was no sign that Lebanon even contemplated doing so, and Mr Hariri told a UN envoy pleading for Lebanese help for the expellees that he was wasting his time.

Suleiman Franjieh, a Maronite leader from the northern town of Zghorta who had been President of Lebanon in 1970–76, died aged 82 on 23 July (see XX:OBITUARY.)

vi.   IRAQ

CAPITAL: Baghdad   AREA: 438,000 sq km   POPULATION: 18,900,000 ('90)
OFFICIAL LANGUAGE: Arabic   POLITICAL SYSTEM: presidential
HEAD OF STATE AND GOVERNMENT: President Saddam Husain (since July '79), also
   Chairman of Revolutionary Command Council and Prime Minister
RULING PARTY: Baath Arab Socialist Party
PRINCIPAL MINISTERS: Muhammad Hamzah al-Zubaydi (prime minister), Tariq Aziz
   (deputy premier), Watban Ibrahim al-Hasan (interior), Muhammad Said Kazim
   al-Sahhaf (foreign affairs), Lt-Gen Amir Hammoudi al Saadi (industry & military
   industrialization), Usamah Abd al-Razzaq Hummadi al-Hithi (oil), Ali Hasan al-
   Majid (defence), Shabib Lazim al-Maliki (justice)
INTERNATIONAL ALIGNMENT: NAM, Arab League, OPEC, OAPEC, ACC, ICO
CURRENCY: dinar (end-'92 £1=ID0.59, US$1=ID0.39)
GNP PER CAPITA: US$3,020 ('80)
MAIN EXPORT EARNERS: oil and gas

DESPITE contrary appearances, little changed during 1992. Iraq's compliance with UN resolutions remained incomplete. The organization continued, under Western pressure but against Arab inclinations, to impose sanctions and a blockade and to seek out and destroy President Saddam Husain's unconventional weapons. The Kurds, partially protected by allied aircraft based in a reluctant Turkey, maintained a precarious hold. Later, a similar umbrella, based on US vessels in the Gulf, gave some protection to anti-Saddam Shias in the south by stopping Iraqi flights there, but could not counter Iraqi pressures on land. President Saddam and his Takriti mafia remained dominant, despite periodic reports of abortive conspiracies and executed conspirators, and were not seriously threatened by Iraqi exiles.

The Iraqi leader persistently rejected the UN's offer to permit limited sales of Iraqi oil to finance essential imports, UN operations and reparations (see also XI.1). His failure to comply fully with UN resolutions left the sanctions in place; Iraq's last unsuccessful attempt to have them lifted was in late November. So the Iraqi people's privations continued to be severe—and fully exploited by official propaganda.

Once the allies had refused to accept Iraq's evasion of its obligations under the ceasefire and threatened to renew hostilities, Saddam allowed the various UN teams to locate and begin destroying his unconventional arsenal, protesting the while that Iraq's sovereignty was being violated. Thus, though the UN's inspectors were harassed by 'spontaneous' demonstrations, they soon began destroying Iraq's chemical weapons stocks. Initially, Iraq asserted its freedom to hold unconventional weapons and to refuse UN inspection, whereupon Washington moved an aircraft carrier to the Gulf. By mid-March Iraq had agreed to the destruction of its missile-making equipment and furnished details of its ballistic and chemical warfare programmes.

Next, UN teams began searching for Scud missiles and destroying chemical rockets. A key nuclear plant was destroyed by 31 May. July saw a similar confrontation over chemical weapons. The Iraqis refused to allow inspection of a suspect building; a US warning followed. Eventually Saddam's chief henchman, Tariq Aziz, suggested that no US or UK inspectors should be included; the search went ahead, but found nothing. Saddam trumpeted this as a triumph.

Similarly, Iraq at first defied, but later accepted, Western demands for compliance with an air exclusion zone, south of the 32nd parallel. This was imposed in August (on the model of one already in force north of the 36th parallel to safeguard the Kurds) as protection for Shias. By 1 September Baghdad had accepted the *fait accompli*. On 27 December an Iraqi fighter crossed the line and was shot down. Other sequences of defiance and eventual compliance concerned Iraq's agreement to the stationing of UN personnel; the northern exclusion zone, which Iraqi air and ground forces entered in late March but evacuated when ordered out; and the proposed new frontier with Kuwait, which deprived Iraq of several oil wells and bisected the new port of Umm Qasr. This frontier was endorsed by the UN Security Council in late August, despite Iraqi protests and threatening behaviour.

Apart from the destruction of Iraq's weapons, the withdrawal of Iraqi forces from Kurdistan and the Kurds' establishment of a joint authority of their own were the most important allied achievements. In February the Kurdish leader, Masud Barzani, helped to secure allied and Turkish agreement to continued stationing of allied aircraft in Turkey to protect the Kurds. This protective shield depended on Turkish goodwill, which was severely tried when Turkish Kurds crossed the frontier and met only half-hearted resistance from their Iraqi kinsmen. Nor were the Iraqi Kurds reliably united. The division between Mr Barzani's Kurdish Democratic Party (KDP) and Jalal Talabani's Patriotic Union of Kurdistan (PUK) was as much tribal as personal. It was reflected in Kurdish relations with Baghdad, with which Mr Barzani was readier to cooperate, and Tehran, where Mr Talabani had the better standing.

Thus the holding in May, after repeated postponements, of elections to a two-party Kurdish assembly (exactly balanced between the KDP and PUK), followed by the establishment in July of a Kurdish government, looked to be considerable achievements, though diminished by Baghdad's continued blockade of Kurdistan. Any Kurdish claim to sovereignty would have aroused universal, especially Turkish and Arab, hostility, and the allies warned against it. A partial solution was found by combining the Kurds' resistance to Saddam with that of other ethnic and religious groups.

Saddam's non-Kurdish opponents met, unimpressively, now in London, now in Vienna, now in Riyadh—one or other group being generally absent from each session. However, after the US Secretary of State had received, on 29 July, a tripartite delegation of Kurds, Shias and Sunnis, September saw comprehensive opposition meetings in Kurdistan. Agreement seemed to have been reached on the concept of a united but federal Iraq. But the Shias, some based in and strongly supported by Iran, were not entirely satisfied that their numerical majority status was being recognized. Moreover, the neighbouring governments of Syria, Iran and Turkey, meeting in Ankara in November, voiced concern about the possible wider ambitions of the new Kurdish authority, which reacted with resentment.

The Security Council had recognized Iraq's need to sell its oil for humanitarian purposes and to finance compensation to its victims. Resolution 706 (see AR 1991, p. 386) had authorized sales up to $1,600 million a year, but throughout 1992 Iraq refused to make such sales. The UN eventually authorized its members to confiscate Iraqi funds within their jurisdiction, which caused a currency crisis and a depreciation of the dinar by over 30 per cent.

Saddam ignored various calls enjoining him to treat his subjects with humanity. One UN inspector described the human rights abuses which he had found; in March these were condemned by the UN's Commission on Human Rights. In May, heedless of these calls, the government began forcibly moving Shias from the marshes and forbidding their return. In July—before the imposition of the southern exclusion zone—UN officials accused Iraq of indiscriminate bombing of Shia villages.

Short of resuming hostilities, the allies could do little against Saddam's tyranny except where allied air power could be reliably deployed against him. In Iraq's central Sunni provinces his grip remained firm. Regular reports spoke of attempted military coups. Reliable information was, as usual, unobtainable, but it was evident that Saddam retained enough loyal supporters to make him formidable. A special unit of 10,000 Takritis was reportedly deployed for his personal protection. Iraqi prisoners-of-war in Saudi Arabia and Iran seemed, understandably, reluctant to return to their homeland.

Saddam could equally defy the world in his treatment of Westerners entering Iraq by mistake. Two Britons and one Swede were condemned to years in prison. A luckier American engineer in Kuwait was quickly released.

The Iraqi government claimed that allied sanctions were imposing great sufferings, and shortages did indeed hit hard, especially outside Baghdad and the main towns. These privations caused massive black-market trading in food and foreign currency; scores of people convicted of such offences were executed, and Saddam himself publicized the fact.

There were still resources to spare. A canal 350 miles long between Baghdad and Basra, begun in early summer, was inaugurated in December. The stated object was to desalinate adjoining land and facilitate its cultivation. Observers noted that it would assist the government to drain the marshes and thus tame the tribes traditionally living there.

3.   SAUDI ARABIA—YEMEN—ARAB STATES OF THE GULF

i.   SAUDI ARABIA

CAPITAL: Riyadh   AREA: 2,150,000 sq km   POPULATION: 13,300,000 ('92 est.)
OFFICIAL LANGUAGE: Arabic   POLITICAL SYSTEM: monarchy
HEAD OF STATE AND GOVERNMENT: King Fahd ibn Abdul Aziz (since June '82), also
    Prime Minister
PRINCIPAL MINISTERS: Crown Prince Abdallah (first deputy premier), Prince Sultan
    (second deputy premier, defence), Prince Nayef (interior), Prince Saud al-Faisal
    (foreign affairs), Muhammad Ali Aba al-Khalil (finance & national economy),
    Hisham Nazer (petroleum), Mohammed ibn Ibrahim ibn Jubair (justice)
INTERNATIONAL ALIGNMENT: NAM, Arab League, OPEC, OAPEC, GCC, ICO
CURRENCY: riyal (end-'92 £1=SRls5.68, US$1=SRls3.76)
GNP PER CAPITA: US$7,050 ('90)
MAIN EXPORT EARNERS: oil and gas

THE most important political event of the year was the publication of a number of royal decrees on 1 March. The King acknowledged that 'momentous events' in the recent past had made administrative reform necessary. As expected, the changes endeavoured to strike a balance between those who sought greater political 'modernization' and the demands of other Saudis who wished to 'protect' Islamic values. The most widely-publicized change was the creation of a 60-member

Consultative Council. The members, who were all to be chosen by the King, would have the power to review the government's foreign and domestic policies, and to propose new legislation but not to pass it. The members of the new Council were supposed to be nominated within six months, but this deadline was not met. By the end of the year only the Speaker, who was the existing Minister of Justice, had been appointed.

Other elements in the royal decrees were also noteworthy. One effectively annulled the automatic right of any future crown prince to ascend the throne (although incumbent Crown Prince Abdullah was confirmed as King Fahd's heir in a separate decree). There was also the first public recognition that the grandsons of the country's first ruler, Abd al-Aziz (Ibn Saud), were eligible to succeed. The effect was that the next king but one would be chosen from, and by, an electoral college of some 500 princes of both generations.

Another significant article stipulated that private homes in Saudi Arabia were sacrosanct and could not be entered and searched without proper legal authority. This was seen as an attempt to curb some of the unpopular activities of the religious police. However, in a speech at the end of March the King warned those expecting further reforms that democratic practices were not suitable for an Islamic society like that of Saudi Arabia. 'Elections', he said, 'do not fall within the sphere of the Muslim religion'. That those remarks were made in an interview with a Kuwaiti newspaper was seen as having considerable regional political significance.

The third set of decrees gave the country's 14 provinces a greater measure of administrative autonomy. Each was to have an 'advisory council', consisting of at least ten appointed members who would meet under the chairmanship of the provincial governor. The members were to be appointed by the governor in consultation with the Minister of the Interior.

While the reforms were seen by many Saudis as a welcome first step, it soon became clear that the opposition of some 'religious radicals' to the ruling family had not been deflected by the changes. Tape recordings of critical speeches and sermons continued to be produced (see AR 1991, pp. 221–2), and a particularly bitter 45-page memorandum was circulated after being signed by over 100 religious teachers and leaders of disparate backgrounds. As well as condemning the incompetence, extravagance, corruption and nepotism of some members of the royal family, the memorandum called for an end to the kingdom's close links with the USA and for the cessation of economic assistance to foreign regimes which 'suppressed' Islam. In addition, the memorandum demanded the creation of a strong army to 'defend' Islam, better social services for less wealthy Saudis and less censorship. The document, as well as other demands for greater restrictions on the social role and educational opportunities of women, angered not only liberal Saudis but also progressive members of the royal family—a reaction again showing the complexity of the country's politics. The most influential religious body in the kingdom, the Supreme Council of Religious Scholars (Ulema), voted to condemn the memorandum; seven of its members who felt unable to do so were asked to 'resign' on the grounds of ill-health.

In foreign affairs, too, the year was far from uneventful. During January Saudi Arabia played host to a delegation from the American Jewish Congress, the first time such a visit had occurred. In late February the government invited Ayatollah Muhammad Bakir al-Hakim, leader of an Iranian-supported Shia opposition movement in southern Iraq, to visit Saudi Arabia; moreover, Riyadh encouraged other Iraqi opposition parties to unite for more effective action against President Saddam Husain. The kingdom's relations with neighbouring Yemen remained strained (see V.3.ii), and at the end of September there was a border dispute with Qatar in which two men were reported to have been killed (see also V.3.iii). At the end of December it was announced that this dispute had been resolved, thanks to mediation by the Egyptian government, but no details were published. More worrying for the government was the plight of the Muslims in Bosnia (see III.1.vi): Riyadh pressed for greater international efforts on their behalf through the United Nations and the Islamic Conference Organization.

The pilgrimage in June passed off peacefully. It was marked by a much greater attendance by Muslims from the former Soviet republics of central Asia, whose visits were made possible by a personal donation from the King.

The economy showed signs of steady growth and oil production remained high throughout the year. The government's budget planned to increase expenditure by 27 per cent compared with 1990 (the Gulf War having seriously distorted the figures for 1991). Priority was again given to arms purchases, but spending on economic development, social services and education also rose, and subsidies for petrol, electricity and telephone services were increased. In September President Bush authorized the sale of 72 F-15 aircraft to Saudi Arabia, but the implementation of the second stage of an earlier arms agreement with Britain experienced some difficulties.

ii.   YEMEN

CAPITAL: Sanaa   AREA: 540,000 sq km   POPULATION: 11,200,000 ('91 est.)
OFFICIAL LANGUAGE: Arabic   POLITICAL SYSTEM: presidential democracy
HEAD OF STATE AND GOVERNMENT: President (Gen.) Ali Abdullah Saleh (since '90)
VICE-PRESIDENT: Ali Salim al-Bid (since '90)
PRINCIPAL MINISTERS: Haidar Abu Bakr al-Attas (prime minister), Hasan Mohammed
   Makki (first deputy premier), Gen. Mujahid Yahya Abu Shawarib (deputy
   premier, internal affairs), Gen. Salih Ubayd Ahmed (deputy premier, defence),
   Abdul Karim al-Iryani (foreign affairs), Alwi Salih al-Salami (finance),
   Abdel Wasi Ahmed Sallam (justice)
INTERNATIONAL ALIGNMENT: NAM, Arab League, ACC, ICO
CURRENCY: rial & dinar (end-'92 £1=YRls25.02 or YD0.71, US$1=YRls16.53 or YD0.47)
GNP PER CAPITA: US$650 ('89)
MAIN EXPORT EARNERS: oil, agricultural products

IN 1992 Yemen continued to suffer the serious economic and political consequences of its stance over the Iraqi invasion of Kuwait (see AR 1990, pp. 222–3). The expulsion of over one million Yemeni workers from Saudi Arabia had caused considerable hardship in 1991 (see AR 1991, p. 223), and the loss of their remittance income and of external Arab financial aid continued to have very damaging effects on the economy. Levels of unemployment and inflation remained high, and government attempts to enforce a series of austerity measures had little apparent success. A new round of price increases in the late autumn provoked much resentment, culminating in rioting which began in Taiz on 9 December. Similar violent anti-government protests followed in several other towns, including Sanaa and Hodeida. Over a dozen people were reported to have been killed and a number of arrests were made.

The political atmosphere was already very tense before the riots occurred. This reflected, in part, the rapidity with which the country had been unified in May 1990. During the year there were several unsuccessful assassination attempts against leading political figures including the Prime Minister, the Minister of Justice, the Speaker of the National Assembly and two other members of the Presidential Council. There were also a number of bomb attacks on the premises of the Yemeni Socialist Party (which had previously governed South Yemen), and on the offices of the General People's Congress (which had been the ruling party in North Yemen). Buildings belonging to various other political organizations, including several Islamically-inspired ones, were also attacked. It was not, therefore, surprising that the general election which was supposed to be held in November was postponed until April 1993. On 30 December there were two bomb attacks on hotels in Aden, and an Austrian tourist was reported to have been killed.

Many Yemenis believed that Riyadh was behind much of the political unrest, and relations with Saudi Arabia remained difficult. On 19 April the Saudi ambassador in Sanaa was held hostage in his office, but was later freed, unharmed, by the security forces. A more serious development had occurred earlier when the Saudi government sent a letter to a number of foreign companies who were exploring for oil in Yemen—both onshore and offshore—warning them not to continue with such ventures in the border region between the two countries. The letters, which in effect amounted to a claim on Yemeni territory, prompted one company to cease its operations; but the others continued and new oil discoveries were made in the vicinity of Shabwa. Other reports also indicated the possible presence of large additional reserves of natural gas. On 20 July Yemeni and Saudi officials met in Geneva for talks on the border dispute, but no official communiques were issued. On 10 October a long-expected border agreement with Oman was signed.

Yemen was the destination for over 50,000 refugees from Somalia (see VI.1.ii), with others also coming from Eritrea and Ethiopia (see VI.1.i). In late June a group of some 3,000 refugees, who had hijacked a ship in Mogadishu harbour, forced its Chinese captain to run his vessel aground at Aden so as to compel the authorities to provide refuge for them. In this task the government received help from several European states and from the United Nations. Discreet talks were held during the year with a number of European organizations on the possible emigration of Yemen's small remaining Jewish population; but little publicity was given to this very sensitive issue.

iii.   ARAB STATES OF THE GULF

United Arab Emirates
CONSTITUENTS: Abu Dhabi, Dubai, Sharjah, Ras al-Khaimah, Fujairah, Umm al-Qaiwin, Ajman
FEDERAL CAPITAL: Abu Dhabi   AREA: 77,000 sq km   POPULATION: 1,600,000 ('90)
OFFICIAL LANGUAGE: Arabic   POLITICAL SYSTEM: federation of monarchies
HEAD OF STATE & GOVERNMENT: Shaikh Zayad bin Sultan al Nahayyan (Ruler of Abu Dhabi), President of UAE (since '71)
CURRENCY: dirham (end-'92 £1=Dh5.56, US$1=Dh3.67)
GNP PER CAPITA: US$19,860 ('90)
MAIN EXPORT EARNERS: oil & gas

Kuwait
CAPITAL: Kuwait   AREA: 18,000 sq km   POPULATION: 1,500,000 ('92)
OFFICIAL LANGUAGE: Arabic   POLITICAL SYSTEM: monarchy
HEAD OF STATE & GOVERNMENT: Shaikh Jabir al-Ahmadal Jabir as-Sabah (since '77)
CURRENCY: dinar (end-'92 £1=KD0.46, US$1=KD0.30)
GNP PER CAPITA: US$16,150 ('89)
MAIN EXPORT EARNERS: oil & gas

Oman
CAPITAL: Muscat   AREA: 300,000 sq km   POPULATION: 1,600,000 ('90)
OFFICIAL LANGUAGE: Arabic   POLITICAL SYSTEM: monarchy
HEAD OF STATE & GOVERNMENT: Shaikh Qaboos bin Said (since '70)
CURRENCY: rial (end-'92 £1=OR0.58, US$1=OR0.39)
GNP PER CAPITA: US$5,220 ('89)
MAIN EXPORT EARNERS: oil & gas

Qatar
CAPITAL: Doha   AREA: 11,400 sq km   POPULATION: 439,000 ('90)
OFFICIAL LANGUAGE: Arabic   POLITICAL SYSTEM: monarchy
HEAD OF STATE & GOVERNMENT: Shaikh Khalifah bin Hamad al-Thani (since '72)
CURRENCY: riyal (end-'91 £1=QR6.81, US$1=QR3.65)
GNP PER CAPITA: US$15,860 ('90)
MAIN EXPORT EARNERS: oil & gas

Bahrain
CAPITAL: Manama   AREA: 685 sq km   POPULATION: 503,000 ('90)
OFFICIAL LANGUAGE: Arabic   POLITICAL SYSTEM: monarchy
HEAD OF STATE & GOVERNMENT: Shaikh Isa bin Sulman al-Khalifah (since '61)
CURRENCY: dinar (end-'92 £1=BD0.57, US$1=BD0.38)
GNP PER CAPITA: US$6,340 ('88)
MAIN EXPORT EARNERS: oil & gas, aluminium

THROUGHOUT 1992 the Arab states of the Gulf consolidated their recovery from the war against Iraq in 1991. As far as regional security was concerned, the Gulf Cooperation Council (GCC), at its annual meeting in Kuwait on 25–26 December 1991, politely buried the idea of joint security structures with Syria and Egypt, as proposed in the Damascus Declaration of March 1991 (see AR 1991, pp. 207, 225–6). A proposal from Oman for a 100,000-strong Gulf defence force was also sidelined. Instead, Gulf states sought bilateral solutions to their future defence needs, while keeping the 10,000-strong Peninsula Shield force in being. Bahrain and Qatar followed Kuwait's lead (given in September 1991) by signing defence cooperation agreements with the USA in the first half of the year. Kuwait also signed similar cooperation agreements with the UK and France in February, while obtaining Patriot missiles from the USA in the early part of the year. The UAE, however, did not extend its defence commitments beyond the agreement with France signed in September 1991. Instead, it and Oman sought to improve relations with Iran as a means of guaranteeing regional security, while Oman also tried to improve relations with Saudi Arabia and Egypt during a visit to both countries by Sultan Qaboos in June.

The UAE's plans in this respect took a severe knock in April, however, when the Iranian authorities on the island of Abu Musa—which had been jointly controlled by Sharjah and Iran since 1971—suddenly threatened to expel all non-UAE and non-Iranian nationals. Despite diplomatic intervention, the crisis erupted again at the end of August when the Iranian authorities on the island turned away a boat carrying 100 Arab non-UAE nationals, many of them teachers resident on Abu Musa. Iran offered to reverse its stand, despite statements by several Iranian officials that Abu Musa was entirely Iranian territory, if the UAE paid compensation for the aid it had offered to Iraq during the Iran-Iraq war. Iran's actions were condemned by the GCC in early September, an action which added fuel to the flames because the GCC also condemned Iran's annexation of the Greater and Lesser Tunbs islands, which had belonged to Ras al-Khaimah, in 1971. The Arab League also backed the UAE and an attempt to resolve the issue through negotiation failed at the end of September when the UAE tried to include the Tunbs issue as the first item on the agenda. In the wake of this failure, the UAE threatened to take the matter to the United Nations.

Despite an agreement at the GCC summit in Kuwait in December 1991 to create a GCC common market and a unified currency within seven years, with a subsequent agreement for unified tariffs by March 1993 in June 1992 as part of an EC-GCC trade agreement, intra-GCC relations were not smooth throughout 1992. Relations continued to be bedevilled by the Qatar-Bahrain dispute over ownership of the Hawwar islands and of offshore reefs such as Fasht al-Dibal. Despite Saudi mediation, neither side was prepared to abandon its claim and Bahrain filed its counter-arguments to Qatar's original claim with the International Court of Justice at The Hague in June. At the same time, Manama rejected Doha's unilateral extension of its territorial waters to 12 miles, with jurisdiction over an additional 12-mile contiguous zone. The Court would eventually hear oral argument by both sides over the disputed areas.

A far more serious dispute developed at the end of September, when Saudi and Qatari forces clashed twice at the al-Khofous border post, in territory formerly part of the UAE but conceded to Saudi Arabia in 1974. In the wake of the first clash, Doha unilaterally abrogated the 1965 agreement which delimited the border between Qatar and Saudi Arabia. In response, Riyadh claimed that Qatar had encroached into Saudi territory over a period of years and that the true al-Khofous site lay 14 km away, inside Qatari territory. Despite apparent Saudi willingness to find a mediated solution to the crisis, the situation worsened in mid-October when the Qatari embassy in London published a document which claimed that Saudi Arabia had breached articles 3 and 5 of the 1965 treaty by not demarcating the boundary. Riyadh protested that it had been Doha which had refused to accept border posts designated in 1968 and had also failed to collaborate in appointing neutral mediators to demarcate the border thereafter. Qatar remained obdurate and refused to participate in the GCC defence ministers' summit in Kuwait in mid-November. By the end of the year, however, Egyptian mediation defused the crisis, with both sides agreeing to accept a neutral mediator to demarcate the border and Qatar agreeing to rejoin GCC deliberations at the annual GCC summit at the end of December.

The crisis in Saudi-Qatari relations revealed some of the underlying stresses in Gulf affairs during the past year. One reason for the tensions was Qatar's growing links with Iran. Early in the year the two countries signed six cooperation protocols which included, inter alia, an agreement to supply Qatar with water via a pipeline. The UAE and Oman, too, had caused considerable anxieties in Riyadh because of their growing links with Iran in early 1992, while Oman also tried to mediate in the crisis between Iran and the UAE over Abu Musa later in the year. Even Bahrain agreed to consider investment in an aluminium plant on Iran's new free trade zone on Qeshm island. Saudi Arabia was also annoyed that its attempts at mediation did not prevent Bahrain and Qatar from taking their border dispute to the International Court of Justice. Further anxiety was caused when Bahrain suggested, in mid-year, that the time had come to consider restoring contacts with Iraq. Although there was a growing tendency in the Gulf to accept this point of view, no government was prepared to do so openly. The surprise was all the greater, therefore, when Qatar completely unexpectedly reopened its embassy in Baghdad on 27 October. Although the move was a deliberate slight to Saudi Arabia (and the Qatari ambassador was quickly recalled to Doha), the point had been made: Iraq was no longer the complete pariah it had been for the previous 18 months.

As far as Kuwait was concerned, however, relations with Iraq continued to be completely frozen. Indeed, tensions rose periodically throughout the year as Iraqi units made a series of incursions across the international border and on Bubiyan island. In April the leaking of the UN border commission's proposals, to modify the Kuwait–Iraq border in Kuwait's favour as a result of its interpretation of the 1932 border treaty between the two countries, raised tensions to new heights. The proposal, which was formally published in July, gave Kuwait access to ten oil-wells in the Rumailah field and ceded large parts of the Iraqi naval base at Umm Qasr to Kuwait. The decision was rejected both by Baghdad and by all the exiled Iraqi opposition groups and seemed likely to afford a new *casus belli* in the future. Kuwait refused to consider any concession and announced that it intended to fortify the new border (due to come into operation on 15 January 1993) and that there would be no border crossing points available.

Kuwait's obdurate hostility towards Iraq was echoed, albeit with increasing misgivings, by the other Gulf states when they supported the Anglo-Franco-American decision to impose a no-fly zone on Iraq south of the 32nd parallel in late August, ostensibly to protect Iraq's Shia population (see also V.2.vi). Persecution of the Gulf's Palestinian population declined markedly during the year, however, as memories of the Iraqi invasion of Kuwait receded. Although Qatar expelled 350 Palestinians, this reflected official anger at a pro-democracy petition signed by 50 leading Qataris in December 1991. In Kuwait the mass expulsions effectively came to an end at the start of the year when the residence permits of 35,000 Palestinians designated for deportation were extended. Kuwait's population had dropped from 2.14 million in 1990 to 1.5 million in 1992, the Palestinian community declining from around 400,000 to 40,000 and the *bidoun* community being cut in half to 100,000. The government also announced that, henceforth, only

40 per cent of the total population would be non-Kuwaiti in origin.

There were also significant political changes throughout the year. On 12 January Kuwait removed censorship restrictions imposed during the Gulf War. Qatar experienced a major cabinet reshuffle in September which considerably increased the power of the crown prince, Shaikh Khalifah bin Hamid al-Thani, and brought ten members of the al-Thani family into the 18-man cabinet. Although Qatar rejected further constitutional change towards greater popular participation, and the UAE avoided the issue, both Bahrain and Oman instituted *majlis ash-shura* consultative councils. The Omani chamber, which had been announced in 1991, actively participated in government, questioning ministers and governmental decisions, to evident official annoyance, as was clear on the live television transmissions of its hearings in May. The Bahraini proposal to appoint a 30-man chamber in November, in emulation of a similar experiment in Saudi Arabia, was met with popular derision. However, the belated elections in Kuwait at the start of October, which took place under the provisions of the 1965 constitution, generated some surprising results. Involving an electorate of 82,000 (7 per cent of the Kuwaiti population), the elections were for 50 seats, of which 35 were won by opposition parties. The combined Sunni and Shia Islamic movements won 19 seats—ten more than in the last elections—while secular groups won 16 seats, including two for the leaders of the Kuwait Democratic Forum, Abdullah Nibari and Dr Ahmad al-Khatib. Although cabinet members were *ex officio* assembly members, it was thought unlikely that the Emir would allow this provision to be used to pack the assembly. Although the incumbent premier, Shaikh Sa'ad al-Abdallah al-Sabah, was retained in office, he appointed a wide-based cabinet, including five members of the ruling al-Sabah family, five ministers from the former government and six oppositionist deputies, of whom four came from moderate Islamic factions. One of the oppositionist deputies, Ali Ahmad Baghli, was appointed Oil Minister in late October.

The aftermath of the Gulf War was also evident in economic affairs. Kuwait announced that the direct costs of Operation Desert Storm had been $22,000 million of which all but $2,000 million had been paid by 1992. Total costs had been $40,000 million and $46,000 million of Kuwait's foreign investments had had to be liquidated as a result. This compared with the cost to Saudi Arabia of around $40,000 million. Kuwait's 1991/92 and 1992/93 budgets reflected the continuing financial strains that its economy faced, as a result of these extraordinary costs and of the loss of oil revenues in the wake of the occupation and the subsequent destruction of Kuwaiti oil-wells. However, the 1992/93 budget, which began in July, reflected the vast improvement in Kuwait's oil revenues in 1992, with average production expected to be 1.05 million barrels per day (b/d) and daily production reaching 1.5 million b/d by the end of the year. Revenues were set at KD 2,218 million—more than twice the previous year's level—and expenditure was expected to reach around US$4 billion. The overall deficit was expected to be KD 1,782 million.

Kuwait's foreign investment programme was marred by difficulties in Spain, where its holding company, the Grupo Torras, had to be put into credit-protected receivership at the end of the year. Nonetheless, some optimism was derived from the recovery of the oil sector. At the end of 1992 Kuwait's Oil Minister announced that the emirate would accept the discipline of renewed OPEC quotas once its production capacity had been restored to its pre-invasion level of 2.5 million b/d.

The UAE, surprisingly, abided by its OPEC quota throughout the year, this having been raised 50 per cent above its July 1990 level to 2.244 million b/d. Production averaged 2 million b/d throughout the year, with Dubai supplying 435,000 b/d and Sharjah 35,000 b/d. The UAE was also able to tie up the embarrassing loose ends of its involvement in the Bank of Credit and Commerce International (BCCI) affair (see AR 1991, pp. 24–5, 229) by proposing a $2,200 million settlement plan to outstanding creditors which would satisfy between 30 and 40 per cent of their claims. The UAE economy also began to rally during the year, with the Jebal Ali free trade zone reporting 350 member companies by the end of 1991, an increase of 80 over the previous year. The UAE also contributed $1,500 million to the Arab Development Programme, a new investment body designed to aid the private sector primarily in Arab countries which had participated in the multinational coalition against Iraq. The other contributors, at $2,500 million each, were Saudi Arabia and Kuwait; a further $3,500 million remained to be found to complete the planned ten-year disbursement programme.

Oman, not an OPEC member, raised its oil output to 700,000 b/d during 1992 and promised to increase it still further to 750,000 b/d. Oman also engaged in a major pipeline programme in the Commonwealth of Independent States (CIS), the Caspian pipeline, which would allow 1.5 million b/d of crude to be transported from Kazakhstan to the Black Sea. The joint venture with Kazakhstan was later joined by Azerbaijan and the Russian Federation. Oman also participated in an oil exploration programme in Kazakhstan and took a 20 per cent stake in a new refinery project in Thailand as part of its economic diversification programme.

The most important economic development of 1992, however, occurred in Qatar, where the North Field gas reserves came on stream. Natural gas was set to displace crude as Qatar's major source of foreign currency over the next decade, with oil production stagnating at around the current OPEC quota level of 377,000 b/d. In addition to a long-term proposal for a 1,600-km gas pipeline to Pakistan, Qatar entered into a series of more immediate natural gas projects during

1992. An agreement to deliver 4 million tonnes a year of liquefied natural gas (LNG) to Japan from 1997 was signed in mid-year. The Mobil Oil Company bought a 10 per cent stake in Qatargas, once the Japanese contract was announced, and a further 30 per cent stake in a new LNG project to supply 2 million tonnes a year of LNG to South Korea. A further joint venture with Bunker Hunt was to supply 6 million tonnes a year of LNG to Italy from 1997 and a fourth joint venture with Sumitomo and Elf envisaged the supply of 4 million tonnes/year to the Far East from the late 1990s. The total cost of these developments was estimated to be in the order of $5,000 million, but they would enable Qatar to escape from its chronic current-account deficit by the middle of the decade.

4. SUDAN—LIBYA—TUNISIA—ALGERIA–MOROCCO–WESTERN SAHARA

i. SUDAN

CAPITAL: Khartoum   AREA: 2,500,000 sq km   POPULATION: 25,100,000 ('90)
OFFICIAL LANGUAGE: Arabic   POLITICAL SYSTEM: military regime
HEAD OF STATE AND GOVERNMENT: Lt.-Gen. Omar Hasan Ahmed al-Bashir,
    Chairman of Revolutionary Command Council (since June '89)
PRINCIPAL MINISTERS: Brig.-Gen. Zubir Mohammed Saleh (deputy premier, interior)
    Ahmad Sahlul (foreign affairs), Abdul Rahman Mahmoud Hamdi (finance &
    economic planning)
INTERNATIONAL ALIGNMENT: NAM, Arab League, OAU, ACP, ICO
CURRENCY: Sudanese pound (end'92 £1=Lsd15.16, US$1=Lsd10.02)
GNP PER CAPITA: US$480 ('88)
MAIN EXPORT EARNERS: cotton, agricultural products

POLITICAL instability, economic decline and continuing civil war in the south were major features of the year. Some leading members of the banned Democratic Unionist Party were arrested for their alleged involvement in a plot to overthrow the government. Two officers were killed and 41 others were arrested on suspicion of planning to bomb the General Staff headquarters. Dismissal of professional people employed by the state continued, allegedly 'for the public good', whereby sympathizers with the regime were appointed in place of those dismissed.

Sudan's economic and military alliance with Iran was strengthened. Iranian revolutionaries were reportedly fighting with the Sudanese troops against the Sudan People's Liberation Army (SPLA). Iran was reported, moreover, to have funded the purchase for Sudan of fighter aircraft, tanks and a multiple launcher rocket system worth $300 million. Iran was given access to many power installations at Port Sudan in return for its help with power transformation equipment and oil supplies. Sudan's fundamentalist regime was favoured by the Iranian government in its ambition to spread Islamic fundamentalism in North

Africa. But Egypt, alarmed by Iran's growing influence in Sudan, accused the Sudanese government of financing and training Egyptian fundamentalists in camps in Sudan. Despite denials by Sudan, relations between the two countries deteriorated, a process further accelerated when Egypt occupied the disputed border area of Halaib.

Sudan expelled the United Arab Emirates (UAE) ambassador and two of his staff in retaliation for the expulsion of the Sudanese ambassador and other diplomats accused of undesirable activities with regard to Sudanese working in the UAE. Tunisia and Algeria also expelled Sudanese diplomats who were accused of supporting Muslim fundamentalists in their countries. Kenya complained of Sudan's support for the Kenyan Islamic Party, which was contesting the multi-party elections in that country (see VI.1.iv). In pursuing the war against the SPLA, Sudan government forces bombed Moyo in northern Uganda. Ethiopia opened its borders with Sudan and Sudanese troops were able to pursue SPLA forces on Ethiopian territory. The Sudan government criticized the sending of American troops to Somalia (see VI.1.ii), but the United States warned against interference.

The weakening of the SPLA as a result of the infighting between its factions led to government gains. Government forces recaptured the towns of Yirol, Pibor, Liria, Pachala, Kapoeta and Bor, whereas the SPLA occupied temporarily the headquarters of the southern military command in Juba. Both sides contributed to the increasing number of refugees fleeing to neighbouring countries. The government and the SPLA factions reached an agreement to guarantee the flow of relief supplies to those affected by the civil war. Nigeria's efforts to mediate between Sudan and the SPLA factions failed. The Sudan government was criticized for the continuation of the civil war in the south and for its policy of 'ethnic cleansing' in the Nuba mountains. This area was closed off and military operations were conducted to remove non-Arab rebel elements accused of supporting the SPLA. In the removal from Khartoum of an estimated half a million refugees from the south and the Nuba mountains, 16 deaths and 81 injured were reported.

In tandem with its Islamic fundamentalist policy, the government decreed the Arabization of universities, the banning of women from working in the markets and other public places after 5 pm, and the closure of all shops for two hours for Friday prayers. The President signed a new national service law which compelled nationals aged from 18 to 33 to serve up to 18 months. To give the regime a democratic facade, the President appointed a 302-member Transitional Assembly composed of members of the Revolutionary Command Council (RCC), federal ministers and state governors. He dissolved all specialized RCC committees and their functions were taken over by the Assembly, which was given the power to propose and pass legislation and vet all RCC decrees. In consequence of the establishment of the Assembly,

Sudan was readmitted to the Inter-Parliamentary Union. The President ordered the release of state security prisoners serving sentences of 15 years or less.

To tackle the growing economic decline, high inflation and shortage of foreign exchange, the government cut subsidies, devalued the Sudanese pound, made budget cuts and increased taxes. Demonstrations in Khartoum and Omdurman followed over the rise in prices of petrol, sugar and bread. The government decided to privatize or liquidate 142 public companies in a three-year programme. The Khartoum-based Concorp International bought Chevron's oil concessions in south-west Sudan for an estimated $23–26 million. Concorp began producing diesel fuel at its refinery at Abu Jabra oilfield in Kordofan. Despite government efforts to stimulate the economy, concern was expressed by the IMF about Sudan's rate of inflation (estimated to be about 150 per cent) and debt arrears of $1,500 million. The 1992/93 budget was estimated by the government to be running a $863 million deficit as a result of a slump in cotton and gum arabic prices. Remittances vital to the country's foreign exchange fell from $440 million in 1987/88 to $106 million in 1991/92 because of the return of some Sudanese working in the Gulf. The European Commission blocked Sudan's allocation of 165 million ecu in view of its lack of respect for human rights, the continuing civil war in the south and lack of progress in free movement of emergency aid to the south. On 4 December the UN General Assembly agreed in committee to pass a resolution criticizing Sudan for its human rights record.

ii. LIBYA

CAPITAL: Tripoli   AREA: 1,760,000 sq km   POPULATION: 4,500,000 ('90)
OFFICIAL LANGUAGE: Arabic   POLITICAL SYSTEM: socialist 'state of the masses'
HEAD OF STATE: Col. Muammar Qadafi, 'Leader of the Revolution' (since '69)
GOVERNMENT LEADERS: Maj. Abdul Salem Jalloud ('Libyan number two'),
    Abu Zaid Omar Dourda (sec.-gen. of Gen. People's Congress), Mohammad
    Bait al-Mal (planning), Omar Mustafa al-Muntassir (foreign affairs & international
    cooperation), Abdullah Salem al-Badri (energy), Ibrahim Mohammad Bakkar
    (justice & public security), Jaddallah Azzouz al-Talhi (industry)
INTERNATIONAL ALIGNMENT: NAM, Arab League, OPEC, OAPEC, AMU, OAU, ICO
CURRENCY: dinar (end-'92 £1=LD0.44, US$1=LD0.29)
GNP PER CAPITA: US$5,310 ('89)
MAIN EXPORT EARNERS: oil and gas

As the year opened, the Lockerbie affair continued to dominate Libya's external relations as both parties in the dispute turned to international organizations to support their case. On 21 January the UN Security Council unanimiously adopted a resolution (731) demanding that Libya fulfil US and UK demands to hand over the two Libyans implicated in the

1988 bombing of the Pan Am airliner and to cooperate with the French
authorities investigating the bombing of the UTA flight over Niger in
1989 (see AR 1991, pp. 234–5). It called on the new UN Secretary-
General, Dr Boutros-Ghali, to try to persuade Libya to comply with
the resolution (see XI.1). On 28 January Abdul Salem Jalloud stated
that two Libyan prosecutors were investigating the incidents but that the
Libyan government was ready to hand over the two Libyan suspects to
an international commission. Officials repeated that under Libyan law
the two men could not be extradited to the USA or UK. On 11 February
Libya told the UN that it was willing to cooperate with France in the
investigation into the explosion aboard the UTA airliner. Early in March
Libya appealed to the International Court of Justice, at The Hague,
for an opinion on which country under international law had the legal
jurisdiction to try the two suspects.

Both the US and the UK governments expressed their determination to
maintain pressure on Libya to comply with resolution 731. Together with
France, they asked the UN Security Council on 17 March to approve a
draft resolution to impose sanctions on Libya. On 31 March the Security
Council approved resolution 748 imposing an air and arms embargo on
Libya if it failed to hand over the two Lockerbie suspects by 15 April.
Efforts by Egypt's President Mubarak and by Dr Boutros-Ghali's
personal envoy, Vladimir Petrovsky, to find a compromise, and a
last-minute proposal by the Arab League that Libya should hand over
the two suspects to a neutral country, failed to stop the implementation
of resolution 748. On 14 April the International Court of Justice had
ruled that it was unable to interfere with the functions and prerogatives
of the Security Council (see also XV.1.i).

In that Libya had a variety of alternative land and sea routes available
to it, and large stockpiles of arms, the UN sanctions failed to force
Libyan compliance, although there were rumours of a rift between
Colonel Qadafi and Major Jalloud over Libya's response to the crisis.
Nevertheless, on 9 June in Geneva, Libyan officials met UK diplomats
and handed over information on Libyan links with the IRA in what
appeared to be an attempt to meet Western demands that it abandon
its support for international terrorism. There were further meetings
in Cairo in August. Debate in the General People's Congress was
dominated by the Lockerbie affair. On 23 June its chairman announced
that the Congress did not object to the investigation and trial being
carried out through the committee of seven constituted by the Arab
League or through the UN before a just and fair court.

On 12 August the UN Security Council announced that existing
sanctions on Libya would continue for a further four months. There was
no immediate official response from Tripoli but in a televised address
to the nation on 31 August, the eve of the 23rd anniversary of the 1969
revolution, Colonel Qadafi stated that the dispute could be resolved

through direct negotiations with America, Britain and France. Britain responded immediately, reiterating the demand that the two suspects be handed over to either a US or a Scottish court. On 27 October the French judge investigating the UTA bombing was refused entry to Libya.

In the run-up to the Security Council's review of sanctions in mid-December, the USA, France and Britain again increased pressure on Libya to comply with resolution 731. In a joint statement issued on 27 November they condemned Libya for attempting to escape its international obligations through 'equivocation and delay' and warned that such actions could only further its isolation from the world community. They stressed that if Libya continued to ignore UN demands then efforts would be intensified to make sanctions more effective. Earlier that month a number of US senators had written to Dr Boutros-Ghali urging him to support a world oil embargo against Libya. But some observers were convinced that Colonel Qadafi would continue to resist pressure from the West over the Lockerbie affair. They argued that the political cost of surrendering the two suspects was too high for the Libyan leader and that he believed that support for an extension of the embargo by the Security Council would be difficult to mobilize. A further renewal of existing sanctions would not seriously damage the Libyan economy and indeed could be used to rally popular support for the Libyan leader.

At a second meeting of the General People's Congress on 8 October a major restructuring of the secretariats within the General People's Committee (cabinet) was approved. It was announced that 14 existing secretariats would be merged into six and that two new secretariats would be formed. In an extensive cabinet reshuffle on 18 November, the moderate Omar Mustafa al-Muntassir, former planning and economy minister, was appointed to head the Foreign Liaison and International Cooperation Secretariat, replacing Ibrahim Beshari, who had been head of intelligence at the time of the Lockerbie bombing. The armed forces remained as before under the General Provisional Committee for Defence and outside the responsibility of the General People's Committee. Most observers were convinced that, although the names had changed, policies would remain the same and that on the Lockerbie affair there would be words but no action. On 9 December the UN Security Council decided to reapply resolutions 731 and 748 for a further four months.

iii. TUNISIA

CAPITAL: Tunis AREA: 164,000 sq km POPULATION: 8,100,000 ('90)
OFFICIAL LANGUAGE: Arabic POLITICAL SYSTEM: presidential
HEAD OF STATE AND GOVERNMENT: Gen. Zayn al-Abdin Ben Ali (since Nov '87)
RULING PARTY: Constitutional Democratic Rally (RCD)
PRINCIPAL MINISTERS: Hamid Qarwi (prime minister), Habib Ben Yahia (foreign
    affairs), Abdullah Khalal (interior), Sadok Chaabane (justice), Abdelaziz
    Ben Dhia (defence), Nouri Zorgati (finance), Sadok Rabah (economy)
INTERNATIONAL ALIGNMENT: NAM, Arab League, OAPEC, AMU, OAU, ICO
CURRENCY: dinar (end-'92 £1=D1.45, US$1=D0.961)
GNP PER CAPITA: US$1,440 ('90)
MAIN EXPORT EARNERS: tourism, oil and gas, phosphates, olive oil

THE prospect of an Islamist victory in the general elections in neighbouring Algeria had strained relations between the two countries,
so that the departure of President Chadli and the cancellation of
the second round of elections came as an immense relief to the
Tunisian regime. President Ben Ali was one of the first leaders to
congratulate Mohammad Boudiaf on his appointment as Algerian
head of state (see V.4.iv). When Mr Boudiaf was assassinated in July,
President Ben Ali blamed Islamic 'fundamentalists', while Tunisian
officials stated that they had warned their Algerian counterparts of
the dangers of legalizing Islamist parties. Suppression of Tunisia's own
Islamist movement, Nahda, continued with widespread arrests and a
large security presence on the streets.

At the end of July more than 100 Tunisians were put on trial at
the Tunis military tribunal accused of belonging to an Islamist terrorist
group called Commandos of Sacrifice, which the authorities claimed
was Nahda's military wing. The accused, who included army, police
and customs officials, were charged with conspiring to take power by
force and plotting to assassinate the President. During the trial Nahda's
official spokesman, Ali Laaridh, insisted that the Commandos of Sacrifice were not part of his movement and that Nahda was committed
to peaceful political action. He denied the existence of any plot to
overthrow the state. Habib Laasoued, alleged to be the leader of the
Commandos, also denied any link with Nahda, which he described as a
rival movement. He admitted calling for a *jihad* (holy war) but claimed
that he was speaking in theoretical terms and had no intention of putting
the threat into practice. At the same time, almost 200 alleged Nahda
members were put on trial for plotting to take power by force.

Throughout both trials there were allegations of irregularities in the
conduct of the hearings and of human rights abuses. Many of the accused
claimed that torture had been used to extract a confession. There were
calls from three international human rights groups for the trials to be
delayed until these allegations could be investigated thoroughly. At
the end of August the courts announced long prison sentences for the
defendants, although demands by the prosecution for death penalties

in 28 cases were rejected. Among those receiving life sentences were three exiled Nahda leaders, Rached Ghannouchi, Salah Karkar and Habib Moknil. In an interview with a Paris newspaper on 3 October, Mr Ghannouchi rejected claims that he had received funds from the governments of Iran, Sudan and Saudi Arabia to overthrow the Tunisian regime and that he was organizing violent Islamist revolution. These mass trials were seen as the culmination of the Tunisian government's long campaign against Nahda, whose organization had been largely stamped out while its leaders had been imprisoned or forced into exile. Some members of opposition parties accused President Ben Ali of using the threat of Islamic fundamentalism as an excuse to delay long-promised democratic reforms.

The Tunisian government remained very sensitive to any criticism of its human rights record and reacted angrily when Amnesty International stated that torture was common in detention centres where some 8,000 Islamist supporters were being held. It complained that opposition leaders were using the Tunisian Human Rights League as a means of attacking the government, and in March introduced legislation which prevented leading members of political parties from occupying positions within organizations such as the league and forcing it to open its membership to all applicants. The league rejected the legislation and was convinced that the new restrictions had been imposed because it had spoken out against human rights abuses in the country. After international pressure was exerted, a compromise was agreed in September to enable the league to hold a congress to explore ways in which it might operate under the new law. However, the congress, originally planned for 31 November, was postponed following a dispute within the leadership over whether the current chairman, Dr Moncef Marzouki, should seek another term of office.

The decision by the UN Security Council in April to impose sanctions against Libya over the Lockerbie affair (see V.4.ii) was reluctantly accepted by Tunisia. But, although flights to and from Libya were suspended, Tunisia acknowledged popular feeling and the close economic ties between the two countries by insisting that land and sea links would remain open. The Libyan sanctions created a mini-boom in southern Tunisia amid a sharp increase in cross-border trade. But relations with Libya deteriorated sharply early in September when Muammar Qadafi, the Libyan leader, remarked that Tunisia had no future and was doomed to unite with either Libya or Algeria. This outburst provoked an indignant response from President Ben Ali, who drew attention to Tunisia's achievements and commented pointedly that the Libyan people were suffering from the consequences of a crisis for which they were not responsible.

Political stability was seen as essential for the country to achieve the ambitious investment targets set by the eighth five-year plan introduced on 4 July. This aimed to transform the economy from state domination to a liberal market system with a fully convertible currency by 1996. A $110 million commercial bank syndication signed at the end of June, the first time Tunisia had returned to international capital markets since 1986, was seen as a sign of confidence in the economy. As a result of a strong economic performance in 1992, Tunisia decided not to apply for a new IMF facility to replace the extended fund facility which expired during the summer.

At the end of the year, President Ben Ali announced that presidential and parliamentary elections would be held in March 1994. Promising a revised electoral law and an up-to-date voting register, the President predicted that the consultation would consolidate political pluralism in Tunisia.

iv. ALGERIA

CAPITAL: Algiers   AREA: 2,382,000 sq km   POPULATION: 25,100,000 ('90)
OFFICIAL LANGUAGE: Arabic   POLITICAL SYSTEM: quasi-military regime
HEAD OF STATE AND GOVERNMENT: Ali Kafi, President of Council of State (since
    June '92)
PRINCIPAL MINISTERS: Belaid Abdesselam (prime minister, economy), Lakhdar
    Brahimi (foreign affairs), Maj.-Gen. Khaled Nezzar (defence), Mohammed Hardi
    (interior), Mohammed Teguia (justice), Abdennour Keramane (mines, industry)
INTERNATIONAL ALIGNMENT: NAM, Arab League, OPEC, OAPEC, AMU, OAU, ICO
CURRENCY: dinar (end-'92 £1=DA33.50, US$1=DA22.131)
GNP PER CAPITA: US$2,060 ('90)
MAIN EXPORT EARNERS: oil and gas

As the year opened, the Islamic Salvation Front (FIS), having taken a commanding lead in the first round of the country's general elections (see AR 1991, p. 242), seemed set to gain an outright majority in parliament in the second round to be held on 16 January. Protest was widespread, led by professional and women's organizations and by secular parties such as the Socialist Forces Front (FFS), which organized a huge march through the centre of Algiers on 2 January in support of democracy. There were fears of civil war and speculation was rife that the army would intervene if the Islamists came to power. But President Chadli reaffirmed that he would respect the election results and indicated that he would be prepared to work with an FIS government.

Such an arrangement was clearly unacceptable to the military, so that when President Chadli suddenly announced his resignation on the 11 January, after 13 years in power, it was widely believed that the army was responsible. As tanks and heavily-armed troops were deployed around key buildings in the capital, people were left in no doubt who was in control. Mr Chadli's dramatic announcement created a power vacuum and plunged the country into political crisis. Since the

National Assembly had been dissolved at the beginning of the year and the constitution in effect suspended, a High Security Council took power with the declared aim of preserving public order and national security. Three of its six members were senior army officers. The Council's first action was to cancel the second round of the general elections.

To give a veneer of constitutional respectability to their intervention, the new authorities set up a five-member Council of State, a sort of collegiate presidency. This body was headed by Muhammad Boudiaf, one of the historic leaders in the war of independence, who was recalled from exile in Morocco. The Council also included the new regime's strongman, Major-General Khaled Nezzar, the Defence Minister. The three major political parties, the FIS, the FFS and the former ruling National Liberation Front (FLN), all condemned the new Council of State, but the deep divisions between them prevented any united opposition.

Although robbed of almost certain victory at the ballot box, the FIS kept its supporters from taking to the streets, fearing that any confrontation with the military-backed regime would result in the banning of the party. Despite this restraint, the new regime moved quickly to try and stamp out the FIS as a political movement. Laws banning the use of religion for political purposes were strictly enforced, and leading FIS officials were arrested. This provoked a series of violent clashes across the country. On 9 February the authorities declared a state of emergency giving the security services sweeping powers of arrest and detention. Thousands of FIS supporters were arrested and held at a number of special detention centres in remote parts of the Sahara. Islamic militants responded with guerrilla attacks on the security forces.

Early in March the authorities began court proceedings which resulted in the FIS being outlawed. In response, the FIS called on its supporters to take up armed struggle against the regime. In May, after military courts had condemned several Islamic militants to death, there was an upsurge of violence across the country, to which police and army units responded vigorously. At the same time, in an attempt to improve its image, the regime freed a large number of detainees in the weeks before the festival of Aid el-Adha on 11 June. But armed attacks against the security forces continued, as the Islamist movement was increasingly forced underground and control passed to the FIS faction advocating violent international revolution.

On 29 June the head of state, Muhammad Boudiaf, was assassinated during an official visit to Annaba. A special commission set up to investigate the killing found that the assassin was a sub-lieutenant in the special anti-terrorist units which had been responsible for the President's security that day. According to the investigators, the assassin had been influenced by Islamist movements at home and abroad; while concluding that he had not acted alone, they declined to state who had ordered the killing. Few people believed that the FIS were responsible, many Algerians being convinced that the assassination had been planned by people within the establishment who felt threatened by President Boudiaf's policies, particularly his campaign against corruption in high places.

Ali Kafi, secretary-general of the Algerian War Veterans' Organization and one of the few surviving guerrilla leaders from the war of independence, succeeded Muhammad Boudiaf as head of state. His appointment was interpreted by many as a sign of continuity in that the military remained effectively in control. Following the resignation of Sid-Ahmed Ghozali on 8 July, Belaid Abdessalam, who had been in charge of the Algerian economy under President Boumédienne, became Prime Minister and appointed a cabinet made up of competent technocrats. Some commentators predicted a radical change in certain aspects of economic policy. The economic and political challenges that confronted the new government were daunting.

In mid-July, at the long-awaited trial of seven FIS leaders, a military court found them guilty of conspiring against the authority of the state, although they were acquitted of the more serious charge of plotting armed insurrection. Abbasi Madani and Ali Belhadj were sentenced to 12 years in prison (the other five receiving lesser terms). The verdicts provoked clashes throughout the country between FIS demonstrators and the security forces.

At the end of August a series of bombings, including an attack on Algiers international airport which killed nine people and injured 100, marked a dangerous escalation in the cycle of violence which undermined efforts to restore confidence at home and abroad. In a further crackdown on armed Islamist groups, a tough new anti-terrorism law was announced on 2 October, but political violence continued across the country. Although Belaid Abdesselam's government promised a new dialogue with the opposition, there were few signs of any revival in the political process and persistent rumours of a power struggle between the military and civilian branches of the regime. Early in November the Prime Minister ruled out early general elections because of the critical security situation. At the end of the month he called for 'total war' against supporters of the banned FIS. Despite the curfew imposed in Algiers and six neighbouring provinces at the beginning of December, clashes between the security forces and Islamist militants intensified.

v. MOROCCO

CAPITAL: Rabat   AREA: 460,000 sq km   POPULATION: 25,100,000 ('90)
OFFICIAL LANGUAGE: Arabic   POLITICAL SYSTEM: monarchy
HEAD OF STATE AND GOVERNMENT: King Hassan II (since '61)
RULING PARTIES: Constitutional Union heads coalition
PRINCIPAL MINISTERS: Mohammed Karim Lamrani (prime minister), Abdel Latif Filali
   (foreign affairs), Mohammed Berrada (finance), Driss Basri (interior,
   information), Moulay Mustapha Ben Larbi Alaiou (justice), Moulay Driss Alaoui
   M'Daghri (energy and mines)
INTERNATIONAL ALIGNMENT: NAM, Arab League, AMU, ICO
CURRENCY: dirham (end-'92 £1=DH12.58, US$1=DH8.31)
GNP PER CAPITA: US$960 ('90)
MAIN EXPORT EARNERS: phosphates, agricultural products, tourism

IN a speech on 3 March marking the anniversary of his accession
to the throne, King Hassan launched a major political initiative by
announcing a referendum on a new constitution, to be followed by
general elections. The king promised that the proposed changes to
the existing constitution, introduced in 1972, would establish a better
balance between the monarch and parliament and by implication allow
the opposition parties a greater voice. The last general elections were
held in 1984 and those planned for September 1989 were postponed
because of the dispute over the Western Sahara. The king called for
free and honest elections and stated that he wanted to see new faces
in the future parliament.

Changes in the electoral system were introduced on 4 June when
parliament passed a new electoral law. The voting age was reduced
from 23 to 20 and the minimum age for candidates from 25 to 23. All
political parties were given equal access to state finance and to radio and
television. Five opposition parties—Istiqlal, the Union Socialiste des
Forces Populaires (USFP), the Organisation de l'Action Démocratique
et Populaire (OADP), the Parti du Progrès et du Socialisme (PPS) and
the Union Nationale des Forces Populaires (UNFP)—formed the Bloc
Démocratique (BD) to coordinate their activities in the run-up to the
general elections. All deputies of the parliamentary opposition boycotted the vote on the new law. They had demanded 18 as the minimum
voting age (21 for candidates), a two-tier voting system, a new all-party
organization to supervise elections and an independent chairman of the
electoral commission. King Hassan rejected these demands.

On 11 August King Hassan announced a new government made up
of ministers without formal party affiliations and appointed Mohammed
Karim Lamrani to the premiership. In an address to the nation on
20 August, King Hassan stated that the revised constitution would
give more responsibilities to parliament but emphasized that this did
not mean a reduction in the sovereign's prerogatives. Under the changes
proposed, ministers would be chosen by the prime minister but approved
by the king (whereas the opposition had demanded that the prime minis-

ter should be appointed by parliament). A new constitutional council of eight members, half appointed by the king, would be created to arbitrate at the request of one-quarter of the parliamentary deputies. The revised constitution also reaffirmed the king's commitment to human rights.

A referendum on the new constitution took place on 4 September, it being officially announced that 99.96 per cent had voted in favour and that 97.25 per cent of the 11 million registered voters had participated. As most of the opposition parties had advised their supporters not to vote, the result was greeted with deep scepticism by the world's press. The opposition claimed that the results made Morocco the 'laughing stock of the whole world' and destroyed all credibility in the democratic process. However, Interior and Information Minister Driss Basri dismissed accusations of irregularities and stated that the government would have been proud of the result even if the vote had been 100 per cent in favour.

Despite their protests over the referendum result, the opposition Bloc Démocratique contested the communal elections which took place on 16 October as the first stage of the electoral process. The Rassemblement Nationale des Indépendents (RNI) led by Ahmed Osman, a former prime minister, became the largest party in local government, winning 18.1 per cent of the vote and 21.7 per cent of the 22,282 seats contested. The independent list, Sans Appartenance Politique (SAP), which despite its name was close to the government, won 13.8 per cent of the vote and the loyalist Union Constitutionelle 13.4 per cent. Istiqlal emerged as the largest opposition party with 12.5 per cent of the vote followed by the USFP, which confirmed its traditional strength in the two major cities, Casablanca and Rabat. But the opposition parties failed to improve on their showing in the last communal elections in 1983, even though they contested many more seats. Despite King Hassan's assurances that the elections would be free and fair, the opposition parties complained of widespread malpractices by local authorities in favour of 'loyalist' parties, especially in rural areas, where caids, mokadems and other local notables continued to dominate political life.

At the end of October Abdesselam Yassine, head of the illegal Islamist group Adl wal Ihsan, was released after almost three years under house arrest.

In December it was announced that the long-awaited parliamentary elections would not be held until 30 April 1993, to allow time for the drawing up of new voting registers. The opposition demanded that electoral lists should be radically revised and the boundaries of constituencies redrawn. The Interior and Information Ministry stated that the new registers would include newly-eligible voters but rejected any other changes. The second stage of the electoral process was set for February 1993, in the form of elections to the three professional chambers.

vi.   WESTERN SAHARA

CAPITAL: Al Aaiún   AREA: 252,000 sq km   POPULATION: 164,000 ('82)
STATUS: regarded as under its sovereignty by Morocco, whereas independent Sahrawi
   Arab Democratic Republic (SADR) was declared by Polisario Front in 1976

ON 1 January the UN Security Council stated that it would ask the new
Secretary-General, Dr Boutros-Ghali, to prepare a new report within
two months establishing voting criteria for the referendum on the future
of the Western Sahara, following allegations that the recommendations made by outgoing Secretary-General Pérez de Cuellar favoured
Morocco (see AR 1991, pp. 246–7). This meant that the referendum,
originally planned for the end of January, had to be postponed. The
Polisario Front accused Morocco of arresting 400 of its supporters
during police raids in the main towns of the disputed territory and of
strengthening its defences there in violation of the UN ceasefire.

In March Dr Boutros-Ghali gave Morocco and Polisario until 31 May
to resolve their differences over the electoral register for the referendum, warning that otherwise the UN would have to adopt a different
approach to the problem. He accused Morocco of committing most of
the ceasefire violations recorded by the UN Mission for the Referendum
in the Western Sahara (MINURSO), of refusing to disclose details of
the strength and location of its military forces in the territory and of
obstructing the deployment of UN peace-keeping forces. At the end
of March only 375 of the 2,700 ceasefire monitors were in place. In
April General Yakoub Khan, a former foreign minister of Pakistan, was
named UN special representative for Western Sahara, an appointment
welcomed by Morocco but not by Polisario. By the end of May
no progress had been made in re-launching the peace process and
Dr Boutros-Ghali gave both parties another three months to resolve
their differences.

The UN-sponsored peace process suffered a new setback when
Morocco announced that it would go ahead with its long-awaited
local and general elections after a constitutional referendum in September (see V.4.v) and that the Western Sahara would be included
in the electoral process. Morocco had previously stated that it would
wait until the UN referendum on the future of the territory before
holding national elections. Polisario denounced Morocco's decision
and threatened to return to armed conflict in the face of this new
provocation. The Moroccan Foreign Minister, Abdel Latif Filali, argued
that there was no link between the UN referendum and the Moroccan
elections because each had fundamentally different objectives. In the
4 September referendum, Morocco claimed that the vast majority of
Sahrawis had voted in favour of the constitutional reforms. Polisario
complained to the UN Security Council that Morocco was conspiring to

change the legal status of Western Sahara. Despite widespread reports of disturbances in the disputed territory during the local elections in October, Morocco announced that parliamentary elections scheduled for April 1993 would extend to Western Sahara.

As the year ended, the UN peace process remained deadlocked, and Morocco appeared to have seized the initiative in the Western Sahara dispute. Special representative Yakoub Khan had failed to resolve the differences between the two sides over voting criteria and there were serious doubts over the fate of the UN referendum on the future of the territory. The impasse weakened Polisario and divisions within the front were highlighted in August by the defection to Morocco of Ibrahim Hakim, its ambassador in Algiers. While Algeria continued to support the UN peace plan, there were reports that unofficially the new Algiers regime did not wish to antagonize Morocco by backing Polisario's claims for an independent state. In the absence of international pressure to resolve the dispute, Morocco continued to strengthen its economic and political control over the territory.

VI EQUATORIAL AFRICA

1. ETHIOPIA—SOMALIA—DJIBOUTI—KENYA—TANZANIA—UGANDA

i. ETHIOPIA

CAPITAL: Addis Ababa   AREA: 1,220,000 sq km   POPULATION: 51,200,000 ('90)
OFFICIAL LANGUAGE: Amharic   POLITICAL SYSTEM: presidential
HEAD OF STATE: President Meles Zenawi (since July '91)
PRINCIPAL MINISTERS: Tamirat Laynie (prime minister), Alemayehu Dhaba (finance),
    Mehitema Solomon (justice), Seyoum Mesfin (foreign affairs), Kuma Demeksa
    (interior), Siye Abraha (defence)
INTERNATIONAL ALIGNMENT: NAM, OAU, ACP
CURRENCY: birr (end-'92 £1=Br7.48, US$1=Br4.94)
GNP PER CAPITA: US$120 ('90)
MAIN EXPORT EARNERS: coffee, agricultural produce

THE interim government dominated by the Ethiopian People's Revolutionary Democratic Front (EPRDF), which had seized power in May 1991 (see AR 1991, pp. 248–9), faced increasing difficulties in establishing its promised democratic structure of government. This was based on the principle of ethnic federalism, in which each of the major nationalities would have the right to internal self-government; 14 new regions based on nationality had accordingly been established late in 1991. At the same time, previously-suppressed data from the 1984 national census gave total numbers of people then identifying themselves with each nationality. The Oromo people, as expected, constituted the largest single group, with 29.1 per cent of the total, but this was much less than the 40 per cent or more claimed by Oromo nationalists, and only slightly more than the 28.3 per cent identifying themselves as Amhara. Other major groups were the Tigrinya-speakers (9.7 per cent), Gurages (4.4 per cent), Somalis (3.8 per cent), Sidamas (3.0 per cent) and Welaytas (2.6 per cent). Nine further groups were each in the 1–2 per cent bracket, and no fewer than 77 had less than 1 per cent. These figures were inevitably subject to dispute, and likely to be inaccurate, especially for northern areas of the country (including Eritrea) where civil war was raging at the time of the census. However, no more accurate or generally-accepted assessment was likely to become available in the near future.

The formation of some 63 political organizations, most of which sought to represent nationality groups, greatly complicated the political process. The most important of these groups were, first, those associated with the EPRDF, including notably the Tigray People's Liberation Front (TPLF), the Ethiopian People's Democratic Movement (EPDM) and the Oromo People's Democratic Organization (OPDO); and second, the

Oromo Liberation Front (OLF). A variety of groups (including the EPDM) claimed to represent the Amharas, while OLF's support among Oromos was disputed not only by the OPDO but by the Islamic Front for the Liberation of Oromia (IFLO). Although OLF representatives had been included in the interim government formed in 1991, its relations with EPRDF remained tense, and fighting between them broke out in the western part of the country early in the year. An open breach was prompted by Ethiopia's first multi-party elections, on 21 June, for officials at district level.

The OLF boycotted the June elections, accusing the EPRDF authorities of intimidation, and disrupted the polls, especially in western parts of the country; Western observers who had been monitoring the elections withdrew from these areas. The elections were also postponed in three eastern regions where the security situation was precarious. The co-chairman of the observer delegation, US congressman Donald Payne, stated that the elections could not be described as completely free and fair. On 23 June the OLF withdrew its representatives from the interim government, and also withdrew its organization from Addis Ababa, in an evident prelude to the resumption of civil war. Though open hostilities were averted, following Western diplomatic pressure, the situation remained tense. As a result, the planned state funeral of the late Emperor Haile Selassie on 23 July (the centenary of his birth) was postponed.

Famine continued to affect millions of Ethiopians, especially in the south-east of the country, where refugees flooded in from the civil war in neighbouring Somalia (see VI.1.ii) and access was restricted by fighting between rival Oromo groups in the region around Harar. In August 1992 relief organizations in the area reported that thousands of people had died, while several relief workers were killed by mines and bandits. Some 8 million people, about one-sixth of the country's population, were said to be at risk from famine, and an appeal for 1.4 million tons of food aid was only very partially successful. The main rains were, however, good throughout the country. Though peaceful conditions prevailed in the north, famine relief was impeded by transport delays from the port at Aseb. Moreover, large numbers of internally-displaced people and farmers returning from the previous government's ill-advised resettlement schemes in the south and west placed further strains on relief services.

In September the Ethiopian birr, which had been held at $1=2.05 birr since the 1950s, was devalued to $1=4.94 birr. An IMF structural adjustment loan amounting to $70 million was approved.

The northern region of Eritrea had effectively become self-governing from May 1991, pending a referendum on the territory's independence which was due to be held in April 1993. In contrast to the rest of Ethiopia, the whole of Eritrea appeared to be firmly under the control of the Eritrean People's Liberation Front (EPLF) led by Isayas Afewerki, which enjoyed considerable support, though an opposition grouping dominated by factions from the Eritrean Liberation Front (ELF) was formed at Jeddah in September. Opposition to the Eritrean referendum was also voiced by groups claiming to represent the Afars of the Red Sea coast, who would be divided from their compatriots in the rest of Ethiopia by Eritrean independence.

The EPLF-led provisional government of Eritrea (PGE) launched a campaign of reconstruction after the 30-year war. The economy remained at a very low level, however, and Eritrea continued to be highly dependent on relief food. Relations with international organizations and other donors were affected by Eritrea's anomalous international status: the territory was not independent but the PGE refused to acknowledge that it was even formally part of Ethiopia. The PGE was nonetheless closely involved in attempts to achieve a peaceful political settlement in Ethiopia, while also maintaining good relations with Sudan.

ii. SOMALIA

CAPITAL: Mogadishu   AREA: 638,000 sq km   POPULATION: 7,800,000 ('90)
OFFICIAL LANGUAGES: Somali & Arabic   POLITICAL SYSTEM: interim government
HEAD OF STATE: Ali Mahdi Mohammed, interim President (since Jan '91)
PRINCIPAL MINISTERS: Umar Arteh Ghalib (prime minister), Mohammed Qanyareh
    Afrah (interior), Abdullah Shaikh Ismail (foreign affairs)
INTERNATIONAL ALIGNMENT: NAM, OAU, ACP, Arab League, ICO
CURRENCY: shilling (end-'92 £1=SoSh3,973.25, US$1=SoSh2,624.34)
GNP PER CAPITA: US$120 ('90)

LATE in 1992 Somalia became the focus of global attention as a massive US-led military intervention took place under UN auspices in an attempt to rescue its people from famine brought about by a collapse of public order and the looting of relief supplies by armed gangs. President Bush visited US forces in Somalia on 31 December.

The main source of conflict was the rivalry between interim President Ali Mahdi Mohammed and General Mohammed Farah Aydid, leaders of clan-based factions within the United Somali Congress. A bewildering variety of other factions, including that loyal to former President Mohammed Siyad Barre, added to the confusion. A visit by UN assistant secretary-general James Jonah in January failed to end the fighting. Although the Security Council imposed an arms embargo in January and sponsored peace talks in February, these moves achieved little. The Security Council agreed on 24 April to send unarmed observers, but deferred a proposal to send troops. On 29 April former President Barre fled to Kenya after the border area where he had taken refuge fell to General Aydid's forces. He was subsequently given asylum in

Nigeria, but fighting continued in western Somalia as well as in the capital, Mogadishu. An Ethiopian attempt to negotiate a ceasefire in June was also unsuccessful.

By May the food situation was giving rise to acute international concern, and three-quarters of the country's people were estimated to be facing starvation. Although several relief agencies sought to bring food into the country, they were obliged to hire local 'guards' in order to protect their supplies, and these extorted half or more of the relief in payment. Unsettled conditions made relief distribution almost impossible. On 10 May the former Algerian UN envoy, Mohammed Sahnoun, arrived as UN special representative; by late July he estimated that 5,000 people were dying daily across the country, with the result that the UN Security Council authorized deployment of a security force (see also XI.1). A detachment of 500 Pakistani troops arrived in mid-September but were unable to prevent widespread looting. General Aydid, whose forces were reported by Amnesty International to have carried out mass executions, opposed any further UN involvement, as an affront to Somali sovereignty. The situation reached its nadir on 27 October, when Mohammed Sahnoun resigned after a reprimand from UN Secretary-General Boutros-Ghali for criticizing the ineffectiveness of the UN operation. By this time an estimated 300,000 Somalis had died, and a million more were refugees.

International pressure grew for humanitarian military intervention, regardless of the issue of sovereignty. On 3 December the UN Security Council approved such intervention under US leadership, with participation by France and other countries. The vanguard of a projected US force of 28,000 landed in Mogadishu on 9 December, while French troops arrived from Djibouti. Despite delays, these forces took over key towns in the south of the country, including the famine epicentres of Baidoa and Bardera, and sought to establish a relief network. In the face of overwhelming force, the faction leaders decided to welcome the intervention, and little resistance occurred. However, the US-led force did not seek to disarm the factions, and they withdrew with their weapons intact. No long-term arrangements were made for a political settlement or the re-establishment of an administration. The length of time for which the intervention force would remain was uncertain.

These developments did not affect the northern part of the country, formerly British Somaliland, which had declared its independence in 1991 (see AR 1991, p. 251). This secession was not recognized by any other state, however, and little information emerged from the area. Despite divisions within the government led by Abdel-Rahman Ahmed Ali, the situation did not descend to the disastrous anarchy of the south.

iii. DJIBOUTI

CAPITAL: Djibouti AREA: 23,000 sq km POPULATION: 427,000 ('90)
OFFICIAL LANGUAGES: Arabic & French POLITICAL SYSTEM: presidential
HEAD OF STATE: President Hassan Gouled Aptidon (since '77)
RULING PARTY: Popular Rally for Progress (RPP)
PRINCIPAL MINISTERS: Barkat Gourad Hamadou (prime minister, planning & land
    development), Ismail Ali Youssouf (defence), Moussa Bouraleh Robleh (finance
    & economy), Moumin Bahdon Farah (foreign affairs), Ahmed Bulaleh Barreh
    (interior), Ougoute Hassan Ibrahim (justice)
INTERNATIONAL ALIGNMENT: NAM, OAU, ACP, Arab League, ICO, Francophonie
CURRENCY: Djibouti franc (end-'92 £1=DF265.00, US$1=DF175.03)
GNP PER CAPITA: US$480 ('81)
MAIN EXPORT EARNERS: agricultural products

LATE in 1991 guerrillas of the Front pour la Restauration de l'Unité et
la Démocratie (FRUD) overran northern areas of the country apart from
the towns of Tadjoura and Obcock. Formed from a coalition of groups
opposed to President Hassan Gouled's ruling Rassemblement Populaire
pour le Progrès (RPP), FRUD was dominated by the Afar ethnic group.
Though President Gouled called for French military assistance under
a 1977 defence treaty, the French treated the conflict as an internal
one and refused to become involved, though they sought to act as a
neutral peace-keeping force. Intermittent clashes between FRUD and
government forces continued throughout the year.

Weakened by the resignation of several ministers, President Gouled
sought to deflect domestic and external opposition by agreeing to a new
multi-party constitution, which was approved by referendum on 4 September. Elections under this constitution were held on 18 December, but
only one opposition grouping, the Parti du Renouveau Démocratique
(PRD), contested them. Less than half the electorate voted, and the
ruling RPP, with 76.7 per cent of the votes cast, won all 65 seats in the
Chamber of Deputies. Earlier, former chief minister Ali Aref Bourhan
and others had been sentenced to ten years' imprisonment in June for
plotting to overthrow the government.

iv. KENYA

CAPITAL: Nairobi AREA: 580,000 sq km POPULATION: 24,200,000 ('90)
OFFICIAL LANGUAGE: Kiswahili & English POLITICAL SYSTEM: presidential
HEAD OF STATE AND PARTY LEADER: President Daniel Arap Moi (since '78)
RULING PARTY: Kenya African National Union (KANU)
PRINCIPAL MINISTERS: George Saitoti (vice-president, finance), Wilson Ndolo Ayah
    (foreign affairs), Davidson Ngibuni Kuguru (home affairs), Zachary Onyonka
    (planning & national development)
INTERNATIONAL ALIGNMENT: NAM, OAU, ACP, Cwth.
CURRENCY: shilling (end-'92 £1=Ksh54.05, US$1=Ksh35.70)
GNP PER CAPITA: US$370 ('90)
MAIN EXPORT EARNERS: coffee, tea, petroleum products, tourism

PRESIDENTIAL and parliamentary elections were held simultaneously on 29 December following an acrimonious campaign in which a number of lives were lost. These multi-party elections—the first to be held since independence in 1963—were forced on a reluctant President Daniel Arap Moi by a combination of domestic and international pressure (see AR 1991, pp. 252–4).

The main opposition party to register was the Forum for the Restoration of Democracy (FORD), whose strength was that it cut across ethnic divisions and united in one organization the Kikuyu (the country's largest ethnic group) and the Luo (the second largest). However, FORD was greatly weakened when one of its leading members—Kenneth Matiba, a wealthy Kikuyu businessman who had resigned as a cabinet minister in 1988—decided to challenge President Moi for the presidency. He thus turned down the possibility of standing as running mate to the (Luo) veteran politician and former Kenyan vice-president, Jaramogi Oginga Odinga, FORD's interim chairman, who had already declared his candidacy.

Following his election as substantive chairman by a party congress in September, Mr Odinga was formally adopted by delegates as FORD's presidential candidate. Attempts to reconcile the two factions failed and FORD split into two parties—Mr Odinga's FORD-Kenya and Mr Matiba's FORD-Asili ('Original FORD'). The opposition was also weakened by the earlier formation of the Democratic Party (DP); its leader was Mwai Kibaki, a former Kenyan vice-president, who probably lost support by accepting demotion to Minister of Health in 1988 and by remaining in government until December 1991.

The split in the opposition vote proved critical. Standing as candidate of the ruling Kenya African National Union (KANU), President Moi received 36.3 per cent (or approximately 1.9 million votes) in a high poll, Mr Matiba 26 per cent, Mr Kibaki 19.5 per cent and Mr Odinga 17.5 per cent. Since President Moi received the constitutionally-required nationwide majority and a minimum of 25 per cent of the votes in five out of the country's eight provinces, there was no need for a run-off contest and he was sworn in for a further term. In the parliamentary elections, KANU finished up with 100 seats (18 were unopposed and 15 cabinet ministers were defeated), while FORD-Kenya and FORD-Asili each won 31 and the DP 23. The smaller opposition parties got nowhere in either election. The President was constitutionally entitled to nominate 12 MPs, bringing KANU's tally to 112 out of 200.

Voting was along ethnic lines: FORD-Kenya swept the board in Nyanza province (Mr Odinga's homeland), while FORD-Asili and the DP shared all the seats in Kikuyuland, notably Central province. KANU won only one seat in Nairobi, the capital, where socio-economic issues predominated. The overall effect of the elections was the virtual exclusion from government of the Kikuyu and Luo.

The opposition parties pointed to 'widespread irregularities' perpetrated by government and KANU in the electoral process; these allegedly included preventing opposition candidates from handing in their nomination papers, bribing and intimidating voters, and inciting ethnic attacks by 'warriors' belonging to President Moi's Kalenjin group on non-Kalenjin (especially Kikuyu) living in Rift Valley province, resulting in many deaths. While considering that some aspects of the elections were not 'free and fair', the Commonwealth observer group and other election monitors thought that, in broad terms, the results reflected the will of the people and should be accepted by the opposition. After some hesitation, the three main opposition parties decided to take up the parliamentary seats won by their candidates, to form a united front and to 'use all legal and non-violent methods to ensure that fresh elections are held'. They were expected to challenge at least 17 results in the courts.

Early in June Professor George Saitoti, Vice-President and Minister of Finance, presented the 1992/93 budget against a background of economic depression, rising inflation, serious shortages of basic foods and political instability. Most commentators agreed that the economy was over-centralized, the parastatal sector costly and inefficient, and corruption rife. Mr Saitoti's object was to restore business confidence and help win back the foreign aid suspended in 1991. To reduce the budget deficit of KSh 2,300 million, he announced stricter spending controls and some revenue-raising measures. He also provided more export incentives and, contrary to expectations, marginally reduced individual and company taxation. The main thrust of his budget was on stronger tax reforms and administration, especially in value added tax (VAT) and customs duties; he was convinced that improved collection rather than higher taxes was the key to increasing revenue. He conceded the need to reduce the size of the civil service and to speed up privatization.

Over 400,000 Somalis and Ethiopians sought refuge in Kenya to escape from civil war, drought and famine in their own countries (see VI.1.i & ii). Kenya itself suffered from prolonged drought and had to import maize for the first time since 1984. Bandits attacked and robbed German and other tourists in the Masai Mara game reserve, where the British tourist Julie Ward was murdered in September 1988. Two game rangers, charged with killing her, were acquitted in the High Court in June, although the presiding judge criticized the police for attempting to cover up the murder. President Moi, on his way to the Earth Summit in Brazil in June, broke his journey in South Africa and met President F. W. de Klerk.

v. TANZANIA

CAPITAL: Dar es Salaam/Dodoma AREA: 945,000 sq km POPULATION: 24,500,000 ('90)
OFFICIAL LANGUAGES: Kiswahili & English POLITICAL SYSTEM: presidential
HEAD OF STATE AND GOVERNMENT: President Ali Hassan Mwinyi (since '85)
RULING PARTY: Chama cha Mapinduzi (CCM)
VICE-PRESIDENTS: John Malecela (prime minister), Salmin Amour (president of
   Zanzibar)
PRINCIPAL MINISTERS: Kighoma Ali Malima (finance), Ahmed Hassan Diria (foreign
   affairs), Augustine Lyatonga Mrema (interior)
INTERNATIONAL ALIGNMENT: NAM, OAU, ACP, Cwth.
CURRENCY: shilling (end-'92 £1=Tsh495.95, US$1=Tsh327.58)
GNP PER CAPITA: US$110 ('90)
MAIN EXPORT EARNERS: coffee, cotton, tropical foodstuffs

IN January the presidential commission established early in 1991 to test
opinion on political change (see AR 1991, p. 255) recommended that
Tanzania should adopt a multi-party system of government. In accepting
this recommendation, the national executive committee of the ruling
Chama cha Mapinduzi (CCM) stipulated that the new political parties
should be 'national parties', taking into consideration the two parts of
the union (mainland Tanzania and Zanzibar), and should not be parties
which favoured one part of the union or divided people along tribal,
religious or racial lines. The adoption of multi-partyism was endorsed
by the CCM national conference in February and was legalized in May,
when parliament amended the constitution to allow the formation of
opposition parties.

   Many parties emerged and obtained provisional registration for
multi-party elections scheduled for 1995, when the current presidential
mandate would expire; several of their leaders were former politicians
and trade unionists. The government indicated that the number of
women in parliament would be 15 per cent of the total number of
MPs. In Zanzibar, despite reservations expressed by Seif Sharif Hamad,
a former chief minister, the house of representatives unanimously
endorsed the multi-party proposals and voted to retain the union.
The island's attorney-general announced that the Zanzibar government
would remain unchanged until multi-party elections were held and that,
in the interim, representatives and elected officials who defected to the
opposition would lose their seats or offices.

   Under the 1992/93 budget, presented to parliament in June, development expenditure was to increase by 164 per cent over 1991/92.
However, mainly because of the fall in world market prices of primary
produce—notably coffee, cotton, sisal and tea—the country faced serious balance-of-payment problems: exports paid for only 29 per cent of
imports, resulting in heavy reliance on donor grants and loans. On the
other hand, inflation fell to under 20 per cent; the currency market was
liberalized; tax concessions were made to boost local industry; and many
new companies were established.

Responding to the urging of the donor community to accelerate the pace of structural reform, the government, despite retaining a formal commitment to socialism, committed itself to cut public expenditure, reduce the size of the civil service (10,000 employees were to go in 1992), improve the social and physical infrastructure (road conditions and telephone services, in Dar es Salaam particularly, were appalling) and expand the private sector's role in stimulating economic growth. In fact, though most maize marketing was in the hands of private traders and cotton ginning was slowly being privatized, significant privatization made little headway; the total debts of the country's 400-plus parastatals were immense.

The failure to maintain (or build new) hotels to an international standard had an adverse effect on the tourist industry. In Zanzibar the government proposed to implement 86 development projects. Reduced export earnings and devaluation and a heavy imports bill meant that the island suffered substantial balance-of-payments and balance-of-trade deficits.

In February the Tanzanian government rejected the demand, which was backed by strike action, of students of Dar es Salaam University that it should scrap a cost-sharing scheme, due to start in August, under which they would have to pay part of the cost of their tuition. It expelled 240 engineering students for intimidating other students who refused to continue the strike. In June the government arrested a group of Burundi refugees who were seeking to overthrow the government of Burundi (see also VII.1.ii). An outbreak of cholera occurred the same month in Zanzibar, where a new bi-monthly government newspaper called *Nuru* was published.

vi. UGANDA

CAPITAL: Kampala   AREA: 240,000 sq km   POPULATION: 16,300,000 ('90)
OFFICIAL LANGUAGE: English   POLITICAL SYSTEM: presidential
HEAD OF STATE AND GOVERNMENT: President Yoweri Museveni (since Jan '86)
RULING PARTY: National Resistance Movement (NRM) heads broad-based coalition
PRINCIPAL MINISTERS: Samson Kisseka (vice-president, internal affairs), George
    Cosmas Adyebo (prime minister), Eriya Kategaya (first deputy premier), Paul
    Ssemogerere (second deputy premier, foreign affairs), Abubakar Mayanja
    (third deputy premier, justice), Joshua Mayanja–Nkangi (finance & planning),
    Richard Kaijuka (commerce, industry & cooperatives)
INTERNATIONAL ALIGNMENT: NAM, OAU, ACP, Cwth.
CURRENCY: shilling (end-'92 £1=Ush1,846.50, US$1=Ush1,219.62)
GNP PER CAPITA: US$220 ('90)
MAIN EXPORT EARNERS: coffee, cotton

IN April President Yoweri Museveni created a new Ministry of Commerce, Industry and Cooperatives. He also combined the Ministry of Planning and Development with the Ministry of Finance, partly to ensure that all parastatal bodies implemented the Economic Recovery

Programme (see AR 1991, p. 257). The constitutional commission, appointed in February 1989, continued to sound out public opinion and was expected to recommend a return to political pluralism. This outcome was favoured by a number of senior members of the government, including Paul Ssemogerere, leader of the Democratic Party (DP), Second Deputy Prime Minister and Foreign Minister.

President Museveni himself, however, did not favour multi-partyism. Though committed to accepting the commission's findings, he believed that parties were 'not synonymous with democracy' and wanted their legalization to be deferred until 1995, when presidential elections were due. The programme for the election of resistance committees, from village to district level, began in late February. If elected to district, town or municipal committees (but not before), civil servants had to resign their posts.

The government depended on external aid to finance 70 per cent of the country's development expenditure. It continued to adhere to World Bank and IMF economic adjustment programmes and was committed to private sector development, the introduction of a market-based exchange rate system, and import and export trade liberalization. In January it devalued the Uganda shilling by just over 8 per cent—the fifth devaluation since the 1991/92 budget in July 1991. Western donors agreed in May to provide $850 million in aid, while the following month the Paris Club of creditor states recommended that Uganda's external debt of $3,000 million should be waived as to 50 per cent to ease balance-of-payments and debt-servicing burdens.

Joshua Mayanja-Nkangi, the Finance Minister, presented an austere budget on 30 June. He announced that 6,000 civil servants were to be laid off and that the 250,000-strong National Resistance Army (NRA) and local defence units were to be reduced in size. He projected that in absolute terms spending in 1992/93 would increase by 56 per cent over 1991/92 and revenue by an estimated 350 per cent, enabling a near 50 per cent cut to be made in the current-account deficit. Higher taxes were imposed on petroleum products and private investment was encouraged, for example by reducing import duties on capital goods. The decline in coffee earnings led the government to allow market forces to determine the price paid to farmers.

In August the Public Enterprises Reform and Divestiture secretariat (PERD), a government body appointed to handle the privatization exercise, published a long list of public enterprises which were being put up for sale. The loss-making companies were of varying size; most of them had been owned by Asian entrepreneurs and investors prior to the 1972 expulsion of Asians by Idi Amin (see AR 1972, p. 234). These and other Asians were encouraged to return and make use of the machinery established to reclaim the property seized illegally by Amin; large property-owners were prominent among the returnees.

AIDS was the leading reported cause of death among the adult population—almost 10 per cent of the total population was HIV-positive, the worst-hit districts being in the south-west. Ecological changes taking place in Lake Victoria seriously threatened the future of the fishing industry. Villagers living near the borders with Rwanda (see VIII.1.ii) and Sudan (see V.4.i) suffered because of the civil war in these countries; Uganda had to accommodate refugees from them and also from Zaïre (see VII.1.i). A military training exchange agreement was signed with Tanzania in October.

2.   GHANA—NIGERIA—SIERRA LEONE—THE GAMBIA—LIBERIA

i.   GHANA

CAPITAL: Accra   AREA: 240,000 sq km   POPULATION: 14,900,000 ('90)
OFFICIAL LANGUAGE: English   POLITICAL SYSTEM: presidential
HEAD OF STATE: President-elect Jerry Rawlings (since Nov '92), previously Chairman
   of Provisional National Defence Council (since '81)
PRINCIPAL MINISTERS: P. V. Obeng (chairman of committee of secretaries),
   Kwesi Botchwey (finance & economic planning), Obed Y. Asamoah (foreign
   affairs), Mahamad Idrisu (defence), Nana Kwesi Obuadum (justice), Col. E. M.
   Osei-Owusu (interior)
INTERNATIONAL ALIGNMENT: NAM, OAU, ACP, Cwth.
CURRENCY: cedi (end-'92 £1=C788.60, US$1=C520.87)
GNP PER CAPITA: US$390 ('90)
MAIN EXPORT EARNERS: cocoa, gold, minerals

THOSE who believed and those who doubted that Ghana was moving towards democracy could both find evidence in the year's events. The country was caught up in election fever once the constitutional commission had adopted (27 March) the final text of what would be the constitution of the Fourth Republic. There was to be an elected president and a parliament of 200 members, but no prime minister. The president would serve for a term of four years, renewable only once. There would be no legally-imposed one-party state, and traditional leaders who wished to stand for election would be required to forfeit their chieftaincy.

On 28 April a referendum was held on whether the country should adopt these reforms. Since all sides were agreed that it should, the number voting was small: 3,680,983 out of 8.5 million electors. There was an overwhelmingly 'yes' vote of 92 per cent. The central question, whether Flight-Lieutenant Rawlings would stand for the presidency, became clear on 10 June when the Provisional National Defence Council (the ruling junta) formed a political party, the National Democratic Congress (NDC). Other parties emerged from the shadows once the

11-year-old ban on politics was lifted (18 May). Eventually, five candidates contested the presidency, and the full panoply of a Ghanaian election—the ninth major contest since 1951 and the first since Flight-Lieutenant Rawlings seized power in 1981—absorbed public interest throughout the rest of the year.

There were 18,000 polling stations under the authority of some 50,000 officials in the 200 single-member constituencies. The register of electors became a focus of great controversy. It had been compiled for district council elections at a time when politics were forbidden under the pretence that Ghana was a 'no party state'. Many, therefore, were not on the register. The main opposition parties—the New Patriotic Party (NPP) led by Professor Adu Boahen, the People's National Convention (PNC) under the former prime minister, Hilla Limann, the National Independence Party (NIP) led by Kwabena Darko and the People's Heritage Party (PHP) of General Emmanuel Erskine—contended that their supporters were not fully registered. Attempted court action failed, as did protest to the chairman of the interim national electoral commission, Justice J. Ofori-Boateng.

The presidential election was held on 3 November. The outcome was not as expected by local pollsters and newspapers, nor by the Accra astrologer Dr Baldwin Baddo. Flight-Lieutenant Rawlings won by a substantial margin (58.3 per cent) against his chief opponent, Professor Boahen (30.4 per cent), while Mr Limann obtained only 6.7 per cent, Mr Darko 2.8 per cent and General Erskine 1.2 per cent.

That there was strong regional bias in both Ashanti and the Volta region surprised no one, but Professor Boahen was shocked by his defeat. He was quoted as saying: 'I am convinced I won the election' adding that there was 'ballot-rigging on a massive scale', coupled with falsification of the results. That was not the view of the Commonwealth observer team, which judged the election to be 'free and fair', nor of those who watched the contest on behalf of the US Carter Center. Both groups, however, were critical of the electoral register.

On 8 December the main opposition parties held a joint rally in Accra. They decided not to appeal to the electoral commission because (said J. Agyenim Boateng, NPP general secretary) they feared a continuation of the violence which had followed the election. They would, however, boycott the parliamentary elections. These were held on 29 December and the result was predictable: the NDC won 189 seats against token opposition, 11 seats going to minor parties and independents. Ghana was now virtually a *de facto* one-party state. The inauguration date for the new President was 7 January 1993.

Among other controversies was the discovery of a cache of weapons, but the arrest on 16 July of Mike Soussidus of the EGLE party—'Every Ghanaian Living for Everybody'—came to nothing. The year was marred by a catalogue of public protests against the effects of the structural adjustment programme. On 2 March the University of Science and Technology at Kumasi was closed after student riots. In June nurses went on protest strike against conditions of work, followed by civil servants and other public employees angered by the curtailment of end-of-service benefits. September–October saw a major interruption of bauxite exports from Tema and Sekondi-Takoradi.

Foreign policy was subordinate to these domestic upheavals but a close watch was kept on disturbances in neighbouring Togo (see VI.3.viii). If Ghana was now a democracy, it was also in disarray.

ii. NIGERIA

CAPITAL: Lagos   AREA: 924,000 sq km   POPULATION: 88,500,000 ('92)
OFFICIAL LANGUAGE: English   POLITICAL SYSTEM: transitional
HEAD OF STATE AND GOVERNMENT: President (Gen.) Ibrahim Babangida (since '85)
PRINCIPAL MINISTERS: Zakari Ibrahim (foreign affairs), Lt-Gen. Sanni Abacha
    (defence), Abubakar Alhaji (finance & economic planning), Chu Okongwu
    (petroleum), Clement Akpamgbo (justice), Tunji Olagunju (interior)
INTERNATIONAL ALIGNMENT: NAM, OAU, OPEC, ICO, ACP, Cwth.
CURRENCY: naira (end-'92 £1=N32.60, US$1=N21.54)
GNP PER CAPITA: US$360 ('92)
MAIN EXPORT EARNERS: oil and gas

IN his budget address on 1 January President Ibrahim Babangida announced that government spending for the year was projected at N 27,594 million compared with N 22,123 million in 1991. Of total spending, N 15,618 million was assigned to current expenditure with the remainder slated for capital projects. Federal government revenue was projected at N 101,201 million, of which central government would retain N 54,307 million, the remainder to be disbursed to state and local governments. Revenue projections were based upon an oil price of US$21 per barrel rather than the then market price of $17. Foreign exchange earnings were projected at $8,998 million of which $2,227 million was assigned to debt servicing, a figure well below scheduled obligations of around $5,800 million. This suggested that the Armed Forces Ruling Council (AFRC) was assuming that it would conclude a debt rescheduling agreement during 1992 and/or that oil earnings would be substantially higher than forecast.

It was commonly held that a rescheduling of Nigeria's $30,000 million total external debt depended in the first instance upon a renegotiated IMF agreement, the last agreement having been suspended because of the Fund's displeasure at Nigeria's significantly overshooting projected budget expenditure during 1991. The Fund and the World Bank had also expressed concern about the employment of unorthodox procedures in national accounting. Against this background, a dramatic step was taken towards placating the IMF when, on 5 March, the multi-tiered foreign exchange system—widely seen as a source of much abuse—was abolished and the naira floated. Within 24 hours the value of the currency had plunged from the pegged central bank rate of 10.5 to 18 per US dollar.

Initial public reaction to the flotation of the naira and its consequences for domestic inflation was surprisingly muted. But two months later a tidal wave of cumulative frustrations burst upon the streets of Lagos in ten days of rioting, burning, looting and killing which left at least 300 people dead. Similar outbursts were reported in three other southern states. The ostensible trigger was a 500 per cent increase in taxi fares provoked by an acute shortage of fuel. The petrol crisis was prompted by significantly reduced capacity due to maintenance work at two of the country's major refineries, exacerbated by large-scale smuggling of Nigeria's cheap fuel into neighbouring countries. A third factor, believed to play a contributory role, was widespread hoarding motivated primarily by the expectation of the removal of the government subsidy on petrol (an IMF demand which in principle the government had accepted). In fact, the fuel shortage had become so acute that by the end of April a government spokesman was forced to admit that Nigeria, the world's 13th largest oil producer and a member of OPEC, was having to import 20 per cent of its domestic needs.

Parallel to, but unconnected with, the Lagos upheavals was a serious outbreak of Muslim-Christian violence in Kaduna state. Originating in a land dispute between minority Christian Kataf people and the majority Muslim Hausas in a village some 250 km from the city of Kaduna, the violence soon spread to the state capital, where several churches were razed and an estimated 300 people killed. The federal government responded by banning all religious, ethnic and tribal groupings as well as announcing the formation of a new National Guard aimed at reducing the role of the army in riot control.

Despite these upheavals the National Assembly elections, brought forward from November to 5 July, proceeded without serious incident. The outcome was that the purportedly leftish Social Democratic Party (SDP) gained a majority in both the Senate and the House of Representatives, although not sufficiently large to be able to override a presidential veto. There was some indication of 'tribal' voting. The allegedly northernist National Republican Convention (NRC) swept the board in the traditional Muslim states of Sokoto, Niger and Kebbi (formerly southern Sokoto—see AR 1991, p. 260), while the 'southern' SDP romped home in the Yoruba west. But political loyalties elsewhere failed to crystallize along clearcut north/south lines.

The success and generally orderly nature of the parliamentary elections no doubt encouraged President Babangida, in an interview with *Newsweek* in August, to affirm that 'the transition programme is very much on course'. However, widespread electoral malpractices during the presidential primaries held in August and September compelled the AFRC to postpone the presidential election scheduled for 5 December and to announce a radically-altered transition programme. Broadcasting to the nation on 16 November, the President earmarked 12 June 1993 as the new date for the presidential election, with the victor being sworn into office on 27 August, more than seven months after the original date of 1 January.

In the meantime, a thorough-going overhaul of the party organizations had taken place, their executive committees being dissolved in October and all 23 existing presidential candidates being disqualified from further participation in the electoral contest. Caretaker committees, under the superintendence of the national electoral commission (NEC), were charged with organizing the printing of party membership cards and the registration of members (the absence of bona fide membership lists having been a major source of irregularities during the primaries), as well as the election of new executives and the screening of presidential candidates. The presidential campaign was now scheduled to take place from 19 April to 11 June 1993.

The President also announced the formation, under his chairmanship, of a new interim executive in the form of a National Defence and Security Council (NDSC) which replaced the AFRC. This would oversee the work of a 29-strong National Transitional Council, comprising bankers, entrepreneurs, legal experts and other professionals, which would supplant the Council of Ministers and be responsible for the day-to-day running of government. In the absence of an elected head of state, any legislation produced by the National Assembly (which was inaugurated on 5 December) would need to be ratified by the NDSC.

At the end of the year Nigeria's fundamental economic problems remained those of chronic over-dependency on oil revenue together with a crippling level of debt servicing (the latter estimated to consume 60 per cent of export revenue). The consequential need to curb public spending was becoming increasingly difficult to reconcile with the political exigencies of an emerging democratic system. Despite the severe hardships that they continued to endure, Nigerians theoretically found themselves suddenly enriched with the publication of the provisional census results in March. The new population figure of 88.5 million, substantially less than the commonly accepted estimate of over 110 million, required that the figure for per capita income be revised up from $250 to $360 per annum.

iii.   SIERRA LEONE

CAPITAL: Freetown   AREA: 72,000 sq km   POPULATION: 4,100,000 ('90)
OFFICIAL LANGUAGE: English   POLITICAL SYSTEM: military dictatorship
HEAD OF STATE & GOVERNMENT: Capt. Valentine E. M. Strasser, Chairman of
   Supreme Council of State (since May '92)
PRINCIPAL MINISTERS: Lt Solomon Musa (first secretary), Col. Alimany Usman
   Kamara (internal affairs, rural development), John Karimu (trade, industry),
   Arnold Gooding (justice)
INTERNATIONAL ALIGNMENT: NAM, OAU, ICO, Cwth.
CURRENCY: leone (end-'92 £1=Le781.00, US$1=Le515.85)
GNP PER CAPITA: US$240 ('90)
MAIN EXPORT EARNERS: diamonds, coffee, cocoa

ON the day of the Gambian elections on 29 April (see VI.2.iv), a coup occurred in Sierra Leone. Despite the introduction of a multi-party constitution the previous October (see AR 1991, pp. 262–3), President Joseph Momoh and his All People's Congress (APC) government were swept from power by middle-ranking officers headed by 28-year-old Captain Valentine Strasser. Mr Momoh escaped to neighbouring Guinea, where he was granted political asylum. What started as a violent but limited protest against pay arrears by soldiers fighting anti-government forces in the districts bordering on Liberia turned into a full-blow insurrection. A 23-member National Provisional Ruling Council (NPRC), comprising civilians and soldiers from all sections of the country, took over the government and committed itself to a programme of political reform and economic recovery. Popular dissatisfaction with the Momoh regime's administrative record and political intentions ensured that the army take-over was well-received, though it went against the recent trend towards elective government in Africa.

Following the refusal of the rebel Revolutionary United Front to surrender despite the overthrow of the APC government, the drawn-out fighting on the Liberian border continued. More positive results were achieved in other areas. Three commissions of inquiry into the assets of former prominent members of government, the civil service and security forces were set up; a recovery budget was introduced in July and civilians were put in control of the day-to-day administration of the country. Also in July, the NPRC was transformed into the Supreme Council of State (SCS) and a 19-member advisory council was set up to consider a transition to civilian rule.

Hopes for a swift end to military rule were not only hampered by continued fighting in the east and the enormity of the task of economic reconstruction. On 28 December there was an attempted coup against the Strasser government, resulting in numerous arrests and the execution of 26 alleged plotters, including a former inspector-general of police. The summary executions threatened desperately-needed international support for Sierra Leone's economic recovery programme, particularly as Britain cut off its aid programme in protest.

iv. THE GAMBIA

CAPITAL: Banjul AREA: 11,300 sq km POPULATION: 875,000 ('90)
OFFICIAL LANGUAGE: English POLITICAL SYSTEM: presidential democracy
HEAD OF STATE & GOVERNMENT: President Sir Dawda Kairaba Jawara (since '70)
RULING PARTY: People's Progressive Party (PPP)
PRINCIPAL MINISTERS: Saihou S. Sabally (vice-president, defence), Bakary Bunja
  Darbo (finance, economy), Omar Sey (external affairs), Lamin Kiti Jabang
  (interior), Hassan Jallow (justice)
INTERNATIONAL ALIGNMENT: NAM, OAU, ACP, ICO, Cwth.
CURRENCY: dalasi (end-'92 £1=D13.26, US$1=D8.75)
GNP PER CAPITA: US$260 ('90)
MAIN EXPORT EARNERS: groundnuts & groundnut products

PRESIDENTIAL and parliamentary elections took place in the Gambia on 29 April. Despite doubts about its electoral prospects, prompted by a revival of the political opposition, the ruling People's Progressive Party (PPP) won the elections for the sixth time since independence in 1965. The President, Sir Dawda Jawara, defeated four rivals in the presidential poll, taking 58.4 per cent of the vote, nearly three times more than his nearest rival, Sheriff Dibba of the National Convention Party (NCP), who managed only a 22 per cent share.

In the parliamentary elections four opposition parties put forward nearly 90 candidates in the 36 constituencies. The PPP did less well than in the presidential contest, ending up overall with 25 seats, six less than in the outgoing parliament. The main beneficiaries were (i) the NCP, which won six seats overall (an increase of one) and returned its leader to parliament after an absence of ten years; and (ii) the Gambia People's Party, which won two seats, although its leader, Assan Musa Camara, was defeated. Neither the recently-established Gambia Democratic Party, led by Dr Lamin Bojang, nor the longer-established radical People's Democratic Organization for Independence and Socialism, won any seats. The results did not generate the usual opposition accusations of electoral malpractices by the PPP, but the disappointingly low turnout of 58.4 per cent suggested a worrying level of indifference on the part of the electorate.

The new cabinet was sworn in on 11 May. Only three new appointments were made, two of them former ministers. The most important change was the exchange of posts between Vice-President Bakary Darbo and Finance Minister Saihou Sabally. The elevation of Mr Sabally—who was now seen as the most likely successor to President Jawara—confirmed earlier press speculation about the declining influence of Mr Darbo. President Jawara announced the creation of a new constitutional review body, opening up the possibility of the revival of an executive prime minister. He also promised measures to ease the hardships resulting from the otherwise successful economic recovery programme. A general amnesty was granted to all those in exile for their part in the abortive coup of July 1981, save its leader, Kukoi Samba Sanyang.

v. LIBERIA

CAPITAL: Monrovia   AREA: 97,750 sq km   POPULATION: 2,600,000 ('90)
OFFICIAL LANGUAGE: English   POLITICAL SYSTEM: presidential
HEAD OF STATE & GOVERNMENT: Amos Sawyer, President of interim government
PRINCIPAL MINISTERS: Peter Naigow (vice-president), Edward Kesselly (defence),
    Gabriel Matthews (foreign affairs), Amelia Ward (economy & planning),
    Philis Banks (justice), James Holder (commerce & industry)
INTERNATIONAL ALIGNMENT: NAM, OAU, ACP
CURRENCY: Liberian dollar (end-'92 £1=L$1.51, US$1=L$1.00)
GNP PER CAPITA: US$450 ('87)
MAIN EXPORT EARNERS: iron ore, rubber, coffee

ANOTHER year passed without any resolution of the political and military impasse in Liberia (see AR 1991, pp. 264–5). Most commentators shared the view of the interim government and the West African Monitoring Group (ECOMOG) that the National Liberation Front of Liberia (NPFL) led by Charles Taylor, who was believed to be backed by Burkina Faso and Libya, was the main obstacle to a negotiated peace settlement and a return to elected civilian government.

For much of the year fighting between warring factions was limited. From October, however, renewed clashes took place around Monrovia, where NPFL forces engaged ECOMOG forces defending the Liberian capital, and on the Sierra Leone frontier, where anti-Taylor United Liberation Movement (ULIMO) forces claimed to have made deep incursions into NPFL territory. Even so, some 75 per cent of the interior was still reported to be under Mr Taylor's control, and he appeared no nearer accepting the Yamoussoukro IV and Geneva conference accords on the disarming of the rival military groups and the reintroduction of national elections under a multi-party constitution.

Frustrated by Mr Taylor's evasiveness and hostility towards ECOMOG forces, the ECOWAS group of states, backed by the UN Security Council in October, declared an arms embargo on the warring factions and backed this up with air strikes against airfields and harbours under NPFL control to prevent arms deliveries. It remained to be seen by late December whether these measures would force Mr Taylor to enter into and honour peace agreements.

3. SENEGAL—GUINEA—MALI—MAURITANIA—CÔTE D'IVOIRE—
BURKINA FASO—NIGER—TOGO AND BENIN—CAMEROON—CHAD
GABON AND CENTRAL AFRICAN REPUBLIC—CONGO—
EQUATORIAL GUINEA

i. SENEGAL

CAPITAL: Dakar   AREA: 196,000 sq km   POPULATION: 7,400,000 ('90)
OFFICIAL LANGUAGE: French   POLITICAL SYSTEM: presidential democracy
HEAD OF STATE & GOVERNMENT: President Abdou Diouf (since '81)
RULING PARTY: Socialist Party (PS) heads coalition
PRINCIPAL MINISTERS: Habib Thiam (prime minister), Famara Ibrahima Sagna
   (economy, finance & planning), Medoune Fall (armed forces), Serigne Lamine
   Diop (justice), Djibo Ka (foreign affairs), Khary Dieng (interior)
INTERNATIONAL ALIGNMENT: NAM, ACP, ICO, Francophonie
CURRENCY: CFA franc (end-'92 £1=CFAF418.25, US$1=CFAF276.26)
GNP PER CAPITA: US$710 ('90)
MAIN EXPORT EARNERS: agricultural products & fish, chemicals

THIS was the year in which the international ambitions of President
Abdou Diouf reached their apogee. While keeping the presidency
of the Islamic Conference Organization (ICO) for the whole year,
as well as the chairmanship of the Economic Community of West
African States (ECOWAS) until July, he also took on the chairmanship
of the Organization of African Unity (OAU) and that of the group of
15 medium-ranking developing countries known as G15. This meant
that Dakar was host to a series of summits during the year, in the
massive King Fahd conference complex built for the Islamic summit
in December 1991. The OAU met in Senegal in June, ECOWAS in July
and G15 in November. Senegal's capital also saw a number of other
meetings, including the annual assemblies of the African Development
Bank and Interpol.

While all this activity enhanced President Diouf's international reputation, it was viewed with mixed feelings by his countrymen. Many of
them felt that he should give more attention to pressing problems at
home, especially as presidential and parliamentary elections were due
early in 1993.

The deaths of Senegalese soldiers of the ECOWAS peace-keeping
force in Liberia in May heightened the disquiet. As a preliminary to
the elections, the coalition between President Diouf's Socialist Party
(PS) and the Democratic Party (PDS) of Abdoulaye Wade came unstuck
with Maître Wade's departure from the government in October. This
followed the announcement of the presidential candidacies of both party
leaders, as well as seven others. By the end of 1992 the country was in
full election fever, especially since a new and fairer electoral code was
expected to produce a more genuine result.

Meanwhile, the problem of the Casamance secessionist movement
flared up again in August with the breakdown of a year-old ceasefire.

In bloody incidents, more than 50 civilians were said to have been killed, mainly by the military in response to secessionist attacks on non-Diola peoples. The ethnic nature of the problem was an increasingly obvious dimension to what had once been seen as a regional revolt against rule from Dakar. On Senegal's northern frontier, formerly the Senegal river, discontent remained high among both the local population and refugees from Mauritania, due in part to rapprochement between President Diouf and the Mauritanian authorities.

ii. GUINEA

CAPITAL: Conakry   AREA: 246,000 sq km   POPULATION: 5,700,000 ('90)
OFFICIAL LANGUAGE: French   POLITICAL SYSTEM: military regime
HEAD OF STATE & GOVERNMENT: Brig.-Gen. Lansana Conté, Chairman of Transitional
    Committee for National Recovery (since '84)
PRINCIPAL MINISTERS: Maj. Ibrahim Sylla (foreign affairs), Maj. Abdourahmane
    Diallo (defence), Soriba Kaba (planning, finance), Salifou Sylla (justice)
    Alseny René Gomez (interior)
INTERNATIONAL ALIGNMENT: NAM, OAU, ACP, ICO, Francophonie
CURRENCY: Guinean franc (end-'92 £1=GF1,231.85, US$1=GF813.64)
GNP PER CAPITA: US$440 ('90)
MAIN EXPORT EARNERS: bauxite, oilseeds

LIKE many of the African countries engaged in transitions to multi-party democracy, Guinea did not find that the road was easy. Although the transition was not scheduled to be completed until 1994, considerable political tension developed in 1992. In February the President, General Lansana Conté, was said to have narrowly escaped death when his car was set upon by student demonstrators. In March there was an outbreak of rioting in the capital Conakry. Even so, in the same month political parties were legalized, these numbering nearly 40 by mid-year.

In May a population census was held as part of the preparations for elections. In September, after a series of party clashes, all meetings and demonstrations were banned. Following a reported attempt on the life of the President in October, elections scheduled for November were postponed to 1993, due to 'material and financial difficulties'. The main alliance of the opposition parties, the Democratic Forum, continued to be recognized by the authorities.

iii.   MALI

CAPITAL: Bamako   AREA: 1,240,000 sq km   POPULATION: 8,500,000 ('90)
OFFICIAL LANGUAGE: French   POLITICAL SYSTEM: presidential
HEAD OF STATE & GOVERNMENT: President Alpha Oumar Konaré (since April '92)
RULING PARTY: Alliance for Democracy in Mali (ADEMA)
PRINCIPAL MINISTERS: Younoussi Touré (prime minister), Mahamar Oumar Maiga
     (economy & finance), Idrissa Traore (justice), Abdoulaye Sekou Sow (defence),
     Mohamed Aloussine Touré (foreign affairs)
INTERNATIONAL ALIGNMENT: NAM, OAU, ACP, ICO, Francophonie
CURRENCY: CFA franc (end-'92 £1=CFAF418.25, US$1=CFAF276.26)
GNP PER CAPITA: US$270 ('90)
MAIN EXPORT EARNERS: cotton, agricultural products

THE main opposition leader, Alpha Oumar Konaré of the Alliance for
Democracy in Mali (ADEMA), coasted to victory in the presidential elections in April. He won over 70 per cent of the votes in the second round,
the rest going to his main rival, Tieoule Mamadou Konaté of the US-RDA
(Union Soudanaise—Rassemblement Démocratique Africaine). In the
first round Mr Konaré had obtained 44.9 per cent and Mr Konaté only
14.5 per cent against seven other candidates. The turnout was about
23 per cent in the first round and 16 per cent in the second. This
low poll was variously attributed to apathy, lack of politicization and
difficulties with the electoral list. Mr Konaré was sworn in as President
on 6 June in succession to Colonel Amadou Toumani Touré, who had
seized power in March 1991 (see AR 1991, p. 268) but who now returned
to private life. The new leader was faced with substantial problems, from
the poverty of the economy to the continued threat of Touareg revolt, in
spite of a peace accord signed in Algeria in April with the main dissident
Touareg groups. The trial of former President Moussa Traoré and 30
members of his regime began in June but had not been completed by the
end of the year. The main charges were of illicit acquisition of wealth.

iv.   MAURITANIA

CAPITAL: Nouakchott   AREA: 1,000,000 sq km   POPULATION: 2,000,000 ('90)
OFFICIAL LANGUAGES: French & Arabic   POLITICAL SYSTEM: quasi-military
RULING PARTY: Democratic and Social Republican Party (PRDS)
HEAD OF STATE & GOVERNMENT: President (Col.) Moaouia Ould Sidi Mohammed
     Taya (since Jan '92), previously Chairman of Military Council of National
     Salvation (since '84)
PRINCIPAL MINISTERS: Sidi Mohammed Ould Babaker (prime minister), Mohammed
     Abdrahmane Ould Moine (foreign affairs), Hasni Ould Didi (interior),
     Sow Adema Samba (justice), Kan Acheikh (finance), Mouhamedou Ould Michel
     (planning), Col. Ahmed Ould Minnih (defence)
INTERNATIONAL ALIGNMENT: NAM, Arab League, ICO, OAU, ACP, AMU, Francophonie
CURRENCY: ouguiya (end-'92 £1=OM160.75, US$1=OM106.18)
GNP PER CAPITA: US$500 ('90)
MAIN EXPORT EARNERS: iron ore, fish

IN January President (Colonel) Ould Taya was re-elected in the country's first multi-party elections, amid opposition charges of rigging. Of over 550,000 votes cast (just over 50 per cent of the electorate), he received 62 per cent. His nearest rival, Ahmed Ould Daddah, received 32 per cent, the remainder going to two other candidates. The six opposition parties rejected the result and boycotted the legislative elections on 6 and 13 March. Of the eight parties which contested the latter, the President's own Democratic and Social Republican Party (PRDS) obtained 67 of the 79 seats in the National Assembly.

v.   CÔTE D'IVOIRE

CAPITAL: Abidjan   AREA: 322,000 sq km   POPULATION: 11,900,000 ('90)
OFFICIAL LANGUAGE: French   POLITICAL SYSTEM: presidential
HEAD OF STATE & GOVERNMENT: President Félix Houphouët-Boigny (since '60)
RULING PARTY: Democratic Party of Côte d'Ivoire (PDCI)
PRINCIPAL MINISTERS: Alassane Ouattara (prime minister, economy & finance),
    Amara Essy (foreign affairs), Léon Konan Koffi (defence), Emile Constant
    Bombet (interior), Jacqueline Lohoues Oble (justice)
INTERNATIONAL ALIGNMENT: NAM, OAU, ACP, Francophonie
CURRENCY: CFA franc (end-'92 £1=CFAF418.25, US$1=CFAF276.26)
GNP PER CAPITA: US$750 ('90)
MAIN EXPORT EARNERS: cocoa, coffee, timber

TENSIONS between government and opposition, simmering since the heavy electoral defeat of the opposition by the ruling Democratic Party of Côte d'Ivoire (PDCI) in late 1990, came to a head in February. The initial cause was the publication of a report on alleged atrocities by security forces against students in May 1991 (see AR 1991, p. 270), which confirmed the events and recommended the removal of the head of the army, General Robert Guei. When octogenarian President Houphouët-Boigny refused to accept the report, the opposition staged a protest march on 18 February. This deteriorated into violence and led to mass arrests, including that of the leader of the Ivorian Popular Front (FPI), Laurent Gbagbo. Mr Gbagbo and several of his colleagues were sentenced to gaol terms of up to two years for involvement in 'acts of violence', even though the defence said that the violence had been stirred up by *agents provocateurs*.

Meanwhile, the President went on his annual extended visit to Europe, where he stayed for four months. Only on his return in June was it decided to amnesty all those convicted after the February riots. There had been considerable international pressure in favour of clemency, but the opposition claimed that the amnesty was intended to short-circuit the detainees' appeals against their imprisonment. The rest of the year was quiet politically. At the end of December 15 opposition parties formed an alliance called the Union of Democratic Forces, although the FPI was not a member.

The country's economic and financial problems continued to be worrying, in spite of World Bank/IMF reforms carried out by the Prime Minister, Alassane Ouattara. There were insistent reports that M. Ouattara was in conflict with the president of the National Assembly, Henri Konan Bedié. Although the latter was designated to take over temporarily in the event of the demise of the President, there was no official successor, and M. Ouattara was seen as an increasingly strong challenger.

vi. BURKINA FASO

CAPITAL: Ouagadougou   AREA: 275,000 sq km   POPULATION: 9,000,000 ('90)
OFFICIAL LANGUAGE: French   POLITICAL SYSTEM: transitional
HEAD OF STATE: President (Capt.) Blaise Compaoré, Chairman of Popular Front
   (since '87)
PRINCIPAL MINISTERS: Youssouf Ouedraogo (prime minister), Thomas Sanon (external
   relations), Roch Christian Kabore (finance & planning), Timothee Some
   (justice),Yarga Larba (defence)
INTERNATIONAL ALIGNMENT: NAM, OAU, ACP, ICO, Francophonie
CURRENCY: CFA franc (end-'92£1=CFAF418.25,US$1=CFAF276.26)
GNP PER CAPITA: US$330 ('90)
MAIN EXPORT EARNERS: cotton, agricultural produce

FOLLOWING the presidential elections of late 1991, which returned President Blaise Compaoré unopposed in the face of an opposition boycott (see AR 1991, pp. 270–1), the country went to the polls again in May for legislative elections. This time the opposition took part, but failed to secure even a substantial minority. The ruling Organization for Popular Democracy—Labour Movement (ODP-MT) won 78 out of 107 seats in the National Assembly, the remaining 29 being shared by eight opposition parties. The latter alleged that there had been 'massive fraud', recalling that in the December presidential elections there had been a 75 per cent boycott, which indicated, they claimed, the true strength of Captain Compaoré's support. Ruling party control of the electoral machine had facilitated fraud, they added. President Compaoré's continued links with Charles Taylor's rebel movement in Liberia, in contravention of ECOWAS resolutions, continued to excite attention. In October the United States withdrew its chargé d'affaires from Ouagadougou in protest.

vii. NIGER

CAPITAL: Niamey   AREA: 1,267,000 sq km   POPULATION: 7,700,000 ('90)
OFFICIAL LANGUAGE: French   POLITICAL SYSTEM: transitional
HEAD OF STATE: President (Brig.) Ali Saibou (since '87)
HEAD OF GOVERNMENT: Amadou Cheiffou, Prime Minister (since Oct '92)
PRINCIPAL MINISTERS: Hassane Hamidou Diallo (foreign affairs), Albert Wright
(communication), Daouda Rabiou (interior), Abdou Tiousso (justice),
Laoual Chaffani (finance & planning), Mohammed Moussa (commerce &
transport)
INTERNATIONAL ALIGNMENT: NAM, OAU, ACP, ICO, Francophonie
CURRENCY: CFA franc (end-'92 £1=CFAF418.25, US$1=CFAF276.25)
GNP PER CAPITA: US$310 ('90)
MAIN EXPORT EARNERS: uranium, metal ores

IT was a troubled year, in which a difficult and uncompleted political
transition was further complicated by a worsening of the Touareg
rebellion in the north. At the end of February the transition came
close to being derailed by an army action against the government of
Prime Minister Amadou Cheiffou, which had been set up after the
long-drawn-out national conference of 1991 (see AR 1991, p. 271). In
the event mutinous soldiers (led by a sergeant) drew back from staging
a coup. After securing a pledge that the near-bankrupt government
would pay January and February salaries immediately, the mutineers
released politicians they had arrested and ended their occupation of the
radio-TV station. Three weeks later M. Cheiffou suddenly dissolved his
government, on the grounds that it had been inefficient and inadequate.
At the same time, the presidential guard, which had been at the centre
of the mutiny, was also dissolved. For various logistical reasons, the
calendar of the transition, which had envisaged a referendum and
elections before the end of the year, was delayed. The referendum on
the multi-party constitution was not held until 28 December, yielding
the expected massive vote in favour.

An attack by Touareg rebels in August led to the initiation of a
'hard-line' policy against the rebellion. This involved the arrest of over
160 people, including prominent political personalities, alleged to be
members of the Front de Libération de l'Air et l'Azawad (FLAA). This
movement favoured the setting up of a separatist 'Azawad Republic'
in league with Touaregs in Mali and Algeria. In October M. Cheiffou
called for the setting up of a 'national reconciliation forum' to discuss
the Touareg problem. Nevertheless, rebel attacks were continuing as
the year ended.

viii. TOGO AND BENIN

Togo
CAPITAL: Lomé   AREA: 57,000 sq km   POPULATION: 3,600,000 ('90)
OFFICIAL LANGUAGES: French, Kabiye & Ewe   POLITICAL SYSTEM: transitional
HEAD OF STATE: President Gnassingbe Eyadema (since '67)
HEAD OF GOVERNMENT: Joseph Kokour Koffigoh, transitional Prime Minister (since
   Aug '92)
CURRENCY: CFA franc (end-'92 £1=CFAF418.25, US$1=CFAF276.26)
GNP PER CAPITA: US$410 ('90)
MAIN EXPORT EARNERS: phosphates, cocoa

Benin
CAPITAL: Porto Novo   AREA: 113,000 sq km   POPULATION: 4,700,000 ('90)
OFFICIAL LANGUAGE: French   POLITICAL SYSTEM: presidential
HEAD OF STATE & GOVERNMENT: President Nicéphore Soglo (since April '91)
CURRENCY: CFA franc (end-'92 £1=CFAF418.25, US$1=CFAF276.26)
GNP PER CAPITA: US$360 ('90)
MAIN EXPORT EARNERS: cotton, palm products

IT was a troubled and disillusioning year for the democracy movement in TOGO, which had entertained such high hopes after the 1991 national conference (see AR 1991, pp. 272–3). Already in December 1991 army elements loyal to President Eyadema had succeeded in intimidating the transitional government of Joseph Kokou Koffigoh into a ministerial reshuffle so that some of the President's men could take key positions. The threat of further army action remained constant through the year, with the result that Mr Koffigoh progressively lost the confidence of the pro-democratic parties. One result of the intimidation was the repeated postponement of the programme of elections envisaged for the transition. It appeared that the pro-Eyadema forces did not want to enter elections until they could be sure of controlling them.

The situation deteriorated amid a series of attacks on opposition figures, including an assassination attempt in May on the son of former President Olympio (assassinated in 1963). Tavia Amorin, the leader of a small political party, was murdered by soldiers in July, and it was rumoured that there was a 'hit list' of all leading opposition figures. Talks between Mr Koffigoh and President Eyadema in August led to a new government further tilted in the latter's favour. This enabled a referendum on the new constitution to be held on 27 September, when there was a large vote in favour.

There followed a bizarre episode on 22 October, when soldiers took members of the interim parliament hostage for several hours, during which they were beaten and humiliated. This incident led to a complete breakdown of trust between the President and the opposition. After elections had been postponed indefinitely, the opposition called a general strike to demand a more balanced government and the establishment of an independent security force. The strike was still in progress as the year ended, although President Eyadema tried to reach an accommodation with the isolated Mr Koffigoh. The President stated that the transition would end on 31 December, as prescribed by the national conference, the implication being that he would then resume his former powers. After the hostage episode, aid was suspended by the USA and Germany, and international protests mounted. Togo's politics seemed set on a collision course.

In BENIN it was a quiet year politically, although there were occasional rumblings from students and trade unions. President Nicéphore Soglo, who had been democratically elected in 1991 (see AR 1991, pp. 273–4), continued to use the 'model multi-party democracy' image to raise more international funds for an economy which, he said, had been 'completely ruined by 17 years of marxism'. Somewhat against his will, he took on the chairmanship of ECOWAS in July, and found himself involved in difficult discussions to do with the Liberian imbroglio (see VI.2.v).

ix. CAMEROON

CAPITAL: Yaoundé AREA: 475,000 sq km POPULATION: 11,700,000 ('90)
OFFICIAL LANGUAGES: French & English POLITICAL SYSTEM: transitional
HEAD OF STATE: President Paul Biya (since '82)
RULING PARTY: Cameroon People's Democratic Movement (RDPC)
PRINCIPAL MINISTERS: Simon Achidi Achu (prime minister), Edouard Akame
    Mfoumou (defence), Antoine Ntsimi (finance), Ferdinand Leopold Oyono
    (foreign affairs), Douala Montome (justice)
INTERNATIONAL ALIGNMENT: NAM, OAU, ACP, ICO, Francophonie
CURRENCY: CFA franc (end-'92 £1=CFAF418.25, US$1=CFAF276.26)
GNP PER CAPITA: US$960 ('90)
MAIN EXPORT EARNERS: oil, cocoa, coffee, aluminium

THE mounting political troubles triggered by the arrival of a multi-party democracy movement reached two turning-points in the course of 1992. These were the parliamentary elections of March and the presidential elections of October. Both were officially won by President Paul Biya and his Cameroon Democratic People's Movement (RDPC), but the victories were so close and surrounded by so many ambiguities that little seemed to be solved in the Cameroon political drama.

The March legislative elections, although slightly delayed, were still too soon for the opposition parties, which claimed that they needed more time to organize. Consequently, some of them, notably the Social Democratic Front (SDF) of John Fru Ndi, boycotted the polling. The results showed that the RDPC had won 88 (i.e. less than half) of the 180 seats in the National Assembly. However, through an alliance with a small non-Fulani northern party led by Dakolé Daissala, the RDPC was assured of a continued majority. The next largest party was the National Union of Democracy and Progress (UNDP), whose main power base was among the Fulani people of its leader, Bello Bouba Maigari.

In September President Biya called a snap presidential election for

11 October, even though one was not due until 1993. Given the first-past-the-post electoral system, and the continued divisions of the opposition, the President had an obvious advantage. But the campaigning skills of the English-speaking Mr Fru Ndi, especially his populist use of 'pidgin' in francophone areas, had the effect of placing the President on the defensive. The official results, delayed for ten days, gave Mr Biya 39.9 per cent and Mr Fru Ndi 35.9 per cent. However, the latter claimed that he had won, with 38 per cent against Mr Biya's 36 per cent, and that the official results had been doctored. Widespread rigging was in fact documented by the US National Democratic Institute, whose report was denounced by the RDPC.

President Biya proceeded to form a new government, which included some members of other parties. At the same time he declared a state of emergency in Mr Fru Ndi's home province in the north-west, placing him under house arrest in Bemenda and detaining hundreds of his supporters. Despite international pressure, this situation still obtained at the end of the year.

x. CHAD

CAPITAL: Ndjaména   AREA: 1,284,000 sq km   POPULATION: 5,700,000 ('90)
OFFICIAL LANGUAGES: French & Arabic   POLITICAL SYSTEM: presidential
HEAD OF STATE & GOVERNMENT: President (Col.) Idriss Deby (since Dec '90)
PRINCIPAL MINISTERS: Joseph Yodemane (prime minister), Mahamat Ali Adoum
    (foreign affairs), Loum Hinassou Laina (defence), Safi Abdelkader (economy &
    finance), Youssouf Togoimi (justice)
INTERNATIONAL ALIGNMENT: NAM, OAU, ACP, ICO, Francophonie
CURRENCY: CFA franc (end-'92 £1=CFAF418.25, US$1=CFAF276.26)
GNP PER CAPITA: US$190 ('90)
MAIN EXPORT EARNERS: cotton, agricultural products

IT was an unstable year for President Idriss Deby, who did well to survive it. The year began with an invasion across the western border (in the vicinity of Lake Chad) by a coalition of opponents, including elements of the former army of ex-President Hissène Habré, who had been deposed in 1990 (see AR 1990, p. 274) and was now living in Dakar. The invasion was contained by President Deby's army, but it was a pattern that was to recur several times during the year. The result was the continuance of war psychosis in the capital, Ndjaména.

In February the assassination of a human rights leader, Dr Joseph Behidi, apparently by unruly elements of President Deby's tribally-based army, provoked substantial protest in the capital, and a renewed commitment by the President to his programme for full multi-party civilian rule by September 1993. As the year wore on, this timetable looked increasingly unlikely, not least because of a further revolt by southern army elements. Even more serious was a quarrel between President Deby and one of his principal lieutenants, Abbas Koty, leader of the hardliners among the President's own people, the Zaghawa. Colonel Koty opposed both democratization and the plan to cut down the 50,000-strong army (many of whom had crossed with Colonel Deby from Sudan in 1990). In April disaffected soldiers surrounded the presidential palace in a pseudo-confrontation, and in June Colonel Koty fled after being accused of staging an attempted coup (although he claimed that he had been framed). His whereabouts with his supporters was a continuing worry for President Deby, until he was detained at Maroua in Cameroon at the end of December. Continuing outbreaks of violence, including an army-led massacre at Doba in the south in August, maintained an atmosphere of insecurity.

The regime's crisis of survival was compounded by continuing problems with the opposition and especially the trade unions. The latter staged a series of strikes in the latter part of the year in protest against attempts to apply structural adjustment policies and serious delays in paying civil servants' salaries. The government was only kept afloat by French subventions, and the French also provided extra funds for the almost impossible task of reducing and reforming the army. Even so, political parties were legalized in March, and preparations for the much-delayed national conference on political change continued.

xi.   GABON AND CENTRAL AFRICAN REPUBLIC

Gabon
CAPITAL: Libreville   AREA: 268,000 sq km   POPULATION: 1,100,000 ('90)
OFFICIAL LANGUAGE: French   POLITICAL SYSTEM: presidential
HEAD OF STATE & GOVERNMENT: President Omar Bongo (since '67)
RULING PARTY: Gabonese Democratic Party (PDG)
CURRENCY: CFA franc (end-'92 £1=CFAF418.25, US$1=CFAF276.26)
GNP PER CAPITA: US$3,330 ('90)
MAIN EXPORT EARNERS: oil & gas, manganese

Central African Republic
CAPITAL: Bengui   AREA: 623,000 sq km   POPULATION: 3,000,000 ('90)
OFFICIAL LANGUAGE: French   POLITICAL SYSTEM: transitional
HEAD OF STATE AND PARTY LEADER: President (Gen.) André Kolingba (since '81)
RULING PARTY: Central African Democratic Assembly (RDC)
CURRENCY: CFA franc (end-'92 £1=CFAF418.25, US$1=CFAF276.26)
GNP PER CAPITA: US$390 ('90)
MAIN EXPORT EARNERS: coffee, diamonds, timber

ALTHOUGH there were periodic strikes and political clashes in GABON during 1992, President Omar Bongo seemed to have mastered the art of living in a multi-party democracy, and of keeping a multitude of opposition parties at bay and warring with each other. Economic restructuring of a basically rich economy continued. In October Libreville was host to the Franco-African summit, part of the President's scheme to project himself as an 'elder statesman' before the 1993 presidential elections.

In the CENTRAL AFRICAN REPUBLIC the hazards of trying, reluctantly, to make a transition from military to multi-party rule became evident in October, when presidential and general elections were cancelled following serious confusion and violence on polling day. The elections had seven candidates, notably the current President, André Kolingba; former president David Dacko; former prime minister Ange Patasse; and long-time opposition leader Abel Goumba. Nearly 30 parties had contested the parliamentary elections, including the 14 parties which made up the Consultation des Forces Démocratiques (CFD), led by Mr Goumba. The cancellation followed the suspension of elections in the capital, Bangui, where the government claimed that the polling operation had been 'sabotaged'. President Kolingba promised that new elections would be held as soon as possible, although no date had been fixed by year's end.

xii. CONGO

CAPITAL: Brazzaville   AREA: 342,000 sq km   POPULATION: 2,300,000 ('90)
OFFICIAL LANGUAGE: French   POLITICAL SYSTEM: transitional
HEAD OF STATE: President Pascal Lissouba (since Aug '92)
INTERNATIONAL ALIGNMENT: NAM, OAU, ACP, Francophonie
CURRENCY: CFA franc (end-'92 £1=CFAF418.25, US$1=CFAF276.26)
GNP PER CAPITA: US$1,010 ('89)
MAIN EXPORT EARNERS: oil & gas, timber

CONTRARY to some expectations, it proved possible both to hold elections in the course of 1992 and to achieve a transition from military to civilian rule. After several delays, a constitutional referendum was held in March, and local elections were held in May. These showed that no party had an overall majority, but that the three most significant were the Union Pan-Africain pour la Démocratie Sociale (UPADS) led by Dr Pascal Lissouba, the former sole ruling Parti Congolais du Travail (PCT) headed by President Denis Sassou-Nguesso; and the Mouvement Congolais de la Démocratie et le Developpement Integré (MCDDI) of Bernard Kolelas. All three had regional bases, in the centre (UPADS), north (PCT) and south (MDCCI).

In parliamentary elections in July UPADS became the largest party in both the National Assembly and the Senate. The pattern of support evident then was largely repeated in presidential elections held on 2 and 16 August. In the first round Dr Lissouba won 35.98 per cent, Mr Kolelas 20.32 per cent, and Colonel Sassou-Nguesso 16.87 per cent (13 other candidates obtaining the remainder of the votes). In the second round, following a pact between UPADS and the PCT, Dr Lissouba came convincingly ahead with 61.1 per cent, against 38.6 per cent for Kolelas. Dr Lissouba accordingly took office as President on 31 August and appointed Stephane Bongho-Nouarra as Prime Minister.

Even before the end of the year, however, there was a confrontation between President Lissouba's supporters and those of the PCT. A vote of no confidence against the government in the National Assembly impelled the President to dissolve the Assembly and to call for fresh elections so that he could seek a majority. This led to riots in Brazzaville and Pointe Noire which left eight dead. Following an army 'intervention', in which all party leaders were brought together to work out a solution, Claude Antoine da Costa, a non-political former international civil servant, was appointed Prime Minister. At the end of the year political discussions were continuing.

xiii.   EQUATORIAL GUINEA

CAPITAL: Malabo   AREA: 28,000 sq km   POPULATION: 417,000 ('90)
OFFICIAL LANGUAGE: Spanish   POLITICAL SYSTEM: military regime
HEAD OF STATE & GOVERNMENT: Col. Teodoro Obiang Nguema Mbasogo, President
    of Supreme Military Council
PRINCIPAL MINISTERS: Siale Bileka Silvestre (prime minister), Miko Benjamin Mba
    Ekua (foreign affairs), Melanio Ebendeng Nsomo (defence), Marcelino Nguema
    Ongueme (economy & finance), Mariano Nsue Nguema (justice)
INTERNATIONAL ALIGNMENT: NAM, OAU, ACP, Francophonie
CURRENCY: CFA franc (end-'92 £1=CFAF418.25, US$1=CFAF276.26)
GNP PER CAPITA: US$330 ('90)
MAIN EXPORT EARNERS: cocoa, timber, coffee

IT was a turbulent and confused year, in which a programme for multi-party civilian rule was delayed because of concern on the part of the ruling junta under President Teodoro Obiang Nguema Mbasogo at the prospect of losing power. A transitional government was established in January, political parties were legalized in April and by the end of the year nine opposition parties had formed a 'joint opposition platform'. They claimed that 'paranoia' was still stifling the move to democracy, and that the President had formed a new paramilitary force for his personal protection. In October two Spanish businessmen were arrested and accused of preparing a coup.

VII CENTRAL AND SOUTHERN AFRICA

1. ZAÏRE—BURUNDI AND RWANDA—GUINEA—BISSAU AND CAPE VERDE—SÃO TOMÉ & PRÍNCIPE—MOZAMBIQUE—ANGOLA

i. ZAÏRE

CAPITAL: Kinshasa   AREA: 2,345,000 sq km   POPULATION: 37,300,000 ('90)
OFFICIAL LANGUAGE: French   POLITICAL SYSTEM: presidential
HEAD OF STATE AND GOVERNMENT: President (Marshal) Mobutu Sese Seko (since '65)
RULING PARTY: Popular Movement of the Revolution (MPR)
PRINCIPAL MINISTERS: Etienne Tshisekedi (prime minister), Mattieu Bossunga
   (interior), Paul Bandoma (defence), Pierre Lumbi (external relations),
   Benoît Atale (finance), Fernand Tala Ngai (economy & industry), Roger Gisanga
   (justice)
INTERNATIONAL ALIGNMENT: NAM, OAU, ACP, Francophonie
CURRENCY: zaïre (end-'92 £1=Z2,960,800, US$1=Z1,955,614)
GNP PER CAPITA: US$220 ('90)
MAIN EXPORT EARNERS: copper, other minerals, oil

SEEN at its simplest, Zaïre's political situation in 1992 featured a long-drawn-out tug-of-war between President Mobutu Sese Seko and his opponents in the national conference which had come together in 1991 to work out the constitutional measures needed in the transition from presidential autocracy to multi-party democracy (see AR 1991, pp. 279–81). By the end of the year the President was still in office, but his position had been gravely weakened.

President Mobutu's obstinate resistance to meaningful reform lost him the last shreds of the support he had once enjoyed from the United States, France and Belgium, whose governments now openly sided with his opponents. To make up for the aid thus lost, he visited Saudi Arabia and Kuwait. But at this stage in the country's fortunes the influence of outsiders seemed of minor significance. The President's power rested more clearly than ever on two military formations largely recruited from members of his own relatively small ethnic group (the Ngbandi), namely the Special Presidential Division (SPD) and the Civic Guard. And he possessed his own powerbase in the sub-region of Ubangi du Nord, in the extreme north of Equateur province, where he had transformed his home village Gbadolite into an ultra-modern town with an international airport. Here he was reported to maintain a massive military arsenal and a treasure trove containing vast sums of foreign exchange and large quantities of gold, diamonds, cobalt and other minerals.

The national conference was attended by 2,800 delegates from a wide range of parties and other organizations. Its three most prominent members were Nguza Karl I Bond, Etienne Tshisekedi and the Catholic archbishop of Kisangani, Mosengwo Pasinya. Mr Nguza, a Lunda from

Shaba, had fallen in and out of favour with the President so often that he was now regarded as 'the chameleon of Zaïrean politics'. Mr Tshisekedi, a Luba from Kasai, was widely respected as the doughtiest of President Mobutu's opponents. Archbishop Mosengwo, who became president of the conference in December 1991, was also held in popular esteem.

The year started with Mr Nguza as Prime Minister, a post to which he had been appointed the previous November. The national conference was reconvened on 14 January, only to come into immediate conflict with the Prime Minister, who ordered its closure on 19 January. This high-handed action led to protest demonstrations in Kinshasa organized by the Sacred Union, the coalition of opposition groups formed in mid-1991 (see AR 1991, p. 280). On 22 January a group of soldiers took over the city's main radio station in what was seen as the first stage of a coup. They were ejected within hours by troops loyal to the President, but discontent continued to simmer. On 16 February thousands of Kinshasa's Catholics, led by a group of radical young priests and carrying candles and prayer books, took part in a peaceful demonstration, only to be fired on by troops of the SPD, with the loss of 30 lives. But in the end the opposition achieved its immediate goal: at the beginning of April the national conference was reconvened and promptly announced that it now possessed 'sovereign status'.

The prestige of Prime Minister Nguza fell very low among the majority of delegates, who saw him as working hand in glove with the President. Accordingly, in August the conference took matters into its own hands by voting on a new government. Having received 1,896 of the 2,651 votes cast, Mr Tshisekedi became Prime Minister and chose as his ministerial colleagues those untainted by corruption (although the President secured a ministerial post for Mr Nguza).

By this time alarming reports were coming in from Shaba of ethnic clashes in which immigrant Luba from Kasai were the victims of Lunda attacks. At the same time members of the old Katangan gendarmerie living in eastern Angola, from where they had launched two near-successful invasions of Shaba in 1977 and 1978, let it be known that they were willing to assist Mr Nguza against his political enemies. From the opposite side of the country came reports that guerrillas, allegedly members of the Congo National Liberation Front, had crossed the border from bases in Uganda.

The last months of the year witnessed a power struggle between the Tshisekedi government and the President. The government had no effective military force at its disposal. Its weakness was shown up when it tried to dismiss the governor of the central bank, regarded as a corrupt crony of President Mobutu's, only to find the latter protecting his friend by sending in tanks to surround the bank's offices. On 6 December the national conference—by now being boycotted by President Mobutu's and Mr Nguza's supporters—completed its work by nominating a High Council of the Republic to serve as a provisional assembly until democratic elections could be held. The President refused to accept this change and sent in troops to prevent the Council from meeting. The year ended with ominous news from Kisangani, where the local garrison had mutinied, arrested the civilian governor and gone on a looting spree. Reports of other disturbances involving soldiers were received from other parts of the country.

This increasingly confusing political situation needed to be set in a context of economic breakdown. In Kinshasa public services no longer functioned, so frequently were schools, hospitals and offices closed by striking staff. With no taxes being collected, the President paid his bills by having new banknotes printed in Germany and flown in by the ton load. The exchange rate for the US dollar depreciated from Z 18,000 in mid-1991 to Z 1 million by mid-1992. Offices and factories looted by the soldiers in September 1991 remained abandoned. Many expatriates and wealthy Zaïreans left the country. In Shaba the revenue produced by the copper mines was reckoned to be no more than one fifth of the 1989 revenue. Zaïreans were paying a very heavy price for what Etienne Tshisekedi described as 'the demystification of Mobutu and the freeing of the people from fear'.

ii.   BURUNDI AND RWANDA

Burundi
CAPITAL: Bujumbura   AREA: 28,000 sq km   POPULATION: 5,400,000 ('90)
OFFICIAL LANGUAGE: French & Kirundi   POLITICAL SYSTEM: presidential
HEAD OF STATE & GOVERNMENT: President (Maj.) Pierre Buyoya, Chairman of
    Military Council for National Salvation (since Sept '87)
CURRENCY: Burundi franc (end-'92 £1=FBu367.15, US$1=FBu242.50)
GNP PER CAPITA: US$210 ('90)
MAIN EXPORT EARNERS: coffee, tea

Rwanda
CAPITAL: Kigali   AREA: 26,300 sq km   POPULATION: 7,100,000 ('90)
OFFICIAL LANGUAGES: French & Kinyarwanda   POLITICAL SYSTEM: presidential
HEAD OF STATE AND GOVERNMENT: President (Maj.-Gen.) Juvénal Habyarimana
    (since '73)
CURRENCY: Rwanda franc (end-'92 £1=RF222.95, US$1=RF147.26)
GNP PER CAPITA: US$310 ('90)
MAIN EXPORT EARNERS: coffee, tea, tin

IN March the people of BURUNDI voted in a referendum on a new constitution designed to create a multi-party democracy under an executive president elected for five years by universal suffrage. Given the country's record of inter-ethnic violence, special significance was attached to the clause which forbade any party to identify itself with any one ethnic group, region or religion. In a 96.7 per cent poll, the constitution was approved by more than 90 per cent of the electorate. The first multi-party election was scheduled for 1993. In April a new government with a majority of Hutu members was formed by President Pierre Buyoya. For the first time the Ministry of the Interior was given to a Hutu.

In March a mutiny by soldiers allegedly acting on behalf of the exiled ex-President Jean Baptiste Bagaza was easily suppressed. In May an Amnesty International report asserted that at least 1,000 Hutu had been executed without trial by the army in operations against Hutu guerrillas in November 1991 (see AR 1991, p. 282). In July 64 Hutu accused of complicity in the guerrilla movement were put on trial and sentenced to varying periods of imprisonment.

Two themes dominated the politics of RWANDA in 1992: the movement from one-party rule towards a more widely-based government and the armed conflict between the Kigali government and the Ugandan-based Rwanda Patriotic Front (FRP). In the more liberal atmosphere encouraged by President Juvénal Habyarimana, at least 12 new parties made their appearance. Four of the new parties—the Democratic Republican Movement, the Christian Democratic Party, the Liberal Party and the Social Democratic Party—were included, together with ministers drawn from the President's Revolutionary National Movement for Democracy and Development, in a new government of national unity formed in April. These developments were not welcome to Hutu extremists, who were thought to have been responsible for a series of massacres in which 300 Tutsi were killed in the southern province of Bugesera in March.

The new government was anxious to enter into negotiations with the FRP, which was now in control of a region north of Kigali and had shown its capacity to outfight the hastily-recruited Rwandan army. In July the two sides met in Arusha for protracted negotiations under the chairmanship of the Tanzanian Foreign Minister and in the presence of observers from neighbouring African states and from France, Belgium and the USA. Agreement was reached on a ceasefire to be monitored by military observers from other African countries. In October President Habyarimana announced his willingness to accept FRP participation in an interim government, although precise details remained to be worked out.

iii.   GUINEA-BISSAU AND CAPE VERDE

Guinea-Bissau
CAPITAL: Bissau   AREA: 36,00 sq km   POPULATION: 980,000 ('90)
OFFICIAL LANGUAGE: Portuguese   POLITICAL SYSTEM: presidential
HEAD OF STATE AND GOVERNMENT: President (Brig.-Gen.) João Vieira (since '80)
RULING PARTY: African Party for the Independence of Guinea and Cape Verde
   (PAIGC)
CURRENCY: peso (end-'92 £1=PG7,582.50, US$1=PG5,008.26)
GNP PER CAPITA: US$180 ('90)
MAIN EXPORT EARNERS: groundnuts, agricultural products

Cape Verde
CAPITAL: Praia   AREA: 4,000 sq km   POPULATION: 371,000 ('90)
OFFICIAL LANGUAGE: Portuguese   POLITICAL SYSTEM: emerging democracy
HEAD OF STATE: President Antonio Mascarenhas Monteiro (since March '91)
RULING PARTY: Movement for Democracy (MPD)
HEAD OF GOVERNMENT: Carlos Veiga, Prime Minister (since Jan '91)
CURRENCY: Cape Verde escudo (end-'92 £1=CVEsc109.75, US$1=CVEsc72.49)
GNP PER CAPITA: US$890 ('90)
MAIN EXPORT EARNERS: cashew nuts, fish

IN GUINEA-BISSAU slow progress continued to be made towards a more democratic regime. In October President Vieira dismissed eight ministers who had held office since 1974 and announced that elections for the presidency and the legislature would be postponed from November 1992 to March 1993. By the end of the year ten opposition parties were in existence and the country had acquired its first independent journal.

CAPE VERDE was facing, according to one outside observer, 'the birth pangs of a fledgling democracy' following the victory of the Movement for Democracy over the African Party for the Independence of Cape Verde (PAICV) in January 1991 (see AR 1991, p. 283). At least one local critic complained that 'the one-party state is being replaced by another one-party state'. But there was clearly greater freedom of expression in the local press—a freedom that permitted the exposure of human rights abuses by the PAICV in the years between 1977 and 1981.

iv.   SÃO TOMÉ & PRÍNCIPE

CAPITAL: São Tomé   AREA: 965 sq km   POPULATION: 117,000 ('90)
OFFICIAL LANGUAGE: Portuguese   POLITICAL SYSTEM: emerging democracy
HEAD OF STATE AND GOVERNMENT: President Miguel Trovoada (since March '91)
RULING PARTY: Democratic Convergence Party (PCD)
PRINCIPAL MINISTERS: Norberto Costa Alegre (prime minister), Evaristo do Espirito
   Santo Carvalho (defence & internal order), Arlino Afonso de Carvalho (economy
   & finance), Albertino Braganca (foreign affairs)
INTERNATIONAL ALIGNMENT: NAM, OAU, ACP
CURRENCY: dobra (end-'92 £1=Db363.95, US$1=Db240.39)
GNP PER CAPITA: US$400 ('90)
MAIN EXPORT EARNERS: cocoa, copra

SÃO TOMÉ was thrown into political crisis in April when President Miguel Trovoada, who had been elected as an independent in 1991 (see AR 1991, p. 284), dismissed the Prime Minister, Daniel Diao, accusing him of causing a 'deadlock between presidency and government'. The Prime Minister's majority Democratic Convergence Party (PCD) strongly protested. This in turn provoked demonstrations by the Movement for the Liberation of São Tomé and Príncipe (MLSTP), which had ruled the islands as a one-party state from 1974 to 1991 and whose members now supported the President's stand. This crisis was resolved when the President accepted as the new Prime Minister the PCD's nominee, Norberto Costa Alegre, the former finance minister.

v. MOZAMBIQUE

CAPITAL: Maputo   AREA: 800,000 sq km   POPULATION: 15,700,000 ('90)
OFFICIAL LANGUAGE: Portuguese   POLITICAL SYSTEM: presidential
HEAD OF STATE AND GOVERNMENT: President Joaquim Chissano (since '86)
RULING PARTY: Front for the Liberation of Mozambique (Frelimo)
PRINCIPAL MINISTERS: Mario da Graça Machungo (prime minister, planning),
    Lt.-Gen. Alberto Joaquim Chipande (defence), Pascoal Mucumbi (foreign
    affairs), Col. José Manuel António (interior), Eneias da Conceiçao (finance),
    Ossmane Ali Dauto (justice)
INTERNATIONAL ALIGNMENT: NAM, OAU, ACP
CURRENCY: metical (end-'92 £1=Mt4,158.50, US$1=Mt2,746.70)
GNP PER CAPITA: US$80 ('90)
MAIN EXPORT EARNERS: sea food, cashew nuts

FOR millions of Mozambicans the miseries of a singularly brutal civil war, which had lasted at least 16 years, were compounded by a terrible drought. Provinces south of the Zambezi lost almost their entire grain harvest and the Limpopo ran dry 90 miles from the sea. But many observers saw in the drought the only really effective means of bringing the two warring sides, the Frelimo government and the rebel National Resistance Movement (MNR or Renamo), to a peace agreement. Such an agreement was eventually signed in Rome on 4 October, in the presence of more than 30 African heads of state or other dignitaries, after more than two years of exceptionally difficult negotiations (see AR 1990, p. 284 and 1991, p. 285).

One reason for the protracted nature of the negotiations lay in the MNR's lack of a clear structure of command. Warlords and gang leaders, each intent on his own narrow interests, dominated the movement. Some warlords were reported to welcome the eventual integration of their forces into a new national army; others pointed to the weakness of the Frelimo government (whose troops were turning to mutiny in protest at lack of pay) and argued that a convincing victory would soon be attainable. But the drought made it increasingly difficult for many MNR bands to extract food from impoverished rural communities. There was no shortage of firearms—a million AK47 assault rifles were reckoned to be circulating in the country—but guns were useless without adequate rations.

In political terms the MNR looked much weaker than it had been before the ending of the Cold War and Frelimo's abandonment of marxism-leninism. In that era the MNR's strident anti-communism had attracted a range of foreign backers, who were now less interested. Without a coherent political programme and with no well-defined power base in one or more of the country's ethnic groups, the MNR was ill-prepared to contest a democratic election. But by objecting to certain clauses in the constitution adopted by Frelimo in 1990, and by spinning out arguments about the exact size of the new national army, MNR negotiators showed themselves exasperatingly competent at drawing out the peace talks.

To these difficulties were added the suspicion and bitterness produced by years of war. So suspicious was the MNR that the government would take advantage of any agreement allowing the aid agencies to move food supplies to famine-stricken areas, by moving its own troops in after the aid convoys, that it for long objected to any such agreement. And, when such an agreement was eventually signed in July, the aid agencies found that MNR obstruction prevented its implementation.

But the MNR's leaders were conscious of the need for some measure of external support. This left them exposed to persuasion by outsiders. In the negotiations a crucial role was played by a British business-man, namely 'Tiny' Rowland, chief executive of Lonrho, which had substantial commercial and agro-industrial interests in Mozambique. Apart from this practical interest, Mr Rowland was on terms of intimacy with many African leaders. So he was able to arrange a meeting between President Mugabe of Zimbabwe and the MNR leader, Afonso Dhlakama. Later, with President Mugabe's backing, he also brought about the first face-to-face meeting between the MNR leader and President Chissano in Rome early in August. Other contributions to the peace process were made by ministers and diplomats from South Africa, the United States, the United Kingdom, Kenya, Botswana and Italy.

The peace treaty of 4 October provided for an almost immediate ceasefire. The armed forces of the two sides were then to move to specially designated but segregated assembly points, while the contingents from Zimbabwe and Malawi withdrew behind their own borders. A general election was to be held by October 1993. The whole process was to be supervised by the United Nations. Initially the UN was ill-prepared to fulfil this role, but a resolution passed unanimously by the Security Council on 16 December set up the United Nations Operation in Mozambique (ONUMOZ) with a peace-keeping force of 7,500 made up of both military and civilian personnel (see also XI.1).

Ominously, within days of the ceasefire coming into force, a number

of serious breaches were reported for which the MNR appeared responsible. Until a measure of security had been established over large areas
of the country, it remained impossible for the aid agencies effectively to
distribute the food on which at least 3 million people were reckoned to
be dependent for survival. 'Fear is what you meet everywhere', wrote a
Western journalist. 'It is what the people feel all the time, . . . it is the
thing which controls them.' In such an atmosphere it was impossible
for most Mozambicans to believe that the war had really come to an
end. The latest developments in Angola (see VII.1.vi) provided a sombre
warning of the fragility of the most elaborate peace negotiations.

vi.   ANGOLA

CAPITAL: Luanda   AREA: 1,247,000 sq km   POPULATION: 10,000,000 ('90)
OFFICIAL LANGUAGE: Portuguese   POLITICAL SYSTEM: presidential
HEAD OF STATE AND GOVERNMENT: President José Eduardo dos Santos (since '79)
RULING PARTY: Popular Movement for the Liberation of Angola-Workers' Party
    (MPLA-PT)
PRINCIPAL MINISTERS: Fernando José França Van-Dúnem (prime minister),
    Col.-Gen. Pedro Maria Tonha 'Pedale' (defence), Lt-Col. Pedro de Castro Van-
    Dúnem 'Loy' (external relations), Lazaro Manuel Dias (justice), Rafael Caseiro
    (planning), Mario de Alcantara Monteiro (finance)
INTERNATIONAL ALIGNMENT: NAM, OAU, ACP
CURRENCY: kwanza (end-'92 £1=Kw861.10, US$1=Kw568.76)
GNP PER CAPITA: US$610 ('89)
MAIN EXPORT EARNERS: oil, coffee, diamonds

THE first general election in the country's history was held on 29–30 September and was declared to have been 'generally free and fair' by UN and
other international observers. The results showed a clear victory for the
MPLA over its leading opponent, Unita, whose leader, Dr Jonas Savimbi,
refused to accept the result. By November fierce fighting was taking
place in many parts of the country between the two rival armies. By
the end of the year Angolans found their country plunged back into
civil war, despite the optimism generated by the Estoril Accord of May
1991 (see AR 1991, pp. 287–8).

   That an election should have been held at all was a remarkable
achievement. The UN Angola Verification Mission (UNAVEM) given
the task of supervising the peace process numbered less than 1,000,
compared with the 6,000 UN personnel deployed in Namibia for the
same purposes in 1989–90 (see AR 1989, p. 288 and 1990, p. 295). This
peace-keeping on the cheap was to have dire consequences.

   The peace accord signed in May 1991 laid down the procedure to be
followed in the creation of a 50,000-strong national army out of the
estimated 200,000 men the two sides had under arms (see AR 1991,
p. 288). But demobilization proceeded very slowly and discontent was

rife at the assembly points. Moreover, Unita managed to maintain many of its detachments intact, their men retaining their arms or burying them in secret caches. By the time of the election, fewer than 7,000 men had been recruited into the new national force.

The election campaign was vigorously conducted, some meetings attracting 100,000 people. But so deep was the hostility between the two main contestants of the past 16 years that tension was often dangerously high. Numerous violent incidents were reported, some ending in the deaths of party activists or government officials. 'Peace hangs by a thread', one correspondent wrote a week before the election.

More than 20 parties contested the election, but the minor parties failed to come together to form the 'third force' that some Angolans hoped would offer them a valid alternative to the MPLA or Unita. The minor parties provided a platform for a number of politicians who had played a prominent part in Angolan politics in the 1970s, notably Holden Roberto and Daniel Chipenda. But the vast majority of Angolans came to accept that the only meaningful choice lay between President dos Santos and the MPLA on one side and Jonas Savimbi and Unita on the other.

For many it was an unenviable choice. 'MPLA robs, Unita kills': this graffito in a Luanda shanty town tersely summed up many voters' feelings. The MPLA was associated with a bureaucratic class whose members had mismanaged the economy for years and were now tarnished with allegations of corruption as they enriched themselves from the oil and diamond industries. Unita was regarded, at least by the urban middle class, as brutal and uncouth in its methods, and too closely associated with a single ethnic group (albeit the largest in the country), the Ovimbundu, and led by a man thought to have totalitarian leanings. Unita's reputation was further blackened by well-confirmed reports of human rights abuses brought out by defectors who had once been among Dr Savimbi's staunchest supporters. This new evidence of abuses of human rights led to a notable cooling-off of support for Unita on the part of outsiders, especially the US government.

Nearly 5 million voters were registered in a total population estimated to number over 10 million. The turnout was an astonishing 91 per cent, some voters from remote areas being brought in by airlift. In the presidential election President dos Santos received 49.57 per cent of the votes cast, just short of the 50 per cent required to avoid a second round of voting, while Dr Savimbi gained 40.07 per cent. Of the 220 seats in the legislature, the MPLA won 129 to Unita's 70.

In the run-up to the election the Unita leader had been supremely confident of victory—a confidence which some competent observers felt was not misplaced. Before a vote had been cast, Dr Savimbi was saying that only by vote-rigging could he lose. Once an MPLA victory appeared probable, Unita spokesmen began denouncing 'generalized systematic fraud', while Unita's military commander announced the withdrawal of the Unita contingent from the new national army.

By the end of October the first shots had been fired in a renewed civil war. Unita forces attacked Luanda airport and government positions in Huambo and a number of southern towns. In Luanda the government, using the newly-formed riot police and armed civilians, fought back. After three days of fighting Unita's power base in the capital had been demolished. A number of leading Unita office-holders were killed and Ovimbundu people living in Luanda were the victims of a pogrom that claimed hundreds, possibly thousands, of lives. By December Unita had captured a number of towns in northern Angola and claimed to control at least 60 per cent of the country. All attempts at mediation by members of the United Nations and the South African Foreign Minister proved fruitless. Meanwhile, in Cabinda, a faction of the Front for the Liberation of the Enclave of Cabinda (FLEC) kept up small-scale guerrilla activity. The year ended on a very gloomy note.

This gloom contrasted sharply with the euphoria expressed in certain quarters before the election. There was renewed interest in the country's huge economic potential: oil production had reached 500,000 barrels per day and was still rising; diamonds would become a major asset if illegal digging could be controlled; food production had started to rise. Commercial links with South Africa were being vigorously resumed, following the resumption of diplomatic relations between Luanda and Pretoria. There was talk of simply refusing to pay the debt of $3,200 million (out of a total debt of $8,000 million) owed to Russia for military equipment. But the renewed civil war put all forms of development in jeopardy.

2. ZAMBIA—MALAWI—ZIMBABWE—NAMIBIA—BOTSWANA— SWAZILAND

i. ZAMBIA

CAPITAL: Lusaka   AREA: 750,000 sq km   POPULATION: 8,100,000 ('90)
OFFICIAL LANGUAGE: English   POLITICAL SYSTEM: presidential
HEAD OF STATE AND GOVERNMENT: President Frederick Chiluba (since Nov '91)
RULING PARTY: Movement for Multi-Party Democracy (MMD)
PRINCIPAL MINISTERS: Levy Mwanawasa (vice-president), Benjamin Y. Mwila (defence), Vernon J. Mwaanga (foreign affairs), Emmanuel G. Kasonde (finance), Newstead L. Zimba (home affairs), Roger Chongwe (legal affairs)
INTERNATIONAL ALIGNMENT: NAM, OAU, ACP, Cwth
CURRENCY: kwacha (end-'92 £1=K498.95, US$1=K329.56)
GNP PER CAPITA: US$420 ('90)
MAIN EXPORT EARNERS: copper, zinc, cobalt

THE first year of the new government formed in November 1991 by the Movement for Multi-Party Democracy (MMD) under President Frederick Chiluba (see AR 1991, pp. 290–1) passed off without any serious political upheavals, although divisive strains became apparent within the ruling party. For most Zambians the new government brought no perceptible improvement. Indeed, most people found their standard of living reduced still further, as devastating drought cut the country's maize harvest from over one million tons to 250,000. After the government had removed subsidies on basic foods, the price of mealie meal increased five times, while the annual inflation rate, though lower than in 1991, was still 100 per cent. Against this background, some observers saw the new government as providing no more than a change of personnel, with wealth being redistributed among the elite but with little filtering down to the majority of Zambians.

Other commentators took a more positive view, praising the government for proving itself to be 'one of the most modern, open and forward-looking in Africa'. They pointed to an impressive range of achievements: a new system for distributing food relief in famine areas, regarded by the aid agencies as one of the most efficient in Africa; a boost to the farming industry by the removal of many bureaucratic restrictions and price controls; the privatization of 130 state-owned companies, including Zambia Consolidated Copper Mines; the creation of a climate more favourable to foreign investors (notably from South Africa); and the negotiation of a new package for debt relief and foreign aid of a kind that could never have been secured by the Kaunda government.

The division within the MMD took the form of a Bemba-Lozi split. The President, himself a Bemba, was surrounded by ministers who were mostly powerful Bemba businessmen. Opposing them was a mainly (but not exclusively) Lozi group. Two of the latter resigned their ministerial posts in July, accusing the government of failing to curb corruption. They went on to convert the Caucus for National Unity, hitherto no more than an inner MMD faction, into an independent party. Many prominent members of the former ruling United National Independence Party (UNIP), which had suffered a crushing defeat in the 1991 election, moved over to the MMD or were given generous pensions or diplomatic posts. Former President Kenneth Kaunda talked of retiring from politics.

ii. MALAWI

CAPITAL: Lilongwe AREA: 118,500 sq km POPULATION: 8,500,000 ('90)
OFFICIAL LANGUAGE: English POLITICAL SYSTEM: presidential, one-party state
HEAD OF STATE AND PARTY LEADER: President Hastings Kamuzu Banda (since '66)
RULING PARTY: Malawi Congress Party (MCP)
PRINCIPAL MINISTERS: Wadson Deleza (without portfolio), Louis Chimango (finance),
    Dalton Katopola (trade & industry)
INTERNATIONAL ALIGNMENT: NAM, OAU, ACP, Cwth.
CURRENCY: kwacha (end-'92 £1=MK6.55, US$1=MK4.33)
GNP PER CAPITA: US$200 ('90)
MAIN EXPORT EARNERS: tobacco, tea, sugar

MALAWI experienced a momentous year. For the first time in his 28 years of highly authoritarian rule, Life President Hastings Kamuzu Banda was faced with open opposition, and so it was possible for outside observers to get some impression of the range and variety of the regime's opponents.

In November 1991 an underground group calling itself the United Democratic Party (or Front) had come into existence, circulating leaflets critical of the regime. Three months later, in a widely-publicized speech, Dr Banda warned his opponents that they would become 'meat for crocodiles'. His speech coincided with an Amnesty International report which drew attention to the atrocious conditions in Malawi's prisons.

On 8 March the regime was presented with its first open expression of dissent when a Lenten pastoral letter signed by seven Catholic bishops was read out in 160 churches throughout the country. The letter drew attention to the 'growing gap between the rich and the poor' and appealed for 'a more just and equal distribution of the nation's wealth'. Claiming that 'bribery and nepotism are growing', the letter added that 'academic freedom is seriously restricted', that 'censorship prevents the expression of dissenting views' and that 'some people have paid dearly for their political opinions'. The letter caused outrage among members of the ruling Malawi Congress Party (MCP). The signatories, denounced as 'Mafia-style crooks' in the official press, were interrogated but not detained by the police, although one of them, Bishop-elect John Roche, was deported. On 17 March students at Chancellor College in Zomba staged a demonstration calling for multi-party democracy.

At the end of March a conference of Malawian political exiles was held in Lusaka. Chakufwa Chihana, secretary-general of the Lilongwe-based Southern African Trades Union Coordination Council, was mandated on his return to Lilongwe to call for 'a conference of democratic forces'. Predictably, Mr Chihana (who had been detained without trial in Malawi for seven years in the 1970s) was arrested the moment he stepped off the plane at Lilongwe on 6 April. But his brave act provided the regime's opponents with a popular hero.

On 6 May strikers at a textile factory in Blantyre took to the streets and were joined by hundreds of other demonstrators, the strike quickly spreading to workers on nearby plantations. The demonstrators smashed a supermarket belonging to the Life President and attacked MCP offices. Order was restored after the police used live ammunition, killing at least 38 people. On 8 May there was a 5,000-strong demonstration in Lilongwe, followed by some looting, in support of the imprisoned Mr Chihana.

On 11 May Western donors meeting in Paris agreed to freeze aid to Malawi, except for sums earmarked for drought relief and humanitarian purposes. The freeze was to last until there was 'tangible and irrefutable evidence of a basic transformation' in the Malawi government's attitude to human rights and basic freedoms. The government introduced some concessions, freeing some long-term political prisoners (although the best-known, Orton Chirwa, died in prison on 18 October) and allowing the Red Cross to visit some prisons. However, as more and more dissident literature spread through the country, the police made hundreds of arrests, concentrating on those with access to photocopiers and fax machines. A general election held on a one-party basis on 27 June suggested that support for the MCP was declining: the official media claimed a turnout of 80 per cent, but independent observers halved that figure.

Faced with clear evidence of discontent, even within the ranks of the MCP, Dr Banda proclaimed on 18 October that a referendum would be held, at a date to be announced, so that the people could decide whether to maintain the one-party state. Shortly afterwards two opposition groups, the United Democratic Front (UDF) and the Alliance for Democracy (AFORD), came out into the open. AFORD took as its leader Chakufwa Chihana, who received a two-year prison sentence for sedition in December, and had the backing of exile groups and the churches. The UDF had at its core former MCP politicians who had fallen foul of the Life President. Appealing first to the urban middle class, both groups claimed 'an astonishing growth in support'. The army was reported to be sympathetic to the democratic movement, while the regime could count on the police and, so it was thought, grassroots support in rural areas. There the Life President, believed to be in his mid-nineties, remained a revered figure.

iii. ZIMBABWE

CAPITAL: Harare AREA: 390,000 sq km POPULATION: 10,400,000 ('92)
OFFICIAL LANGUAGE: English POLITICAL SYSTEM: presidential
HEAD OF STATE AND GOVERNMENT: President Robert Mugabe (since Dec '87,
  previously Prime Minister)
RULING PARTY: Zimbabwe African National Union-Patriotic Front (ZANU-PF)
PRINCIPAL MINISTERS: Simon Muzenda (vice-president), Joshua Nkomo (vice-
  president), Didymus Mutasa (senior minister, national affairs), Bernard Chidzero
  (senior minister, finance, planning & development), Nathan Shamuyarira
  (foreign affairs), Emmerson Munangagwa (justice), Moven Mahachi (defence),
  Dumiso Dabengwa (home affairs)
INTERNATIONAL ALIGNMENT: NAM, OAU, ACP, Cwth.
CURRENCY: Zimbabwe dollar (end-'92 £1=Z$8.28, US$1=Z$5.47)
GNP PER CAPITA: US$640 ('90)
MAIN EXPORT EARNERS: tobacco, gold, tin

THE drought of 1991–92, the most severe since records began, affected almost every aspect of Zimbabwe's life. Most immediately it threatened to derail the Economic Structural Adjustment Programme (ESAP) launched by Robert Mugabe's ZANU-PF government in January 1991 in an attempt to revive the country's flagging economy and reduce its fiscal debt (see AR 1991, pp. 292–3). In the budget of 30 July, Z$2,000 million, or 15 per cent of GDP, was designated for drought relief, to be financed through a special tax levy of 5 per cent of income. Nearly half the country's estimated 10.4 million population was dependent on food aid.

The impact of the drought, on an already fragile economy, contributed to an estimated 11 per cent decline in real economic growth, and pushed annualized inflation to a peak of 48 per cent in November, the highest level in the country's history. One-fifth of government expenditure during the 1992–93 financial year was expected to be met through foreign subsidy or external borrowing. Zimbabwe's military expenditure, however, remained the third highest in Africa.

ESAP continued to find strong support within the international community. In January the World Bank and the African Development Bank agreed loans totalling US$360 million, while the International Monetary Fund pledged $484 million over three years. At a second donors' conference in Paris at the close of the year, the World Bank released an additional $160 million in recognition of Zimbabwe's progress in implementing fiscal reform. During the year further grants or low-interest loans came from Japan, Belgium, Germany, the United States and the European Community. In the short term the receipt of aid totalling over Z$7,000 million for the year expedited urgently-needed capital projects. In the longer term, of course, the loans would need to be repaid, or Zimbabwe would fall victim to the debt-trap from which few third-world countries escaped.

The primary casualty of the drought was agriculture, the country's largest revenue earner. Output was down by 40 per cent in 1992, production of maize, the principal food crop, falling most dramatically, from 1.6 million tonnes to fewer than 300,000. For the second successive year the importation of substantial quantities of maize—this time yellow maize from Argentina—was necessary to avert widespread famine, particularly in rural areas. The sorghum, wheat and cotton harvests were also low, while the deterioration of pasture posed a long-term threat not only to livestock levels but also to wildlife, one of the country's greatest tourist attractions. Only tobacco withstood the drought, production rising to another annual record of 180,000 tonnes, earning more than Z$1,500 million.

Power supply interruptions were a common feature during the year. More a consequence of mismanagement of Zesa, the country's power authority, than of heavy dependence upon hydro-electricity, the failures had an especially damaging impact on the mining and manufacturing sectors. Mining output, normally responsible for 7 per cent of the country's wealth, declined and income from manufacturing industry, already weakened by low domestic demand, fell by 5 per cent. In turn, fading productivity increased unemployment and exacerbated the country's visible trade deficit. On the other hand, trade with South Africa boomed, rising to Z$3,000 million for the year. Increasingly seen as politically legitimate, Zimbabwe's southern neighbour reached an agreement in April with the former 'front-line states' of the Southern African Development Co-ordination Conference (SADCC) on moves to combat malnutrition across the sub-continent.

The deterioration of the economy provoked generalized attacks on the government's record and competence. As in earlier years, students at the University of Zimbabwe in Harare led the protest. Following marches, demonstrations and pitched battles with security forces in May, the university was closed for a week. More significantly, a month earlier, combat veterans of the former ZANLA and ZIPRA guerrilla armies accused Mr Mugabe of having betrayed the aims of ZANU-PF and of the liberation struggle. 'The party', they declared, 'is dead'. Also for the first time, divisions emerged within the parliamentary party itself, and indeed within the cabinet, over issues such as restrictions on press freedom and persistent waste and excess within the still-bloated public sector. In May opposition groups established a Forum for Democratic Reform, with the former chief justice, Dr Enoch Dumbutshena, as patron. Its declared objectives were the retrieval of democratic principles, an accountable, multi-party government, the separation of legislature and judiciary, an efficient civil service and recognition of basic human rights.

The long-threatened Land Acquisition Bill (see AR 1991, p. 294) finally became law in March. Some 5.5 million hectares of predominantly white-owned land were compulsorily appropriated for redistribution to landless black peasants, rectifying an historic inequality under which less than one per cent of the population owned more than a third of the arable land. Describing it as 'a do-or-die issue', Mr Mugabe declared that 'we cannot run a society of haves and have-nots'. The problem was that the white-owned land earned 42 per cent of the country's foreign trade revenue and also created the major proportion of agricultural employment. Though welcomed by impoverished Zimbabweans, the new law was widely expected to damage foreign investor confidence.

For ordinary Zimbabweans the experience of rapidly-rising prices, higher interest rates, random power-cuts and queues for basic foodstuffs contrasted sharply with conspicuous government spending on ceremonial display and ministerial perks, self-enrichment by ZANU-PF officials and manifest administrative incompetence. This led to widespread public scepticism of the government's fitness to rule. For the first time in 12 years the President failed to attend the traditional May Day rally at Harare's Ruffaro stadium. To a vociferous crowd, the president of the Zimbabwe Congress of Trade Unions, Gibson Sibanda, described the depletion of Zimbabwe's food reserves as 'a national crime' and called for the removal from office of those responsible.

AIDS remained the country's hidden nightmare. Research published at the end of the year estimated that 1.5 million Zimbabweans already carried the HIV virus and that one in six babies were born with the infection.

iv. NAMIBIA

CAPITAL: Windhoek   AREA: 824,000 sq km   POPULATION: 1,800,000 ('90)
OFFICIAL LANGUAGES: Afrikaans & English
POLITICAL SYSTEM: presidential democracy
HEAD OF STATE: President Sam Nujoma (since March '90)
RULING PARTY: South West Africa People's Organization (SWAPO)
PRINCIPAL MINISTERS: Hage Geingob (prime minister), Theo-Ben Gurirab
    (foreign affairs), Peter Mueshihange (defence), Hifikepunje Pohamba (home
    affairs), Ngarikutuke Tjiriange (justice), Gerhard Hanekom (finance),
    Andimba Toivo ja Toivo (mines & energy)
INTERNATIONAL ALIGNMENT: NAM, OAU, SADCC, Cwth.
CURRENCY: South African rand (end-'92 £1=R4.63, US$1=R3.06)
GNP PER CAPITA: US$1,030 ('89)
MAIN EXPORT EARNERS: minerals

THE ruling party of Namibia, SWAPO, won a sweeping victory in regional and local elections in December over the Democratic Turnhalle Alliance (DTA) and the United Democratic Front. It was the first time Namibians had gone to the polls since the country gained independence from South Africa in 1990 (see AR 1990, pp. 295, 393).

SWAPO took control of nine of the 13 regional councils and was the winner in 31 contests out of 48 at local authority level, with the DTA winning eight and no overall majority being recorded in the remaining nine. The average turnout was 80 per cent and in some areas as much as 94 per cent of the electorate went to the polls. Official observers sent by the German government praised the way in which the elections had been conducted.

Namibia's third year of independence was peaceful but the country suffered as a result of a slump in demand for its main exports, uranium and diamonds. Unemployment was estimated at 40 per cent.

Foreign investment and support from the international community were not forthcoming on the scale that Namibia had hoped would happen. A World Bank report in April concluded that the country would have to slash its civil service wage bill by 20 per cent over the next four years, diverting expenditure into capital expenditure which would underpin economic growth. It was announced in the annual budget statement that the government intended to create further incentives to stimulate economic development in general and industrial development in particular.

In August Namibia and South Africa agreed to implement a joint administration for Walvis Bay, the disputed enclave which was annexed by Britain in 1878 and transferred to the Cape Colony in 1884; together with certain offshore islands, the enclave had remained under South African control after Namibian independence. In terms of UN resolutions, Walvis Bay was to be reintegrated with Namibia. Observers believed that the final settlement of the dispute over sovereignty depended on the outcome of constitutional negotiations in South Africa (see VII.3).

Norway and Sweden, supporters of SWAPO from its days as a liberation movement, cancelled emergency drought aid for the country in August in protest against Namibia's purchase of a jet aircraft for President Nujoma at a cost of R 75 million. The Norwegian view was that if Namibia had funds to buy presidential jets then it had no need of emergency drought aid. The Namibian Information Minister, Hidipo Hamutenya, said that the President required rapid transport to reach outlying areas of the huge country.

v. BOTSWANA

CAPITAL: Gaborone AREA: 580,000 sq km POPULATION: 1,300,000 ('90)
OFFICIAL LANGUAGE: English POLITICAL SYSTEM: presidential democracy
HEAD OF STATE & GOVERNMENT: President Quett Masire (since '80)
RULING PARTY: Botswana Democratic Party (BDP)
PRINCIPAL MINISTERS: Festus Mogae (vice-president, finance, development &
    planning), Gaositwe Chiepe (external affairs), Patrick Balopi (home & labour
    affairs)
INTERNATIONAL ALIGNMENT: NAM, OAU, ACP, Cwth.
CURRENCY: pula (end-'92 £1=P3.41, US$1=P2.25)
GNP PER CAPITA: US$2,040 ('90)
MAIN EXPORT EARNERS: diamonds, copper-nickel, beef

A commission of inquiry into the Botswana Housing Corporation
(BHC) reported in December that a former assistant minister of local
government and lands had been given a R 675,000 bribe to ensure
that a contract would be awarded to Spectra Botswana, a construction
company partly owned by the Premier Group of South Africa. The
chairman of Premier announced that he had appointed a team of
lawyers to investigate and that action would be taken if any impropriety
were found. He said the payment appeared to be sinister but was not
necessarily so.

Earlier, in March, Vice-President Peter Mmusi and Agriculture
Minister Daniel Kwelagobe resigned after they had been severely
criticized by the Kgabo commission of inquiry into land allocations.
At the same time, President Quett Masire reshuffled his cabinet and
appointed Finance Minister Festus Mogae as Vice-President.

Discussing Botswana's 1992–93 budget, Mr Mogae said a fiscal surplus
was envisaged for the tenth year in a row. He called for renewed
commitment to disciplined economic management, efforts to stamp
out corruption and steps to promote the private sector. Although
Botswana had maintained an average growth rate of 13 per cent a
year since independence in 1966, growth slipped to 3.5 in 1992 (from
8.7 per cent the previous year) as a result of a fall in demand for its
three major commodities, diamonds, copper and beef.

It was reported in February that completion of Botswana's multi-
million dollar air base had been delayed by more than two years, until
1995, because of budgetary problems and construction work difficulties
caused by bad roads.

vi.   LESOTHO

CAPITAL: Maseru   AREA: 30,000 sq km   POPULATION: 1,800,000 ('90)
OFFICIAL LANGUAGES: English & Sesotho
POLITICAL SYSTEM: monarchy, under military rule
HEAD OF STATE: King Letsie III (since (Nov '90)
HEAD OF GOVERNMENT: Maj.-Gen. Elias Ramaema, Chairman of Military Council
   (since April '91)
PRINCIPAL MINISTERS: A. L. Thoalane (finance, planning & economy), Tokonye
   Kotelo (foreign affairs), Mohalefi Bereng (interior), A. K. Maopoe (justice)
INTERNATIONAL ALIGNMENT: NAM, OAU, ACP, Cwth.
CURRENCY: maloti (end-'92 £1=M4.63, US$1=M3.06)
GNP PER CAPITA: US$530 ('90)
MAIN EXPORT EARNERS: diamonds, wool

IN May the exiled King Moshoeshoe II announced that his return to
Lesotho was imminent. However, negotiations between his supporters
and the ruling Military Council became bogged down over the terms of
his return, the Council insisting that he could not come back as king
and that his son, Letsie III, who had been installed after Moshoeshoe's
deposition in February 1990 (see AR 1990, p. 297), should not abdicate.
There were also conditions that he should accept a pension and not interfere with the elections—then scheduled for October/November—which
would restore Lesotho to civilian rule.

It was not until July that Moshoeshoe arrived in Maseru, to an
emotional welcome from his supporters and amid some fears that his
return would inflame the political climate. Meanwhile, Lesotho was
facing a critical water shortage. No rain had fallen in some areas since
the previous November and streams and springs in large parts of the
country had dried up. With farmers producing only a quarter of the
maize necessary to feed the population, it was announced that Lesotho
would approach the government of South Africa for emergency aid.

In November the chairman of the Military Council, Major-General
Ramaema, announced that the planned general elections had been
postponed, it being announced subsequently that they would be held
in March 1993. General Ramaema had taken over from the ousted
Major-General Justin Lekhanya as head of the Military Council in
April 1991 (see AR 1991, p. 297), committing the Council to return
Lesotho to civilian rule.

The possible integration of Lesotho into a post-apartheid South Africa
was discussed at a meeting in August between a delegation from the
National Union of Mineworkers of South Africa and representatives
of political and other organizations.

In May Amnesty International published a report expressing concern
about the failure of the Lesotho government to take adequate steps to
investigate and prevent torture and alleged extra-judicial execution.

vii.   SWAZILAND

CAPITAL: Mbabane   AREA: 17,350 sq km   POPULATION: 797,000 ('90)
OFFICIAL LANGUAGES: English & Siswati   POLITICAL SYSTEM: monarchy
HEAD OF STATE & GOVERNMENT: King Mswati III (since '86)
PRINCIPAL MINISTERS: Obed Dlamini (prime minister), Sibusiso Barnabas Dlamini
   (finance), Sir George Mbikwakhe Mamba (foreign afairs), Prince Sobandla
   (interior), Zonke Amos Khumalo (justice)
INTERNATIONAL ALIGNMENT: NAM, OAU, ACP, Cwth.
CURRENCY: emalangeni (end-'92 £1=E4.63, US$1=E3.06)
GNP PER CAPITA: US$810 ('90)
MAIN EXPORT EARNERS: sugar, agricultural products

PRESSURES mounted in Swaziland during 1992 for the kingdom's traditional political system to be replaced by a modern democracy. All parties had been banned in Swaziland for nearly 20 years and the king ruled as an absolute monarch, although there was an indirectly-elected traditional parliament. Traditionalists continued to maintain that a multi-party system was unsuitable for Swaziland, but King Mswati III announced in April that there would be an investigation into the country's traditional system. Eventually, in October, it was announced that direct elections by secret ballot would replace the traditional electoral system. Any individual citizen (but not political parties) who was nominated by 15 other citizens would be able to stand for election. The announcement was seen as a dramatic advance by an ultra-traditionalist society in the direction of multi-party democracy. Elections were to be held in March 1993.

    In March it was announced that four senior officials of Swaziland's central bank had been suspended in connection with an R 3.8 million fraud.

3.   SOUTH AFRICA

CAPITAL: Pretoria   AREA: 1,220,000 sq km   POPULATION: 35,900,000 ('90)
OFFICIAL LANGUAGES: Afrikaans & English
POLITICAL SYSTEM: presidential, under white minority rule (democracy for whites,
   partial representation for coloureds and Asians)
HEAD OF STATE & GOVERNMENT: President F. W. de Klerk (since Sept '89)
RULING PARTY: National Party (NP)
PRINCIPAL MINISTERS: R. F. ('Pik') Botha (foreign affairs), Roelf Meyer (constitutional development), Gene Louw (defence), George S. Bartlett (minerals &
   energy), Kobie (H.J.) Coetsee (justice), Derek Keys (finance), Louis Pienaar
   (home affairs)
CURRENCY: rand (end-'92 £1=R4.63, US$1=R3.06)
GNP PER CAPITA: US$2,530 ('90)
MAIN EXPORT EARNERS: precious & base metals, minerals

SOUTH Africa approached the threshold of a negotiated settlement of its constitutional future in 1992 and then relapsed into the worst bout of civil strife in its history. By the end of the year more than 3,500 people had died in political violence, much of it in the course of hostilities between supporters of Nelson Mandela's African National Congress (ANC) and Chief Mangosuthu Buthelezi's Zulu-dominated Inkatha Freedom Party. As in the previous year (see AR 1991, pp. 299–304), there was also a great deal of random terrorism directed at the black population, apparently designed to poison the climate for negotiation.

There was no longer much doubt that elements in the clandestine arm of the security forces hostile to President de Klerk's reforms were actively undermining the negotiating process. There were again mysterious attacks at regular intervals in which railway commuters from the black townships on their way to work were mowed down by automatic fire from masked gunmen. The motive for these attacks was clearly not robbery. Although hundreds of commuters died from gunshot or stabbing attacks, or were hurled to their deaths out of train windows, very few arrests were made in these cases during the year and not a single prosecution for murder was recorded.

Evidence came to light in court hearings and in media investigations of the activities of Military Intelligence operatives which strengthened the conviction that there was a so-called 'third force' at work in the country bent on destabilizing the ANC and wrecking the chances of a settlement. President de Klerk denied any knowledge of such a force and a commission headed by Mr Justice Goldstone was at first unable to find conclusive proof of its existence. In December, however, following a raid by Goldstone commission investigators on a Military Intelligence covert operations centre in Pretoria, Mr de Klerk announced that illegal activity and malpractices on the part of senior officers of the South African Defence Force (SADF) were under investigation. Twenty-three members of the SADF, including two generals, were placed on compulsory leave or early retirement, pending the outcome of the investigation. Almost all the officers in question were connected with the Division of Military Intelligence or its covert operations centre. There was some scepticism among observers about the chances of the offenders being brought to court and widespread expectation of yet another cover-up of security force complicity in political violence. By year's end no arrests had been made. It was noted that Mr de Klerk had pushed legislation through parliament earlier in the year extending existing indemnity legislation and providing for the maintenance of secrecy.

Although these developments confirmed ANC suspicions of what had been happening, Mr Mandela did not seem disposed to pursue the matter to a point which would imperil the fragile negotiating process, as long as Military Intelligence was brought under proper multi-party control. The ANC was reluctant to weaken Mr de Klerk's position as leader of the ruling National Party (NP) by insisting on punitive steps, because the consequences of his departure from the scene would be incalculable, as they saw it, and the ANC was on the point of joining the NP in an interim government of national unity.

As the year was ending, bilateral NP–ANC discussions resumed, partly in the realization by both camps that the country's economy was drifting into a dangerous state of stagnation. Economic activity was slowing down as a result of a lack of business confidence, which, in its turn, was attributed to the violence and the continuing failure to make headway in negotiations. With unemployment soaring, a political settlement was seen on all sides to be a matter of the utmost urgency. Crime was rampant throughout the country, cities such as Johannesburg being plagued by bank robberies, hold-ups and motor vehicle hijackings. In the rural areas there was a spate of murderous attacks on isolated farm houses in the Orange Free State and elsewhere in which robbery was apparently the motive.

There had been steady progress in the early months of 1992 in the proceedings of the Convention for a Democratic South Africa (CODESA). The country's political parties came close to formal agreement on constitutional principles and transitional arrangements for governing the country in the run-up to the first non-racial one-person-one-vote general election. But by mid-year the negotiations had collapsed. Both major parties appeared to have run into difficulties with their supporters, some of whom seemed to feel that the negotiations were going ahead too quickly. There were mistrustful elements on both sides which questioned so rapid a rapprochement between traditional political foes and believed that more time was needed to prepare for elections.

President de Klerk reshuffled his cabinet after the breakdown in negotiations, moving the liberal-minded Minister of Defence, Roelf Meyer, who had served very briefly in that portfolio, into the key position of Minister of Constitutional Development, in which he replaced Dr Gerrit Viljoen, who had been leading the negotiating team and now became Minister of State Affairs without departmental responsibilities. A recruit from the private sector, Derek Keys, became Minister of Finance, replacing an exhausted Barend du Plessis, who retired on grounds of ill-health. Gene Louw became Minister of Defence. Mr Viljoen later left the cabinet and retired from politics on grounds of ill-health, as did another colleague, the NP secretary-general, Stoffel van der Merwe.

In the same month the Pickard commission of inquiry revealed fraud, corruption and maladministration on a massive scale in the Department of Development Aid. Later in the year a further commission of inquiry, chaired by the chief magistrate of Johannesburg, reported gross corruption in the administration of the Lebowa tribal homeland, while a third inquiry, the Parsons commission, disclosed serious irregularities in the KwaNdebele tribal homeland. The image of the government was harmed by these disclosures and by the rapid turnover in cabinet posts.

However, much of the maladministration had taken place in the term of the previous government headed by P. W. Botha.

Mr de Klerk's position amongst his own NP followers appeared to weaken during the year. In February he lost a white parliamentary by-election to the ultra-right-wing Conservative Party in Potchefstroom, western Transvaal, by a landslide. But in the following month, on 17 March, he succeeded in winning an overwhelming majority from the white electorate, including many English-speaking voters, at a referendum which approved his plans for negotiating a constitutional settlement. In a turnout of 85 per cent of eligible voters, 68.6 per cent voted in favour.

By mid-year it was apparent, however, that there was a division of opinion between hawks and doves at the NP leadership level. The ANC leadership was divided on similar lines and the CODESA negotiations eventually broke down in June. In the ANC, militants who favoured increasing pressure on the government by means of general strikes, marches and mass rallies were increasingly setting the tone. A campaign of mass action was announced by the ANC and its Communist Party and trade union allies.

At this point (17 June) there was a midnight massacre at Boipatong township in the Transvaal in which 40 men, women and children were butchered by panga-wielding assassins. Most blacks in the region blamed the killings on the de Klerk government and on the reluctance of the security forces to act against the Zulu impis supporting Inkatha, which was seen as the ally and surrogate of the government. President de Klerk was booed and driven away by angry crowds when he sought to visit the scene of the massacre. He went ahead with plans to visit Spain but was compelled to return home after a few days for urgent cabinet discussions. Feelings were inflamed in the black community, with the result that the ANC's mass action campaign was given further impetus.

Mr Mandela went to New York in mid-July to urge the UN Security Council to send a special envoy to Pretoria to investigate violence against blacks and to seek ways of reviving the negotiations. Early in August the ANC and its allies mounted an impressive show of strength when at least four million of the country's six million workers—according to the ANC's count—took part in a two-day general strike. In some areas between 80 and 95 per cent of workers stayed away from work.

The campaign of mass action had a tragic sequel in September, when a march of 50,000 members of the ANC and its allies was fired upon by troops of the pro-apartheid military regime of the so-called independent Ciskei homeland at its capital, Bisho, near Kingwilliamstown. At least 28 people were killed and more than 200 injured in the shooting, which took place when a group of young blacks led by a Communist Party militant, Ronald Kasrils, broke away from the agreed route of the march and rushed in the direction of the Ciskei government buildings.

Paradoxically, the incident advanced the prospects of a negotiated settlement in that it discredited the militants in the ANC and enabled the pro-negotiation leadership group around Mr Mandela to seize the initiative. The Bisho incident also led to sharpened international pressures on the major parties in South Africa to end the violence and return to negotiations. An advance party of 18 UN observers arrived in South Africa, the first of a complement of 50 who were to monitor the violence. Earlier, following a visit by an EC delegation, it was announced that the Community would send 15 peace monitors and five other experts to help the Goldstone commission in investigating the violence. A personal representative of the UN Secretary-General arrived on 16 September on a week-long mission to promote resolution 722 of the Security Council (which called on all parties to end the violence and resume negotiations).

Eventually, on 26 September, President de Klerk and Mr Mandela met at a 'peace summit' and signed a bilateral 'record of understanding', noting their agreement on the need for a democratically-elected parliament and an interim government of national unity. There were also provisions designed to curb the violence, including the fencing of the hostels housing Zulu migrant workers (in which much of the violence was originating) and the prohibition of the carrying of dangerous traditional weapons.

These provisions were not acceptable to Chief Buthelezi, who as Inkatha leader was also head of the Kwazulu government and enjoyed influential support among conservative whites in Natal. He rejected the bilateral understanding between the ANC and the NP and said that he was withdrawing from multi-party discussions. He also announced plans for a federal constitution for Natal-Kwazulu—a move which was seen in some quarters as an implicit threat of secession which could lead to further violence. At the same time, having made what some people saw as a unilateral declaration of regional autonomy, he joined in an alliance with white right-wingers and the apartheid-era leaders of the Bophuthatswana and Ciskei homelands who sought to maintain their autonomy under a new constitution. However, most observers were confident that Chief Buthelezi's resistance to a resumption of negotiations was tactical and would not be sustained.

Both the ANC and the South African security forces were censured during the year in reports by Amnesty International on human rights abuses. In June an Amnesty report analysed the violence in which more than 7,000 people had died between January 1990 and March 1992, concluding that the police had passively, and at times actively, colluded in Inkatha attacks on people believed to be ANC supporters. In November Amnesty reported on documented incidents of torture, ill-treatment and executions in ANC detention camps in Angola, Zambia, Tanzania and Uganda, calling for the prosecution of ANC officials guilty of human rights abuses. The findings of the ANC's own internal commission of inquiry had been disclosed by Mr Mandela in the previous month. He said that he accepted full responsibility on behalf of the ANC and would appoint an independent and impartial body to investigate the allegations. Most of the victims in the detention camps, it appeared, had been rebellious members of the ANC or its armed wing and those suspected of espionage on behalf of the Pretoria government.

In December the developing NP-ANC understanding became explicit following a three-day meeting between the leaders of both parties at a secret venue in northern Transvaal. After the meeting, Mr Mandela said that 'real progress' had been achieved. It appeared that the parties had agreed to speed up a resumption of multi-party discussions to pave the way for elections before the end of 1993 or soon thereafter. The hope was that, with agreement reached between the leaderships of the major parties on transitional arrangements pending elections, their followers and the other political parties would quickly fall into line. Some difficulties on the extreme left and right flanks of the political spectrum were foreseen, however. This was underlined in the final weeks of the year when units of the Azanaian People's Liberation Army (APLA), the military wing of the Pan-Africanist Congress, claimed responsibility for a campaign of terrorist attacks on soft targets in the eastern Cape which seemed to be aimed specifically at whites.

As the year ended, it was plain that a new spirit of cooperation had taken hold between the leaderships of the NP and the ANC. Hopes were strong that with the active assistance of the international community decisive steps would be taken in 1993 to resolve the constitutional impasse.

VIII   SOUTH ASIA AND INDIAN OCEAN

1.   IRAN-AFGHANISTAN-CENTRAL ASIAN REPUBLICS

i.   IRAN

CAPITAL: Tehran   AREA: 1,650,000 sq km   POPULATION: 56,800,000 ('92)
NATIONAL LANGUAGE: Farsi (Persian)   POLITICAL SYSTEM: Islamic republic
RELIGIOUS LEADER: Ayatollah Seyed Ali Khamenei (since June '89)
HEAD OF STATE AND GOVERNMENT: President (Hojatolislam) Hashemi Ali Akbar
   Rafsanjani (since July '89)
OTHER SENIOR LEADERS: Hossain Moussavi (presidential adviser), Hassan Ebrahim
   Habibi (vice-president), Seyed Mohajerani (vice-president, legal and parlia-
   mentary affairs), Massoud Roghani Zanjani (vice-president, planning and
   budget), Raza Amrollahi (vice-president, atomic energy), Mansour Razavi
   (vice-president, state employment), Mehdi Manafi (vice-president, environment),
   Hassan Ghafurifard (vice-president, physical education)
PRINCIPAL MINISTERS: Ali Akbar Velayati (foreign affairs), Gholamreza Agazadeh
   (oil), Abdollah Nouri (interior), Mohsen Nourbakhsh (economic affairs and
   finance), Hojatolislam Ismail Shostari (justice)
INTERNATIONAL ALIGNMENT: NAM, OPEC, ICO, ECO
CURRENCY: rial (end-'92 £1=Rls2,267.00, US$1=Rls1,497.36)
GNP PER CAPITA: US$2,490 ('90)
MAIN EXPORT EARNERS: oil and gas, carpets

IRAN was praised in February, in a report by the UN Commission on Human Rights, for its humanitarian treatment of refugees but severely criticized for maltreatment of its own nationals, especially for a high number of executions, the use of torture and practice of religious discrimination. A second UN sub-commission report in August issued a judgment against Iran for the execution of political prisoners and punishment of women under the Islamic dress code.

A general election for the fourth Majlis (Islamic assembly) since the revolution took place in 270 constituencies in April and was completed in May. Turnout in the poll was low, probably less than half of the electorate. It was estimated that two-thirds of the elected representatives were supporters of President Rafsanjani, the remainder being radicals. Many hardline radical leaders, such as Hojatoleslam Mohteshami and the Majlis speaker, Mehdi Karrubi, were either excluded as candidates or failed to get elected. Nevertheless, the expected strengthening of the President against the hardliners failed to materialize after the elections. The regime as a whole remained heavily influenced by radical Islamic groups, to the extent that decision-making by the Rafsanjani government continued to be slow and uncertain.

The Islamic regime was deeply shaken in May by a series of riots in the important urban centres of Meshhed, Shiraz, Tabriz and Arak. Meshhed was taken over by anti-government rioters for several days;

official buildings were destroyed and many deaths were reported before order was restored. The ostensible cause for the riots was grievance against local authorities who attempted to remove shanty dwellings in areas forbidden for housing. In fact, the unrest also arose from frustration among the mass of poor people at deteriorating economic conditions, high costs of housing and inequalities in income. Immediately following the riots the government gave new powers to the *baseej* (Islamic volunteer brigades) to act as front-line troops to enforce security in urban areas.

Iranian foreign policy met with few successes. On 2 April Iranian jets attacked an opposition Mujahideen Khalq army base inside Iraqi territory, causing some damage but violating Iraqi air space and costing the loss of an aircraft. Demonstrations by the Mujahideen against Iranian embassies and offices abroad ensued, causing further embarrassment. Relations with the government in Baghdad were poor. Iran was concerned at the harassment of Iraqi Shias by the forces of Saddam Husain (see V.2.vi) and was obstructed in getting a *de jure* end to the Iran-Iraq war under UN resolution 598 of 1987. Iran opposed the imposition of a 'no-flying zone' in southern Iraq and was fearful that Iraqi territorial integrity would be put at risk by Western intervention there and in support of Kurdish national claims in the north of Iraq.

Iran sought to develop its interests in Transcaucasia and central Asia during 1992. Special trade links were constructed with five republics of the former Soviet Union in February within the Economic Cooperation Organization (ECO), which included Turkey and Pakistan. Bilateral links with the new states to the north were also strengthened through official agreements for the expansion of commerce and cultural exchanges. Promises of aid in the development of oil and gas resources and offers to set up rail and road connections between the landlocked republics via Iran to the Persian Gulf were also made. Iran was inhibited in its bid for influence in the new republics by its lack of economic strength and by competition from Turkey and others. Iran had successes, however, in mediating an end to all-out war between Armenia and Azerbaijan, protecting the independence of Nagorno-Karabakh and fostering pan-Islamic sentiment in the region (see also III.2.i).

In the Persian Gulf there were setbacks to Iran's policy of establishing close links with the Arab peninsula states. In April a local dispute on Abu Musa, where Iranian officials expelled workers sent by Sharjah, put into question the Iran-Sharjah arrangement for joint control of the island instituted in 1971 at the time of the British military withdrawal. When the problem recurred in September, the matter was taken up for Sharjah by the UAE and rapidly became a major international issue when the UAE also demanded a review of Iran's occupation of two other islands, Greater and Lesser Tunb (see also V.3.iii). Iran was also embroiled later in the year on Qatar's side in an inter-Arab dispute with

Saudi Arabia, raising future fears in the Arab countries, particularly Saudi Arabia, concerning Iran's ambitions in the Gulf (ibid. and V.3.i). Iranian support for the Islamic regime in Sudan together with alleged succour for the Islamic opposition movements in Algeria and Egypt added to Arab antipathies towards Iran. Moreover, Iranian involvement with the Hamas Islamic organization in Lebanon and the West Bank hardened fears that Iran was again exporting Islamic revolution.

Iranian relations with European states were strained. In June a British diplomat in Tehran was accused of spying and later expelled. The British government protested and on 24 July expelled two Iranian embassy officials from London on grounds of national security. This in turn provoked retaliation from Tehran, which deported three British businessmen. Iran also had difficulties with other West European states, including Germany, over its failure to complete the Bushire nuclear power plant. There were also strains with France on the matter of the implication of an Iranian official in the assassination of Shapour Bakhtiar in Paris in August 1991 (see AR 1991, pp. 99, 306, 569) and with Switzerland over the extradition of this same suspect. Diplomatic links with the USA remained broken. Only China, which moved closer to Iran through arms supplies, was an exception to the international isolation which increasingly enfolded Iran in 1992. President Rafsanjani paid an official visit to China and other states of the Far East and South-East Asia in late August and early September.

The Iranian government was much concerned with events in Bosnia–Hercegovina (see III.1.vi). It recalled its mission from Belgrade in May in protest against alleged Serbian atrocities and attempted to dispatch arms to Muslim partisans. Iran also used its position in the Islamic Conference Organization to demand military intervention to stop Serbian attacks on Muslims. On several occasions Iranian Islamic leaders threatened to take unilateral action by sending volunteer troops to assist the Bosnian Muslims, although at year's end this remained only a threat.

Many of Iran's problems centred on economic affairs. Oil production rose during the year to more than 3.5 million b/d by December, following an energetic expansion of production facilities. An ambitious development programme to restore war damage and bring the offshore zone back to full capacity was also set in train. However, Iran's inability to persuade fellow OPEC members to restrain output led to falling crude prices. Oil income for 1992 was estimated at $15,000 million, 25 per cent below budget forecasts, though non-oil exports of $2,500 million gave some small compensation. Rising imports, which totalled $28,000 million in the Iranian year to 20 March 1992, forced Iran to delay foreign payments in July and led to a growing foreign debt, estimated at more than $30,000 million by year's end, when the five-year economic development plan was tacitly abandoned because of shortages of foreign exchange resources. The short-lived economic boom came to an end and an ad hoc austerity programme put into effect. Inflation rose to more than 40 per cent on an annual basis, a situation exacerbated by the uncertain international value of the rial, which by end-December fell to a floating rate against the US dollar of Rls 1,497, compared with an official rate of Rls 67. Economic successes were won in petrochemicals, where expansion of capacity continued and in areas of light industry. Agriculture fared well in most areas after plentiful rains in spring.

ii. AFGHANISTAN

CAPITAL: Kabul   AREA: 650,000 sq km   POPULATION: 15,000,000 ('88 est.)
OFFICIAL LANGUAGES: Pushtu, Dari (Persian)   POLITICAL SYSTEM: presidential
HEAD OF STATE AND GOVERNMENT: President Burhanuddin Rabbani (since June '92)
PRINCIPAL MINISTERS: Ahmad Shah (deputy premier, home affairs), Sayd Solayman
    Gaylani (foreign affairs), Gen. Khodad Hazareh (interior), Lt-Gen. Hamidollah
    Rahimi (finance), Ahmed Shah Masud (defence), Mawlawi Jalaloddin Haqani
    (justice)
INTERNATIONAL ALIGNMENT: NAM, ICO
CURRENCY: afghani (end-'92 £1=Af99.25, US$1=Af65.55)
GNP PER CAPITA: US$168 ('82)
MAIN EXPORT EARNERS: agricultural products

THIS was the year which actually saw the long-predicted and long-delayed downfall of President Najibullah, the man the USSR had left in charge in Kabul when Soviet forces withdrew in 1989. His fall followed the collapse of the Soviet Union in late 1991. In his last year in office, General Najibullah tried desperately to gloss over his own past as a ruthless secret service chief and protégé of Moscow. Increasingly critical of his former ally towards the end, for provoking the uprising in his country, the President declared 15 February as Afghanistan's national day to celebrate the final withdrawal of Soviet troops.

President Najibullah and his highly-factionalized Pushtu-based regime were overthrown in late April, as a broad front of mujahideen leaders and their followers patched together a coalition against their common adversary. Events were soon to show, however, that this coalition was virtually incapable of sustaining stable coalition government. The rest of the year was punctuated by manoeuvrings, skirmishes, disagreements and fighting. Those who had helped to overthrow the Najibullah regime could not agree on who should compose the government, for how long and with what aims.

The virtual bankruptcy of the country and the flight of many skilled personnel undoubtedly contributed to the inability of successive 'governments', preoccupied by power struggles, to define clearly, still less to implement, coherent policies. A murderous power struggle raged, the various mujahideen groups being reluctant or unwilling to accept the necessary compromises of coalition government, even though a coalition was the only realistic prospect if the country was to have any semblance of a national government. More citizens of Kabul died within a few months of the eviction of the Najibullah regime than during the 14 preceding years of civil war.

Throughout the year Iran, Saudi Arabia and Pakistan competed and jostled inconclusively for influence in Kabul. As the capital became gripped by discords and rivalries, its importance for the rest of the country declined. Ethnic, linguistic and sectarian centres formed, and in some cases re-formed, to make new administrative centres in Afghanistan. Despite the political fragmentation of the country, however, and the continued fighting that convulsed Kabul, hundreds of thousands of Afghan refugees returned home, not so much to the country of Afghanistan as to their villages, families and tribes.

Fighting between rival mujahideen factions continued intermittently throughout the second half of the year. The main clashes were between the forces of Gulbuddia Hekmatyar, leader of the fundamentalist Hezb-i-Islami faction, and those of General Abdul Rashid Dostam, the Uzbek warlord and *de facto* leader of northern Afghanistan.

Compounding Afghanistan's problems were some 100,000 refugees who had fled across the Oxus river into the north to escape bitter fighting in the central Asian republic of Tajikistan (see VIII.1.iii). In late December relief coordinators reported that three or four children were dying every night in freezing temperatures in one makeshift camp. These displaced people were mainly Tajiks from the mountainous north who were settled in the south of Tajikistan under Stalin to grow cotton. They were described in 1992 as victims of 'ethnic cleansing' by lowland Tajiks and Uzbeks seeking to reclaim what they regarded as their ancestral lands. Having fled across the Oxus, they became entangled in Afghanistan's chronically unstable politics.

At the end of the year an assembly of over 1,300 tribal and religious leaders approved the creation of a parliament and a new army in Afghanistan. The assembly also laid down strict Islamic guidelines for the country. Afghanistan was one of seven new member-states admitted to the Economic Cooperation Organization (ECO), the association of central-south Asian countries, at an extraordinary meeting held in Islamabad on 28 November.

One indicator of the depressed economy and low public morale was the sinking unofficial exchange value of the national currency, the afghani. In April there were about 500 afghanis to the US dollar; by end-December there were over 1,100, compared with an official rate of US$1=65.55 afghanis.

iii.   KAZAKHSTAN—TURKMENIA—UZBEKISTAN—
KIRGHIZIA—TAJIKISTAN

Kazakhstan
CAPITAL: Alma Ata   AREA: 2,717,300 sq km   POPULATION: 17,000,000 ('92)
OFFICIAL LANGUAGE: Kazakh   POLITICAL SYSTEM: republic
RULING PARTY: Socialist Party of Kazakhstan (SPK)
HEAD OF STATE AND GOVERNMENT: President Nursultan Nazarbayev
CURRENCY: rouble   GNP PER CAPITA: US$1,464 ('90 est.)

Turkmenia
CAPITAL: Ashkhabad   AREA: 448,100 sq km   POPULATION: 3,600,000 ('92)
OFFICIAL LANGUAGE: Turkmenian   POLITICAL SYSTEM: republic
RULING PARTY: Democratic Party of Turkmenia (DPT)
HEAD OF STATE AND GOVERNMENT: President Saparmurad Niyazov
CURRENCY: rouble   GNP PER CAPITA: US$1,082 ('90 est.)

Uzbekistan
CAPITAL: Tashkent   AREA: 447,400 sq km   POPULATION: 20,000,000 ('92)
OFFICIAL LANGUAGE: Uzbek   POLITICAL SYSTEM: republic
RULING PARTY: People's Democratic Party (PDP)
HEAD OF STATE AND GOVERNMENT: President Islam Karimov
CURRENCY: rouble   GNP PER CAPITA: US$830 ('90 est.)

Kirghizia
CAPITAL: Bishkek   AREA: 198,500 sq km   POPULATION: 4,400,000 ('92)
OFFICIAL LANGUAGE: Kirghizian   POLITICAL SYSTEM: republic
RULING PARTY: Democratic Movement of Kirghizia (DMK)
HEAD OF STATE AND GOVERNMENT: President Askar Akayev
CURRENCY: rouble   GNP PER CAPITA: US$996 ('90 est.)

Tajikistan
CAPITAL: Dushanbe   AREA: 143,100 sq km   POPULATION: 5,300,000 ('92)
OFFICIAL LANGUAGE: Tajik   POLITICAL SYSTEM: republic
RULING PARTY: Communist Party of Tajikistan (CPT)
HEAD OF STATE: Acting President Imamuli Rakhmanov
HEAD OF GOVERNMENT: Abdumalik Abdulllojanov, acting Prime Minister
CURRENCY: rouble   GNP PER CAPITA: US$1,705 ('90 est.)

IN the immediate aftermath of the abortive Soviet coup of August 1991,
four of the five Central Asian republics (Uzbekistan, Kirghizia, Tajikistan
and Turkmenia) made declarations of independence. However, these
were generally perceived to be tactical manoeuvres on the part of the
regional leaders—a means of distancing themselves from the factional
in-fighting in Moscow. There was no popular demand for secession.
Indeed, many of the parliamentary deputies were taken by surprise by
the announcements that were presented to them by the ruling elites as
virtual *faits accomplis*. Subsequently, little action was taken to create the
technical mechanisms that would give political and economic substance
to independence. The Central Asian states were thus in no way prepared
for the demise of the Soviet Union at the end of 1991 (see AR 1991,
pp. 177–88). Kazakhstan belatedly proclaimed its independence on
16 December. Shortly afterwards, at a summit meeting held in Alma
Ata on 20–21 December, it was agreed that the new Commonwealth
of Independent States (CIS) should include not only the three Slav

republics, but also eight other members, amongst them all five Central Asian states.

Without warning, and without preparation, the newly-independent Central Asian states had suddenly to assume full responsibility for a daunting array of economic, social and environmental problems. Partly because of their lower level of development, partly because of their physical remoteness, the five republics were far more dependent on USSR structures and subsidies than the other republics. Consequently, the shock waves from the collapse of the union were felt more acutely. The abrupt termination of budgetary subsidies from the centre (one of the principal sources of funding for the welfare services), the dislocation of inter-republican trade, the shortage of banknotes (Moscow retained the monopoly of cash emission) and soaring inflation caused serious distress in a region where poverty was already endemic. Some 60 per cent of the indigenous population of Tajikistan and Kirghizia were reported to be below the official poverty line in 1990.

Market-oriented reforms were set in motion in all the Central Asian republics in 1992. Progress, however, was slow and tortuous. The liberalization of prices in January provoked serious civil disorders throughout the region; worst affected was Tashkent, where several student protesters were killed. Privatization programmes proved to be even more difficult to implement here than in other parts of the former Soviet Union. Not only was there a chronic shortage of professional expertise in such essential fields as law, insurance, accountancy and taxation, but cultural and social factors compounded the technical problems. The formerly nomadic peoples were reluctant to acquire shares in immovable property and regarded the whole process of privatization with deep suspicion. Such obstacles meant that even in Kazakhstan and Kirghizia, ostensibly the most committed to privatization programmes, there was very little genuine progress in this field.

Economic reform was further hampered by the threat of mass unemployment. The high rate of demographic increase (2.2 per cent per annum in Kazakhstan, 3 per cent and above in the other four republics) required a constant increase in job opportunities. This was difficult to satisfy in the last years of the Soviet regime. Now, with the sharp decline in industrial production, the disbanding of many enterprises (particularly those of the military-industrial complex) and attempts to curb over-manning, it was impossible to maintain existing levels of employment. This was of major concern in a region where families with many dependants, both young and old, and few wage earners, were the norm. Moreover, unemployment played a significant role in the growth of crime, especially by gangs of youths. The dramatic increase in illegal trafficking in narcotics, some produced locally, some imported from neighbouring countries for onward dispatch, exacerbated the situation. UN officials estimated that in 1992 some four-fifths of the drugs imported into Europe came from Central Asia.

Another problem was the increase in ethnic, clan and regional tensions. Since the late 1980s old rivalries over land and water rights had re-emerged and competition for jobs and housing had become steadily fiercer. By 1990 the general climate had become so tense that Slavs and other immigrants (such as Germans) had started to leave. This trend increased in 1992, causing serious industrial disruption. Clan and regional rivalries also became more acute, turning into an open struggle for political power. This trend was most pronounced in Tajikistan, where by March factional confrontation was already slipping into civil war. In September President Nabiyev was forced to resign by a coalition of opposition forces. Government control of Dushanbe, the capital, was re-established in December, but fighting continued in many areas. Similar tendencies were to be found in the other republics. On the surface, ideological differences appeared to be the main cause, although these often reflected older, local allegiances. Thus in Tajikistan the struggle appeared to be between ex-communist hardliners, Islamic activists of various complexions and secular democrats, but in fact these groupings represented regionally-based factions with a long pre-Soviet history of animosity.

Islam gained new significance following independence. Under Soviet rule knowledge of Islam had been reduced to such a low level that for the great mass of the population it consisted of little more than the random observance of a few traditional rites. In the late 1980s, however, Islam began to re-emerge as a potential force in society. At the same time nationalist tendencies began to cause deep rifts. Hitherto there had been a single, unified Muslim administration, based in Uzbekistan but serving the region as a whole. Shortly before the collapse of the Soviet Union the other republics demanded their own administrations. In 1992, the fissiparous tendencies grew stronger. The 'official' Muslim clerics became more overtly nationalist, while rivalries between followers of the various 'informal' local leaders became more acrimonious. The only formal Muslim political party was the Islamic Revival Party (officially registered in Tajikistan since 1991 but not in the other republics). It enjoyed little support outside the Ferghana Valley and some rural areas and was much distrusted by other Muslim factions. Senior government officials, until recently solid Communist Party functionaries, were now careful to stress their Islamic credentials, thereby attempting to establish a new form of legitimacy with which to replace the discredited Soviet legacy. Fledgling democratic groups, too, resorted to Islam as a means of strengthening their own appeal to the masses. Thus, paradoxically, although adherence to Islam as a religion was still far from widespread, as a political symbol it had already acquired considerable power.

The economic, transport, communications, defence and administrative ties between Central Asia and the other republics, especially Russia, were too close to be broken overnight. However, during 1992 considerable strides were made in all five republics towards establishing independent national institutions (for example, national central banks) and formulating economic and foreign policy agendas that answered their particular needs. The President of Kazakhstan was a strong advocate of a 'common economic space' for CIS members, serviced by inter-republican institutions similar to those of the European Community. The other Central Asian republics showed a preference for more focused bilateral and multilateral agreements to safeguard common interests, for example in the area of defence.

Relations between the Central Asian states and the international community developed rapidly in 1992. A number of airlines established direct flights to Central Asian cities, while satellite links improved communications by telephone. By year's end each republic had established diplomatic relations with over 100 countries. All five were accepted as members of the United Nations on 2 March and began the process of joining the specialized agencies. They also joined regional groupings such as the Economic Cooperation Organization (with Turkey, Iran and Pakistan), while Kazakhstan and Turkmenia joined the Caspian Sea Group (with Russia, Iran and Azerbaijan).

The opening-up of the region attracted much commercial interest, particularly with regard to its vast mineral and hydrocarbon resources. Logistical problems, lack of an adequate legal infrastructure and a cumbersome bureaucracy presented serious obstacles to foreign investment, however, and there was as yet more curiosity than active involvement. Nevertheless, Kazakhstan succeeded in securing agreements on a number of major projects, including that with Chevron for the development of the Tengiz oil field and with the British Gas/AGIP consortium for the Karachaganak field.

It was a year of fundamental readjustment for the Central Asian republics. They weathered the collapse of the Soviet Union better than might have been anticipated, but there remained great uncertainties about their futures. Although they were rich in human and material resources, decades of uneven development—extreme overspecialization in some fields, neglect in others—had left them highly vulnerable. In the face of growing social tensions, the republican governments were attempting to maintain control by resorting to authoritarian, at times highly repressive, measures. Moreover, international rivalries were being projected into the region, as countries to the west, south and east all sought to establish competing spheres of influence. The Central Asian governments repeatedly stated their determination to follow their own models of political and economic development and to reject the advances of prospective 'elder brothers'. Only time would tell whether they could succeed in preserving such an independent stance.

2. INDIA—PAKISTAN—BANGLADESH—SRI LANKA—NEPAL—BHUTAN

i. INDIA

CAPITAL: New Delhi   AREA: 3,287,000 sq km   POPULATION: 844,000,000 ('91)
OFFICIAL LANGUAGES: Hindi & English   POLITICAL SYSTEM: parliamentary democracy
HEAD OF STATE: President Shankar Dayal Sharma (since July '92)
RULING PARTIES: Congress (I) forms minority government
HEAD OF GOVERNMENT: P. V. Narasimha Rao, Prime Minister (since June '91)
PRINCIPAL MINISTERS: Manmohan Singh (finance), Sharad Pawar (defence),
   S. B. Chavan (home affairs), K. Vijaya Bhaskara Reddy (justice)
INTERNATIONAL ALIGNMENT: NAM, SAARC, Cwth.
CURRENCY: rupee (end-'92 £1=Rs43.63, US$1=Rs28.82)
GNP PER CAPITA: US$350 ('90)
MAIN EXPORT EARNERS: precious stones, textiles, tea, tourism

SUPERFICIALLY 1992 was a year in which India's overall political status quo appeared to be preserved. At year's end the same government and the same Prime Minister were in office in New Delhi. In reality, however, both the Union government and the Prime Minister were much diminished in authority, principally because of viciously spiralling inter-communal violence in December. Even before the ignominious end of the year, however, sick jokes about the Prime Minister's alleged indecisiveness were circulating widely. In particular, many informed Indians, as well as foreign commentators, were saying that the earlier, much-lauded liberalization of the economy was more words than deeds.

To a considerable extent the decline in the ruling Congress (I)'s authority and self-confidence, so marked in the last month of the year, was the obverse of the fortunes of the main opposition party, the Hindu revivalist Bharatiya Janata Party (BJP). For most of 1992 the BJP seemed to have lost the impetus it had built up for the 1991 elections (see AR 1991, pp. 310–1). In January the new BJP president, Murti Manohar Joshi, attempted to organize a 'march for unity' to Srinagar, capital of Kashmir (the only Muslim-majority state in India), to demonstrate the BJP's mass following and discipline and to raise the national flag on 26 January (Republic Day). The exercise ended somewhat in anti-climax, in that Mr Joshi was airlifted into Srinagar by an army helicopter for the final stage of his 'march', while his flag-raising ceremony had to be performed within a protective ring of armed troops far outnumbering BJP supporters. By the end of the year, however, the BJP was experiencing an upsurge of Hindu support over the vexed question of the mosque at Ayodhya, in Uttar Pradesh, northern India.

In April a Congress (I) plenary session at Tirupati (in the south) conducted the first internal party voting for many years. Prime Minister Narasimha Rao's apparent commitment to open party debate and elections was qualified in the event by his understandable desire to see his preferred candidate win. To prevent his rivals, notably Human Resources Minister Arjun Singh, from making gains at his expense, the Prime Minister sanctioned procedural devices to ensure the nomination of sympathetic members to the party's central committee.

The Bofors scandal (see AR 1987, pp. 294–5; 1989, p. 303), involving accusations of bribery at the higher levels of government in connection with a large arms deal with Sweden, resurfaced actively, despite efforts by the government to discourage any further publicity or proceedings in the case. A maladroit attempt in February by the Minister of External Affairs, Madhavsinh Solanki, to persuade the Swedes to end their part in the inquiries misfired, and he was forced to resign in April. In September a court decision made it even less likely that the Bofors case would be speedily and unambiguously resolved.

India's serving Vice-President, Shankar Dayal Sharma, became the country's ninth President since independence in 1947. A former Cambridge law don, Mr Sharma began his five-year term on 25 July, when President R. V. Venkataraman retired. At the electoral college contest on 16 July, Mr Sharma, the ruling Congress (I) and the Left Front nominee, had secured 67 per cent of the votes, against 33 per cent for George Gilbert Swell (a former diplomat and the deputy parliamentary speaker). The electoral college consisted of some 700 Union parliamentarians and about 4,300 state legislators, who were ballotted in New Delhi and the state capitals respectively. The President's functions were mainly ceremonial, although minority governments at the centre and many centre-state tussles in recent years had enhanced his role as a political referee. There was general agreement in political circles that Mr Sharma would make a good head of state despite his loyalty to the Congress Party and to the Nehru-Gandhi family which had dominated it for most of India's post-independence history.

The Ayodhya question centred on the Hindu demand for the construction of a temple on the site of the reputed birthplace of the god Rama and for the consequential demolition of the ancient (and disused) Babri mosque dating from the Mogul Empire. The long-simmering issue came to a head when Hindu militants invaded the site on 6 December and destroyed the mosque. This action not only caused much Hindu-Muslim blood-letting but also precipitated a political showdown between Congress and the BJP, amid speculation that there would be a snap general election early in 1993.

Having immediately dismissed the BJP ministry in Uttar Pradesh, on 15 December the Prime Minister also dismissed three other BJP-controlled state governments, charging that their constitutional machinery had broken down. These dismissals had been widely expected, as was the defiant BJP reaction that the law-and-order situation in these states was no worse than those run by the Congress. In a direct challenge to the Prime Minister, a senior BJP leader (and former minister of external affairs), A. B. Vajapayee, said: 'If he is so sure of his stand, let him dissolve the parliament and seek a fresh mandate. The Indian people will give a fitting reply.'

It became clear in the week after the mosque attack that Mr Narasimha Rao faced no immediate challenge from within Congress. However, his authority and reputation were seriously weakened by the impression of indecisiveness he gave as mob fury swept nearly all corners of the country, particularly the northern Hindu belt. Within five days the death toll from communal violence had risen to over 1,200. There were many reports that the violence was aggravated by criminals taking advantage of the turmoil to loot, extort and grab land by driving out Muslims. Muslims claimed that the police often stood aside, giving Hindu mobs free rein.

The Prime Minister's credibility depended critically on whether the government could succeed in proving the legal culpability of eight top BJP and other Hindu leaders arrested and charged with stirring up religious hatred. Much also depended on whether he could carry through the two-year bans announced on 10 December against three BJP-associated organizations.

On the economic front, and in large measure because of the mounting communal problems, the Congress government failed to give a positive impetus to its economic reform programme. Since taking office, the government had liberalized imports, lowering tariff barriers, improved the scope for foreign investment, eased foreign exchange controls and made the rupee partially convertible. It also began the process of privatizing state-owned companies and making the rupee fully convertible in the medium term. Even so, no real consensus seemed to have been created for the cause of economic reform.

Left-wingers and domestic vested interests denounced the economic reforms, while many reformists complained that the pace of change was too slow. Bills to amend the foreign exchange regulations, to institute structural changes to nationalized banks and to de-license some industries were scheduled to be tabled in parliament in December. Each had to be deferred when the legislature was adjourned in the wake of the Ayodhya clashes. Most of these measures had been instituted administratively but they lacked statutory sanction.

During the year groups in India and abroad contended that government forces frequently, and sometimes blatantly and brutally, violated the human rights not only of political activists and militants but also of innocent spectators. The Indian government and much of the media were critical of such accusations, notably those made in a much-publicized report by Amnesty International. It was announced in September that a human rights commission would be appointed.

At the end of the year investigators into a major banking scandal nearly doubled their estimate of the amounts missing, to $2,000 million. Stockbrokers and bank officials had allegedly colluded to direct money illegally from the bond market to boost share prices.

In its annual report to India's aid donors, the gist of which was released to the press on 19 August, the World Bank forecast that India's external debt would rise to $93,000 million in five years, from $74,000 milllion at present. The Bank said India would need about $60,000 million a year over the next five years to finance its current-account deficit, repay its debt and increase foreign exchange reserves. The report added that India's current-account deficit was expected to double in 1992/93 to $6,000 million (from $3,000 million in the previous year), mostly due to the lifting of import curbs imposed in April 1991.

The declaratory dimension of India's foreign policy in 1992 was intended to convey the impression that economic considerations were uppermost. On this view, foreign economic policy was seen as an extension of the domestic economic motif of liberalization. In practice, communalism within India and the banking scandal greatly inhibited new investment. Furthermore, India's relations with its partners in the South Asian Association for Regional Cooperation (see XI.6.ii), especially with Pakistan, Bangladesh and Sri Lanka, became more strained, notably over the Ayodhya mosque episode and ensuing repercussions.

With Pakistan, relations remained tense, accusations and counter-accusations being batted back and forth concerning Kashmir and the Punjab. India remained convinced that the Pakistanis were backing its Sikh and Kashmiri dissidents. Pakistan accused India of fomenting or exacerbating trouble in Sindh (see VII.2.ii). Even so, official-level talks were held in a low-key manner on specific matters, such as the dispute over the proper line of control on the Siachen glacier in the north-west corner of Kashmir. (For relations with Sri Lanka, see VIII.2.vi.)

More widely, India sought rather tentatively to adjust its relations with a number of countries, amid the fluidities of the post-Cold War world. In general, relations with the United States were better than for many years, though there were several specific disagreements, most notably over the GATT Uruguay Round negotiations and nuclear matters. Joint Indo-American naval exercises were held in the Indian Ocean, the first such for more than 30 years. There were mutually guarded but basically cordial relations with China. India's Defence Minister visited China in July and talks between officials on the Sino-Indian border dispute and related matters were held in Beijing in early November, though without any breakthrough resulting. Prime Minister Rao paid a five-day visit to Japan in June. In September an extradition treaty was signed with Britain. During the year relations with post-Soviet Russia were carefully reviewed and somewhat realigned, especially in trade, payments and weapons supplies.

ii. PAKISTAN

CAPITAL: Islamabad   AREA: 804,000 sq km   POPULATION: 112,400,000 ('90)
OFFICIAL LANGUAGE: Urdu   POLITICAL SYSTEM: nominal parliamentary democracy
HEAD OF STATE: President Ghulam Ishaq Khan (since Aug '88)
RULING PARTY: Islamic Democratic Alliance (IJI), dominated by Muslim League
HEAD OF GOVERNMENT: Nawaz Sharif, Prime Minister (since Nov '90)
PRINCIPAL MINISTERS: Sayed Ghaus Ali Shah (defence), Choudhry Shujat Hussain
    (interior), Sartaj Aziz (finance & economy), Hamid Nasir Chattha (planning &
    development), Choudhary Abdul Ghafoor (justice)
INTERNATIONAL ALIGNMENT: NAM, ICO, SAARC, Cwth., ECO
CURRENCY: rupee (end-'92 £1=PRs38.68, US$1=PRs25.55)
GNP PER CAPITA: US$380 ('90)
MAIN EXPORT EARNERS: cotton, textiles, rice

STALEMATE persisted in Pakistan's politics throughout 1992. Within the ruling triumvirate of Prime Minister, President and Chief of the Army Staff, no-one was able to make a decisive move. Outside the government the Pakistan People's Party (PPP) and the Mohajir Qaumi Movement (MQM)—the latter in opposition from June—used their street power to embarrass but not to dislodge their opponents. Short-term calculations and dispositions produced a rapid succession of alliances of convenience.

Prime Minister Nawaz Sharif and the Islami Jamhoori Ittehad (IJI), itself an alliance of parties, not only maintained their majority in the National Assembly but were also represented in the ruling coalitions in all the provinces. However, their position was weakened by lacklustre performance in office and allegations of corruption, by internal dissension within the alliance and within its major element, the Muslim League, and by the loss of the Jamaat-i-Islami (which left the IJI in May) and then the following month of its coalition partner, the MQM. There was a greater emphasis during the year on Islamic themes, in some cases at the expense of religious minorities, as a way to gain popular support. President Ghulam Ishaq Khan retained the discretionary powers inherited from the late General Zia-ul-Haq, under which, for example, he had dismissed the PPP government in August 1990 (see AR 1990, pp. 316–7). But he was distrusted by a wide swathe of political opinion, which felt that his main concern was to manoeuvre himself into a further presidential term from 1993 onwards. It was in his interests, therefore, to practise divide and rule between the political parties. The army, under General Asif Nawaz Janjua, maintained its interest in a stable, pro-military central government, but seemed less willing to consider direct intervention than previously.

The PPP, under the leadership of Benazir Bhutto, continued throughout the year to call for fresh elections under neutral auspices. It was able to demonstrate its popular support through a series of public meetings and other activities. These came to a head in November when the PPP leader announced a 'long march' to the National Assembly in

Islamabad in order to rally her supporters and destabilize the Nawaz Sharif government. She had the support of a number of other opposition leaders, notably the former prime minister, Ghulam Mustafa Jatoi, who had formed his own National Democratic Alliance, allegedly with the backing of the President. The government responded with a massive show of strength. Islamabad was effectively cut off from the rest of the country on 18 November, and Benazir Bhutto herself was placed under house arrest for a while. There were widespread clashes on the streets of Lahore and other cities between the police and PPP supporters. However, the PPP was itself under pressure throughout the year, as the government used various means at its disposal to harass it, including amendments to legal procedures. Benazir Bhutto's husband remained under detention for the whole year. Like other political parties, the PPP was further hindered by internal factional conflicts.

At the end of May the army was sent in to Sindh province with a mandate to restore law and order, which had largely broken down under the combined impact of rural banditry and conflict in Karachi between ethnically-based political parties. The decision was made by the triumvirate, but it was clear that there had been differences of expectation between them. The Prime Minister was principally concerned at the effect on his position in the National Assembly, while the President appeared to be motivated by his own political calculations. The impact of the army's action was felt immediately in the rural areas, but in Karachi it proved more difficult to act effectively in a highly-politicized situation. The immediate effect of the army action was to force the official MQM leadership into hiding or voluntary exile, while a breakaway faction, the MQM Haqiqi, enjoyed support from the army intelligence agencies. MQM members of the National Assembly and the Sindh assembly resigned in the hope of making political capital, although the net result was to further muddy the waters and to make any sort of government initiative harder to implement.

There were a number of thinly-veiled calls during the year from politicians, particularly from the PPP, for the army to intervene in order that fresh elections could be held under neutral auspices. Although the army showed no overt sign of responding, it kept in close touch with political developments and with politicians of all parties. General Asif Nawaz Janjua was known to have had differences with the Prime Minister over appointments and other matters. Although the army's actions in Sindh were popular in many quarters, there were also allegations that it had abused its powers in trying to restore law and order.

According to official figures, the economy grew by 6.4 per cent in the financial year ended 30 June, despite the political uncertainties. Structural problems persisted, however, particularly in the areas of exports, where low world prices cancelled out the record cotton crop, and of public finance, where the fiscal deficit remained well above the target agreed with the IMF. The privatization programme initiated in 1991 continued, amid allegations of favouritism and corruption in the way in which it was being implemented. In November 1991 the Federal Shariat Court had ruled that all forms of interest were repugnant to Islam and would have to be phased out by 30 June 1992. However, the government succeeded in side-stepping the issue. In May the federal budget made some changes to the tax system but did not address the major issue of how to extend the very narrow base of direct tax-payers.

In September massive floods led to a substantial death toll and serious economic losses. Some 400 cultivators were swept away from a river island when the gates of the Mangla dam were opened without proper warning.

For most of the year relations with India remained icy but polite. In February an attempt was made by the Jammu and Kashmir Liberation Front to force the government's hand by sending marchers to cross the 'line of control' from Pakistani-held to Indian-held Kashmir. Concerned at the unpredictable consequences of such an action, the Pakistan government took steps to halt the march just short of the border, a small number of marchers being shot dead in the process. In October a similar attempt was made, although it was stopped with less difficulty. Talks were held at official level, and in September the Prime Ministers of the two countries were able to hold informal discussions at the Non-Aligned Movement's meeting in Jakarta (see XI.4.ii).

An entirely new strain on Indo-Pakistan relations developed in December when Hindu extremists demolished a mosque at Ayodhya (see VIII.2.i). The majority of those killed in subsequent riots belonged to India's Muslim minority. The backlash in Pakistan was predictable and to some extent beyond the capacity of the government to control. Mobs systematically demolished Hindu temples in Lahore, Karachi and elsewhere, often with the connivance of politicians and local authorities. However, there were only stray attacks on Pakistan's small Hindu minority, and the government made a determined effort to protect Indian high commission buildings, although not with total success.

Relations with the United States remained at a low ebb and the US arms embargo imposed in 1990 remained in force. Nawaz Sharif visited Kabul in April to mark the installation of a mujahideen government in Afghanistan (see VIII.1.ii), in whose formation he had played a major role. An agreement was reached with Bangladesh in July on the longstanding issue of the Biharis (Urdu-speaking minority) who were to be allowed to migrate to Pakistan.

iii. BANGLADESH

CAPITAL: Dhaka AREA: 144,000 sq km POPULATION: 108,000,000 ('90)
OFFICIAL LANGUAGE: Bengali POLITICAL SYSTEM: parliamentary democracy
HEAD OF STATE: President Abdur Rahman Biswas (since Oct '91)
RULING PARTIES: Bangladesh National Party (BNP)
HEAD OF GOVERNMENT: Begum Khaleda Zia, Prime Minister (since March '91)
PRINCIPAL MINISTERS: Mirza Gholam Hafiz (justice), A. S. M. Mustafizur Rahman
   (foreign affairs), Saifur Rahman (finance), Abdul Matin Choudhry (home),
   Maj.-Gen. Majedul Haq (agriculture, irrigation & flood control)
INTERNATIONAL ALIGNMENT: NAM, ICO, SAARC, Cwth.
CURRENCY: taka (end-'92 £1=Tk58.95, US$1=Tk38.94)
GNP PER CAPITA: US$210 ('90)
MAIN EXPORT EARNERS: jute, fish

THE often feverish quality of parliamentary life in Bangladesh was evident throughout the year. Nevertheless, the Bangladesh Nationalist Party (BNP) government of Begum Khaleda Zia, which had come to office in March 1992 (see AR 1991, p. 317), remained firmly in power, although it faced a worrying escalation of terrorist violence.

Pandemonium prevailed for over an hour on the opening day of the winter session of the Jatiya Sangsad (parliament) on 4 January. The two main opposition groups, the Awami League (AL) and the Jatiya Party (JP), staged three walk-outs and then boycotted the inaugural address of President Abdur Rahman Biswas. Of the many complaints voiced against the BNP government, the most vigorously pursued involved opposition to ten ordinances promulgated by the President after the previous parliamentary session. AL and JP spokesmen claimed that these ordinances violated democratic norms and practices by bypassing parliament, which was now supposed to be sovereign. The Jatiya Party also complained bitterly about the government's abrupt abolition of the *upazilla* system of elected local government councils.

Later in the year, other issues took the attention of parliamentarians. Opposition parties again boycotted parliament in June in protest against the government's decision not to appoint a special tribunal to try Gholam Azam, leader of the Jamaat-i-Islami Bangladesh, for war crimes allegedly committed during the 1971 war of independence. A controversial new law enacted on 29 October provided that schoolchildren found cheating in examinations would be liable to imprisonment for up to ten years, as would teachers found guilty of leaking examination questions.

Foreign policy matters continued to be dominated principally by relations with adjoining India. At the same time, Bangladesh continued to participate actively in the Islamic Conference Organization, the Non-Aligned Movement and the South Asian Association for Regional Cooperation (SAARC). A protocol establishing diplomatic relations with Armenia was signed in the Armenian capital, Yerevan, on 14 November. During talks in Dhaka on 3–5 November between the Bangladesh

Foreign Minister and China's Vice-Minister for Foreign Affairs, China offered to help in the matter of securing humane treatment and right of repatriation for the tens of thousands of Muslim refugees (the Rohingyas) who had fled from Myanmar (Burma) into Bangladesh (see AR 1991, pp. 318, 330).

Acts of terrorism increased in severity during the first nine months of the year, to the extent that the government warned that the country's recently-renascent democracy was under serious threat. Violence was often convulsive on university campuses. Consequently, a new anti-terrorist bill was adopted by parliament on 1 November in an amended form. The amended bill, which was to be in force for two years in the first instance, stipulated the death sentence or 20 years in gaol (with minimum of five years' rigorous imprisonment) for terrorist offences. A total of 168 cases were registered under the new law from 15 September to 20 October, out of 255 people arrested for suspected terrorist offences. The highest concentration of such cases were the 48 recorded in Dhaka.

About 400 demonstrators fought with police and smashed vehicles on 27 December, protesting over the arrest of Khaledur Rahman, the JP secretary-general. Mr Rahman had been detained three days earlier after he had led about 50 supporters in the storming of a sealed building in Dhaka, claiming that it was rightfully the property of his party.

iv. NEPAL

CAPITAL: Kathmandu   AREA: 147,000 sq km   POPULATION: 18,900,000 ('90)
OFFICIAL LANGUAGE: Nepali   POLITICAL SYSTEM: parliamentary democracy
HEAD OF STATE: King Birendra Bir Bikram Shah Deva (since '72)
RULING PARTY: Nepali Congress Party (NCP)
HEAD OF GOVERNMENT: Girja Prasad Koirala, Prime Minister (since May '91)
PRINCIPAL MINISTERS: Sher Bahadur Deupan (home affairs), Maheshwore Prasad
    Singh (justice)
INTERNATIONAL ALIGNMENT: NAM, SAARC
CURRENCY: rupee (end-'92 £1=NRs70.71, US$1=NRs46.71)
GNP PER CAPITA: US$170 ('90)
MAIN EXPORT EARNERS: agricultural products, tourism

THE year began with a new cabinet, following a major reshuffle on 30 December 1991. Having dropped six ministers from rival groups, Prime Minister Girja Prasad Koirala inducted 12 new members from amongst his own followers, within the ruling Nepali Congress Party (NCP), thus strengthening and consolidating his political position. This was the first reshuffle of the seven-month-old Koirala government voted into power in the multi-party elections of May 1991 (see AR 1991, p. 319). The six deposed ministers belonged either to the camp of the NCP president, Krishna Prasad Bhattarai, or to that of the main party manager, Ganesh Man Singh.

Internal NCP divisions were apparent at the party's national convention, the first for 32 years, held at Jhapa in mid-February. Following
the convention a former prime minister, Maitrika Prasad Koirala,
announced the formation of a new party, the Rashtriya Janata Parishad,
to provide a democratic alternative to the NCP.

Voters went to the polls in May and June to elect about 44,000
local government officials, including town councillors and mayors, for
a five-year term. The results confirmed the dominance of the NCP,
especially in rural areas, although the elections were preceded by
unrest and some strikes in protest against economic hardship. Earlier, in
February, the government had set up a ten-member commission under
the chairmanship of the then Finance Minister, Mahesh Acharya, to
recommend programmes and priorities for the privatization of existing
state undertakings.

By the middle of the year it had become apparent that an intra-party
struggle in the so-called United Communist Party of Nepal (Marxist
and Leninist) was in progress. The eventual outcome, despite desperate
efforts to patch up the divisions, was a vertical split in the party, which
formed the main opposition group in the Nepalese parliament.

The substance of Nepal's foreign policy continued to revolve around
relations with its two giant neighbours, India and China. Prime Minister
Koirala paid an official visit to China on 16–31 March. India and Nepal
took a number of joint decisions on water resources development during
the year, continuing their quiet, mostly technical, discussions on this
subject. The two governments also cooperated in the presentation of
a number of development projects in the eastern Himalayan border
region for assistance under Japan's global infrastructure fund (GIF).
India's Prime Minister visited Nepal on 19–20 October, the first such
visit for 15 years.

v. BHUTAN

CAPITAL: Thimphu   AREA: 46,500 sq km   POPULATION: 1,400,000 ('90)
OFFICIAL LANGUAGES: Dzongkha, Lhotsan, English   POLITICAL SYSTEM: monarchy
HEAD OF STATE AND GOVERNMENT: Dragon King Jigme Singye Wangchuk (since '72)
PRINCIPAL MINISTERS: Dawa Tsering (foreign affairs), Namgyel Wangchuk (home
    affairs), Dorji Tsering (finance)
INTERNATIONAL ALIGNMENT: NAM, SAARC
CURRENCY: ngultrum (end-'92 £1=N43.63, US$1=N28.82)
GNP PER CAPITA: US$190 ('90)
MAIN EXPORT EARNERS: tourism, cement, timber

THE government had two major concerns in 1992: first, to maintain the
political and administrative status quo against challenges from members
of the banned Bhutan People's Party (BPP); second, to implement the

seventh five-year plan (1992–97) despite the efforts of militants to destroy development infrastructure in the south.

Many of the militants were ethnic Nepalese advocating a 'greater Nepal'. Others adhered to the notion of 'Gorkaland', an entity that would include parts of India, Bhutan and Nepal. Linked with these phenomena was the demand that immigrants from Nepal should have the freedom to express their Hindu culture, especially in the southern districts of Bhutan, where they probably outnumbered native Bhutanese. During the year exiled Bhutanese opposition groups accused the Bhutan government of forcing ethnic Nepalese to accept Bhutanese culture and religion or leave the country.

Bhutan's foreign and economic affairs during 1992 were, as usual, dominated by its ties with India, as was illustrated in the number of visits made by high-level Bhutanese officials to New Delhi. There was no change in the longstanding arrangement under which the Bhutan ngultrum was pegged to the Indian rupee. Otherwise, there were only limited opportunities to promote Bhutan's interests with its regional neighbours in the South Asian Association for Regional Cooperation. Trade arrangements continued with Nepal and Bangladesh, although difficulties arose periodically because of the lawless border situations.

In early November there were press reports that the King of Bhutan had moved out of his grand fortress-palace outside Thimphu, Bhutan's capital, and was living ascetically in a two-room log cabin. The monarch was said to be working hard to set a good example to his subjects, aiming in particular to combat corruption.

vi. SRI LANKA

CAPITAL: Colombo   AREA: 64,500 sq km   POPULATION: 17,000,000 ('90)
OFFICIAL LANGUAGES: Sinhala, Tamil, English
POLITICAL SYSTEM: presidential democracy
HEAD OF STATE AND GOVERNMENT: President Ranasinghe Premadasa (since Feb '89)
RULING PARTY: United National Party (UNP)
PRINCIPAL MINISTERS: Dingiri Banda Wijetunge (prime minister, finance),
    Harold Herath (foreign affairs), A. C. S. Hameed (justice), Festus Perera (home affairs)
INTERNATIONAL ALIGNMENT: NAM, SAARC, Cwth.
CURRENCY: rupee (end-'92 £1=SLRs68.55, US$1=SLRs45.28)
GNP PER CAPITA: US$470 ('90)
MAIN EXPORT EARNERS: tea, rubber, tourism

SRI LANKA entered its tenth year of civil war without any resolution of the military situation. The Jaffna peninsula remained under the control of the Liberation Tigers of Tamil Eelam (LTTE). There were several successful attacks on military personnel, including leading officers, and massacres of civilians, mainly of east coast Muslims, continued. The international situation was complicated when official charges were laid by the Indian government against the LTTE leader, Vellipullai Prabhakaran, in connection with the assassination of Rajiv Gandhi (see AR 1991, pp. 310, 321). Mr Prabhakaran continued to operate openly in Jaffna peninsula beyond the grasp of the Sri Lanka government. The United National Party (UNP) government remained in office despite the creation of a new Democratic United National Front under the leadership of a former UNP minister, Lalith Athulathmudali. The opposition remained relatively ineffective, partly because of struggles within the Sri Lanka Freedom Party (SLFP) between Sirimavo Bandaranaike's son, Anura Bandaranaike, and her daughter, Chandrika Kumaranatunga.

The year began with the abandonment of an attempt to negotiate with the LTTE by the Minister for Tourism and Rural Industries Development, Sauvmiamoorthy Thondaman, who was also leader of the Ceylon Workers' Congress. Organized Buddhist and Sinhalese nationalist objections to Mr Thondaman's proposed visit to Jaffna forced him to cancel the plan on 31 January, though it was not clear that his proposal for maximum autonomy for the north and east would have been acceptable to the LTTE leaders (who favoured complete independence). For most of the rest of the year the emphasis was on military operations, though these had little success in changing the battle lines of the past few years.

Indian concern over the influence of Tigers in Tamil Nadu, and their alleged involvement in Mr Gandhi's assassination, led to the outlawing of the LTTE in India on 13 May. On 31 January a Madras court ordered Mr Prabhakaran to appear before it by the end of February. On his failure to do so he and 40 other named LTTE members were formally charged with the assassination on 13 May and India requested his extradition from Sri Lanka to face the charges. A second Indian response was to expedite the repatriation of Tamil refugees, a process which began with a shipload of 614 to Trincomalee on 22 January, followed by a further 659 on 29 January. By the end of August it was officially announced that 30,000 had been repatriated. This process, administered under the supervision of the United Nations High Commissioner for Refugees (UNHCR), was severely criticized as putting the returnees in danger, and the programme was suspended between May and August. There were already 30,000 refugees living in camps in Trincomalee. Repatriation was assisted by a grant to UNHCR of $1.6 million from Australia, Canada, the United States, France and Britain. European states began to tighten restrictions on Tamil asylum seekers, a voluntary return programme being launched by Switzerland on 22 June.

Several military offensives were organized during the year. On 16 March the Mullaitivu area was targeted and on 28 May government forces captured the Tiger stronghold of Tellippalai. In June a massive operation began against the Jaffna peninsula which lasted into July without regaining the city or its surroundings. The city was sealed off, but the army announced that in the first half of the year it had lost 507 soldiers, as against 350 civilians killed and 1,153 identified Tigers killed. Although a further campaign to retake Jaffna was launched on 18 September, the situation at the end of the year was still not resolved in the army's favour. Meanwhile, the forces had lost some of their leading members. On 8 August the northern army commander and nine other senior officers were killed by a landmine on Kayts island near Jaffna. On 16 October a suicide bomber killed the commander of the navy, Vice-Admiral Clancy Fernando, close to navy headquarters in the middle of Colombo.

Massacres of civilians continued. In January the presidential commission of inquiry found that soldiers had killed 67 civilians at Kokkaddicholai in the previous year (see AR 1991, p. 321). In late April 57 Muslims and 53 Tamils were killed in inter-communal clashes near Batticaloa. The largest massacre took place in Medirigiriya, where 190 Muslims were killed. Although the Tigers denied involvement in these attacks on Muslims, they were generally condemned for this local variant of 'ethnic cleansing' which was becoming increasingly common in areas where Muslims and Tamils lived in close proximity.

While the situation in the Sinhalese south was now more peaceful, previous mass murders were referred to by a former deputy inspector-general of police, Premadasa Udugampola, who in April detailed the organization of death squads against suspected supporters of the militant Janatha Vimukthi Peramuna (JVP). These revelations led the opposition parties to call for the resignation of President Premadasa. On 21 May the SLFP boycotted the parliamentary select committee on ethnic issues in protest against the revelations, as did other opposition parties.

The validity of President Premadasa's election in December 1988 was upheld by the Supreme Court in September against a petition by his defeated opponent, Sirimavo Bandaranaike. The ruling closed what had proved to be the longest court case in Sri Lankan history. On 23 September the President began a tour of the capitals of the South Asian Association for Regional Cooperation (SAARC) nations, including a three-day visit to India, in his first trip overseas since 1989. Prime Minister Dingiri Banda Wijetunge presented his 1993 budget on 6 November, envisaging a deficit of Rs 91,000 million but also forecasting an economic growth rate of 5.3 per cent and an inflation level of 12 per cent. On 13 October the International Monetary Fund had approved the SDR 112 million second tranche of a three-year structural adjustment loan granted in September 1991 in support of Sri Lanka's economic reform programme.

Sri Lanka was badly affected by drought in March and April, by severe rain in Colombo on 5 June, which killed 14 people, and by a cyclone on the east coast in November, which destroyed over 10,000 houses. These natural disasters, combined with the civil war, left most of the major rice growing area out of cultivation.

3. INDIAN OCEAN STATES

i. MAURITIUS

CAPITAL: Port Louis   AREA: 2,040 sq km   POPULATION: 1,100,000 ('90)
OFFICIAL LANGUAGE: English   POLITICAL SYSTEM: parliamentary democracy
HEAD OF STATE: President Cassam Uteem (since June '92)
RULING PARTIES: coalition of Mauritian Socialist Movement (MSM), Mauritian Militant
   Movement (MMM) and Organization of the Rodrigues People (OPR)
HEAD OF GOVERNMENT: Sir Anerood Jugnauth (MSM), Prime Minister (since '82)
PRINCIPAL MINISTERS: Prem Nababsing (MMM/deputy premier, health), Paul Bérenger
   (MMM/foreign affairs), Jean-Claude de l'Estrac (MMM/planning & development)
INTERNATIONAL ALIGNMENT: NAM, OAU, ACP, Cwth., Francophonie
CURRENCY: rupee (end-'92 £1=MRs25.83, US$1=MRs17.06)
GNP PER CAPITA: US$2,250 ('90)
MAIN EXPORT EARNERS: sugar, textiles, manufactured goods, tourism

FOLLOWING two previous attempts, Mauritius at last became a republic on 12 March, the 24th anniversary of independence. The government of Sir Anerood Jugnauth, commanding a substantial parliamentary majority, had no difficulty this time in legislating for the necessary changes which gave Mauritius a constitution broadly akin to the Indian model. Governor-General Sir Veerasamy Ringadoo, a veteran former politician, became the first President of Mauritius; Cassam Uteem, a Muslim and a member of one of the governing coalition parties, the Mauritian Militant Movement (MMM), replaced him in July.

During the Mauritius republic debate in the British House of Commons, Tam Dalyell (Labour) raised the question of the Ilois, the displaced population of Diego Garcia. The Diego Garcians were removed by the British government as part of a pre-independence deal. Part of the Diego Garcia atoll became an American military base, under a British-US defence agreement due to expire in 2016, with an option to renew for a further 20 years. The Mauritian Foreign Minister, Paul Bérenger, also raised the question of Diego Garcia at the United Nations but there seemed no likelihood that the archipelago would be returned to Mauritian sovereignty in the foreseeable future.

Prime Minister Jugnauth warned in March that the country faced an economic recession following the boom years of 1984–90. In the event, there were only limited signs of a downturn during 1992. Trade with the United Kingdom and France increased, while Mauritius kept its enviable record in prompt debt repayments, as its external borrowing grew but represented an increasingly smaller share of export revenues.

Some textile factories and hotels closed and there was concern that the planned change from a largely unskilled workforce, employed in the textile factories, to skilled workers trained in more sophisticated industries might mean the end of full employment. But the Mauritian Central Statistical Office reported that the real income of the average household had risen by 25 per cent since 1987, explained by the larger number of incomes per household as a result of full employment and more opportunities for women to take paid work.

Mauritius retained the right of appeal to the Privy Council in London under the new constitution and in July five English law lords sat in judgment on a case brought by two Muslims against the government of Mauritius. They claimed that they were being deprived of their rights to the practice of Islam unhindered. Before the judicial committee of the Privy Council heard the case the Mauritian government brought in new legislation enabling Muslims to marry according to their religion, while a Muslim Family Council was established to make rules about marriages, divorce and inheritance. The law lords found for the government but did not award costs against the two appellants. The case reflected the underlying religious tensions in a country with a 60 per cent Hindu population.

In October the opposition leader, Dr Navin Ramgoolam, left Mauritius and returned to London to complete his bar exams. He left no designated member of parliament to take his place but said that the opposition would be 'collective'. As his Labour Party/Mauritian Social Democratic Party opposition group held only seven seats against the governing coalition's 59 seats, the dominance of the Jugnauth government became even more apparent.

ii.   SEYCHELLES, COMOROS AND MALDIVES

Seychelles
CAPITAL: Victoria   AREA: 454 sq km   POPULATION: 68,000 ('90)
OFFICIAL LANGUAGE: Creole   POLITICAL SYSTEM: presidential
HEAD OF STATE AND GOVERNMENT: President France-Albert René (since '77)
RULING PARTY: Seychelles People's Progressive Front (SPPF)
CURRENCY: rupee (end-'92 £1=SR7.86, US$1=SR5.19)
GNP PER CAPITA: US$4,670 ('90)
MAIN EXPORT EARNERS: tourism, copra, fish

Comoros
CAPITAL: Moroni   AREA: 1,860 sq km   POPULATION: 475,000 ('90)
OFFICIAL LANGUAGES: Arabic & French   POLITICAL SYSTEM: presidential
HEAD OF STATE AND GOVERNMENT: President Said Mohammed Djohar (since '89)
CURRENCY: CFA franc (end-'92 £1=CFAF418.25, US$=CFAF276.26)
GNP PER CAPITA: US$480 ('90)
MAIN EXPORT EARNERS: vanilla, agricultural products, tourism

Maldives
CAPITAL: Malé AREA: 300 sq km POPULATION: 214,000 ('90)
OFFICIAL LANGUAGE: Divehi POLITICAL SYSTEM: presidential
HEAD OF STATE AND GOVERNMENT: President Maumoun Abdul Gayoom (since '78)
CURRENCY: ruffiya (end-'92 £1=R18.16, US$1=R11.99)
GNP PER CAPITA: US$450 ('90)
MAIN EXPORT EARNERS: tourism, fish, coconuts

THE people of SEYCHELLES responded quickly to President René's December 1991 announcement of a return to a pluralist political system after 15 years of one-party rule (see AR 1991, p. 325). Eight parties registered for the elections and a year of intense political activity began. The elections were to be held in three stages: first, the election of the members of a constitutional commission, second a referendum on the constitution they would prepare and finally elections at the end of the year for a new parliament and President under the new constitution.

James Mancham, who had been ousted from the presidency in 1977 by the coup which had brought France-Albert René to power, returned to lead his revived Seychelles Democratic Party (SDP). Rev Wavel Ramkalawan, an Anglican priest who had been an outspoken critic of the ruling Seychelles People's Progressive Front (SPPF), formed the Parti Seselwa (Seychellois Party). Former ministers led some of the other parties. Press restrictions were relaxed and a number of new papers and broadsheets were launched. The government established a new independent Seychelles Broadcasting Corporation.

Traditional open-air rallies were held by all the parties, the SPPF attracting the biggest attendance. There were a few incidents of violence at some meetings but the crowds were for the most part well-behaved and good-humoured. On the last weekend in July, the SPPF won 58.4 per cent of the votes for membership of the constitutional commission and the SDP 33.7 per cent; the Parti Seselwa came third. It was clear that the SPPF's extensive organization, built up over many years, had been decisive, despite the renewed attraction of Mr Mancham and his SDP.

The SPPF and the SDP were the only parties represented on the constitutional commission, although members of other parties were invited to join the delegations as observers from time to time. The SDP objected to the speed with which the SPPF members of the commission were pushing through the discussions. It also objected to the sessions being held in secret. In September the SDP pulled out of the meetings altogether, leaving the SPPF, with more than the 12-member quorum required, to continue on its own. Meanwhile, André Sauzier, the Mauritian-born director of the electoral committee, called for changes to be introduced without waiting for the new constitution to come into force. However, in the November referendum the new constitution failed to get the 60 per cent approval needed; in an 81.9 per cent turnout, only 53.7 per cent voted in favour. There was no statutory provision for the time-limit needed to prepare a revised constitution, but the commission was expected to finish its work in March 1993.

Some businessmen privately expressed approval that the René government was to continue, as this would give the country some stability in a time of change and uncertainty, when the economy, dependent almost entirely on tourism for its foreign exchange earnings, was under pressure following the recession in the West. But the leaders of the opposition parties believed that the delay in the electoral process gave them a chance to build up their followings, in a political atmosphere where personalities counted for more than ideologies.

THE difficulties of organizing a multi-party democracy in the COMOROS were more than apparent during a troubled and unstable year, which had begun optimistically enough with the installation of a transitional government including the main political groupings. The 'Coordinator' (Prime Minister) was Mohammed Taki, who had been beaten by President Said Mohammed Djohar in the 1990 presidential elections. A national conference held in February approved a new constitution and a transition programme, but in a surprise reshuffle in May Presiden Djohar marginalized Mr Taki by eliminating many of his supporters from the government and consolidating the power of the Magwazu Party of Finance Minister Mohammed Mchangama. The Udzima, which had been the ruling party in the days of the one-party state, was also excluded from the government. It recommended a 'no' vote in the constitutional referendum in June, but received only 23.7 per cent of the vote, which was massively in favour of the new multi-party constitution.

Mr Mchangama, now perceived as the country's 'strong man', encouraged President Djohar to restructure the government again and to dismiss Mr Taki as Coordinator. It was alleged that Mr Mchangama had recruited Patrick Klein, a mercenary known as 'Mytho', as a special adviser. This heralded a new wave of mercenary neurosis, recalling the fact that mercenaries, led by the notorious Bob Denard, had dominated the political life of the islands in 1977–89. Documents were circulated claiming that President Djohar had been negotiating a return of Mr Denard. Although strongly denied by the President, the tension generated formed the background to a coup attempt by junior officers on 16 September. This was followed by the arrest of many leaders of Udzima, who were said to have been involved. An unsuccessful attempt in mid-October to free these prisoners—who included two sons of former President Ahmed Abdallah, assassinated by mercenaries in 1989—led to a genuine rebellion of rank-and-file troops, which was suppressed with heavy loss of life.

All this took place during the campaign for multi-party general elections in November. Not surprisingly these were held amid a great deal of confusion. They were boycotted by some opposition parties, including Udzima, and voting had to be postponed until mid-December in the capital, Moroni. At the end of the year the victors were still uncertain, as not all results had been announced.

IN November the 200,000th tourist to visit the MALDIVES in 1992—an Italian on his honeymoon—was greeted with a special welcome at the airport. Although tourist numbers had been steadily increasing, their presence put pressure on the environment. Sewage dumped at sea competed for oxygen with the coralline rocks surrounding the country's many islands, and reefs were plundered for material to build hotels and better housing for the Maldivians. Without the reefs the islands could not survive, especially in view of rising sea levels. This threat was emphasized by President Maumoun Abdul Gayoom at the Earth Summit in Rio de Janeiro in June (see also XIV.3) and also in his discussions with US Secretary of State James Baker, who visited the Maldives on 24 July. Mr Baker noted that the Maldives had supported UN resolutions during the 1990–91 Gulf crisis.

The government declared 1992 the Year of the Maldivian Youth, and a public holiday on 1 March celebrated the commencement of a number of special events for young people. The government announced that the national literacy rate had risen to 98 per cent and that 11 islands had eliminated illiteracy.

Although inflation rose during the year, the costs of basic foodstuffs remained low compared with the figures for 1989. Tourism remained the main foreign exchange earner but the President, in his budget presentation as Minister of Finance, said that earnings from fish exports had doubled over the previous five years. Government expenditure was greatest on education (18 per cent), followed by health (9 per cent), while ten major development projects were continued with the help of external grants and loans.

On 11 November President Gayoom celebrated 14 years in office and expressed his willingness to continue after his current term expired in 1993. There were indications, during the year, that the government's conservative and authoritarian policies were holding firm.

iii. MADAGASCAR

CAPITAL: Antananarivo   AREA: 587,000 sq km   POPULATION: 11,700,000 ('90)
OFFICIAL LANGUAGES: Malagasy & French   POLITICAL SYSTEM: presidential
HEAD OF STATE AND GOVERNMENT: President (Adml.) Didier Ratsiraka (since '75)
PRINCIPAL MINISTERS: Guy Razanamasy (prime minister), Ceasire Rabenoro (foreign affairs), Armand Rajaonarivelo (justice), Col. Sylvain Rakotoarison (interior), Evariste Marson (finance), Gen. Philippe Ramakavelo (armed forces)
INTERNATIONAL ALIGNMENT: NAM, OAU, ACP, Francophonie
CURRENCY: Malagasy franc (end-'92 £1=FMG2,751.85, US$1=FMG1,817.60)
GNP PER CAPITA: US$230 ('90)
MAIN EXPORT EARNERS: coffee, vanilla, cloves

ALTHOUGH a major movement for democracy had been operating in Madagascar since 1989, the process was not an easy one. President Didier Ratsiraka proved to be particularly adept at clinging to power, in spite of the strength and persistence of the movement against him. The year began with hopes that an orderly transition might yet take place, and by December major advances had been made. After the first round of presidential elections, Admiral Ratsiraka seemed on the brink of leaving office.

In January a power-sharing arrangement had been introduced, with four main institutions: the presidency, the High Authority of State (with opposition leader Professor Albert Zafy as its president), the Committee for Economic and Social Revival and the government of Premier Guy Razamanasy. This was followed in February-March by a national forum to draft the new constitution, involving the two major political groupings, the 'Living Forces' of Professor Zafy and the Militant Movement for Socialism in Madagascar (MMSM) of the former presidential majority. The forum approved a unitary constitution, although it ended amid a certain amount of violence from 'federalists' who enjoyed the support of the MMSM.

Nonetheless, the country proceeded with the transition. After some delays and an abortive coup attempt, a referendum to approve the new constitution was held in August. The proposed text was supported by just over 70 per cent of the 60 per cent of the electorate who cast valid votes. The coup plotters had succeeded only in taking over the radio station for three hours, in the name of a mysterious Pastor Fety (said to be an extremist supporter of the Living Forces). Their failure was followed by a wave of occupation of towns by federalists, which were mostly suppressed by supporters of Living Forces. However, violence connected to federalist activity continued to mark the run-up to the crucial first round of the presidential elections in November. At the same time four regions—Antsiranana in the north and Toamasina, Toliagnaro and Fianarantsoa in the south—unilaterally declared themselves federal states. However, after the government had pronounced them illegal, the movement petered out.

In the presidential elections eight candidates stood, but as expected only Professor Zafy and Admiral Ratsiraka went through to the second round to be held in February 1993. Professor Zafy received 45.2 per cent and President Ratsiraka 29.2 per cent: the other candidates came a long way behind.

IX SOUTH-EAST AND EAST ASIA

1. MYANMAR (BURMA)—THAILAND—MALAYSIA—BRUNEI— SINGAPORE—INDONESIA—PHILIPPINES—VIETNAM— CAMBODIA—LAOS

i. MYANMAR (BURMA)

CAPITAL: Yangon (Rangoon)   AREA: 676,500 sq km   POPULATION: 41,600,000 ('90)
OFFICIAL LANGUAGE: Burmese   POLITICAL SYSTEM: military regime
HEAD OF STATE AND GOVERNMENT: Gen. Than Shwe, Chairman of State Law and
    Order Restoration Council and Prime Minister (since April '92)
PRINCIPAL MINISTERS: U Ohn Gyaw (foreign affairs), Maj.-Gen. Phone Myint (home
    affairs), Brig.-Gen. David Ábel (trade, planning & finance)
CURRENCY: kyat (end-'92 £1=K9.85, US$1=K6.50)
GNP PER CAPITA: US$200 ('86)
MAIN EXPORT EARNERS: teak, rice, minerals

THE political stalemate between the military State Law and Order Restoration Council (SLORC) and the country's pro-democracy political parties continued in 1992. In April, following the departure of SLORC Chairman Saw Maung, the government made several concessions to its opponents in the lead-up to constitutional meetings. Political prisoners (including former premier U Nu) were released, and 1991 Nobel Peace Prize winner Daw Aung San Suu Kyi was again permitted to see her family.

In June meetings were held between the SLORC and seven political parties, including the majority National League for Democracy (NLD), in order to prepare a draft constitution. Critics, however, dismissed these televised meetings as a charade. The new NLD leaders, under former army brigadier Aung Shwe, lacked the credibility of the imprisoned leadership—Tin U, Kyi Maung and Suu Kyi. Nevertheless, amid national and international protest, the government pressed on with its constitutional reform, and set 9 January 1993 as the date for the opening of a national convention to establish the basic principles of the new constitution. At the close of the year, however, this forthcoming event was overshadowed by Suu Kyi's decision not to accept outside support, which was taken to mean that she was starting a hunger strike.

International opposition to the regime continued, Myanmar's neighbours being particularly uneasy over the apparent intransigence of the military. The crisis with Bangladesh over Arakanese refugees (see AR 1991, p. 330) prompted growing international criticism as well as a visit in April from the UN under-secretary-general for humanitarian affairs, Jan Eliasson. Myanmar's subsequent decision to receive Arakanese refugees seemed unlikely to resolve this intractable conflict or to placate the distrust of the region's Muslim countries.

Meanwhile, relations with Thailand suffered a setback during the year. The military's incursions into disputed territory claimed by Thailand in pursuit of Karen insurgents worried and angered Thai politicians and military spokesmen. The occupation of a disputed hill (Hill 491) in Chumphon province by a battalion of Burmese troops was the occasion of an unprecedented intervention by Thailand's King Bhumibol Adulyadej in early December, designed to diffuse the growing confrontation (see also IX.1.ii). Subsequently, the visit of a Thai military delegation to Yangon led to an agreement to use a boundary commission to settle the issue. In contrast, close relations with China persisted in 1992 (see AR 1991, p. 330) as trade, and Chinese supplies to the military, grew.

The year was also marked by changes in government leadership. In a widely-predicted move, the ailing and increasingly erratic Senior General Saw Maung was replaced as SLORC Chairman in April by General Than Shwe, who had assumed the defence portfolio in March. If the 81-year-old Ne Win was believed to continue to exert an influence over events, the SLORC appeared to be concerned over who would ultimately take Ne Win's place after his death. As a result of various government and military changes, the chief of military intelligence, Brigadier-General Khin Nyunt, appeared to consolidate his position.

The war against the various insurgents continued in 1992. Myanmar's increasingly well-equipped 250,000-man army stepped up its campaign against the Karen National Union (KNU), and in February the Karen base of Ye Gyaw was captured after an attack from the Thai side of the border. However, by April, with the approach of the rainy season, the military offensive against the KNU was halted as insurgent resistance stiffened. A resolution to the ongoing civil war appeared as far away as ever at year's end.

Government plans to develop a viable petroleum industry received a setback during the year as two foreign firms abandoned oil and gas exploration work in the country. By December other firms appeared set to follow suit, though a French firm took up contracts for off-shore exploration. Generally, the economy continued to suffer from the effects of the country's international ostracism and political troubles.

ii. THAILAND

CAPITAL: Bangkok   AREA: 513,000 sq km   POPULATION: 55,800,000 ('90)
OFFICIAL LANGUAGE: Thai   POLITICAL SYSTEM: constitutional monarchy
HEAD OF STATE: King Bhumibol Adulyadej (Rama IX) (since June '46)
RULING PARTIES: Democrat Party heads coalition
HEAD OF GOVERNMENT: Chuan Leekpai, Prime Minister (since Sept '92)
PRINCIPAL MINISTERS: Banyat Banthatthan, Amnuai Wirawan, Bunchu Rotchanasathian,
   Suphachai Panitchaphak (deputy premiers), Gen. Wichit Sukmak (defence),
   Tharin Nimmanhemin (finance), Squadron Ldr. Prasong Sonsiri (foreign affairs),
   Gen. Chaovalit Yongchaiyut (interior), Suwit Khunkitti (justice)
INTERNATIONAL ALIGNMENT: ASEAN
CURRENCY: baht (end-'92 £1=B38.60, US$1=B25.49)
GNP PER CAPITA: US$1,420 ('90)
MAIN EXPORT EARNERS: textiles, rice, tapioca, rubber, tourism

THAILAND experienced its most tumultuous year since 1973. During 1992 there were four governments, two general elections, widely-reported demonstrations and associated killings in May and the almost unprecedented intervention of King Bhumibol Adulyadej in the political process.

The first general election on 22 March was contested by 15 parties vying for seats in the 360-member House of Representatives. On the same day the ruling military junta appointed a 270-member Senate dominated by serving or retired military men and police officers. The military-backed Samakkhi Tham Party won the largest number of seats (79) in the House and formed a coalition with three other pro-military parties—Chart Thai (74), the Social Action Party (31) and Prachakorn Thai (7)—giving a majority of 11 seats. On 25 March Rassadorn (4 seats) also joined the coalition.

Narong Wongwan, the leader of Samakkhi Tham, was proposed as Prime Minister, but his nomination was withdrawn after it became clear that the US State Department had denied him a visa on suspicion of involvement in drug-trafficking. Under pressure from leaders of the coalition, General Suchinda Kraprayoon, effective head of the military junta which had taken power in February 1991 (see AR 1991, p. 331), accepted the premiership and was appointed on 7 April. His appointment contrasted starkly with his November 1991 vow never to accept the post.

Some 50,000 demonstrators congregated in Bangkok on 20 April calling for General Suchinda, as a non-elected Prime Minister, to resign. On 4 May Major-General Chamlong Srimuang, leader of the opposition Palang Dharma Party (41 seats), announced that he was beginning a fast to the death unless General Suchinda resigned. Despite attempts by the military to defuse the situation, 70,000 joined a rally on 7 May in the heart of Bangkok, in support of Major-General Chamlong. On 9 May House Speaker Arthit Urairat announced that the government and opposition parties had agreed on a number of constitutional revisions and Major-General Chamlong called off his fast. But later the government appeared to go back on its promises, and Major-General Chamlong denounced General Suchinda at a rally on 17 May attended by an estimated 150,000. Clashes between demonstrators and army paratroopers on the night and early morning of 17/18 May resulted in some deaths as soldiers fired into the crowd. Major-General Chamlong appealed for calm, but his arrest—along with other 'agitators'—inflamed the situation still further. The government announced a state of emergency in Bangkok and four surrounding provinces and imposed a media blackout. Troops fired on demonstrators in the early morning of the 19 May while trying to seal off the city centre, also arresting large numbers of protesters. Estimates of the death toll ranged from 50 to several hundred. By the end of the year it was still unclear how many had died. The Interior Ministry listed 117 people as 'missing' (and expected this to fall to 40–60) in addition to the 52 confirmed casualties; the Mahidol University 'hotline' centre put the former figure at 192.

On 20 May King Bhumibol summoned Major-General Chamlong and the Prime Minister to an audience in his palace. The televised encounter was widely interpreted as a rebuke for General Suchinda. The next day the Prime Minister announced that those arrested would be released and on 24 May he resigned, later leaving the country—but not before ensuring that the King declared an amnesty for those military personnel involved. In October the newly-elected House of Representatives voted unanimously to revoke the amnesty, although this action was later ruled illegal by the Constitutional Tribunal.

After a period during which Thailand was effectively leaderless, on 10 June Anand Panyarachun was appointed again as interim Prime Minister. Fresh elections were set for 13 September. Mr Anand's cabinet contained many figures who served in the highly-regarded so-called Anand I government of March 1991 to April 1992. Significantly, the Ministry of the Interior was given to respected police general Pow Sarasin while the defence portfolio was awarded to the uncontroversial retired General Banchop Bunnak. General Vimol Wongwanich was appointed as the new army commander. The Anand II government took quick action to curtail the power of the military by dissolving the Capital Security Command and the Internal Peace-Keeping Force, moving those held responsible for the recent killings to inactive posts, and removing military men from the boards of state-run enterprises. On 12 July former Prime Minister Chatichai Choonhaven became leader of the new Chart Pattana (National Development) Party.

The year's second general election on 13 September was widely touted as a contest between 'angel' (pro-democracy) and 'devil' (pro-military) parties. The 'angel' parties secured only a bare majority. The Democrat Party, with 79 seats, formed a coalition with three other 'angel' parties—the New Aspirations Party (51), Palang Dharma (47) and

Ekkaparb (8)—but was forced to include the Social Action Party (22) to secure a working majority. 'Clean' Democrat leader Chuan Leekpai was appointed the year's fourth Prime Minister on 23 September, his cabinet including a number of non-elected technocrats. General Wichit Sukmak, a respected soldier, was appointed Defence Minister. The leader of the Palang Dharma Party, Major-General Chamlong, refused a cabinet post despite having played a leading role in the May demonstrations. Prime Minister Chuan announced that his government would concentrate on promoting rural development. In December the government passed a bill abolishing the Internal Peace-Keeping Directorate Act, thereby reducing the ability of the military to mount another operation similar to the May crack-down.

On 4 December, King Bhumibol intervened for a second time, when he called for a peaceful settlement to a conflict with Myanmar (Burma) over a hill on the Thai-Myanmar border (see also IX.1.i). After Myanmar troops had occupied the hill in April, the King called for the area to be declared a neutral zone and a joint survey to be conducted. Forces withdrew and a meeting between the parties was held in Yangon on 8 December.

Despite the year's tumultous political scene, and widely-expressed fears that the violent scenes of May might curtail foreign investment and confidence, the economy continued to perform well. Economic growth for the year was 7.5 per cent. AIDS continued to be a topic in the news, official figures recording that as many as 400,000 Thais might be HIV-positive.

iii.   MALAYSIA

CAPITAL: Kuala Lumpur   AREA: 132,000 sq km   POPULATION: 17,900,000 ('90)
OFFICIAL LANGUAGE: Bahasa Malaysia   POLITICAL SYSTEM: federal democracy
SUPREME HEAD OF STATE: Sultan Azlan Muhibuddin Shah of Perak (since '89)
RULING PARTY: National Front coalition
HEAD OF GOVERNMENT: Dr Mahathir Mohamad, Prime Minister (since '81)
PRINCIPAL MINISTERS: Abdul Ghafar Baba (deputy premier, development),
    Abdullah Ahmad Badawi (foreign affairs), Najib Tun Razak (defence),
    Anwar Ibrahim (finance), Hamid Albar (justice)
INTERNATIONAL ALIGNMENT: NAM, ASEAN, ICO, Cwth.
CURRENCY: ringitt (end-'92 £1=M$3.96, US$1=M$2.62)
GNP PER CAPITA: US$2,320 ('90)
MAIN EXPORT EARNERS: oil, palm oil, timber, rubber, tin

IN a constitutionally-unprecedented measure on 10 December Malaysia's parliament unanimously approved a motion censuring the Sultan of Johor, Mahmood Iskandar ibni Al-Marhum Sultan Ismail, for having allegedly assaulted Douglas Gomez, a college field-hockey coach. Sultan Mahmood had served as King of Malaysia between 1984 and 1989. Mr Gomez had been critical of a decision by the Johor education department in November to withdraw the team which he coached from a national schools competition only hours before it was due to play a semi-final match. The decision was linked in the press to the prior suspension for five years by the Malaysian Hockey Association of one of the Sultan's sons, Tunku Abdul Majid Idris, who in July had assaulted the opposing goalkeeper after a national final in which Johor had lost to Perak. After his criticism to state athletic officials became known, Mr Gomez was summoned on 30 November to the Sultan's palace, where he was allegedly beaten up.

On 12 December the government announced that it would convene special sittings of both houses of parliament in January 1993 to remove from the federal constitution the immunity from prosecution enjoyed by the hereditary rulers reigning in nine of Malaysia's 13 states. The Deputy Prime Minister, Abdul Ghafar Baba, explained that the aim of a proposed amendment to article 181(2) of the constitution was not to turn the country into a republic. Such amendment would require the consent of the Conference of Rulers, whose objections to the proposed removal of the King's prerogative to assent to bills approved by parliament had caused a constitutional crisis in 1983 (see AR 1983, p. 279). At the end of the month Prime Minister Mahathir Mohamad informed members of the ruling United Malays National Organization (UMNO) that additional amendments would be introduced removing the right of the rulers to reject legislation affecting their interests, as well as curbing their powers to pardon themselves or members of royal families.

The episode involving Sultan Mahmood brought to a head the issue of abuse of power and privilege, especially in business matters, by members of Malaysia's royal families. Earlier in the year the government had sought to curb such abuses by introducing a voluntary code of conduct. In July, however, the Sultans of Johor and Kelantan had been two of three rulers who had refused to sign the code when it came before the Conference of Rulers. Sultan Ismail Petra of Kelantan had also aroused controversy by refusing to pay duty on a Lamborghini sports car which he had imported.

In May the USS *Tuscaloosa* became the first American warship to undergo repairs at the Lumut naval dockyard under an agreement designed to provide alternative facilities following the US withdrawal from military bases in the Philippines (see IX.1.vii). A series of collisions from June between vessels in the Strait of Malacca, with loss of life and spillage of oil, prompted Dr Mahathir to call in September for users of the strait to pay a toll to finance measures to ensure safety of navigation. The Defence Minister, Datuk Seri Najib Tun Razak, announced at the end of November that Malaysia would give up using the Woodlands naval base in Singapore in 1997 because of proposed new rental charges.

In mid-August Malaysia broke off diplomatic relations with the federal Yugoslav government in protest at Serbian attacks on Bosnian Muslims (see III.1.vi). Its government sought also, without success, to deny Yugoslavia representation at the meeting of heads of governments of Non-Aligned states which convened in Indonesia in September (see XI.4.ii). In March strong protests had been made to Myanmar over the flight to Bangladesh of tens of thousands of Rohingya Muslims (see VIII.2.iii).

In December Lorrain Osman, the former non-executive chairman of Bumiputera Malaysia Finance, was extradited from Britain to Hong Kong after a record seven-year legal battle. He faced 41 criminal charges relating to the collapse in 1983 of the property group Carrian Investments, of which Bumiputera Malaysia Finance was the biggest creditor.

iv.   BRUNEI

CAPITAL: Bandar Seri Bagawan   AREA: 5,765 sq km   POPULATION: 256,000 ('90)
OFFICIAL LANGUAGES: Malay & English   POLITICAL SYSTEM: monarchy
HEAD OF STATE AND GOVERNMENT: Sultan Sir Hassanal Bolkiah (since '67)
PRINCIPAL MINISTERS: Prince Mohammed Bolkiah (foreign affairs), Prince Jefri
   Bolkiah (finance), Pehin Dato Haji Isa (internal affairs), Pengiran Bahrin (law)
INTERNATIONAL ALIGNMENT: NAM, ICO, ASEAN, Cwth.
CURRENCY: Brunei dollar (end-'92 £1=B$2.48, US$1=B$1.64)
GNP PER CAPITA: US$15,390 ('87)
MAIN EXPORT EARNERS: oil and gas

SULTAN Hassanal Bolkiah celebrated the 25th anniversary of his accession to the throne on 5 October in lavish regal splendour. At a ceremony attended by royalty and heads of government from Asia, the Middle East and Europe, the Sultan extolled the virtues of Brunei's national ideology, namely 'Malay Islamic monarchy'. He also announced a personal donation of US$1 million to the 'betrayed and oppressed' Muslims in Bosnia-Hercegovina. In Jakarta in September the Non-Aligned Movement admitted Brunei to full membership (see XI.4.ii).

v. SINGAPORE

CAPITAL: Singapore   AREA: 620 sq km   POPULATION: 3,000,000 ('90)
OFFICIAL LANGUAGES: Malay, Chinese, Tamil, English
POLITICAL SYSTEM: parliamentary
HEAD OF STATE: President Wee Kim Wee (since '85)
RULING PARTY: People's Action Party (PAP)
HEAD OF GOVERNMENT: Goh Chok Tong, Prime Minister (since Nov '90)
PRINCIPAL MINISTERS: Lee Kuan Yew (senior minister), Ong Teng Cheong (deputy
    premier), Lee Hsien Loong (deputy premier), Wong Kan Seng (foreign affairs),
    Richard Hu Tsu Tau (finance), Shanmugam Jayakumar (home affairs, law),
    Yeo Ning Hong (defence)
INTERNATIONAL ALIGNMENT: NAM, ASEAN, Cwth.
CURRENCY: Singapore dollar (end-'92 £1=S$2.48, US$1=S$1.64)
GNP PER CAPITA: US$11,160 ('90)
MAIN EXPORT EARNERS: machinery & equipment, petroleum products, financial
    services, tourism

COMMONLY-held assumptions about political succession were thrown into disarray on 16 November when it was announced that both Deputy Prime Ministers, Lee Hsien Loong and Ong Teng Cheong, had been diagnosed as suffering from cancer. Lee Hsien Loong, the elder son of former prime minister Lee Kuan Yew, had been regarded as the most likely successor to Prime Minister Goh Chok Tong. He gave up his trade and industry portfolio while undergoing treatment, his office being filled temporarily by Suppiah Dhanabalan (who had relinquished responsibility for national development three months earlier to return to the private sector).

On 19 December a by-election was held in the four-member Marine Parade constituency which had returned Goh Chok Tong to parliament in 1991. In calling the by-election, the Prime Minister was fulfilling a campaign pledge made the year before and was also seeking to test voter confidence in his leadership at a time of national anxiety. He took the opportunity to strengthen his team through the nomination of the Singapore navy commander, Commodore Teo Chee Hean. The convincing majority for the ruling People's Action Party (PAP) candidates, of 72.9 per cent in a constituency of some 75,000 voters, was less than the 77.2 per cent recorded in the general elections in 1991. Prior to the by-election, Lee Kuan Yew had stepped down as secretary-general of the PAP in favour of Goh Chok Tong (although he remained Senior Minister in the government).

In August members of the Internal Security Department searched the offices of the newspaper *Business Times* to investigate possible violations of the Official Secrets Act. The search was prompted by the newspaper's publication on 29 June of estimates of economic growth for the second quarter of 1992 which were allegedly obtained from a government source. In a public comment on the episode, Lee Kuan Yew expressed doubt as to whether the *Business Times* would have used illegally-obtained or leaked official figures had he still been head of the government. After the investigation had been extended to the offices of Merrill Lynch, in December, charges were brought under the Official Secrets Act against the editor of *Business Times*, a government monetary official and two private-sector economists.

Employing powers from legislation enacted in 1990, a parliamentary committee in September appointed six non-elected independent members with full voting rights on all matters except amendments to the constitution, confidence motions and supply bills. One of these members, Walter Woon, a lecturer in law at the National University of Singapore, provoked a stormy public debate with a newspaper article in which he challenged the conventional wisdom of government by arguing that core Asian values could be passed on perfectly adequately through the English language.

President George Bush visited Singapore in early January. An agreement was concluded to move a US logistics facility to the island-state from the Philippines under a memorandum of understanding of November 1990. At the end of January the fourth summit of the Association of South-East Asian Nations (ASEAN) convened in Singapore, where an agreement was reached to establish an ASEAN free trade area within 15 years (see XI.6.iii). In September the fourth Asia-Pacific Economic Cooperation (APEC) conference, meeting in Bangkok, approved the establishment of a permanent secretariat in Singapore.

vi. INDONESIA

CAPITAL: Jakarta   AREA: 1,905,000 sq km   POPULATION: 178,500,000 ('90)
OFFICIAL LANGUAGE: Bahasa Indonesia   POLITICAL SYSTEM: presidential, army-backed
HEAD OF STATE AND GOVERNMENT: President (Gen. rtd.) Suharto (since '68)
RULING PARTY: Joint Secretariat of Functional Groups (Golkar)
PRINCIPAL MINISTERS: Lt-Gen. (rtd.) Sudharmono (vice-president), Adml. (rtd.)
   Sudomo (political affairs & security), Radius Prawiro (economy, finance,
   industry & development), Ali Alatas (foreign affairs), Gen. Rudini (internal
   affairs), Gen. Beny Murdani (defence & security), J. B. Sumarlin (finance),
   Lt-Gen. (rtd.) Ismail Saleh (justice)
INTERNATIONAL ALIGNMENT: NAM, ASEAN, ICO, OPEC
CURRENCY: rupiah (end-'92 £1=Rp3,121.98, US$1=Rp2,062.07)
GNP PER CAPITA: US$570 ('90)
MAIN EXPORT EARNERS: oil and gas

INTERNATIONAL criticism of Indonesia's human rights record continued in 1992 as the uproar over the army's shooting and beating of unarmed demonstrators in Díli (the capital of East Timor province) in November 1991 persisted. Three Western countries (Canada, Denmark and the Netherlands) suspended new aid programmes in protest, but an official inquiry and the removal of two generals by President Suharto (see AR 1991, p. 337) warded off the prospect of stronger international action.

In a move that won widespread popular support at home, the

Indonesian government took advantage of divisions among Western aid donors to confront its erstwhile colonial ruler and one of its most outspoken contemporary critics, the Netherlands. In March it disbanded the Inter-Governmental Group on Indonesia (IGGI), the Netherlands-headed consortium which coordinated aid to the country, and rejected all further aid from the Dutch. In April this ban was extended to assistance received by Indonesian non-governmental organizations (NGOs) from Dutch NGOs. The strategy of isolating the Dutch apparently succeeded, as aid amounting to some US$4,800 million was confirmed by a new aid consortium formed by the World Bank, excluding the Netherlands. Despite continued criticism—notably in the US Congress, where in October $2.3 million in military aid to Indonesia was frozen—Indonesia emerged from this latest crisis over its human rights record relatively unscathed.

However, international attention was once again focused on East Timor province following the capture of insurgent leader, Xanana Gusmao, on 20 November in the city of Lahane. Damaged by the capture of Gusmao, Fretilin (the group fighting for East Timorese independence) appeared incapable of sustaining its armed struggle against an Indonesian military that was tightening its hold on the troublesome territory. On the other hand, the capture of Xanana Gusmao invited renewed international criticism of Indonesia's treatment of political prisoners. At year's end the Suharto government had yet to escape this latest twist in the East Timor saga.

Politically, attention during the year centred on the parliamentary elections of 9 June and the forthcoming election of a vice-president in March 1993. As expected, President Suharto in October accepted the nomination of Golkar (his political party) for a sixth term, making the presidential election a foregone conclusion. However, given that the 72-year-old leader would be unlikely to run again in 1998, and perhaps would not complete his latest five-year term, attention focused on the selection of a vice-president as being the person who would be best-placed to succeed him. While the military favoured the armed forces (ABRI) chief, General Try Sutrisno, with a view to entrenching the army's control over Indonesian politics, the possibility of a civilian leader was also mooted. The civilian front-runner, Minister of Research and Technology Bacharuddin Jusuf Habibie, was known to have a close and longstanding friendship with President Suharto.

If speculation over President Suharto's choice of running-mate remained intense, the results of the elections on 9 June confirmed the dominant political position of Golkar. Although its share of the vote fell from 73 per cent (in 1987) to 68 per cent, and its number of parliamentary seats declined to 282 from 299, Golkar retained a commanding lead over its two rivals, the Partai Persatuan Pembangunan (PPP) and the Partai Demokrasi Indonesia (PDI). The PPP's position, at 17 per cent of the vote and 62 seats, was essentially unchanged, whereas the PDI increased to 15 per cent of the vote and 56 seats (up from 40).

Indonesia's economic performance continued to be good in 1992. Economic growth at about 5.5 per cent was down from the 1991 rate of 7 per cent, but inflation was also down, from 9.5 per cent in 1991 to 7.8 per cent in 1992. In what economists termed a 'prudent' budget, the Indonesian government in 1992 continued its quest for economic stability by emphasizing cost restraints and improved tax collection. The year also witnessed new banking legislation, the ongoing privatization of the troubled Jakarta Stock Exchange and a liberalized investment law, as part of Indonesia's attempt to respond to changing international economic conditions and to improve its global competitiveness.

vii.   PHILIPPINES

CAPITAL: Manila   AREA: 300,000 sq km   POPULATION: 61,500,000 ('90)
OFFICIAL LANGUAGE: Filipino   POLITICAL SYSTEM: presidential democracy
HEAD OF STATE AND GOVERNMENT: President Fidel Ramos (since May '92)
RULING PARTIES: Lakas ng Edsa/National Union of Christian Democrats heads coalition
PRINCIPAL MINISTERS: Salvador Laurel (vice-president), Roberto Romulo (foreign affairs), Gen. Renato de Villa (defence), Franklin Drilon (justice), Ramon del Rosario (finance), Salvador Enriquez (acting) (budget)
INTERNATIONAL ALIGNMENT: NAM, ASEAN
CURRENCY: peso (end-'92 £1=P35.78, US$1=P23.63)
GNP PER CAPITA: US$730 ('90)
MAIN EXPORT EARNERS: electrical goods, textiles, agricultural products, minerals

THE domestic political scene in 1992 was dominated by the May elections, the first regular polls since the fall of President Ferdinand Marcos in 1986. At issue was the presidency as well as 17,000 other posts, ranging from mayor and provincial governor to congressional representative. Eight major candidates (including Imelda Marcos, wife of the former incumbent) sought President Corazon Aquino's job.

By February the presidential campaign had boiled down to a three-way race between former House Speaker Ramon Mitra of the Lakas ng Democratikong Pilipino (LDP), Eduardo Cojuangco of the Nationalist Party and Fidel Ramos of the Lakas ng Edsa/National Union of Christian Democrats. Not running herself, President Aquino threw her support behind Mr Ramos, who was also favoured by the country's big business elite. Benefiting from such support as well as a lacklustre campaign performance by Mr Mitra, Mr Ramos was the clear relative winner on election day, receiving 30 per cent of the votes cast. But the LDP also did well, winning 17 of 24 Senate seats and 75 of 200 House seats. As a result, post-election politics centred on the ability of Mr Ramos to build and sustain a congressional coalition. An important step in that process was the election of Mr Ramos's assistant, Jose de Venecia, as new Speaker of the House of Representatives.

The new President, who began his six-year term of office on 30 June, faced a daunting political and economic challenge. The task was to restore economic growth in a country in which up to 70 per cent of the population was below the poverty line, in a context of severe government spending restraints. Inheriting a structural adjustment programme worked out between the Aquino government and the IMF, the Ramos government needed to earmark 40 per cent of the 1993 budget for debt repayment. After government salaries were allowed for (38 per cent), little was left for spending on infrastructure and other capital projects.

Nevertheless, the year was also marked by positive economic news. An annual inflation rate of 20.4 per cent in March 1991 had been reduced to 8.7 per cent by October, and the growth rate of exports climbed from 5.7 per cent to 13 per cent between April and September. If the economy was still not out of trouble at year's end, it was nevertheless in better shape than it had been in for years.

Largely overshadowed by domestic political events, the departure of the last US Marines from Subic Bay naval base in November signalled the close of a long and tumultuous chapter in Philippine history. Fittingly, the US withdrawal (which followed a decision by the Philippine Senate in September 1991 to reject a new 10-year treaty with the USA—see AR 1991, p. 339) was the subject of further wrangling, as the US Navy's departure plans clashed with Philippine plans to convert the base into a maritime industrial estate.

As the US withdrawal was achieved, the Ramos government moved to end the 23-year-long Communist insurgency. In September, in goodwill gestures, two high-ranking members of the Communist Party of the Philippines (CPP) were released and the ban on the CPP was lifted. However, disagreement between and within both the government and the CPP over the site and purpose of negotiations indicated that a resolution to the conflict would not be easy.

By year's end the Ramos government was looking increasingly beleaguered. A power struggle developed between the military faction (headed by ex-General Jose Almonte), the business and technocratic faction (led by Finance Secretary Ramon del Rosario and Foreign Secretary Roberto Romulo) and the professional politicians (represented by House Speaker Jose de Venecia and congressman Edelmiro Amante). The government's credibility was further damaged by its inability to resolve the country's serious crime problem and by the frequent power shortages that afflicted the Manila area. Under pressure from the opposition and media, the President ordered an inquiry in October into a series of questionable state loans made to business during the Marcos era. The inquiry appeared set to implicate senior government officials.

While the May elections showed a level of political stability that was a refreshing departure from the tumult of the Marcos and Aquino years, the subsequent difficulties of the Ramos regime indicated the tenuous nature of that achievement. At the end of the year, Philippine politics remained as complex and volatile as ever and the ability of government to address the underlying problems of society seemed to be as constrained as at any time this century.

viii.   VIETNAM

CAPITAL: Hanoi   AREA: 330,000 sq km   POPULATION: 66,300,000 ('90)
OFFICIAL LANGUAGE: Vietnamese   POLITICAL SYSTEM: socialist republic
RULING PARTY: Communist Party of Vietnam (CPV)
HEAD OF STATE: President (Gen.) Le Duc Anh (since Sept '92)
PARTY LEADER: Do Muoi, CPV general secretary (since June '91)
PRINCIPAL MINISTERS: Gen. Vo Van Kiet (premier), Nguyen Manh Cam (foreign affairs), Lt-Gen. Bui Thien Ngo (interior), Gen. Doan Khue (defence), Ho Te (finance), Nguyen Dinh Loc (justice)
INTERNATIONAL ALIGNMENT: NAM
CURRENCY: dong (end-'92 £1=D16,241.70, US$1=D10,727.70)
MAIN EXPORT EARNERS: coal, agricultural products, seafood

THE year saw evidence of further rapprochement between Vietnam and the USA. In February presidential envoy General John Vessey announced that the USA would provide humanitarian assistance to typhoon victims, while on 13 April the USA lifted its embargo on telecommunications links. At the end of April restrictions on US NGO contact with Vietnam, and on trade in food, medicines and agricultural supplies, were also lifted. In an interview President Bush said that significant progress had been made towards meeting the preconditions for normalization of relations. In November a US congressional team led by Senator John Kerry visited Vietnam, delivering a letter from President Bush to President Le Duc Anh. On 14 December the Bush administration gave permission to US companies to sign contracts to be implemented after the US embargo was lifted, raising the possibility of a change of policy by the new Clinton administration.

As part of the process of normalization of relations with Beijing, the Chinese Foreign Minister, Qian Qichen, visited Hanoi on 12–15 February. He and Vietnam's Foreign Minister, Nguyen Manh Cam, signed two agreements and discussed the peace process in Cambodia and the long-standing territorial dispute over the Spratly and Paracel islands in the South China Sea. On 1 April China and Vietnam formally reopened the Friendship Pass border crossing. On 30 November Chinese Premier Li Peng began a five day visit to Vietnam, the first by a Chinese premier for 21 years. The talks again focused upon the territorial disputes in the South China Sea, but failed to reach a resolution.

The Malaysian Prime Minister, Dr Mahathir Mohamad, and the former Singapore premier, Lee Kuan Yew, visited Vietnam in April. On 13 April Australia resumed official aid to Vietnam, and in October

Japan followed suit. In late May Nguyen Manh Cam began a tour of European capitals. In January ASEAN invited Vietnam to accede to the association's 1976 Treaty of Amity and Cooperation, as a first step towards full membership of the grouping.

On 15 April the National Assembly unanimously approved a new constitution. The new text reaffirmed the commitment to economic reform but also reiterated the leading political role of the Communist Party of Vietnam. It also specified that a president, elected from the National Assembly, would replace the collective Council of State, while a cabinet headed by a prime minister would replace the council of ministers. Reference to Vietnam's wars against the USA, China and France were dropped from the constitution. On 19 July elections were held to the 395-seat National Assembly, on a one-party basis. The first meeting of the National Assembly opened on 19 September and elected General Le Duc Anh and Vo Van Kiet to the new posts of president and prime minister respectively. The Assembly dissolved the National Defence Council (which had played an important role in the management of the Vietnam War), replacing it with the National Defence and Security Council. In late October Vo Van Kiet was named as the fourth member of the influential standing committee of the politburo.

In October the Montagnard United Front for the Liberation of Oppressed Races (FULRO), fighting for self-government in Vietnam's central highlands, surrendered to officials of the UN High Commissioner for Refugees. A record grain harvest of perhaps 24 million tonnes was expected, as were rice exports of up to 1.9 million tonnes. On 23 December the National Assembly amended the foreign investment law.

ix.   CAMBODIA

CAPITAL: Phnom Penh   AREA: 181,000 sq km   POPULATION: 8,500,000 ('90)
STATUS: under administration of UN Transitional Authority in Cambodia (UNTAC);
    Supreme National Council (SNC), representing four different factions, formed Sept
    '90 to embody Cambodian 'independence, sovereignty and unity' and represent
    the country at the UN
HEAD OF STATE: Prince Norodom Sihanouk, 'Legitimate Head of State' and President
    of SNC (since Nov '91)
SUPREME NATIONAL COUNCIL FACTIONS: State of Cambodia (SOC), Khmers Rouges
    (KR), Khmer People's National Liberation Front (KPNLF), Sihanoukists
MEMBERS OF SUPREME NATIONAL COUNCIL: Hun Sen (SOC), Gen. Tea Banh (SOC),
    Hor Nam Hong (SOC), Maj.-Gen. Sin Sen (SOC), Dit Munty (SOC), Im Chhunlim
    (SOC), Norodom Ranaridh (Sihanoukist), Khieu Samphan (KR), Son Sen (KR),
    Son Sann (KPNLF) Ieng Muli (KPNLF)
CURRENCY: riel (end-'92 £1=R3,033.00, US$1=R2,003.30)

IN January Yasushi Akashi (Japan) was appointed to head the UN Transitional Authority in Cambodia (UNTAC) charged with realizing the objectives set out in the peace agreement of October 1991 (see AR 1991, pp. 343–4). The first military contingent of UNTAC's 22,000-member peace-keeping force was deployed in Cambodia on 11 March. A notable feature was the arrival of Japanese troops in September, these being the first to be deployed overseas since World War II. Mr Akashi had arrived in Phnom Penh on 15 March, thus formally establishing the UNTAC presence. The probable cost of the operation was put at $1,900 million. At the end of May the UN began the process of repatriating the estimated 380,000 Cambodian refugees living in camps along the Thai border. By September 115,000 had been repatriated. In October UNTAC began to compile lists of voters for the elections scheduled for May 1993. During the year there were visits by numerous foreign ministers and diplomats to witness the UN's largest-ever peace-keeping mission, including Chinese Foreign Minister Qian Qichen in February and UN Secretary-General Boutros-Ghali in April.

Clashes between State of Cambodia (SOC) and Khmers Rouges (KR) forces occurred throughout the year. Khieu Samphan, *de jure* head of the KR, denied UN peace-keepers access to KR-controlled areas until the UN agreed to set up check-points on the Vietnam-Cambodia border to ensure that no Vietnamese troops or supplies crossed into Cambodian territory. The second phase of the UN operation, involving the assembling and disarming of the 200,000 militiamen in the three guerrilla factions, should have started in June. However, the KR refused to cooperate, claiming that the UN had not verified the withdrawal of Vietnamese forces from Cambodia and that the Supreme National Council (SNC), comprising members from all four factions, had not been empowered as agreed in the 1991 agreement.

By mid-year Mr Akashi and many Western governments were becoming increasingly critical of the intransigence of the KR. On 13 October the UN Security Council unanimously agreed a deadline of 15 November for the KR to begin cooperating fully with UNTAC. Talks held in Beijing on 7 November failed to break the impasse. On 30 November the Security Council adopted a resolution threatening sanctions from 31 December and the possibility of elections without KR participation should they not allow UNTAC access to KR-controlled areas by 31 January 1993. Strong resistance to sanctions came from Thailand, where local businessmen, military leaders and politicians had benefited from the timber and gem trade with the KR. On 31 December Thailand yielded to UN demands and officially closed its borders to trade with KR-controlled areas.

The formation of the National Unity of Cambodia Party, headed by Khieu Samphan and Son Sen, was announced by the KR on 30 November. In December, UNTAC expressed concern over the rising level of political violence and harassment, as the bodies of ten executed men were discovered. Twice in December Prince Norodom Sihanouk threatened to stop cooperating with UNTAC and the SOC government, in protest at the 'political terrorism' directed at his and former prime minister Son Sann's supporters. By the end of the year, commentators were beginning to wonder whether the peace process was on the verge of unravelling.

x. LAOS

CAPITAL: Vientiane   AREA: 237,000 sq km   POPULATION: 4,100,000 ('90)
OFFICIAL LANGUAGE: Laotian   POLITICAL SYSTEM: people's republic
RULING PARTY: Lao People's Revolutionary Party (LPRP)
HEAD OF STATE: President Nouhak Phoumsavan (since Nov '92)
HEAD OF GOVERNMENT: Gen. Khamtay Siphandon, LPRP chairman (since Nov '92)
   and Prime Minister (since Aug '91)
PRINCIPAL MINISTERS: Gen. Phoune Sipaseuth (vice-premier, foreign affairs),
   Khamphoui Keoboualapha (vice premier, economy, planning & finance),
   Brig.-Gen. Choummali Saignakong (defence), Asang Laoli (interior), Kou
   Souvannamethi (justice)
INTERNATIONAL ALIGNMENT: NAM
CURRENCY: new kip (end-'92 £1=KN1,084.30, US$1=KN716.18)
GNP PER CAPITA: US$200 ('90)
MAIN EXPORT EARNERS: minerals, timber, coffee, electricity

PRESIDENT Kaysone Phomvihane died on 21 November aged 71 (see XX: OBITUARY). He had led the ruling Lao People's Revolutionary Party (LPRP) from its foundation in ·1955 and had dominated Lao politics since the final victory of the communist Pathet Lao in 1975. Commentators thought that Mr Kaysone's death was unlikely to cause Laos to deviate from its established path of economic reform. The Lao Premier, 68-year-old Khamtay Siphandon, replaced Mr Kaysone as leader of the LPRP, while the 78-year-old National Assembly chairman, Nouhak Phoumsavan, was elected state President.

On 6–15 January Mr Kaysone had visited Thailand, paving the way for the signing of a treaty of friendship and cooperation on 19 February. In January Laos was invited to accede to ASEAN's 1976 Treaty of Amity and Cooperation, as a first step towards full membership of the grouping (see XI.6.iii). On 10 June an agreement on border demarcation was signed between China and Laos in Vietnam. During the year there were visits by an official delegation from Vietnam in February and by the US Assistant Secretary of State for East Asian and Pacific Affairs, Richard Solomon, in March. On 29 October the US Information Service announced that it would be opening an office in Vientiane, after a 15-year absence.

During the course of the year there were reports of sporadic fighting between rebels and the government in Vientiane province and in the north-east of the country. In December it was announced that two former deputy ministers and an official had been given 14-year gaol sentences for calling for multi-party democracy.

2. CHINA—TAIWAN—HONG KONG—JAPAN—
SOUTH KOREA—NORTH KOREA—MONGOLIA

i. PEOPLE'S REPUBLIC OF CHINA

CAPITAL: Beijing AREA: 9,600,000 sq km POPULATION: 1,158,230,000 ('91)
OFFICIAL LANGUAGE: Chinese POLITICAL SYSTEM: people's republic
HEAD OF STATE: Yang Shangkun, President (since April '88)
RULING PARTY: Chinese Communist Party (CCP)
PARTY LEADER: Jiang Zemin, CCP general secretary (since June '89)
CCP POLITBURO STANDING COMMITTEE: Jiang Zemin, Li Peng, Qiao Shi, Li Ruihuan,
    Zhu Rongji, Liu Huaqing, Hu Jintao
CCP CENTRAL COMMITTEE SECRETARIAT: Hu Jintao, Ding Guangen, Wei Jianxing,
    Wen Jiabao, Ren Jianxin
CENTRAL MILITARY COMMISSION: Jiang Zemin, chairman (since Nov '89)
PRINCIPAL MINISTERS: Li Peng (premier), Zhu Rongji, Zou Jiahua, Yao Yilin,
    Wu Xueqian & Tian Jiyun (vice-premiers), Qian Qichen (foreign affairs),
    Liu Zhongli (finance), Qin Jiwei (defence), Jia Chunwang (state security),
    Tao Siju (public security), Cai Cheng (justice)
INTERNATIONAL ALIGNMENT: independent, orientated towards the Third World
CURRENCY: renminbi (RMB) denominated in yuan (end-'92 £1=Y8.67, US$1=Y5.73)
GNP PER CAPITA: US$380 ('91 est.)
MAIN EXPORT EARNERS: petroleum & petroleum products, chemicals, agricultural
    products, textiles, light manufactured goods

DEVELOPMENTS in China during 1992 confirmed that, although without formal office for more than two years, Deng Xiaoping continued to enjoy supreme authority within both party and state. A tour of southern China in January and February provided him with a platform to air his views on China's current situation. His subsequent calls for accelerated reform and the further opening-up of the economy in the interests of modernization were endorsed both by the National People's Congress (NPC) and, above all, by the 14th national congress of the ruling Chinese Communist Party (CCP). His remarks were swiftly incorporated into official policy, enshrining a new goal of establishing a 'socialist market system' in China.

Such radical initiatives were absent in China's foreign relations, where continuity was more in evidence during 1992. A major event was the unprecedented state visit to China by Emperor Akihito of Japan. Also significant, and symbolic of the emergence of new relationships in the wake of the break-up of the Soviet Union, was the arrival in Beijing of the Russian President, Boris Yeltsin. By contrast, there were fewer signs of a resumption of closer ties between China and the United States. Perhaps most vexatious of all, Sino-British relations deteriorated seriously amid growing differences over how to handle transitional developments in Hong Kong prior to the restoration of Chinese sovereignty in 1997.

During his visit to southern China (18 January–21 February), Deng Xiaoping commended the achievements of Zhuhai and Shenzhen special economic zones (SEZs) and urged Guangdong province—which he described as the 'leading force for economic development' in China—to emulate the achievements of Hong Kong, Taiwan, South Korea and Singapore. He insisted that economic construction remained China's topmost priority and, to this end, called for new measures to accelerate the twin process of reform and modernization. He was disdainful of those whose ideological convictions led them to oppose reform and suggested that fears of corrosive capitalist influences were unfounded as long as political power remained in the hands of the CCP. Indeed, it was later to be argued in ruling circles that China should itself borrow from the experience of capitalist countries in order to share the economic advantages which had accrued to them.

Li Peng's government work report, delivered to the fifth NPC congress at the end of March, gave a favourable account of China's economic situation. The Chinese Prime Minister cited growth rates of 7 per cent (GNP), 14.2 per cent (industry) and 3 per cent (agriculture) as evidence of China's economic achievements during 1991. He spoke, too, of further organizational improvements in agriculture (including the establishment of special grain reserves), price rationalization, better enterprise management and the achievement of greater control over planning, finance and distribution as further proof of economic progress. Even allowing for other outstanding economic difficulties, Prime Minister Li insisted that the retrenchment policies, introduced at the end of 1988 under the guise of 'improving the economic environment and rectifying the economic order', had fulfilled their objectives. In short, the stage was now set for renewed expansion on the basis of intensified reform of the kind being advocated by Deng Xiaoping.

By mid-May proposals for the implementation of Deng Xiaoping's economic demands had found expression in a policy document, calling for the opening-up of cities along the Yangtze river, as well as in south-west and north-west China. These areas were intended to benefit from the same preferential policies as had already been implemented in the SEZs and open coastal areas. Links between coastal and inland areas would also be strengthened in an effort to accelerate the development of China's interior.

Claims that China's economy was booming were borne out in a report by Vice-Premier Zou Jiahua to the effect that GDP had grown by 12 per cent (and industry by a remarkable 17.5 per cent) in the first half of 1992, as compared with the same period of the previous year. No less noteworthy was the 28.5 per cent expansion of domestic fixed capital formation. The growth in China's foreign trade had also been maintained, exports and imports increasing by 28.5 and 19.2 per cent respectively. Against this background, there were widespread calls to scale up the growth targets contained in the original formulation of the current (eighth) five-year plan. These were to find expression in the report of the CCP general secretary, Jiang Zemin, to the opening session of the 14th CCP congress (on 12 October). This endorsed an upward revision of anticipated annual GNP growth from 6 to 8 or 9 per cent for the rest of the 1990s.

Jiang Zemin's speech was especially significant for containing an explicit and authoritative affirmation of the new Deng line. Echoing the latter's impatience with abstract arguments about whether current strategy was 'socialist' or 'capitalist', the party leader urged that the focus of structural reform be urgently directed towards the establishment of a 'socialist market economic system' in China. This was inherently an ambiguous term, but its advocacy clearly presaged an extension of price and market signals in the search for greater economic efficiency and higher productivity.

The market orientation was expected to embrace state-owned enterprises, as well as facilitating the development of commodity, securities and money markets. It also implied a diminution of government economic functions and promised to promote the reform of labour and wage systems and of arrangements for tax and profit-sharing. Such domestic adjustments would meanwhile be complemented by efforts to deepen China's participation in the international economy, not only through an expansion of merchandise trade but also through the further encouragement of foreign investment and programmes of technological transfer.

Significantly, if predictably, Jiang Zemin's report gave no hint of political liberalization. To this extent, it subscribed to the Dengist belief that economic liberalization did not require a counterpart in the political sphere. Hence the Prime Minister's insistence that, far from fostering 'the multi-party and parliamentary systems of the West', accelerated reform measures sought to provide a firmer foundation for the establishment of 'Chinese-style socialist democracy'.

The policies enunciated at the 14th party congress—the first to be held since the political upheavals of 1989—undoubtedly represented a triumph for Deng Xiaoping and his reformist colleagues. The same could be said of the amendments to the party constitution and of the organizational and personnel changes confirmed by delegates to the congress. A significant development was the abolition of the central committee's central advisory commission, hitherto headed by Chen Yun, a vigorous conservative opponent of Dengist reform measures. Within the new, expanded central committee itself, the waning power of the conservative faction was evidenced in the fact that some 47 per cent of members were elected to the body for the first time. Many of these were young, professionally-trained technocrats, sympathetic towards the Dengist imperatives of reform and economic modernization, although there was also increased representation by the military establishment. The composition of the new politburo (which included the party secretaries of Guangdong, Shanghai and Shandong amongst its membership) reflected similar realignments.

The most spectacular individual demotions were those affecting the 'Yang brothers'. The Chinese state President, Yang Shangkun, was not re-elected to the politburo, nor was he reappointed to the Central Military Commission (CMC), of which he had been first vice-chairman. Meanwhile, his younger half-brother, Yang Baibing, also suffered demotion, losing his positions as secretary-general of the CMC and director of the general political department of the People's Liberation Army (PLA), as well as his membership of the central committee's secretariat. These changes were widely interpreted as attempts to counter the growing influence of the Yang clique within the PLA.

Speculation about the possible re-emergence of the former Chinese premier and party general secretary, Zhao Ziyang, proved unfounded. The final meeting of the 13th central committee, held on the eve of the new congress, upheld the earlier verdict that Mr Zhao's activities in 1989, when he had shown sympathy with pro-democracy demonstrators, had lent support to the 'turmoil' and had split the party. It confirmed that the former premier would be allowed to retain his membership of the CCP and would face no further charges. But the decision effectively ruled out any chance of his early reappointment to senior office.

The fifth session of the seventh NPC, held in Beijing between 20 March and 3 April, also gave formal approval of a motion to undertake construction of the Three Gorges (Sanxia) dam on the Yangtze river. This decision finally ended years of debate and controversy inspired by concerns about the project's cost and environmental implications. It was revealed that water storage capacity of the dam would be 39,300 million cubic metres, whilst the associated hydropower station complex would, on completion, generate some 84,000 million kWh of electricity a year—one-eighth of China's current annual production level. Energy supplies from the dam would facilitate economic development in eastern and coastal regions of China, as well as meet some of the needs of Sichuan province. Improvements in navigation along the Yangtze and Yichang waterways would enable 10,000-ton class ships to sail as far as Chongqing (Sichuan), raising annual shipping capacity from 10 to 50 million tonnes.

The anticipated cost of the Three Gorges project was enormous, total investment requirements being initially estimated at 67,000 million yuan (1990 constant prices). Construction work would result in 140 towns and 4,500 villages under the jurisdiction of 19 countries or cities in Sichuan and Hubei being submerged. More than one million people were expected to be displaced, at a cost of 18,500 million yuan. Construction of the principal section of the project was scheduled for completion within 15 years, although electricity generation would begin in the ninth year.

A recurring theme in accounts of China's domestic development in recent years (see AR 1991, p. 349) had been the serious state of social order. If anything, that situation deteriorated still further in 1992. Such at least was the message of Ren Jianxin, president of the Supreme People's Court, in his address to delegates attending the seventh NPC. He drew particular attention to the threat posed by economic crimes and demanded severe sentences for offenders. Statistics cited by Ren Jianxin revealed that in the first 11 months of 1991 Chinese courts had handled over 2,470,00 cases of first instance, including 360,000 criminal cases and 470,000 economic disputes. Of the 1.9 million civil suits filed during the entire year, 90 per cent involved divorce, debt or demands for compensation. Subsequently, a senior official drew attention to the 'grim' state of national public security and admitted that international narcotics rings had begun to infiltrate China for the first time since the 1950s.

The minority regions of China were also the source of increasing concern to the central authorities. It was perhaps no coincidence that 1992 should have seen the first 'nationalities work conference' ever to be convened under the joint auspices of the CCP central committee and State Council. In his speech to the conference (held in January), Jiang Zemin noted that China contained some 55 minority peoples, with a total population of over 100 million people, mostly living in remote agricultural border regions. His remarks were a conventional rehearsal of the economic and social achievements of official party policy on minorities and contained no hint of difficulties being experienced. In other sources, however, such difficulties were more readily apparent. For example, reports spoke of sabotage activities in Xinjiang, allegedly undertaken by 'national splittists', the seriousness of which was suggested in official denials of the growing momentum of an independence movement in the region. Elsewhere, there was reference to 'violent riots' and other forms of protest having occurred in Inner Mongolia.

But most persistent of all, the activities of Tibetan 'separatists' attracted the greatest attention. Against a background of widespread criticism overseas of Chinese policies in Tibet, it was not coincidental that September should have seen the publication of a State Council white paper on human rights and other aspects of recent developments in the region. No more surprising was the document's insistence on the historical precedents of China's claims to sovereignty over the region, nor its condemnation of 'the so-called "Tibetan independence" which the Dalai [Lama] clique and overseas anti-China forces fervently propagate'. In short, the paper provided a pretext for a vindication in familiar terms of China's claim to the inalienability of Tibet from the People's Republic.

A number of veteran figures died during 1991. They included Marshall

Nie Rongzhen (14 May; aged 93), who had participated in the 1919 May Fourth Movement and subsequently risen to the highest ranks in both army and party; Li Xiannian (21 June; 83), a veteran of the Long March and state president between 1983 and 1988; Deng Yingchao (11 July: 88), widow of the former prime minister, Zhou Enlai, and herself a former member of the CCP politburo; and Hu Qiaomu (28 September: 81), a senior figure in ideological and theoretical circles. In August it was also announced that Wang Hongwen, a member of the 'gang of four' (or in official terminology 'a principal culprit of the Lin Biao-Jiang Qing counter-revolutionary clique'), had died of a liver complaint at the age of 68. (For Nie and Li, see XX: OBITUARY.)

EXTERNAL RELATIONS. Jiang Zemin's report to the 14th CCP congress, also contained a statement on China's foreign relations. The Chinese party leader drew attention to new political alignments emerging out of what he described as the increasing multi-polarization of the international community. In the face of the considerable risks inherent in the uncertain conditions of the post-Cold War world, China was determined to maintain its independent and peaceful foreign policy—a policy which was 'opposed to all forms of hegemonism, power politics, aggressive conduct and expansion'. Jiang was also at pains to reaffirm the Chinese government's commitment to the role of the United Nations in safeguarding world peace and promoting international disarmament. He added that it also remained determined to strengthen its ties with Third World countries.

The importance which China attached to increased cooperation with Western Europe was reflected in a number of visits which senior Chinese officials (including Li Peng, Qian Qichen and Zhu Rongji) made to individual European Community countries during the year. In general, Sino-European relations improved and economic cooperation was strengthened. However, the potential fragility of such ties was demonstrated at the end of 1992 when French participation in the construction of Guangzhou's underground railway system was suspended in protest against the French government's decision to sell Mirage fighters to Taiwan (see also II.1.i).

Growing differences between the Chinese and British authorities over financial arrangements for the construction of a new airport in Hong Kong continued to impede the smooth implementation of the project throughout 1992. But conciliatory remarks made by both sides early in the year, and the warmth of official praise of Lord Wilson's efforts to promote mutual trust and cooperation during his governorship of Hong Kong, suggested that Sino-British relations might show some improvement. Certainly there was no hint of the serious deterioration which in fact took place during the second half of the year, following the appointment of Chris Patten as Lord Wilson's successor (see IX.2.iii).

If Sino-British relations reached a low ebb during 1992, those between Beijing and Washington showed few signs of real improvement. Suggestions by members of the US House of Representatives that China be granted only conditional renewal of its most-favoured-nation status, as well as the same body's adoption of a US–Hong Kong Policy Act, were condemned by official Chinese sources. A spokesman for the State Education Commission also demanded that the US Senate should revoke its Chinese Students' Protection Act (1992), arguing that such legislation was a mere pretext for preventing overseas Chinese students from returning home. There was anger, too, over an American decision—allegedly in violation of agreed principles governing bilateral relations—to sell F-16 fighter aircraft to Taiwan.

Following protracted but fruitless negotiations on market access, it seemed likely that the US authorities would have no alternative but to impose punitive tariffs on Chinese imports currently valued at almost $4,000 million a year—action which could only have led to Chinese retaliation. Such an outcome was avoided when an eleventh-hour comprehensive trade agreement was reached on 11 October. Chinese sources hoped that the memorandum of understanding would mark the beginning of a new era in bilateral economic and trade relations and expressed satisfaction that the USA had committed itself to support China's application to join GATT.

Positive progress was evident in China's relations with the former republics (now independent states) of the Soviet Union. Most significant of all was the growing political and economic rapprochement between China and the Russian Federation, which also embraced hopes for arms and troop reductions along the two countries' common border. To these ends, high-level contacts took place throughout the year, culminating in a state visit to China by President Yeltsin on 17–19 December (see also III.2.i). Although cut short by the pressure of domestic events in Russia, the visit appeared to have achieved its goals. There was reference to a 'new model of friendship and cooperation' and it was revealed that a package of more than 20 agreements had been signed, embracing cooperation in economic, commercial, military and cultural spheres.

Emperor Akihito arrived in Beijing on 23 October. His visit to China—the first ever by a Japanese monarch—was, like that previously made to Japan by Jiang Zemin (in April), officially part of the celebrations surrounding the 20th anniversary of the normalization of China's relations with Japan. It was also symbolic of the continuing process of China's international diplomatic rehabilitation, the Japanese Emperor being the most senior foreign figure to travel to China since June 1989. In a speech at a welcoming banquet, the Emperor expressed his deep regret for the suffering which Japan had inflicted upon China during the 'unfortunate period' of its wartime occupation. A Chinese Foreign Ministry official was later quoted as saying that such remarks had fallen short of a full apology.

Two diplomatic initiatives in 1992 represented watersheds in what, historically speaking, had been uneasy, even at times hostile, relationships. The first, in January, was the visit to Beijing by the then Israeli Foreign Minister and Deputy Prime Minister, David Levi. It was the first time such a senior Israeli official had travelled to China and it marked the establishment of formal diplomatic relations between the two countries (see also V.1). In September Qian Qichen made a reciprocal visit to Israel, where he was received by Mr Levi's successor, Shimon Peres.

Even more significant was the visit to China in August of the South Korean Foreign Minister, Lee Sang Ok, during which a long-anticipated announcement of the establishment of bilateral diplomatic relations was made. It was agreed that the two countries should open embassies and consulates as quickly as possible, and the two sides moved quickly to further strengthen rapidly-developing trade and economic ties.

Official comment surrounding these developments stressed Israel's and South Korea's recognition of the PRC as the sole legal government of China and the inalienability of Taiwan as part of Chinese territory. Both countries undertook to develop only economic and cultural ties with Taiwan.

Finally, the wish to establish closer ties with South-East Asian countries (see AR 1991, p. 352) was again in evidence in 1992. Of particular significance were Yang Shangkun's visits to Singapore and Malaysia at the beginning of the year—the first to the region ever undertaken by a Chinese head of state. The Laotian President and the Indonesian Vice-President were also visitors to China during the year. The prime motivating force behind all these exchanges was no doubt the potential benefits available to China from increased economic cooperation with the region. In contrast, reciprocal visits by senior Chinese and Vietnamese officials and one to Phnom Penh undertaken in February by Qian Qichen were no doubt inspired more, if not exclusively, by political considerations.

ii.   TAIWAN

CAPITAL: Taipei   AREA: 35,981 sq km   POPULATION: 20,540,000 ('91)
OFFICIAL LANGUAGE: Chinese   POLITICAL SYSTEM: presidential
HEAD OF STATE & GOVERNMENT: President Lee Teng-hui (since Jan '88)
RULING PARTY: Kuomintang (KMT)
PRINCIPAL MINISTERS: Gen. Hau Pei-tsun (premier), Frederick Chien (foreign affairs),
    Wu Po-hsiung (interior), Vincent Siew (economic affairs), Pai Pei-ying (finance),
    Chen Li-an (defence)
CURRENCY: New Taiwan dollar (end-'92 £1=NT$38.47, US$1=NT$25.41)
GDP PER CAPITA: US$8,800 ('91)
MAIN EXPORT EARNERS: manufactured goods, machinery

AN official investigation of the '28 February incident' (the 1947 uprising which led to the massacre and execution of many thousands of
Taiwanese citizens by government troops) criticized Chiang Kai-shek
for his failure to punish those responsible for the killings. The report's
publication was accompanied by expressions of regret from KMT leaders
and an undertaking to consider granting compensation to victims'
families.

Constitutional reform proposals, submitted by President Lee Teng-
hui, were the focus of debate during a meeting of the KMT central
committee on 14–16 March. In the absence of agreement on the
means—though not the principle—of popular election of the president,
members called for further discussion in order that detailed measures
could be formulated by 1996. A consensus was reached on a reduction
of the presidential term from six to four years and on measures designed
to strengthen the role of the National Assembly. The following month
these and other proposals were placed before the Assembly. There
followed weeks of acrimonious discussion, culminating in the formal
adoption of the constitutional amendments—albeit only after vain
attempts to have alternative ideas discussed had led to a premature
exit from the debate by 75 opposition members.

Government revisions of laws on human rights and political freedoms were reflected in changes to Taiwan's sedition law. Henceforth
discussion of Taiwanese independence and the advocacy of communism
would be permitted, punishment being reserved only for those who
advocated acts of seditious violence. In line with the new legislation,
a number of people were released from gaol, including Huang Hwa
(Taiwan's most prominent dissident). Later in the year another leading
dissident, Peng Ming-min, returned to Taiwan after more than 20 years
of exile in the USA.

The importance of these political and constitutional initiatives notwithstanding, they were overshadowed by the legislative elections held
on 19 December. The forced retirement of elderly delegates originally
elected in 1947 (see AR 1991, p. 353) made this the first occasion
on which all the successful candidates could be selected from within
Taiwan itself. It also provided the Democratic Progressive Party (DPP)

with a further opportunity to test support for its oppositionist policies. Dominating the campaign was the question of Taiwan's relations with the mainland. This was an issue on which the KMT's attempt to maintain a unified stand in favour of its traditional 'one China' policy was undermined by intra-party factional differences with those who favoured dual recognition of the Beijing and Taipei governments (and who contested the election without official KMT endorsement). Greater unity was displayed by the DPP opposition, which campaigned on the basis of a 'one China, one Taiwan' platform.

In contrast to its strong showing in the 1991 National Assembly elections, in which it took 72 per cent of the popular vote, the KMT's performance in the elections to the Legislative Yuan was disappointing. Although it won 96 out of the 161 contested seats, its share of the popular vote fell to a record low of only 53 per cent (from 61 per cent in 1989), compared with a record high of 31 per cent for the DPP. To what extent the KMT result reflected intra-party factionalism, electoral opposition to its policies or mere disenchantment with its ties with the corporate business sector awaited further analysis. It was beyond doubt, however, that these elections heralded a new era of political pluralism in Taiwan and the emergence of a legitimate two-party system.

The process of continuing rapprochement between Taiwan and the PRC was indicated by several developments. These included a visit by mainland Chinese scientists (in June), official approval of financial measures to facilitate cross-strait links (in September) and the holding of more talks between representatives of the two agencies responsible for mediating bilateral relations (in October). Most symbolic of all, on 7 November martial law on the two offshore islands of Matsu and Chimen (Quemoy) was lifted after more than 40 years.

Other developments were more divisive in their impact. Above all, in September separate arms deals concluded by Taiwan with the USA and France were denounced by the authorities in Beijing. The first, worth an estimated $6,000 million, provided for the sale by the US government of 150 F-16 warplanes. The second, valued at $2,600 million, involved the sale 60 French Mirage fighters.

But even these developments were no obstacle to the further expansion of trade and investment ties between Taiwan and the mainland. It was predicted that bilateral trade through Hong Kong would rise by over 20 per cent to reach $7,000 million in 1992. Meanwhile, annual Taiwanese investment on the mainland was expected to reach $1,500 million.

Having driven Taiwan's remarkable post-war record of economic growth, the continued strength of its trade sector was apparent in the record trade surplus of $13,300 million which Taiwan enjoyed in 1991, during which merchandise trade grossed $139,000 million. It was, however, noticeable that Taiwan surplus with the USA had fallen to $9,800 million.

Controversy surrounded the six-year economic development plan announced in 1991 (see AR 1991, p. 354). Some critics expressed concern that the level of government spending which it embodied could cause Taiwan's public debt, currently amongst the lowest in the world, to rise to over 50 per cent of GNP, thereby threatening its ability to sustain high economic growth.

An agreement with Russia to exchange unofficial representative offices and meetings with senior Japanese and German economic officials were among the more important developments affecting Taiwan's foreign relations in 1992. The Latvian Prime Minister visited Taiwan in September.

iii.   HONG KONG

CAPITAL: Victoria   AREA: 1,073 sq km   POPULATION: 5,822,500 ('91)
STATUS: UK dependency due to revert to Chinese sovereignty on 1 July 1997
GOVERNOR: Chris Patten (since July '92)
CURRENCY: Hong Kong dollar (end-'92 £1=HK£11.73, US$1=HK$7.75)
GDP PER CAPITA: US$14,210 ('91)
MAIN EXPORTS: manufactured goods, textiles, financial services

A period of uncertainty and intense speculation followed the British government's announcement on 30 December 1991 that a new governor would be appointed to replace Sir David (now Lord) Wilson at some point during 1992. Not until after the British general election, however, was it finally disclosed that the new appointee would be Chris Patten, a professional politician (and current chairman of the Conservative Party), who had lost his parliamentary seat in the recent UK general election. The appointment was generally welcomed, not least by those who felt that Mr Patten's access to government leaders in London would serve Hong Kong's political and business interests. Some pro-Chinese elements did express doubts, although the official Chinese response was more measured.

The new governor's intentions were outlined in his address at the opening of the 1992/93 session of the Legislative Council (LEGCO) on 7 October. Side-by-side with a commitment to low taxation, it contained a comprehensive package of social and economic reforms. These included the establishment of advisory bodies for the maintenance of monetary stability and economic growth; the implementation of higher spending on social welfare, education and the environment; the introduction of a 'citizens' charter'; and the abolition of capital punishment.

A significant administrative initiative was the intended separation of LEGCO from the Executive Council (EXCO), which would prevent any member of either body from simultaneously serving on the other. Membership of the new EXCO, which had traditionally fulfilled the role of a cabinet in Hong Kong, revealed a mix of familiar and new faces, the latter including leading lawyers and academics. Evidence of a more open approach was apparent in the introduction of a formal mechanism to monitor government business and the institution of a monthly governor's question time in LEGCO.

The most radical element in Mr Patten's address, however, concerned his remarks on the 1995 elections. The governor revealed that Qian Qichen had rejected a formal proposal from the British Foreign Secretary that the number of directly-elected members of LEGCO be raised, on the grounds that such a move would be contrary to the Basic Law. Accordingly, he (Mr Patten) had formulated an alternative electoral package, designed to raise the degree of democratization in Hong Kong. Through a reduction in the voting age from 21 to 18 and, critically, an extension of the scope of the so-called 'functional constituencies' (including their voter base), the new measures would extend the franchise to 'all eligible voters in our working population of 2.7 million'. In addition, it was proposed that direct election to district boards and municipal councils should be increased from the current one-third to all members by 1995.

The immediate official Chinese response to the proposals was condemnation of the constitutional package as 'irresponsible and imprudent'—a statement which set the scene for increasing acrimony in Sino-British relations throughout the last quarter of the year. The depth of feeling was apparent from accusations, made shortly after Mr Patten's first gubernatorial visit to China (on 20–23 October), that he had violated the Basic Law for the future Hong Kong special administrative region (SAR). Interestingly, Chinese spokesmen also claimed that he had reneged on a series of secret bilateral UK-China agreements on 'convergence' between Hong Kong's current political system and its post-1997 status as an SAR.

On 11 November LEGCO voted by 32 to 21 in favour of the reforms. Those in favour included liberal and independent members, who under the previous governor had expressed strong criticism of British policy towards Hong Kong. By contrast, the colony's business community had by now emerged as opponents of the package, its representatives in LEGCO arguing that implementation of the measures must be conditional upon full Chinese support. Meanwhile, Chinese sources sought to invalidate the debate by arguing that LEGCO was only a 'consultative body' without power to approve any resolution that was contrary to earlier bilateral governmental agreements. Such a view was clearly not supported in London, where both John Major and Douglas Hurd expressed their personal support for Mr Patten. At year-end no resolution of the crisis was in sight, as both sides awaited

the outcome of further LEGCO deliberations on the legislation early
in 1993.

The increasing rancour of Sino-British relations was reflected in more
acrimonious exchanges over plans to construct a new airport at Chek
Lap Kok. In the face of escalating costs, Chinese sources expressed
concern that the consequent debt might threaten Hong Kong's post-1997
reserves, as guaranteed by the British and Chinese governments in 1991
(see AR 1991, p. 355). Nor were they persuaded that private investment
would cover any rise in construction costs, one senior Chinese official
even accusing the Hong Kong government of deceit in making such a
suggestion.

Chinese opposition notwithstanding, the Hong Kong government
made clear its own determination to press ahead with its plans, not
only for construction of the new airport but also for a new container
port terminal. China's response, interpreted by some as an attempt to
link political and economic issues in its opposition to Mr Patten, was
to threaten that after 1997 it would not honour these, or any other,
contracts, which had been signed without China's prior approval.

In his presentation of the budget on 4 March, the financial secretary,
Hamish Macleod, predicted a surplus of HK$5,000 million during fiscal
1992/93 (against a surplus of HK$14,000 million in 1991/92, albeit
largely in consequence of delays in airport construction work). Key
elements in the budget embraced a number of tax changes, the most
significant of which was a 1 per cent rise in the corporate tax rate.
Underlying the fiscal projections was a forecast that GDP growth in
1992 would reach 5 per cent (compared with 3.9 per cent in 1991).
Mr Macleod also predicted that Hong Kong's fiscal reserves would
reach HK$71,600 million by 1997—well in excess of the agreed level
for that date, although some 20 per cent below the current level.

The year saw a major reduction in the number of Vietnamese refugees
arriving in Hong Kong. In May a Sino-Vietnamese agreement was
signed providing for the forcible repatriation of all 'economic refugees'
from the colony. Almost half of the 55,000 'boat people' currently in
Hong Kong had been screened and the overwhelming majority of them
had been classified as 'economic migrants'. There was a suggestion that
the repatriation process could be completed by 1995.

iv. JAPAN

CAPITAL: Tokyo   AREA: 378,000 sq km   POPULATION: 123,500,000 ('90)
OFFICIAL LANGUAGE: Japanese   POLITICAL SYSTEM: parliamentary democracy
HEAD OF STATE: Emperor Tsugu no Miya Akihito (since Jan '89)
RULING PARTY: Liberal-Democratic Party (LDP)
HEAD OF GOVERNMENT: Kiichi Miyazawa, Prime Minister (since Oct '91)
PRINCIPAL MINISTERS: Michio Watanabe (deputy premier, foreign affairs),
    Masaharu Gotoda (justice), Yoshiro Hayashi (finance), Yoshiro Mori
    (international trade & industry), Keijiro Murata (home affairs)
INTERNATIONAL ALIGNMENT: OECD, security pact with USA
CURRENCY: yen (end-'92 £1=Y189.00, US$1=Y124.84)
GNP PER CAPITA: US$25,430 ('90)
MAIN EXPORT EARNERS: transport & electronic equipment, other manufactured goods,
    financial services

DURING 1992 the Japanese were preoccupied with signs of economic recession and persistent political scandals. The economy was at the top of the agenda, as it experienced difficulties following the speculative boom of the 1980s. Stock market prices crashed: the Nikkei index fell from a peak of 38,000 in December 1989 to below 20,000 in March and close to 17,000 in August. After the bubble economy of the 1980s, land prices had collapsed and banks had so many bad debts on their books that they were unwilling to make new loans. The result was a lack of confidence among managers, of an order probably not seen since the first oil shock of the 1970s.

After an extended boycott of the Diet by the opposition parties, the budget was passed in April despite the fact that it had been rejected by the House of Councillors (upper house). At the end of March the government published a modest set of emergency measures involving construction projects which were to be funded from central sources. But the moves did not result in an improvement in the Tokyo stock market. The government's alleged inactivity was regarded as a factor contributing to the Prime Minister's unpopularity in the polls and the poor performance of the ruling Liberal-Democratic party (LDP) in by-elections.

January saw a fresh wave of scandals affecting political leaders. In that month Fumio Abe, a former minister of state and organizer of the Miyazawa faction, was arrested for allegedly accepting bribes from Kyowa, a steel frame manufacturer. This was a rare case of a Diet member being arrested and was particularly damaging for Prime Minister Kiichi Miyazawa, who had been in office for only three months (see AR 1991, p. 360). Meanwhile, Tokyo Sagawa Kyubin, one of the largest trucking companies in Japan, was said in press reports to have paid substantial sums to some 200 politicians and to be linked to organized crime. With the arrest of the company's chief executives, the rumours grew and implicated many top LDP politicians. As a result, the opposition Social Democratic Party of Japan (SDPJ) said that its deputies would boycott sittings on the budget until some of those implicated testified before the Diet. Press publicity for these scandals inevitably weakened the standing of the Miyazawa cabinet.

The political atmosphere was much affected by the prospect of the election for half the seats in the upper house in July. Since the LDP had lost its majority in that House in 1989, for the first time in 34 years (see AR 1989, p. 351), the government had been in difficulties over getting its legislation through the Diet. With so many top-level scandals in the air, many speculated that the LDP would make further losses. The ruling party had a mixed performance in by-elections, losing at Nara (9 February) and Miyagi (8 March) but winning two seats at Gumma (29 March).

Although Prime Minister Miyazawa was low in the public opinion polls, he managed in June to steer through the Diet the Peace-Keeping Operations (PKO) Bill, which his more popular predecessor, Toshiki Kaifu, had not succeeded in doing. The opposition deputies of the SDPJ and the Communist Party employed the celebrated 'ox-shuffle' in order to delay, and give publicity to, the legislation. But this tactic failed, having in any case probably been counter-productive in that filibustering was widely seen as an abuse of parliamentary procedures.

Mr Miyazawa paid a successful visit to President Bush in early July and created a good impression at the G7 summit in Munich. These successes probably had an effect on the upper house elections when they took place on 26 July. The LDP won 69 of 127 contested seats, a considerable improvement on the 36 seats it took in 1989. This was insufficient to restore its majority in the upper house but was a better performance than had been foreseen in advance. By contrast, it was a disappointing outcome for the SDPJ and the Rengo-no-kai, the union-based party, which failed to secure representation.

The LDP's political fortunes having been partly restored by its electoral performance, Finance Minister Tsutomu Hata announced on 28 August a comprehensive package of emergency fiscal measures totalling 10,700,000 million yen, including 8,600,000 million yen for expenditure on public works. These were intended to cover an increase in public works spending, both central and local, as well as land acquisition, expansion of housing investment, revitalization of small and medium-sized companies, and activation of the stock market. It was hoped that the measures would reinvigorate economic growth and recreate confidence. They were not likely to solve the short-term problems of banks, nor were they primarily intended to deal with the country's surging overseas trade surplus, about which foreign countries, notably the United States, were complaining. Washington reminded Japan of its commitment under the Structural Impediments Initiative (see AR 1990, p. 362) that imports should be encouraged as part of Japan's long-term strategy. As a result, some provision was made for public procurement to be explicitly opened to international tender.

These economic measures were, however, obscured by the dramatic news that Shin Kanemaru, long understood to be the king-maker within the LDP, had admitted that his office had accepted money from Sagawa. While continuing to hold his Diet seat, Mr Kanemaru resigned as vice-president of the LDP on 27 August. Further allegations in October forced him to retire from the Diet and later to give up his leadership of the Takeshita faction in the LDP, on which Mr Miyazawa's support largely depended. This led to a bitter struggle within the faction, the largest within the LDP. At the end of the year a fullscale split took place and a rival faction under Mr Hata was created.

In spite of a great deal of backstage consultation, relations with Russia deteriorated during 1992. On 19–22 March the Russian Foreign Minister paid a visit to Japan and announced that Russia would honour the undertakings given in 1956 in the long dispute over the of 'northern territories'. This was seen as equivalent to a Russian undertaking to return two of the four island groups claimed by Japan. It was hoped that the issue would come closer to a solution when the Russian President, Boris Yeltsin, paid a long-planned visit to Japan in September. However, four days beforehand he cancelled the trip abruptly, to the natural annoyance of the Japanese. It was not immediately apparent whether the cancellation resulted from the domestic difficulties Mr Yeltsin was experiencing or from his distaste for the Japanese stance over the northern territories issue. However, when President Yeltsin later fulfilled the other part of his schedule by visiting South Korea, it seemed to be clear that he had felt that discussions in Tokyo were not likely to lead to fruitful results. Russo-Japanese relations had been cooling since the days of Mikhail Gorbachev and Eduard Shevardnadze. Mr Yeltsin later stated that the initiative on this issue rested with Japan, which should soften its demand for the return of the southern Kuriles.

In Japanese eyes the northern territories issue had a financial dimension. When the Munich G7 summit in July agreed to give Russia $24,000 million, Japan succeeded in inserting in the communique a demand that Russia should take action on the territorial dispute. At the Tokyo conference on international assistance to the former Soviet republics on 29 October, Japan insisted on the same point. Nevertheless, the meeting ended with the United States and Japan announcing additional humanitarian and technical aid to the region.

On 8 September the problem of Cambodia came to the fore, when the Japanese cabinet agreed to send some 1,800 ground troops (mainly engineers) to assist with UN peace-keeping operations over the next year (see also IX.1.ix). This was the first result of the peace cooperation legislation passed by the Diet in June. In response to a direct appeal from the UN Secretary-General and the UN Transitional Authority in Cambodia (UNTAC), the first contingents arrived in October. According to the guidelines prepared by the Defence Agency, Japanese troops could open fire if their lives were in danger or if their equipment was damaged by the firing of others.

After elaborate diplomatic preparations, the visit of the Emperor and Empress to China took place in October (see also IX.2.i). Disagreements on both sides had held up the implementation of such a visit for years, notably over the events in Tienanmen Square in 1989. More recently, the Japanese had moderated their criticisms of the Chinese leadership, while the Chinese had sought an imperial visit which would overcome their post-Tiananmen isolation in the world. During the summer Prime Minister Miyazawa gradually overcame most of the resistance to a China visit from loyalist imperial groups, the pro-Taiwan lobby and the right wing of the LDP. Timed to coincide with the 20th anniversary of the restoration of Sino-Japanese diplomatic relations in 1972, the visit by the Emperor began on 23 October and lasted six days.

During a speech at a banquet hosted by the Chinese President in Beijing, Emperor Akihito said that he deeply deplored the period when Japan had inflicted great suffering on the Chinese people. He pledged that Japan would follow the paths of a peaceful nation and act as a good neighbour to China. In a similar speech in Shanghai, the Emperor repeated the sentiments he had articulated in the capital. These amounted to a deeper apology than the Japanese court had previously offered, though it left some in China and Japan disappointed. Apart from his official engagements, the Emperor visited the Academy of Sciences and met scholars, artists, journalists and students. In spite of earlier anxieties, the visit passed off successfully and without incident. It was probably an important signpost to improving Sino-Japanese commercial relations.

Towards the end of the year the Japanese economy gave grounds for concern. Stock prices had declined dramatically since March, business conditions had deteriorated and economic activity had slowed down. Growth of GNP in 1992 was estimated at only 1.6 per cent, while the number of job-seekers greatly exceeded the number of vacancies available. To counter the recession, the government pushed through a supplementary autumn budget containing the proposals to stimulate the economy which had been announced during August. Because of opposition tactics, the budget was not passed until 1 December, although some aspects of government intervention had already taken effect. State investment in public works increased by some 13 per cent, and government low-interest loans for private housing made some contribution towards a recovery in residential construction. In contrast to private bodies, government institutions extended loans to small- and medium-scale enterprises and increased their procurement of land in an attempt to stimulate real estate transactions.

Amid party and economic problems, Prime Minister Miyazawa carried out a radical cabinet reshuffle in December. He retained only two ministers, namely Michio Watanabe, the Foreign Minister and Deputy Prime Minister, and Masami Tanabu, the Agriculture Minister (who was trying to resolve the sensitive problem of Japanese rice imports in the GATT talks). But the Prime Minister continued to rely heavily on the support of the LDP's Takeshita faction whose members were strongly represented in the new cabinet.

An issue which caused great anxiety to public opinion in Japan in the last quarter of 1992 was the movement of the *Akatsuki Maru*, a ship carrying over a ton of plutonium from France to Japan. The shipment was part of the Japanese government's project to import some 30 tons of plutonium during the 1990s as an energy stockpile for a trial fast-breeder nuclear reactor. From 7 November, when it slipped out of Cherbourg, the vessel was closely protected on its non-stop passage to Japan but attracted much opposition in countries on its route. At the end of the year, as it approached the Japanese port of Tokai, hostile demonstrations broke out in Japanese cities.

v. SOUTH KOREA

CAPITAL: Seoul   AREA: 99,143 sq km   POPULATION: 43,674,117 ('92)
OFFICIAL LANGUAGE: Korean   POLITICAL SYSTEM: presidential
HEAD OF STATE & GOVERNMENT: President Roh Tae Woo (since Feb '88)
PRESIDENT-ELECT: Kim Young Sam (from Feb '93)
RULING PARTY: Democratic Liberal Party (DLP)
CURRENCY: won (end-'92 £1=SKW1,191.27, US$1=SKW786.84)
GNP PER CAPITA: US$6,498 ('91)
MAIN EXPORT EARNERS: electronics, automobiles, ship-building, steel, textiles, footware

IN 1992 the affairs the Republic of Korea (ROK) were characterized externally by further diplomatic and economic success compared with North Korea, and internally by a peaceful transition from a government led by former military figures to a truly civilian-led administration.

In the field of the ROK's international relations, an ever-deepening relationship with Russia and recognition by the People's Republic of China (PRC) were the two most important features of South Korean diplomatic success in 1992. There continued to be a stream of Korean and Russian delegations coming and going between Seoul and Moscow, to discuss fishing rights (mid-January), the development of the mouth of the Tumen river as an industrial and export zone (27–28 February), commercial trade (4 March), Korean development of industrial sites in Siberia (13–26 April) and Russian repayment of Korean loans to the USSR (late May). These and other meetings culminated in a state visit by Boris Yeltsin on 18–20 November, during which the Russian President addressed the National Assembly and handed over the flight recorder of the Korean airliner shot down in 1983 by Soviet aircraft (see AR 1983,

p. 300). In mid-December, however, it was learned that, unbeknown to President Yeltsin, the Russian military had withheld the most sensitive material from the flight data recorder.

Diplomatic recognition by the PRC on 24 August (see also IX.2.i) was a major coup for the ROK, although it created problems with the Taiwan government in that the latter immediately broke off relations with its former longstanding ally. Over the following weeks, Taiwan cold-shouldered Korean representatives sent to smooth relations. Immediately after formal ROK-PRC diplomatic ties were established, a Chinese trade delegation arrived in Seoul. On 27–30 September President Roh made a state visit to China, where he signed trade and scientific exchange agreements.

In February full diplomatic relations were established with former republics of the Soviet Union, including Turkmenia, Ukraine and Belorussia, in addition to which an ROK embassy was established in Vietnam on 22 December. Formal state visits to South Korea were undertaken by President Bush of the USA (5–8 January), who urged the removal of all 'non-trade' barriers, President Václav Havel of Czechoslovakia (late April), the President of Uzbekistan (16–19 June), King Baudouin of the Belgians (12–18 October) and the Prince and Princess of Wales (2–5 November). In mid-September President Roh spoke to the UN General Assembly, where he proposed a conference to discuss a lasting peace in north-east Asia.

Relations with Japan in 1992 were characterized by two features. One was South Korea's concern that the Japanese should not grant full diplomatic recognition to North Korea unless the Pyongyang regime agreed to international inspection of its nuclear facilities. President Roh's informal visit to Japan in mid-November focused on this issue. The second feature was the revelation of the extent to which the Japanese military had enslaved Korean 'comfort women' in military brothels during World War II. A South Korean organization brought this issue before the UN Human Rights Commission on 27 February. It continued to sour Korean-Japanese relations to the end of the year.

Internal politics achieved a greater state of maturity in 1992 than ever before. Elections to the National Assembly on 24 March showed decreased support for the ruling Democratic Liberal Party (DLP), which won only 149 of the 299 Assembly seats (i.e. less than a two-thirds majority). Kim Dae Jung's Democratic Party (DP) took 97 seats, the Unification National Party (UNP) 31 and other parties and independents 22. Much intra-party wrangling eventually resulted in Kim Young Sam, for many years a prominent dissident politician, being selected as the DLP's presidential candidate in May, and as party president in early September. In the elections on 18 December the DLP candidate was duly elected as South Korea's first civilian President since the 1961 military revolution, receiving 41.9 per cent of the votes against 33.8 per cent for Kim Dae Jung (DP), his erstwhile opposition colleague. An important feature of the contest was that all the candidates were genuine civilians. Of five other contenders, Chung Ju Yong (UNP) took 16.3 per cent and Park Chan Jong (New Political Reform) 6.4 per cent.

The sixth, seventh and eighth meetings of the prime ministers of the two Korean states were held in Pyongyang (18–21 February), Seoul (6–7 May) and Pyongyang again (16–17 September). The sixth session marked the ratification by the two sides of two agreements concluded in December 1991 (see AR 1991, p. 362), one providing for reconciliation, non-aggression and cooperation and the other for the denuclearization of the Korean peninsula. Nevertheless, North Korean intransigence on the issue of nuclear inspection remained a major obstacle to closer relations, while other unresolved questions included the exchange of separated families and projected investment in North Korea by the South Korean conglomerate Daewoo. There was a skirmish in the demilitarized zone (DMZ) on 22 May in which three North Korean infiltrators were killed.

A new domestic issue in 1992, was the concern expressed by the Korean Justice Ministry about illegal guest workers from other parts of Asia. The protection of the environment also became a keen domestic issue. In early June major business groups adopted a seven-point 'businessmen's environment declaration', and on 5 June President Roh issued a 'national declaration on environmental conservation' to mark the 20th World Environment Day. The significance of Korea on the world stage was highlighted in July by the inclusion of the Korean alphabet in the latest generation of the international language-coding system for computers. On 11 August South Korea launched its first information satellite from French Guiana. Korean teams did very well in the Barcelona Olympic Games, winning 29 gold medals.

vi. NORTH KOREA

CAPITAL: Pyongyang   AREA: 123,370 sq km   POPULATION: 21,815,000 ('91)
OFFICIAL LANGUAGE: Korean   POLITICAL SYSTEM: people's republic
RULING PARTY: Korean Workers' Party (KWP)
HEAD OF STATE AND PARTY LEADER: Kim Il Sung, President of Republic and KWP
    general secretary (since Dec '72 and June '49 respectively)
PRINCIPAL MINISTERS: Kang Song San (premier), Kim Yong Nam (vice-premier,
    foreign affairs), Kim Tal Hyon (vice-premier, chairman of state planning
    commission), Vice-Marshal Oh Jin Wu (armed forces), Yung Ki Chong (finance)
CURRENCY: won (end-'92 £1=NKW1.69, US$1=NKWO.97)
GNP PER CAPITA: US$1,038 ('91)
MAIN EXPORT EARNERS: minerals, metallurgical products, cement, agricultural
    products, textiles & clothing

THE economic decline of the Democratic People's Republic of Korea (DPRK) was graphically shown in figures revealed by a South Korean government agency in August 1992. Due to shortages of energy resources and of raw materials, along with the collapse of its most important economic partner (the Soviet Union) in 1991, North Korea experienced two years of negative growth: minus 3.7 per cent in 1990 and minus 5.2 per cent in 1992. The overall scale of the economy in 1992 was one-twelfth the size of South Korea's and GNP one-sixth as large. Especially indicative of this trend was a 3.4 per cent decline in the North Korean construction industry in 1992. Military spending as a proportion of the GNP was 22.5 per cent for North Korea and only 3.8 per cent for South Korea. Most worrying for the North was the ratio of foreign debts to GNP, which was 40.5 per cent for North Korea and only 13.9 per cent for South Korea.

These economic problems were mirrored by grave problems in the diplomatic sphere. While South Korea achieved recognition in August from China (see IX.2.v and IX.2.i), North Korea was unable to gain full diplomatic recognition from Japan in spite of years of protracted negotiations. This failure was due largely to Japan's insistence that North Korea must first submit its nuclear installations to international inspection. Likewise, although the North/South prime ministerial meetings continued, there was no tangible outcome due to the nuclear inspection issue.

Notwithstanding these diplomatic and economic reverses, the state chose to host numerous lavish events, including the celebration of the 80th birthday of Kim Il Sung (13–17 April), the 60th anniversary of the Korean People's Army (25 April), the 44th anniversary of the foundation of the state (8 September) and the 47th anniversary of the foundation of the party (10 October). The leadership also loaded itself with honours: Kim Il Sung was made a generalissimo (13 April) and his son and designated successor, Kim Jong Il, a marshal (20 April). A special event was held for 'intellectuals' on 9–12 December, when the 6,000 representatives present pledged their eternal support for the party.

The shaky internal political situation was further indicated by two meetings of the ninth Supreme People's Assembly on 8–10 April and 11 December. At the latter meeting, Kim Il Sung requested that four key figures, including Prime Minister Yon Hyong Muk, be 'relieved' of their duties. The new Prime Minister was Kang Song San, a Moscow-trained economic technocrat who had previously held the premiership in 1984–86.

vii. MONGOLIA

CAPITAL: Ulan Bator   AREA: 1,565,000 sq km   POPULATION: 2,156,300 ('92)
PRINCIPAL LANGUAGE: Halh (Khalkha) Mongolian
POLITICAL SYSTEM: republic ruled by reformed communist party
HEAD OF STATE: President Punsalmaagiyn Ochirbat (since Sept '90)
RULING PARTY: Mongolian People's Revolutionary Party (MPRP)
PARTY LEADER: Büdragchaagiyn Dash-Yondon, MPRP secretary-general
PRINCIPAL MINISTERS: Puntsagiyn Jasray (prime minister), Choyjilsürengiyn Pürevdorj
   (deputy prime minister), Lhamsürengiyn Enebish (deputy prime minister,
   administration), Tserenpiliyn Gombosüren (foreign relations), Lt-Gen. Shagalyn
   Jadambaa (defence), Tsevegmidiyn Tsogt (trade & industry)
INTERNATIONAL ALIGNMENT: NAM
GNP PER CAPITA: US$110 ('91)
MAIN EXPORT EARNERS: livestock, agricultural products, copper ore

UNDER the new constitution which came into force on 12 February the country's name was changed from the Mongolian People's Republic to Mongolia, the red star was removed from the national flag and a flying horse and Buddhist symbols formed the new national emblem. The People's Great Hural and Little Hural were replaced by the Mongolian Great Hural, a 76-member single-chamber assembly elected directly for a four-year term.

In Hural elections on 28 June 293 candidates, including 82 from the ruling MPRP, stood in 26 constituencies, formed by the 18 provinces, Darhan and Erdenet towns, and Ulan Bator city (six). Each constituency had two, three or four seats according to the size of the electorate, and candidates were elected by a simple majority. The MPRP won 70 seats (71 including a pro-MPRP independent) with 56.9 per cent of the votes countrywide, while the opposition parties, with a combined total of 40 per cent, managed to get five candidates elected. These five represented the Democratic Association, the Democratic Party, the National Progress Party, the Social Democrats and the United Party (formerly the Republican Party).

At its first session on 20 July the Great Hural elected as its chairman Natsagiyn Bagabandi, a vice-chairman of the MPRP presidium. Under the new constitution he would act as head of state if the President became indisposed. The President's nominee for Prime Minister was rejected and the MPRP's nominee, Puntsagiyn Jasray (58), was appointed. Mr Jasray, president of the Association of Production and Services Cooperatives and not a current member of the MPRP central committee, had been elected to the Great Hural in an Ulan Bator constituency. A former deputy chairman of the Council of Ministers and alternate member of the MPRP politburo, Mr Jasray had resigned with the rest of the politburo in March 1990 following the challenge from the democracy movement (see AR 1990, pp. 368–9). Meanwhile, plans to try the former politburo members for abuse of office were abandoned, on the grounds that they had acted constitutionally.

Because the Great Hural examined each ministerial candidate, the formation of Mr Jasray's government was a protracted affair. The drafting of the government's programme also took time, and in the event was lacking in specific targets. The MPRP emphasized its nature as a parliamentary 'liberal-democratic party' and its willingness to cooperate with other parties for the sake of national unity, but the opposition leaders rejected this proposal. The Democratic, National Progress, United and Renaissance parties amalgamated in October to form the National Democratic Party (NDP) led by Davaadorjiyn Ganbold. Under a concurrent restructuring of the MPRP, an enlarged central committee was renamed the MPRP little hural, the presidium (former politburo) became the leadership council, and the chairman was appointed secretary-general.

Dashiyn Byambasüren, the former prime minister, expressed much public disapproval of the policies of his successor, and then resigned from the MPRP and the Great Hural in December in protest against what he called the party leadership's reversion to marxism-leninism. Mr Byambasüren had resigned from the post of Prime Minister on 16 January, saying that the government was ineffectual and unpopular, but had been persuaded by the MPRP to soldier on until the June elections.

While in Moscow in March for trade and economic cooperation talks, Mr Byambasüren secured a resumption of Russian oil shipments, which had been suspended because of the breakdown of an agreement to credit Mongolia's foreign exchange earnings with Russian oil suppliers. At the first meeting of a new intergovernmental commission on trade, economic, scientific and technical cooperation, held in Ulan Bator in June, Russia agreed to supply 800,000 tonnes of oil in 1992 and granted Mongolia credit of US$38.7 million.

Mr Byambasüren had talks in Beijing in May on Mongolian freight transit through Tianjin port and signed an economic cooperation agreement. China granted Mongolia a 30 million yuan interest-free loan, promised to help build a sugar refinery and paper mill in Mongolia, and agreed to supply 50,000 tonnes of oil in exchange for copper concentrate.

At the second international aid conference held in Tokyo in May, Mr Byambasüren estimated Mongolia's trade deficit for 1992 at $160 million and sought new loans in addition to the $159 million pledged by the September 1991 Tokyo aid conference and a subsequent donors' meeting in Ulan Bator. The total additional aid pledged for 1992/93 amounted to $320 million. However, in September the IMF expressed dissatisfaction with Mongolia's slow progress towards market reform and some donors then suspended their aid packages. Mongolia's chronic shortage of hard currency prevented the purchase of enough oil to meet basic needs, cutting motor transport, grounding the airline, halving the harvest, closing mines and threatening electricity and urban heating supplies during the severe winter period.

The Mongolian Foreign Relations Ministry issued a statement in May denying foreign press reports about a Chinese 'movement against unification of the three Mongolias' as a 'provocation' and saying that Mongolia had friendly ties with China and Russia. The reports had given details of a document said to have been circulated by the Inner Mongolia branch of the Chinese State Security Bureau. It accused the Dalai Lama, some Japanese academics and US officials of colluding with 'separatists' to 'unify the three Mongolias' in a Greater Mongolia, and went on to claim that independent Mongolia, Inner Mongolia and the Buryat republic (in the Russian Federation) belonged to China. It also asserted that Inner Mongolian dissidents arrested in 1991 had been inspired by literature smuggled in from Ulan Bator.

Asked about the reports on his return from Beijing, Mr Byambasüren said that China respected Mongolia's sovereignty and independence; similar assurances were given during the visit by Premier Li Peng and CCP leader Jiang Zemin. While in Beijing Mr Byambasüren exchanged views on border cooperation, including marking the border, withdrawing military forces and opening new crossing-points for citizens of the two countries. Mongolia was increasingly concerned about better control of international traffic and reducing illegal crossings of its borders.

In June the government newspaper *Ardyn Erh* published an article by Lt-Colonel S. Bat-Ochir of the Mongolian border troops which included a list of territories Mongolia had 'lost' to Russia and China between 1915 and 1980. Presidential aide Ravdangiyn Bataa told journalists in September, however, that such views did not represent the state's position and that 'our country has no border disputes with neighbouring countries'.

The withdrawal of Russian troops from Mongolia was completed in 1992, the last train-load of equipment leaving in June and the last soldier in September, although talks on the hand-over of barracks and other facilities continued. Mr Byambasüren said that the Treaty of Friendship, Cooperation and Mutual Aid signed with the USSR in 1966, under whose terms the troops had been stationed in Mongolia, would be annulled, although a new treaty of friendship and cooperation should be concluded. Russia appointed a new ambassador to Mongolia in April.

Diplomatic relations were established and ambassadors exchanged with the new republics of the former USSR. More Kazakh families emigrated from Bayan-Ölgiy in western Mongolia to Kazakhstan. Cultural and economic relations were strengthened with the Tuva, Kalmyk and Buryat republics within Russia, each having close historical ties with Mongolia.

X AUSTRALASIA AND SOUTH PACIFIC

1. AUSTRALIA—PAPUA NEW GUINEA

i. AUSTRALIA

CAPITAL: Canberra   AREA: 7,687,000 sq km   POPULATION: 17,100,000 ('90)
OFFICIAL LANGUAGE: English   POLITICAL SYSTEM: federal parliamentary democracy
HEAD OF STATE: Queen Elizabeth II   GOVERNOR-GENERAL: William Hayden
RULING PARTY: Australian Labor Party (ALP)
HEAD OF GOVERNMENT: Paul Keating, Prime Minister (since Dec '91)
PRINCIPAL MINISTERS: John Dawkins (treasurer), Ralph Willis (finance), Gareth Evans
    (foreign affairs, trade), Robert Ray (defence), John Button (industry, technology,
    commerce), Michael Duffy (attorney general), Brian Howe (health, housing),
    Simon Crean (primary industry, energy)
INTERNATIONAL ALIGNMENT: ANZUS, OECD, Cwth.
CURRENCY: Australian dollar (end-'92 £1=A$2.20, US$1=A$1.45)
GNP PER CAPITA: US$17,000 ('90)
MAIN EXPORT EARNERS: minerals, meat & agricultural products, basic manufactures

THE Australian economy remained depressed in 1992. Unemployment approached one million by the end of the year (over 11 per cent) and was higher than at any time since the depression of the 1930s. The only compensation was a historically low level of inflation. Several major banks recorded large losses during the year. Despite this, the Australian Labor Party (ALP) government remained in office and its opinion poll support passed that of the Liberal-National opposition in October. Labor lost control of Victoria, which meant that the majority of the population lived under Liberal-National state governments. During the year four of the six states changed their premier. The two Labor governments of Western and South Australia faced serious economic crises and declining support. There was, however, no massive swing away from the ALP in national politics, and the opposition modified some of its policies at the end of the year in the belief that it was not effectively marketing them to the voters.

One of the most difficult policies for the opposition to advocate remained its proposal for a goods and services tax (GST). In February the ALP launched its own alternative programme, One Nation, favouring an injection of A$2,300 million into the economy and the creation of 800,000 new jobs over four years. This marked a widening of the gap between the free market approach of the Liberals and a pump-priming approach by Labor. However, this difference was diminished towards the end of the year by greater Liberal responsiveness to approaches over tariff reductions and some regressive aspects of the proposed GST, including the taxing of food. The Labor government continued its sale of public corporations, 25 per cent of Qantas being sold to British

Airways in December. Competition with the two major domestic airlines was resumed by Compass under new management (see AR 1991, p. 371). Competition between the publicly-owned Telecom and a private company, Optus, began at the end of the year, giving Australia two telecommunications systems for the first time.

There were few major innovations at the national political level. The High Court ruled that attempts to limit political advertising during elections were unconstitutional, thus implying in a novel departure that an element of civil rights was protected by the constitution. After a long controversy between the defence establishment and the Attorney-General's department, the cabinet agreed that homosexuals should be permitted to serve in the armed forces. This decision was welcomed by the homosexual rights lobby but criticized by the Returned Services League. The government organized a 'Vietnam homecoming' march in Canberra during the unveiling of a Vietnam war memorial, and this decision was welcomed by ex-service organizations as ending the long controversy about Australian involvement. Australian troops were sent to Cambodia and Somalia as part of UN peace-keeping activity and an offer to conciliate in Sri Lanka was made but not taken up. Australia recognized Croatia and Slovenia, but not Macedonia, and established a diplomatic mission in Ukraine. Large demonstrations were held from time to time over Macedonia, Croatia, Bosnia, East Timor and Burma (Myanmar), but without significant violence.

The Victorian election of 3 October saw the landslide defeat of Joan Kirner's ALP government and the return of a Liberal-National coalition led by Jeff Kennett. In contrast to other states, this was the first such coalition to govern in Victoria for over 40 years, as the two conservative parties had a long history of tension, which now seemed to have passed. The results for the legislative assembly gave the Liberals 52 seats, the National Party 9 and the ALP 27, while the legislative council (upper house) outcome was Liberals 24, National Party 6 and ALP 14. Five ministers were defeated but Joan Kirner remained as ALP state leader. With clear majorities in both houses, the Liberal-National coalition set about implementing radical changes in public policy, some of them necessitated by the serious budgetary problems left by the outgoing government.

In Queensland on 19 September the ALP government of Wayne Goss was easily returned, as expected. The result in the unicameral parliament was ALP 54 seats, National Party 26, Liberals 9. In Tasmania the Liberal Party, led by Ray Groom, had a convincing victory over the ALP government on 1 February, winning 19 seats against 11 for Labour and 5 for the Greens.

There was a surprising reversal in the Wills national by-election on 11 April caused by the resignation from parliament of the former Labor prime minister, Bob Hawke (see AR 1991, p. 369). This former safe

ALP seat in a Melbourne industrial suburb was won by an independent, Phil Cleary. However, in November the High Court, sitting as a court of disputed returns, ruled that Mr Cleary held an 'office of profit under the crown' as he was a state school teacher on unpaid leave. The Court also advised, under the constitution, that neither the ALP nor the Liberal candidate was eligible to replace Mr Cleary, as they 'owed allegiance to a foreign power', being former Greek and Swiss citizens respectively. This latter finding raised many issues, including the status of a number of parliamentarians holding dual British and Australian citizenship.

The new Victorian government attracted strong opposition from the trade unions to its attempts to replace arbitration with individual contracts and to cut costs in public transport, schools and hospitals. On 10 November over 100,000 marched in Melbourne's largest demonstration for over 20 years. The sudden reversal of the popularity of the Victorian Liberals was seen as one of the major factors influencing declining support for the party at the national level. However, support was starting to return to Mr Kennett by the end of the year.

New South Wales politics saw the resignation of the premier, Nick Greiner, on 24 June and his replacement as Liberal leader and premier by John Fahey. In an attempt to strengthen his small majority, Mr Greiner had supported the public service appointment of a former Liberal minister, Dr Terry Metherell, who had become an independent and vacated a formerly safe Liberal seat. (see AR 1991, p. 369). The State Independent Commission Against Corruption ruled on 19 June that the appointment was impermissible and that Mr Greiner and another minister, Tim Moore, had acted corruptly. This finding was reversed by the state supreme court later in the year but too late to save Mr Greiner's political career. A major factor in his downfall was the refusal of three independent parliamentarians to support him, a rare instance of political leadership being determined from outside the major parties.

In South Australia Labor premier John Bannon resigned on 1 September after ten years in office and was replaced by Lynn Arnold. Mr Bannon's reputation had been damaged by the huge indebtedness of the State Bank (see AR 1991, p. 369). In continuing repercussions of the speculative boom of the previous decade, the commission of inquiry into the collapse of the Tricontinental merchant bank in Melbourne ruled on 6 September that, despite serious failings leading to the loss of A$2,500 million, no charges should be laid against former directors (see AR 1990, p. 373).

More serious consequences arose in Western Australia, where various charges were laid against several prominent businessmen and politicians, who had worked together in what became known as WA Inc. An inquiry into the relationships between business and government in Western Australia found in October that three former premiers were guilty of improper conduct but that there was little evidence of corrupt or illegal activity. However, the general atmosphere surrounding the inquiry was damaging to the state Labor government, which was consistently behind in opinion polls. The bankrupt Western Australian businessman Alan Bond (see AR 1991, p. 371) was imprisoned for dishonesty on 29 May, but released on appeal three months later.

Visitors during the year included George Bush on 1 January, paying the first visit by an American President for 25 years. In February Queen Elizabeth attended the 150th anniversary of Sydney municipal government, a visit noteworthy for the British media's focus on Prime Minister Keating's 'familiarity' in placing his arm on Australia's head of state. Mr Keating continued his sympathy for eventual republican status, and at the end of the year a proposal for a new oath of allegiance removing references to the monarchy was floated by the Commonwealth government.

An important development in Aboriginal affairs was the High Court's decision in June, in the *Mabo* v *Queensland* case, that native land right had not been expunged in part of the Torres Strait Islands. This gave strength to further claims by mainland Aboriginal land councils and ended the legal fiction of *terra nullius*, i.e. that Australian land had no ownership prior to the British settlement of 1788. The Commonwealth continued in conflict with the High Court and the legal profession over the rights of illegal immigrants. Several hundred, mainly from Cambodia, were detained at a remote camp in Port Hedland and faced delays of up to two years in the processing of their claims for refugee status; of those heard to date, virtually all had been rejected, leaving the detainees open to deportation. The immigration programme continued to be restricted, largely due to economic circumstances. The Commonwealth withdrew financial support from the War Crimes Commission, though some trials of former East European immigrants continued on the basis of its previous work.

Canberra was host to the World Council of Churches in January. The long struggle to ordain women as priests of the Anglican Church was finally resolved and 12 women were ordained in Melbourne on 13 December (see also XIII:RELIGION). However, the Sydney diocese remained hostile, as did several other provincial bishops. Sporting history was made when the Perth West Coast Eagles won the Australian football league premiership on 26 September, the first such victory for a team from outside Victoria, the original home of Australian Rules football. Australia won seven gold, nine silver and 11 bronze medals in the Barcelona Olympics in July, its best performance for over 35 years (see also XVII:SPORT). The tunnel under Sydney harbour was opened on 29 August, finally bringing relief to the 60-year old bridge.

The renowned artist, Sir Sydney Nolan, died in London on 28 November aged 75 (see XX:OBITUARY); in June another well-known artist,

Brett Whiteley, died in Sydney. The inquest on the murder of Canberra police commissioner Colin Winchester was reopened in December and the prime suspect was arrested and released on bail in July (see AR 1991, p. 371). The abduction of two children in July by their father, a Malaysian prince, raised issues of relations with Malaysia and of the capacity of Australia to protect decisions made by its courts, which had granted custody of the children to their mother in 1985. Malaysia claimed that under state and Islamic law the father had the right to custody, while Australia officially saw the matter as a private dispute which could not be resolved between governments.

ii. PAPUA NEW GUINEA

CAPITAL: Port Moresby   AREA: 463,000 sq km   POPULATION: 3,900,000 ('90)
OFFICIAL LANGUAGES: Pidgin, Motu, English
POLITICAL SYSTEM: parliamentary democracy
HEAD OF STATE: Queen Elizabeth II   GOVERNOR-GENERAL: Wiwa Korowi
RULING PARTIES: People's Democratic Movement (PDM) heads coalition
HEAD OF GOVERNMENT: Paias Wingti, Prime Minister (since July '92)
PRINCIPAL MINISTERS: Sir Julius Chan (deputy prime minister, finance & planning),
      Paul Tohian (defence), John Kaputin (foreign affairs), Philemon Embel (Justice),
      Andrew Posai (home affairs)
INTERNATIONAL ALIGNMENT: NAM, ACP, Cwth.
CURRENCY: kina (end-'92 £1=K1.49, US$1=KO.9831)
GNP PER CAPITA: US$860 ('90)
MAIN EXPORT EARNERS: copper, coffee, palm oil, cocoa

THE two dominating features of 1992 in Papua New Guinea were the fourth post-independence elections for the 109-seat national parliament, and the gradual unwinding of the secession crisis on Bougainville (see AR 1991, p. 373).

   The elections, held over two weeks in June, brought a change of prime minister with the return of Paias Wingti of the People's Democratic Movement (PDM). Mr Wingti's nomination and the success of his coalition were secured in July only by the casting vote of the parliamentary Speaker. The outgoing prime minister, Pangu Pati leader Rabbie Namaliu, only narrowly held his own East New Britain seat amidst widespread claims of ballot-rigging. In August Mr Namaliu was replaced as leader of the opposition on an interim basis by the Pangu veteran, Michael Somare, who had led the country to independence in 1975.

   Despite Mr Wingti's characteristic commitment to bring a new reforming energy to the country's affairs, there was widespread scepticism about the degree of change achievable by any government in Port Moresby. The fragility of coalitions, and indeed of the parties and factions which composed them, had become a major constraint on government action. One of the most radical of Mr Wingti's plans involved the drastic reform, even the abolition, of Papua New Guinea's highly decentralized provincial government system. Wracked by continuing corruption scandals and debilitated by general incompetence, the system had nevertheless survived as the price of the tenuous national unity enjoyed since independence. It remained to be seen whether the extension from six to 18 months of the new government's immunity from removal by no confidence vote would significantly increase room for manocuvrc in this or other areas (see AR 1991 p. 373).

The composition of Mr Wingti's coalition attracted some interest. As expected, the former prime minister and leader of the People's Progress Party, Sir Julius Chan, was named as Deputy Prime Minister and Minister for Finance and Planning. Among the more surprising appointments, however, was that of Paul Tohian, the former police commissioner who had faced treason charges for an inept 'coup attempt' in 1990 (see AR 1990, p. 377). He became Defence Minister in the new administration.

The new government's prospects were improved by the gradual unravelling of the Bougainville secession. A piecemeal reoccupation of the island by central government forces continued throughout the year, culminating in October with the securing of the main town, Arawa. It was hoped that the evident collapse of the rebellion would discourage others with micro-nationalist tendencies beyond Bourgainville. The government's success perhaps enhanced the security of lucrative mining ventures in other parts of the country, but it was unclear whether it would ever be possible to resume copper production at Panguna in Bougainville, the trigger of the revolt and a major source of national income since independence.

The passing of the crisis also promised to ease recent discomforts in PNG's regional international relations. An end seemed in sight to the stream of criticism, particularly from Australia and New Zealand, of the human rights abuses associated with the anti-secessionist campaign. Incursions by the PNG Defence Force had also caused a sharp deterioration in the hitherto amicable relationship with neighbouring Solomon Islands during 1992.

2.   NEW ZEALAND—SOUTH PACIFIC

i.   NEW ZEALAND

CAPITAL: Wellington   AREA: 270,000 sq km   POPULATION: 3,400,000 ('90)
OFFICIAL LANGUAGE: English   POLITICAL SYSTEM: parliamentary democracy
HEAD OF STATE: Queen Elizabeth II   GOVERNOR-GENERAL: Dame Catherine Tizard
RULING PARTY: National Party (NP)
HEAD OF GOVERNMENT: Jim Bolger, Prime Minister (since Oct '90)
PRINCIPAL MINISTERS: Don McKinnon (deputy prime minister, external relations),
    Ruth Richardson (finance), Paul East (attorney-general), Warren Cooper
    (defence), Doug Graham (justice)
INTERNATIONAL ALIGNMENT: ANZUS (suspended), OECD, Cwth.
CURRENCY: New Zealand dollar (end-'92 £1=NZ$2.95, US$1=NZ$1.95)
GNP PER CAPITA: US$12,680 ('90)
MAIN EXPORT EARNERS: meat & meat products, wool, dairy products, manufactures

SIGNS of a long-awaited economic recovery finally began to emerge. Helped by price stability (increases for the year were never above 2 per cent) and by benchmark 90-day interest rates consistently at 6–7 per cent, the government claimed that inflation had been effectively tamed. Notwithstanding recession among major trading partners, exports grew by 13 per cent, showing strong returns for dairy products, fish, timber and manufactures. Imports increased only marginally less, leaving the overall balance of payments running at a small deficit. Investment picked up, while housing, services, tourism and export-oriented enterprises all indicated positive growth.

Nevertheless, New Zealand saw 14 per cent of its public spending allocated to servicing a public debt that stood at 5.6 per cent of gross domestic product. Although it did not increase, unemployment remained at 11 per cent of the potential work-force. A raft of charges for hospital care, prescriptions, accident compensation and higher education curtailed discretionary spending. The effects of the 1991 Employment Contracts Act (see AR 1991, pp. 376–7) dampened pressure for upward pay adjustments, while the cumulative impact of several years of economic contraction limited the recovery.

In a July budget Finance Minister Ruth Richardson forecast a deficit of NZ$3,000 million, tightened tax on companies operating overseas and cut public spending. A three-year transition in fiscal management was completed which placed the government's accounts on an accrual rather than a cash-based system. Departments of state were required to pay a 13 per cent charge on any capital assets, this being designed to extract better fiscal information and control on spending.

Public health management proved controversial, the government announcing in December a major reorganization due for full inception in July 1993. Four regional health authorities were established with overall responsibility for the provision of core services and allocation of public money. Former public hospitals were reorganized as crown health enterprises and required to tender for funds from their relevant authority. The aim was to separate funding from provision of services. This reorganization was attacked by health professionals for its proliferation of administrative overheads and the unproven capacity of competitive bidding to proceed as envisaged. Also stressed by critics was the likely reluctance of specialists to perform as health entrepeneurs within an ostensibly public system.

The government's objectives were not helped when the Health Minister, Simon Upton, faced strong pressure to resign following revelations that, in July, he had been explicitly warned by a health professional, Dr Elizabeth Berry, about the dangers of continuing to use suspect blood supplies carrying the risk of infection from hepatitis C. Ignoring this warning until it was aired on television in November, the minister maintained that he had not been negligent. A government-appointed inquiry subsequently identified a failure of communication within Health Department systems of advice.

Adverse winter weather conditions not only hit farming returns but also helped to precipitate a major power shortage. The state-owned enterprise Electricorp ignored warnings about autumn drought conditions that left it short of water supplies for its major South Island hydroelectricity-generating facilities. This resulted in a restriction of operations by the aluminium-processing plant Comalco, and also widespread cuts to domestic users. Following claims that the power crisis had occurred through undue attention to profit at the expense of conservation, the government established a monitoring unit for state-owned enterprises. It also continued to divest itself of state assets, announcing in December the sale of the Railways Corporation (the state's sole remaining transport interest). There were also moves to sell the national electricity grid company, Trans Power, but with the government keeping a controlling share.

In September the government struck an important fisheries deal with representatives of a number of leading South Island tribes concerned to maintain Maori access to fishing quotas allocated by the crown. The government advanced NZ$150 million to enable Maori interests to buy into the country's largest inshore fishing enterprise, Sealord—this in settlement of any further Maori claims to fishing quotas under the 1840 Treaty of Waitangi. Through subsequent legislation, existing traditional Maori access to fishing grounds for non-commercial tribal purposes was guaranteed. The crown also provided substantial funding for the Maori Fisheries Commission.

Not all tribes accepted the Sealord deal, some making accusations of non-consultation and attacking the government at an indigenous peoples conference held under UN auspices in New York. Nor did Maori MPs support the initiative, claiming the relevant legislation had been ill-timed and hasty.

In September a significant indicative referendum was conducted on electoral practice. In a 55 per cent turnout of registered voters, 85 per cent indicated, first, that they wanted a change from the existing 'first-past-the-post' system of parliamentary representation. Given a choice of four alternative options in part two, 70 per cent of voters chose the recommendation of the 1986 royal commission that favoured the German mixed-member system of proportional representation. In December the government responded by introducing legislation setting out the terms for a binding referendum due to be held concurrently with the 1993 general election. Voters would have a choice of either the existing plurality system or a mixed-member system under which 60 representatives would be elected from individual constituencies and a further 60 from party lists to ensure proportionality. A threshold of 4 per cent would apply, although this would be waived for parties representing Maori interests.

These developments encouraged a continuing growth in support for Jim Anderton's Alliance, a coalition united by its hostility to the two major parties, National and Labour. Polling respectably but without success in by-elections the Alliance called for tax increases for the better paid, repeal of the Employment Contracts Act, major public spending for job creation, tariff protection for industry, a freeze on state asset sales and an impost on financial transactions to replace the existing goods and services tax. By the end of the year, the Alliance was attracting 30 per cent opinion poll support, although continued Green Party affiliation to the coalition was in doubt.

Within the National parliamentary caucus, the maverick behaviour of Winston Peters remained an embarrassment to the government. Using parliamentary privilege, Mr Peters named and attacked leading business and banking figures for what he claimed was collusion and fraud involving the management and financial restructuring of the Bank of New Zealand. He claimed that the Bank of New Zealand had avoided its revenue responsibilities by use of tax haven facilities in the Cook Islands and overlapping board memberships involving UK-based banking interests. Forced out of the National parliamentary caucus Mr Peters continued as an independent, attracting continued constituency and wider public support.

A single trans-Tasman Sea aviation market was advanced, in that Australia and New Zealand agreed to deregulate bilateral flights and allow each other's airlines to pick up passengers en route to third-country destinations. This cooperation was offset, however, by a sourness in the political relationship. The ruling Australian Labor Party attacked its Liberal opponents for propounding deregulation policies and a goods and services tax akin to those adopted in New Zealand (see X.1.i). Prime Minister Bolger told his Australian counterpart, Paul Keating, that he did not appreciate New Zealand being characterized in this way.

In its wider foreign relations, New Zealand emphasized the development of closer ties with Asia—particularly for trade purposes—through a project entitled 'Asia 2000'. After extensive lobbying, New Zealand succeeded in winning election to the UN Security Council for a non-permanent seat for 1993–94. In doing so, it emphasized its Pacific area, small state and good UN credentials.

New Zealand's relations with France improved. This followed an April announcement in Paris of a one-year moratorium on nuclear testing in the Pacific (see II.1.i). There was also bilateral cooperation in disaster relief and development assistance planning. The year also saw the resumption of New Zealand's sporting ties with South Africa.

Towards the United States there was little movement on the outstanding issue of nuclear ship visits. A government commission of inquiry on nuclear-propelled ships visiting New Zealand reported in December that such visits presented no hazard on grounds of their method of propulsion. Responding to the report, Mr Bolger said that his government would be in no haste to alter existing anti-nuclear legislation.

In other spheres, the government abolished the legal requirement for comprehensive cover for personal injury, thus restoring liability for damages on these grounds. Consumer protection in respect of quality, liability for repairs and 'reasonable' pricing was introduced. Within the governing caucus there was conflict over the terms of planned amendments to human rights legislation—in particular the inclusion of sexual orientation as a ground of unjustified discrimination. Although the bill that emerged excluded sexual orientation, the responsible minister, Katherine O'Regan, indicated that she would move amendments to have this provision included.

ii. SOUTH PACIFIC

Fiji
CAPITAL: Suva   AREA: 18,375 sq km   POPULATION: 744,000 ('90)
OFFICIAL LANGUAGE: Fijian & Hindi   POLITICAL SYSTEM: republic
HEAD OF STATE: President Sir Penaia Ganilau (since '87)
HEAD OF GOVERNMENT: Maj.-Gen. Sitiveni Rabuka, Prime Minister (since May '92)
CURRENCY: Fiji dollar (end-'92 £1=F$2.38, US$1=F$1.57)
GNP PER CAPITA: US$1,780 ('90)
MAIN EXPORT EARNERS: sugar, agricultural products, tourism

Tonga
CAPITAL: Nuku'alofa   AREA: 750 sq km   POPULATION: 99,000 ('90)
OFFICIAL LANGUAGES: Tongan & English   POLITICAL SYSTEM: monarchy
POLITICAL SYSTEM: King Taufa'ahua Tupou IV (since '65)
HEAD OF GOVERNMENT: Baron Vaea, Prime Minister
CURRENCY: pa'anga (end-'92 £1=T$2.20, US$1=T$1.45)
GNP PER CAPITA: US$1,010 ('90)
MAIN EXPORT EARNERS: agricultural products, tourism

Western Samoa
CAPITAL: Apia   AREA: 2,830 sq km   POPULATION: 165,000 ('90)
OFFICIAL LANGUAGES: Samoan & English   POLITICAL SYSTEM: monarchy
HEAD OF STATE: Susuga Malietoa Tanumafili II (since '62)
HEAD OF GOVERNMENT: Tofilau Eti Alesana, Prime Minister (since '88)
CURRENCY: tala (end-'92 £1=ws$3.83, us$1=ws$2.53)
GNP PER CAPITA: us$730 ('90)
MAIN EXPORT EARNERS: cocoa, copra, agricultural products, tourism

Vanuatu
CAPITAL: Port Vila   AREA: 12,000 sq km   POPULATION: 151,000 ('90)
OFFICIAL LANGUAGES: English, French & Bislama   POLITICAL SYSTEM: parliamentary
HEAD OF STATE: President Fred Timakata (since Jan '89)
HEAD OF GOVERNMENT: Maxime Carlot, Prime Minister (since Dec '91)
CURRENCY: vatu (end-92 £1=vt181.85, us$1=vt120.11)
GNP PER CAPITA: us$1,100 ('90)
MAIN EXPORT EARNERS: copra, agricultural products, tourism

Nauru
CAPITAL: Domaneab   AREA: 21.4 sq km   POPULATION: 9,100 ('90)
OFFICIAL LANGUAGES: Nauruan & English   POLITICAL SYSTEM: presidential
HEAD OF STATE AND GOVERNMENT: President Dowiyoga (since Dec '89)
CURRENCY: Australian dollar
GNP PER CAPITA: us$20,000 ('89)
MAIN EXPORT EARNER: phosphates

Solomon Islands
CAPITAL: Honiara   AREA: 28,000 sq km   POPULATION: 316,000 ('90)
OFFICIAL LANGUAGE: English   POLITICAL SYSTEM: parliamentary democracy
HEAD OF STATE: Queen Elizabeth II   GOVERNOR-GENERAL: Sir George Lepping
HEAD OF GOVERNMENT: Solomon Mamaloni, Prime Minister (since '86)
CURRENCY: Solomon Islands dollar (end-'92 £1=si$4.53, us$1=si$2.99)
GNP PER CAPITA: us$590 ('90)
MAIN EXPORT EARNERS: timber, copra, fish, tourism

Niue
CAPITAL: Alofi   AREA: 250 sq km   POPULATION: 2,700 ('88)
STATUS: self-governing associated territory of New Zealand

Tuvalu
CAPITAL: Fongafle   AREA: 26 sq km   POPULATION: 9,000 ('90)
OFFICIAL LANGUAGES: Tuvaluan & English
POLITICAL SYSTEM: parliamentary democracy
HEAD OF STATE: Queen Elizabeth II   GOVERNOR-GENERAL: Toalipi Lati
HEAD OF GOVERNMENT: Bikenibeu Paeniu, Prime Minister (since Sept '89)
CURRENCY: Australian dollar (end-'92 £1=a$2.20, us$1=a$1.45)
GNP PER CAPITA: us$680 ('81)
MAIN EXPORT EARNERS: copra, tourism

Cook Islands
CAPITAL: Avarua   AREA: 4,200 sq km   POPULATION: 20,000 ('90)
STATUS: New Zealand associated territory

New Caledonia
CAPITAL: Nouméa   AREA: 19,000 sq km   POPULATION: 165,000 ('90)
STATUS: French overseas territory

French Polynesia
CAPITAL: Papeete   AREA: 4,200 sq km   POPULATION: 197,000 ('90)
STATUS: French overseas territory

American Samoa
CAPITAL: Pago Pago   AREA: 197 sq km   POPULATION: 39,000 ('90)
STATUS: unincorporated territory of USA

Guam
CAPITAL: Agana   AREA: 542 sq km   POPULATION: 137,000 ('90)
STATUS: Unincorporated territory of USA

Belau
CAPITAL: Koror   AREA: 500 sq km   POPULATION: 8,500 ('86)
STATUS: republic with US commonwealth status
HEAD OF STATE: President Kuniwo Nakamura (since Nov '92)

Marshall Islands
CAPITAL: Dalap-Uliga-Darrit   AREA: 200 sq km   POPULATION: 34,000 ('90)
STATUS: free association with USA
HEAD OF STATE: President Amata Kabua (since '87)

IN FIJI, a May general election resulted in the 1987 coup leader, Major-General Sitiveni Rabuka, emerging as Prime Minister. His Fijian Political Party won 30 of the 37 seats allocated to native Fijians, while the 27 seats allocated to voters of Indian origin were won by the National Federation Party (14) and the Labour Party (13). For other voters (i.e. part-European, European and Chinese), the General Voters Party won all five seats involved. A number of Fijian elected representatives favoured a proven administrator and financial expert, Jo Kamikamica, as head of government, but he lacked Major-General Rabuka's popular appeal. The latter was able to cobble together sufficient support to form a government by making various promises to the Labour Party. The pledges were to revise unpopular labour decrees and value-added tax measures, to protect land tenancy arrangements and, above all, to reform the 1990 constitution to provide for fairer representation. In office, Major-General Rabuka proved as unpredictable as expected. Initially he denied any commitment to constitutional reform, but in December surprised colleagues and opponents alike by calling for the formation of a government of national unity. His government dropped controversial plans to import its own petroleum. Despite a continued growth in tourism, Fiji faced future economic difficulties on account of EC plans to curtail imports of tropical sugar.

In TONGA, continuing pressure for democratization culminated in a major conference in November which voiced recommendations for constitutional reform allowing enhanced popular representation and accountability of the executive to an elected body.

WESTERN SAMOA concentrated on economic recovery following the cyclone devastation of late 1991 (see AR 1991, p. 379), gaining assistance from Australia and China (a US$7 million interest-free loan), as well as help from New Zealand in infrastructure rebuilding. The country also sought investment for its manufacturing industry by offering tax holidays for up to ten years.

In VANUATU, the Carlot government came under pressure from its opponents over its links with France, while relations with Australia deteriorated following the government's expulsion of an Australian diplomat. This official had voiced his government's concerns about Vanuatu's proposals to issue, revoke or refuse business licences without right of appeal.

In NAURU, the death occurred of former President Hammer deRoburt, who led his country to independence in 1968 and was the dominant political figure for the next two decades (see XX:OBITUARY). President Dowiyogo called on all members of the South Pacific Forum to refuse extended economic zone entry to a Japanese vessel carrying plutonium, while the International Court of Justice paved the way for Nauru to pursue its claim against Australia for A$72 million for the rehabilitation of lands damaged by phosphates mining prior to the country's independence.

In the SOLOMON ISLANDS, relations with Papua New Guinea remained tense and difficult following incursions by the latter's defence forces into Solomons territory (see also X.1.ii). These actions were directly related to continuing strife on the neighbouring island of Bougainville, under Papua New Guinea's jurisdiction. The Solomons claimed loss of life and material damage, calling on the UN Security Council to investigate these grievances. The Solomons also suspended defence cooperation arrangements with Australia on the grounds that these programmes were not meeting its immediate security requirements regarding Bougainville.

In NIUE, the death occurred of 84-year-old Robert Rex, the island's leader for 40 years and its Premier since 1974, when Niue gained self-government in free association with New Zealand (see XX: OBITUARY). He was succeeded by Young Vivian.

TUVALU's Prime Minister, Bikenibeu Paeniu, expressed disappointment, during a visit to the United Kingdom in October, that London was providing insufficient development assistance despite commitments made at the time of Tuvalu's independence.

In the COOK ISLANDS, a meeting was held in January of leaders of the Small Island States (SIS) organization, consisting of the Cook Islands, Kiribati, Tuvalu and Nauru. Joint approaches were formulated regarding (i) negotiations with distant-water fishing nations on access to the SIS extended economic zones; (ii) surveillance and exploitation, of SIS seabeds; and possible restrictions on the use of SIS airspace. An arson attack, for which a culprit was convicted, resulted in substantial property damage to government offices, law courts and the Prime Minister's facilities in Avarua, the main centre of the Cook Islands.

In NEW CALEDONIA, France continued to supply investment and public infrastructure in a continuing implementation of the 1988 Matignon accords. Representatives of the pro-independence Front (FLNKS) bought into tourism developments in the Northern province, while a ten-year contract was signed between a major Japanese nickel smelting interest and New Caledonia's South Pacific Mining Company. In FRENCH

POLYNESIA, territorial president Gaston Flosse called on Paris to spell out compensation terms for the territory, given the economic and social dislocations caused by the April decision to suspend French nuclear-weapons-testing in the Pacific for at least 12 months. Paris took direct control of the territorial budget and decreed substantial cuts—steps which M. Flosse saw as a violation of the spirit, if not the letter, of the 1984 statute of autonomy. (See also II.1.i.)

In the US South Pacific territories, the Democrats won key posts in the November elections. In AMERICAN SAMOA, long-serving governor Peter Coleman was defeated by A. P. Lutali. In GUAM (which was twice hard hit by hurricanes during the year), Ben Blaz was defeated by Robert Underwood for the post of delegate to the US Congress.

In November elections in BELAU, Vice-President Kuniwo Nakamura, was elected to the presidency by a narrow majority. In a simultaneous referendum, a 62 per cent majority favoured reducing the existing constitution's 75 per cent requirement to 50 per cent concerning the support needed in any future referendum on changes to the territory's existing nuclear-free status. This was regarded as a step towards a final determination of decolonization from the United States through settlement of the relevant Compact of Association. The neighbouring MARSHALL ISLANDS sustained serious hurricane damage in November, with the result that international relief efforts were mounted.

XI INTERNATIONAL ORGANIZATIONS

1. UNITED NATIONS AND ITS AGENCIES

ON 1 January Dr Boutros Boutros-Ghali, hitherto Deputy Prime Minister of Egypt, began a five-year term as the sixth Secretary-General of the United Nations (see AR 1991, p. 383). An Egyptian Coptic Christian with a Jewish wife, Dr Boutros-Ghali became the first African to achieve this high office. Over the course of the year he oversaw an initial restructuring of the UN secretariat and a remarkable expansion of UN peace-keeping and enforcement activities.

AN AGENDA FOR PEACE. Reflecting the enhanced international position now enjoyed by the United Nations, the first-ever meeting of the Security Council at the level of heads of state and government took place in New York on 31 January. This historic summit expressed optimism 'that the world now has the best chance of achieving international peace and security since the foundation of the United Nations'. The summit requested Dr Boutros-Ghali to prepare recommendations on strengthening the capacity of the UN for preventive diplomacy, peace-making and peace-keeping.

The subsequent report, issued in June 1992 and entitled *An Agenda for Peace*, opened up a major debate on the future work of the organization. The 53-page document placed emphasis on conflict-prevention through enhancing the early-warning capacity of the UN and through the preventive deployment of UN personnel in the field. It called for improved training and better logistical support for UN peace-keeping operations. More controversially, the Secretary-General proposed that article 43 of the UN Charter should be applied in practice, i.e. member states should make troops available to the UN on a permanent basis. The mounting arrears of the UN were dealt with in a chapter containing specific recommendations to address the financial problems of the organization. While the report was well received and extensively considered by both the General Assembly and the Security Council, a number of developing countries raised fears over national sovereignty and the possible marginalization of economic development issues.

47th GENERAL ASSEMBLY. The Assembly began its 47th session on 15 September and elected Stoyan Ganev, the Bulgarian Foreign Minister, as its president. In his opening address Mr Ganev spoke of the historic transformations taking place in the world and of his desire to facilitate a dialogue to advance the reform of the United Nations. On 11 December the General Assembly took this theme forward, adopting

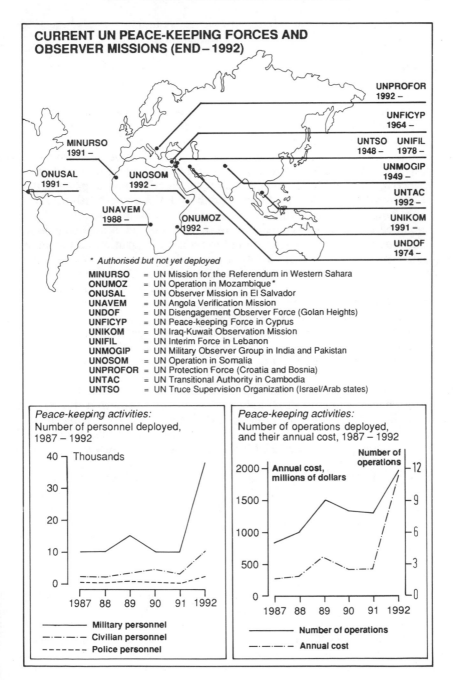

CURRENT UN PEACE-KEEPING FORCES AND
OBSERVER MISSIONS (END – 1992)

UNPROFOR
1992 –

UNFICYP
1964 –

UNTSO   UNIFIL
1948 –   1978 –

UNMOGIP
1949 –

UNTAC
1992 –

UNIKOM
1991 –

UNDOF
1974 –

MINURSO
1991 –

ONUSAL
1991 –

UNOSOM
1992 –

UNAVEM
1988 –

ONUMOZ
1992 –

* Authorised but not yet deployed

MINURSO	=	UN Mission for the Referendum in Western Sahara
ONUMOZ	=	UN Operation in Mozambique*
ONUSAL	=	UN Observer Mission in El Salvador
UNAVEM	=	UN Angola Verification Mission
UNDOF	=	UN Disengagement Observer Force (Golan Heights)
UNFICYP	=	UN Peace-keeping Force in Cyprus
UNIKOM	=	UN Iraq-Kuwait Observation Mission
UNIFIL	=	UN Interim Force in Lebanon
UNMOGIP	=	UN Military Observer Group in India and Pakistan
UNOSOM	=	UN Operation in Somalia
UNPROFOR	=	UN Protection Force (Croatia and Bosnia)
UNTAC	=	UN Transitional Authority in Cambodia
UNTSO	=	UN Truce Supervision Organization (Israel/Arab states)

Peace-keeping activities:
Number of personnel deployed,
1987 – 1992

40 – Thousands
30 –
20 –
10 –
0 –
1987 88   89   90   91 1992

——— Military personnel
—·—·—· Civilian personnel
- - - - - Police personnel

Peace-keeping activities:
Number of operations deployed,
and their annual cost, 1987 – 1992

Number of operations
2000 – Annual cost, millions of dollars – 12
1500 – – 9
1000 – – 6
500 – – 3
0 – – 0
1987 88   89   90   91 1992

——— Number of operations
—·—·—· Annual cost

a resolution inviting states to submit written comments by 30 June 1993 on the possible review of Security Council membership.

UN SECRETARIAT. On 7 February Dr Boutros-Ghali announced sweeping changes to the structure of the UN secretariat, cutting the number of main departments from 20 to eight and reducing the number of high-level posts from 48 to 32. The head of each department was given the position of under-secretary-general.

In his report to the 47th General Assembly, the Secretary-General explained that this streamlining would create 'a more effective and efficient secretariat' with 'clearer and more direct lines of responsibility'. Effective from 1 March, these changes created a new department of political affairs headed by James Jonah and Vladimir Petrovsky. The former economic and social divisions in the secretariat were merged into one department under Ji Chaozhu. Marrack Goulding remained head of a renamed Office of Peace-keeping Operations, legal affairs came under Carl-August Fleischhauer, information under Eugeniusz Wyzner, and administration and budget under Dick Thornburgh. In a move reflecting the increased importance given to issues of humanitarian assistance by the UN in 1992, Dr Boutros-Ghali also appointed Jan Eliasson as the first under-secretary-general for humanitarian affairs.

In November three additional departments were added covering development, support and management services; policy coordination; and sustainable development.

MEMBERSHIP. There were 179 member states of the UN at the close of 1992. This total included 12 new states admitted during the year; namely Armenia, Kirghizia, Uzbekistan, Moldova, Kazakhstan, Tajikistan, Azerbaijan, Turkmenia and San Marino (2 March); Bosnia-Hercegovina and Croatia (22 May); and Georgia (31 July).

FINANCE. While member states voted for a significant expansion in the activities of the UN during 1992, they did not show a corresponding willingness to finance the work of the organization. According to official figures, the regular UN budget was owed US$500 million at 31 December. UN peace-keeping operations were also in substantial arrears: in particular, UNIFIL (Lebanon) was owed a total of $228 million, UNCTAC (Cambodia) $163 million and UNPROFOR (Yugoslavia) $61 million. The situation reached a crisis point in August 1992 when the Secretary-General was able to pay the salaries of the regular UN staff only by borrowing from peace-keeping funds.

ANGOLA. The adoption of resolution 747 by the Security Council on 24 March expanded the mandate of the UN Angola Verification Mission (UNAVEM II) to include an electoral division, which assisted in the elections held in September (see VII.1.vi). However, although the UN validated the results, fighting continued between Unita and government forces. Marrack Goulding went to Angola on 6 November to try to find a way of halting the renewed civil war, while in New York the UN's special representative, Margaret Anstee, called attention to the difficulties suffered by the UNAVEM operation on the ground.

On 17 November, following discussions with Mr Goulding and Ms Anstee, Unita leader Jonas Savimbi finally accepted the election results, paving the way for a UN-sponsored meeting between representatives of the Angolan government and Unita in the city of Namibe on 26 November. Under the Namibe declaration both parties accepted the Angolan peace accords as 'the only way of solving the Angolan problem' and called for a larger quantitative and qualitative involvement by UNAVEM II. Nevertheless, serious outbreaks of violence continued. Subsequent action by the Security Council extended the UNAVEM mandate until 31 January 1993.

MOZAMBIQUE. UN participation in the conflict in Mozambique (see VII.1.v) deepened during the year, culminating in the authorization of the UN Operation in Mozambique (ONUMOZ) under Security Council resolution 797, adopted on 16 December. The ONUMOZ mandate was described by the Secretary-General in his report of 3 December as including the disarming and demobilizing of government and opposition forces and providing assistance for democratic elections scheduled for autumn 1993. Dr Boutros-Ghali stated in his report to the General Assembly that the 'the organization's efforts with Mozambique will be important in the region as a whole and the measures required must be approached as a comprehensive package'.

HORN OF AFRICA. The Secretary-General issued an updated appeal for the region on 15 July, requesting a total of $541 million. An earlier appeal to the international community (in February) for $621 million had fallen short of its target by over $100 million. The revised appeal included the outstanding requirements of Ethiopia, Eritrea, Sudan, Somalia, Djibouti and Kenya, where some 18 million people were potentially affected by drought. UN agencies were stretched by the twin evils of the scale of the drought and the flight of thousands of refugees from the numerous civil wars in the area. Humanitarian assistance was accompanied by political initiatives, promoted by the Secretary-General. These efforts focused on preparing for a transition to democracy and the organization of regional elections.

SOMALIA. With no end in sight to the civil war around Mogadishu, Somali Prime Minister Omer Arteh Ghalib appealed in January for the Security Council to consider the situation in the city and to take appropriate action on the cessation of hostilities (see also VI.1.ii). A ceasefire was agreed on 3 March, though it was barely observed by the opposing factions. Later that month a UN technical team arrived in Mogadishu to monitor the ceasefire and to look into the requirements of a peace-keeping operation. This was authorized by the Security Council in resolution 751 of 24 April, whereupon UN Operation in Somalia (UNOSOM) began to arrive in the Somali capital on 5 July, initially consisting of 50 ceasefire observers. Although by 10 November 500 Pakistani UNSOSOM troops had secured Mogadishu airport, the situation had deteriorated to such a level that James Kunder, director of the US Office of Disaster Assistance, described Somalia as 'the single worst humanitarian crisis in the world'.

In October Mohammed Sahnoun, the Secretary-General's special representative to Somalia, said that 'a whole year slipped by, as the organization [UN] and international community watched Somalia descend into hell'. He was addressing an aid donors' conference in Geneva, at which the UN and NGOs launched a 100-day Action Programme for Accelerated Humanitarian Assistance for Somalia. The same month the World Bank approved a $20 million grant in support of the programme. Prompted by the scale of the human disaster and the endless fighting between Somali warlords, the Security Council made a historic decision by adopting resolution 794 on 3 December. This authorized the Secretary-General and member states to 'use all necessary means' to establish as soon as possible a secure environment for humanitarian relief operations.

Resolution 794 provided that a 'unified command and control' should be established between the UN and those forces involved, though the force would not be under UN command. The United States spearheaded the international force, subsequently sent to Somalia, contributing about 28,000 troops, accompanied by a further 17,000 from 20 other countries. While the deployment of Pakistani troops in Mogadishu had been a peace-keeping operation, resolution 794 and the subsequent deployment of an international force were aimed at peace-enforcement. Dr Boutros-Ghali said that he hoped that the action in Somalia would set a precedent in the post-Cold War era.

SOUTH AFRICA. Following the Boipatong massacre and suspension of constitutional negotiations in June (see VII.3), the Security Council adopted resolution 765 inviting the Secretary-General to appoint a special representative to South Africa. Cyrus Vance was chosen and he immediately visited the country. Also at the request of the parties, 30 UN observers were dispatched to witness mass protest action during the week commencing 3 August. The adoption of Security Council resolution 772 on 17 August made provision for the deployment of 50 UN observers in South Africa. Two other special envoys carried out missions, namely Virendra Dayal in September and Tom Vraalsen in November/December.

WESTERN SAHARA. The UN Mission for the Referendum for Western Sahara (MINURSO) continued to monitor the ceasefire, while the Secretary-General's special representative sought agreement between the two parties on the interpretation of the criteria relating to voter eligibility in the proposed consultation to decide the territory's status. Despite regular reports by the Secretary-General to the Security Council, the plan remained in deadlock at the end of 1992 (see also V.4.vi).

AFGHANISTAN. The under-secretary-general for humanitarian affairs, Mr Eliasson, declared at a donors' conference in New York on 2 November that some $17.8 million was required to meet the winter emergency needs of the UN relief and repatriation programme for Afghanistan (see also VIII.1.ii). During the year the programme succeeded in repatriating over a million people from Pakistan and 200,000 from Iran. In addition, 135,000 internally-displaced Afghans were in need of assistance. On 10 November the World Food Programme (WFP) approved three projects worth $171,359,000 for Afghanistan and Afghan refugees. In parallel political moves during the year, the Secretary-General's representative in Afghanistan and Pakistan, Benon Sevan, engaged in intensive consultations with all segments of the Afghan people. In April Mr Sevan told the warring parties that there was 'no viable alternative' to a political solution.

CAMBODIA. The Security Council's adoption of resolution 745 on 28 February established the UN Transitional Authority in Cambodia (UNTAC). The proposed force of 22,000 personnel, the largest peace-keeping operation in the organization's history, began arriving in Phnom Penh on 15 March (see also IX.1.ix). Despite the reluctance of the Party of Democratic Kampuchea (PDK), i.e. the Khmers Rouges, to comply with the 1991 Paris peace accords, UNTAC proceeded in June to disarm forces of the other three factions in the conflict. In early July UNTAC moved to take over the civil administration in the country, including foreign affairs, national defence, finance, security as well as public municipal administration.

Concern continued at the PDK's obstruction of UNTAC's mandate, however. On 13 October the Security Council unanimously adopted resolution 783 by which it demanded that the PDK should fulfil its obligations under the Paris agreements and facilitate the full deployment of UNTAC in areas under its control. Stronger measures against the PDK were threatened on 30 November with the adoption of resolution 792 whereby the Security Council called for sanctions to be imposed on any party which did not comply with the peace plan. By the end of the year UNTAC had helped to register over 4 million Cambodians for the elections scheduled for May 1993, while the UN High Commissioner for Refugees (UNHCR) had succeeded in repatriating over 100,000 Cambodian refugees.

EL SALVADOR. Dr Boutros-Ghali attended the signing of the peace agreements between the government of El Salvador and the Farabundo Martí Liberation Front (FMLN) in Mexico on 16 January (see IV.3.xiii). These had been brokered by his predecessor, Javier Pérez de Cuellar, at the end of 1991 (see AR 1991, p. 83). Two days earlier the Security Council had adopted resolution 792 which expanded the mandate of the UN Observer Mission in El Salvador (ONUSAL), to include the verification and monitoring of the implementation of the subsequent peace agreements. Despite the delay in implementing these agreements, President Alfredo Cristiani in November reaffirmed his support for the UN peace initiative.

CYPRUS. On 18 June the two Cypriot communities entered into further talks, initiated by the UN Secretary-General, on a 'set of ideas' for an overall framework agreement on Cyprus (see II.3.vi). Adopted on the 26 August, Security Council resolution 774 reaffirmed that a settlement must be based upon 'a state of Cyprus with a single sovereignty and international personality and single citizenship'. The two parties adjourned the talks on 11 November, without agreement, although negotiations were scheduled to be resumed in March 1993.

FORMER SOVIET UNION. The United Nations found itself embroiled in international efforts to resolve a catalogue of civil and ethnic conflicts which, having erupted during the twilight years of the Soviet Union's existence, intensified after its final disintegration in December 1991 (see II.2.i). Concern over the deteriorating situation in Nagorno-Karabakh prompted the Secretary-General to send two fact-finding missions to the area on 16–21 March and 21–28 May. A third mission was sent on 4–10 July to investigate Azerbaijani claims that Armenia had used chemical weapons. The UNHCR launched a $6 million operation to bring humanitarian aid to more than 750,000 refugees and internally-displaced persons in Armenia and Azerbaijan. A fact-finding mission to Moldova on 25–29 August reported that the situation had greatly improved and that the parties were adhering to the provisions of the peace agreement signed on 21 July. Against the backdrop of unrest in his own Georgian republic, President Eduard Shevardnadze warned Dr Boutros-Ghali, in a letter dated 11 November, of the broadening of the conflict zone in the Caucasus.

FORMER YUGOSLAVIA (BALKAN CONFLICT). The UN presence in former Yugoslavia was characterized by an ever-changing mandate in response to the civil and ethnic conflict which worsened in intensity as the year proceeded (see III.1.vi). UN liaison officers had already been monitoring ceasefire arrangements between the Yugoslav Federal Army and the Croatian People's Guard for over a month when the Security Council adopted resolution 743 of 21 February approving the establishment of the UN Protection Force (UNPROFOR). Under the command of Lieutenant-General Satish Nambir (India), an advance party of the 15,000-member force began to deploy in Belgrade on 9 March. On 23 March advance infantry and support contingents moved to secure UN protection areas in Krajina and in eastern and western Slavonia (i.e. in three Serb-held enclaves in eastern and southern Croatia). This was in preparation for the arrival of the full force, whose deployment was confirmed by Security Council resolution 749, adopted on April 7. In May the UN high commissioner for refugees, Sadako Ogata, called attention to the humanitarian tragedy unfolding in Bosnia-Hercegovina. She described the creation of thousands of Yugoslav displaced persons by the spread of ethnic violence as the worst refugee problem in Europe since World War II. Continued Serbian aggression in Bosnia prompted the international community to ostracize the Serbian-dominated Federal Republic of Yugoslavia, culminating in UN-imposed sanctions during May.

On 8 June the Security Council adopted resolution 758 extending the UNPROFOR mandate to Bosnia-Hercegovina and authorizing the deployment of 60 military observers to the besieged Bosnian capital, Sarajevo. Throughout June the force commander, General Louis McKenzie, attempted to broker a durable ceasefire to allow the opening of Sarajevo airport and ensure the unimpeded delivery of aid to the civilian population. During June and July the Security Council strengthened this presence by authorizing, through resolutions 761 and 764, the deployment of additional UNPROFOR contingents to the city.

The continued deterioration of the humanitarian situation prompted the adoption of two further Security Council resolutions on 13 August which aimed at strengthening the international community's relief efforts. Resolution 770 called upon 'all states to take all measures to facilitate, in coordination with the UN, humanitarian assistance to Sarajevo and, where needed, to other parts of Bosnia-Hercegovina'. This was widely interpreted as authorizing the use of force. During August the UN met with representatives of the North Atlantic Treaty Organization (NATO), the Western European Union (WEU) and the Conference on Security and Cooperation in Europe (CSCE) on the practicalities of international military intervention in former Yugoslav republics. Moreover, resolution 771 demanded that the International Committee of the Red Cross (ICRC) and other relevant agencies be admitted to all camps, detention centres and prisons in the former Yugoslavia. Attached to these resolutions was the warning that failure to comply with their provisions would prompt further action to be taken under chapter VII of the UN Charter.

Co-chaired by the UN and the European Community, the London conference of 26–27 August established a 'steering committee' jointly headed by Cyrus Vance and Lord (David) Owen charged with powers to seek a political settlement in former Yugoslavia and to find ways of implementing the provisions of the conference's final declaration. Subsequently, Mr Vance and Lord Owen became the co-chairmen of the Permanent Conference on Yugoslavia, which opened in Geneva on 3 September. During that month the UN moved towards a more interventionist policy with the adoption of Security Council resolution 776 on 14 September. This approved the Secretary-General's proposal to strengthen the UN force by up to 6,000 troops and to allow it to provide armed escort for UNHCR aid convoys. The UNPROFOR mandate was extended to allow its members to use force in self-defence and in situations where they were prevented from carrying out their duties.

On 10 November the Security Council adopted resolution 786 establishing a team of 75 military observers to monitor the no-fly zone over Bosnia-Hercegovina which the Council had invoked through its previous resolution (781) adopted on 9 October. On 18 December the General Assembly urged the Security Council to authorize member states 'to use all necessary means', in the event of Serb and Montenegrin non-compliance with UN resolutions, to restore the sovereignty of Bosnia-Hercegovina. Faced with a further escalation of the Balkan conflict, the Security Council adopted resolution 795 on 11 December authorizing the deployment of an UNPROFOR presence in Macedonia. A monitoring team of 14 members went to Macedonia at the end of November ahead of the UNPROFOR deployment. On 31 December Dr Boutros-Ghali visited Sarajevo, where he told his Bosnian hosts that 'sooner or later you will have to coexist and there is no alternative but to talk to your enemies'.

IRAQ. Iraq continued to defy Security Council resolution obligations imposed in the wake of the 1991 Gulf War (see AR 1991, pp. 385–6, 550–5). Tensions over UN inspections of Iraq's weapons programme came to a head during the summer when the Iraqi authorities refused inspectors from the International Atomic Energy Agency (IAEA) entry to the Ministry of Agriculture and Irrigation in Baghdad (see also V.2.vi). On 6 July the Security Council demanded that the Iraqi authorities admit the inspectors, who had maintained a constant vigil outside the ministry; however, on 22 July the team was forced to withdraw in the face of anti-UN and anti-Western demonstrations. As tensions rose, the USA and its Western allies engaged in a form of sabre-rattling, in what became the most serious incident since the end of the Gulf hostilities. It was eventually resolved only after intense diplomatic manoeuvring in New York. Subsequent IAEA inspections of the Iraqi ministry on 28 July uncovered no illegal documents or materials.

Various Iraqi military facilities had already been destroyed earlier in the year under UN auspices, including the Al Atheer Weapons Centre. The UN special commission on Iraqi disarmament declared on 25 August that, after inspections of eight sites, no evidence had been found to suggest that Iraq had the capability to produce complete guidance and control systems for ballistic missiles. A further 50 sites were inspected between 16 and 30 October but weapons inspectors failed to locate any of Iraq's estimated 100 Scud missiles.

Following the failure during the summer of negotiations between the Iraqi government and the UN to resolve the issue of Iraqi oil exports (see AR 1991, p. 386), the Security Council adopted resolution 778 on 20 October impounding Iraqi oil assets worth $500–800 million. These monies were transferred to the UN 'escrow account' which would be used to provide humanitarian relief in Iraq, facilitate the destruction of Iraq's weapons programme and fulfil the obligations of the UN Compensation Fund for Gulf War victims.

The UN relief operation in northern Iraq continued to be harassed by the Iraqi authorities during 1992. The destruction of six trucks belonging to the World Food Programme on 29 November prompted the Secretary-General to strengthen the UN guard contingent protecting relief convoys.

ISRAEL-PALESTINE. Security Council resolution 726 of 6 January condemned Israel's deportation of 12 Palestinians from the Israeli-occupied territories, invoking the Fourth Geneva convention. On 17 January US Secretary of State James Baker met the Secretary-General to discuss the future role of the UN in the Arab-Israeli peace process, although at Israel's insistence the UN as such continued to play no role during 1992 (see V.2.i).

In resolution 799 of 18 December, the Security Council again found itself strongly condemning Israel, this time for the collective deportation of 415 Palestinians (see V.1). UN political affairs head, James Jonah, went to Israel in late December to seek a resolution of the issue, which sparked a renewed wave of violence and tension in the occupied territories.

LEBANON. An escalation of violence in southern Lebanon following Israel's assassination of Sheikh Abbas Musawi (see V.ii.v) prompted a meeting of the Security Council on 19 February at the request of the Lebanese delegation. The Council deplored the violence, reiterated its call for restraint and reaffirmed resolution 425 of 1978. Nevertheless tensions continued to rise, as Israeli troops broke through checkpoints of the UN Interim Force in Lebanon (UNIFIL) on 20 February and took control of villages north of Israel's 'security zone'. In this engagement UNIFIL suffered one soldier killed (and six injured), this bringing the number of UNIFIL fatalities to 185 since 1978.

LIBYA. The United Nations' relations with Libya in 1992 centred on the organization's demands that Tripoli should cooperate with investigations into the bombing of Pan Am flight 103 in 1988 and the destruction of UTA flight 772 in 1989 (see V.4.ii). The failure of British, French and US efforts to secure the extradition of Libyan nationals accused of involvement in these acts prompted the Security Council to adopt resolution 731 on 21 January, deploring the reluctance of the Libyan government to cooperate fully. The Security Council pursued a tougher stance with its adoption of resolution 748 on 31 March, imposing mandatory sanctions against Libya, including an air and arms embargo. Sanctions came into effect on 15 April. Despite Tripoli's assertions that it had distanced itself from terrorism, and further negotiations with a UN special envoy, the Council renewed the sanctions on 12 August for a further 120 days.

DISARMAMENT. The UN Secretary-General commemorated Disarmament Week 1992 on 28 October by presenting a report setting out his vision of the UN's potential role in disarmament in the post-Cold War world. The report called for 'universal adherence' to the recently-finalized draft international treaty banning chemical weapons (see XII.1) and said that the Non-Proliferation Treaty should be 'indefinitely and unconditionally extended' in 1995. The UN Conventional Arms Register came into effect from January 1992.

ENVIRONMENT AND DEVELOPMENT. Dr Boutros-Ghali opened the special summit of the UN Conference on the Environment and Development (UNCED) in Rio de Janeiro, Brazil, on 3 June (see XIV.3 & XIX.1). At its close on the 14 June a framework convention on climate change and a convention on biological diversity had been signed by 153 countries. In addition, negotiating process for a convention on desertification was mandated and a non-binding plan for environmental action (Agenda 21) was approved. A proposal to set up a UN Commission on Sustainable Development was adopted at the General Assembly later in the year.

WOMEN. Prompted by research findings that over half of agricultural workers in less developed countries were women, a World Summit for Women was convened in Geneva in February–March under the auspices of the International Fund for Agricultural Development (IFAD). Marking International Women's Day on 8 March, the Secretary-General expressed concern that progress on the advancement of women had visibly slackened and that the gap between equality before the law and equality in practice was growing.

2. THE COMMONWEALTH

WHILE the global news focus was on conflict in Yugoslavia, Somalia and the Middle East, the Commonwealth was busy developing the new 'good offices' role on which heads of government had launched it at their summit in Harare in 1991 (see AR 1991, pp.392–3).

It was a year of many elections in Commonwealth countries, mainly in Africa, where the change to multi-partyism gathered speed in the wake of Western economic and political pressures. The Commonwealth role was to advise on the constitutional and legal preparations and then to observe the polling. In 1992 this process took place in five countries. Each involved difficult diplomatic interventions by the Commonwealth Secretary-General, Chief Emeka Anyaoku, before, during and after the election. In each country the preparation of the voters' register proved the most difficult exercise.

For the first of three elections in Seychelles—that for the election of a constitutional commission (23–26 July)—a 12-strong team of observers was sent, led by Henry de B. Forde, opposition leader in Barbados. It adjudged the poll free and fair, 'notwithstanding some shortcomings'. A smaller team returned for the referendum on 15 November, which resulted in rejection of the draft constitution (see VII.3.ii).

In Guyana 26 observers and support staff led by David R. Peterson, former premier of Ontario, found the much-delayed election on 5 October free and fair, although 'a significant number' of voters had not been able to find their names on the list. The People's National Congress government, led by Desmond Hoyte, accepted the verdict and went into opposition after 26 years in power, making way for the People's Progressive Party, under Cheddi Jagan (see IV.4.ii).

The Ghana presidential election (3 November), bringing back civilian rule, proved more difficult for the observers (see VI.2.i). The team of 24, chaired by Sir Ellis Clarke, former attorney-general of Trinidad & Tobago, found many imperfections in the polling, including the fact that there could have been up to 1.5 million errors in the voters' roll. They concluded that these did not detract from 'the overall freeness and fairness of the process'. The opposition parties, which lost by a wide margin to the former military ruler, Jerry Rawlings, rejected the result and boycotted the parliamentary elections on 29 December, despite attempts by Commonwealth officials to persuade them to take part. The Secretary-General decided not to send an observer group for the second poll.

The Kenya elections on 29 December proved even more difficult (see VI.1.iv). Dispatch of a 40-strong observer group, led by Mr Justice Telford Georges (Trinidad & Tobago), was preceded by months of diplomatic contact between Chief Anyaoku, President Daniel Arap Moi and the divided opposition parties. The Commonwealth group's report exceeded previous criticism by saying that the election could not be given an unqualified rating as free and fair, although it added: 'We believe the results in most instances directly reflect, however imperfectly, the expression of the will of the people.' The main opposition parties rejected the result and at year's end Chief Anyaoku flew to Nairobi to persuade their leaders not to boycott parliament.

Elections in Lesotho, transferring power from a military to a civilian government, were postponed until 1993 following several visits by Commonwealth officials to advise on constitutional and polling arrangements. In June Chief Anyaoku acted as mediator in talks in London between the military ruler, Major-General Elias Ramaema, and the exiled King Moshoeshoe II. A formula was devised that led to the return home of the King a few weeks later (see VII.2.vi).

The Commonwealth also played an observer role in South Africa for the first time (see VII.3). In October it sent 18 observers to help in the quest to stem the worsening violence, including Canadian and British police chiefs, a retired Nigerian general and a former supreme court judge from Ghana. Working alongside UN and EC teams, the team proved the most effective at grassroots level. It mediated in local disputes involving the South African police and defence force and helped the work of the committees set up under the 1991 peace accord, mainly in the most violent areas of Natal and Kwazulu. In addition, there was frequent high-level contact throughout the year between the Commonwealth secretariat and the government and political parties in South Africa. Sanctions having ceased to be a controversial issue, sporting contacts with South Africa were quickly resumed by Commonwealth countries following the lifting of African National Congress (ANC) objections. Although the Commonwealth (except Britain) continued to support economic sanctions in line with ANC policy, governments began openly dealing with Pretoria. President de Klerk visited Nigeria in April, while Kenya opened formal relations later in the year.

The long process of 'high-level appraisal' of the Commonwealth, begun at the Kuala Lumpur summit in 1989, came to fruition at the biennial meeting of senior officials held in Kampala on 16–18 November. The meeting approved a major restructuring of the secretariat. The 16 divisions would be reduced to 12 and the Secretary-General would have three deputies instead of, as hitherto, two deputies, an assistant and a managing director of the Commonwealth Fund for Technical Cooperation (CFTC), which post would disappear. The deputies' duties would be categorized as: political, economic, and social and development cooperation. One important change was that the Secretary-General would now appoint his deputies from government nominations; hitherto they had been chosen by governments.

On the retirement of 'Inoke Faletau (Tonga) as director of the Commonwealth Foundation, Dr Humayun Khan, recently Pakistan's high commissioner in London, was appointed to succeed in 1993. Commonwealth ministerial meetings in 1992 brought together government members responsible for health (Geneva, 3 May), youth affairs (Malé, Maldives, 10–12 May) and finance (New York, 16–17 September).

The Commonwealth Games Federation, meeting in Barcelona at the time of the Olympic Games, decided that Malaysia would host the 1998 Commonwealth Games—only the second developing country ever to do so (after Jamaica in 1966). Earlier, the Secretary-General set up a four-year committee on Commonwealth cooperation in sport under Roy McMurtry, deputy chief justice of Ontario.

3. EUROPEAN COMMUNITY

HOPES that the 1991 Maastricht Treaty on European Union would be ratified by all member states by 1 January 1993 ebbed away during the year. National economies slipped into recession and public scepticism about European integration increased. Europe's political establishment had been almost unanimous in approving the deal struck in Maastricht at the end of 1991 (see AR 1991, pp. 400–2, 465–7, 561–6), but voters had their doubts. On 2 June the Danes voted against ratification in a national referendum (see II.2.i). Three months later the French public gave only a 'petit oui'—a wafer-thin majority in favour of the treaty (see II.1.i). In November the British government just scraped through in a parliamentary vote on the intention to proceed to ratification (see I.5).

The Danish vote precipitated a major crisis which worsened as the British took over the Community presidency from Portugal for six months beginning on 1 July. Political uncertainty and economic slowdown were building up to a major currency crisis which threatened the future of the European Monetary System (EMS). The EC's impotence in former Yugoslavia further soured public opinion.

There was accordingly much relief among governments when the December European Council in Edinburgh reached agreement on a range of issues, including a formula to suit the Danes, a seven-year budget package, a commitment to begin accession talks with Sweden, Finland and Austria and plans for economic stimulus (see XIX.3:

DOCUMENTS). Expectations had been much reduced in the 12 months since Maastricht, but there was a feeling that one of the Community's most testing periods had been successfully weathered.

RATIFYING MAASTRICHT. Ratification by all 12 EC member countries was necessary before the Maastricht treaty could come into effect. The target date was 1 January 1993, to coincide with the inauguration of the single European market. Denmark and Ireland had always intended to hold a referendum before formal ratification. The vote in the Danish parliament was convincingly in favour (130 votes to 25), so the shock was all the greater when, on 2 June, the Danish people voted by a narrow majority to reject the treaty. Two days later EC foreign ministers, at a NATO meeting in Oslo, announced that they intended to press ahead with ratification by the end of the year 'on the basis of the existing text', while stressing that 'the door for Denmark's participation in the union remains open'. President Mitterrand then announced that France would also hold a referendum.

The Danish vote unleashed political forces in several member states which had until then been subdued. In Britain those hostile to the Maastricht process were given new heart and there was increasing support for a referendum. German public opinion polls also showed pressure for a popular vote as the implications of economic and monetary union (EMU) for the Deutschmark sunk in. A positive Irish vote on 18 June was some consolation (see II.1.vii), but on 20 September the French voted for ratification by the smallest of margins. Thereafter, it became clear that the treaty would not come into effect by the end of the year.

The British presidency convened an extraordinary summit in Birmingham in October. The meeting reaffirmed government commitment to the Maastricht treaty, asserting: 'We need to make progress towards European union if the Community is to remain an anchor of stability in a rapidly changing continent, building on its success over the last quarter of a century.' Nevertheless, most member states did ratify by 31 December. There was understanding for the Danish government's aim of holding a new referendum in the summer of 1993, but consternation among other EC governments when it became known that UK Prime Minister John Major had promised some Conservative MPs that final ratification at Westminster would have to await the outcome of the Danish vote. This was the price he had to pay for the 319:316 government victory in the House of Commons on 4 November on a 'paving motion' towards ratification. This was the first time since British accession that a substantive European vote had been carried in the House of Commons without bipartisan support.

The European Council in Edinburgh on 11–12 December agreed a text to calm Danish fears without requiring treaty modifications (see

XIX.3). Denmark would be able to opt out of the single currency and the defence provisions of Maastricht, with the right to change its mind later, so taking early advantage of provisions already in the treaty. There was also an affirmation that European citizenship would in no way change nationality law. Most Danish political parties welcomed the package as a reasonable basis on which to conduct a new referendum. It highlighted the trend towards an *à la carte* Community, where member states would choose which policy initiatives to accept.

It was clear that in many countries the Community was unpopular. This gave new force to 'subsidiarity', the concept of devolving power to the most appropriate level, which was already a key element in the Maastricht text. For Germany this meant giving substantial new powers to the Bundestag and the German *Länder* for overseeing new Community legislation and deciding on the final move to EMU. For many in Britain it implied the repeal of much existing EC legislation and a reduction in the power of the Commission. The French government underlined the need to bring the Community closer to the people, in which vein the Birmingham summit declared that 'as a Community of democracies we can only move forward with the support of our citizens'.

This all reinforced trends which were already evident: strengthening the Council of Ministers at the expense of the Commission and giving national parliaments a bigger role. The European parliament was no longer seen as the route to greater democracy. Commission president Jacques Delors, addressing the parliament on its 40th anniversary, spoke of the end of the 'sweet tyranny' of the Community institutions, which could take decisions in the face of popular indifference, often with the complicity of governments.

The Edinburgh summit spelt out the principles of subsidiarity (see XIX.3). National decisions should be the rule and Brussels action the exception, said the communique. While the EC Commission would retain its sole right to propose legislation, it would have to demonstrate that action at EC level was strictly necessary. A formula for applying subsidiarity would be worked out between all the EC institutions. The workings of the Council of Ministers would become more open.

CURRENCY CRISIS. The draft Maastricht treaty set the timetable for EMU and laid down strict economic criteria to be met by member states before they could embark on the third phase. These provisions had an immediate effect. Inflation, public borrowing, exchange rate and interest rate targets all provided discipline for member states as they tried to reform their economies. The draft treaty reassured markets that governments really were committed to tough policies. The Danes, Belgians and Italians all introduced new taxation proposals in the first part of the year designed to achieve the EMU targets. The EMS exchange rate mechanism (ERM) limited currency fluctuations. German interest rates were high, but hopes of future convergence allowed some relaxation in rates for the weaker EC economies. In April the Portuguese joined the ERM, leaving only the Greek drachma outside. In May some French bankers were calling for a revaluation of the franc against the Deutschmark to reflect good French economic performance.

It was in June that things began to go wrong (see also XVIII). The vote in Denmark cast doubt on the future of the Maastricht treaty and EMU; President Mitterrand's decision to call a referendum in France compounded the uncertainty. The German Bundesbank put up interest rates just as the Americans were reducing theirs. As the surge in the German money supply showed no sign of abating, it became clear that the Bundesbank would not relax its policy. The Community was therefore at the mercy of an autonomous German central bank battling against a domestic inflation crisis brought about by unification. The high level of interest rates was damaging for all EMS members, but particularly serious for the British, slipping into renewed recession and already suffering high levels of personal and corporate debt, and the Italians, who were obliged to fund a massive level of government debt.

The pressures were contained until August, when currency values became more volatile. As the interest rate differential between the US dollar and the Deutschmark widened, reaching nearly 7 per cent, so the scramble to buy the German currency and to sell the weaker ones began in earnest. A statement by the EC monetary committee on 28 August ruled out an EMS realignment. On 3 September the British government raised a 10,000 million ecu loan to defend the pound.* Next day the Italians announced that they would resort to an unlimited EMS borrowing facility to support the lira. Finance ministers met in Bath on 4–5 September, together with central bank governors. Discarding routine business, they spent all their energies on the currency crisis. The UK Chancellor of the Exchequer, Norman Lamont, tried to persuade the Bundesbank president, Helmut Schlesinger, to reduce interest rates, but like all his fellow ministers refused to countenance any realignment. Herr Schlesinger's only concession was to say that German rates would not go higher.

On 13 September the pressure became too great. In return for a 0.25 per cent reduction in German interest rates, the Italians devalued by 7 per cent. To French Prime Minister Pierre Bérégovoy, just seven days before the French referendum, this was 'the embodiment of the spirit of Maastricht'. However, the markets then turned even more fiercely on sterling. By 16 September its ERM parity could no longer be sustained, despite heavy intervention and a short-lived hike in UK

---

*At end-1992 1 ecu=£0.79 or US$1.21.

interest rates to 15 per cent. Both the British and the Italian currencies were forced to float free (and the Spanish peseta was devalued by 5 per cent), in what became known in Britain as 'Black Wednesday'. The British government blamed the Bundesbank, first for a newspaper interview given by Herr Schlesinger which implied that the pound was overvalued, and then for not committing sufficient reserves to support sterling. The Bundesbank issued a rebuttal, saying that it had spent DM$44,000 million on defending the pound and the lira, most of it on the pound. The British government spoke of the need to repair what Mr Major described as the 'fault-lines' of the EMS.

There was much talk of the imminent collapse of the EMS. On 22 November the peseta (again) and the Portuguese escudo were devalued by 6 per cent. The acid test remained the French franc value. Finance Minister Michel Sapin referred to a battle plan drawn up by Germany and France and said that currency speculation was deliberately aimed against the EMS. As it turned out, the franc was successfully defended for the rest of the year.

For some the September crisis proved that a system of pegged exchange rates could never work. For others, including M. Delors, it was proof of the need to move faster to full monetary union.

EC BUDGET. The EC's current five-year budget programme expired at the end of 1992. Agreeing budget plans for the following years promised bitter arguments in an already difficult period for the Community. Economic slowdown and the cost of German unification made the net contributor countries less willing to agree higher spending. Yet the Maastricht treaty envisaged a major increase in resources for the poorer member states, among which Spain in particular would settle for nothing less. Britain was determined to preserve the formula for limiting its contributions which had operated for the five previous years.

The EC Commission unveiled the so-called Delors II proposals in February. They envisaged a 5 per cent annual increase in the budget over the five years to 1997; a doubling of funds going to the four poorest countries (Greece, Ireland, Spain and Portugal); new resources to help European industry; and a special budget allocation for helping countries outside the EC. The Commission proposed that the budget ceiling should rise from 1.2 per cent of GNP in 1993 to 1.37 per cent in 1997. Calculation of the British contribution would be left until later. Presenting these proposals to the European parliament, M. Delors spoke of the three central aims behind the programme: to create the conditions for economic convergence which would allow member countries to move to full economic and monetary union; to make member countries' economies and business more competitive; and to give the Community the resources needed to conduct a common foreign policy.

At the European Council in Lisbon in June EC leaders agreed that there should be 'an adequate increase' in the total amount of EC funding and reaffirmed their commitment to a fund to help the poorer member countries (the Cohesion Fund). However, Britain and Germany won support for postponing any detailed budget decisions until the end-year summit. It was therefore up to the British to deliver a budget package in Edinburgh, at the end of an EC presidency which was beset by crisis. A budget settlement was crucial to the success of the Edinburgh meeting as a whole and was achieved as part of a complex overall package. The basis of the compromise was a seven-year plan, retaining the 1.2 per cent GNP ceiling for total EC expenditure for three years (1.14 per cent in 1993), but allowing it to rise to 1.27 per cent over the subsequent four years to 1999. On the basis of these figures, the summit set out the financial perspectives for the main policy areas, including a Cohesion Fund beginning at 1,500 million ecu rising to 2,600 million by 1999. The total spending ceiling would rise from 66,800 million ecu in 1992 to 84,000 million in 1999. The British contribution formula was untouched.

Once agreement had been reached in Edinburgh, the European parliament approved the 1993 budget and the presidency began to seek consensus between Council, parliament and Commission on the seven-year financial perspectives.

SINGLE MARKET. By the end of 1992 almost all the EC measures needed to achieve a genuine European single market without internal barriers had been agreed. This represented a remarkable legislative achievement. Since the publication of the 1985 proposal some 500 pieces of legislation had been proposed by the Commission and adopted by the Council of Ministers. The most sensitive areas of policy, such as public procurement and financial services, were covered. It was estimated that 60,000 customs officials might lose their jobs as a result of the single market.

Tax harmonization proved a most difficult issue. Governments had rejected the Commission's original idea of a Community VAT regime in favour of a transitional scheme, running until 1997, under which goods traded between member countries would be zero-rated in country of origin and taxed in the country of sale. In June they agreed on a 15 per cent 'minimum' VAT rate, although lower rates were permissible for certain goods and services. They also set minimum rates for excise duties which effectively confirmed duty levels currently exacted by member states.

Details were worked out for the application of VAT on internal trade in a Community where customs barriers would no longer exist. A data network was established between national tax authorities which would allow any trader to confirm the VAT details of customers in other member states and include these on returns made to the domestic authorities. The tardiness of national administrations in introducing the necessary administrative arrangements for applying the new system was a major worry for business in the closing months of the year.

The downside was that certain member countries were slow to enact EC single market legislation at national level. By end-1992 implementation ranged from 73 per cent in Italy to 96 per cent in Denmark. In areas such as banking much remained to be done in adapting national legislation, while major changes were still needed in the national public tendering rules to comply with single market requirements. Although the Commission believed it to be contrary to the principles of the single market, frontier checks on the movement of people were expected to continue, especially in the UK, Ireland and Denmark.

AGRICULTURE AND GATT. Major changes in the common agricultural policy (CAP) were agreed after intense negotiations between agriculture ministers in May. The most fundamental reform was a 29 per cent cut in cereal prices over three years, which would bring EC grain prices closer to world market levels and reduce costs for the consumers of grain. Grain producers were to be compensated for loss of income by direct payments, as long as they took at least 15 per cent of their land out of production (set-aside). Milk prices were to be cut by 5 per cent over two years and quotas to be reduced, while limits were to be imposed on the number of cattle and sheep which a farmer could keep on a given area and still receive subsidy. Beef guarantee prices would also fall.

The immediate aim of these measures was to contain budgetary costs, which would otherwise continue to soar. However, the agreement also had major implications for the GATT Uruguay Round negotiations, which had long been blocked by disagreements over agriculture. Fitful attempts were made during the year to bring the GATT talks back on track. An agreement between the Community and the United States on aircraft subsidies defused one difficult area, but the EC system for supporting domestic oilseeds production continued to cause major problems. M. Delors met President Bush in April to try to move the talks along, but a series of deadlines came and went. In June the Americans increased the pressure by threatening tariffs on $1,000 million of Community food exports in retaliation for the oilseeds regime. The EC Commission described this threat as 'totally without justification since it lacks any legal basis' within the GATT.

In further talks in Washington in November, Ray MacSharry, the EC commissioner responsible for agriculture, appeared to be getting close to a compromise agreement. The talks were then abruptly broken off and Mr MacSharry resigned, claiming informally that his position was being undermined by M. Delors. There followed intense lobbying by the rest of the Commission and by member states, as well as discussion in London between M. Delors and Prime Minister Major. The outcome was that Mr MacSharry withdrew his resignation and returned to Washington, where a GATT deal was quickly struck.

The French government was furious, however, and argued that the settlement went far beyond the CAP reform programme agreed in May. There were widespread farmers' demonstrations in France. The EC Commission disingenuously maintained that the deal did not go beyond the reforms. In fact, it tied down the May agreement in a new way, since it involved cuts in the level of subsidized grain exports (21 per cent by volume over six years and 36 per cent by value) and limits on the area planted to oilseeds in the Community. The May reforms had only concerned prices: their real effect on production could only be guessed at.

The provisional EC–US agreement was only a stage in the difficult quest for a GATT accord. Attempts were then made to speed up negotiations between the 108 GATT members on the whole range of Uruguay Round issues. However, by the end of the year talks seemed bogged down and the Community's top negotiator, Frans Andriessen, had announced that he would not stand for reappointment.

ENLARGEMENT. Prior to the Lisbon summit in June M. Delors promised a Commission report on enlargement which would be a 'political, intellectual and institutional shock' for governments. He believed that changes would be needed in the way the Community worked and, in particular, foresaw a new presidency system which would protect the interests of smaller member states against the dictatorship of the big countries. This message, interpreted as a Delors bid for power, was a factor in the Danish 'no' vote on 2 June. The report was never presented.

Austria and Sweden having applied for EC membership in 1991, Finland put in its application in March 1992, the Swiss in May and the Norwegians in November. All were party to the European Economic Area (EEA) agreement which dealt with many of the economic and industrial problems of accession by bringing the EFTA countries into the single European market (see AR 1991, pp. 403, 416–7). The EEA agreement was signed on 2 May in Oporto after European Court of Justice misgivings had been resolved (see XI.5.iv & XV.1.ii). The target date of implementation of the EEA was 1 January 1993, but a Swiss referendum on 6 December rejected Swiss membership (see II.2.vii). This decision necessitated some rebalancing of the agreement, particularly as regards the financial contributions foreseen under it.

The British were keen for enlargement negotiations to begin as quickly as possible, but could get no firm commitment until the Edinburgh summit, when it was agreed that talks should start at once with Sweden, Finland and Austria, and then include Norway. It was clear, however, that the negotiations could not be concluded until after ratification of the Maastricht treaty. Meanwhile, the Swiss were reconsidering their EC membership application in light of the EEA referendum result.

FORMER YUGOSLAVIA. A helicopter of the EC monitoring mission was shot down by the Yugoslav army in the first week of 1992, killing four Italian soldiers and a French officer (see III.1.vi). The Community said that 'it was 'appalled and dismayed' by the incident, but that it should not be allowed to jeopardize the peace process. On 15 January the EC presidency formally granted Community recognition to Slovenia and Croatia, in deference to German pressure and against the better judgment of those who wanted greater prior assurances of protection for minorities. Lord Carrington, the would-be EC peacemaker, continued his search for a negotiated settlement in former Yugoslavia.

A peace formula was agreed for Croatia, and the Community fully supported the sending of a UN peace-keeping force in parallel with the EC-sponsored peace conference. In March the Community agreed a declaration with the United States underlining the principles that no changes should be made in borders by force and that there should be strong protection of human and minority rights in all the republics. The EC and USA undertook to coordinate their approach to Serbia and Montenegro and laid particular emphasis on their support 'for the territorial integrity of the other republics and for the rights of minorities on their territory'.

In April the Community and its member states condemned 'the violence that is now spreading in Bosnia-Hercegovina at the hands of various armed elements with the support of regular forces'. On 4 June it imposed a trade embargo on Serbia and Montenegro and urged the UN Security Council to adopt similar measures. There was deep concern that the conflict might spread to Kosovo and Macedonia. EC recognition of Macedonia was held up by the determination of Greece that the name of Alexander the Great's birthplace should not be used by an independent state to the north of Greek Macedonia.

The Lisbon summit used tough language about the siege of Sarajevo, saying that it 'did not exclude' the use of force to ensure that humanitarian aid could be delivered. This, together with Security Council pressure, brought about a temporary ceasefire. President Mitterrand made a flying visit to the Bosnian city to underline the point (see also II.1.i).

The British presidency convened a further peace conference in London in the second half of August to try to stop the carve-up of Bosnia-Hercegovina into separate states. This made only limited progress, and Lord Carrington resigned as EC representative, to be replaced by Lord Owen. He worked with UN representative Cyrus Vance throughout the autumn in trying to find a settlement (see also XI.1). All this time the Community faced the dilemma of whether to intervene or not. In October it took a number of steps to help the people of former Yugoslavia to cope with the winter (providing 213 million ecu in aid) and tried to maintain pressure on the Serbs in the run-up to their elections. Sanctions assistance missions were sent to Bulgaria, Hungary and Romania for a trial period to help the local authorities to enforce the trade embargo.

EASTERN EUROPE AND THE CIS. The Community continued to develop its financing programmes for the East European countries (PHARE) and the ex-Soviet Union (TACIS), putting them on a longer-term basis. The 1992 budgets were respectively 1,000 million and 450 million ecu. In July the Commission proposed agreements with the CIS countries and Georgia which would offer them closer links with the Community. Each agreement would follow similar principles, although the content would be adapted to the needs of each partner. Commercial and economic agreements were signed with Albania, Estonia, Latvia and Lithuania in May, while an agreement with Bulgaria was initialled in December.

EC INSTITUTIONS. The Edinburgh summit took a definitive decision on the location of the main EC institutions, which had been provisional since the formation of the Community. Strasbourg was confirmed as the seat of the main European parliament sessions and Brussels as the home of the Council of Ministers and the Commission, subject to some meetings and offices remaining in Luxembourg. This agreement ended the long battle of some parliamentarians to move parliament business to Brussels. It was also agreed that the number of MEPs would be increased from 518 to 567 to allow representation for the new German states. This expansion would take effect from 1994.

4. OECD—NON-ALIGNED MOVEMENT

i. ORGANIZATION FOR ECONOMIC COOPERATION AND DEVELOPMENT (OECD)

FOR the OECD 1992 was, like 1991 (see AR 1991, pp. 404–5), overshadowed by the continuing global recession, as monitored in the principal OECD reports, and by the GATT deadlock which persisted late into the autumn and beyond.

The annual ministerial meeting, in Paris on 18–19 May, urged vigilance on members running large budget deficits, encouraged policies to promote medium-term growth and called on countries with external trade deficits to stimulate internal demand. Combating unemployment—high on the agenda at the urging of France and the USA—was nevertheless not seen as justifying the relaxation of fiscal rigour. Ministers stressed instead the contribution of training, wage flexibility and 'active' labour market policies to increase the incentive for the unemployed to seek jobs, and backed away from calls by the OECD trade union advisory committee for 'vigorous government action'. At this time the OECD was forecasting a decline in unemployment in 1993; in December 1992, however, the gloomier forecast was that unemployment in member countries would rise further, from 32,300,000 to 33,800,000 (8.3 per cent) by the end of 1993.

This latest projection, contained in the 52nd semi-annual OECD *Economic Outlook* published on 16 December, was based on the 'relatively sombre' expectation that aggregate OECD growth would pick up only slowly, from 1.5 per cent in 1992 to around 2 per cent in 1993 (2.4 in the USA, 2.3 in Japan, but only 1.2 in Europe), while inflation would fall from 3.5 to 3.2 per cent (2.3 in the USA, 1.7 in Japan, but 4.9 in Europe). The global picture was brightened, however, by developments outside the OECD area. The 'dynamic Asian economies' (DAEs)—South Korea, Taiwan, Hong Kong, Singapore, Thailand and Malaysia—currently averaged 7 per cent annual growth, and there were 'signs that output declines are coming to an end' in those central and east European countries 'most advanced in the reform process'.

As regards eventual widening of OECD membership, South Korea became the first of the DAEs to express its aspirations officially. In June a letter to OECD secretary-general Jean-Claude Paye described South Korean membership as an objective 'during the seventh five-year economic development plan' (1992–96). On 17–18 June Seoul hosted a workshop on trade policy developments as part of the OECD-DAE dialogue which had been under way since 1990. In July President Salinas of Mexico, visiting Paris, used the occasion to stress his interest in early OECD membership.

Representatives of Russia, Czechoslovakia, Poland and Hungary attended an OECD meeting for the first time, as observers, on 10–11 March in Paris, at a special conference on science policy and the problems of 'brain drain' to the West. As regards former Yugoslavia, the OECD council concluded on 27 November that the 1961 agreement granting Yugoslavia special status was extinct. The agreement, said the council, was 'not in force between the Organization and any of the states emerging from the former Socialist Federal Republic of Yugoslavia (SFRY)'.

Considerable emphasis was given to re-examining 'the basic rationales and orientations for aid' in the post-Cold War era. The OECD's development assistance committee (DAC)—which now, with the addition of Luxembourg, consisted of 21 countries plus the European Commission—held its annual high-level meeting in Paris on 30 November–1 December, together with representatives of the World Bank, the IMF and the UNDP. It agreed to classify Kazakhstan, Kirghizia, Tajikistan, Turkmenia and Uzbekistan as developing countries. It also decided to remove from this list, from 1996, the Bahamas, Brunei, Kuwait, Qatar, Singapore and the UAE. A DAC review of the definition of official development assistance (ODA) was to be completed in 1993.

Total ODA from DAC members in 1991, the committee's report showed, increased in real terms by 3.3 per cent on the previous year, reaching $57,000 million. Japan, the largest donor, accounted for much of this growth, but its ODA, at 0.32 per cent of GNP, was still just below the OECD average of 0.33 per cent. Finland joined Norway, Denmark, Sweden and the Netherlands above the 0.7 per cent level which had long been set as a target by the UN.

An OECD report on the external debt of developing countries, published on 14 September, welcomed some landmark agreements, notably between commercial banks and some Latin American debtor countries, but noted the particularly critical situation of sub-Saharan Africa, which was now almost totally dependent on official development finance for external capital. Overall debt of developing countries rose 2.5 per cent in 1991 to $1,478,000 million, with new net lending largely offset by debt reorganizations. Aggregate debt service payments by developing countries were down by $8,000 million to $151,000 million, continuing their gradual downward trend since 1988.

ii.   NON-ALIGNED MOVEMENT

DESPITE some Western media incomprehension that the Non-Aligned Movement (NAM) should still exist after the Cold War had ended, the tenth NAM summit conference took place in Jakarta (Indonesia) on 1–6 September. The attendance included 100 of the 108 member countries, eight observers and 21 guest countries. Brunei, Guatemala, Papua New Guinea, the Philippines and Uzbekistan became members at the summit, while Myanmar (Burma) resumed its membership, having left in 1979. The Cambodians were represented for the first time since their seat had been held vacant because of their civil war. Notable additions to the observers included Armenia, China and Croatia, while Germany, Bosnia-Hercegovina and Slovenia were among the guests.

It was a strange twist to the pattern of historical events that Yugoslavia, the country which had provided the leadership to create the NAM in 1961, generated such an intense level of conflict within the Movement in 1992. In May a dispute over whether to allow the Federal Republic of Yugoslavia (Serbia and Montenegro) to continue to hold the seat of the former Yugoslavia was so disruptive that a ministerial meeting of the NAM Coordinating Bureau in Bali failed to begin work on preparing for the summit. In general the African countries were more sympathetic to the new Yugoslavia, while the Malaysians and the Iranians led the attack of the Muslim countries incensed by events in Bosnia-Hercegovina. The Indonesians in September carefully steered a compromise through the summit. The Yugoslavs were allowed to keep their seat, pending a decision by the UN General Assembly, but they refrained from taking the traditional role of the outgoing chairman at the opening of the summit. The Jakarta final document 'strongly condemned the obnoxious policy of ethnic cleansing by Serbs' but did not explicitly blame the Belgrade regime. In positive terms, the summit affirmed the territorial integrity of Bosnia-Hercegovina, called for a wider deployment of UN forces, endorsed the work of the London peace conference and appealed for relief assistance to Sarajevo.

For a grouping founded on the belief of its members in sovereignty and independence, the summit showed a remarkable concern for the 'inter-dependence, integration and globalization of the world'. It was strongly argued that the new world order, recently proclaimed by President Bush, was so far 'little more than a new international realignment'. The new order should cover economic and social justice, as well as security, and be based on a strengthened United Nations rather than 'the unilateral use of force' and 'claims to exercise extra-territorial rights'. The latter comments were a thinly-veiled attack upon the United States, but implied rather than explicit. When it came to Somalia, gratitude was expressed to the United States and the European Community for their humanitarian assistance. Moreover, concern with famine, violence, death and destruction was seen as a global responsibility to the ordinary people of Somalia, without reference to their political leaders. Tensions and inconsistencies, between the commitment to a global community and the assertion of independence, appeared most evident in the response to regional conflicts, human rights and the environment. However, in all fields the Movement's change of style and change of priorities included much greater internationalism than had been the case in the 1970s and the 1980s.

The summit gave high priority to reform of the United Nations. The participants wanted to reduce the dominance of the five permanent members of the Security Council, to review their veto power and to expand the elected membership. Second, they sought to strengthen the General Assembly, arguing that it should become the central coordinating organ for the UN, with an enhanced status. Third, they advocated greater political independence and administrative support for the UN Secretary-General, as well as a more balanced secretariat in geographical and gender terms. Finally, they wished to increase the financial independence of the UN, by reducing the level of voluntary funding and the proportion of contributions coming from the major countries. Few specific proposals were made as to how these aims might be achieved, but a working group was established to pursue these themes in New York after the summit. The Indonesians were left with responsibility for deciding the composition of this group and convening its meetings.

Economic issues were again very high on the Movement's agenda. There was optimism over the potential benefits of the GATT Uruguay Round, including liberalization of agriculture and an end to Western protectionism against developing country exports. The commitment to international commodity agreements was strongly reaffirmed, including a special plea for the re-establishment of an agreement on coffee with economic provisions. The position on financial assistance was somewhat incoherent. On the one hand, the official development assistance (ODA) target of 0.7 per cent of developed countries' GNP was reasserted (see XI.4.i). On the other, the significance of ODA was belittled in the summit's assertion that Western restrictions, 'particularly in trade relations', caused annual losses for the developing world 'equivalent to ten times the amount of ODA accorded parsimoniously to them'. One of the main mechanisms suggested to reduce the debt burden and to provide liquidity for trade was a substantial allocation of IMF special drawing rights for developing countries, with the distribution of the SDRs being linked to development needs.

The influence of the Rio Earth Summit (see XIV.3 & XIX.1) was apparent in a section of the final document covering the global environment, referring vigorously to the need 'to save planet Earth from self-destruction'. The concept of sustainable development was endorsed, it being seen as 'imperative that environmental and developmental concerns be fully integrated'. However, these positions were totally negated by the following paragraphs attacking environmental considerations as leading to interference in the internal affairs of developing countries, as a new form of aid conditionality and as barriers to trade. The section on the North-South dialogue contained no positive mention of environmental issues.

The Jakarta summit endorsed the recommendations of the ministerial committee on methodology which had been working under Cypriot leadership since 1988 to review the cumbersome and ineffective institutional machinery of the Movement. Since the Coordinating Bureau had become too large to operate as an executive committee, a much smaller 11-member committee was designated to assist the NAM chairman in his political role. Alternatively, the chairman could choose to operate in a troika of the previous, the current and the next holders of the chair. The minority opposition, which for two decades had blocked the creation of a secretariat, was still able to prevent explicit endorsement of such a body. However, it was agreed that there must be a 'back-up system' consisting of a small committee of officials in New York and ad hoc groups to work on specific topics. The work of 'coordinating countries' (which had been very active in the 1970s on economic topics) was to be reactivated and steps taken to ensure regular consultations between the leadership of the Group of 77 and of the Non-Aligned.

5. OTHER EUROPEAN ORGANIZATIONS

i. CONFERENCE ON SECURITY AND COOPERATION IN EUROPE (CSCE)

AT the beginning of 1992 the CSCE was struggling hard to remain relevant to a Europe increasingly racked by armed conflicts and nationalist excess. With the end of the Cold War, the CSCE had been relaunched in November 1990 as the institutional forum for pan-European cooperation in a continent which was expected to enjoy a 'new era of democracy, peace, and unity' (see AR 1990, pp. 438, 569–76). However, this euphoric mood quickly evaporated in 1991 and 1992 as a series of bitter conflicts broke out amidst the ruins of communism. The newly-institutionalized CSCE found itself confronted by awesome problems which its embryonic structures were ill-equipped to manage, let alone resolve. For the CSCE, therefore, 1992 was a year characterized above all by the search for structures and processes which would allow it to play a more effective role in conflict prevention and crisis management.

Some progress in this area was made at the second meeting of the CSCE council of foreign ministers (held in Prague on 30–31 January), which modified the process of unanimous decision-making by endorsing the principle of 'consensus minus one' for most decisions. Under another decision, the Office of Free Elections, based in Warsaw, was renamed the Office of Democratic Institutions and Human Rights (ODIHR) and given a central role in the sphere of civil liberties, constitutional government and the rule of law. With the Russian Federation having taken the USSR seat in the CSCE, membership was increased in Prague from 38 states (the original 34 Final Act signatories plus Albania, Estonia, Latvia and Lithuania) to 48 by the admission of the other 10 CIS republics. Later in the year Georgia (not a CIS member), Croatia, Slovenia and Bosnia-Hercegovina also became full CSCE members, while federal Yugoslavia (i.e. Serbia/Montenegro) was suspended (see below). At year's end the admission of the Czech and Slovak republics (in place of disappearing Czechoslovakia) restored effective CSCE membership to 52 states.

The third CSCE foreign ministers' council, held in Helsinki on 24–26 March, was notable for the signature of an 'open skies' treaty facilitating reconnaissance flights over each other's territories. Heralded as the first arms control agreement of the post-Cold War era, the treaty would in particular enable countries without satellite capability to obtain information on military movements in other CSCE members. Prior to the Helsinki session, on 4 March, the CSCE states had agreed a wide range of other confidence-building measures, including exchange of military data and restrictions on the size and frequency of military activities (see also XII.2).

The March session initiated the fourth CSCE follow-up meeting (in Helsinki), which lasted until 8 July and proved to be the key event for the CSCE in 1992. The process concluded with the adoption of a major reformulation of aims and structures entitled *The Challenges of Change*. This document was then ratified by the third summit of CSCE heads of state and government held in the Finnish capital on 9–10 July. Arguing that the CSCE's task was now 'managing change', the Helsinki document stated that summit meetings were 'to set priorities and provide orientation at the highest level' and that review conferences were to be 'operational and of short duration'. The council of foreign ministers was confirmed as the 'central decision-making and governing body of the CSCE', whilst the committee of senior officials (CSO) was to be responsible between meetings of the council for 'overview, management and coordination' of CSCE activities. Indeed, the CSO now emerged as a key body within the CSCE, particularly in the areas of conflict prevention, crisis management and dispute settlement. At the same time, a 'troika' arrangement was confirmed whereby the current chairman-in-office would be assisted in carrying out 'entrusted tasks' by the immediate past and prospective chairmen.

Of particular importance was the summit's decision to create the post of high commissioner on national minorities, in recognition that problems of national minorities and their collective rights constituted a major threat to the security of Europe. The role of the high commissioner was to provide 'early warning' and, as appropriate, 'early action' in regard to 'tensions involving national minority issues that have the potential to develop into a conflict within the CSCE area'. It was subsequently announced that Max van der Stoel, a former Dutch foreign minister, had been appointed to the post.

Another key initiative of the Helsinki meeting was the decision to provide the CSCE with the capability to undertake peace-keeping operations, which meant that for the first time the CSCE would acquire operational functions. CSCE peace-keeping operations were to conform to UN principles and resolutions, and no operation would be undertaken without an effective ceasefire, written agreement between the CSCE and the parties concerned, and guarantees of safety for CSCE personnel. Such operations would require unanimous approval by the council or CSO and would be supervised by the CSO. It was also stated that CSCE peace-keeping operations could draw upon the experience and resources of organizations like the EC, NATO, the WEU and the CIS and could, if appropriate, be placed under UN authority.

Finally, the Helsinki session decided to establish a Forum for Security Cooperation, with an ambitious 'programme for immediate action'. This Forum, which met for the first time on 22 September in Vienna, was allocated three priority tasks: negotiating new disarmament and confidence-building measures; harmonizing existing obligations; and formulating 'codes of conduct' on civil-military relations.

Apart from the Helsinki summit, there were other significant CSCE meetings in 1992. The inaugural meeting of the CSCE Parliamentary Assembly took place in Budapest on 3–5 July, while on 12–23 October an important meeting on the peaceful settlement of disputes took place in Geneva. The latter created two new mechanisms (in addition to the Valletta mechanism for the peaceful settlement of disputes agreed in January 1991—see AR 1991, pp. 410–11), namely (i) 'directed concili-ation', by which the CSO could rule on disputes without the consent of the disputing parties; and (ii) a 'court of conciliation' based on a legally-binding international convention. On 14–15 December the CSCE council, meeting in Stockholm, endorsed the results of the Geneva meeting and agreed to establish the post of secretary-general, responsible for following-up the implementation of CSO decisions.

During the year the CSCE was particularly involved in four major conflicts. The first was Yugoslavia, where the CSCE, although it took a back seat to the EC and UN, did provide a valuable pan-European frame-work for discussing the civil war (see III.1.vi & XI.1). It also deployed monitoring teams in Yugoslavia and 'sanctions assistance teams' in countries bordering on Yugoslavia to ensure compliance with UN sanc-tions. Moreover, from September a CSCE mission was based in Belgrade with the task of reporting on the human rights situation in Kosovo, the Sanjak and Vojvodina, and promoting dialogue between the Serbian authorities and the ethnic communities. A mission was also sent to Macedonia (whose application for CSCE membership was deferred in view of Greek objections to its name—see also II.3.v; XI.3). The CSCE explicitly attributed responsibility for the Bosnia-Hercegovina conflict to Serbia/Montenegro, in which light rump Yugoslavia was excluded from participation in CSCE meetings from 8 July. In November the CSO published a report recommending the creation of an international tribunal to try war crimes alleged to have been committed in former Yugoslavia.

The burgeoning conflicts in the ex-USSR (see III.2.i) were also the subject of CSCE concern and diplomatic activity. On Nagorno-Karabakh, the 'Minsk conference' was established on 24 March with a view to providing a negotiating framework to help diffuse deep-seated hatreds and tensions. However, although some preparatory meetings were held in Rome, at year's end they had not yet reached a stage where convening the conference would be worthwhile. A six-person CSCE mission led by the chairman-in-office's personal representative arrived in Georgia on 6 December, its aim being to promote negotiations between the Georgian authorities and disaffected groups in Ossetia. Another CSCE good-offices mission was sent to Moldova.

The efforts of the CSCE at conflict management and crisis resolution bore no fruit in 1992. Nonetheless, the organization ended the year with new structures and mechanisms which could allow it to play a more constructive role in the future. For its proponents, CSCE remained a valuable and flexible forum for consultation and dialogue on a comprehensive range of issues affecting the area stretching from Vancouver to Vladivostok.

ii. EUROPEAN BANK FOR RECONSTRUCTION AND DEVELOPMENT (EBRD)

THE European Bank (as the EBRD had come to be known, in symmetry with the short title of the World Bank) held its first annual meeting in Budapest on 13–14 April with a certain panache. In reporting on the year then completed, its president, Jacques Attali, could point to the funding of 20 projects aggregating a commitment of 621 million ecu.* That was, of course, only a start. The Finance Minister of Czechoslovakia, Václav Klaus, observed that 'so far the role of the EBRD in our part of the world has been no more than marginal'.

Expansion on two fronts was on the agenda for the second operational year. One was formal, to take account of the division of states initially admitted as single countries. The three Baltic states had applied for membership in September 1991 immediately after achieving independence (see AR 1991, p. 413). The procedure of admission took time and their effective dates of membership were in February 1992 for Estonia and in March for Latvia and Lithuania. On 28 March the board of governors approved the division of the 6 per cent of capital stock previously held by the USSR and prepared the way for the several admissions of the post-Soviet states. The Russian Federation and Uzbekistan obtained a quick entry (each during April). Moldova followed in May, Belorussia, Kirghizia and Turkmenia in June,

---

*At end-1992 1 ecu=£0.79 or US$1.21.

Kazakhstan in July, Ukraine in August, Azerbaijan and Georgia in September and Armenia in November.

The board of directors recognized on 27 July that the former federal Yugoslavia no longer existed and that it had 'no sole successor to its membership of the bank'. Of the once-constituent republics, only Slovenia had achieved membership by the end of the year (on 23 December); on 15 December the board recommended admission of Croatia 'after consultations with the two chairmen of the peace conference'. The Bank would in due course provide separate membership for the Czech Republic and for Slovakia.

The second front was in substantive business, where policy was divided into two lines. One was to formulate and publish (after intensive consultation with the national authorities) a strategy document upon which the EBRD's operations in each country would be based. They followed a fairly standard pattern, covering perceived needs in financial sector reform and privatization, in agriculture and agrobusiness, in energy, in transport and in environmental protection. For external oversight of policy-making, the bank created a business advisory council (of 26 eminent industrialists and financiers from the private sector), an economic advisory council (ten prominent academics) and an environmental advisory council (of 15 members drawn from research, government and business).

The other line was the concrete response to Mr Klaus's comment: approval of 26 projects (against 12 in calendar year 1991). In the period from foundation to end-1992 899 million ecu of the bank's funds had been committed within a total project investment, i.e. including co-investors, of 3,109 million ecu. In addition, by the same date 260 technical cooperation schemes had been committed. Of the latter, 49 were regional rather than national, and much was expected of a payments arrangement supporting trade among the European states of the former Council for Mutual Economic Assistance (CMEA). The International Bank for Economic Cooperation (IBEC), previously a CMEA construct, continued its activities. Its council as usual met twice during the year. On 9 April report was made that a current-account turnover of close to 3,000 million ecu had been effected for commercial clients during 1991 (against 30 million ecu in 1990) and on 19-20 October that Hungary was withdrawing from membership. The latter meeting declared that an improvement in the bank's financial position was needed.

iii.   COUNCIL OF EUROPE

FOR the Council of Europe the year began and ended with a British presidency. Sir Geoffrey Finsberg, leader of the UK delegation to the Parliamentary Assembly, became its first British president for almost 30 years, after Anders Björck had resigned on being appointed Minister of Defence in the Swedish government. Sir Geoffrey held office for the remainder of Mr Björck's term, i.e. until the opening of the new Assembly session in May.

Whereas the UK delegation was customarily appointed by the Prime Minister to serve for the forthcoming Assembly session, Mr Major refused to name a new contingent until after the April general election. He then made the announcement by press release rather than the usual formal statement to parliament. Re-elected members were reappointed to the delegation, as was Sir Geoffrey, who was also reappointed leader, despite having stood down from the House of Commons. Labour members of the delegation, angered by the non-reappointment of any of their own retiring MPs (which left them under-represented in terms of party proportions), challenged the credentials in protest. Following an inquiry by the Assembly's committee on rules of procedure, the Assembly accepted that the UK government had acted within the provisions of the statute, but urged that steps be taken to bring the method of appointing the delegation more into line with its spirit by allowing parliament a greater role. The two houses proceeded to pass resolutions approving the existing method by which the UK delegation was appointed, and the credentials of the reconstituted delegation were subsequently approved by the Assembly on 30 June in Budapest—at its first-ever session outside Strasbourg. Lord Finsberg (as he had now become) continued as leader.

The geographical expansion of the Council of Europe continued to be a major preoccupation, Bulgaria being welcomed as a full member. The Russian Federation was accepted as the successor to the former Soviet Union's special guest status, although not without some dispute. The committee of ministers invited the Assembly to express its opinion on the accession of Russia, but for the first time also asked for specific issues to be taken into consideration. Belorussia and Ukraine successfully applied for special guest status, and other applications were in progress. The three Baltic states signed the European Cultural Convention, an important landmark on the road to membership. However, doubts were cast as to whether their electoral legislation met the requirements of the Council of Europe's democratic standards. The Council of Europe continued to provide practical help to the emerging democracies, particularly through the Demosthenes Programme, which was expanded to include training for civil servants, the judiciary and local government staff.

While holding the chairmanship-in-office, Turkey made a particular effort to raise the awareness of European governments concerning the problems facing the Transcaucasian republics. It organized a special ministerial conference on the subject in Istanbul, as well as a fact-finding tour for the secretary-general and the chairman. The secretary-general and the Swiss chairman also visited the USA in February, for talks with President Bush as part of an effort to improve relations with North America.

President Mitterrand visited Strasbourg in May to lay the foundation stone of the Council's new human rights building. In an address to the Assembly, the French President coupled praise with the suggestion that the organization was in need of structural reform. The judicial mechanism was the prime example among several of the Council's institutional mechanisms seizing up through overwork: it now took an average of five years to obtain a decision from the European Court of Human Rights. M. Mitterrand proposed that a summit of heads of government of member states should be called to examine the issues facing the organization. This was later scheduled to take place in Vienna in October 1993. President Mitterrand also urged greater cooperation and complementarity between European institutions, as all worked towards the construction of the 'new Europe'.

The Council of Europe spent much time and effort building up relations with the EC (see XI.3) and the CSCE (see XI.5.i) at governmental, institutional and parliamentary level. Lord Owen, co-chairman of the peace conference on Yugoslavia, urged the Assembly to seek a means by which those countries which were not yet members could afford themselves the judicial protection of the mechanisms attached to the European Convention on Human Rights. The United Kingdom took up the chairmanship-in-office in its rotational turn on 5 November.

iv.   EUROPEAN FREE TRADE ASSOCIATION (EFTA)

THE year held some promise of being one of fulfilment for EFTA, in its current dual role in the European integration process. First, the European Economic Area (EEA) was due to become a reality at the end of the year, as the world's largest free trade area (see AR 1991, p. 416), embracing the seven EFTA member countries and the 12 of the European Community (EC). Secondly, there was the opening to the east, developing relations with central and eastern Europe and creating a new set of free trade agreements.

Paradoxically, had 1992 seen confident progress on 'building Europe', then even the fullest achievement of EFTA objectives would have seemed a modest and secondary element in that process. The central Europeans already looked beyond EFTA to their links with the EC. Moreover, for EFTA's own larger members the EEA embrace seemed no more than a prelude to a full marriage with the EC, for which Austria, Sweden, Switzerland, Norway and Finland had all applied.

In the event, it was not achievements but unfinished business which stood out at the end of 1992. The 20–21 May ministerial meeting in Reykjavik marked the high point under Iceland's six-month chairmanship (which passed to Norway on 1 July). The EEA agreement had just been signed, albeit belatedly, in Oporto on 2 May after a formula had been found to handle disputes without affronting the insistence of the (EC) European Court of Justice on its supreme right to interpret EC law (see also XV.i.ii). Ratification procedures stretched through late autumn. By November the EFTA country parliaments had delivered the large majorities their governments sought, with the exception of Iceland (where ratification would come in January 1993). However, the requirement of referenda, in Switzerland (on 6 December) and Liechtenstein (13 December), meant that the timetable became too tight for the EEA to take effect on 1 January 1993 as planned.

Despite the 'no' vote in Switzerland (see II.2.vii) the other participants declared that they would press ahead with the EEA. Liechtenstein's electorate delivered a 'yes' vote (see II.2.viii), implying some severing of its umbilical connection with Swiss foreign policy. But Swiss non-participation left a hole in the EEA. Most immediately, it made a hole the size of 27 per cent of the 2,000 million ecu Cohesion Fund which EFTA members were to contribute for the advancement of poorer EC countries (see also XI.3). It remained to be resolved whether the other EFTA countries would pay more, or the poorer EC countries receive less. This, and the need for formal modification of the EEA treaty, put back its entry into force, the new target being mid-1993.

At the EFTA annual autumn meeting, held in Geneva on 10–11 December in the wake of the Swiss referendum, the Swiss stood down from the rotating chairmanship, which passed to Sweden. The meeting was able to record the signature of free trade agreements with Poland and Romania. EFTA's earlier free trade agreement with Czechoslovakia, signed on 20 March, would be applied on an interim basis from January 1993 in the separate Czech and Slovak republics. EFTA's intended free trade agreement with Hungary was not yet ready, although Hungary had been one of the first former communist countries to sign a joint declaration with EFTA back in June 1990. The three Baltic states and Bulgaria, which had all signed joint declarations with EFTA in 1991, were also some way from concluding free trade agreements. Meanwhile, EFTA signed two new joint declarations, with Slovenia on 20 May and with Albania on 10 December.

Extending for the first time beyond Europe itself (except insofar as it had signed a free trade agreement with Turkey in December 1991—see

AR 1991, p. 417), EFTA also concluded a free trade agreement with Israel. Initialled on July 16 after 13 months of negotiation (building on a 1975 association agreement), it was signed on 17 September in Geneva, to enter into force (subject to ratification) on 1 January 1993.

On the administrative side, EFTA switched to a January-December budgetary year, with an interim budget covering July-December 1992. It also began transferring some staff to Brussels to meet new bureaucratic requirements of the EEA.

v.   NORDIC AND BALTIC ORGANIZATIONS

THIS was a year of adapting existing Nordic institutions to member states' changing relations with a wider Europe, and creating new institutions of cooperation for the post-Cold War Baltic region.

The inter-parliamentary Nordic Council met in Helsinki on 3–6 March. It simultaneously celebrated its 40th anniversary and debated the radical changes in structure and priorities consequent on the establishment of the European Economic Area (EEA) and the prospect of Swedish, Finnish and perhaps Norwegian EC membership (see also XI.3 & IX.4.iv). The members had before them for consideration the council of ministers' proposed programme for cooperation after 1992; members' recommendations for action; and the interim report on the future of Nordic cooperation prepared by the Nordic Prime Ministers' personal representatives following their Mariehamn meeting in November 1991 (see AR 1991, pp. 418–9).

The cooperation programme foresaw a greater concentration on cultural, environmental, social and employment issues. Other traditionally important areas of cooperation would in future be dealt with primarily within the EEA institutions, including economic and financial policy, trade, energy and transport. The aim would be to strengthen the regional sense of identity, including the network of cooperation existing outside the institutions of official cooperation. The official level would require rationalization and adaptation. The interim report proposed a leading role in future cooperation for the Nordic Prime Ministers, a rotating presidency on the EC model, and more emphasis on cooperation in foreign and security policy. The institutions of Nordic cooperation should be adapted to those of wider European cooperation.

The Nordic Council adopted 31 recommendations for action by the council of ministers. They included adopting a new social security convention and a fisheries programme for 1993–96; extending the scope of the working environment convention; and strengthening the Nordic industrial and development funds. It also recommended assisting the three newly-independent Baltic states with investment, legislative expertise and medical cooperation.

At Bornholm, on 17 August, the Prime Ministers approved the final report of their personal representatives. This followed the interim version in proposing a concentration on strengthening the Nordic cultural community and home market; cooperation within wider European institutions; a more prominent role for the prime ministers; and rationalizing the network of secretariats and committees. It also proposed that the Nordic Council itself should meet in full session twice a year.

On 25–26 January the Baltic Assembly, grouping parliamentarians from Estonia, Latvia and Lithuania, held its inaugural session in Riga. Its main purpose was described by Latvia's President as establishing democratic principles for the member states' development and decision-making processes. Unlike the Nordic Council, members represented national parliamentary committees; decisions were reached by consensus; and voting was along national lines. In May the Assembly concluded a formal agreement with the Nordic Council providing the basis for close cooperation between the two institutions.

The second Baltic Parliamentary Conference, involving representatives from all Baltic parliaments, was held in Oslo on 22–24 April. It called on the Baltic governments to produce a long-term plan for developing the Baltic region's transport and telecommunications infrastructure. It requested that government representatives should participate in the next conference and report steps taken to implement the conference's recommendations.

The parliamentarians in Oslo particularly welcomed the founding of the Council of the Baltic Sea States by foreign ministers meeting in Copenhagen on 5 March. The aim was to create the political and economic preconditions for a distinct Baltic region based on free-market principles and democratic institutions and closely linked to existing European organizations. Areas of cooperation would include the development of democratic institutions, regional infrastructure and communications, and environmental protection. The Council was intergovernmental and would meet annually.

6.   AFRICAN, ASIAN, PACIFIC AND AMERICAN
REGIONAL ORGANIZATIONS

i.   AFRICAN CONFERENCES AND ORGANIZATIONS

THE Organization of African Unity (OAU) continued to be on the defensive over its inadequate responses to the variety of crises shaking

the African continent, notably the collapse of Somalia into anarchy (see VI.1.ii) and the inability to resolve the civil war in Liberia
(see VI.2.v). The annual OAU summit was held from 29 June to 1 July
in Dakar, capital of Senegal, and passed resolutions on both subjects,
though in the case of Somalia the African leaders supported initiatives
taken by the United Nations and in Liberia backed the efforts of
the Economic Community of West African States (ECOWAS) to find
a solution. On Somalia there was a deafening silence over the de
facto secession of former British Somaliland (now the self-proclaimed
independent Somaliland republic), just as the OAU chose to ignore
the impending secession of Eritrea from Ethiopia (see VI.1.i). These
developments ran right against the grain of the OAU rule on the
inviolability of the frontiers which obtained on independence.

The problem of Liberia was somewhat more digestible for OAU
members, since the ECOWAS Monitoring Group (ECOMOG) at least
represented an African attempt to find a solution. Dr Amos Sawyer,
President of Liberia's interim government, told the Dakar summit that
he thought that an ECOMOG force which evolved from peace-keeping
into peace-enforcement could serve as a model for the OAU. The
most significant debate at the summit, indeed, was precisely on the
question of an African role in peace-keeping on the continent. The
secretary-general, Salim Ahmed Salim, put up a proposal for an embryo
African 'security council' which might eventually have a mandate to
mobilize peace-keeping forces. However, the idea of interventionism
alarmed some African states experiencing their own civil conflicts,
such as Sudan and Rwanda, and the secretary-general was sent away to
produce a complete report on the matter for the 1993 summit, to be held
in Cairo. Thus the other iron rule of the OAU, that of non-intervention
in the internal affairs of member states, remained intact, despite looking
increasingly threadbare.

President Ibrahim Babangida of Nigeria, handing over the chairmanship
of the OAU after a year's incumbency to President Abdou Diouf of
Senegal, made a heartfelt observation on the 'futility of mindless
violence in the resolution of political disputes and conflicts' compared with armed struggle for liberation where no other option was
available. President Diouf himself, in his acceptance speech, asserted
that self-confidence was the primary condition for Africa's success in
coping with its challenges. He also made a reference to an increasingly
important African theme (even if the OAU was wary of trying to establish
collective positions in it) when he said that 'the search for a model of
democracy suited to the values of African societies' was one of the
challenges facing Africa in a changed world situation.

Apart from the standard resolution on South Africa (broadly supporting
ANC positions in its protracted dialogue with the de Klerk government—see
VII.3), the summit produced a programme of action on AIDS. This was

the first time that the OAU had ever given serious consideration to this major scourge, which was having grave social and economic consequences across the continent. The OAU document, said to have been pushed through very much on the initiative of the Senegalese President, predicted that by the year 2000 some 20 million Africans would be HIV-positive, leading to a million deaths a year. The programme sought particularly to secure a commitment from each African government (some of which had buried their heads in the sand when confronted with the problem) to join in international efforts to combat and limit 'the twentieth-century plague'.

Other African conferences and institutions continued to struggle to find solutions to the continent's economic problems, notably through the recommended path of regional integration—so much supported on paper but so little implemented on the ground. The UN Economic Commission for Africa (ECA), which over the past 20 years had provided much new thinking about the continent's economic problems, experienced a change at the helm. The crusading executive secretary, Professor Adebayo Adedeji of Nigeria, had bowed out in 1991 (after 17 years in the post) and his stop-gap replacement, Issa Diallo of Guinea, had not made his mark. Accordingly, a new substantive replacement was found in the person of the former Algerian trade minister, Layachi Yaker, although it was reckoned that Professor Adedeji would be a hard act to follow. On leaving the ECA Professor Adedeji had set up a Nigeria-based think-tank, which organized its first international conference in 1992 on the topical subject of the 'marginalization of Africa'.

One regional grouping which seemed to be genuinely trying to put its house in order was ECOWAS. At its summit at the end of July (also held in Dakar), a report by 16 'wise men' under the former head of state of Nigeria, General Yakubu Gowon, was approved in principle. Assembled leaders also made provisions for a new revised ECOWAS treaty to be signed at an extraordinary summit in Abuja, Nigeria's recently-established federal capital. If this seemed to underline Nigeria's crucial role in the grouping, President Babangida nonetheless conspicuously declined to take back the chairmanship from President Diouf, even for six months, preferring to pass it to the Benin President, Nicéphore Soglo. The key elements in the new treaty were a stronger emphasis on the political side of the Community, including the setting up of a foreign ministers' council, the introduction of a 'binding' content to Community decisions and a less dilatory method of financing operations. The political emphasis was no doubt a by-product of the political cooperation in which the Community was engaged over Liberia (not without upsets). The summit produced a strong resolution calling for sanctions against the rebel movement of Charles Taylor unless he complied with the 1991 ECOWAS peace initiative (see AR 1991, p. 421), including disarmament of all factions, which was further endorsed at another ECOWAS-sponsored peace discussion in Geneva in April 1992. By the end of the year, in spite of a Taylor counter-offensive on Monrovia in October, ECOWAS sanctions were said to be biting, and were even being cautiously applied by Côte d'Ivoire, whose long border with Liberia had been the main base for rebel activity.

Among other groupings which showed signs of life in 1992 was the Organization for the Development of the Senegal River, which had been moribund since 1989 because of tension between Senegal and Mauritania. A summit was held in August at which the three members (Senegal, Mauritania and Mali) pledged to reactivate the organization, which had already built two dams on the river (contributing to the member countries' enormous foreign debt). The Southern African Development Coordination Conference (SADCC) changed its name to the Southern African Development Community (SADC), a response to the changed situation in the region, where the Community no longer had as its principal vocation economic survival without South Africa. The consolidation also seemed to be a riposte to those who were pressing for the grouping to be merged into the ECA-sponsored Preferential Trade Area (PTA) covering 18 countries of eastern, central and southern Africa, excluding South Africa. As the year ended, this bone of contention was becoming acute.

While Africa's relationship with the European Community (through the Lomé Convention) was in a quiescent period, the same could not be said of Africa and France. Through the year increased pressure was reportedly applied by the IMF and the World Bank for a change in the parity of the overvalued (CFA) franc used by most former French colonies in Africa. Denials that devaluation was contemplated, from both African and French leaders, occurred with increasing regularity, culminating in one issued by the Franco-African summit held in Libreville (Gabon) in October. Reforms to strengthen the African franc zone were mooted at the summit, but doubts persisted as to the viability of a parity which had remained unchanged, at 50 CFA francs to the French franc, since 1948.

ii. SOUTH ASIAN ASSOCIATION FOR REGIONAL COOPERATION (SAARC)

THIS was another year in which SAARC failed to hold a summit meeting at heads of state or government level, although SAARC's founding charter of 1985 specified annual summits. Tension between India and several other members over the destruction of a mosque in the Indian city of Ayodhya (see VIII.2.i & VIII.2.ii), and the ensuing communal strife throughout much of the northern sub-continent, led to the non-convening of the planned 1992 summit in Dhaka, capital of Bangladesh, and to its postponement until January 1993. Similar tensions had previously prevented a SAARC summit from being held in 1989 (see AR 1989, pp. 406–7) and had almost stopped the 1991 gathering (see AR 1991, pp. 421–2). SAARC did, however, convene meetings at senior official and ministerial levels and thus demonstrated that a still young regional association could continue with its rather unspectacular progress away from the limelight of high-level political encounters.

The Independent South Asian Commission on Poverty Alleviation completed its work in late November in readiness for the summit meetings originally scheduled for early December. The commissioners sounded a word of caution to their member-governments, warning that the poor would be hard hit by the initial impact of the structural adjustments demanded by the opening-up of their economies. The commission had been set up after the sixth SAARC summit, held in Colombo in December 1991. Its chairman was K. P. Bhattarai, a former prime minister of Nepal.

The commission outlined a broad strategy for the member-countries to adopt, claiming that much of the mass poverty of the SAARC nations could be alleviated within ten years. It proposed institutional arrangements to ensure that the poor could participate in development, estimating that the region had about 450 million poor people, or about 40 per cent of the total population. Briefing reporters as they completed their report, the commissioners said that the ailing economies in the region had no option other than to accept conditions imposed by the International Monetary Fund (IMF) and the World Bank. They warned, however, that structural adjustments would have an adverse effect on the poor, whose uplift would therefore need to be included in the national plans of governments.

Shivraj Patel, Speaker of India's Lok Sabha (lower house), whilst on a visit to Nepal in late November, told Indian journalists based in Kathmandu that India was prepared to help South Asian countries if they wished to emulate India's 'time-tested system of parliamentary democracy'. He added in qualification: 'We are not going to impose our ideas on anybody . . . There is no question of India giving a lead.' Mr Patel cautiously endorsed the idea of launching an Association of SAARC Speakers and Parliamentarians (ASSP).

iii. SOUTH-EAST ASIAN ORGANIZATIONS

DURING 1992 ASEAN took its first genuine steps towards regional free trade. The heads of government of the six member states gathered in Singapore in January for the organization's fourth summit, the first since 1987. The summit ended with the signing of a mutual tariff reduction agreement under the terms of which an ASEAN Free Trade Area (AFTA) would be in place by the beginning of 2008. AFTA would be implemented through an impressive two-track (one fast, one slow) common effective preferential tariff (CEPT) mechanism which aimed to reduce tariffs to 5 per cent or less within 15 years. The CEPT mechanism applied to manufactures, processed agricultural products and capital goods, but not to agricultural raw materials. It included an opt-out clause which allowed individual countries temporary exemptions. Analysts expected Indonesia and the Philippines—both of which had expressed some concern about their potential exposure to regional competition—to maintain the highest number of exemptions. ASEAN economic ministers, meeting in Manila in October, agreed to implement the CEPT mechanism on 1 January 1993.

A variety of other issues were discussed at the Singapore summit. The six agreed that ASEAN should intensify debate on security and political issues through the mechanism of post-ministerial conferences (PMCs) with the organization's 'dialogue partners'. The designation of China and India as 'dialogue partners' was approved in principle. Vietnam and Laos were invited to accede to ASEAN's 1976 Treaty of Amity and Cooperation (TAC) as a first step towards full membership (it being envisaged that Cambodia would also be invited to accede following elections and the formation of a new government). Vietnam and Laos formally acceded to the TAC at the 25th annual ASEAN foreign ministers' meeting held in Manila in July. The move effectively signalled an end to more than a decade of hostility between the Indo-Chinese states and their non-communist neighbours. For the first time China and Russia attended the meeting as observers.

A special declaration adopted at the Manila meeting urged all countries involved to settle the dispute over conflicting claims to the Spratly Islands in the South China Sea 'in a peaceful manner'. The Spratly islands were claimed by three ASEAN members—Brunei, Malaysia and the Philippines—and by China, Taiwan and Vietnam. The dispute had come to a head in early 1992 after China and Vietnam awarded contracts separately to Western companies to drill for oil in the disputed archipelago. A joint communique on closer economic cooperation between developed and developing countries expressed the customary 'dismay' over the failure to conclude the GATT Uruguay Round.

A meeting between ASEAN foreign ministers and their EC counterparts in Manila in October was largely dominated by the divisive issue of East Timor, the Portuguese colony forcibly annexed by Indonesia in 1976. Portugal had initially threatened to block the release of a joint communique unless specific reference was made to its former colony. In the event, the Portuguese accepted a compromise whereby both sides pledged their commitment to human rights and fundamental freedoms and 'agreed to continue their dialogue and cooperation on these issues'. The meeting ended with only general agreement on enhancing trade and investment between the two regions.

Ministers from all 15 member countries attending the fourth Asia-Pacific Economic Cooperation (APEC) conference in Bangkok in September made the first serious move towards formalizing the loose APEC forum by approving the establishment of a permanent secretariat in Singapore. It was envisaged that the secretariat would coordinate APEC activities, including research projects and work programmes. Asian countries attending the meeting expressed concern that the North American Free Trade Agreement (NAFTA) linking Canada, the USA and Mexico (see IV.1 & IV.2) might divert investment away from Asia. However, US and Canadian delegations at the conference apparently provided assurances that Asian interests would not be harmed.

The 48th session of the UN Economic and Social Commission for Asia and the Pacific (ESCAP) was held in China in April. A resolution was passed on social development strategy for the Asia-Pacific region in the year 2000 and beyond. In addition, the decade 1993–2002 was proclaimed as the Asian and Pacific decade of disabled persons. A number of new members were admitted, including North Korea, Azerbaijan, Kirghizia, Turkmenia, New Caledonia and French Polynesia. Associate membership was afforded to the Marshall Islands and the Federated States of Micronesia.

iv.   SOUTH PACIFIC REGIONAL COOPERATION

THE 23rd South Pacific Forum heads of government meeting was held in the Solomon Islands in July, where it heard environmental concerns amplified. Concern was expressed at the failure of the recently-concluded UN Rio Earth Summit (see XIV.3) to address population issues fully, while global warming and sea-level rise were stressed as continuing concerns for the South Pacific. The suspension of French nuclear weapons testing in the South Pacific was welcomed, although the Forum wrote to President Mitterrand urging that this moratorium should become a permanent ban. Also discussed were the rights of indigenous peoples, the special needs of smaller states and economic trade concerns. The communique asserted that 'sustainable development will only be realized in full if developing countries are able to benefit from responsible management of their resources through more open and fairer trading conditions'.

The Forum agreed to Taiwan's becoming a 'dialogue partner', but without full sovereign status. Those Forum members who spoke with Taiwan's representatives would do so in their own right, not as representing any joint position.

Immediately prior to the Forum meeting, a fisheries surveillance and law enforcement treaty was signed in Niue by 11 Forum member countries. This provided for cooperation in surveillance of fisheries and law enforcement measures designed to combat drug-trafficking or other organized criminal activities in the region.

Parties to the Nauru agreement (Nauru, Federated States of Micronesia, Papua New Guinea, Tuvalu, the Marshall Islands, the Solomons and Kiribati) signed a treaty for new fishery management arrangements in the central and western Pacific. This sought to control the allocation of licences to foreign fleets, aiming to reduce foreign fleet numbers by 20 per cent, protect tuna stocks and maximize returns through fees.

The October meeting of the South Pacific Commission in Fiji was marked by tension over the appointment of ex-President George Sokomanu of Vanuatu to the post of secretary-general. This decision was deemed unsatisfactory by some delegations on account of Mr Sokomanu's previous political record in Vanuatu (see AR 1988, p. 373; 1989, p. 369). The meeting also heard serious concerns voiced about the financial management of the organization. A US$22 million budget was approved, but made conditional upon implementation of improved financial management measures. Australia indicated that, unless such improvements were instituted, it would be forced to reconsider its extra-budgetary contribution of A$2 million.

v. LATIN AMERICAN ORGANIZATIONS

EFFORTS by the Organization of American States (OAS) to negotiate a return to democratic government in Haiti continued, following the rejection by military and congressional leaders in the country of a settlement agreed on 8 January (see IV.3.xii). At Nassau on 17–18 May OAS foreign ministers agreed to tighten trade sanctions, despite evidence that the existing restrictions had created widespread poverty in Haiti and that the elite had prospered by evading them. The new measures banned the transport of goods to Haiti by sea and air. Moreover, by ending the issue of travel visas, they had the effect of halting the exodus of Haitian refugees to the United States. On 28 May President Bush announced that the 'boat people' already intercepted by the US Coastguard would be returned to Haiti forthwith, without a hearing. In mid-August the US Coastguard reported that 27,440 of the 37,381 Haitians who had fled since the fall of President Aristide in September 1991 (see AR 1991, p. 79) had already been repatriated. The OAS secretary-general, João Baena Soares, again visited Haiti on 18–21 August, at the head of a 13-member OAS delegation. On 17 September a small permanent OAS mission arrived to evaluate progress, a move generally taken as confirmation that the OAS had accepted *de facto* the military-backed government of Marc Bazin.

The report of the OAS commission on the coup by President Fujimori of Peru on 5 April was non-committal (see also IV.3.viii). The President himself had defended his actions to the meeting, having already given pledges to hold a plebiscite and to allow local elections to go ahead as planned; though Venezuela had suspended diplomatic relations with Peru, and Colombia trade links, no other action had followed. Now, following warnings both from the US government and the OAS itself, President Fujimori agreed to an elected constituent assembly within five months and to allow OAS observers to oversee the elections. In return, the meeting urged a swift return to democracy in Peru and did not impose economic sanctions. On 18 June the new Peruvian Prime Minister, Oscar de la Puente Raygada, travelled to Washington to explain his government's plan to postpone the municipal elections due on 8 November to March 1993. The subsequent OAS decision, announced on 28 August, to send observers to the congressional elections was generally seen as acceptance of President Fujimori's position. However, the Peruvian government's intention to reintroduce the death penalty was foreshadowed when it gave notice on 15 October of its intention to withdraw from the 1978 American Convention on Human Rights.

Amendments presented on 28 August to the general conference of the Organization for the Prohibition of Nuclear Weapons in Latin America and the Caribbean (OPANAL) opened the way for the full compliance of Argentina, Brazil and Chile with the terms of the Treaty of Tlatelolco banning nuclear weapons in Latin America. Protocol No. 1 of the treaty was ratified by France.

The San José Group, consisting of the foreign ministers of Central America and Panama, met in Lisbon on 25–26 February, together with representatives of Colombia, Mexico and Venezuela and the European Community, and agreed to more extensive cooperation over the coming four years. In May the Presidents of Costa Rica, Honduras and Panama again visited Europe to protest against proposals to introduce a quota on 'dollar bananas'. This protest was reiterated at the six-nation regional summit held in Managua on 4–5 June, which also called on President George Bush to unblock much-needed aid to Nicaragua. On

20 August the economy ministers of Central America and Mexico (but not Panama), meeting in Managua, agreed to form a regional free trade area by 1996. The foreign ministers of the Rio Group countries (less Panama and Peru) met in Santiago de Chile on 28–29 May to sign four agreements with Ireland, Portugal, Spain and the United Kingdom on joint investment, training and technology transfer in the region.

The Presidents of Argentina, Brazil, Paraguay and Uruguay (with the President of Bolivia present as an observer) met on 26–27 June at Las Lenas, Argentina, to concert arrangements for the implementation of the South American Common Market (Mercosur) by 31 December 1994, as scheduled. On 26 August the government of Peru announced its temporary withdrawal from the Andean Pact because of its continuing failure to obtain multilateral aid. Given the earlier announcement that Bolivia had applied to join Mercosur, the outlook for the pact looked doubtful.

The second Ibero-American Summit was held in Madrid on 23–14 July, attended by the heads of state or heads of government of 17 Spanish and Portuguese-speaking countries. At the instance of President Jaime Paz Zamora of Bolivia, the delegates signed an agreement to create a Fund for the Development of the Indigenous Peoples of Latin America and the Caribbean. In a final declaration they confirmed their support for democracy, human rights and the peaceful settlement of disputes, as well as concern about foreign debt and the dangers of protectionism. They also agreed to ask the International Court of Justice to rule on the US Supreme Court judgment of 15 June which authorized the US government to kidnap foreign nationals abroad.

vi.   CARIBBEAN ORGANIZATIONS

FOR the 13 member states of the Caribbean Community (CARICOM), 1992 was an anxious year. Familiar issues dominated the agenda: for small countries, dependent on primary commodity exports and tourism, the industrialized world's recession bit deep.

The year ended with uncertainty about whether preferential access for the CARICOM countries' key export crop, bananas, could survive in a unified EC market. Post-colonial relationships and the Lomé Convention distorted the international market. France and Britain argued for quotas but settled in December for high tariffs to protect their present and former territories. German and Benelux importers of cheaper Latin American 'dollar bananas' objected to the concessionary regime, which was also open to challenge in the GATT talks.

The process of regional integration plodded on, the main sticking-point being still the CARICOM common external tariff (CET). The CET, designed to stimulate industry by taxing non-CARICOM imports, was opposed by Jamaica and others because of its possible inflationary effects and for fear of US retaliation in kind. Caribbean exporters felt threatened by the North American Free Trade Agreement (NAFTA), and Jamaica was already finding that some textile plants were relocating to Mexico. The Organization of Eastern Caribbean States (OECS) said that NAFTA created an 'uneven playing field', and the incoming CARICOM secretary-general, Edwin Carrington, complained of 'bullying'. The United States responded that all 24 countries benefiting from its Caribbean Basin Initiative (CBI) should abandon protectionism and embrace free competition. In October a special CARICOM meeting resolved to complete implementation of the CET by mid-1993, then phase out the protection over several years.

In July the annual CARICOM summit in Trinidad had received the report of the West Indies Commission (WIC), established in 1989. Its 225 recommendations included freedom of travel, CARICOM entry into NAFTA (while retaining CBI benefits) and monetary union within eight years. A recommendation for the creation of a Caribbean Commission with executive powers was overturned at the October meeting, in favour of the establishment of a bureau consisting of the Community's chairman along with his or her predecessor and successor. The Community postponed a decision on Cuba's application for observer status, although a joint commission on cooperation was established.

Meetings of the OECS in January and November achieved modest progress, with the harmonization of marine fees and agreement on joint diplomatic representation. In February a meeting of CARICOM and Central American foreign ministers in Honduras heard the host country call for a free trade zone of 48 million consumers. Other evidence of continuing commitment to the integration concept came in the fields of Windwards unification, transport and tourism.

The final report of the Windward Islands Regional Constituent Assembly advocated a unitary state for Dominica, Grenada, St Lucia and St Vincent, with an executive presidency and a bicameral legislature; the four governments undertook a public relations programme to promote the merger. Two Caribbean airlines, BWIA and LIAT, decided to coordinate schedules and marketing and consider a merger, but a joint shipping venture between Jamaica, Trinidad and Barbados was wound up. For the second year running, tourist arrivals were down in 1992, but the Caribbean Tourism Organization—expanded with the admission of Cuba—reported some success in a late marketing drive.

XII SECURITY, ARMS CONTROL AND DISARMAMENT

IN the fields of security and arms control, 1992 was a year in which the United States and Russia (as principal successor to the Soviet Union) continued the long process of dismantling the military structures of the Cold War. Yet it was also a year in which it seemed easier to reduce the old structure of strategic nuclear deterrence than to establish new mechanisms and processes for crisis prevention, crisis management, peace-keeping or peace-making. Nowhere was this more evident than in the Balkans, where the conflict in former Yugoslavia not only took on new dimensions but also proved resistant to external efforts at mediation and pacification (see III.1.vi). Considerable discussion about possible military intervention to impose peace in the Balkans was not accompanied by commensurate action. There was little enthusiasm for efforts to go beyond the deployment of limited peace-keeping forces and actually to become involved in peace-making. Towards the end of the year, however, the United States engaged in a form of humanitarian military intervention in Somalia (see VI.1.ii). Under UN auspices, US marines were deployed to end the disruption of relief food supplies by local warlords and armed gangs. However, even this limited military involvement sparked off a vigorous debate in the United States about the circumstances under which—and the interests for which—military force should be used.

The deployment of US troops in Somalia was a particularly striking event, highlighting as it did the United States' new status as the world's only military superpower. It came towards the end of a year in which efforts to enhance peace-making capabilities had been at the forefront of the agenda. Yet individual nations and international institutions had been wary of becoming deeply involved in internal military conflicts that might prove resistant to external efforts to restore peace and stability. In 1990 and 1991 a great deal had been made of the new European security architecture and its 'complementary overlapping institutions'. The expectation was that the Conference on Security and Cooperation in Europe (CSCE), the European Community (EC)/Western European Union (WEU) and the North Atlantic Treaty Organization (NATO) would provide a comprehensive approach to security in Europe and would be able to engage in effective crisis prevention and crisis management. However, in 1992 (as in much of 1991) these institutions simply engaged in collective 'buck-passing', as the conflict in Yugoslavia intensified and Serb forces engaged in 'ethnic cleansing' in Bosnia. At the same time the United Nations, which throughout the Cold War had been relegated to the periphery, emerged as the most important institution in relation to peace-keeping and peace-making. But even here the gap between the aspirations of UN Secretary-General Boutros-Ghali and the response of the member nations was pronounced. The record of peace-keeping and peace-making looked even more dismal when set against the major achievements of the year in the continued efforts to dismantle Cold War military structures.

START-II TREATY. The most important progress in arms control during 1992 was in the area of strategic forces, where the United States no longer had to deal with the Soviet Union but with the newly-independent Russian state. Set against a background of continued concern over both the ultimate fate of internal reform and the possibility of a nuclear arms bazaar in the former Soviet Union, drastic reductions in strategic forces became a high priority even for a Bush administration seeking re-election amid intractable domestic economic problems. The commitment of the new Russian government under Boris Yeltsin was equally strong.

The progress in arms control and disarmament in 1992 came after something of a hiatus, following the signature of the first Strategic Arms Reduction (START) Treaty in July 1991 (see AR 1991, pp. 436–7, 555–7). Progress between the United States and the Soviet Union towards agreement on post-START reductions was temporarily derailed by the August 1991 coup attempt in Moscow and the subsequent disintegration of the Soviet state. However, the emergence of Boris Yeltsin as the leader of an independent Russia opened the way for the resumption of serious negotiations, which led to far-reaching agreement on changes in the level and structure of strategic nuclear forces.

The year began on a positive note when the United States proposed to reduce its strategic forces to a total of 4,700 warheads, of which 3,600 would be accountable under START. Although this proposal went well beyond the reductions contemplated in the 1991 START treaty, it did not satisfy the new Russian government. Following the pattern of arms control and disarmament 'one-upmanship' established by Mikhail Gorbachev, the new Russian President proposed going down to a limit of 2,000–2,500 nuclear warheads, while also suggesting that the United States and Russia should work jointly towards a global defence shield. This was discussed in broad terms by Presidents Bush and Yeltsin during a meeting in February at Camp David, but the gap between the American and Russian positions remained large. With the US Defence Secretary, Dick Cheney, stressing the importance of providing sufficient forces to maintain deterrence, it was far from certain that further negotiated reductions would be possible. The end of the Cold War and the change in the political relationship, however, meant that both sides could afford to be much more relaxed about strategic force structures and the overall balance.

In March 1992 US Secretary of State Baker and Russian Foreign Minister Kozyrev, while in Brussels for a North Atlantic Cooperation Council meeting, agreed to try to bridge the gap between the American and Russian positions on both timing and the 'exact mix' of the reductions. The United States continued to focus on the heavy ex-Soviet land-based MIRVed missiles which had been seen as the major threat to strategic stability since the late 1970s, while Russia was reluctant to concede too much without receiving commensurate concessions by Washington. In effect, the ministers faced one of the most enduring problems in superpower arms control efforts: the need to balance and reconcile asymmetrical force structures. Moreover, although there was a willingness in both Moscow and Washington to abandon contentious notions of strategic parity, each side still had domestic constituencies to be satisfied.

In spite of the difficulties, the pace of the negotiations quickened in May and June, as the summit meeting planned for 15–18 June provided additional impetus. Mr Baker and Mr Kozyrev met in Washington on 8–9 June, when they agreed to cut to a level of 4,700 warheads each, even as the United States still pressed for the elimination of land-based MIRVs. The next Baker–Kozyrev meeting, in London on 12 June, made further progress, as the United States proposed to cut its SLBM force by 50 per cent in return for Russian agreement to the elimination of land-based MIRVs. This opened the way for a successful meeting and the release on 17 June of a joint understanding on reductions in strategic offensive arms.

Under this document, Presidents Bush and Yeltsin accepted a framework which was to be translated into a formal treaty as soon as possible. They agreed that, within the seven-year period following entry into force of the 1991 START treaty, they would implement further substantial reductions in strategic forces. By the end of this period each state could have somewhere between 3,800 and 4,250 warheads, consisting of 1,200 MIRVed warheads, 650 heavy ICBM warheads and 2,160 SLBM warheads. These limits, however, represented only an interim stage. It was also agreed that, by the year 2003 (or by 2000 if the United States contributed to the financing of the destruction of Russian forces), the warhead limits would be reduced to between 3,000 and 3,500; all MIRVed ICBMs would be eliminated; and SLBM warheads would be reduced to 1,750 or less. A major change in the rules was also instituted whereby the number of warheads counted for heavy bombers was to be the number of bombs they actually carried. Previous counting rules had been far less stringent.

The framework highlighted the trade-off between US SLBMs, which Washington would cut by half (whereas Moscow would not have to cut its SLBM force at all), and Russian land-based MIRVed missiles. The United States had also accepted the principle that it would consider helping to pay for the destruction of Soviet MIRVs. Other issues agreed on at the summit included the notion of an international protection centre as part of a 'global defence system' (GDS) in which the United States and Russia would share technology and consult extensively about deployment of strategic defences.

The framework agreement was warmly welcomed in at least some quarters in the United States. Senator Joseph Biden, for example, noted that President Bush had struck 'what may be the best deal in the history of arms control'. Part of the enthusiasm came from the expectation that the proposed reductions would save the United States considerable amounts of money—assessments ranging from $1,000 million to $40,000 million over the next 15 years depending on what was counted. In Russia, however, the reaction was rather more critical, as conservative voices argued that President Yeltsin had given in to American demands and agreed to abandon one of the main residual sources of Russian power and status, i.e. its land-based large MIRVed missiles. Even those Russians who were more sympathetic to the new framework not only put limits on the reduction process but also argued that there should be 'a rehabilitation of nuclear weapons' in Russia and an abandonment of Mr Gorbachev's ideas of a nuclear-free world.

In spite of this domestic opposition, rapid progress was made, with the result that before the end of July the United States submitted a draft of the proposed treaty to Moscow. The Russians raised over 20 substantive questions about the draft. Not surprisingly, as the issues moved from the level of political decision-making to that of the experts, the problems multiplied. Although steady progress continued to be made in resolving a series of complex and specialized issues, the presidential election in the United States added another obstacle. With the election over, the pace of negotiations increased, especially when President-elect Clinton publicly supported the Bush administration's efforts to complete the agreement.

Nevertheless, there were still important, if rather esoteric, issues to resolve. The Russian desire to convert the SS-18 silos for single-warhead missiles, rather than destroying them, had to be reconciled with the American desire to deal once and for all with the land-based MIRVed missile threat. In the end, the United States agreed that Russia would be allowed to keep 90 of the 154 SS-18 silos left to it after the first START treaty had been implemented. For their part, the Russians agreed to pour five metres of concrete on the bases of the silos to ensure that they could not easily be reconverted. The United States also agreed to allow Russia to convert 105 of its 170 six-warhead SS-19 missiles to single-warhead projectiles, with the proviso that these missiles and warheads would be subject to inspection. For their part, Russian inspectors would be given one-time access for a partial inspection of the B-2 Stealth bomber.

These issues were resolved partly because of presidential involvement. In early December President Bush initiated another round of personal negotiations with Mr Yeltsin, it being announced later that there would be a summit between the two leaders in January 1993. On 29 December agreement was announced on the terms of a second START treaty (see III.2.i & IV.1) Although this instrument would not be formally signed until early January 1993, it meant that the 1992 arms control and disarmament negotiations ended on a high note, as most of the elements established by the June framework were retained and formalized.

In many respects, the START-II agreement was a remarkable achievement. At the beginning of 1992 it had been hard to believe that Washington and Moscow would agree that by 2003 Russia would reduce its forces to 3,000 warheads and the United States to 3,500. Significant though the agreement was, however, there was little euphoria. First, there were continued question-marks about the future direction of Russian politics and the fate of the Yeltsin regime. Second, there was an even bigger question-mark about implementation. Each of the other three former Soviet republics with nuclear weapons—Belorussia, Kazakhstan and Ukraine—had to ratify START-I before START-II could come into force. The START-I treaty was approved by the US Senate on 1 October by 93 votes to 6 and by the Russian legislature on 4 November by a vote of 157 to 1 with 26 abstentions. However, both the US and the Russian governments reiterated that they were unwilling to implement fully START-I (let alone START-II) until it was clear that Belorussia, Kazakhstan and, most importantly, Ukraine would also dismantle their nuclear weapons. Indeed, much of the commentary on the impending START-II agreement suggested that it symbolized not only the triumph of traditional arms control but also its limits.

Even so, START-II provided the big arms control achievement of the year. Considerable progress was also made towards the signing of an international chemical weapons convention, while efforts to maintain limits on proliferation of nuclear weapons took on a new urgency in view of the doubts about both the physical security and the command and control mechanisms of the nuclear weapons possessed by the states of the former Soviet Union. Even these concerns could not overshadow the achievements of START. In other security areas, however, the accomplishments were less obvious than the limits, in that the dismantling of Cold War security structures was not matched by the creation of effective new international security mechanisms and procedures.

UNITED NATIONS: FROM PEACE-KEEPING TO PEACE-MAKING? There was a great deal of discussion in 1992 about strengthening UN capabilities for peace-keeping, peace-making and deterrence. These were prompted partly by the new opportunities that arose as a result of the end of the Cold War and partly by the new instabilities which became an increasingly salient aspect of the international scene. The new threats and the new opportunities were reflected in a major report entitled *An Agenda for Peace: Preventive Diplomacy, Peace-making and Peace-keeping* issued on 17 June by the UN Secretary-General, Boutros Boutros-Ghali (see also XI.1). It recommended that the Security Council should be provided with a permanent armed force which could operate under article 43 of the UN Charter for the enforcement of peace. Noting that 'the longstanding obstacles to the conclusion of such special agreements no longer exist', the Secretary-General emphasized the need to make the 'hard decisions demanded by this time of opportunity'. The report argued that a standing UN force would help to deter breaches of the peace, and advocated the activation of the UN's military staff committee as a step towards this. In addition, Dr Boutros-Ghali asked that governments provide the Security General with timely warning of problems to allow for better crisis prevention and crisis management efforts. He also recommended that the UN should consider deploying forces in tension areas, including inside the frontiers of states threatened by their neighbours. Recognizing the difficulties imposed by the mounting costs of existing UN peace-keeping operations (let alone the implementation of the more ambitious programme he had outlined), the Secretary-General proposed that contributions to peace-keeping should come out of national military budgets rather than foreign policy budgets. He also advocated the formation of regional risk reduction centres.

This ambitious plan to give the United Nations a major role in maintaining international peace and security, when juxtaposed with events in both Yugoslavia and Somalia, highlighted the continued gap between aspirations and achievements. Yet at the end of the year it was clear that progress had been made, especially in dealing with the situation in Somalia, where a new form of humanitarian intervention was being attempted.

The US intervention in Somalia (see also IV.1 & VI.1.ii) came at the end of a year in which humanitarian missions and small UN peace-keeping actions had proved wholly inadequate to deal with a situation in which even the semblance of government had disappeared. The deployment of US forces was a reflection of the failure of previous efforts to restore order and ensure food supplies. On 23 January the UN Security Council adopted a resolution imposing an arms embargo. This had little impact on the ground in Somalia, however, where the problems of refugees, famine and feuding became inextricably linked. Moreover, although the United Nations sponsored peace negotiations in New York on 14 February, the resultant ceasefire agreement had little impact. The situation worsened through the spring and summer, as food supplies provided by relief agencies were stolen. In August an agreement was signed which permitted 500 armed UN guards to be deployed in Mogadishu in order to prevent the disruption of efforts to distribute food. Nevertheless, by late August around 2,000 people were dying daily. A series of resolutions to deploy additional armed troops to Somalia had little effect. The peace-keeping forces remained relatively weak and were inhibited by restrictive rules of engagement, while the anarchy and violence intensfied.

The desperate plight of the refugees and the starving in Somalia was highlighted by increased television coverage in the United States, which not only brought the issue to public attention but placed it very squarely on the post-election political agenda. Ironically, as a 'lame-duck' President, George Bush was able to take decisive action. As the issue of humanitarian intervention became more insistent, the President, although sensitive to CIA assessments that the prospects for the restoration of stable government were bleak, decided to propose to the United Nations that US troops be sent to Somalia on a short-term basis to restore order and ensure the delivery of aid. This plan was presented to the United Nations on 25 November. By 1 December broad agreement had been reached that the operation should be under American command, albeit with close links to the United Nations, and two days later the UN Security Council authorized a new peace-keeping effort in Somalia (see XI.1). Against a background of intense debate about US objectives and the dangers of being sucked into a quagmire, the first detachments of a 28,000-strong US force arrived in Somalia on 9 December in what was termed 'Operation Restore Hope'. Although these forces also had restrictive rules of engagement, their presence seemed to have a significant impact in restoring order, at least in the short term. By the end of December it was having a positive effect on food distribution.

Although the US contingent in Somalia was the cornerstone of the operation, French and Italian forces were also involved. Moreover, on 17 December Chancellor Kohl announced that he wanted to send 1,500 German troops to Somalia in early 1993, subject to appropriate amendment of the German constitution (see II.1.ii). By then there was a clear recognition that the restoration of order would not necessarily solve the problems of what some observers described as the prototype of the 'failed nation state'. Nevertheless, the Bush administration's decision to intervene in Somalia provided at least some hope that the international community—with the United States still in a leading role—was willing to be more activist in dealing with local and regional security problems. There were others, however, who saw the US intervention in Somalia as allowing Washington to avoid confronting the even more intractable conflict in former Yugoslavia.

If military intervention in Somalia was undertaken very hesitantly, there was even greater reluctance to intervene in the conflict in

Bosnia-Hercegovina (see III.1.vi). This reluctance was shared by the United States and the Europeans, although there were times, especially in December, when the United States seemed to be pressing its allies to take a stronger line. Ultimately, the issue was one of political will: for Washington and its NATO allies the stakes were limited, while the prospects for successful military intervention were uncertain at best. Within this constrained framework, collective efforts to deal with the evolving crisis continued throughout the year. The efforts to negotiate a settlement, the imposition of sanctions and the deployment of peace-keeping forces had limited success. In the words of James Goodby, these efforts were 'too little too late'.

The first phase of the conflict in Yugoslavia was brought to an end with a ceasefire between Serbia and Croatia in January 1992. In February, after vigorous discussion, the UN Security Council agreed on a plan to send 14,000 troops to Croatia. This force, known as the UN Protection Force or UNPROFOR, began arriving in early April. Ironically, as one conflict subsided, an even more intractable one began. The declaration of independence by Bosnia-Hercegovina sparked off a conflict in which Serbian 'ethnic cleansing' of Muslim areas gave rise to growing public pressure in the West for military intervention. However, the European and US governments preferred a low-risk strategy of diplomatic pressure, economic sanctions and limited military involvement to ensure the flow of humanitarian aid.

The diplomatic isolation of Serbia/Montenegro (i.e. rump Yugoslavia) was followed by the imposition of sanctions on 30 May under UN Security Council resolution 757. On 10 July NATO and the WEU agreed to police UN-imposed sanctions by means of an air and sea operation in the Adriatic, although without authorizing forcible stopping of vessels suspected of breaking sanctions. The NATO naval force in question had been set up by the NATO military committee in April, the resultant fleet being based in Naples and consisting of Italian, Greek and Turkish warships (US, UK and other NATO navies being expected to participate if required). Although this force moved from monitoring to blockade in November, the escalation of pressure seemed to have little effect on Serbian behaviour. There were also limited peace-keeping actions. In the summer the United Nations authorized all measures necessary to deliver relief to Sarajevo. By the end of the year there were about 7,000 UN peace-keeping forces in Bosnia, made up largely of British and French contingents. Ironically, the presence of peace-keeping forces was double-edged, as Britain in particular was reluctant to take any action which might further jeopardize the safety of these forces.

This was perhaps most evident in the deliberations about enforcing a 'no-fly' zone. In October the UN Security Council banned all flights in Bosnia-Hercegovina except for those by relief groups and UNPROFOR. This ban, however, had limited impact, and some observers estimated that there were over 200 violations well before the end of the year. Consequently, much of the discussion in December concerned the need for enforcement. US efforts to obtain agreement to shoot down military aircraft which violated the 'no-fly' zone encountered British concerns that this would lead to retaliation against the peace-keepers. Nevertheless, on 20 December President Bush and Prime Minister Major issued a joint statement calling for UN enforcement of the ban.

This call symbolized a toughening of policy provoked partly by the failure to influence Serbian actions in Bosnia and partly by fears that the war might expand to Kosovo, a development with the potential to embroil Albania, Bulgaria, Greece and Turkey in a major Balkan conflict. It was revealed on 28 December that the previous week President Bush had warned the Serbs that the United States would intervene militarily if Serbia attacked the Albanians in Kosovo. The United States also made clear its willingness to enforce the ban on Serbian flights over Bosnia and that it would respond to any Serb attack on its peace-keeping forces.

Another positive development in relation to peace-keeping was the announcement on 18 December that NATO and the former Warsaw Pact countries had agreed on 'joint sessions on planning of peace-keeping missions, joint participation in peace-keeping training and consideration of possible joint peace-keeping exercises'. Reached within the framework of the 37-nation North Atlantic Cooperation Council (NACC), of NATO and former Warsaw Pact members, this agreement symbolized the continuing efforts to transcend the old Cold War divisions. The problem was that 1992 had not only underlined the need to go beyond peace-keeping and engage in peace-making, but had also shown that this was less a matter of capability than of political will. And in 1992 in Europe that will was lacking.

XIII RELIGION

WOMEN PRIESTS. On 11 November the General Synod of the Church of England, at Church House, Westminster, voted by the two-thirds majority needed to allow the ordination of women to the priesthood (see AR 1988, p. 436). Bishops approved the change by 39 votes to 13, clergy by 176 to 74 and laity by 169 to 82. The presiding Archbishop of Canterbury, Dr George Carey, made a strong plea for female ordination and for tolerance; 1,300 women had already been ordained as deacons but their priesting also required approval by both houses of parliament and royal assent, which could not happen for over a year. The Anglican Church claimed apostolic and episcopal succession as well as close connection with Roman Catholics and the Eastern Orthodox, both of which restricted ordination to men. The Vatican stated that 'a new and grave obstacle to unity' had been created, but Cardinal Basil Hume of Westminster said that 'it does not signal a breakdown in ecumenical relations'. The Anglo-Catholic group in the Synod reacted variously: John Gummer (Minister of Agriculture) resigned from the Synod; the bishop of Sheffield, David Lunn, indicated that he might resign his orders; and a former bishop of London, Graham Leonard, suggested collective transfer of objecting priests to Roman obedience. But a new organization, Forward in Faith, explored ways of staying in the Anglican Church while rejecting women priests, and the Vatican gave a cool response to suggestions of breakaway groups. There were indications of sympathy for female orders in some quarters in the Roman Catholic Church. A poll of Catholics in the USA showed 67 per cent support for women priests and 70 per cent for married priests. Catholic Archbishop Rembert Weakland, in the *New York Times*, deplored the church's failure to grant women higher status and ordination. He was contradicted four days later by Cardinal John O'Connor in *Catholic New York*, 'without malice' but insisting that women were excluded from priesthood 'because they are women, not because they are inferior'.

The Church of England was the elder of the worldwide Anglican communion but only one member, and many other churches had gone ahead with female ordination. On 7 March Archbishop Peter Carnley of Perth, Australia, ordained ten women deacons as priests, and on 21 November a special Australian synod gave a two-thirds vote in all three houses, of bishops, clergy and laity, to enable dioceses to ordain women if they wished (though the large and wealthy diocese of Sydney opposed change). In August the provincial synod of the Anglican Church in southern Africa voted for female ordination by 166 votes to 45, after an impassioned plea for justice to women from Archbishop Desmond Tutu. In the universal Anglican communion the USA had 1,031 women priests, Canada 158, New Zealand 120, Uganda 36, Australia 10, Ireland seven and 10 other countries smaller numbers. Moreover, there were only 70 million Anglicans worldwide within the total of over 370 million Protestants, most of whom had women ministers. In June Rev Kathleen Richardson, married with three daughters, was inducted as first female president of the British Methodist Conference, 20 years after this church first approved female ordination. She presided over a debate on feminine imagery for God in prayers, hymns and liturgy. In the Lutheran Church in Germany Rev Maria Jepsen became the first woman to be elected bishop for the diocese of Hamburg.

MORALITY. On 7 May Dr Eamonn Casey resigned as Roman Catholic bishop of Galway, Ireland, after admitting a 15-year relationship with an American woman and acknowledging their son, to whose maintenance he had contributed. A popular figure, active in social reform, Dr Casey went abroad for missionary work. There was shock in Ireland but recognition that the problem was not uncommon. It was claimed that in the past 20 years the Catholic Church worldwide had lost 100,000 priests, mostly for marriage. In Canada a two-year-old committee was still considering charges of sexual abuse of women and children by priests and laity. At Larne in Northern Ireland Fr Pat Buckley defied church law by marrying divorcees, mostly from the Irish Republic.

The Vatican remained rigid. In January it rebuked Fr André Guindon of St Paul's University, Ottawa, for his book *The Sexual Creator: An Ethical Proposal for Concerned Christians*, requiring him to 'bring his position on sexual morality into harmony with church teaching'. Professor Guindon directly criticized statements in the papal encyclical *Humanae Vitae* (see AR 1968, pp. 499–504) that artificial contraception was unlawful. Also in January the Archbishop of Paderborn, Germany, suspended theologian Fr Eugen Drewermann from the priesthood for denying the dogmas of the virgin birth and the inauguration of the sacraments. On 17 May Pope John Paul II announced the beatification of Mgr Josémaria Escrivá, Spanish founder of the conservative pressure group Opus Dei in 1927. There was criticism of the speed of this action, the first step towards canonization, and of failure to listen to critics. Opus Dei existed in 60 countries, with a membership of 75,000, including 1,500 bishops and priests.

Debate raged over abortion in several countries. In the USA outgoing President Bush opposed it with support from the religious right, while Bill Clinton, the successful Democratic challenger, backed the rights of individuals. On 26 June the German parliament voted a new law establishing the right to abortion during the first 12 weeks of pregnancy, despite opposition from the Roman Catholic Church and Chancellor Kohl's Christian Democratic Union. In Poland Catholics and secularists clashed over a tough new proposal for an anti-abortion law, and hospitals banned abortion because of church pressure. In Ireland debate was intense after the Attorney-General in February sought to prevent a 14-year-old girl, pregnant after alleged rape, from travelling to England for abortion (see II.1.vii). After the Attorney-General had been overruled by the Supreme Court, a referendum on 25 November found Irish Catholic bishops divided in their advice to voters. They agreed that the destruction of any human life 'at any stage from conception to natural death' was 'gravely wrong', but were imprecise on whether there should be rights to receive information about abortion or to go elsewhere for a termination. The electorate's verdict was to endorse the existing basic prohibition on abortion but to approve information-dissemination on the subject as well as the right of travel for an abortion.

In July the Congregation for the Doctrine of the Faith issued an advisory document declaring that 'there is no right' to homosexuality, which it described as an 'objective disorder'. But a homosexual Catholic association in Britain criticized the document as 'more evidence of homophobia', and the American New Ways Ministry claimed that the Vatican statement was based on 'myths and stereotypes'.

Visiting Angola in June, the Pope reaffirmed his opposition to artificial birth control. He was criticized by Baroness Chalker (UK Overseas Development Minister) and by the Archbishop of Canterbury, who said that population control was essential to world peace.

On 27 June the Brazilian liberation theologian, Leonardo Boff (see AR 1991, p. 441), announced his resignation from the priesthood and the Franciscan Order 'to be free to work without impediment', signing himself 'brother, minor theologian and sinner'. Swiss theologian Hans Küng declared that Dr Boff was a 'victim of the Rome inquisition', which he described as the 'last authoritarian absolutist institution in Europe'. In October Dr Boff was appointed to the chair of ethics and spirituality in the State University of Rio de Janeiro.

STRUGGLE. In Malawi the seven Roman Catholic bishops published a pastoral letter in March, to be read in all churches, criticizing public injustice and corruption. As a result, they were detained for three days by police. Despite an official denial that arrests had been made, Bishop John Roche was deported in April and further arrests of Catholics and Presbyterians were reported in August. In October five American nuns were murdered by Liberian rebels near their convent in Monrovia. In Sudan many Christians were killed in the civil war between the Islamic north and the tribal and Christian south. Sudanese bishops appealed to the UN on 26 August against persecution, 'genocide' of non-Muslims, closure of places of worship, forced conversions to Islam and expulsion of missionaries.

Celebrations of the 500th anniversary of the landing of Christopher Columbus in the Americas were mixed. Bishops in Guatemala issued a pastoral letter asking for forgiveness of past wrongs on indigenous peoples. On 12 October, Columbus Day, the Pope opened the fourth conference of Latin American bishops in Santo Domingo, calling for 'new evangelization'. But local bishops, protesting that Curia officials had manipulated the conference, demanded a system of 'collegiality' under which the Pope would remain their head but would recognize local differences.

After a rupture of diplomatic relations for over a century of militant anti-clericalism, Mexico and the Holy See agreed to exchange ambassadors (see II.2.viii & IV.3.xiv). Some 93 per cent of Mexicans were baptized Catholics.

The French Dominican priest, Fr Gilles Danroc, sent an open letter to the Vatican in July claiming that the Catholic Church supported the illegal government of Haiti, since the coup which had ousted President Aristide (see AR 1991, p. 79). The Vatican was the only power that recognized Haiti's new government, which had the support of most bishops but had imprisoned priests and lay workers (see also IV.3.xii).

In Northern Ireland Bishop Edward Daly and Presbyterian church leaders held secret talks with Sinn Féin in April and June in efforts to solve communal differences (see also I.10).

During the communist era secret ordinations of priests and bishops had been performed in Czechoslovakia, where about 260, estimated at two-fifths of the total, now sought Vatican approval. Some of the clandestine clergy were married and one bishop had three children. But Rome refused to make exceptions to its celibacy law, offering reordination only to celibate priests and suggesting that married clergy might be reordained in Eastern-rite churches which allowed a married priesthood. There was bitterness and opposition from the clergy concerned, among whom married Bishop Fridolin Zahradnik insisted on his valid ordination by continuing to celebrate Mass.

ORTHODOX DIVISIONS. The Ukrainian Orthodox Church (formerly under the control of the Moscow patriarchate) and the previously-banned Ukrainian Autocephalous Church decided on union under the leadership of 94-year-old Patriarch Mstyslav and Metropolitan Filaret of Kiev. The latter had long been a supporter of the 'one, indivisible' Soviet Union but was now declared deposed by Moscow, amid unsavoury reports about his uncanonical wife and previous links with the KGB. In December Patriarch Mstyslav, from his home in the USA, repudiated the union, but Filaret and his supporters, pointing to the Patriarch's residence abroad and advanced age, called for his resignation and a new synod.

In Bulgaria a parliamentary commission, led by Fr Hristofor Subev (see AR 1990, p. 445), ruled that the election of Patriarch Maxim in 1971 had been illegal and that he had collaborated with the former communist regime. Metropolitan Pimen and two others called for Maxim's resignation, formally seceded from the Holy Synod, seized its offices in Sofia and consecrated Fr Subev as bishop. Patriarch Maxim appealed to the courts, but they ruled that they could not interfere in church affairs and that it was for the Orthodox Church to decide between the two synods.

In March the Russian parliament ruled that the feast on 24 May of Saints Cyril and Methodius, apostles to the Slavs, should be a national holiday. In November the Georgian leader and former Soviet foreign minister, Eduard Shevardnadze, announced his conversion; his baptism took place in a Georgian Orthodox cathedral. A survey in Belorussia found that 60 per cent of the population considered themselves to be Orthodox, 30 per cent atheists and 8 per cent Roman Catholics.

JEWISH CONCERNS. On 29 July Israel and the Vatican agreed to establish official relations (see also V.1), Israel being recognized *de facto*. A working commission considered church issues in Israel and the occupied territories but was unable to discuss the rights of Palestinians or the status of Jerusalem. On 31 March a ceremony of reconciliation was held in a Madrid synagogue, attended by King Juan Carlos of Spain and President Chaim Herzog of Israel, deploring the expulsion of Jews from Spain five centuries previously. There were now 15,000 Jews and 14 synagogues in Spain.

Struggles of women elsewhere were reflected in British Judaism when the orthodox Chief Rabbi and his court, Beth Din, refused to authorize a women-only prayer meeting in the united synagogue at Stanmore, Middlesex. Reform and liberal synagogues granted women full equality (and ordained women as rabbis), but in orthodox congregations men and women still sat separately, the latter usually in a ladies' gallery or behind a thick curtain. Chief Rabbi Jonathan Sacks launched an inquiry into 'women in the community', but there were fears of ultra-orthodox reaction. A 300-page review of Anglo-Jewry asserted that 'the united synagogue must change if it is to survive'.

In March the Archbishop of Canterbury broke with custom by declining patronage of the Church's Mission Among the Jews, on the grounds that he was bound 'to encourage trust and friendship' between different faiths. The Chief Rabbi praised this as a 'courageous act', while the Muslim, Dr Zaki Badawi, described it as 'a wonderful development.'

COMMUNAL TENSIONS. The shame of the year was the 'ethnic cleansing' of Muslims from parts of Bosnia-Hercegovina (see III.1.vi). Descended from a medieval dualistic sect of Bogomils, persecuted by Orthodox and Catholic, they had adopted Islam readily when the

Ottoman Turks conquered the Balkans in the fifteenth century. Now forming some 43 per cent of the population, Bosnian Muslims stressed their Slav-European identity; before the current conflict they had been fully integrated and had allowed frequent inter-marriage. Attacked by Serbs and Croats, and with restricted access to arms, they were seen in the Islamic world as the victims of a latter-day crusade by Christians against an Islamic people. By August Turkey and Iran were calling for military aid to the Bosnian Muslims, as several Islamic conferences urged action. There were protests from Christian and Jewish leaders against the atrocities, and criticism in former Yugoslavia itself. At Pentecost the Serbian Orthodox Church organized processions and tolled bells for peace, and Patriarch Pavle begged forgiveness for the warfare. In October the Patriarch joined with the Catholic Archbishop of Zagreb to appeal for an end to all destruction of Christian and Muslim sanctuaries and 'a stop to the inhuman practice of ethnic cleansing'.

As regards developments in the Islamic world, the term 'fundamentalism' was used by outside observers to suggest backward-looking ideologies, although some preferred 'Islamicism' for the application of Islamic principles to modern government. Existing Islamicist states were Saudi Arabia (which had applied Sunni sharia law since 1932), Iran and Sudan, while Pakistan was moving in the same direction. In Algeria an army takeover in January prevented the election victory of the Islamic Salvation Front (see V.4.iv), which controlled 8,000 of the country's 10,000 mosques. The assassination of President Muhammad Boudiaf on 29 June led to further repression of Islamic activists. Also in June, Dr Farag Fouda, an outspoken Egyptian critic of extremism, was shot dead in a Cairo street, against a background of mounting attacks on Coptic Christians and foreign visitors by a Jamaat Islami group. The Muslim Brotherhood made sweeping gains in the Egyptian elections in October and was the first organization to provide help for the homeless after a devastating earthquake (see V.2.ii).

A 'Muslim Parliament' was convened in Britain, composed of 155 members nominated by interested groups. Its leader, Dr Kalim Siddiqui, declared opposition to 'any public policy or legislation that we regard as inimical to our interests'. A 'decade of Islamic revivalism' was announced to counter the Christian churches' 'decade of evangelism', although leaders of most religious faiths came out against over-zealous proselytism.

Ayodhya in northern India was again the centre of widespread conflict between Hindus and Muslims (see VIII.2.i & VIII.2.ii). One of the seven most holy Hindu places and centre for groups of sacred actors, Ayodhya was also the site of the Babri mosque, opposition to which was whipped up by militant Hindu nationalist organizations. On 6 December huge crowds broke through lines of police and soldiers and tore down the walls and three domes of the mosque. Violence erupted throughout

India, temples and mosques being attacked or destroyed from Bombay to Calcutta (and also in Pakistan). Eventually over 1,000 deaths were reported. The rapid spread of the news overseas led to the fire-bombing of Hindu temples in Britain and the destruction of the Sri Krishna temple in West Bromwich.

BOOKS OF THE YEAR. There were several criticisms of traditions of the life of Jesus: *Jesus* by the novelist A.N. Wilson; a novel *Live from Golgotha* by Gore Vidal; *Jesus the Man* by B. Thiering; *Born of a Woman* by Bishop J.S. Spong; and *Son of Joseph* by Geoffrey Parrinder. A prayer book for homosexuals, *Daring to Speak Love's Name*, was refused publication by a religious firm after disapproval by the Archbishop of Canterbury but was published elsewhere with a preface by Dr David Jenkins, bishop of Durham. *Catholics and Sex* by K. Saunders and P. Stanford (former editor of the *Catholic Herald*) criticized church teaching, and in *Wrestling with the Church* Mary Levison described struggles for female ordination in the Church of Scotland. *Opus Dei: An Open Book* was a reply by W. O'Connor to the critical *Secret World of Opus Dei* by M. Walsh (1989). *Religious Policy in the Soviet Union*, edited by S.P. Ramet, discussed the Christian churches but said little of other religions, and *Salvation Outside the Church?* by F.A. Sullivan sketched the history of Catholic attitudes to other faiths. The massive *Judaism* by Hans Küng emphasized common ethical traditions but was questionable on the Holocaust and the state of Israel, while E.P. Sanders's *Judaism, Practice and Belief 63BCE–66CE* gave this great scholar's favourable assessments of the Pharisees and other traditional groups. *Women and Islam* by F. Mernissi and *Women and Gender in Islam* by L. Ahmed provided new light on Islamic tradition, and in *Tears of Blood* M. Craig described repression in Tibet.

XIV THE SCIENCES

1. MEDICAL, SCIENTIFIC AND INDUSTRIAL RESEARCH

PHYSICS AND ASTRONOMY. By far the greatest sensation of the year was provided by data from the 'cosmic background explorer' (COBE) satellite operated by the US National Aeronautics and Space Administration (NASA). In April the news was released that the satellite had detected what newspaper headlines called 'ripples from the dawn of time'. Respectable scientists described the findings as the Holy Grail of cosmology.

COBE had been launched to search for irregularities in the microwave radiation which had been emitted very early in the history of the universe and had been travelling around the universe ever since, gradually cooling. Before COBE's launch, less sensitive instruments on earlier satellites had failed to find any such irregularities, returning data that seemed to show that the cosmic background radiation was perfectly smooth in all directions. This in turn implied that at the time that the background radiation was produced the matter in the universe must also have been completely smooth and featureless, in contrast to today's tight clumping into stars and galaxies with vast expanses of empty space between. Cosmologists had become increasingly concerned by the mystery of what had caused these irregularities to appear, and when. COBE had been launched in search of the first discontinuities in the early universe which, it was hoped, would have survived in the form of irregularities in the cosmic background radiation.

After many months in orbit, COBE eventually reported minute variations in temperature in the background radiation. These variations were only thirty millionths of a degree but still enough to confirm that irregularities which could have grown into stars and galaxies were present in the very early universe. Theorists now began a renewed search to explain the origin of such discontinuities.

On 12 October, 500 years after Columbus had discovered the Americas, NASA switched on an electronic ear consisting of two radio telescopes to intensify SETI—the 'search for extra-terrestrial intelligence'. The telescopes targeted 1,000 stars resembling our own Sun in the hope of receiving signals sent out by other civilizations.

There was already some evidence of planets orbiting other stars, though this was somewhat controversial. In 1991 radio astronomers at Britain's Jodrell Bank observatory had reported that planets were orbiting a pulsar, one of the cinders left after a supernova explosion (see AR 1991, p. 445). This very surprising conclusion—a supernova would have been expected to have destroyed any such planets—had been based on the discovery of minute irregularities in the timing of the normally ultra-regular flashes coming from the pulsar. Subsequently, another team of radio astronomers using the radio telescope at Arecibo on Puerto Rico had reported the discovery of similar evidence for planets orbiting a pulsar. But then the Jodrell Bank team wrote to the journal *Nature* to say that a second check of their calculations had shown that the irregularities they had thought they had observed in their pulsar's movements did not really exist. So neither did the planets.

This confession cast doubt on the reality of the planets whose existence had been predicted by the team at Arecibo. Nevertheless the Arecibo team (from Cornell University) defended their calculations, in the belief that they had genuine evidence of planets probably formed from material sucked from a companion star by the powerful gravitational pull of the pulsar. More evidence to support the theory was produced during the year, though it remained controversial.

A Mars observer probe was launched by NASA in September, designed to fly to Mars to map the planet in preparation for a possible later manned mission. In July *Giotto*, the European space probe that had already survived an encounter with Halley's Comet in 1986, made a rendezvous with another comet, Grigg Skjellerup, during one of that comet's periodic visits to the Solar System.

During the year the hadron electron ring accelerator (HERA) came into use at Hamburg in Germany. Two different kinds of sub-atomic particles, protons and electrons, were for the first time smashed into each other head-on, both travelling at near to the speed of light. It was hoped that HERA would show whether protons and electrons were composed of truly fundamental particles, i.e. 'quarks'.

MOLECULAR BIOLOGY AND MEDICINE. Early in the year an international team led by scientists of the University of Manchester's Institute of Science and Technology reported in *Nature* their achievement in being the first completely to sequence all the bases (sub-units of DNA) in an entire chromosome (one of those of yeast.) Besides demonstrating that very effective international collaboration was possible in such a competitive area, the project revealed that there were many more genes in the chromosome than had been expected, most of them with functions which remained unknown.

Later in the year other scientists announced the successful high-resolution mapping of two human chromosomes, the Y chromosome (distinguishing males from females) and chromosome 21. The mapping demonstrated that the Human Genome Project, begun in 1990, was living up to its promise and proceeding ahead of schedule. Two other groups, in the USA and Paris, completed larger-scale maps of almost the entire human genome, the totality of human DNA. The maps were prepared by 'cloning' (i.e. using genetic engineering to copy repeatedly) overlapping fragments of DNA which each contained at least one known sequence, and then arranging the known sequences in order. In this way the vast stretches of unknown DNA were divided up into shorter sequences arranged in the right order ready to be parcelled out to eager laboratories round the world for more detailed sequencing. Mapping of the important genes in the human chromosome was expected to be completed by 1995, and complete sequencing of the entire human genome, with every base pair in its right place on every chromosome, by 2005 at the latest.

From the beginning of molecular biology in the 1950s scientists had developed theories that DNA had been the original self-replicating molecule that had created more complex life forms to protect it while it replicated. But in the early 1990s evidence emerged that RNA, the similar molecule into which form DNA is copied to carry its messages into the cell for translation into proteins, might have been the original replicator from which DNA evolved. In other words, there might have been an 'RNA world' before there was a DNA world. This evidence came from the discovery of 'ribozymes', RNA molecules which were able to act as catalytic enzymes. Much more was discovered about the functions of these molecules in 1992, giving promise that some of them might be developed into therapeutic agents. Research revealed that ribozymes could link amino-acids, the sub-units of proteins, to form new protein molecules and that they could specifically make or break bonds between nucleic acids and proteins; they could therefore be involved in the control of gene expression, which depends upon the masking or unmasking of DNA by proteins. The primitive power of ribozymes was being intensively researched by a number of private biotechnology companies in 1992. The companies hoped to develop ribozymes into new medical drugs able to attack such targets as the human immune virus (HIV) responsible for AIDS, while leaving host cells intact.

The enormous power of genetic engineering in areas beyond medicine was demonstrated by the success of Florida University scientists, reported in the journal *Biotechnology* in June, in inserting foreign genes into wheat plants to make them resistant to a particular herbicide. The genes were implanted by shooting them into the nuclei of cells in cell cultures in the laboratory, the genes being carried on the surfaces of tiny tungsten or gold balls. Subsequent tests showed that a small proportion of the plants which grew from the cells treated in this way were resistant to the chosen herbicide. Earlier work had succeeded in developing techniques for introducing alien genes into one of the two great groups of plants, the dicotyledons, but not into the other group, the monocotyledons, to which most of the world's main crops and all the cereals belong. But finding ways genetically to engineer cereals had proved unexpectedly difficult. Rice had succumbed in 1989 and maize in 1991; wheat completed the trio in 1992.

Some environmentalists were concerned that the first use for the new technique was in making wheat resistant to herbicides. As they pointed out, this would add to the quantity of chemicals sprayed onto the land rather than decreasing it, although the herbicide used in this first experiment was biodegradable and harmless to most forms of life. On the other hand, the achievement opened up the prospect of endowing crops with genes for such properties as resistance to viruses, fungi and insect pests. This could be achieved far more rapidly using genetic engineering than was possible by conventional plant-breeding technology. In some cases, genetic engineering was allowing breeders to add in genes which could not be provided at all by conventional breeding techniques, because the genes were simply not found in any members of a crop species but only beyond it in other species accessible only through genetic engineering.

While herbicide manufacturers were prepared to pay for research to develop herbicide-resistant crops, there were fewer companies prepared to pay for the development of crops made resistant to pests or viruses; nor was there much interest in more nutritious or drought-resistant crops. However, one commercial company, Monsanto, had provided the technology needed to create virus-resistant potatoes free of charge to Mexico, where 60 per cent of the potato crop had been destroyed by virus disease. Whether this example would be followed by other companies so as to make the benefits of genetic engineering available to the developing world was an open question.

Cambridge scientists revealed one remarkable breakthrough in genetic engineering when they reported that they had succeeded in engineering plants to produce vaccines to protect against disease, including foot and mouth disease in animals. The work involved taking genes for individual antigens (proteins able to stimulate a strong immune response) from disease organisms and inserting them into plant cells. The work held considerable promise because of the ability of plants to produce such vaccine material in large quantities and at low cost.

Equally important in a different area was work in Cambridge, at Addenbrookes Hospital and elsewhere, in which pigs were being genetically engineered so that their organs could potentially be used as transplants for humans without their being rejected. In Britain and some other countries there were waiting lists of people in need of kidneys and other organs for transplant, as a consequence of a general shortage of organs from people who had died in accidents. Pig organs which would not be rejected were being developed as a possible, though controversial, solution to the problem. The technique being developed depended upon the discovery that rejection was largely dependent upon the part of the immune system known as complement. The Cambridge group demonstrated that, by engineering genes for proteins able to inactivate human complement in mice, they could make the mice able to accept foreign grafts without rejecting them.

The Cambridge team pointed out that it would be some years before genetically-engineered pig organs were widely available for use as transplants, leaving ample time for public debate of the issues involved. But ethical questions were raised more immediately by the use in the USA of a baboon's liver as a transplant for a man for whom an appropriate human liver could not be found in time. The operation appeared successful, although the patient died several months later. Several objections to the use of organs from baboons were mooted: the animals were not bred nor available naturally in large numbers; they were closely related to humans and highly intelligent; and their organs were considerably smaller than the human equivalents. None of these objections applied to pigs. The Cambridge team accepted that those opposed to any use of animals by humans would strongly oppose their proposal and even find it abhorrent, but they felt that any objector who ate ham or bacon was being somewhat hypocritical.

Genetic engineering techniques were making their mark in a growing number of new drugs and approaches to therapy. Notable among those which held out clear promise in 1992 were new approaches to the treatment of multiple sclerosis and rheumatoid arthritis and to the prevention of cholera. The results of trials published in September showed that an oral vaccine, made by engineering genes from cholera bacteria into other bacteria already used in oral vaccinations, was potentially cheap and provided high levels of protection. Hopes were high for a vaccine which would be suited for use in poor countries in the developing world, for whom no appropriate form of protection against cholera existed.

In November encouraging first results were announced from trials in the USA using a new anti-arthritis drug based on a wholly new approach to the disease. The new drug was composed of molecules designed to block so-called cell adhesion molecules, becoming known as CAMs. White cells, called T-cells, caused inflammatory arthritis by leaving blood vessels and attacking the lining of joints in self-destructive auto-immune reactions. In order to push their way out of blood vessels the T-cells had to obtain leverage by attaching themselves to CAMs in the walls of blood vessels, using them as a kind of molecular velcro. The drug molecules fastened onto the CAMs, blocking them so the T-cells were unable to fasten to them. First tests on severe and advanced cases of rheumatoid arthritis, who were not benefiting at all from conventional drastic treatments such as steroids or gold injections, showed substantial improvements.

Cells of the immune system were also prevented from leaving blood vessels in an experimental treatment for multiple sclerosis which was successfully tested in rats during the year. The treatment involved the making of antibodies which reacted specifically with the group of T-cells responsible for the auto-immune reaction against the sheaths of nerves which caused the symptoms of MS. The treatment was highly effective in a condition mimicking MS in mice. Human trials were expected in 1993.

So-called 'anti-sense' technology was used for the first time to treat humans in 1992. Anti-sense DNA was synthetic DNA comprising a sequence of bases designed to be precisely complementary to the sequence of bases in some chosen harmful gene, such as that of an invading virus. During 1992 anti-sense technology was used experimentally to attack HIV (the AIDS virus), to treat leukaemia and to attack the papilloma virus which is the prime cause of cervical cancer. Tests of anti-sense DNA against lung cancer were approved, to start in 1993.

Some surprising species of living or extinct organisms were discovered during the year. A forest goat found in Vietnam appeared to be a member of a species previously unknown to science. The remains of a dinosaur (nicknamed 'superslasher' because of the half-metre-long claws on its hind feet) became famous because palaeontologists calculated that an utahraptor (its proper name) would have won a battle with a tyrannosaurus rex (although the two creatures had not lived at the same time). The largest living organism ever found was identified in the USA in March, and named armillaria bulbosa. This was a single fungus, the size of 20 football pitches, composed of a vast underground network of microscopic strands.

During the year the much-debated cause of the extinction of the dinosaurs was confirmed, at least to most people's satisfaction, when two groups of scientists independently dated rock from a 180-km diameter crater in Mexico, formed by the impact of an asteroid, as having been formed 65 million years ago, the time of the extinction not only of the dinosaurs but of many other plants and animals. The impact would have caused climatic changes sufficient to have been responsible for massive changes in terrestrial ecology.

At the end of the year *Science* magazine announced the winner of its 'molecule of the year' contest, which had become a keenly-awaited event since its launch in 1989. The editor of *Science*, Daniel Koshland, explained that the idea behind the award was to draw people's attention not to personalities, for whom there were already plenty of awards, but to the areas of science where new and rapid progress had been made which would probably have a major impact on human affairs and on how humans viewed the world. The 1992 winner was nitric oxide (NO), chosen because research, largely completed during the year, had identified it not only as a multi-purpose 'messenger molecule' within the body, helping to control functions as diverse as respiration, memory and immunity, but also specifically as the agent directly stimulating the erection of the penis. It was hoped that new treatments for impotence might be developed from the discovery. Runners-up in the contest included the enzyme nitrogenase, responsible for the natural fixing of atmospheric nitrogen and its reincorporation into living organisms in the nitrogen cycle. The precise structure of nitrogenase was elucidated in 1992. It was hoped that this success would lead to more cost-effective means of fixing nitrogen artificially and so lead to a reduction in the cost of fertilizer.

NOBEL PRIZES. The 1992 Nobel Prize for Medicine was awarded to two US scientists, Edwin Krebs and Edmund Fischer, at the University of Washington in Seattle, for work carried out in the 1950s and 1960s which, by revealing how hormones stimulate muscle cells to burn chemical fuel, had laid the foundations for modern understanding of cellular responses to all kinds of chemical messages and of the ways in which the malfunctioning of such responses could cause cancer.

The Nobel Prize for Chemistry was awarded to Professor Rudolph Marcus of the California Institute of Technology, for his work on electron transfer reactions in chemical systems, which laid the foundations for modern understanding of processes including corrosion and photosynthesis, both of which involved the flow of currents of electrons.

The Nobel Prize for Physics was awarded to Professor Georges Charpak (France) of the CERN international particle physics laboratory near Geneva, for his development, in 1968, of the particle detector called the 'multiwire proportional chamber'. The device had enabled physicists to collect data from atom-smashing experiments a thousand times faster than had previously been possible, and so had greatly speeded the progress of research into the ultimate structure of matter.

2. INFORMATION TECHNOLOGY

OF potentially great strategic import was the election in November 1992 of Senator Albert Gore Jr as the next Vice-President of the United States (see IV.1). Prior to his election, in addition to interests in the environment and 'family values', Senator Gore had demonstrated a greater awareness of both information and technology than perhaps any other figure in a position of such prominence on the world stage.

Initiatives with which Vice-President-elect Gore had been associated included the High Performance Computing Act (1991), which promoted the development by 1996 of a national research and educational network (NREN); the Information Infrastructure and Technology Bill, introduced in July 1992 in order to extend electronic information dissemination to the tiers of education below university level; and the GPO Gateway to Government Bill, introduced in June 1992 and aimed at making the

Government Printing Office (GPO) responsible for wide networking of federal electronic information. Some of these measures were controversial, perceived by the private sector as government interference in the information market-place. Whether Mr Gore would wish, or be able, to pursue this particular line of interest in the new administration remained to be seen.

DIGITAL VIDEO. An important theme very much to the fore in a number of areas in 1992, notably personal computers (PCs) but also consumer multimedia and high-definition television (HDTV), was that of digital video. In the PC field, the announcement in November of a product called *Video for Windows* by the US software company Microsoft made a major impact. Microsoft's existing *Windows* software, effectively a graphical user interface (GUI) extension to the MS-DOS operating system for PCs, already held a dominant position in the commercial PC market-place and had been reported during 1992 as selling more than 500,000 copies per month. *Video for Windows* incorporated video compression/decompression (codec) algorithms, enabling any PC operating under version 3.1 of *Windows* to integrate moving picture sequences into any application running on that PC.

Before the advent of *Video for Windows*, motion video had been the last remaining element of 'multimedia' (i.e. the seamless integration of text, sound, graphics, animation, still photographs and motion video) not readily accessible to the generality of PC users. One remarkable characteristic of the new Microsoft product was 'scalability', in that the software automatically adapted to the power of the PC running it. Thus digital video sequences would be played at only 15 frames per second (fps) on one-tenth of the screen on a 386 machine but at 24 fps on one-quarter of the screen on a 486 machine. With the assistance of an accelerator card using the i750 video processor (see AR 1990, p. 461), produced by the US chip manufacturer Intel, the same sequence could be displayed in full-screen, full-motion mode. Interestingly, although Microsoft had collaborated with Intel in producing *Video for Windows*, the new software effectively undermined the future viability of Intel's own DVI (digital video interactive) technology, which required mainframe compression facilities.

To be fair, it should be pointed out that about a year earlier the US company Apple Computer had brought to market a software product called *QuickTime*, which permitted real-time decompression of moving digital pictures and worked in tandem with compression software. Apple microcomputers, however, whilst technologically advanced, were an élite product and Apple had nowhere near the market dominance for software enjoyed by Microsoft in relation to International Business Machines (IBM) and IBM-compatible PCs. At much the same time as Microsoft announced its new product, Apple released a version of

QuickTime for PCs operating under *Windows*, but Microsoft inevitably had a considerable advantage in its traditional market.

CONSUMER MULTIMEDIA. Despite expectant articles in the press, the elusive full-screen full-motion video (FSFMV) failed to become available for consumer multimedia devices. Premature announcements by the Dutch company Philips, the main contender in this field with its CD-I (compact disc interactive) technology, had created expectations in previous years too, but once again the launch of FSFMV for CD-I was put back (see AR 1991, p. 452). In the meantime, another CD-based consumer multimedia technology, VIS (*Video Information System*), was brought out by the US company Tandy.

HIGH-DEFINITION TELEVISION. The year was not a good one for HDTV in Europe. In December compromise proposals for a five-year action plan failed to win approval. The plan had effectively been promised in December 1991 at the time of the final approval of the EC's Satellite Broadcasting Directive (see AR 1991, p. 454) when the EC Commission had stated that it would adopt 'appropriate measures' to encourage the use of HDTV standards before they became obligatory in 1995. This lack of progress was particularly disappointing given that broadcasters and equipment manufacturers, who had been implacably opposed to one another prior to the approval of the directive, had agreed on a common HDTV strategy in June.

Opposition to the action plan had been led by the UK, which had finally found itself isolated against its 11 EC partners. The UK opposition had every appearance of obstinacy over budgetary issues and industrial policy in the face of the vested national interests of France and the Netherlands, the homes, respectively, of major HDTV equipment manufacturers Thomson and Philips. Nevertheless, there was at least one substantive technical issue, on which the UK had earlier gained support from other member states. This was whether the EC Commission was correct to foster analogue HDTV or whether it was better to adopt a more far-sighted strategy taking account of developments in digital HDTV in Japan, the United States and Sweden.

Meanwhile, an interesting experiment, successfully carried out in November 1992, pointed to the potential of digital HDTV techniques. The BBC (UK) and Thomson (France) demonstrated that digital HDTV could be broadcast via a standard eight-megahertz channel, as currently used for conventional terrestrial analogue transmissions. Compression techniques used in the experiment were developed by Thomson and the transmission facilities were provided by the BBC. Previous HDTV experiments had tended to focus on satellite rather than terrestrial transmission. Another experimental project suggested that digital channels could be broadcast alongside conventional services without causing interference.

CHIP TECHNOLOGY. Volume production of 16-megabit DRAM (dynamic random access memory) devices, superseding 4-megabit DRAMs which had been in production since 1989, commenced during 1992, but manufacturers were already focusing on subsequent generations. The soaring costs of developing new generations of chips had already brought together companies from different parts of the world for the purposes of developing 64-megabit technology, including IBM (USA) and Siemens (Germany), Texas Instruments (USA) and Hitachi (Japan), and AT&T Microelectronics (USA) and NEC (Japan). In 1992 Toshiba (Japan) joined IBM and Siemens in order to develop a 256-megabit DRAM, production of which was predicted for around 1996–97. IBM was reported to be already working on a 1-gigabit DRAM.

One valuable side-effect of these global alliances was that they helped to heal US-Japanese antagonism in the semiconductor industry, which had arisen in the first half of the 1980s as a result of Japanese companies flooding the US market. Constantly rising development costs were not, however, the sole motivation for such alliances. At much the same time, the prices of 4-megabit devices were falling, largely as a result of over-supply. Moreover, new competitors, in the form of South Korean companies, of which the leader was Samsung, were able to undercut the Japanese companies which had hitherto dominated the sector.

A major international alliance, in a different part of the semiconductor industry, was announced in July. The US firm Advanced Micro Devices (AMD) and Fujitsu (Japan) embarked on a joint venture to manufacture 'flash' memory chips (see AR 1991, p. 453). These devices were expected eventually to supplant hard and floppy discs which somewhat incongruously relied upon mechanical drives. In another announcement, Fujitsu also claimed to have built the world's most powerful super-computer, thereby seizing the initiative in this field from US companies, such as Cray, which had hitherto built the largest commercially-available hardware of this type. According to Fujitsu, its VPP500 machine was capable of 355 gigaflops (355,000 million floating point operations) per second. Two technical points worth noting were the use of gallium arsenide chips and of vector parallel processing (VPP). These chips were roughly three times faster than silicon chips, although they were more difficult to make and more expensive. VPP combined the existing super-computer techniques of vector (effectively serial or sequential) processing and parallel processing.

SUBSIDIARITY IN EUROPEAN COMMUNITY R&D. In October the EC Commission published its proposals for a 'fourth framework programme of Community activity in the field of research and technological development', covering the five-year period 1994–98. A major segment of the programme was devoted to information and communication technologies. Because it was anticipated that the Maastricht Treaty on European Union would be ratified before final approval of the programme (or, at the latest, during the period covered by it), the plan took full account of the provisions of the treaty. Accordingly, the document defined the types of R&D activity which, having regard to the key principle of subsidiarity (see XIX.3), were appropriate for an EC-level programme, as follows: (i) 'big science', consisting of very large-scale projects requiring commitment and coordination at a European level; (ii) long-term, cross-sector ('generic') projects, often involving collaboration with non-EC countries; (iii) actions contributing to the establishment of the single market; and (iv) pre-normative research in support of norms, standards and regulations.

The total budget proposed by the EC Commission for the fourth framework programme was 14,700 million ecu. It was difficult to compare this proposed provision with the 5,700 million ecu approved for the third framework programme in April 1990 (see AR 1990, p. 462), since, in line with requirements in the Maastricht agreement, the scope of the framework programme had been much extended.

EUROPEAN COMMUNITY REGULATORY ISSUES. Following a process of consultation which had culminated in consideration by the European Parliament, the EC Commission issued an amended proposal for a data protection directive in October. The revised proposal claimed to have taken account of many of the 131 amendments approved when the parliament had debated the original draft directive in March. In fact, the previous draft, which had been issued in July 1990, had been the subject of serious concern within the information industry and had resulted in much lobbying and many representations to MEPs. According to the Commission, the amended proposal contained two major changes at the behest of the parliament, namely (i) the distinction between rules applying in the public and private sectors was dropped; and (ii) the provisions on the procedures for notification and on codes of conduct were expanded. Furthermore, the title of the directive was modified by the addition of the words 'and on the free movement of such data' in order to emphasize that the proposal aimed to stimulate the single market as well as to protect individuals.

INTERNATIONAL REGULATION. The Geneva-based International Telecommunication Union (ITU), the specialized UN agency charged with the international coordination and regulation of telecommunications (including radio and television), held an additional plenipotentiary conference in December. More than 800 delegates attended from 140 countries and approved a radical revision of the constitution intended to make the ITU better able to respond to the increasing demands placed upon it to keep pace with ever-accelerating progress in telecommunications. Under the ITU's new structure, three sectors were established covering, respectively, development, standardization and radio communication. In creating the development sector, the ITU recognized the crucial role of telecommunications for developing countries.

3.   ENVIRONMENT

ENVIRONMENTAL events in 1992 were dominated by the UN Conference on Environment and Development (UNCED), the so-called Earth Summit, which was held in Rio de Janeiro on 3–14 June and was said to be the biggest-ever gathering of heads of government. The meeting, which came 20 years after the UN Conference on the Human Environment in Stockholm, was hailed as a triumph by many and as a failure by many, with all blends of these extremes also available in commentaries.

The Rio UNCED summit approved a number of documents, of which the conventions on biological diversity and climate change were the only legally-binding instruments. The centre-piece text was the Rio Declaration, setting out the broad principles of environmentally sound development (see XIX.1). This 27-page document was originally envisaged by the UNCED secretary-general, Maurice Strong, as a one-page text which could be hung on the wall, but it grew during protracted debate and was weakened by compromises.

Also adopted was Agenda 21, a 720-page, 40-chapter 'blueprint for action' detailing how and, in some cases, when to carry out the UNCED resolutions. It was the best representation to date of where government thinking stood on environment/development issues providing a comprehensive inventory of the issues pertinent to sustainable development, highlighting linkages between them and suggesting principal action programmes. Nevertheless, developing world delegates criticized it for being weakest on the issues the UN resolution calling for the conference had stressed the most: financial and institutional arrangements and technology transfer. Moreover, there was virtually no agreed funding of the actions for which the Agenda called and no attempt to set priorities among those actions. The UNCED secretariat estimated that the total Agenda would cost $600,000 million yearly, of which $125,000 million could be covered by foreign aid.

The Biological Diversity Convention was designed to protect ecologically-important animal and plant species and wild areas. It called for developing countries to receive financial and technical help in their conservation efforts and for them to be compensated when their genetic resources were turned into commercial products. The convention would come into force when 30 states had ratified it. The United States was the only country in Rio which refused to sign, in light of concern over the treaty's effects on the US biotechnology industry.

The Framework Convention on Climate Change required states to limit emissions of 'greenhouse' gases, especially carbon dioxide, but it did not contain any specific targets. It recommended that industrial nations should stabilize CO_2 emissions at 1990 levels by the year 2000. The EC agreed to this target in 1991. Scientists argued that, even if this target were achieved, warming between 1992 and 2100 would have been reduced by only 5 per cent or so. The treaty did require governments to gather and report their emission levels regularly. And it was expected that this framework convention would be followed by more specific protocols. The United States fought hard to keep specific targets out of the treaty, and was supported by some oil-producing nations. Yet the United States was among the 15 states which had signed the accord by the end of the Rio summit.

Also adopted was a Statement of Forest Principles, which was appended to the Rio Declaration after a failed attempt to agree a binding forest convention. Certain nations which exported tropical wood saw such a convention as threatening their sovereignty over their natural resources. The principles were aimed primarily at protecting tropical forest ecosystems and at encouraging their sustainable use. They also called for technical and financial help in forest conservation efforts.

The Earth Summit brought together over 100 national leaders, produced two treaties and an international agenda. The simultaneous meeting in Rio of non-governmental organizations in the so-called Global Forum brought together some 2,000 such groups. Taken together, the two meetings could be seen as very important in terms of creating political momentum. However, many observers claimed that UNCED provided good evidence that the former East-West divide had been replaced by a North-South divide, and that neither industrial nor developing nations showed seriousness about working separately or together on global environment and development issues. By the end of 1992 few if any governments or multilateral organizations had taken any credible steps towards turning the Rio documents into policies.

The autumn UN General Assembly passed seven resolutions having to do with UNCED, the most important creating a 53-member Commission on Sustainable Development, which would meet once a year to monitor how governments and the UN system were implementing the Rio texts. The members were to be elected by, and to report to the UN Economic and Social Council (ECOSOC), a body not known for a high level of activity in the UN system. Thus the success of the Commission would depend in large part on the Secretary-General's success in reforming the UN in general and ECOSOC in particular (see also XI.1). The General Assembly also decided to establish a High-Level Advisory Board of 'eminent persons' with expertise appropriate to the Commission's needs. UNCED had been notable for allowing greater participation than in previous UN conferences by non-governmental groups, and the Assembly's resolution language suggested that this level of participation might be encouraged in the workings of the Commission.

The final communique of the Group of Seven summit held in Munich in July called upon governments 'to direct policies and resources towards sustainable development which . . . safeguards present and future generations'. It also called for the creation of a $100 million multilateral fund to make safe the many old, badly-designed and badly-maintained nuclear reactors of Eastern Europe. In October the US and Russian governments signed an accord by which the United States would provide up to $15 million in technical assistance to help Russia safely store nuclear material from scrapped weapons.

Concern for the ozone layer gathered momentum during the year. In February the United States, Britain and the EC announced (on different days) bans on production of most of the gases causing ozone depletion from the end of 1995. These announcements, in response to evidence that such gases existed in record quantities in the northern hemisphere, moved forward by five years the date of a production ban agreed in the 1987 Montreal Protocol (which entered into force in 1992). Then, at the fourth meeting of the parties to the protocol in late November, ministers from 91 nations and the EC agreed to a complete phase-out of ozone-depleting chlorofluorocarbons (CFCs) and carbon tetrachloride by 1 January 1996. This was accompanied by a pledge by the industrial nations to add $500 million to the $240 million already committed to help developing nations meet the new target. The UN Environment Programme's executive director, Mustafa Tolba, warned that the new agreement did not go far enough, adding that the ozone damage allowed by even the tighter timetable was unfair to future generations.

Meeting in Paris in September, representatives of 13 European nations signed a Convention on Marine Pollution. This Paris Convention was based on the principle that nothing unhealthy for marine species or the human species should be dumped into the seas. It was meant to reduce discharges of toxic wastes to harmless levels by the end of the century, and to ban the dumping of radioactive wastes for 15 years. The Scandinavian governments wanted a permanent ban; Britain and France preferred to leave the option open.

The Presidents of the Amazon states of Bolivia, Brazil, Colombia, Ecuador, Guyana and Suriname, together with representatives of Peru and Venezuela, held a two-day 'forest summit' in Manaus (Brazil) in February to call for financial and technical aid from Northern countries in return for their efforts to protect the forest. Their declaration also reasserted their view that the biological resources of the forests were the property of the countries which exercised sovereignty over the forests. In an effort to conserve forests, the Vietnamese government announced in March a ban on the export of all raw and sawn timber. Industry was to be encouraged to use coal rather than wood or charcoal, and export permits were to be withdrawn.

The science working group of the UN Intergovernmental Panel on Climate Change (IPCC) announced at a January meeting that it was more certain than ever that global warming was happening. But they said that the process might be delayed by other pollutants such as sulphur dioxide, which had a cooling effect in that it reflected back into space some of warming solar radiation. Most sulphur dioxide pollution, also associated with acid rain, came from the burning of fossil fuels. The meeting predicted that global warming would increase rapidly from the middle of the 21st century.

In May the European Commission approved proposals for an energy tax to reduce carbon dioxide emissions. The tax would be equivalent to US$3 per barrel of oil in 1993, and rise by $1 a year to a maximum of $10 per barrel in the year 2000. However, the tax was conditional on other industrialized nations, particularly the United States, following suit, and would not come into force until approved by member governments. Industrialists and some oil-producing nations protested. Many environmentalists argued that a tax on carbon-based energy (fossil fuels) was needed to cut carbon emissions by encouraging efficient energy use and the development of new and renewable energy sources such as solar and wind energy.

A March meeting in Kyoto, Japan, of the 114 signatory states of the convention on International Trade in Endangered Species (CITES) resisted efforts by five southern African countries to weaken the ban on trade in ivory and other elephant parts begun in 1989. Delegates from Botswana, Malawi, Namibia, South Africa and Zimbabwe argued that their elephant herds were being well managed, that numbers were increasing and that trade should be resumed gradually. Most Western countries supported the continuation of the ban. A report to the meeting listed 135 infractions of CITES trade restriction, more than half involving EC nations.

The 44th annual meeting of the International Whaling Commission held in Glasgow on 29 June–3 July, agreed in effect to maintain the present ban on commercial whaling for at least another year. During the year a new catch monitoring system and quotas were to be worked out, so that commercial whaling was expected to resume in 1993 or 1994. However, Iceland withdrew from the Commission on the day before the meeting, and Norway announced a unilateral resumption of commercial whaling in 1993. In September Iceland, Norway, the Faroe Islands and Greenland announced the establishment of a pro-whaling body called the North Atlantic Marine Mammals Commission.

In March the French government announced that it was suspending its

Pacific Ocean nuclear weapons tests for the rest of the year (see II.1.i). It said that this decision was meant to discourage nuclear proliferation, and called upon other nuclear nations to make balanced reductions in their arsenals. Since 1966 the French had exploded some 200 nuclear devices above and below ground at Fangataufa and Mururoa atolls in French Polynesia. The tests had produced a steadily rising tide of opposition throughout the Pacific and internationally.

The marine environment laboratory of the International Atomic Energy Agency reported in August that pollution of the Gulf as a result of the 1991 war was far less serious than originally feared. In fact, according to the laboratory, there was less oil pollution in the waters around Bahrain than before the conflict, apparently because the war had decreased tanker traffic. Severe oil pollution had affected 400 km of the Saudi coastline south of Kuwait, but most of the oil had been digested by microbes and levels of cancer-causing chemicals left by burning oil were no higher than those in UK estuaries.

A relatively new environmental issue quietly came to the fore in 1992, as negotiators laboured to complete the GATT Uruguay Round trade liberalization negotiations. Many environmentalists feared that more liberal trade would weaken restrictions on unhealthy or environmentally-unsound goods. This fear was particularly prevalent in the United States and Canada with reference to the new North American Free Trade Agreement (see IV.1 & IV.2). But European groups were also beginning to oppose free trade, given their concerns about the environmental effects of the new single European market.

The US Vice-President-elect, Senator Al Gore, could claim to be the first holder of the post to have written a major book on the environment, one which called for urgent action (see also XIV.2). US environmentalists had regarded the Republican administrations of Ronald Reagan and George Bush as anti-environment. They looked for bold new initiatives from the Clinton-Gore team.

XV THE LAW

1. INTERNATIONAL LAW—EUROPEAN COMMUNITY LAW

i. INTERNATIONAL LAW

THE UN-authorized action in Somalia (see VI.1.ii and XI.1) and in former Yugoslavia (see III.1.vi) raised important legal questions about the scope of UN peace-keeping and enforcement powers. The UN was also still seeking compliance by Iraq with the ceasefire agreed in 1991 (see AR 1991, pp. 550–5). To ensure compensation by Iraq of the victims of its unlawful invasion and occupation of Kuwait in 1990–91, the UN Compensation Commission was established as a subsidiary organ of the UN Security Council and began to make decisions (see AR 1991, p. 386). In that the number of potential claims was enormous, it was unlikely that they would be met in full. The Commission made arrangements to act fast but on the basis of principle. It consisted of three bodies: a governing council, a secretariat and a panel of commissioners. Charged with deciding questions of policy, the governing council had, by end-1992, issued 13 decisions on procedure, funding and the criteria for the different categories of claims. The structure of the Commission and the decisions of its governing council represented important developments in the resolution of international disputes.

The International Court of Justice (ICJ) continued to be busy. Four new cases were brought. Libya made two separate applications against the USA and the UK under the Montreal Convention for the Suppression of Unlawful Acts against the Safety of Civil Aviation. The USA and the UK had charged two Libyan nationals with blowing up Pan Am flight 103 over Lockerbie on 21 December 1988 (see AR 1988, p. 38) and were pressing Libya to surrender them for trial; they had rejected Libyan requests to resolve the matter under the Montreal convention. Libya asked the ICJ to declare that it had complied with its obligations under the convention and that the USA and the UK were in breach of the convention and under a duty to cease all threats against Libya. Libya also requested the Court to indicate provisional measures enjoining the USA and UK from taking any coercive action to compel Libya to surrender their nationals and to ensure that no steps be taken to prejudice the rights of Libya with respect to the merits of the case.

The USA and the UK had been using the Security Council to put pressure on Libya. On 21 January resolution 731, a non-binding resolution under chapter VI of the UN Charter, expressed concern that Libyan officials were implicated in the terrorist act and urged Libya to respond to US and UK requests for the surrender of the two accused

Libyan nationals. While the request for provisional measures was still under consideration by the ICJ, the USA and the UK on 31 March secured the passing of resolution 748, which was binding under chapter VII of the UN Charter. This determined that Libya's failure to respond to the requests in resolution 731 constituted a threat to international peace and security and decided that Libya must comply with that resolution.

This recourse to the UN Security Council while the ICJ was still considering the request for provisional measures attracted considerable criticism. The Court was left with little alternative other than to hold that Libya, as a member of the UN, was obliged to carry out Security Council decisions, and that this *prima facie* extended to resolution 748. In accordance with article 103 of the UN Charter, obligations of UN membership prevailed over any other treaty, including the Montreal convention. By 11 votes to 5, the Court held that the rights claimed by Libya under the Montreal convention could not be protected by provisional measures (see V.4.ii & XI.1 for subsequent developments).

Two other new cases were brought to the Court, one by Hungary against Czechoslovakia over the projected diversion of the Danube and one by Iran against the USA with respect to the destruction of Iranian oil platforms during the Iran-Iraq war. And two cases were withdrawn. Following last year's withdrawal of its case against the USA (see AR 1991, p. 462), Nicaragua withdrew its claim against Honduras in the case concerning *Border and Trans-border Armed Actions* on 11 May. Finland and Denmark settled their dispute concerning passage through the Great Belt and this case was also discontinued.

In *Certain Phosphate Lands in Nauru*, the Court gave judgment on the preliminary objections. Nauru claimed that Australia was responsible for breaches of its trusteeship agreement with Nauru and of international obligations on self-determination and permanent sovereignty. Australia made several preliminary submissions challenging the jurisdiction of the Court, which Nauru claimed was based on article 36(2) of the ICJ Statute. Australia argued that, because of its reservation to article 36(2), the Court did not have jurisdiction over any dispute in regard to which the parties had agreed to some other method of peaceful settlement; any dispute that had arisen in the course of its trusteeship should be regarded as having been settled by the termination of the trusteeship. The Court found no evidence of any agreement to settle the dispute about the rehabilitation of the phosphate lands by means other than resort to the Court. Nor had Nauru waived its claims.

Australia also argued that since Nauru did not formally raise its claim until nearly 20 years after its independence (in January 1968), the claim was inadmissible. The Court accepted that delay could render an application inadmissible but held that on the facts this had not occurred. However, the judges unanimously accepted Australia's objection that Nauru's claim to legal entitlement to the Australian allocation of the overseas assests of the British Phosphate Commissioners was inadmissible because this was in form and substance a new claim which appeared for the first time in the Nauru memorial. The Court rejected Australia's argument that because the other administering powers, the UK and New Zealand, were not parties to the proceedings the claim could not proceed against Australia alone.

A chamber of the Court gave a decision on the merits of the *Land, Island and Maritime Frontier Dispute* between El Salvador and Honduras (see also IV.3.xiii). In each of these areas, land, island and maritime, the chamber applied the *uti possidetis juris* principle: colonial boundaries were transformed into international frontiers on the independence of El Salvador and Honduras. As regards the land area, there were difficulties in identifying these colonial boundaries; no legislative material was available but the chamber looked at land grants and the conduct of the administrative authorities as proof of the effective exercise of territorial jurisdiction during the colonial period. As regards the islands in the Gulf of Fonseca, the evidence on *uti possidetis* was again fragmentary and ambiguous, and the chamber had to turn to the conduct of the parties to determine title. Finally, on the Gulf of Fonseca the parties disagreed whether their special agreement empowered the chamber to delimit a maritime boundary or simply to determine the legal status of the Gulf. The chamber held that the absence of any specific reference to delimitation in the special agreement was decisive. On the basis of the *uti possidetis* principle, because the Gulf had not been divided at the time of independence from Spain, it continued to be an historic bay to which El Salvador, Honduras and Nicaragua (which had intervened in the case on this point—see AR 1991, p. 469) succeeded jointly. That is, El Salvador's claim that the Gulf was a condominium and that delimitation was inappropriate was upheld by 4 votes to 1.

An important arbitral award on maritime delimitation between Canada and France was made on 10 June (see also II.1.i & IV.2). A five-person court of arbitration was established to determine a single maritime boundary in accordance with international law. The dispute concerned the French islands of St Pierre and Miquelon, situated near the coast of Newfoundland. Canada argued for a 12-mile enclave for the islands; France supported a median line. The tribunal followed earlier jurisprudence in holding that geographical features were at the heart of the delimitation process, and that international law required the application of equitable principles taking account of relevant circumstances in order to achieve an equitable result. The tribunal regarded the claims of both parties as exaggerated and held that neither of the proposed solutions provided even a starting-point for the delimitation. In the area westward of the islands it held that the equitable solution would be to grant the islands an extra 12 nautical miles from the limit of their 12-mile territorial sea as an exclusive economic

zone. In the second sector the tribunal found that, as the French islands
had a coastal opening towards the south unobstructed by any Canadian
coast, they were entitled to a frontal seaward projection of 200 nautical
miles. The tribunal thus rejected the Canadian argument made on the
basis of earlier jurisprudence that the status of political dependency of
the French islands justified less extensive maritime rights than if they
were independent. Much of this award was legally controversial and,
significantly, the Canadian and French aribtrators both dissented.

Several important treaties were concluded on environmental matters.
These included the UN Convention on Biological Diversity and the
Framework Convention on Climate Change, emanating from UN Conference on the Environment and Development held in Rio de Janeiro
(see XIV.3 & XIX.1). The Basle Convention on Control of Transboundary Movements of Hazardous Wastes and their Disposal entered
into force on 5 May. In the area of human rights, the USA finally ratified
the 1966 International Covenant on Civil and Political Rights on 8 June.
This had been signed by President Carter on 5 October 1977 and at
year's end had over 100 states parties.

ii.   EUROPEAN COMMUNITY LAW

THE EC's Maastricht treaty was duly signed on 7 February 1992 (see
also XI.3). Although it had been negotiated throughout 1991, and
finally agreed at the December 1991 Maastricht summit (see AR 1991,
pp. 400–2, 465–7, 561–6), in the form of two separate treaties, it had by
February been transformed into a single text, of particularly monstrous
size. The treaty itself was quite short. But it contained in its middle a
huge article which made massive and fundamental amendments to the
EEC treaty and was quite incomprehensible until the EEC treaty itself
had been reprinted with all the amendments incorporated into it. This
was promptly done a month later by *Common Market Law Reports*.

That, however, was not the end of the enormity. Tacked on to the
Treaty of Union (the Maastricht treaty proper) were 17 protocols, many
of them of crucial importance, and 33 declarations. And to compound
the offence the texts on economic and monetary union (EMU), which
constituted the core of the innovation and which, more than any of
the other provisions, formed a coherent and well-drafted whole, were
split between four of the protocols to the Treaty of Union, on the one
hand, and 27 brand-new articles of the EEC treaty (comprising a new
title divided into four chapters), on the other. No wonder the Danish
people threw up their hands in horror when their government unwisely
distributed to them thousands of free copies of the raw, unedited treaty,
and then in a referendum on 2 June went on to vote (narrowly) against
ratification (see II.2.i).

As a result, the Danish government went into shock and the remaining member states (except Britain) jumped up and down uttering wild threats to expel the Danes or to go ahead regardless. The trouble was that not only did article R of the Maastricht treaty require ratification by all 12 EC states before it could come into force, but also the EEC treaty itself could not be amended except by a similarly-unanimous 12-fold ratification. If Denmark failed to ratify, the treaty would be dead. All efforts were therefore directed to finding a formula which would persuade enough Danish voters to switch sides to produce a vote in favour of the treaty. At the Edinburgh summit just before Christmas such a formula was agreed and a second Danish referendum was planned for mid-1993, in which it was hoped that a positive vote would be obtained.

But the farce started well before the Danish referendum. In the closing stages of negotiation on the Union treaties, in the autumn of 1991, the European Court had ruled, in *SPUC* v. *Grogan* (see AR 1991, p. 467), that the anti-abortion provision in the Irish constitution (article 40.3.3) might in certain cases have to give way to the right of free movement under the EEC treaty. Although the actual case before it did not fall into that category (and the Irish government won), it feared that one day there might be a damaging constitutional clash with Community law. (One Irish Supreme Court judge, in the *Grogan* case, had threatened that if the European Court held against Ireland the Supreme Court might, when the case came back to it from Luxembourg, refuse to follow Community law.) And so the Irish government persuaded the other member states to insert a special one-sentence protocol in the Maastricht treaty placing article 40.3.3. of the Irish constitution beyond the reach of any Community law. A month after signature of the treaty the Irish Supreme Court gave judgment in another abortion case, *Attorney General* v. *X*, where it held that in certain very exceptional cases (and the case before it was just such a one) an Irish woman might be entitled to travel abroad to obtain an abortion notwithstanding article 40.3.3 (see also II.1.vii). The government took the view that this softening of the Supreme Court's position might be frustrated by the 'abortion protocol' in the Maastricht treaty and sought the agreement of the other member states to remove or alter it. The latter refused to reopen the treaty for fear of it unravelling. Instead, they agreed to make a 'solemn declaration'—which they hoped would be legally binding—that the protocol was not intended to hinder the EEC right of free movement between member states.

The second big constitutional legacy from 1991 paralleled the fate of the Maastricht treaty uncannily. The European Economic Area (EEA) treaty was hastily redrafted after the European Court had, just before Christmas 1991, rejected its creation of a special EEA court as harmful to the special character of the EEC treaty and the

standing of the European Court itself (see AR 1991, p. 465). To replace
the EEA court a 'two pillar' system was worked out, whereby EFTA
would have its own court and enforcement agency, equivalent to the
European Court and the Commission, each acting in its own area.
Complex provisions were included to cover a possible divergence of
interpretation between the two pillars (EFTA and EC) of the EEA. In its
main part the treaty provided that all the *acquis communautaire*, i.e.
the Community law which existed at the date of signature of the EEA
treaty, and particularly the 'four freedoms' (of movement of goods,
persons, services and capital), together with 'flanking' rules such as
those on competition, should apply throughout the EEA—in effect that
Community law should apply to the EFTA countries without their being
members of the Community and so without their taking part in the
creation of that law.

   This was all ready by 14 February, when agreement on the EEA treaty
was formally reached at official level, one week after the Maastricht
treaty had been signed. However, the European Parliament was not
happy with it and persuaded the Commission to refer the revised
version of the treaty to the European Court once again for a ruling
on its compatibility with the EEC treaty. The Court gave its favourable
response in April and the EEA treaty was duly signed on 2 May. It
was even more monstrous than the Maastricht treaty. It contained
not only 129 articles but also 49 protocols, 22 annexes listing the
Community law which the EFTA countries undertook to make part
of their own domestic law, 30 joint declarations and a further 41
unilateral declarations, the whole covering 1,000 pages of text (see
XIX.2 for introductory articles). On the same day the EFTA states
signed their own parallel EFTA Surveillance Agreement which would
set up the EFTA court and surveillance authority, i.e. the EFTA pillar
under the two-pillar system.

   These two texts then set off on their ratification journey; and, like
the Maastricht treaty, were intended to come into force on 1 January
1993. But just as Maastricht was thrown off course, temporarily at least,
by the Danish referendum, so the EEA treaty suffered similarly from a
negative Swiss referendum on 6 December (see II.2.vii). Just as exactly a
year previously the EEA treaty had had to be redrafted following the first
European Court ruling, so now it was subjected to further redrafting to
adapt it to the absence of Switzerland. This was possible because, unlike
Maastricht, its ratification was not subject to a unanimity rule.

   By the end of the year, therefore, none of these treaties was ready
to come into force on the intended date of 1 January 1993, although they
had all been ratified by most of the contracting parties. In order to get
that far, five of the EC member states had found it necessary to amend
their constitutions: Ireland, Spain, France, Portugal and Germany,
even though all except Ireland had not thought it necessary when

they first joined the Community. Also during the year three further EFTA countries (Finland, Switzerland and Norway) applied for full membership of the EC, following the earlier applications by Austria and Sweden. To some extent, therefore, the EEA negotiations had acted as a trial run for the membership negotiations to come.

Finally, both groupings began to creep eastwards. EFTA entered into free trade agreements with Turkey, Czechoslovakia, Poland and Romania; and the EC concluded 'Europe agreements' (in reality, association agreements) with Bulgaria and Romania, to add to those it had agreed with the three Visegrad countries (Czechoslovakia, Hungary and Poland) at the end of 1991.

While all this constitutional high drama was taking place, the Community legislative machine was steadily working its way through the 1992 programme of legislation and virtually completed it by the appointed date of 31 December 1992. One of the most important texts was a VAT directive which set out new rules to cope with the abolition of intra-Community frontiers after 1992 as a result of article 8a of the EEC treaty. Because even then each member state would remain a separate tax territory, with its own rates of VAT, the existing system, whereby zero-rated goods leaving one member state were liable to local VAT on entering another, would be impossible to sustain. To replace it, a complex and heavily bureaucratic scheme was introduced. Consumer sales would be taxed where they took place and thereafter be outside the tax system; but the states, fearing loss of revenue, were unwilling to allow this simple system to be applied to trade sales and distance sales. For these, tax would be levied in the destination country but it would then be shared out with the state of origin through an inter-state clearing house based on detailed statistical information to be supplied by traders for every inter-state transaction they carried out.

Judicial highlights included the European Court's final ruling that national restrictions on Sunday trading did not infringe article 30 of the EEC treaty (*Stoke on Trent* v. *B & Q plc*); and a reversal of the previous understanding of 'reverse discrimination' so that citizens in their own member state would enjoy Community rights in their own country if they had as it were 'activated' their Community status by going to work in another member state and then returned home (*R.* v. *Surinder Singh*).

2.   LAW IN THE UNITED KINGDOM

PARLIAMENT enacted three important consolidating statutes. The long-overdue consolidation of the law relating to social security was achieved by the *Social Security Contributions and Benefits Act*, while the administration of the system was streamlined by the *Social Security*

Administration Act, giving effect to recommendations of the Law Commission made in 1991.[1] The *Trades Union and Labour Relations (Consolidation) Act* brought together in a single statute all of the legislation relating to trades unions and other collective labour organizations; and the *Tribunals and Inquiries Act* similarly re-enacted the *Tribunals and Inquiries Act* of 1971, which had undergone considerable amendment in the intervening two decades. The *Local Government Finance Act* replaced the widely-disliked community charge (poll tax) with a council tax assessed by reference to the value of the property in which the taxpayer lived. The powers of the Charity Commissioners to monitor the activities of charities were considerably strengthened by the *Charities Act*, largely giving effect to the recommendations of a White Paper of 1989.[2] The *Transport and Works Act* gave greater powers to the government to regulate transport operations; in particular, part II of the act introduced measures designed to give greater safety on railways, including the prohibition of the use of drink and drugs by responsible employees.

In the courts, the Secretary of State's decision to close a number of collieries without adequate consultation was held to be unlawful by the Court of Appeal[3]; and the decision of Browne-Wilkinson V.-C. that a government minister might be under a common law duty to take reasonable care in the exercise of his statutory functions was upheld.[4] The Queen's Bench Division held that a policy of selective prosecution by the Inland Revenue was lawful, refusing to rule that they should prosecute all or no offenders in a particular category.[5] It also ruled that the Law Society was acting properly in adopting a policy limiting the compensation which they would pay to clients who had suffered loss at the hands of dishonest solicitors.[6]

Both parliament and the courts put down markers in favour of the free flow of information. The *Human Fertilization and Embryology (Disclosure of Information) Act* relaxed the restrictions on disclosure of information relating to individuals conceived as a result of artificial insemination,[7] where it was desirable that this information should be available for legal or medical reasons. The Court of Appeal held that it was wrong to prevent the publication of a newspaper article describing how a ward of court had been fostered with a homosexual couple;[8] while the Divisional Court ruled that a newspaper should not be liable for contempt of court for publishing facts relevant to a trial, unless there was a real, rather than a hypothetical, risk that a fair trial would be prejudiced by the publication.[9] A local authority was held not to be entitled to use the law of libel to prevent criticism of its activities by the press.[10]

The House of Lords adopted a benign approach to the interpretation of legacies intended to be charitable, holding that a gift 'for a purpose in connection with sport' did not attract liability to capital transfer tax.[11]

In another case of enormous practical and theoretical importance, the House of Lords decided against the Inland Revenue, upholding the decision of the Court of Appeal to the effect that a taxpayer who had paid tax wrongfully demanded was entitled to recover the amount paid plus interest.[12] On the other hand, the House reiterated the traditional view that where the wording of a statute was unambiguous it was not open to the courts to read words into it in order to prevent the occurrence of unforeseen anomalies.[13]

In the wake of public disquiet over dangerous joy-riding in stolen cars, the *Aggravated Vehicle Taking Act* introduced more stringent penalties for cases where cars were taken without the consent of the owner and subsequently driven in a reckless manner; criminal liability was also attached to passengers in such vehicles. As one of a series of responses to the prison riots which occurred in 1990, the *Prison Security Act* introduced a new offence of prison mutiny, slightly wider than the older offences of riot and violent disorder.[14]

The statutory anonymity granted to complainants of rape was extended to the victims of other sexual offences by the *Sexual Offences (Amendment) Act*. On several occasions the courts considered the question of whether a woman who killed her husband after having suffered prolonged domestic violence at his hands had a defence to a charge of murder. In *Thornton*[15] the Court of Appeal held that the defence of provocation was not normally available; but in *Ahluwalia*[16] a move was made towards the recognition of the defence by the ruling that the fact that a woman was suffering from battered wives' syndrome was a relevant factor which should be taken into account in assessing the seriousness of any allegedly provocative acts on the part of the victim. The well-established rule that the defence of duress was not available to a charge of murder was extended by the House of Lords to cases of attempted murder.[17]

The definition of 'appropriation' in the Theft Act[18] continued to give the courts enormous difficulty. In *Stringer and Banks*[19] the Court of Appeal held that the signing of false invoices was a sufficient appropriation of the property to which they referred. In *Nadir*, Tucker J. held that an act could not amount to an appropriation if it was done with the consent of the owner.[20] Finally, the House of Lords in *Gomez*[21] ruled that there had been an appropriation when property had been taken dishonestly notwithstanding that the owner had consented to the taking.

In an important case on the freedom of the individual, the Court of Appeal held that the full consent of the victim to a beating was no defence to a charge of assault and battery or unlawful wounding;[22] the case was subsequently argued at length in the House of Lords. The Court of Appeal[23] and the House of Lords[24] confirmed that an objective test of recklessness should be applied in cases of causing death by reckless driving, spurning the opportunity to depart from their own previous decision on the point. An ambiguity in the *Computer Misuse Act* of 1990 was resolved by the decision of the Court of Appeal that an offence had been committed by a person who used one programme of a computer to gain unauthorized access to another programme on the same computer.[25]

A computer print-out was held to be inadmissible as evidence of liability to pay community charge on the grounds that it was hearsay;[26] in order to avoid the practically disastrous effects of this ruling, the government hurriedly reversed it by statute.[27] In another, very difficult, case on the scope of the admissibility of hearsay evidence, the House of Lords by a majority held that telephone calls made to the appellant's home requesting that he sell drugs to the callers were inadmissible in a prosecution for the possession of drugs with intent to supply.[28] On the other hand, the potential evidentiary difficulties flowing from the increasing use of computers in retail sales were avoided by the decision of the House of Lords that evidence of the proper functioning of the computer could be given by any person familiar with its operation—in the instant case, a store detective—even if that person was not a computer expert.[29]

Detailed regulations were made preparatory to the coming into force of the Child Support Act 1991.[30] In the meantime, the Court of Appeal gave effect to the policy behind the act, holding that a father who wanted custody of his child should normally be granted it even though the mother might have wished to place the child for adoption;[31] that a father whose behaviour was eccentric and bizarre should not automatically be denied access to his children;[32] and that a father who requested access after some years' absence should normally be granted it.[33] In the same way, the policy of the Children Act 1989 was furthered by a ruling that the wardship jurisdiction should not be used to bypass the statutorily-conferred jurisdiction of the Home Secretary and immigration officials.[34]

While a traditionally tentative attitude continued to be taken towards the redistribution of property rights between unmarried partners,[35] a more radical approach was visible in dealing with other points of dispute between cohabitants. Scott-Baker J. was willing to take cognizance of a claim for the redistribution of property where the parties had only entered into an agreement to marry, even where at the time of the agreement one of them was married already;[36] and the joint intention of cohabiting parties was held to determine the destination of moneys payable under a policy of life insurance, notwithstanding the express terms of the policy.[37] Similarly, a wide approach to the phrase 'living together as husband and wife' was taken by the Court of Appeal in *City of Westminster* v. *Peart*[38], though on the facts the court held that it was not possible to extend the definition to cases where one party retained a separate home.

In the *Carriage of Goods by Sea Act*, giving effect to the recommendations of the Law Commission,[39] parliament took the opportunity of removing a range of anomalous situations in which the consignee of goods had been prevented from recovering compensation when the goods had been damaged. Commercial certainty was furthered by the courts' continued refusal to impose liability in negligence for pure economic loss,[40] and their narrow view of the circumstances in which liability would be imposed for negligently causing nervous shock.[41] The House of Lords declined to undermine the traditional principles of certainty in contracts, refusing to hold that an undertaking to negotiate with only one other person for an unspecified period was unenforceable.[42] Less restrictively, the Court of Appeal held that a child had a right of action at common law for injuries suffered while it was still in the womb.[43]

The House of Lords held that a lease of land had to be for a fixed term, and hence a purported lease for an uncertain period was void, giving expression to a conclusion which had been argued to be law for several centuries.[44] Similarly, the Court of Appeal finally gave authoritative recognition to the medieval rule that where bailed property was damaged either the bailor or bailee, but not both, might sue in respect of it.[45] The boundary between the lease and the licence was further considered by the House of Lords in *Westminster City Council* v. *Clarke*,[46] holding that an agreement to occupy a room in a local authority hostel for the homeless was a licence.

The equal treatment provisions of the Sex Discrimination Act 1975 continued to give difficulty. In *Webb* v. *EMO Air Cargo (UK) Ltd*[47] the House of Lords concluded, subject to a reference to the European Court, that it was not unlawful discrimination to dismiss a trainee who had recently become pregnant on the grounds that by the time she had been trained she would not be capable of performing the duties for which she had been employed. Employment in universities was held to be governed by potentially different rules: in *R* v. *Hull University ex parte Page*[48] the House of Lords held that the courts had no power to review the decision of the university visitor unless she had clearly acted in excess of her powers under the university's statutes. There was further exploration of the powers of the courts to approve the cessation of medical treatment to a hopelessly incurable patient; the Court of Appeal upheld the decision of Sir Stephen Brown P. that effect should be given to informed medical opinion that it would not be in the patient's interests that his life be prolonged further.[49]

1   (1991) Cm 1726. Related statutes brought about similar results in Northern Ireland.

2 'Charities: A Framework for the Future' (1989) Cm 694.
3 *R* v. *Secretary of State for Trade, ex parte Vardy and others, The Times* 30 December.
4 *Lonrho* v. *Tebbit* [1992] 4 All ER 280.
5 *R* v. *Inland Revenue Commissioners, ex parte Mead and Cook* [1992] STC 482.
6 *R* v. *Law Society, ex parte Reigate Projects* [1992] 3 All ER 232.
7 *Human Fertilization and Embryology Act* 1990, s. 35(5).
8 *re W (a minor) (Wardship: Restrictions on Publication)* [1992] 1 WLR 100.
9 *Attorney-General* v. *Guardian Newspapers* [1992] 3 All ER 38.
10 *Derbyshire County Council* v. *Times Newspapers* [1992] 3 WLR 28.
11 *Guild* v. *Inland Revenue Commissioners* [1992] 2 All ER 10.
12 *Woolwich Building Society* v. *Inland Revenue Commissioners* [1992] 3 WLR 366.
13 *BP Oil Development* v. *Inland Revenue Commissioners* [1992] STC 28.
14 *Public Order Act* 1986, s. 1(1) and s. 1(2).
15 [1992] 1 All ER 306.
16 *The Times*, 8 September.
17 *R* v. *Gotts* [1992] 1 All ER 832.
18 *Theft Act* 1968, s. 1.
19 (1992) 94 Cr.App.Rep. 13.
20 *The Independent*, 24 June.
21 [1992] 3 WLR 1067.
22 *R* v. *Brown and others* [1992] WLR 441.
23 *R* v. *Fisher* [1992] Criminal Law Review 201.
24 *R* v. *Reid* [1992] 1 WLR 793.
25 *Attorney-General's Reference (no. 1 of 1991)* [1992] 3 WLR 432.
26 *R* v. *Coventry Justices, ex parte Bullard* [1992] RA 79.
27 *Local Government Finance Act*, Schedule 4, paragraph 14.
28 *R* v. *Kearley* [1992] 2 All ER 345.
29 *R* v. *Shephard, The Times*, 17 December.
30 See [1992] *Family Law* 448.
31 *Re O (a minor) (Custody; Adoption)* [1992] 1 FLR 77.
32 *Re B (Minors: Access)* [1992] 1 FLR 140.
33 *Re H (Minors: Access)* [1992] 1 FLR 148.
34 *Re K and S (Minors) (Wardship: Immigration)* [1992] 1 FLR 432.
35 *Springett* v. *Defoe* (1992) 24 HLR 552; *H* v. *M (Property: Beneficial Interest)* [1992] 1 FLR 229.
36 *Shaw* v. *Fitzgerald* [1992] 1 FLR 357.
37 *Smith* v. *Clerical, Medical and General Life Assurance Society* [1992] 1 FCR 262.
38 (1992) 24 HLR 389.
39 'Rights of Suit in Respect of Carriage of Goods by Sea' (1991) Law Com no. 196.
40 *Nitrigin Eireann Teoranta* v. *Inco Alloys* [1992] 1 All ER 854; but see *Keckskemeti* v. *Rubens Rabin & Co, The Times* 31 December, for a more generous approach by a judge of first instance.
41 *Ravenscroft* v. *Rederiaktiebolaget Transatlantic* [1992] 2 All ER 470.
42 *Walford* v. *Miles* [1992] 1 All ER 453.
43 *Burton* v. *Islington Health Authority; de Martell* v *Sutton Health Authority* [1992] 3 All ER 833.
44 *Prudential Assurance Co* v. *London Residuary Body* [1992] 3 WLR 279.
45 *O'Sullivan* v. *Williams* [1992] 3 All ER 385.
46 [1992] 1 All ER 695.
47 (1992) 142 *New Law Journal* 1720.
48 [1992] 3 WLR 1112.
49 *Airedale National Health Service Trust* v. *Bland* (1992) 142 *New Law Journal* 1755.

3.   UNITED STATES LAW

THE Supreme Court's decision in *Planned Parenthood* v. *Casey* signified a conservative retreat in what became dubbed as the 'year of the woman'. In the wake of a prior decision of the Court in 1989, Pennsylvania had enacted a law which required that a woman who had decided to have an abortion should notify her husband of her intent, be informed of the procedure and be told that the father was liable for child support; a minor seeking an abortion was required to obtain her parents' consent or an order of court waiving such consent. These limitations on the liberty to abort a foetus were clearly inconsistent with the celebrated 1973 *Roe* v. *Wade* decision, which held that a woman's constitutional right of privacy included having an abortion in the first trimester and, subject to limitations, in the second as well. Conservatives hoped, and liberals feared, that the Supreme Court would reverse that decision, leaving states free to curb the right to abortion. In the event, three conservative justices joined with liberal justices in holding invalid the requirement that a woman must notify her husband; they suggested that respect for precedent barred their reversing the landmark 1973 decision. This ruling marked a compromise appropriate for the political temperament of the country, characterized as the 'Year of the Woman'. In the 1992 elections, women candidates campaigning against conservative men were elected to a number of offices, including both Senate seats in California and one in Illinois, thus doubling the number of women in the Senate. The background scenario included the 1991 Senate hearings on the confirmation of Justice Clarence Thomas and the attempted charge of sexual harassment (see AR 1991, pp. 52–3), as well as Supreme Court decisions significantly limiting the right to abortion under *Roe* v. *Wade*.

New chapters were written in the history of asbestos and cigarette litigation, the former a growth industry for the plaintiff's bar in the last decade and the latter a potential growth area despite firm resistance from the tobacco industry. A total of 8,555 claims against a number of asbestos manufacturers were consolidated into a single trial of six 'sample' cases in which the jury found for three plaintiffs against four manufacturers. After devising a formula for determining damages applicable to all cases, the three successful plaintiffs were awarded $11.5 million in compensatory damages and some $29 million in punitive damages. The remaining 8,549 cases were scheduled to proceed in 'mini-trials' of 10 to 12 claims. *Cipollone* v. *Liggett Group*, the first verdict against a cigarette manufacturer for causing the death of a smoker, had been reversed by an appeal court because the trial judge had not properly instructed the jury. The defending cigarette manufacturer had argued (unsuccessfully) that a federal law requiring a warning about cigarette smoking to be printed on the packet pre-empted state law and governed liability. The plaintiff won the argument in the Supreme Court, which held that the federal law did not pre-empt state liability laws. However, his (and his attorney's) resources were exhausted by the lengthy litigation and appeals, with the result that he abandoned the suit.

The mass failure of savings and loan (S & L) institutions (see AR 1989, pp. 51–2; 1990, p. 62) generated high jury awards against their owners, and extensions of liability to lawyers and accountants for their services to such owners. In a lawsuit by 20,000 plaintiffs against Charles Keating, owner of Lincoln S & L (the insolvency of which was expected to cost taxpayers $2,600 million), the jury awarded $600 million in compensatory damages for alleged losses of $288.7 million as well as punitive damages of $3,300 million against Mr Keating and another $5,000 million against co-defendants. Both awards were expected to be reduced on appeal. More significantly, the regulatory Federal Deposit Insurance Corporation was permitted to sue a major California law firm for its alleged negligence in failing to detect its client's fraud when preparing documents about the client's real-estate transactions, which documents were sent to the client's investors. The Office of Thrift Supervision, another regulatory agency, pursued a $275 million law suit against a major New York law firm which represented Lincoln S & L by issuing an asset preservation order intended to prevent the defendants from hiding or dissipating their assets. These assets were principally the firm's bank accounts for paying bills, employees' salaries and partners, so that, with its operations effectively paralysed, the firm was forced to settle with the governmental agency for $41 million. The precedent for law and accounting firms was widely recognized.

The legal atomization of the family into individuals, each with their own rights against the others, reached new levels. In a Florida case an 11-year-old boy successfully petitioned a court to terminate his relationship with his mother, against her wishes and those of the state department responsible for the well-being of children, so that he could be adopted by parents of his choice. In Tennessee a divorced woman sought to have implanted in her womb seven frozen embryos which she had created with her ex-husband during their marriage. The state's supreme court, finding that the embryos had no rights, characterized the dispute as essentially contractual and held that, in the absence of an agreement between the parties as to how the embryos should be disposed of upon divorce, the ex-husband could not be compelled to become a father. In California the state supreme court held that an unwed father had a right to veto the adoption of his child.

Enactments and decisions in criminal law, often perceived as a litmus test of a court's conservative or liberal values, attracted less attention in 1992. The Supreme Court's decision that the abduction of a suspect in Mexico by federal law enforcement officers in order to bring the suspect to trial in the United States did not violate the suspect's rights provoked unhappy reactions in Latin America, where the decision was seen as legitimizing the violation of national sovereignty. The decision was expected to result in revisions to extradition treaties with the United States to prevent such action. The Court also narrowed somewhat the availability of the writ of habeas corpus in federal courts reviewing convictions in state courts. In a dramatic expression of its dislike of such reviews, the Court issued successive orders to the federal appellate court which had stayed the execution of a prisoner in California (who had been sentenced to death in 1979). The appellate court had agreed that there was an issue of whether execution by cyanide gas might be cruel and unusual. The Court, in a short decision, held that, since that claim could have been made more than a decade ago, it was an abuse to now raise the issue. The subsequent execution of the prisoner was the first in California for more than 20 years.

XVI THE ARTS

1. OPERA—MUSIC—DANCE/BALLET—THEATRE—CINEMA —TELEVISION & RADIO

i. OPERA

DURING the year two much-heralded reports on the Royal Opera House were delivered. One, an appraisal by an Arts Council team under the chairmanship of Baroness Warnock, criticized the management but praised the company's recent artistic achievements. The other, commissioned from a firm of management consultants by the Royal Opera House itself, not surprisingly criticized the Arts Council strongly for not providing adequate subsidy. Subsequent action taken by the Royal Opera House board included making seventy employees redundant, renewing the contract of the general director, Jeremy Isaacs, to 1995, and announcing that the planned redevelopment of the building would go ahead even though the money to pay for it had still not been found.

The Royal Opera's artistic standards actually varied widely, primarily because directors of productions were not always wisely chosen. The Mozart cycle entrusted to Johannes Schaaf concluded with *Don Giovanni*, an opera which fared almost as badly at this director's hands as *Cosi fan tutte* and *Le Nozze di Figaro* in previous years. It was played in a series of black boxes open to a sky on which stars, clouds and a thunderstorm were projected, and most of its important dramatic points were either passed over or clumsily mismanaged. Fortunately the musical performance was for the most part superb. The slow pace forced upon the singers in recitative by the director was forgotten in Bernard Haitink's generally brisk tempi, and the tension lacking on stage was admirably conveyed by the orchestra. Though well sung, Thomas Allen's Giovanni was oddly bland, but Carol Vaness brought a creamily rich voice and a convincing characterization to the role of Donna Anna.

The Royal Opera had considerably more triumphs than disasters. One of its most successful new productions was of Benjamin Britten's *Death in Venice*, a work which, when it was first staged at the Aldeburgh Festival in 1973, was greeted with no more than cautious respect. But the director (Colin Graham) and conductor (Steuart Bedford) of that first production returned to the opera in 1992 with perhaps a deeper understanding of it. As Aschenbach, the role composed for Peter Pears, Philip Langridge gave what was surely the finest in his long series of Britten characterizations, and the Royal Opera Orchestra made the score sound richer and more sparkling than before. The opera, which was once generally thought to be the work of a composer in decline, may well turn out to have been Britten's crowning achievement.

Bellini's final opera, *I Puritani*, which had been missing from the Royal Opera's repertoire since 1964 when the role of Elvira was sung by the incomparable Joan Sutherland, returned in a production by Andrei Serban (borrowed from Welsh National Opera) which made the most of the work's dramatic impact without doing violence to the music. Indeed, as opera productions went nowadays, it was a veritable model of sense and sensibility. The casting of the four leading roles was almost a vindication of international opera, with an American soprano (June Anderson), an Italian tenor (Giuseppe Sabatini), a Siberian baritone (Dmitri Hvorostovsky) and a British bass (Robert Lloyd) combining to present a unified style of performance. The brittle radiance of June Anderson's voice may have lacked the heart-stopping magic of Sutherland's, but in all other respects she was an ideal Elvira, and her colleagues were all first-rate. A new young conductor, Daniele Gatti, achieved a powerful account of the score with no sacrifice of its elegance.

In his otherwise perfectly competent new staging of Wagner's *Der Fliegende Holländer*, Ian Judge ignored Wagner's important stage direction requiring the transfigured forms of the Dutchman and his beloved Senta to be seen in close embrace, soaring upwards. An especial glory of this production was the décor by John Gunter, beautifully designed to enable the seamless one-act version of the opera to move with magical ease from scene to scene. James Morris's Dutchman was powerfully sung and acted with conviction, and Christoph von Dohnanyi conducted with strength and sensitivity. Although it was extravagant of the Royal Opera to bring Norbert Balatsch from the Vienna State Opera to train the chorus, it certainly paid off.

Thanks to the discovery of an IRA bomb in the nearby Transport Museum, the Royal Opera's revival of *I Capuleti e i Montecchi*, Bellini's version of the Romeo and Juliet story, not only began twenty minutes late on its first night, but was also denuded of its decor. The conductor and most of the cast were new, with Anne Sofie von Otter as Romeo producing beautiful, if slightly cool, tone, looking thoroughly convincing, and acting the part to perfection. Two unusual additions to the repertoire during the year were of works not previously performed at Covent Garden. Rossini's *Il Viaggio a Reims*, staged to celebrate its composer's 200th birthday and to mark the United Kingdom's presidency of the European Community, was a slight but engaging *pièce d'occasion* which would have benefited from stronger casting. Gershwin's *Porgy and Bess*, however, was sheer delight, gloriously sung by a black, mainly American cast. Trevor Nunn's production, adapted from his Glyndebourne staging, brought the inhabitants of

Charleston's Catfish Row to exuberant life, and Willard White—the only performer to have triumphed as both Shakespeare's Othello and Gershwin's Porgy—was a tower of strength in the title-role.

English National Opera maintained during the year its reputation for combining high musical standards with aggressively modish stage productions. Humperdinck's *Königskinder* was disappointing both musically and dramatically. The piece itself was unsatisfactory, its score alternating between sub-Wagnerian meandering and folk-like simplicity, and not even the excellent Mark Elder could coax his orchestra into making it sound at all flavoursome. David Pountney's production did its best to alleviate much of the tedium of act one, parted company with the work in the second act to substitute a coarse and uncalled-for parody of Bavarian village life, and went badly and distastefully off the rails in act three, in which the village children were dressed as inmates of the concentration camps of a later age and made to drop dead, one by one, in the opera's last bars. (The children were meant to be sorrowful surviving onlookers of the fate of the young lovers.)

By Verdi's standards, *Don Carlos* was a long opera, and made even longer in ENO's new production by the inclusion of music which the composer removed from the score before the 1867 premiere. But it was one of Verdi's greatest works, gripping from its first bar to its last, and the ENO cast did it full justice. Unfortunately the production was much less satisfactory visually than aurally. David Fielding's designs resembled the window displays of a trendy boutique, and David Pountney's direction ranged from the inept, through the misguided, to the deranged. Later in the year, Nicholas Hytner's account of another Verdi opera, *La Forza del Destino*, was considerably better, even though this time the permanent set looked like a fashionable New York discotheque.

Glyndebourne's final season in its old opera house opened with a fine production of Britten's *Peter Grimes*. Despite their allegiance to the currently fashionable concept of the sloping stage, particularly inappropriate to an opera set in the very flat county of Suffolk, John Gunter's designs succeeded in evoking the small fishing community of the Borough (Aldeburgh in disguise), and the director, Trevor Nunn, staged the work with intelligence and flair. The company's other new production was of *Queen of Spades*, Tchaikovsky's somewhat problematical opera which, gripping in its finest moments, could often defeat directors with its formlessness and its stop-go attitude to dramatic narrative. Graham Vick's production worked well, and had the benefit of a remarkably strong cast, headed by an American soprano, Nancy Gustafson, and a Russian tenor, Yuri Marusin.

Among those who died in 1992 were: Stella Roman, the Romanian-born American soprano, a noted exponent of Verdi and Puccini at the Metropolitan Opera in the 1940s; Ronald Eyre, the British director who turned to opera comparatively late in a distinguished career in the straight theatre; Alfreda Hodgson, the English contralto who appeared with the Royal Opera, ENO and Opera North; Sir Charles Groves, the English conductor who worked with Welsh National Opera for many years; Margarita Wallmann, the Austrian director, who was one of the most famous opera directors of the twentieth century; Dorothy Kirsten, the American soprano who sang leading roles at the Metropolitan Opera over a period of 30 years; Ina Souez, the American soprano who was Glyndebourne's first Fiordiligi and Donna Anna in the mid-1930s, and who became a soloist with Spike Jones and his City Slickers in the 1940s; and Sir Geraint Evans (see XX: OBITUARY).

ii. MUSIC

AFTER the splendour of Mozart's music the previous year, 1992 lacked any such focus. Nevertheless the musical calendar was full to saturation point, with occasional moments of distinction to lift the daily offerings of classical concerts above the level of ordinariness and routine. The New York Philharmonic, under Kurt Masur, infused fresh life into their series, meeting the challenge of the new as well as giving the familiar a refurbished look. In Britain the new Symphony Hall in Birmingham not only proved acoustically a successful home for its resident orchestra under Simon Rattle, whose speciality was the late romantic repertoire, but also attracted star performers. Otherwise there was a certain sameness to the London concert scene, marked only occasionally by moments of colourful variety. One such was a season of South American music, contributed by the Latin American and Caribbean Cultural Society, which introduced unknown music from Mexico, Brazil, Paraguay, Argentina and the Caribbean. Based mainly on the guitar and the vihuela, it proved a rich repertoire, old and new.

An equivalent variety in the New York season was provided by the American Ballet Theatre. In an already overcrowded dance scene, where only very special productions could expect to be noticed, a strong impression was created, at one end of the spectrum, by Kenneth MacMillan's *Romeo and Juliet*—largely because of Rudolf Nureyev's conducting debut—and at the other end by *Serious Pleasures*, to an electronic score by Robert Ruggieri, in which a sexually explicit dance for men led to a mass audience exit.

Performances of new and living composers' music accounted for a tiny proportion of musical output in Europe and America. A figure of under 4 per cent was suggested in one magazine. Yet this very small output, representing as it did the chief challenge of the times, could be seen as the seed-corn of the future. Moreover the trend in contemporary Western style in 1992, as far as art music was concerned, continued to move away from the radical avant-garde and towards more accessible idioms which could be expected to communicate more directly with the listener. Serialism had long since been pronounced outdated, and given way to minimalism, various forms of neo-modalism, or other such linear styles.

The high-priests of the European avant-garde, Boulez and Stockhausen, were less in evidence in 1992 than in previous years. The former was concerned with deciding on, and conducting, the definitive versions of already existing works; the latter with a project for recording his entire output, of which the first CD was issued in 1992. The chief exponents of American minimalism on the other hand—John Adams, Philip Glass, Steve Reich—all had a busy year, as did those whose style could loosely be bracketed under the heading 'neo-romantic'—David del Tredici, Aaron Jay Kernis, Ned Rorem and Leonard Bernstein. Indeed a performance of the latter's *On the Town* at the Barbican in July was one of the highlights of the London season. Other American composers whose works enjoyed prominence were John Corigliano and Elliott Carter. Corigliano won the prestigious and lucrative Grawemeyer Award for his First Symphony, thus adding to the great success already achieved by his opera *The Ghosts of Versailles*, which was a hit when it was produced at the Met in New York. 'An adventurous opera for unadventurous ears' was the verdict of one seasoned critic. Adventurous ears were certainly required for the music of Elliott Carter, whose four string quartets were performed and recorded by the Juilliard String Quartet, to be followed by the première of his new work *Quintet for Piano and Winds*, given by Hans Holliger and Kölnmusik.

In England the trend away from radicalism and experiment was plain. Birtwistle and Maxwell Davies yielded several points in the fashion stakes to their less aggressive rivals Holloway and Tavener, both of whom were much in evidence; the former with his violin concerto *Hymn to the Senses* and *Entrance–Carousing–Embarkation* for wind band, the latter with *The Last Sleep of the Virgin* and *Mary of Egypt*. This last piece, which was described by one unimpressed listener as '110 uninterrupted minutes of agonizing in slow motion', was upstaged at its performance at the Aldeburgh Festival by Copland's early piece *Gröhg*.

The cause of the living composer was better served at festivals and special events than in regular concert series. In many cases composers acted as festival directors; Menotti for instance, who in Charleston, South Carolina, directed the American Spoleto Festival, consisting mainly of opera, but with a contrasting focus also placed on young performers from many countries. In Munich Hans Werner Henze directed the Third Biennale, with 20 world premières and six German premières. Many of the theatre pieces, by Rihm, Stabler, Knussen, were poorly performed and attended; a much stronger impression was made by Peter Lieberson's *King Gesau*. Henze himself presented a new version of his 1960 opera *Der Prinz von Homburg*, and the theatrical emphasis of the festival was offset by Schubert songs, performed by Dietrich Fischer-Dieskau.

The equivalent event in Britain was Maxwell Davies's St Magnus Festival in the Orkneys. 1992 saw the 16th such event, and a mellower, much less abrasive Maxwell Davies than the composer of some earlier works such as *Eight Songs for a Mad King* or *Taverner*. Now he reflected the small, close-knit Orcadian community, whether in his piece for local school-children, or in *An Orkney Wedding with Sunrise*. A number of works by his contemporaries as well as jazz, Haydn and Mozart completed the fare.

At a host of other festivals many new or newly-discovered works were performed. In Madrid Roberto Gerhard's *La Duena* at last reached production, 45 years after completion. At the Innsbrück Early Music Festival an early 18th-century opera, *Don Chisciotte in Sierra Morena* by Francisco Conti, proved successful; while at Salzburg Olivier Messiaen's enormous opera *St Francis* was produced, a tribute to the death of the 83-year-old composer during the summer (see XX: OBITUARY). Finally, following the opening-up of the countries of Eastern Europe, there were many folk festivals, or at least they were better publicized, notably a Bulgarian Festival in Sofia, and an eight-day festival of folk and choral music in Moscow.

The year's crop of anniversaries failed to lead to any spectacular discoveries. The much publicized quincentenary of Columbus's landing in the New World perhaps influenced obliquely the London concerts of South American music already mentioned; and the New London Consort produced a strange disc, on 'period instruments' called *Music from the time of Columbus*. But generally it was an anniversary which failed to excite musicians. 1992 was the 250th anniversary of the first performance in Dublin of Handel's *Messiah*, so two new but conflicting versions were brought out, which served only to underline the fact that in 1992 the search for 'authenticity' was still a growth industry. The centenaries of Milhaud and Honegger fell during the year, and the bicentenary of Rossini. Among living musicians, Milton Babbitt, the pioneer of electronic music in America in the 1950s, was still going strong at 75, and the conductor Georg Solti was 80. The latter celebrated his birthday by conducting a star-studded performance of Verdi's *Otello* at Covent Garden, and this glittering occasion, in the presence of the Prince and Princess of Wales, contrasted markedly with another celebratory occasion in 1992, a memorial concert for the composer Andrzej Panufnik, given by Rostropovich and the London Symphony Orchestra at the Barbican. Some of the glitter went from the occasion when it became clear that the two late Panufnik works, which were receiving their London premières, the *Cello Concerto* and the *Tenth Symphony*, were aesthetically slight; the three-note cells were inadequate as material, the geometric symmetries merely mechanical. What was new was not exciting, while what was exciting was not new, to judge from that occasion.

If the effects of the recession led to the tired greyness of the London concert scene in 1992, nothing reflected this more clearly than the policy of the BBC during the year. Its annual contemporary music festival at the Barbican in January was given over to the music of Alban Berg, since, in the words of its head of music, John Drummond, London had 'exhausted the supply of major living composers'. Hardly surprisingly the Promenade Concerts, of which he had sole direction, also were the fruit of this philistine viewpoint.

As for the record industry, 1992 was an active year. The CD was by this time established as the best means of exposure and publicity for the performing artist, and a torrent of releases and re-releases of familiar classics were marked by some memorable achievements. Among the most notable were Elgar recordings of his own work, particularly the Second Symphony; Schubert Sonatas played by Schnabel; a new interpretation of Stravinsky's *Rite of Spring* by Kent Nagano. Recordings of contemporary composers followed the trend in performances generally, away from extremes of avant-garde style. Those works were successful whose idiom was accessible to the public, and which could be apprehended by the 'unadventurous ear'. Such a work was Tavener's *The Protecting Veil*. The most spectacular issue of the year, going back over many decades of the composer's work, was the 17-disc set from Erato of the works of Messiaen.

Among others who died in 1992 were the composers John Cage, William Mathias, and Maurice Ohana, the singer Susan Kessler, and the conductor Sir Charles Groves.

BOOKS OF THE YEAR. *Arthur Honegger* by Harry Halbreich; A *Jazz Retrospect* by Max Harrison; *Satie* by Robert Orledge.

iii.   BALLET & DANCE

A conspicuous feature of the dance year was the emphasis on making dance accessible to all. In Britain companies such as Candoco mixed trained dancers with the physically-disadvantaged, and age was certainly no longer a barrier. In The Hague, Netherlands Dance Theatre 3 was set up for dancers over the age of 40 who wanted to continue their careers, and elsewhere senior citizens were being employed; Michael Clark cast his mother (63), topless, in *Mmm*, while DV8 flung around the frail-looking 64-year-old Diana Payne–Meyers in *Dead Fish*. Australian Ballet's repertory for their London visit included Stanton Welch's *Of*

Blessed Memory, a tribute to an ongoing mother-and-child relationship, choreographed to Canteloube's *Chants d'Auvergne* for which he persuaded his own mother, the ballerina Marilyn Jones (a mere 52), to return to the stage. Maya Plisetskaya needed no encouragement to continue to find vehicles for her stage presence and most recently, at 67, took the title role in Gigi Caciuleanu's *The Mad Woman of Chaillot* in Paris.

The main highlight of 1992 was undoubtedly the second Bournonville Festival held in Copenhagen in April to celebrate the 150th anniversary of the creation of his greatest and most joyful ballet, *Napoli*. The festival included a new, sympathetic, staging by Dinna Bjørn, Henning Kronstam and Frank Andersen featuring both young soloists (Nikølaj Hubbe and Lis Jeppesen alternating with Lloyd Riggins and Heidi Ryom) and incomparable, more mature mimes (Niels Kehlet, Michael Bastian, Fleming Ryberg and, at the gala, Niels Bjørn Larsen to bring to life the on-stage Italian community). During the festival audiences saw most of August Bournonville's surviving ballets; well-known works including *La Sylphide, Flower Festival Pas de Deux* and the classroom scene of *Konservatoriet*. Other remarkable gems of nineteenth-century stage-craft such as *Far from Denmark* revealed attitudes so out of step with twentieth-century 'political correctness' that they were unlikely to be shown abroad. The week-long festival gave visitors the opportunity to immerse themselves in the work of a single choreographer and enjoy lectures, demonstrations, classes and exhibitions which enriched their appreciation of his work.

Inevitably, the 500th anniversary of Columbus's voyage to America, Expo '92 and the Olympics in Madrid encouraged Hispanic themes for productions and festivals in Spain and elsewhere. None of the Columbus-based ballets was of lasting value. Spanish dance troupes toured internationally (Ballet Cristina Hoyos, for example, returned to the Edinburgh Festival) but without notable additions to their repertory; and well-known ballets on Spanish themes (including the Massine/Picasso *Three-Cornered Hat*) were revived by many companies. This 1919 work was the least successful revival on the 'Picasso and the Dance' programme of the Paris Opéra although the only one for which Picasso was completely responsible for the design. He only contributed front cloths for the other two ballets, Bronislava Nijinska's operette dansée *Le Train bleu* from 1924 (acceptably revived by Frank Ries), and the highlight of the programme, Roland Petit's dramatic 1945 portrayal of love and death in the back-streets of Paris, *Le Rendezvous*. The availability of the choreographer to adapt his ballet for contemporary dancers and audiences may have contributed to the success of this revival.

The other memorable reconstruction at the Opéra came in October with Rudolf Nureyev's staging of *La Bayadère*. Possibly less complete than it might have been if Nureyev had not been ill, it was nevertheless a magnificent staging, with décor by Ezio Frigerio, based on the Soviet revisions to Petipa. Complete with hunted tiger, processional elephant, parrots and blacked-up children, it maintained the emphasis on spectacle and the cast were first-class.

La Bayadère also featured on the Maryinsky (formerly Kirov) Ballet's North American tour and attracted most of the attention, along with the revival of Leonid Lavrovsky's landmark *Romeo and Juliet* and newly-mounted ballets by western choreographers. One of the most significant North American ballet events was New York City Ballet's adventurous week-long workshop, the Diamond Project. Eleven ballets by eleven choreographers, all using classical technique, were premiéred. Not all were equally successful but such a showcase by established and emerging talent was necessary for the art to develop, and works by Forsythe, Alleyne and Tanner continued in New York City Ballet's repertory and/or were mounted elsewhere.

Britain generally had a dull year. Choreography of quality could be found at Rambert whose new repertory included Merce Cunningham's first creation for a British company. Having established movement ideas with the aid of his computer Cunningham choreographed *Touchbase* on three groups, one from Rambert and two from his own company on a rota basis, so that he first created movement on the first group who then taught it to be second group while he himself worked with the third. Rambert premiéred *Touchbase* in June together with the first London showing of Siobhan Davies' superb non-representational *Winsboro' Cotton Mill Blues* within which, nevertheless, the dancers conveyed images of workers, machinery and woven fabric. In spite of being the only major British company with a clear policy the company's board gave way to commercial pressure and in December Richard Alston stepped down as artistic director.

Elsewhere box-office concerns already dominated. English National Ballet's main production was an over-decorated *Cinderella* in addition to amusing but slight works by David Parsons, a standard Robert North creation, *A Stranger I Came*, and the dramatic *White Nights* by Kim Brandstrup which showed Josephine Jewkes and Kevin Richmond to advantage. The Royal Ballet produced Forsythe's best-known ballet *In the Middle, Somewhat Elevated* to show off Sylvie Guillem (for whom it was created) and Darcey Bussell, and premiéred Kenneth MacMillan's distasteful *The Judas Tree*, a violent work about rape and suicide (to an original score by Brian Elias) which revealed the strength of the company's male dancers. A more significant tribute to the late Sir Kenneth was his lively choreography for the National Theatre's *Carousel* that he was creating at the time of his sudden death (see XX:OBITUARY). The Royal had a real box-office winner in *The Tales of Beatrix Potter*, adapted from the film which Frederick Ashton had choreographed. It was now more a pageant of masks and costumes with banal music than a ballet. Fortunately, two of Ashton's masterworks, *The Dream* and *Cinderella*, were revived at the same time. In the latter Nina Ananiashvalli showed once again that, although she had adopted a globe-trotting career as a guest artist, she took care to study the style of the choreography she performed. Birmingham Royal Ballet added to their repertory a freshly-designed production of MacMillan's *Romeo and Juliet* and a notable revival of the sadly still-relevant political ballet, Kurt Jooss' *The Green Table.*

London Contemporary Dance Theatre found itself again leaderless but marked time with popular productions, notably Christopher Bruce's *Rooster* (to music by the Rolling Stones) and Mark Morris' *Motorcade.* The year at least gave British audiences the opportunity to see a range of choreography by Morris, who provided much the best material for the visit of the White Oak Project with Mikhail Baryshnikov. Morris also brought his full company to the Edinburgh Festival, where his *Dido and Aeneas* (in which he played both Dido and the Sorceress himself) completely lived up to its reputation. Other welcome visitors to Britain were Netherlands Dance Theatre in musically ambitious works by Kylián, Forsythe and van Manen at the Alhambra, Bradford, and the Ballet du Rhin whose period reconstruction of the 1789 *La Fille mal gardée* had great charm.

The other companies that induced real excitement and queues for tickets were Michael Clark's—whose *Mmm*, in spite of an ear-splitting soundtrack, was superbly danced by the four principals—and the highly theatrical DV8. The latter toured internationally with their physically and visually surprising *Dead Fish*, an examination of loneliness, friendship and faith that, with its ever adaptable setting, was constantly rich in imagery and visual metaphors. A similarly adventurous production, inspired by the life of Kaspar Hauser and performed on a revolving stage and in an adaptable cuckoo-clock house by the Barcelona-based company Danat Danza, deserved similar recognition.

BOOKS OF THE YEAR. *The Legat Saga* by John Gregory; *Striding Out: Aspects of Contemporary and New Dance in Britain* by Stephanie Jordan; *Satie et la danse* by Ornella Volta; *Prodigal Son: Dancing for Balanchine in a World of Pain and Magic* by Edward Villella with Larry Kaplan; *Out of Line: The Story of British New Dance* by Judith Mackrell; *Push Comes to Shove* by Twyla Tharp.

iv. THEATRE

THEATRE in Britain continued to suffer from the recession, and in London the efforts of terrorists to disrupt life cannot have been beneficial to theatre box offices. Nevertheless, attendance figures appear not to have fallen below the 1991 level. Few theatres remained dark for long and there was no noticeable fall in the number of productions offered, although many theatres found it necessary to woo their audiences with discounts and offers of two seats for the price of one. Research by the British Tourist Authority indicated that overseas visitors were becoming less willing to pay top prices, yet the average ticket price increased by 11 per cent over the previous year.

So much for the theatre as an industry. What of the theatre as an art form? 1992 was hardly a vintage year for new plays: in most parts of the country the really successful productions were of classics or revivals of well-established modern plays. Some of the finest revivals were of Irish plays. Brien Friel's popular *Philadelphia, Here I Come* moved into the West End from the enterprising King's Head Theatre in Islington. One of the earlier plays of the contemporary Irish Chekhov, this affectionate depiction of Irish village life might lack the exuberance of Friel's more recent *Dancing at Lughnasa*, but it exuded a more affecting humanity and warmth. Another play by Friel, *Faith Healer*, a story of obsession and delusion, was revived, all too briefly, at the Royal Court Theatre. It contained superb performances by Donal McCann, Sinead Cusack and Ron Cook.

A prestigious revival at the Almeida Theatre of *No Man's Land*, arguably Harold Pinter's finest play, starred the playwright himself, in the role so memorably created in 1975 by Ralph Richardson, and Paul Eddington in the Gielgud role. Peter Hall's elegant staging of Oscar Wilde's *An Ideal Husband* (Globe Theatre), David Thacker's revealing account of Arthur Miller's *All My Sons* (Young Vic) and Trevor Nunn's richly satisfying production of Bernard Shaw's *Heartbreak House* (Haymarket Theatre) were among the most enjoyable theatrical events of the year, while the National Theatre also mounted excellent revivals of Tennessee Williams' *The Night of the Iguana*, Shaw's *Pygmalion* and Chekhov's *Uncle Vanya*.

However, the theatre needed new plays if it was to remain healthy. The National Theatre fared less well in this area than with revivals, its only new play of any substance being *Angels in America* by Tony Kushner, the lengthy (three-and-a-half hours) first section of a two-part play. This vast survey of modern American society took in AIDS, Mormons, Judaism and Roy Cohn in its attempt to pinpoint the reasons for what the playwright obviously saw as the greed and selfishness of the Reagan years. It was competently staged by Declan Donnellan and well acted by its large cast, but the Sunday newspaper critic who described it as the most overblown piece of far-Left propaganda he had encountered for many years came closest to a rational assessment of its aesthetic value.

Tom Murphy's enthusiastically heralded *The Gigli Concert*, first performed in Dublin in 1983 but given its British première at the Almeida in 1992, turned out to be interesting but uneven. Alan Bennett's *Talking Heads* (Comedy Theatre), adapted from his television monologues, functioned well as a comfortable vehicle for the playwright himself and for Patricia Routledge, but made less impact on the stage than on the small screen. John Osborne's *Déjàvu* (Comedy Theatre), the long-awaited sequel to his 1956 *Look Back in Anger*, was little more than a monologue for the character of Jimmy Porter, the original angry young man now found in late middle age to be still stuck in his attitudes of thirty-five years ago. Considerably more impressive was Frank McGuinness's *Someone Who'll Watch Over Me* (Hampstead Theatre), set in a cellar in Beirut in which three hostages, an American doctor, an Irish journalist and an English lecturer, were imprisoned. The performances of Hugh Quarshie, Stephen Rea and Alec McCowen were exemplary.

A new play from Chile which arrived in London, preceded by much favourable publicity, turned out to be disappointing. Ariel Dorfman's *Death and the Maiden* (transferred to the Duke of York's Theatre from the Royal Court where it had opened late in 1991), well acted by Juliet Stevenson and Michael Byrne, resorted to implausible melodrama to deal with its examination of torture, delusion and revenge. An American import, *Six Degrees of Separation* by John Guare, was a chic piece of Broadway fluff posing as something deeper. As a frivolous satire on wealthy white liberalism its story of a young black confidence trickster might have passed muster, but its air of bogus profundity kept getting in the way.

The Shakespeare play which dominated the year was *As You Like It*, perhaps the most delightful of the Bard's comedies, certainly the one with the least malice flavouring its wit. The Royal Shakespeare Company (RSC) at Stratford-on-Avon did well by the play, with Samantha Bond as a most engaging Rosalind, but the company which performed in Regent's Park during the summer made extraordinarily heavy weather of a play which ought to have suited the venue admirably. The director, Maria Aitken (who later in the year distinguished herself as Judith Bliss in a West End revival of Noël Coward's enchanting *Hay Fever*), chose to present *As You Like It* as though it were being filmed by a group of louche amateurs in the 1930s. The melancholy Jaques became the film director because he had, after all, observed that 'All the world's a stage'. Jaques was played by a 'drag queen' named Bette Bourne, and there were hints that the character's melancholy was due to the fact that he was suffering from a certain prevalent sexually-transmitted disease. A production of the same play at the Greenwich Theatre was ploddingly charmless except for the Welsh Phoebe of Buddug Morgan.

At the Young Vic, the director Trevor Nunn put *Measure for Measure*, Shakespeare's celebrated problem play, 'under the moral microscope', updating its action to the Vienna of Sigmund Freud and reclaiming the emotion in a text that can often seem to be about the manipulation of emotion. An *Othello*, presented by a group called the

Deconstruction Theatre Company, did a neat job of deconstructing the play at the Baron's Court Theatre. With the action moved from Venice and Cyprus to an autonomous sultanate off the coast of present-day Africa, all of the characters were black except for Colonel Othello, a white European mercenary: an amusing concept until one began to think about it, which apparently no-one connected with the production bothered to do.

However, the greatest damage was done to Shakespeare during the year not by a small group in the suburbs but by the National Theatre, whose staging of *A Midsummer Night's Dream* drained the play of its verbal magic by casting it with actors who were unable to speak the lines clearly, and who compounded the felony by setting it in what seemed the depths of winter in a muddy pool in whose stagnant waters most of the characters at one point or another were forced to splash about. Since this wet *Dream* was directed by Robert Lepage, thought by some to be the Peter Brook of the nineties, a number of critics appeared to find the production illuminating. It was left to the Open Air Company in Regent's Park to present the play with love and respect, and also with a much better cast than the National Theatre was able to assemble.

The year began badly for London's fringe theatre with *The Marvellous Boy* (at the Bush Theatre), an account of the brief life of the eighteenth-century teenage poet and forger Thomas Chatterton improvized by its highly untalented cast; *Knit One, Murder One* (at the Old Red Lion), a pointless parody of the Agatha Christie-type murder mystery, performed by a two-woman team called Lip Service; and *The Chance*, a tedious morality play adapted from a novel by Peter Carey. But thereafter the fringe recovered, presenting perfectly respectable productions of plays by the kind of dramatist whom commercial theatre tended to neglect, such as Lorca, Wedekind, or Dürrenmatt, as well as introducing a few new playwrights, though none of potential importance.

It was not a good year for new musicals. *Moby Dick* (Piccadilly Theatre) was a damp squib of a show about a group of St Trinian's-like schoolgirls adapting Herman Melville's novel and mounting it as an end-of-term production in the school's swimming pool. Book, lyrics and music were alike dreadful, and the performance of Tony Monopoly as the head mistress who took the role of Captain Ahab was both clearly embarrassed and dreadfully embarrassing. *Grand Hotel* (Dominion Theatre), a Broadway import, was slickly staged by Tommy Tune, and well performed by a cast headed by Liliane Montevecchi in Garbo's old role (for the plot was based on the film version of Vicki Baum's novel), but lacked a single good tune. Its composers were Robert Wright and George Forrest, best known for *Kismet* and *Song of Norway* and obviously only at their best when adapting the music of composers such as Borodin and Grieg. *Some Like It Hot* (Prince Edward Theatre), a musical based on a famous Marilyn Monroe film, had been seen briefly on Broadway in 1972, but was at least new to London. Tommy Steele, in the Tony Curtis role, remained Tommy Steele of the flashing teeth, and Jule Styne's music was instantly forgettable. Vastly superior to all of these was Stephen Sondheim's *Assassins* (Donmàr Warehouse), though it was by no means an example of this composer at his remarkable best.

The two most enjoyable musicals of the year were both revivals. *Spread a Little Happiness* (King's Head Theatre) was actually a compilation, devised by the critic Sheridan Morley, of tunes from the delightful twenties and thirties shows of Vivian Ellis, the eighty-eight-year-old composer who wrote a new song for the occasion. Rodgers and Hammerstein's magnificent 1945 musical, *Carousel*, was revived in exemplary fashion by the National Theatre in a production by Nicholas Hytner.

NEW YORK THEATRE. At least four good new American plays appeared during the year, and surprisingly three of them were produced not off- but on-Broadway. John Guare's *Four Baboons Adoring the Sun* (Vivian Beaumont Theatre) was perhaps the least successful of the four, a curious amalgam of classical myth and modern family life. *Conversations With My Father* by Herb Gardner (Royale Theatre) was a memory play, but its memory was not falsely sentimental as in Brian Friel's *Dancing at Lughnasa*. It was instead lyrical and poetic, as in the best of O'Neill. Peter Parnell's *Flaubert's Latest* (Playwrights Horizons) was a sharp and witty piece about a blocked writer who, obsessed with Flaubert, wanted to complete the French novelist's *Bouvard et Pécuchet*: many of the best lines were borrowed from Flaubert. A new Neil Simon play, *Jake's Women* (Neil Simon Theatre), was about an aging writer trying to come to terms with the women in his life, past and present. Though hardly vintage Simon, it was full of funny lines, most of them admirably delivered by Alan Alda as the protagonist who spends much of his time talking to the audience or to characters who are present only in his memory. Better than any of these was a revival of Arthur Miller's *The Price* (Criterion Theatre) with Hector Elizondo and, as the old furniture dealer, the superb Eli Wallach.

London provided New York with one new musical, the ebullient *Five Guys Named Moe*, a celebration of the work of the American song-writer, Louis Jordan. The only other musical of substance to open during the year was a lively revival, directed by Jerry Zaks, of Frank Loesser's near-perfect *Guys and Dolls*.

v.   CINEMA

WITH costs increasing at an alarming rate and a worldwide recession to counter, it was a difficult year for most film-makers. But Hollywood— which spent upwards of $25 million, almost all on star vehicles—could look back on 1992 with some satisfaction. There was no real fall in film-going in the USA, the biggest single market in the world, and Europe and Japan, in particular, remained highly profitable for American films. This was particularly true of Oliver Stone's audaciously-structured *JFK*. The conspiracy theories about the assassination of President Kennedy were attacked hard enough to prevent the film reaching its target of $100 million in the USA but it still did well enough worldwide to be accounted a commercial success.

Another triumph was Clint Eastwood's *Unforgiven*, a classic Western, which not only got into most critics' ten-best lists of the year, but also proved that a genre once thought to be dead, or at least dying, still had a lot of life in it. This was all the more surprising since its cast hardly looked likely to be a major attraction for today's young audiences. Eastwood himself, Gene Hackman, Morgan Freeman and Richard Harris were veterans who could almost be the grandfathers of the young actors and actresses known as the 'bankable brat pack'.

However, these were not by any means the biggest box-office attractions of the year. The Dutch director Paul Verhoeven's *Basic Instinct*, which made over $300 million all over the world, proved that a flashy and stylish mixture of sex, violence and thrills was still a potent force. It was, of course, made in Hollywood. By contrast, a film at the family viewing end of the scale, Disney's *Beauty and the Beast*, did almost as well, just when the orthodox view was that full-length animated features had, like Westerns, passed their prime. It was by far the best Disney animation for a long time and, closely followed by the almost equally clever *Aladdin*, seemed to revive animation in a very big way.

The rest of the year's successful Hollywood product was less distinctive, though Jonathan Demme's *The Silence of the Lambs*, which won all four of the top Oscars, was both a skilful and successful horror thriller. Steven Spielberg's *Hook* cost so much that even its box-office success could not put this disappointing epic, updated from J.M. Barrie's story, into the black. But Robert Altman, one of the most admired directors in America, at least enjoyed critical and commercial success with *The Player*, in which a large cast of Hollywood regulars engaged in a biting satire of the studio system as it was now, run by businessmen rather than film enthusiasts. Another fine director who had success was Woody Allen. But his intelligent and extremely well-played *Husbands and Wives* got as many into the cinema because its subject matter was very close to home—the court case in which his partner Mia Farrow and he would dispute their lives together would probably run throughout 1993—as because of its quality. Hollywood, in fact, had reason to feel quietly pleased with itself at the end of the year. People were not only going to the cinema in very large numbers in the US, but its tentacles reached across the world, gripping distribution and exhibition systems as tightly as ever.

This presented an increasingly intractable problem for European film-makers in particular. Production was down almost everywhere, especially in Britain and eastern Europe. In Britain there was little government help in terms of increasing very small state subsidies or of meaningful tax incentives. In the former communist countries, where the once-widespread state help was now virtually non-existent, American films held sway at the box office and local product was virtually decimated. Various EC schemes, covering all aspects of film-making, from script-development and production to distribution and exhibition, were beginning to foster some hope. Meanwhile, the European cinema, which could once supply Hollywood with half its talent and still maintain itself at home, looked to be hospitalized and preparing itself for a major operation.

Britain, however, still had the language factor to its advantage and James Ivory's *Howards End*, an elegant and subtle adaptation of E.M. Forster's novel, did as well in the USA as elsewhere. Another much less highly-regarded period piece, Mike Newell's *Enchanted April*, made more money in the US than its strongest advocates could have dared to hope.

Other European films also broke down what looked like insurmountable barriers. *Schtonk!*, a comedy about the fake Hitler diaries, did immensely well in the German market; Bille August's *Best Intentions* from Sweden and taken from a script by Ingmar Bergman about his parents, won the Palme d'Or at Cannes; another Swedish film, *House of Angels* (written and directed by an expatriate Briton, Colin Nutley) was highly successful in Scandinavia; and *Johnny Stechino*, an Italian Mafia comedy, did better in its own country than most of the big American blockbusters. But it was another Italian film, Giorgio Amelio's *The Stolen Children*, which won the European Felix (the equivalent to a Hollywood Oscar) in 1992, awarded at Berlin's famous Babelburg Studios, now at last ready to function again under the management of the German director and producer Volker Schlöndorff, who expressed the hope that big-budget European films, quite unlike the small Amelio film, could once again be mounted there.

Elsewhere there was little movement by comparison with the previous year, though in French-speaking Africa there was an increased number of new films hoping to attract African audiences as well as critical praise at Western festivals. But the outlook was not good for them on their own continent. Outside America, only the Indian and Chinese film industries prospered, largely because film-goers in those countries went to see them in the absence of Hollywood product. The huge Indian industry produced its usual quota of massive hits from Bombay and Madras. But the Indian film community was much saddened by the death of Satyajit Ray (see XX:OBITUARY), its most towering artistic figure and creator of the classic *Apu Trilogy*. Before he died, he received, at his hospital bedside, a Hollywood Oscar for his lifetime's work, which he deemed one of his greatest honours.

China seemed to have forgiven its blue riband director, Zhang Yimou, for making politically-doubtful films and sent his latest, *The Story of Qui Ju*, to the Venice festival. A depiction of ordinary life in China, very different from his more spectacular previous efforts, the film won the Golden Lion and as much praise as his *Raise the Red Lantern*, which also had worldwide critical success in 1992. Other good Chinese films were shown to home audiences as well as those abroad and, though state censorship was still a problem, it seemed to be less stringent than before.

Japan, where American films held sway, though not in so widespread a fashion as in Europe, produced a fair quota of highly commercial and mostly violent films but little of real distinction for the outside world. Latin American film-makers, beset by economic problems, found it as difficult as ever to break through. Here too Hollywood predominated, even on television. But Mexico's young directors, given more government help than elsewhere in the region, seemed to be asserting themselves both at home and in festivals abroad.

It was, more than ever, the festival circuit, growing year by year, which nurtured non-English-language films and the better-class English-speaking productions too. How to translate critical and public praise into commercially-meaningful sales during recession was the biggest problem of the year. For a great many film-makers, the festival circuit was the only real hope and would probably remain so in the immediate future. However, the constant increase in television channels and the burgeoning video market did at least allow further outlets if cinema sales were not forthcoming. And there was still the occasional highly successful small film, such as Australia's cheerful dance drama, *Strictly Ballroom*, which attracted very large audiences in its home territory and was bought by practically every major country in the world.

Meanwhile, those who regretted the dominance of Hollywood would have to reflect that without such 'jackpot' movies as *Lethal Weapon III*, *Sister Act* and a dozen others, there would be virtually no cinemas open in vast tracts of the world. What 1992 proved beyond doubt, however, was that a substantial minority of film-goers wanted wider choice. France, where the Minister of Culture was pretty high in the pecking order and film was regarded as art rather than commerce, gave them that choice. Not many other countries had either the will or the means at present to do so.

Among others who died during the year were the performers Marlene Dietrich, José Ferrer, Paul Heinreid, Anthony Perkins, Denholm Elliot, Robert Morley and Sandy Dennis, and the film-makers John Sturges, Richard Brooks and Hal Roach. (For Dietrich, Ferrer, Morley and Roach, see XX:OBITUARY.)

vi. TELEVISION & RADIO

THE launch of the new BBC soap opera *Eldorado* could stand as a metaphor for the state of British broadcasting during the year. As the soap which promised 'sex, sun and sangria' and a large prime-time audience for the Corporation failed to reach its target, there was great uncertainty, leading characters disappeared overnight and ultimate survival was very much in doubt.

The fate of broadcasting was not quite as bad as the likely fate of *Eldorado*. ITV in fact assembled record audiences against the BBC mainly through the continued success of its popular dramas such as *Inspector Morse, Poirot, London's Burning* and *The Darling Buds of May* and of soaps such as *Coronation Street* and *The Bill*. There was, however, great uncertainty among the ITV companies, as those which had lost their franchises prepared for oblivion as broadcasters and the winners planned for the big 1 January 1993 switch-on. Throughout the system jobs went by the hundred, particularly at those companies that had bid high to keep their franchises. At the BBC work went on all year in an attempt to produce a coherent vision of the future of public service broadcasting in an age of increasing commercial competition—a vision that would continue to justify the institutional survival of the BBC and in particular the universal licence fee that financed it. Its report was unveiled just after the government published a green paper on the Corporation, a discussion document designed to lead a wide-ranging debate on the future of the BBC in advance of the renewal of its royal charter.

But it was the 'disappearance' of a leading character in the real, as opposed to the fictional, world of broadcasting that was perhaps the defining event of the year. On 3 February David Plowright, chairman of Granada Television and a man associated with programmes as diverse as *Coronation Street, Disappearing World, Jewel in the Crown* and *Brideshead Revisited* was forced to resign by the new Granada Group chief executive, Gerry Robinson. Mr Plowright, who had come almost to personify the spirit of public service broadcasting in ITV, made no attempt to disguise the manner of his leaving. 'There is a fundamental disagreement between myself and the board of Granada about how to manage the change into the new broadcasting environment', he said. Stars of *Coronation Street* protested and the actor John Cleese sent a memorable fax to Mr Robinson, who had previously run an industrial catering group, denouncing him as 'an ignorant caterer'.

Mr Plowright's departure was a powerful symbol of change in ITV, a system that was fundamentally reorganized during the year. A network centre was set up, with an annual budget of £515 million, to commission the national ITV network from both the ITV companies and independent producers. Another clue to the changing nature of ITV came from its first chief executive, Andrew Quinn, who said there was no doubt that ITV would inevitably be more commercial in future. Current affairs programmes such as *World In Action* would have to be able to get audiences of 8 million to 9 million to keep their place in prime time. But while Carlton, Good Morning Television, Meridian and Westcountry prepared to replace respectively Thames, TV-am, TVS and Television South-West, the only noticeable programme casualties were the Thames current affairs programme *This Week* and the early Sunday evening religious programme (which was moved out of prime time). There was even uncertainty about the future of Independent Television News (ITN) when a consortium led by Carlton and including Reuters, the international news and information group, bid successfully for ITN. There was less uncertainty about the quality of its journalism in 1992. Reports on Serbian detention camps by ITN journalist Penny Marshall changed the attitude of world leaders to intervening in former Yugoslavia.

The biggest row between the authorities and broadcasters came as usual over Northern Ireland. Channel 4, which in 1993 would have to sell its advertising in competition with ITV, got into trouble over a documentary alleging organized collusion between the security forces and loyalist terrorists. Channel 4 refused to reveal the identity of the main source behind the programme and was prosecuted under the Prevention of Terrorism Act. The threats included sequestration of all Channel 4's assets. Instead Lord Justice Woolf imposed only a moderate fine.

Life at the BBC was no less fraught than at ITV, as the debate began on the renewal of its royal charter at the end of 1996. The debate opened against an uncertain BBC performance in the ratings. There were programme high spots, such as the innovative drama about corrupt policemen, *Between The Lines*, but overall the Corporation was regularly trounced in the ratings, the combined BBC share of viewing often dropping to around 40 per cent.

The government formally opened the debate on 24 November with its green paper which offered a continuing commitment to public service broadcasting but insisted that the BBC would have to become more efficient. In many ways, the government said, 'the BBC had both embodied and communicated our national heritage'. But the

Corporation could not pretend that nothing had changed since the present royal charter was granted in 1981. The options for consideration included a smaller BBC with a more narrowly-defined public service remit and privatizing or contracting-out many of the Corporation's services. There was also the possibility of creating a public service broadcasting council to handle licence fee money but distribute it to a variety of public service broadcasters and not just the BBC. The proposals were markedly less hostile and the approach more open-minded than the way in which ITV had been tackled by Mrs Thatcher when she called it 'the last bastion of restrictive practices'.

The BBC's reply, long in the preparation, came on 26 November from John Birt, the new director-general-in-waiting. The BBC, he said, had to face up to the reality of winning about a third of broadcasting funding and a third of the radio and television audience as commercial broadcasting inevitably expanded throughout the 1990s. The average British household would still watch or listen to BBC services for something like 24 hours a week, the Corporation forecast. The BBC ought to survive as a single integrated institution, providing all its present services funded by a universal licence fee. The main change would come in the type of programmes offered and the efficiency with which they were made. The BBC would continue to try to educate, inform and entertain but, Mr Birt said, 'in ways which press forward; which break new ground; which pioneer; which innovate and challenge the audience; which are marked by intelligence, invention and wit; which strive for quality and excellence'. The aim in future would be to complement the schedules of the commercial sector rather than imitate them.

Earlier, in October, feathers flew at the BBC when the outgoing director-general, Sir Michael Checkland, attacked his chairman, Marmaduke Hussey, in public and suggested that he was too old to lead the Corporation into the next century. He wanted a younger and more representative board of governors so that when he talked about FM (radio) they knew it stood for frequency modulation and not 'fuzzy monsters'. Sir Michael left the BBC just before Christmas, two months earlier than previously announced.

One of the most dramatic signs of change was the announcement, in May, that British Sky Broadcasting (BSkyB), the six-channel satellite television system, had outbid ITV in a £304 million five-year agreement for live rights to the new Premier football league. The presence of the BBC in the deal—the Corporation got the right to show highlights and revived its old *Match of the Day* programme—was controversial. Some saw this as an example of the Corporation selling out to Rupert Murdoch, who owned 50 per cent of BSkyB. During the year the satellite company moved into operating profit (excluding interest charges), turned its sports channel, Sky Sports, into a subscription channel, and added a third film channel to replace the unsuccessful comedy channel. The number of homes with satellite receiving dishes continued to grow. According to Continental Research, the total number of dish homes, was 2.59 million by the end of the year, although other estimates were as low as 2 million. Cable television continued to expand, backed by large North American cable and telephone groups. By the end of the year nearly 500,000 homes had signed up for multi-channel cable and there was also rapid growth in the number of homes using cable networks for their telephone services.

In November Thames Television and the BBC combined to launch their own satellite channel, UK Gold, a channel devoted to repeats from their programme libraries. Re-showings of early *Neighbours* and editions of *The Bill* and *Porridge*, the classic comedy series, were moderately successful.

In December further Thames plans for life after ITV came unstuck. A Thames-led consortium, including Time Warner of the USA, was turned down for a new national fifth television channel, even though it was the only applicant. The Independent Television Commission cited insufficient shareholder commitment and expressed doubt about the consortium's business plan. The ITC would now review what should be done with the Channel 5 frequencies.

One of the surprising successes of the year was BCC World Service Television, which continued to expand in Asia via satellite and was also now carried on cable networks in Canada. The aim was to make it available all round the world by the end of 1994. In December the Prince of Wales was fulsome in his praise of BBC World Service Radio, which celebrated its 60th anniversary. The service had 120 million regular listeners around the world.

In UK radio the big event was the launch of Classic FM, the first of the three planned national commercial radio stations. Contrary to most expectations the station looked like being a considerable success, most estimates putting the audience at more than 4 million a week, double that of the BBC's Radio 3. The second licence, for a national pop station was awarded to a Virgin-TV-am joint venture and the station was scheduled to be launched in late spring 1993. The launch of the third, mainly speech-based station, was delayed until 1995, partly because of recession and partly to allow an orderly introduction of competing stations.

One of the biggest rows of the year was created by BBC plans to replace Radio 4 broadcasts on long-wave with a 24-hour news and current affairs service. In future Radio 4 would be available only on FM. The protests came from those who did not get good FM reception, or indeed any at all, and from expatriates in continental Europe who could receive long-wave but not FM. The BBC decided to go ahead with the plan and set a launch date of April 1994, while promising that listeners would not lose Radio 4 on long-wave before improvements were made to the FM transmitter network.

Outside the UK the patterns were similar. New channels were launched, not all successfully, and technology and business enterprise promised more—many more. In the United States Time Warner launched the first 150-channel cable system in New York, while Direct-TV, a Hughes Aircraft-backed consortium, pushed ahead with plans to deliver 150 channels by satellite, many devoted to pay-per-view movies. TCI, one of the largest US cable operators, announced that it was planning the first 500-channel system, using digital techniques to squeeze four or five channels into the space presently occupied by one.

In Europe the main development was the collapse of the French fifth channel, La Cinque. It was replaced by Arte, an arts television channel funded by the French and German governments. Dreams of launching a European news channel, Euronews, were finally realized with the support of members of the European Broadcasting Union and the European Community (EC). In December the EC adopted a green paper, *Pluralism and Media Concentration*, designed to see whether there should be harmonization of laws restricting media ownership or whether nothing should be done on the issue at the Community level.

The most nostalgic moment of the year—at least for middle-aged listeners—came on New Year's Eve. Fabulous 208, the English-language service of Radio Luxembourg, was finally overwhelmed by the competition after 60 years of broadcasting.

2. ART—ARCHITECTURE

i. ART

EVERYTHING was the same, and everything different. Recession took its toll, as a number of commercial galleries closed their public spaces, retreating into bankruptcy and/or private dealing without a public shop window. Many living artists, art galleries and the auction houses (which imposed a buyer's premium of 15 per cent while announcing staff cuts and redundancies galore) were affected, sometimes devastatingly so, by the dismal economic climate. On the other hand, the public was apparently as well-treated as ever, with remarkable and outstanding exhibitions, international blockbusters and the results of ardent scholarship in the publication of as many distinguished art books as ever.

In London alone, art galleries which closed their public premises in 1992 included the Heim, the Albemarle, Fischer Fine Art, Odette Gilbert, Nigel Greenwood, and Knoedler Kasmin, while Scotland witnessed the closing of the Fine Art Society in Edinburgh and Glasgow, its operations being consolidated in the historic London premises. In several instances, the proprietors, fed up with West End rents and overheads, became private dealers. The same pattern was repeated in several Western capital cities of art dealing. On the other hand, a number of dealers flourished critically and commercially, including Nicholas Logsdail of the Lisson and Anthony d'Offay. Some even made a living out of contemporary art, although this sector was the hardest-hit by the recession after the boom of the 1980s.

The end of the year was marked, in London at least, by increasingly acrimonious debates, mostly in the media, about contemporary art. A majority of commentators, in an echo of the architectural debates of the 1980s sparked off by the Prince of Wales, claimed that the 'cutting edge' of contemporary work amounted to a conspiracy run by art world mandarins to defraud the public aesthetically. This debate was set to run and run. The tone was set by *The Independent*, an august newspaper which normally delighted the audience for art by its extensive coverage of the subject: its anonymous profile of the high-profile director of the Tate was headed 'Nicholas Serota, who once had no enemies'.

The debate in Britain was fuelled by the annual round of the Turner Prize, which again managed to enrage just about everybody. In 1992 four sculptors/installation artists were on the short-list, the most avidly-courted figure being Damien Hirst, who became notorious and/or famous when exhibiting a tiger shark caught to order (not by the artist) in Australia and preserved in formaldehyde. The Turner Prize was won by Grenville Davey, an abstract sculptor; like the 1991 winner, Anish Kapoor (see AR, 1991, p. 502), Davey exhibited with the Lisson Gallery.

An unforeseen disaster in Britain was the fire at Windsor Castle in November, which destroyed several irreplaceable (though not crucial) works of art. The episode raised questions about responsibility for the upkeep and accessibility of both the Castle and the royal collections, generating a discussion to which constitutional historians contributed but which by year's end had produced no consensus nor any authoritative answers. The most important single painting lost to the ravages of the fire was Sir William Beechey's portrait of George III on horseback. But the Windsor losses were perhaps more important as a dramatic symbol of Britain's decline, having a resonant effect not only on national feeling but also more subtly on attitudes to the royal family.

However, the most serious loss to the European art heritage undoubtedly arose from the horrifying and continuing civil war in what had been Yugoslavia, to which the crusading *Art Newspaper* (edited by Anna Somers Cock) called attention. In Eastern Europe, in spite of some heroic efforts in the reclamation and restoration of country estates, the manifold problems of dealing with the heritage were low on the agenda of countries grappling with devastating economic problems and soaring crime rates.

In Britain one political promise was at last fulfilled. After the Conservative election victory in April (see I.2) a Department of National Heritage was created, covering the arts, broadcasting, the media and tourism. The seat in the cabinet attached to the portfolio went to the music-loving David Mellor, but he was forced to resign after a summer of revelations about his personal life and was succeeded by Peter Brooke.

If the mood in Britain seemed scratchy and irritable, elsewhere things were more optimistic. In New York, after years of controversy, the revamped and expanded Guggenheim Museum, the last masterpiece of Frank Lloyd Wright, reopened in June after two years' restoration and expansion, and received almost universal praise. The first special exhibition was an enormous compilation called *The Avant-Garde in Russia 1915–32*. Guggenheim Soho, in a converted warehouse, also opened to praise, and had a run of outstanding small exhibitions, including Rauschenberg and the murals of Chagall from Moscow's Jewish Theatre, which were seen for the first time in America. In December the Guggenheim announced the establishment of a collection of modern and contemporary photography, initiated with a gift in cash and kind of $5 million from the Robert Mapplethorpe Foundation. (Mapplethorpe had died of AIDS in 1988 at the age of 42.)

The exhibition of the year, in terms of critical praise and ecstatic public response, was the Matisse at New York's Museum of Modern Art. Conservatively estimated to have cost at least $5 million to mount, it was the most comprehensive anthology of Matisse's art ever offered to public view, including masterpieces from Russia. The show was seen by approximately 900,000 people over four months, admissions being limited to 6,900 per day, with the result that touts were able to sell tickets to the queuers for about $100. However, the Matisse exhibition was far from being the only blockbuster. The Magritte retrospective, seen to acclaim and crowds at London's Hayward Gallery in the spring, transferred to the Metropolitan Museum in New York and attracted 450,000 visitors.

An exquisite and powerful anthology of an aspect of the work of Picasso was seen in Paris and Cleveland. Called *Picasso & Things*, it explored the art of the great 20th-century polymath as manifested in his still-life works: never can *nature morte* have been so lively. A surprise in Paris was the autumn exhibition—outdoor, free and for everybody—of enormous and humorous bronzes by Botero, up and down the Champs-Elysées.

Other major exhibitions again included Rembrandt (at both the British Museum and the National Gallery in 1992). The painting show was all about reattribution and disattribution, the visible sign of the Rembrandt Project based in Amsterdam, which brought to bear a combination of scientific expertise, historical research and plain old-fashioned connoisseurship (using the eye) in the work of authentication.

Italian Old Master painting was also reassessed. Jacopo Bassano was shown both in his home town, Bassano del Grappa (more famous perhaps for liquor than for art), and at the Kimbell, Fort Worth (Texas), while Jusepe de Ribera (1591–1652) had a major retrospective in Madrid, Naples and New York (at the Metropolitan) marking the 400th anniversary of his birth.

Even in Europe there were unexpected 'firsts', including perhaps the largest-ever exhibition devoted to German Expressionism in Paris. Staged at the city's Museum of Modern Art, it was given the Prix Ptolemée for the best exhibition in Paris of 1992. And there were, as always, some wonderful re-evaluations of artists who had long been somewhere in the canon, notably a showing of the art of the 18th-century portraitist Allan Ramsay in Scotland and England.

In Madrid the Thyssen Collection opened in a building once destined for the expansion of the Prado; the collection was on a ten-year loan to the government of Spain, although negotiations had opened for its sale to Spain, at a price much lower than market rates. In Bonn two new museums opened: the Bonn Art Museum, concentrating on contemporary German art, and the Federal Art and Exhibition Centre.

The year witnessed, in both Europe and North America, a stronger presence of art that was not necessarily Western in its origins. For example, the art of Islamic Spain was explored in the *Al-Andalus* exhibition, shown with enterprising imagination in Granada, at the Alhambra, and then at the Metropolitan in New York. The most spectacular affirmation of the glories of Asian art was revealed at the British Museum, where in November the Queen opened the Hotung Gallery, a major refurbishment made possible by a £2 million donation to the British Museum by Joseph Hotung, a Hong Kong businessman. For the first time in decades the Amaravati Marbles from India, as great an achievement as the Elgin Marbles from the Parthenon, were displayed in a grand hall at the end of the Hotung, itself the largest single gallery in any British museum, the size of two football pitches. The arts of China and South-East Asia were also newly displayed in the Hotung.

The National Gallery had an outstanding year, securing the marvellous Holbein painting, *A Lady with a Squirrel and a Starling*, for £10 million, rehanging to excellent effect its 19th-century galleries and displaying a rediscovered Raphael, *Madonna with the Pinks*, owned by the Duke of Northumberland and authenticated by Nicholas Penny, Clore curator of Renaissance art. A surprise hit show in both London and New York (at the Royal Academy and Metropolitan respectively) was the art of that most intellectual of Renaissance masters, Andrea Mantegna, which in London included the ravishing display of the *Triumph of Caesar*, the sequence of grand paintings removed from Hampton Court for the special showing.

Impressionism still reigned supreme, however. The Sisley exhibition held at the Sackler Galleries at the Royal Academy was a success with the public, and the Sackler Galleries themselves, designed by Sir Norman Foster and partners, won numerous awards for building of the year, including the RIBA award.

Celebrated painters who died in 1992 included the Britons Francis Bacon and John Piper, Viera da Silva of Portugal and Paris and Sir Sydney Nolan of Australia (see XX:OBITUARY).

BOOKS OF THE YEAR. *Magritte* by David Sylvester; the first volume of the *Magritte Catalogue Raisonné* by David Sylvester and Sarah Whitfield; *The Colour of Time: Claude Monet* by Virginia Spate; *Picasso & Things* by Jean Sutherland Boggs et al.; *Watteau's Painted Conversations* by Mary Vidal; *German Expressionism: Primitivism and Modernity* by Jill Lloyd (which won the first National Art Collections Fund/Waterstone's National Art Book Prize); *Corot in Italy* by Peter Galassi; and *Caspar David Friedrich and the Subject of Landscape* by Joseph Leo Koerner. (The last two were 1992 Mitchell Prize winners.)

ii. ARCHITECTURE

THE year saw more disasters than triumphs, and all against a backlog, once again, of declining workload and straightened circumstances. This relatively sorry picture of architecture in Britain was exemplified by the fire at Windsor Castle, which destroyed much of St George's Hall and prompted a debate on how exactly it should be replaced, and by the tragic and untimely death of Sir James Stirling, only days after he had received a richly-deserved knighthood (see XX:OBITUARY). Both events were entirely unexpected, both tragedies. The substantial obituaries which followed Stirling's death suggested that at last he was being accorded the honours due as possibly the greatest British architect of the century.

Regrettably, Stirling's was not the only premature death during the year. The other was that of Peter Rice, an engineer who had a major impact on some of the great post-war buildings produced by a range of British architects (see XX:OBITUARY). The only consolation for his friends and admirers was the award to him of the Royal Institute of British Architects' gold medal for architecture, a rare honour for a non-architect and one which Rice greatly appreciated only months before his death. Two other deaths should be noted: Fred Lloyd Roche, an architect whose main contribution (though not the only one) was to have worked as chief executive of Milton Keynes Development Corporation during its early days; and Sir John Summerson, a beacon of architectural scholarship for 60 years, world authority on John Nash and for several decades curator of the Sir John Soane Museum in London. He, alone of the quartet mentioned here, lived to a ripe old age.

But 1992 had its bright moments too, as the country's leading architects saw major projects taking shape or reaching completion, and also won fresh commissions, including several enormous jobs in the Far East. Most notable was Sir Norman Foster & Partners' victory in the competition to design Hong Kong's Chek Lap Kok airport terminal, one of the biggest projects in the world (even if beset with problems due to tension between Britain and China—see IX.2.iii). Also in Hong Kong, Scott Brownrigg & Turner won a major airport building commission, while Terry Farrell obtained a huge commission to master-plan a mixed-use development around a new transport interchange. In mainland China, Richard Rogers Partnership emerged as the favoured designers of a new development in the suburbs of Shanghai, comprising 4 million square metres of space.

At home, the Rogers firm was confirmed in the role as designers for a large-scale expansion at Heathrow airport. While budget cuts took their toll on architectural commissions for public works, some transport projects continued to make headlines during the year. Gathering shape was Nicholas Grimshaw's Euro-terminal for the cross-channel high-speed rail link at Waterloo Station. Passing through Waterloo, coincidentally, would be the extension to London's Jubilee Line underground route, comprising a dozen stations linking the West End to Stratford in east London (and the City to the huge Canary Wharf development on the Isle of Dogs). Many of the best architects in the capital designed stations for the controversial route; by the end of the year, the government had decided it should proceed, subject to private-sector financial contributions being forthcoming.

Elsewhere in the capital, architects competed for the commissions to design stations on the new Crossrail route, designed to provide speedy links between the west and east sides of London. Notable winners were Will Alsop (Paddington) and Michael Hopkins (Tottenham Court Road and Westminster). Indeed, it was something of an *annus mirabilis* for Hopkins. His first big success during the year was to win a limited competition to design a new headquarters for the Inland Revenue in Nottingham. This competition had been launched as a result of criticisms of an earlier competition based on speed and cost rather than the best possible design. Hopkins also won a commission to produce a new master-plan, for the area around Paddington Station in London, and charmed MPs with his proposals for a parliamentary building above the planned new underground station at Westminster (also designed by him). Meanwhile, his plans for the new Glyndebourne opera house were under construction.

In Seville Nicholas Grimshaw unveiled his UK pavilion for the International Expo, to great acclaim. Meanwhile his former partner,

Terry Farrell, saw the completion of a major City of London office tower, and received more publicity for his riverside building at Vauxhall, to be occupied, it was announced, by MI6. Another government body, English Heritage, organized a competition for a visitors' centre at Stonehenge, which was won by Edward Cullinan.

On the professional front the future of architecture looked likely to change. A report into the privileged position of architects in respect of their legal role suggested to government that it was time for a change. Meanwhile, RIBA campaigned vigorously against government policies aimed at forcing public authorities to appoint architects on the basis of the lowest fee. More than 60 practices signed a statement condemning the growing practice of fee-cutting. The effects of that fee-cutting became more and more apparent: by the end of the year it was estimated that nearly half of the architects employed in private practice had lost a job during the previous two years.

The Pritzker Prize for architecture was won by Kevin Roche of the USA; a new biennial award sponsored by Carlsberg had as its first recipient the Japanese architect Tadao Ando.

3. LITERATURE

IT said something for the reading tastes of the public, not only in Britain but in the English-speaking world as a whole, that the most successful book of the year, selling over 4 million copies, was *Diana: Her True Story*, a biography of the Princess of Wales, told, it was assumed, with the subject's collusion. Andrew Morton was a previously-unknown journalist who almost certainly, through his revelations and the process by which he acquired them, consolidated the marriage breakdown between the Prince and Princess of Wales which his book was largely dedicated to exposing. When works of such dubious motivation not only earned their authors vast publicity and money but also achieved some constitutional significance, publishers of serious literature could be forgiven for concluding that they were plying the wrong trade. Beset by the trade-winds of recession, which saw several famous companies struggling for survival, the old-fashioned literary publisher was fast becoming a being of the past, obliged to popularize or perish.

It was thus that Secker enjoyed unprecedented publicity for *Sex*, a self-advertising display of the pop singer Madonna's supposedly erotic attractions; that Methuen jumped on the mechanical digger undermining the royal family with Sue Townsend's irreverent and hugely popular novel *The Queen and I*; and that even Faber could not resist bringing out an edition of Philip Larkin's letters in advance of Andrew Motion's biography. The latter would have much ground to make up if it was to redeem the curmudgeonly and racist image of

the poet now firmly etched by the letters. It was difficult to imagine
that any of these books would have appeared in quite the way they
did in the days when publishing houses were less commercially-driven,
more dignified and perhaps more learned. In 1992 the pressures for
restructuring appeared to be irresistible, manifest in the continuing
carousel of takeovers and management changes. Of these, the most
significant, because it indicated the virtual impossibility in Britain of
establishing a new mainstream independent publishing company, was
the completion early in the year of Reed International's buy-out of
Sinclair-Stevenson, a company launched to many fanfares less than two
years earlier.

In a publishing climate where staff redundancies were many and
cynical commercial commitments rife, there seemed to be a special role
for the major literary prizes. These reminded us that good writing was
still produced, that publishers would sometimes take a risk on it and that
traditional values might not after all be dead. It required real courage
for Harper Collins to give the previously-unpublished Jung Chang the
scale she required for *Wild Swans*. This autobiographical account of
three generations of Chinese women, the author's herself, her mother's
and her grandmother's, told an epic tale of the transition from imperial
to modern China via the brutality of the Cultural Revolution. It was
hugely popular and led to an exhausting year of personal appearances
for Jung Chang, including a tour organized by the Arts Council of Great
Britain in the company of three other writers of Chinese origin. *Wild
Swans* won the NCR (National Cash Register) Award for biographical
writing against strong competition from more celebrated purveyors
of the genre. The latter included Michael Holroyd, whose *Bernard
Shaw: The Lure of Fantasy, 1918–1950,* completed the main arc of
his magnificent life of the playwright, and John Richardson, whose
The Life of Picasso, Volume 1, 1881–1906 was a major revisionist
assessment which achieved overall success in the Whitbread Awards.

For the first time since the award was split between Nadine Gordimer
and Stanley Middleton in 1974 (see AR 1974, pp. 459–60), the jury of
the Booker Prize (for fiction) found itself unable to agree on an outright
winner. To the despair of its veteran *éminence grise*, Martyn Goff,
the prize was shared between Michael Ondaatje's elegant and poetic
The English Patient and Barry Unsworth's passionate response to
eighteenth-century slavery, *Sacred Hunger*. The two novels could not,
on the face of it, have been more different, but both were products of
a wider vision than was characteristic of modern fiction, especially
in Britain, and reached for the common humanity which crossed
national frontiers. Other leading literary awards included that given
by W.H. Smith for, simply, the Best Book of the Year, deemed to
be Thomas Pakenham's *The Scramble for Africa*. The Smarties Prize
for children's literature went to Gillian Cross for *The Great Elephant*

Chase, at a ceremony where the standard of some children's writing (though not Cross's) was taken to task for its sloppiness and even illiteracy. In a year when the government became increasingly vocal in its denunciations of teaching standards, asserting that schools were producing a generation of teenagers deficient in grammar, this reproof from the Smarties jury gained a lot of public attention. So, too, did the announcement that a new award had been devised to recognize a lifetime's achievement by a major British writer, to be known on account of its sponsorship as the David Cohen British Literature Prize. Administered by the Arts Council, it was quickly dubbed the 'British Nobel prize for literature' and unashamedly sought to be the supreme accolade for a British author, offering the largest prize money and gathering together a pre-eminent jury to decide its first award early in 1993.

The Nobel Prize itself went to Derek Walcott—recognition at last for a Caribbean writer and a rare acknowledgment that a small state, in this case St Lucia, could produce a major literary figure. Walcott's writing had contributed significantly to the widening recognition that great literature in the English language could absorb an almost infinite amount of cultural influences, in his work ranging from Greek classicism to French West Indian patois.

The state of poetry in Britain was the subject of debate in a special symposium of views solicited by *Poetry Review* from leading practitioners and literary people, who were asked to respond to a controversial article by the American critic Dana Gioia on poetry in the United States. The main burden of Gioia's argument was that poetry was becoming an ivory tower pursuit. The evidence in Britain went the other way: there were increasing audiences for live poetry readings, culminating towards the end of the year in the successful Poetry International festival at the South Bank Centre in London.

Among the liveliest new poetry collections of the year were two by Jeremy Reed, *Black Sugar: Trisexual Poems* and *Red-haired Android*. Reed's bold sexuality and crystalline imagery were often accompanied on the poetry circuit by flamboyant public appearances which tended to detract from a serious evaluation of his talent; but he undoubtedly emerged as one of the most individually impressive younger poets. There were in fact many of these, and in 1992 several confirmed their talent, including Jo Shapcott with *Phrase Book*. Shapcott was the only poet to have won the National Poetry Competition twice (the rules calling for anonymous entries, of which there were over 13,000). Her title poem 'Phrase Book' was a witty comment on cultural exchange against an implied background of the Gulf War. Other newer names producing good new collections in the year included Robert Crawford (*Talkies*), Glyn Maxwell (*Out of the Rain*) and 1991 Booker prize-winner Ben Okri (*An African Elegy*). It was also, however, a year in which some poets of established reputation greatly extended their range. Perhaps Thom Gunn's *The Man with Night Sweats* was the most admirable of these, being a compassionate and fully-controlled response to the AIDS epidemic. The most ambitious poem of the year was Sebastian Barker's *The Dream of Intelligence*, a philosophical narrative epic built around the madness of Nietzsche.

During 1992 there was, for the first time, a serious move by mainstream publishers to bring out original fiction in paperback. Such a sensible step in the middle of a recession, taken by Secker among others, seemed to some commentators like the coming of Armageddon—a moment of destruction for all that the publishing industry held dear. It certainly challenged the norms of literary reviewing in the quality press, which had almost never strayed out of the hardback market. Time would tell whether the move away from hard covers was merely a temporary experiment, similar to half-hearted attempts in London's West End to play matinée performances on Sunday afternoons, or here to stay. If it was to be the latter, book-buying habits in British bookshops really could change, as many more new books became affordable. On the other hand, there were gathering fears during the latter part of the year that the government might, under guidance from the European Community, impose value-added tax on books and journals. This would affect everyone's book budget, whether as an individual or within an institution. As a consequence, the high-profile 'hands off reading' campaign, which had lain dormant for a couple of years, again marshalled its forces. The average number of books bought in Britain in 1992 dropped for the first time since the recession began.

Fears about reading standards were rife throughout 1992. When Book Trust published a report on the dismal state of school libraries, it confirmed the evidence of public libraries—that money was now so tight that much smaller quantities of new writing were being purchased for any kind of loan service. Up and down the country public librarians reported drastically-curtailed opening hours in response to reduced local authority funding. Meanwhile, the tabloid press became more frenzied in its exposure of the pecadilloes of public figures, the prose it employed making its own contribution to the decline in balanced reading. There was much debate in educational circles about the literature elements in the new national core curriculum, a clear majority of teachers disliking the threatened emphasis on prescribed reading and what they considered an old-fashioned hagiographical approach to 'great writers of the past' rather than to the living energy of contemporary authors.

The most favourably-reviewed new fiction of the year not to win a major award was *Ulverton*, a first novel (a disappearing genre, some people claimed) by Adam Thorpe. This was the story of an English village told over several generations in a variety of voices. The elements of pastiche were conscious and the scope of the book adventurous, clearly announcing a major talent. Was the English novel retreating once again, however, into a kind of parochialism? Among the major novels of the year, Peter Ackroyd's *English Music* suggested that this might be so. Malcolm Bradbury's excursion round Europe in *Doctor Criminale* or Jeanette Winterson's excursion round the female body, *Written on the Body*, did not contradict this impression. On the other hand, some novelists who were sometimes thought to be formulaic in their methods branched into courageous new territories. P. D. James's *The Children of Men* was this author's first foray away from detective stories into a form of moral fantasy, posing the condition of humankind nearly 40 years into the future, when environmental catastrophe had rendered the race infertile. Another novel to explore the implications of societies which had lost the capacity to feel was Jim Crace's *Arcadia*, which at times seemed like an amalgam of Kafka and Hardy, but whose distinctive voice in the end confirmed its author as one of the best of his generation.

The novel was sometimes said to be a defeated art form—the capacious relic of an imperialist age in which it had been the natural habitat of people with leisure. If it was on the way out, it was, like Charles II, taking a long time a'dying. The new year saw major new novels from some of the form's best practitioners, among them Rose Tremain (*Sacred Country*), Graham Swift (*Ever After*), Stanley Middleton (*A Place to Stand*), Michael Frayn (*Now You Know*) and Marina Warner (*Indigo*). The foremost American novel of the year was Toni Morrison's *Jazz*. There were outstanding new novels from Africa, including the Booker short-listed *Serenity House* by South Africa's Christopher Hope. The young Nigerian writer Biyi Bandele-Thomas, showing that there was a generation succeeding Ben Okri, emerged in the Heinemann African Writers Series with *The Man Who Came in from the Cold*. This series moved into its 30th year by confirming its ability to go on discovering new talent, its influence over the development of African literature being almost incalculable. New names were published in the parallel Caribbean Writers Series, among them the Trinidadian Clem Maharaj (*The Dispossessed*). Plans were announced by Heinemann to begin an Asian Writers Series to complement the other two.

For some people the publishing event of the year was Iris Murdoch's *Metaphysics as a Guide to Morals*, a disquisition on ethics, religion and morality; for any other writer this book would have been considered a life's work, but it hardly seemed appropriate to speak in such terms of Britain's most prolific senior novelist. At the other end of the intellectual spectrum was John Mortimer's amusingly-anecdotal anthology *The Oxford Book of Villains*. This paled, however, beside the achievement of Seamus Deane in editing *The Field Day Anthology of Irish Writing*, one of the key compilations of modern times, matched in importance only by Margaret Busby's *Daughters of Africa*, which collected together utterances by black women over a thousand years. Facile by contrast, an anthology entitled *The Literary Companion to Sex*, compiled by Fiona Pitt-Kethley, grimly extracted sexual episodes from complex lives and contexts.

Victoria Glendinning wrote an outstanding life of John Major's favourite novelist, Anthony Trollope, and Miranda Seymour an equally good life of Ottoline Morrell, Nigel Jones rediscovered one of the neglected 'might-have-been-great' writers of the century, Patrick Hamilton, in his biography *Through a Glass Darkly*. Vanessa Redgrave, Lauren Bacall and Peter O'Toole were among the most popular writers of entertainment autobiographies. The correspondence of Rupert Brooke and Noel Oliver aroused much interest, as did the publication, under the editorship of Anna MacBride White and A. Norman Jeffares, of the correspondence between Maud Gonne and W.B. Yeats.

Among the writers who died in 1992 was Angela Carter, aged 51. Regarded by many as possessing the most brilliantly creative imagination of her generation, she was at the peak of her powers. The internationally-known science fantasist Isaac Asimov died at 72, and among other celebrated writers who died in the year were the poets George MacBeth and Ruth Pitter, the biographer Robert Gittings, the black American author of *Roots*, Alex Haley, the playwright and novelist Bill Naughton, the children's writers Mary Norton (creator of *The Borrowers*) and Rosemary Sutcliffe, and the influential theatre critic Harold Hobson. (For Asimov and Haley, see XX: OBITUARY.)

On 31 December, Salman Rushdie spent his 1,416th day in hiding, following the February 1989 Iranian *fatweh* calling for his death (see AR 1989, pp. 493–4, 538). During the course of the year Iranian threats against his life were reiterated and the bounty on his head was doubled to \$2 million. Emerging in public more than at any previous time since the pronouncement of the *fatweh*, Rushdie actively lobbied on his own behalf in several countries.

Among interesting new books published during the year were the following:

FICTION. Peter Ackroyd, *English Music* (Hamish Hamilton); Kingsley Amis, *The Russian Girl* (Hutchinson); Beryl Bainbridge, *The Birthday Boys* (Duckworth); Iain Banks, *Crow Road* (Scribners); A. L. Barker, *Zeph* (Hutchinson); Rachel Billington, *Bodily Harm* (Macmillan); Dirk Bogarde, *Jericho* (Viking); Malcolm Bradbury, *Doctor Criminale* (Secker); Melvyn Bragg, *Crystal Rooms* (Hodder & Stoughton); Christine Brooke-Rose, *Textermination* (Carcanet); Anita Brookner, *Fraud* (Cape); George Mackay Brown, *Vinland* (John Murray); A. S. Byatt, *Angels and Insects* (Chatto); Katie Campbell, *Live in the Flesh* (Lime Tree); Jim Crace, *Arcadia* (Cape); Andrew Davies, *B Monkey* (Lime Tree); Lisa St Aubin de Teran, *Nocturne* (Hamish Hamilton); Michael Dibdin, *Cabal* (Faber); Sebastian Faulks, *A Fool's Alphabet* (Hutchinson); Michael Frayn, *Now You Know* (Viking); Alasdair Gray, *Poor Things* (Bloomsbury); Christopher Hope, *Serenity House* (Macmillan); Janet Turner Hospital,

The Last Magician (Virago); Dan Jacobson, *The God-fearer* (Bloomsbury); P. D. James, *The Children of Men* (Faber); Thomas Keneally, *Woman of the Inner Sea* (Viking); Doris Lessing, *London Observed: Stories and Sketches* (Harper Collins); Clem Maharaj, *The Disposssssed* (Heinemann); Hilary Mantel, *A Place of Greater Safety* (Viking); Patrick McCabe, *The Butcher Boy* (Picador); Ian McEwan, *Black Dogs* (Cape); Stanley Middleton, *A Place to Stand* (Hutchinson); Rohinton Mistry, *Tales from Firozsha Bagg* (Faber); Toni Morrison, *Jazz* (Chatto); Edna O'Brien, *Time and Tide* (Viking); Michael Ondaatje, *The English Patient* (Bloomsbury); Michele Roberts, *Daughters of the House* (Virago); Paul Sayer, *The Absolution Game* (Constable); C. K. Stead, *The End of the Century at the End of the World* (Harvill); Graham Swift, *Ever After* (Picador); Adam Thorpe, *Ulverton* (Secker); D. M. Thomas, *Flying in to Love* (Bloomsbury); Gillian Tindall, *Spirit Weddings* (Hutchinson); Sue Townsend, *The Queen and I* (Methuen); Rose Tremain, *Sacred Country* (Sinclair-Stevenson); Barry Unsworth, *Sacred Hunger* (Hamish Hamilton); Kurt Vonnegut, *Fates Worse than Death* (Cape); Marina Warner, *Indigo* (Chatto); Nigel Williams, *They Came from SW19* (Faber); Jeanette Winterson, *Written on the Body* (Cape).

POETRY. Simon Armitage, *Kid* (Faber); Simon Armitage, *Xanadu* (Bloodaxe); John Ashbery, *Flow Chart* (Carcanet); George Barker, *Street Ballads* (Faber); Sebastian Barker, *The Dream of Intelligence* (Little Arc); Kamau Brathwaite, *Middle Passages* (Bloodaxe); Charles Causley, *Collected Poems 1951–92* (Macmillan); Wendy Cope, *Serious Concerns* (Faber); Iain Crichton Smith, *Collected Poems* (Carcanet); K. N. Daruwalla, *Crossing of Rivers and The Keeper of the Dead* (OUP); C. Day Lewis (posthumous), *Complete Poems* (Sinclair-Stevenson); Seamus Deane (ed.), *The Field Day Anthology of Irish Writing* (Field Day/Faber); U. A. Fanthorpe, *Neck Verse* (Peterloo); Thom Gunn, *The Man with Night Sweats* (Faber); David Hartnett, *Dark Ages* (Secker); Ted Hughes, *Rain Charm for the Duchy* (Faber); George MacBeth, *The Patient* (Hutchinson); Roger McGough, *Defying Gravity* (Viking); Glyn Maxwell, *Out of the Rain* (Bloodaxe); Graham Mort, *Snow from the North* (Dangeroo); Ben Okri, *An African Elegy* (Cape); Peter Porter, *The Chair of Babel* (OUP); Peter Redgrove, *Under the Reservoir* (Secker); Jeremy Reed, *Red-haired Android* (Paladin); Eva Salzman, *The English Earthquake* (Bloodaxe); Jo Shapcott, *Phrase Book* (OUP); Pauline Stainer, *Sighting the Slave Ship* (Bloodaxe); David Wright, *Poems and Versions* (Carcanet); Daniel Weissbort (ed.), *The Poetry of Survival: Post-War Poets of Central and Eastern Europe* (Anvil).

BIOGRAPHY/AUTOBIOGRAPHY. Brian Boyd, *Vladimir Nabokov: The American Years* (Chatto); Jung Chang, *Wild Swans* (Harper Collins); Jonathan Coe, *Humphrey Bogard: Take It and Like It* (Bloomsbury); Pauline Collins, *Letter to Louise* (Bantam); Michael Coveney, *Maggie Smith, A Bright Particular Star* (Gollancz); Antonia Fraser, *The Six Wives of Henry VIII* (Weidenfeld); P. N. Furbank, *Diderot: A Critical Biography* (Secker); Jonathan Gathorne-Hardy, *The Interior Castle: A Life of Gerald Brenan* (Sinclair-Stevenson); Victoria Glendinning, *Trollope* (Hutchinson); Pippa Harris (ed.), *Song of Love: The Letters of Rupert Brooke and Noel Oliver (1909–1915)* (Bloomsbury); Denis Healey, *My Secret Planet* (Michael Joseph); Richard Hough, *Edward and Alexandra; Their Private and Public Lives* (Hodder & Stoughton); Nigel Jones, *Through a Glass Darkly: The Life of Patrick Hamilton* (Scribner); Michael Kurtz (translated by Richard Toop), *Stockhausen: A Biography* (Faber); John Lahr, *Dame Edna Everage and the Rise of Western Civilization* (Bloomsbury); Doris Lessing, *African Laughter: Four Visits to Zimbabwe* (Harper Collins); Margaret Lewis, *Ngaio Marsh* (Hogarth Press); Andro Linklater, *Compton Mackenzie: A Life* (Hogarth Press); Madonna, *Sex* (Secker); David Marr, *Patrick White: A Life* (Arrow); Anna MacBride White and A. Norman Jeffares, *The Gonne-Yeats Letters 1893–1938* (Hutchinson); Andrew Morton, *Diana: Her True Story* (Michael O'Mara); Ben Pimlott, *The Life and Times of Harold Wilson* (Harper Collins); Vanessa Redgrave, *An Autobiography* (Hutchinson);

Miranda Seymour, *Life on the Grand Scale: The Life and Times of Ottoline Morrell* (Hodder & Stoughton); Eduard Shevardnadze, *The Future Belongs to Freedom* (Sinclair-Stevenson); Martin Stannard, *Evelyn Waugh: No Abiding City (1939–66)* (Dent); Flora Veit-Wild, *Dambudzo Marechera: A Source Book on His Life and Work* (Hans Zell); Michael White and John Gribbin, *Stephen Hawking: A Life in Science* (Viking); Fred Zinnemann, *An Autobiography* (Bloomsbury).

HISTORICAL AND LITERARY WRITINGS. Derek H. Aldcroft *Education, Training and Economic Performance: 1944 to 1990* (Manchester University Press); John Berger, *Keeping a Rendezvous* (Granta); J. I. Catto and T. A. R. Evans (eds.), *The History of the University of Oxford Vol. 2* (OUP); C. E. Challis (ed.), *A New History of the Royal Mint* (Cambridge); Janet Coleman, *Ancient and Medieval Memories: Studies in the Reconstruction of the Past* (Cambridge); Ted Hughes, *Shakespeare and the Goddess of Complete Being* (Faber); John Mortimer (ed.), *The Oxford Book of Villains* (OUP); Iris Murdoch, *Metaphysics as a Guide to Morals* (Chatto); Roland Oliver, *The African Experience* (Weidenfeld); Thomas Pakenham, *The Scramble for Africa* (Weidenfeld); Tom Paulin, *Minotaur: Poetry and the Nation State* (Faber); Fiona Pitt-Kethley (ed.), *The Literary Companion to Sex: An Anthology of Prose and Poetry* (Sinclair-Stevenson); Anthony Thwaite (ed.), *Selected Letters to Philip Larkin 1940–1985* (Faber); Mark Tully, *No Full Stops in India* (Viking).

XVII SPORT

THE POLITICS OF SPORT. Sport continued to be kicked around by politicians, notably in that Yugoslavia was put on the UN blacklist as South African came off it. The first casualty was the Yugoslav football team, which was banned from the finals of the European championship for which they had qualified. That had an unexpected effect as Denmark was promoted to take the vacant place and ended as European champions. One who ignored the blacklisting was the eccentric American chess player, Bobby Fischer, who restaged in Yugoslavia his historic 1972 match against Boris Spassky of Russia. Fischer won again, but faced charges on returning home.

The Olympics at least were for once free of political gestures in either the winter events or the main games. Indeed, even Yugoslavs were allowed to compete provided they paraded under the Olympic flag dressed in white. But the long-running drugs saga continued to cause problems. The most notable casualty was the German sprinter Kristin Krabbe, who withdrew from the Olympics amid much confusion as to whether she had faked a drugs test. At the summer games the British Amateur Athletic Association sent four competitors home for alleged earlier drugs offences, including the sprinter Jason Livingstone. The two weightlifters involved were however later reinstated by their own sport's official body, because of the confusion over what drugs were permitted and when. The war against drugs was a worthy one, but most commentators agreed that the authorities needed to play fair by making it quite clear which drugs were banned and in what circumstances.

The break-up of the Soviet Union produced several new Olympic entrants, including the newly-independent Baltic states. But the core of the old Soviet team competed under the title of 'Unified' team of the Commonwealth of Independent States (CIS) and proved as powerful as ever. The unified German team was not quite as successful as when East and West competed separately.

Cricket had in the past come near to causing political crises, as when the notorious 'bodyline' Test series of 1932/33 strained relations between Australia and England, or when the New Zealand Prime Minister told his Australian counterpart that his team was 'yellow' after an incident in a one-day international. In 1992 an explosive situation involving Pakistan was more delicately handled—too delicately, many thought. After the umpires had changed the ball during the Test-match interval, without any public explanation, England's Allan Lamb gave the press an exposé on how the Pakistanis were unfairly roughing up the ball to make it swing more sharply. This was a new concept to cricketers, though well-known in baseball. Lamb was heavily fined, but no action was taken against Pakistan or the bowlers concerned. Later the Surrey County Cricket Club was also heavily fined for ball-tampering during the season. As their main bowler was the Pakistani Waqar Younis, whom Lamb had nominated, the implication was obvious. Many therefore felt that Lamb had been badly treated and that the handling of the Test problem had been pusillanimous, possibly because of the legal and political implications of revealing the truth.

The 40th year of her reign proved a sombre one for Queen Elizabeth. However, one event which gave her great pleasure was a garden party for all Britain's world and Olympic champions.

WINTER OLYMPICS. The winter Olympics were staged in France based on Albertville in the Val d'Isère. The central event as always was the men's downhill. On a new course Austrian Patrick Ortlieb was first down and set a time no-one else could match. Frenchman Frank Piccard, starting much later, came very close to take the silver, only 0.05 seconds behind Ortlieb. The most charismatic of the skiers was Italy's Alberto Tomba, winner of two slalom golds in the previous games. In the giant slalom Tomba was again a comfortable winner, to become the first Alpine skier to retain a title. After a poor first run in the slalom, he seemed set for another gold until the final skier, Norway's Finn Christian Jagger, narrowly beat him. Among the women skiers, Austria's Petra Kronberger reigned supreme, winning golds in the combined and the slalom and finishing high up in two other events.

The outstanding champion of the games, however, was a 16-year-old Finn, Tony Niemenen. His exceptional ski-jumping promoted his team to the gold medal and himself as individual champion, the youngest person to win a winter Olympic event. The Unified CIS team was as prominent as ever, dominating the ice-skating events; their gold-medal winners were Viktor Petrenko in the men's figure skating, and Marina Klimova and Sergei Pomonorenko in the ice dance with a theatrical but controversial programme. The Unified ice hockey team might no longer be called the 'red machine' but whatever its name it remained peerless, beating Canada in the final.

SUMMER OLYMPICS. Barcelona's splendid staging of the main Olympic Games was a tribute to the IOC president, Jan Samaranch. It also inspired all the competitors, but especially the Spaniards. Having won only four golds in previous summer Olympics, Spain now collected 13. Their winners included Firmin Cacho in the prestigious 1,500 metres while for the home crowds a last-minute winning Spanish goal in the football final was a special attraction.

As always, there were unexpected losers and winners. Sergei Bubka (Unified team), having set more than 30 world records, failed even to qualify for the final stage of the pole-vault. In the women's 10,000 metres, for which Liz McColgan (Britain) was favourite, an Ethiopian, Derartu Tulu, was the surprise winner, while Elena Meyer gained reinstated South Africa's first silver medal. Of the bitter British disappointments, an abiding picture was of Derek Redmond's father helping him limp to the line after he pulled a hamstring in the 400 metres. Perhaps the most memorable sight was the spontaneous tribute which bronze medallist Kris Akabusi (Britain) paid to Kevin Young (USA) after he had set a remarkable world record in the 400-metre hurdles.

Britain had the great prize of Linford Christie winning the 100 metres, regarded as the most important event and carrying the title of fastest man on earth (although he did not break the world record). For Christie, the oldest athlete ever to win this title, the gold was reward for perseverance. His, main stroke of fortune was the absence of Carl Lewis (USA) who had been ill when the American trials were held. Yet Lewis still remained one of the outstanding athletes, winning the long jump by just three centimetres in another epic battle with fellow American Mike Powell and then getting his eighth Olympic gold in the world record-breaking American 4×100 metres relay team. The Americans set another world record in the 4×400 metres relay.

Sally Gunnell did a captain's job in the 400-metre hurdles, winning only the fifth Olympic gold for a British woman in track events. Other notable British golds were the rowing triumphs of Steven Redgrave (his third gold) with Matthew Pinsent in the coxless pairs and the dramatic final surge to victory over the world champion Abbagnale brothers (Italy) by the Searle brothers, Greg and Jonny, guided by Garry Herbert in the coxed pairs. Chris Boardman, in partnership with a revolutionary new 17-lb carbon-fibre bicycle designed by Lotus, swept to gold in the 4,000 metres pursuit, Britain's first cycle win for 72 years.

The United States, the Unified team and Germany took most of the medals. America was outstanding in the athletics events, but not in its overall medal haul, because in some peripheral events it was possible for one individual to win up to six golds, as Unified team member Vitali Sherbo did in gymnastics.

Other highlights included seven boxing golds for Cuba and outstanding successes in swimming for the Unified team, the Americans, the Hungarians, the Australians and the Chinese (who took four golds, their first in Olympic pools). Alexi Popov was the fastest man, winning the 50 and 100 metres freestyle, but the outstanding individual world record was that of Australia's Kieran Perkins in the 1,500 metres.

In the all-important athletics Kenyan men dominated the 800 metres and the steeplechase. Devers Roberts of America unexpectedly won the women's 100 metres, then fell at the last when leading in the sprint hurdles. That allowed Paraskevi Patoulido to win Greece's first-ever Olympic gold medal for a woman. World champion Hassiba Boulmerka of Algeria duly won the women's 1,500 metres and the young Ellen Van Langen of Holland took the 800 metres in style.

The so-called amateurism of the games was made to look even more hypocritical by the inclusion of the millionaire basketball players of the USA's 'dream team', which duly annihilated all opposition. The millionaires in the men's tennis tournament did not exert themselves to the same degree, the final being contested between two low-ranked players. In all other respects these Olympics were rated the best yet. An equally happy event followed, namely the Paraplegic Olympics, in which British sportsmen were outstanding as were those of the USA, Germany and the Unified team.

ASSOCIATION FOOTBALL. The European Nations football finals in Sweden had a surprise ending. The team which took part only because of the banning of Yugoslavia ended as worthy winners. Denmark had been eliminated in the qualifying matches, but was now brought in as substitute. They played England in their first match and came near to winning the drawn game to give notice of their quality. England could then only draw with France and needed to win their last group match against the host country. David Platt did indeed give them the lead, but two second half goals sent Sweden through to the semi-final round, together with Denmark. Gary Lineker was substituted in the Sweden game, after failing to score the goal which would have given him the highest overall total for any Englishman in internationals. Captain Lineker's relations with manager Graham Taylor had not been happy, a factor which fuelled further criticism of Taylor for the disappointing results.

In the semi-finals Denmark faced Holland (one of the two favourites) and against the odds went through to a final with Germany, who had disposed of Sweden. Despite West Germany's outstanding record in world and European competition, the German team were not at their best in this competition. They were fortunate not to be beaten by the Unified CIS team and only went through because Scotland soundly beat the latter after losing their first two games. Scotland indeed played some of the best attacking football and were very unlucky to lose to both Holland and Germany. The Germans were expected to win the final, but a devastating early strike by the Danes and a clinching goal later gave them a victory which sparked huge celebration throughout Denmark and delight in the hearts of many 'neutral' observers.

In the English League, Manchester United had the most talented team and led for most of the season, until their high-priced players succumbed to nerves or tiredness in the final stretch. As the goals dried up for the Manchester side, they were caught and passed by unfancied but determined Leeds United. Leeds owed most to their inspirational captain, Gordon Strachan, whose energy belied his years.

In Lee Chapman they also had a striker with a talent for scoring, and in Howard Wilkinson a perceptive manager. Leeds won the last old-style first division championship, the start of the 1992/93 season marking the introduction of a new Premier League. This had been billed as an important development to improve English soccer, but sadly the wrangles attending its formation meant that it was merely a richer version of the old first division involving just as many clubs and just as tiring a season for the players.

Liverpool were no longer the dominant force in English football and manager Graeme Souness had to cope with a heart operation as well as injuries to key players as he struggled to emulate the success of his predecessor, Kenny Dalgleish, who now piloted second division Blackburn into the Premier League. But Souness did have the pleasure of watching Liverpool lift the FA Cup by beating second division Sunderland at Wembley. That win was comfortable enough, but it had been a hard struggle all the way there, especially in a replayed semi-final with Portsmouth, another second division club.

The relative decline in the standard of English football was reflected in disappointing results of English teams in European events. England also had a stuttering start to their World Cup qualifying matches, before the ebullient Paul Gascoigne drove them to a convincing win over Turkey. For Spain, however, all sporting occasions went right this year: Barcelona won the European Cup, defeating Sampdoria of Italy by the only goal of the final.

RUGBY FOOTBALL. Nothing better expressed England's dominance of Rugby Union in Europe than the final 24-0 victory over Wales in the five nations championship. This completed the first back-to-back 'grand slam' since 1924, against a Welsh team battling desperately to restore pride to a country which not so long ago ruled the sport in Britain. Yet that final performance at Twickenham was generally judged to have been below England's exceptional standards, despite the margin of victory. As rugby commentator Eddie Butler put it: 'They failed to sign off with the glorious flourish which would have added tributes of greatness to statistical majesty.' What the critics had begun to expect was not just greatness but impossible perfection, and that in itself was the greatest tribute to this splendid team. Their two toughest opponents had to be played on their own soil, Scotland being humiliated at Murrayfield and the French disgraced in Paris as their violent response to being totally outplayed ended with two men being sent off. The 118 points England scored in this championship set a record, while full-back Jonathan Webb's personal tally of 67 points (making 246 in his international career) took him beyond the previous records set by Simon Hodgkinson and Dusty Hare respectively.

Webb was one of England's many outstanding players, although

Rory Underwood remained their try scorer supreme. Behind the scrum captain Will Carling was an inspiration and Rob Andrew an astute prompter of his dominant pack, while Jeremy Guscott combined lancing attacks with lethal tackling when danger threatened. But throughout it was the forwards' disciplined mastery in all situations which ensured the succession of convincing victories.

By defeating France 10-6 in a tense match at Murrayfield, Scotland proved the best of the also-rans, while Wales at last gave some hint of a resurgence and Ireland became everyone's whipping boy. South Africa made a muted return to international rugby, winning their first match against France then losing four games in succession there before being beaten in an international match against England at Twickenham.

In English club rugby Bath were again outstanding, winning the league and then beating Harlequins with the last kick of extra time in a tense cup final. In Rugby League Wigan continued to dominate, winning the league and crushing all opposition in the cup. At Wembley Castleford made a fight of the cup final, but two tries by Martin Offiah meant that they were always trailing. In the final of the world Rugby League championship at Wembley Great Britain were narrowly defeated 10-6 by the physically more powerful Australians.

CRICKET. The World Cup matches came to their climax in Australia, where the home team surprisingly failed to reach the semi-finals. In the preliminary rounds New Zealand and England had been the outstanding sides, but at this stage England had the narrowest of wins over South Africa, while Pakistan's brilliant batting overcame the New Zealanders after the latter had set an exceptionally difficult target. In the final the Pakistani batsmen were tied down for a time. But once Graham Gooch had dropped the opposing captain, Imran Khan, they accelerated so well that their final total proved beyond England's capability in the face of fine bowling, particularly by Wasim Akram.

Pakistan's tour of England soon followed and in the five one-day internationals the roles were reversed: England won four of them, making a record one-day international score in one of them. In the more highly valued Test matches, however, England found scoring much more difficult against the fine fast bowling of Wasim and Waqar Younis, both of whom made the old ball swing in a way that raised awkward questions later about illegal tampering. Pakistan took an early lead by winning the Lord's Test, despite some devastating bowling by Chris Lewis, who nearly swung it England's way in the final innings. England squared the series at Headingley, thanks to a fine innings by Gooch, but in the final Oval Test Wasim and Waqar spearheaded a comfortable 10-wicket win for Pakistan, which thus took the series 2-1.

David Gower was reinstated in the England side and this elegant player responded with some excellent and responsible innings which took him well past Geoffrey Boycott's record Test run total for England. When the selectors then failed to include Gower in the tour party for India the outrage was such that MCC members forced an extraordinary general meeting to complain about the selectors. This represented an unprecedented rebuke for the selectors, though there was no prospect of changing their decision.

A new development was the entry of Zimbabwe into Test cricket. They proved that the promotion was deserved, getting draws against India and New Zealand in their first two matches. Durham's first season in English country cricket was reasonably successful, but the county champions were again Essex, who owed much to skipper Gooch and the shrewd management of Keith Fletcher. In the final of the NatWest Trophy Northamptonshire had an easy win over Leicestershire.

GOLF. England's Nick Faldo confirmed his rating as the world's best present-day golfer with a season of consistently high performances interspersed with some memorable achievements. Runner-up to Nick Price of South Africa in the US PGA championship, he became British Open champion again, won the World Matchplay title in style, then climaxed his season by winning the World Championship in December. For that event in Jamaica it was entirely appropriate that Faldo should succeed Fred Couples (USA) as champion, these being currently the two best players in the world. It was, however a hard-won victory, as Greg Norman (Australia) took Faldo to a play-off in a remarkable final round.

So difficult was this Caribbean course in the high winds that only Faldo and Norman were below par, while Seve Ballesteros finished the four rounds 26 over par. A course record 65 in the third round gave Faldo a five-stroke lead and the likelihood of a runaway win. But Norman then went two better with a fabulous new record of 63. Despite another fine round of 68, Faldo had seemed certain of defeat on the final hole: Norman was a stroke ahead and only four feet from the flag in two, while Faldo was on the edge of the green. But Faldo holed bravely and Norman missed his short putt. Norman's two-year barren period had ended with victory in the Canadian Open which qualified him for this event. However, his record of missing out in tight finishes in major events continued, as a bad lie cost him a stroke at the first extra hole. So Faldo's steady par there won him the title he fully deserved and another $550,000 as well.

Faldo made a similar drama of the last round of the 121st British Open at Muirfield. Again he started the final round well ahead and poised for an easy win, but for once he seemed ill at ease and let strokes slip away. That allowed American John Cook, one of the season's most successful golfers, to pass him and build a significant lead. 'I knew I had to play the best last four holes of my life to win', said Faldo afterwards. He did just that, as Cook missed a short putt and dropped a shot at the last, enabling Faldo to win by a stroke with a four-round total of 272. In the World Matchplay at Wentworth Faldo beat Nick Price 2 and 1 in the semi-finals, in which the American, Jeff Sluman, beat Sandy Lyle (Britain). Faldo then destroyed Sluman with a crushing 8 and 7 victory in the final.

This was England's year for victory in the Dunhill Nations Cup at St Andrews, despite the absence of Faldo. The English team of Steve Richardson, Jamie Spence and David Gilford beat America 2-1 in the semi-final, and then beat Scotland's Gordon Brand Jr, Colin Montgomerie and back-to-form Sandy Lyle 2½ to ½ in the final. England's Laura Davies headed the women's professional golf European tour money list and led Europe's women to a conclusive 11½ to 6½ win over America in the Solheim Cup at Edinburgh's Dalmahoy course. English and Irish women amateurs also beat the Americans to retain the Curtis Cup.

Nick Faldo topped the European tour money list with £708,522, while Bernhard Langer (Germany) trailed behind on £488,912, followed by Colin Montgomerie and Sweden's Anders Forsbrand. Fred Couples won the US Masters at Augusta and headed the US tour money list with $1,344,188, followed by Davis Love III, John Cook, Nick Price, Corey Pavin and Tom Kite. Having accumulated the highest-ever aggregate total of golf winnings, Kite at last won the US Open in 1992.

MOTOR SPORT. The 16 Grand Prix races were dominated from the start by Nigel Mansell and Cannon-Williams-Honda. The Williams cars proved more powerful and better balanced than any other, totally reversing their previous inferiority to the McLarens. This, coupled with Mansell's more consistent brilliance, gave the English driver a new record of starting the season with five consecutive wins, one better than Ayrton Senna (Brazil) in 1991. Senna remained outstanding as a driver, but with the McLarens no longer so reliable, or so fast, he depended on others' errors to win races and was often pressed hard by the daring young German, Michael Schumacher, in a Benetton-Ford. Another Englishman, Martin Brundle, also had considerable success for Benetton-Ford after a disappointing start.

Such was Mansell's superiority that he clinched his first world championship title with five races still to run. That was in Hungary in a race won by Senna, who had earlier come first at Monaco after a loose wheel-nut had forced Mansell to make a pit stop. At the start of the Hungarian Grand Prix only Mansell's team-mate, Ricardo Patrese (Italy), could have caught him, having underlined the Williams' command by regularly finishing second. Patrese was in fact well in the lead when he spun off and had to retire with an engine problem. Mansell then had a puncture which dropped him from second to seventh place with only 14 laps left on a circuit where passing was a major problem. Undaunted, Mansell weaved past all but Senna with one of his typical charges. That second place gave Mansell an unassailable 92 points to Patrese's 40, Senna's 34 and Schumacher's 32. By the season's end Manscll had set new records with nine wins and a record point score. Yet Mansell and controversy remained inseparable. His season climaxed not only in triumph but also in a row with Senna (who crashed into him in the final race) and a more prolonged battle with Frank Williams. This resulted in Mansell abandoning Grand Prix racing and signing up instead for the 1993 Indy car racing circuit in America. As some compensation, he was voted the BBC sports personality of the year.

TENNIS. American Jim Courier began the season as the top man in tennis and his early victories in the Australian and French Opens seemed to confirm his superiority. With his sights set on the first 'grand slam' since Rod Laver's in the 1960s, it was a shaking experience for him to be ejected from the Wimbledon singles by an unseeded Russian, who made no further impression. That opened the way for others to take over for the rest of the season.

The immediate gainers were Goran Ivanisevich (Croatia) and André Agassi (USA) whose contrasting talents took them through to an intriguing Wimbledon final. The tall Ivanisevich possessed the most powerful serve in the game and his profusion of aces overwhelmed such leading players as Stefan Edberg (Sweden) and Pete Sampras (USA). Agassi, however, had the reputation of being the best returner of service and now added new purpose and perception to his clever play in the rallies. His good looks and distinctive appearance had already made him the heart-throb of the courts, but his performances in play had rarely matched his natural ability. Now he won the hearts of the crowd as much as by the style and skill of his ebullient tennis, which brought him convincing wins over a rejuvenated John McEnroe (USA) and Boris Becker (Germany) as he swept to the final. There his ability to return the devastating Ivanisevich serve proved decisive in a hard-fought match.

Courier had the satisfaction later of piloting the United States to a Davis Cup final victory over Switzerland, but the nearest he came again to individual success was as losing finalist to Becker in the round-robin tournament for the top ten players. Stefan Edberg returned to his best form in time to retain the US title, while Michael Stich (Germany) beat Michael Chang (USA) to win the Grand Slam Cup. Stich's most memorable performance, however, was as McEnroe's partner in his fifth doubles win at Wimbledon after a marathon final of record duration.

Monica Seles (Yugoslavia) also began with early victories to confirm her number one status. When she beat Steffi Graf (Germany) in the tense final of the French Open the 'grand slam' appeared a reasonable target. A decisive Wimbledon semi-final win over Martina Navratilova (USA) kept her on course. But her style of play included loud grunts as she hit the ball and opponents began to remonstrate that this put them off their game. After Navratilova had made a formal complaint, Seles was obliged to tone down her grunting in the final. Her play was toned down too, so that a confident Graf outplayed her in a final three times interrupted by rain. The sad end to the season was the death of Dan Maskell, a fine player and commentator supreme (see XX:OBITUARY).

THE TURF. Sunday racing was successfully introduced, but the sport in England still suffered from financial problems which led some leading owners to look elsewhere. On the flat the 57-year-old Lester Piggott rode Rodrigo de Triano to two outstanding victories, the first of which was his 30th classic winner in England over a remarkable career. Then, in Florida, he fell so badly when his horse broke a leg that it was feared that his racing career was finally over. However within weeks this indomitable and dedicated man was back in the saddle.

Michael Roberts became the first South African to be champion jockey, piloting 206 winners from his punishing schedule of over a thousand rides in the season. St Jovite was rated the best horse of the year after winning the Irish Derby by 12 lengths from Doctor Devious. The roles were reversed, however, as Doctor Devious won the Irish Champion stakes by a short head in a desperately close finish with St Jovite. User Friendly proved an outstanding filly, achieving three classic wins.

In National Hunt racing Martin Pipe, with 224 wins, and Peter Scudamore (174) were again an unbeatable combination as leading trainer and jockey. The Grand National was won by Party Politics partnered by Carl Llewellyn, who only got the ride because of an injury to Andy Allen. Party Politics finished well clear of Romany King, but there was an enthralling finish to the Cheltenham Gold Cup as three raced for the line together. Cool Ground, whose jockey Adrian Maguire was later suspended for four days for illegal use of the whip, was driven home just ahead of The Fellow and Docklands Express. Champion two-mile chaser Remittance Man was the horse of the year, but novice Royal Gait created the surprise of the season by winning the Cheltenham Champion Hurdles on only his fourth trip over these fences.

AMERICAN ASPECTS. A depressing economic year for Americans also brought sporting tribulation in their own special event of baseball. The World Series had always seemed a misnomer because it had been purely an American concern. That changed dramatically, as the Toronto Blue Jays from Canada took on the Atlanta Braves in a best-of-seven encounter between the season's two most successful teams. Against all expectations, it was the Blue Jays who triumphed, winning one of the most entertaining of recent series by 4-2. In a thrilling final game which went to an 11th inning, failure by inches to reach first base by the final Atlanta batter was the difference between defeat and levelling the series. In the midst of bitter divisions over their proposed new constitution (see IV.2), Canada was briefly united in celebration, while Americans took little comfort from the fact that all the Blue Jays players were American imports.

Basketball's importance nationally continued to be evident in the tradition that the new season was launched by the President pitching the first ball. However, in a depressing end to a disappointing season owners and players became locked in dispute over money, a strike being threatened.

The other annual sporting event of outstanding importance, the American football Super Bowl, took place in Minnesota's Hubert Humphrey Metrodome. The Washington Redskins dominated the 26th final, handing the Buffalo Bills their second successive defeat on this prestigious occasion. The Redskins' superior teamwork was a credit to their coach, Joe Gibbs, and their power proved crushingly effective. The main gainer from the protection this afforded was quarterback Mark Rypien, whose masterminding of their 37-24 win earned him the 'most valuable player' award. The main sufferer was the Bills' quarterback, Jim Kelly, who had a bruising game, being 'sacked' or knocked down on numerous occasions. As a result, Kelly never achieved the same rhythm as Rypien, but he proved a tough and courageous player who battled bravely to the end. In the last six minutes of the game Kelly threw two touchdown passes which made the Redskins' win look less overwhelming. However there was never any doubt that the Redskins would cruise to victory after they led 17-0 at half-time and had shown themselves to be much the stronger side.

To no-one's surprise America retained the America's Cup, the yacht race for rich people and masochists ready to squander a lot of money in coming second to the Americans. The only surprise was that this time an Italian boat, *Il Moro di Venezia*, was the challenger, having defeated various other contenders, including the New Zealand entry.

XVIII ECONOMIC AND SOCIAL AFFAIRS

1. THE INTERNATIONAL ECONOMY

THE economies of the industrialized world expanded by an estimated 1.5 per cent on average in 1992, according to the OECD, but with very strong variations among individual countries (see also XI.4.i). This compared with revised growth of only 0.8 per cent in 1991, the slowest performance for a decade. Western economies were almost everywhere in recession (i.e. growing too slowly to prevent unemployment from rising) as they adjusted to the excesses of the previous decade which had been characterized by high indebtedness and an inflation of property and share prices. The ratio of household debt to GDP rose to its highest level for 20 years in the USA, Japan, Australia, Canada, the UK and Sweden. This trend was especially sharp in the UK, where the ratio of debt to GDP doubled during the decade. In response, people and companies felt obliged to use their cash flow to reduce debts rather than to invest or spend on consumption. This was a major factor retarding the international recovery, aggravated by the past failure of governments to take appropriate action once they had realized the unexpected consequences of the financial liberalization unleashed earlier in the 1980s.

At first, monetary policy had been kept tight (through the medium of high interest rates) to discourage further borrowing. In Japan and the USA, however, monetary policy was progressively eased during 1992 to prevent asset deflation from turning into a full-blooded slump. It was less easy in Europe, where the level of interest rates was kept much higher than the domestic situation warranted because of the need to sustain exchange rates at the levels agreed within the European Community's exchange rate mechanism (ERM)—until the strains of doing that became too great for Italy and the UK (see I.4; II.1.iii; and XI.3). The recession was particularly severe in Eastern Europe, where the teething troubles associated with adapting from communism to capitalism caused most economies to contract quite sharply.

Although 1992 was a year of sluggish growth, it was marked by structural changes all over the world as the main players grouped into three Orwellian super-zones, in a search for global supremacy which was likely to have a profound effect on future patterns of trade. The USA, Canada and Mexico joined together to form the North America Free Trade Agreement (NAFTA), creating a market of 363 million people and per capita incomes ranging from $2,500 a year in Mexico to $21,800 in the USA (see also IV.1 & IV.2). In the Far East, Japan and the nearby 'tiger' economies maintained their inexorable rise, despite the international recession, and continued the process of drawing China into a new Asian 'co-prosperity sphere'. In Europe the year was dominated by preparations for the start of the single European market on 1 January 1993, effectively covering both the 12 European Community (EC) member states and the seven European Free Trade Area (EFTA) countries.

Europe's moves to improve its competitive position in the world economy had three main strands. First, the EC signed a treaty with the seven EFTA countries (Austria, Finland, Iceland, Liechtenstein, Norway, Sweden and Switzerland) providing for the formation of the 19-nation European Economic Area (EEA) (see XI.3, XI.5.iv & XIX.2). Under its provisions, the EFTA members would adopt the 'four freedoms' of the Community: free movement of capital, goods, services and people. They would also accept the EC's common external tariff (currently around 6 per cent) levied on a large number of imports into the Community, although they would not adopt the common agricultural policy (CAP) or some other internal EC programmes. By year's end five of the EFTA countries (Austria, Finland, Norway, Sweden and Switzerland) had in fact applied to become full EC members. But pending the lengthy process of entry negotiations, the EEA was heralded as an important staging-post towards broader West European economic integration. One late snag cropped up on 6 December, when Swiss voters rejected EEA membership in a national referendum (see II.2.vii). This decision meant that the formal inauguration of the EEA would be delayed into 1993 while the other six EFTA countries made appropriate adjustments to their side of the treaty.

Second, there was to be a deepening of the existing Community when the 12 member countries became a single European market, the second largest industrialized market in the world after the newly-formed NAFTA, with over 360 million consumers. This process entailed sweeping away all remaining internal barriers to trade (as opposed to external barriers like tariffs) and marked a milestone on the road towards economic union, which remained the goal of the EC despite the problems surrounding implementation of the Maastricht treaty. It would not suddenly happen with a 'big bang' on 1 January 1993, because most of the 282 measures needed to form a single market had already been implemented in advance under the Single European Act of 1986 (see AR 1987, pp. 535–548).

As a result Community residents would, from the start of 1993, be free to work or live in other EC countries, to move across national boundaries without passports and to carry vegetables and plants without certificates. Lorry drivers, hitherto needing 30 pieces of paper to cross a national frontier, would now need none. For the first time companies would be free to pitch for business on equal terms in other EC countries in the £4,000 million-a-year market for public sector contracts hitherto largely reserved for indigenous companies. As citizens of the Community, everyone would be required to pay the same minimum rates of VAT (15 per cent) and would be able to vote, or even stand, in municipal and European elections in other countries. EC economists reckoned that the removal of all these barriers would boost employment and raise economic wealth (GDP) by 4 to 7 per cent in the medium term.

The third thing which had been due to happen in Europe on 1 January 1993 was implementation of most of the provisions of the Maastricht treaty in fulfilment of the original vision of the framers of the Treaty of Rome. The aim was to move ever closer to monetary union through the creation of a European central bank and—by 1999 at the latest—a single European currency replacing the pound, the franc and all national money issued in the EC. In order to qualify, countries pledged themselves to satisfy tough 'convergence' criteria, including low inflation rates and budget deficits no bigger than 3 per cent of GDP. Britain had negotiated an opt-out clause on the single currency and would not adhere to the so-called Social Chapter, which standardized working hours and conditions in the EC to eliminate unfair competition between countries and companies. To overcome UK opposition the other 11 had taken the Social Chapter out of the main treaty and agreed a separate protocol themselves (see AR 1991, pp. 561–6). As it turned out, ratification of the Maastricht treaty had not been accomplished by Denmark or the UK, but Community governments remained committed to implementation as quickly as possible in 1993.

While the EC was reconstructing itself at home it was also negotiating to finish the GATT Uruguay Round of trade talks which should have been concluded two years earlier. By the end of the year the EC and the USA had agreed a deal (after the USA had threatened sanctions against EC products) to cut export subsidies by just over 20 per cent by the end of the decade. However, as the new year began, France was threatening not to ratify the deal.

In 1992 the economies of the EC countries were held back by the consequences of high German interest rates. These forced all other members of Europe's fixed exchange rate mechanism (ERM) to keep their interest rates high to prevent their currencies from falling below the permitted floor levels in the ERM. As the year wore on speculators and other international investors became convinced that current ERM parities could not be maintained and were prepared to speculate against the Italian lira and the pound. As a result of the turmoil Italy was forced to devalue in the middle of September, then Britain was forced to suspend the pound from membership of the ERM (see also I.7).

This had a cathartic effect on UK policy. Sterling fell 15 per cent in two months and interest rates were lowered (both in absolute terms and relative to those of other European countries), enabling British industry to become more competitive. As a result the first shoots of a possible recovery were evident at the end of the year in Britain, while Germany was facing stagnation or even negative growth. This was a mixed blessing for the UK Chancellor of the Exchequer, Norman Lamont, because the improved prospects for the economy depended on policies which he had opposed earlier in the year, until they were thrust on him by the weight of speculation against the pound.

One of the UK government's fears was that devaluation might reignite inflation through higher import prices which, in turn, would form the basis for higher wage claims. By the end of 1992 this fear had not materialized. The annual rate of price increases had fallen to 2.6 per cent (or 3.7 per cent after excluding mortgage interest). Average earnings, at 5.0 per cent were still high, compared with other European countries, but they had come down from 7.25 per cent at the beginning of the year and were still falling. While the UK economy appeared to have stopped contracting by the end of the year, there was no sign of an end of the rise in unemployment, which increased by almost 422,000 in the year to December to stand at 2,974,000.

The Anglo-Saxon and other Western countries, having led the world into the industrial revolution 200 years ago, were by now finding it difficult to keep up with the information technology revolution. The economies of Western Europe grew by only one per cent during 1992 as their problems of technological competitiveness were compounded by the need to adopt strong deflationary policies (as manifested in high interest rates) in order to meet their obligations under the ERM. In practice this meant keeping interest rates high to match those of Germany even though domestic factors demanded much lower rates. Germany faced severe digestion problems following reunification. The normally strong Germany economy contracted by 1.5 per cent between the second and third quarters of 1992. Inflation remained at the very high (for Germany) level of 3.8 per cent in December and was expected to climb above 4 per cent in the new year to reflect a one per cent increase in VAT. Predictions of economic growth for 1993 varied between minus one per cent and plus one per cent.

While the UK was showing signs of escaping from negative growth of 3.6 per cent (cumulatively) during 1991 and 1992, France was still struggling to emerge from a less serious recession. Although the French electorate appeared to be very unhappy with its government's performance no-one could deny that, compared with most of its neighbours, France was not doing badly. The economy expanded by 1.6 per cent in 1992 and inflation was kept down to only 2.0 per cent. But France could not escape the deflationary effects of being tied in the ERM to high German interest rates. This was reflected in unemployment, which reached the UK level of 10.2 per cent of the working population.

The US economy started to crawl out of recession in 1992 following the 1.2 per cent contraction in 1991 (see also IV.1). As in Europe the pace of recovery (normally brisk in the USA) was held back by the overhang of household debt, defence cut-backs resulting from the end of the Cold War and the crisis in the property markets. The scope for using fiscal policy as a stimulant for recovery was limited by another rise (from $269,000 million to $290,000 million) in the size of the federal deficit. Monetary policy continued to be governed by the need to massage the recovery without rekindling inflation. Short-term interest rates were cut to 3 per cent, the lowest level for 30 years. This easing of monetary policy, buttressed by a parallel tightening in Europe, led to a 7 per cent fall in the value of the dollar against other currencies between the spring and autumn—before the movement was largely reversed in the final quarter. The annual rise in retail prices fell to 3 per cent in November.

Meanwhile, in the Pacific Basin, a number of countries were experiencing an economic convergence towards a de facto trade block. The so-called 'dynamic Asian economies' (DEAs) were being seen increasingly as part of the newly-born 'Chinese economic area'. By 1992 they accounted for half of all the exports of developing countries and their combined share of world export markets was on a par with Japan's. These 'tiger' economies managed to grow by between 5 and 9 per cent in 1992 despite a recession in the key US market. One of the most important developments in recent years was the way that the East Asian economies had assumed a self-reinforcing life of their own, apparently immune from recessions in the rest of the world. With the exception of Japan, their performance was not recorded in the OECD figures (covering 24 nations), which had consequently become less representative of trends in the world economy than they once were.

Malaysia, South Korea, Taiwan and Thailand grew by 7 to 8.5 per cent while mainland China managed 11 per cent. Taiwan had the biggest reserves of foreign exchange ($88,000 million) of any country in the world, including Japan. The 'mature' economies of Singapore and Hong Kong expanded by 5 per cent, although Japan managed only 3.5 per cent. In 1992 the economy of mainland China was taken seriously even by previously-sceptical economists, having achieved growth of an average rate of 9 per cent a year for the previous 14 years. By the end of 1992 it had, on some measures, become the third or fourth biggest economy in the world (in absolute terms, not per capita) after the USA and Japan but possibly ahead of Germany. The year also witnessed a revival of growth in Vietnam, which recorded a 5.3 per cent expansion of GDP despite the evaporation of Soviet aid and the continuing US boycott.

There could be no greater contrast than with Eastern Europe, which continued to contract quite sharply. The economies of the ex-Soviet republics shrank by an estimated 18 per cent in 1992 following a similar fall the previous year. This was caused partly by the shortage of raw materials and components following the demise of central planning; partly by the inevitable post-Cold War contraction of the giant military/industrial complex; partly by government efforts to prevent companies selling to each other using inter-company credit which was unlikely to be repaid; and partly by the chaos of hyper-inflation. Bulgaria, Romania and the Czech and Slovak republics scarcely did better, suffering economic contractions of between 14 and 17 per cent. The only glimmer of hope was in the slightly more experienced economies of Hungary and Poland, which recorded falls of only 9 to 10 per cent amid tentative signs that they might be starting to emerge from the worst of their teething troubles as they journeyed from communism to capitalism. The eastern part of Germany recorded growth of 5 per cent in 1992 after massive injections of capital and credit from the west.

The transition from communism to capitalism was proving to be far more difficult than the countries themselves had imagined when they embarked on the changes; and they had not received as much help as they had anticipated from the Western world. Indeed, it was unfortunate that the end of communism in Eastern Europe coincided with a crisis among the capitalist countries of the West, as they struggled with an unexpectedly steep recession and levels of unemployment not seen since before World War II. Even those countries favourably disposed to help their Eastern cousins were constrained by high budget deficits and the demands of domestic voters.

The economies of the Middle East had a mixed performance. According to provisional estimates assembled by the Economist Intelligence Unit, Syria expanded by 7 per cent (against 5 per cent in 1991), while Saudi Arabia recorded growth of 4.5 per cent compared with 10 per cent the previous year. Over the same period inflation in Saudi Arabia dropped from 4.4 per cent to only 2.5 per cent in 1992. Egypt expanded by 2.8 per cent in 1992 (with inflation of 15 per cent), Jordan by 11.7 per cent and the UAE by 3.5 per cent (down from 7.5 per cent the previous year).

ECONOMIC SUMMIT. The economic summit of the seven leading industrialized democracies (G7), held in Munich in July, was one of the least productive since this series of meetings began. The final communique pledged support for the economically-disintegrating territories of the former Soviet Union and also pledged governments to complete the stalled GATT trade talks and to promote conditions for lower interest rates. These were worthy aims, but were exactly the same as the pledges of the previous year, on which no significant progress had been made on any front. Boris Yeltsin, President of Russia, left the summit with a promise of $1,000 million in Western aid, but this was small beer compared with the $24,000 million requested.

By the end of the year the GATT talks were still stalled, the Russian economy was still deteriorating and the problems of the German economy were still keeping European interest rates much higher than they ought to have been, given the severity of the recession. For the first time, the summiteers included strong references in the communique to the need to bring down unemployment. This expressed the depth of feeling on the subject rather than the discovery of a solution to the problem. Unemployment in the OECD area was forecast to increase to 34 million by the end of 1993.

NOBEL PRIZE FOR ECONOMICS. The 1992 prize was awarded to Gary Becker, the third in succession to have gone to an economist from the laissez-faire school at the University of Chicago. He made his name by applying economic techniques to the decisions made by people in their everyday lives, like having children, smoking, taking drugs, marriage and education. One of his discoveries was that smokers, far from being uncontrollably addicted, responded like most other people to the pricing signals of the market. He and his colleagues found that a 10 per cent increase in the price of cigarettes led to a long-term decline of 7.5 per cent in consumption.

2. ECONOMIC AND SOCIAL DATA

The statistical data on the following pages record developments from 1987 to the latest year, usually 1992, for which reasonably stable figures were available at the time of going to press. Year headings 1987 to 1992 are printed only at the head of each page and are not repeated over individual tables unless the sequence is broken by extending series of figures over a longer period than elsewhere on the page.'

Pages to which the point is relevant include a comparative price index, allowing the current-price figures to be adjusted in accordance with changing values of money.

Unless figures are stated as indicating the position at the *end* of year, they should be taken as annual *totals* or *averages*, according to context.

Tables 2, 3, 4 and 5. Statistics which are normally reported or collected separately in the three UK home jurisdictions (England and Wales, Scotland, and Northern Ireland) have been consolidated into UK series only to show general trends. As the component returns were made at varying times of year and in accordance with differing definitions and regulatory requirements, the series thus consolidated may therefore be subject to error, may not be strictly comparable from year to year, and may be less reliable than the remainder of the data.

Symbols: — = Nil or not applicable .. = not available at time of compilation.

SOURCES

A. **THE UNITED KINGDOM**
GOVERNMENT SOURCES
Annual Abstract of Statistics: Tables 1, 2, 3, 4, 5.
Monthly Digest of Statistics: Tables 1, 11, 17, 18, 23, 24, 25.
Financial Statistics: Tables 9, 11, 12, 13, 14, 15, 16, 26.
Economic Trends: Tables 6, 7, 8, 9, 11, 26.
Social Trends: Tables 2, 3, 4, 5, 10.
Department of Employment Gazette: Tables 19, 20, 21, 22.
Housing and Construction Statistics: Table 5.
ADDITIONAL SOURCES
National Institute of Economic and Social Research, *National Institute Economic Review*: Tables 6, 7, 8.
United Nations: *Monthly Bulletin of Statistics*: Table 1.
The Financial Times: Tables 13, 15.

B. **THE UNITED STATES**
GOVERNMENT AND OTHER PUBLIC SOURCES
Department of Commerce, *Survey of Current Business*: Tables 27, 28, 29, 30, 31, 32, 37, 38, 40.
Council of Economic Advisers, Joint Economic Committee, *Economic Indicators*: Tables 30, 36.
Federal Reserve Bulletin: Tables 33, 34, 35.
ADDITIONAL SOURCES
A. M. Best Co.: Table 35.
Insurance Information Institute, New York: Table 35.
Monthly Labor Review: Tables 38, 39.
Bureau of Economic Statistics, *Basic Economic Statistics*: Table 39.

C. **INTERNATIONAL COMPARISONS**
United Nations, *World Economic Survey*: Table 44.
UN, *Monthly Bulletin of Statistics*: Tables 41, 42.
World Bank, *World Development Report*: Table 41.
IMF, *International Financial Statistics*: Tables 41, 43, 45, 46, 47, 48, 49.
OECD, *Main Economic Indicators*: Table 42.
Stockholm International Peace Research Institute, *Yearbook:* Table 50.
OECD, *Labour Force Statistics*: Table 51.

ECONOMIC AND SOCIAL DATA

2A. THE UNITED KINGDOM

SOCIAL

1. Population	1987	1988	1989	1990	1991	1992
Population, mid-year est. ('000)	56,930	57,065	57,236	57,411	57,561	..
Crude birth rate (per 1,000 pop.)	13·6	13·8	13·6	13·9	13·8	..
Crude death rate (per 1,000 pop.)	11·3	11·4	11·5	11·2	11·2	..
Net migration ('000)	+2	−21	+44	+36	+28	..

2. Health

Hospitals:						
staffed beds, end-year ('000)	388·7	372·9	362·5	337·0	..	..
waiting list, end-year ('000)(1)	806	828	827·0	841·2	830·1	..
Certifications of death ('000)(2) by:						
ischaemic heart disease	173·6	171·0	173·4	169·5	171·2	..
malignant neoplasm, lungs and						
bronchus	39·4	39·4	39·6	39·3	39·2	..
road fatality	5·4	5·1	5·5	5·7	5·2	..
accidents at work (number)	525	610	475	433	..	..

(1) End Sept. except 1991, March.
(2) Great Britain.

3. Education

Schools ('000)	35·4	35·2	34·9	34.8	34·6	..
Pupils enrolled ('000) in schools	9,246	9,101	9,023	9,010	9,062	..
Primary	4,550	4,599	4,663	4,747	4,812	..
Secondary	3,902	3,701	3,552	3,492	3,473	..
Pupils per teacher	17·2	17·1	17·1	16·9	17·2	
Further education: institutions (number)	3,252	3,356	3,508	3,318	..	..
full-time students ('000)	624	633	646	690	..	..
Universities	46	46	46	46	46	..
University students ('000)	316	321	334	351	370	..
First degrees awarded (number)	71,817	73,756	74,953	77,163	..	..
Open University graduates ('000)	8·0	8·0	8·1	8·1	8·3	..

4. Law and Order

Police ('000)						
Full-time strength(1)	136·2	137·3	138·0	139·6	139·2	..
Ulster, full-time strength	8·2	8·2	8·3	8·2	8·2	..
Serious offences known to police ('000)(2)	4,437	4,241·7	4,419·4	5,090·1	5,879·1	..
Persons convicted, all offences ('000)(2)	1,779	1,777	1,744	1,731	..	..
Burglary or robbery(3)	61·4	54·5	49·6	49·9	52·3	..
Handling stolen goods/receiving, theft	180	167	138	137·7	136·8	..
Violence against person	49	64	57·1	54·3	48·7	..
Traffic offences	795	774	760	788	744	..
All summary offences	1,202	1,204	1,224	1,203	1,192	..
Prisons: average population ('000)	56·4	57·1	55·41	52·15	52·5	..

(1) Police full-time strength: Great Britain only. (2) Because of differences in juridical and penal systems in the three UK jurisdictions, totals of offences are not strictly comparable from year to year: they should be read only as indicating broad trends. (3) Specific offences: England, Wales and N. Ireland.

Overall price index (1985=100)	107·8	114·8	123·7	133·6	142·0	148·5

	1987	1988	1989	1990	1991	1992

5. Housing

Dwellings completed ('000)

by and for public sector(1)	33	33	31	33	30	30
by private sector	184	199	179	156	148	138
Homeless households ('000)(2)	118	123	135	151	160	..
Housing land, private sector,						
weighted ave. price (£/hectare)	334,070	438,370	435,964	394,525	398,397	..
Dwelling prices, average (£)(3)	44,220	54,280	62,134	66,695	66,744	63,425

(1) Including government departments (police houses, military married quarters, etc.) and approved housing associations and trusts Great Britain. (2) Accepted by local authorities as in priority need. (3) Of properties newly mortgaged by building societies.

PRICES, INCOME AND EXPENDITURE

6. National Income and Expenditure
(£ million, 1985 prices)

	1987	1988	1989	1990	1991	1992
GDP at factor cost	334,407	349,698	356,698	358,980	350,182	348,549
GDP at market prices (1)	423,500	471,342	515,317	550,350	573,343	595,209
Volume index (1985 =100)	109·1	114·0	116·4	117·0	114·4	113.6
Components of gross domestic product:						
Consumers'expenditure	243,279	261,330	270,575	273,204	269,083	269,575
General government						
consumption	76,034	76,486	77,182	79,513	82,282	82,092
Gross fixed investment	67,753	76,648	81,845	80,040	72,529	72,063
Total final expenditure	501,318	531,645	550,199	556,042	543,741	548,050
Stockbuilding	1,158	4,031	2,668	−374	−3,418	−1,323
Adjustment to factor cost	55,539	58,312	59,974	60,586	58,375	57,467

(1) Current prices, £ 000 million. "Money GDP".

7. Fixed Investment
(£ million, 1985 prices, seasonally adjusted)

	1987	1988	1989	1990	1991	1992
Total, all fixed investment	67,753	76,648	81,845	80,464	72,529	72,063
Dwellings	13,475	15,548	15,296	13,594	10,832	10,619
Private sector	55,807	65,614	68,907	66,701	59,733	58,076
manufacturing	10,048	11,198	12,386	11,759	10,655	10,313
other	45,759	54,416	56,521	54,942	49,078	47,763
Government and public corporations	11,946	11,034	12,938	13,817	12,796	13,987

8. Personal Income and Expenditure
(£ million, seasonally adjusted, current prices unless otherwise stated)

	1987	1988	1989	1990	1991	1992
Wages, salaries and forces' pay	200,143	223,250	248,537	275,257	288,766	299,370
Current grants	52,494	54,087	56,793	61,942	71,701	..
Other personal income(1)	74,561	87,045	100,662	115,085	118,914	..
Personal disposable income	284,608	315,983	351,438	383,020	407,226	437,330
Real personal disposable income(2)	261,301	276,628	291,266	299,685	298,148	304,944
Consumers' expenditure	264,120	296,165	324,348	349,108	367,527	386,606
Personal savings ratio(3)	6·9	5·4	6·6	8·3	9·7	11.6

(1) From rent, self-employment (before depreciation and stock appreciation provisions), dividend and interest receipts and charitable receipts from companies. (2) At 1985 prices. (3) Personal savings as % of personal disposable income.

Overall price index (1985=100)	107·8	114·8	123·7	133·6	142·0	148·5

	1987	1988	1989	1990	1991	1992
9. Government Finance(1)						
(£ million)						
Revenue(2)	158,801	174,457	191,371	206,209	218,084	224,129
taxes on income	52,464	58,459	63,015	71,030	77,438	75,957
corporation tax	13,495	15,734	18,537	21,495	21,495	18,263
taxes on expenditure	63,881	69,780	77,190	81,455	75,095	85,681
value added tax	21,377	24,067	27,328	29,483	31,006	35,335
taxes on capital(3)	3,034	3,733	4,118	4,120	4,065	3,323
Expenditure(4)	168,829	177,754	184,592	206,977	223,879	243,980
net lending(5)	−3,918	−5,231	−5,354	−6,172	−6,610	−7,884
Deficit(−) or surplus	−10,028	−3,297	+6,779	−768	−5,795	−19,851

(1) Financial years ended 5 April of year indicated. (2) Total current receipts, taxes on capital and other capital receipts. (3) Capital gains, capital transfer tax, estate duty. (4) Total government expenditure, gross domestic capital formation and grants. (5) To private sector, public corporations, and overseas.

10. Public Expenditure
(£ billion, constant 90–91 prices)

Health and personal social services	30·3	31·2	32·0	33·0	34·9	..
Social security	60·3	57·7	57·5	58·8	64·8	..
Education	26·8	27·0	28·4	28·4	29·0	..
Housing	5·2	3·8	5·7	4·9	5·5	..
Defence	23·3	22·0	22·5	21·8	21·4	..
Law and order	9·8	10·1	10·9	11·4	12·0	..

11. Prices and Costs (index 1985=100)

Total UK costs per unit of output(1)	107·8	114·8	123·7	133·6	142·0	148·5
Labour costs per unit of output	108·5	115·8	126·3	138·5	149·8	..
Mfg. wages/salaries per unit of output	105·9	108·6	113·6	123·2	132·6	135·0
Import unit values	98·2	97·5	103·2	107·9	108·4	108·5
Wholesale prices, manufactures	108·3	113·2	119·0	126·0	133·0	138·0
Consumer prices	107·7	113·0	121·8	133·3	141·2	146·5
Tax and prices	104·5	107·5	115·0	124·5	126·2	129·8

(1) Used as 'Overall price index' on all pages of UK statistics.

FINANCIAL

12. Monetary Sector(1)
(£ million, amounts outstanding at end of period)

Notes and coins in circulation	13,592	14,755	15,362	15,256	15,716	16,968
M_0(2) (average)	15,894	16,377	17,312	18,293	18,867	19,426
M_2(3)	187,104	213,678	234,814	253,403	276,390	372,910
M_4(4)	303,753	357,218	424,017	473,349	500,957	518,047
Deposits						
domestic	210,720	252,108	336,108	372,783	365,519	285,545
overseas	474,211	511,672	610,069	588,277	562,187	677,994
Domestic lending						
private sector	250,782	318,763	432,941	470,461	466,142	474,742
public sector	17,021	15,153	15,140	14,252	14,499	19,445
Overseas lending	460,772	483,726	566,377	545,186	516,100	646,736

(1) Institutions recognized as banks or licensed deposit-takers, plus Bank of England banking dept. and other institutions adhering to monetary control arrangements. (2) M_0=Notes and coins in circulation plus banks' till money plus bankers' balance with Bank of England. (3) M_2=Notes and coin plus sterling retail deposits with banks and building societies. From 1992, retail deposits and cash in M_4 (4) M_4= Notes and coin plus all sterling deposits held with UK banks and building societies.

Overall price index (1985=100)	107·8	114·8	123·7	133·6	142·0	148·5

	1987	1988	1989	1990	1991	1992
13. Interest Rates and Security Yields(1)						
(% per annum, end of year)						
Treasury bill yield	8·37	12·91	14·63	13·44	11·00	6.54
London clearing banks base rate	8·50	13·00	15·00	14·00	10·50	7·00
2½% consols, gross flat yield(2)	9·31	9·12	9·22	10·84	9·98	9·17
10-year government securities(2)	9·57	9·67	10·18	11·80	10·11	9·07
Ordinary shares, dividend yield(2)	3·50	4·32	4·24	5·03	4·93	4·85
Interbank 3-month deposits	8·87	12·94	15·13	14·03	10·94	7·00
Clearing bank 7-day deposits	3·58	5·97	6·59	5·11	4·00	4·00

(1) Gross redemption yields, unless stated otherwise. For building societies see Table 16. (2) Average during year.

	1987	1988	1989	1990	1991	1992
14. Companies						
(£ million unless stated)						
Total income	86,812	99,429	111,603	116,462	110,140	108,789
Gross trading profit in UK	63,289	70,900	74,446	77,597	77,760	78,178
Total overseas income	11,366	13,827	18,124	18,428	16,276	15,661
Dividends	11,123	14,812	19,026	20,671	22,132	24,850
Net profit	42,395	45,559	39,372	39,467	36,485	38,565
Companies taken over (number)	1,527	1,499	1,337	779	506	426
Total take-over consideration	16,486	22,742	27,250	8,329	10,354	5,725
Company insolvencies (number)(1)	11,439	9,427	10,456	15,051	21,827	24,424
Individual insolvencies (number)(1)	7,427	8,507	9,365	13,987	25,640	36,794

(1) England and Wales.

	1987	1988	1989	1990	1991	1992
15. The Stock Market						
(£ million unless stated)						
Turnover (£000 mn.)	1,757·5	1,602·8	1,627·3	1,655·0	1,814·0	2,100·8
ordinary shares (£000 mn.)(4)	496·1	405·2	564·6	316·0	360·5	432·8
New issues, less redemptions (value)						
Government securities	5,425	−266	−14,113	−8,824	6,384	18,480
Local authority issues(1)	−177	−34	−11	−35	−2	−38
UK companies	15,376	6,693	6,827	4,221	12,142	7,003
FT ordinary share index (1935=100)(2)	1,600·01	1,448·73	1,781·41	1,749·4	1,921·9	1,951·9
FT-Actuaries index (750 shares)(3)	1,025·07	931·67	1,110·29	1,092·4	1,187·3	1,224·2
Industrial, 500 shares	1,133·51	1,019·76	1,221·71	1,199·1	1,316·5	1,375·4
Financial, 100 shares	725·37	679·99	763·45	761·6	784·3	743·4

(1) Includes public corporation issues. (2) Average during year. (3) 1962=100 (4) From 1990, UK and Irish only.

	1987	1988	1989	1990	1991	1992
16. Building Societies						
Interest rates (%): end year:						
Paid on shares, ave. actual	6·51	8·38	9·96	10·06	7·27	4·72
Basic rate	4·02	5·59	6·57	5·77	2·35	0·79
Mortgages, ave. charged	10·34	12·75	14·44	14·34	11·39	8·98
Basic rate	10·30	12·77	14·42	14·48	11·52	8·98
Shares and deposits, net (£ min.)	7,561	13,214	7,735	6,562	6,006	4·99
Mortgage advances, net (£ min.)	15,390	24,737	24,041	24,090	21,039	14,909

	1987	1988	1989	1990	1991	1992
Overall price index (1985=100)	107·8	114·8	123·7	133·6	142·0	148·5

	1987	1988	1989	1990	1991	1992
17. Industrial Production						
(Index, average 1985=100, seasonally adjusted)						
All industries	105·8	109·6	110·0	109·3	106·1	105·7
Energy and water	103·9	99·3	89·8	89·0	92·2	..
Manufacturing industries	106·6	114·2	119·0	118·5	112·2	111·3
Food, drink and tobacco	103·2	105·3	105·4	106·3	106·2	107·6
Chemicals	109·0	114·1	119·2	118·3	121·6	123·4
Metal manufacture	108·5	122·0	124·8	121·3	109·9	104·7
Engineering and allied	103·9	112·6	120·3	119·7	111·0	108·3
Textiles	103·9	102·1	98·4	95·9	87·8	87·8
Intermediate goods	106·4	107·9	104·2	103·1	101·7	101·5
Consumer goods	106·8	112·4	114·7	114·0	109·6	110·9
Paper, printing, publishing	114·4	125·0	131·9	133·9	129·1	..
Construction	111·4	119·5	124·5	125·7	114·5	..
Crude steel (million tonnes)	17·4	18·9	18·7	17·8	16·5	16.2
Man-made fibres (million tonnes)	0·27	0·28	0·27	0·27	0·27	..
Cars ('000)	1,143	1,227	1,299	1,296	1,237	1,292
Motor vehicles, cars imported ('000)(1)	1,041	1,250	1,310	1,190	821	..
Commercial vehicles ('000)	247	318	327	270	217	248
Merchant ships(2) completed ('000 gr.t)	247	31	106	133	110	..

(1) Including imported chassis. (2) 100 gross tons and over.

18. Energy						
Coal, production (mn. tonnes)	104·4	104·1	101·1	94·4	96·1	..
Power station consumption (mn. tonnes)	86·2	82·5	80·6	82·6	82·0	..
Electricity generated ('000 mn. kwh.)	282·7	288·4	292·9	298·5	300·4	..
by nuclear plant ('000 mn. kwh.)	44·8	51·7	59·3	55·0	58·5	..
Natural gas sent out (mn. therms)	19,814	18,655	18,748	19,373	20,974	..
Crude oil output ('000 tonnes)(1)	123,600	114,375	91,800	91,600	91,100	..
Oil refinery output (mn. tonnes)(2)	67·7	72·3	73·0	73·9	74·4	..

(1) Including natural gas liquids. (2) All fuels and other petroleum products.

LABOUR

19. Employment						
(millions of persons, in June each year)						
Working population(1)	28·21	28·26	28·50	28·51	28·27	28·03
Employed labour force(2)	24·68	25·92	26·75	26·89	26·03	25·35
Employees: production industries	5·54	5·59	5·55	5·51	5·15	4·91
Manufacturing	5·04	5·12	5·10	5·07	4·72	4·52
Transport and communications	1·33	1·35	1·34	1·35	1·33	1·31
Distributive trades	3·29	3·32	3·41	3·48	3·36	3·28
Education and health	2·91	3·09	3·13	3·16	3·21	3·24
Insurance, banking, financial	2·30	2·44	2·59	2·70	2·65	2.60
Public service	1·98	2·02	1·87	1·89	1·92	1·91
Total employees	21·82	22·10	22·23	22·33	21·70	21·21
of whom, females	9·93	10·16	10·53	10·81	10·37	10·21

(1) Including registered unemployed and members of the armed forces. (2) Including employers and self-employed.

Overall price index (1985=100)	107·8	114·8	123·7	133·6	142·0	148·5

	1987	1988	1989	1990	1991	1992
20. Demand for Labour						
Average index of weekly hours worked, manufacturing industry, 1985=100	96·1	97·2	97·1	90·9	79·8	75·0
Manufacturing employees:						
Total overtime hours worked ('000)(1)	12,680	13,976	13,380	12·43	9·82	9·72
Short time, total hours lost ('000)(1)	364	249	302	396	813	620
Unemployment, excl. school-leavers, adult students (monthly ave. '000)(2)	2,822·3	2,294·5	1,795·5	1,662·7	2,287·4	2,767·4
Percentage of working population	10·1	8·1	6·4	5·8	8·1	9·7
Unfilled vacancies, end-year ('000)	235·0	238·3	195·4	133·5	123·7	109·1
Work-related training programmes ('000)	311	343	450	418	354	334

(1) Great Britain. (2) Seasonally adjusted.

	1987	1988	1989	1990	1991	1992
21. Industrial Disputes						
Stoppages (number)(1)(2)	1,004	770	693	620	369	240
Workers involved ('000)(3)	884	759	727	285	176	144
Work days lost ('000), all inds., services	3,546	3,702	4,128	1,903	761	523

(1) Excluding protest action of a political nature, and stoppages involving fewer than 10 workers and/or lasting less than one day except where the working days lost exceeded 100. (2) Stoppages beginning in year stated. (3) Directly and indirectly, where stoppages occurred; lay-offs elsewhere in consequence are excluded.

	1987	1988	1989	1990	1991	1992
22. Wages and Earnings						
Average earnings index (1985=100)						
Whole economy	116·3	126·5	138·0	151·4	163·5	173·5
Manufacturing	116·3	126·2	137·2	150·2	162·5	173·2
Average weekly earnings(1)(2)						
Men						
Manual	185·5	200·6	217·8	237·2	253·1	268·3
Non-manual	265·9	294·1	323·6	354·9	375·7	400·4
All occupations	224·0	245·8	269·5	295·6	318·9	340·1
Women						
Manual	115·3	123·6	134·9	148·0	159·2	170·1
Non-manual	157·2	175·5	195·0	215·5	236·8	256·5
All occupations	148·1	164·2	182·3	201·5	222·4	241·1
Average hours(3)	40·4	40·6	40·7	40·5	40·0	39·9

(1) In all industries and services, full time. From 1991, manual and non-manual based on new standard occupational classification. (2) April. (3) All industries and services, all occupations, men and women over 18 years.

	1987	1988	1989	1990	1991	1992
23. Productivity						
(Index of output per head 1985=100)						
All production industries(1)	110·1	113·2	113·7	115·6	119·7	126·3
Manufacturing	109·7	116·2	120·8	122·8	124·6	130·8
Minerals	118·3	129·5	128·1	119·4	115·5	..
Metal manufacture	131·8	157·2	151·2	135·3	132·0	..
Engineering	107·6	115·1	122·9	124·6	123·1	..
Textiles	104·4	102·0	102·8	104·8	101·9	..
Chemicals	114·8	118·7	122·1	122·0	129·5	..

(1) Excluding extraction of mineral oil and natural gas.

Overall price index (1985=100)	107·8	114·8	123·7	133·6	142·0	148·5

TRADE

24. Trade by Areas and Main Trading Partners

(£ million; exports fob; imports cif)	1987	1988	1989	1990	1991	1992
All countries: *exports*	79,848	81,475	93,771	103,882	104,724	..
All countries: *imports*	94,023	106,412	121,888	126,135	118,780	..
E.E.C.: *exports*	39,415	40,932	47,540	55,071	59,449	..
E.E.C.: *imports*	49,555	55,785	63,807	65,955	61,370	..
Other Western Europe: *exports*	7,621	7,412	7,987	9,041	8,679	..
Other Western Europe: *imports*	12,884	13,943	15,155	15,745	14,300	..
North America: *exports*	12,992	12,623	14,437	14,973	13,151	..
North America: *imports*	10,781	12,899	15,929	16,751	15,733	..
Other developed countries: *exports*	4,046	4,496	4,519	4,824	4,010	..
Other developed countries: *imports*	7,283	8,505	8,514	8,414	8,094	..
Oil exporting countries: *exports*	5,223	5,021	5,831	5,575	5,756	..
Oil exporting countries: *imports*	1,700	2,087	2,313	2,974	2,787	..
Other developing countries: *exports*	8,549	8,630	11,185	12,189	12,130	..
Other developing countries: *imports*	9,284	10,471	13,557	13,855	14,155	..
Soviet Union and E. Eur.: *exports*	1,571	1,623	1,473	1,480	1,260	..
Soviet Union and E. Eur.: *imports*	2,099	2,039	1,781	1,797	1,689	..
Balance of trade in manufactures	−8,254	−9,961	−19,567	−13,722	−6,045	−10,057

25. Terms of Trade
(Index 1985=100)

	1987	1988	1989	1990	1991	1992
Volume of exports(1)	109·2	112·0	117·3	125·1	126·9	130·7
manufactures	111·3	118·9	132·1	141·4	144·7	148·3
Volume of imports(1)	114·3	130·1	140·9	142·7	138·6	147·4
Unit value of exports(1)	94·3	94·7	101·3	107·0	107·3	108·7
manufactures	106·0	110·0	116·0	121·0	122·0	125·0
Unit value of imports(1)	98·2	97·5	103·2	107·9	108·4	108·5
Terms of trade(2)	96·0	97·1	97·9	99·2	98·9	100·2

(1) Seasonally adjusted: Overseas Trade Statistics basis. (2) Export unit value index as percentage of import value index, expressed as an index on the same base.

26. Balance of Payments
(£ million: current transactions seasonally adjusted; remaining data unadjusted)

	1987	1988	1989	1990	1991	1992
Exports (f.o.b.)	79,421	80,772	92,792	102,036	103,413	106,775
Imports (f.o.b.)	89,594	101,587	116,632	120,653	113,703	120,546
Visible balance	−10,174	−20,815	−23,840	−18,167	−10,290	−13,771
Invisible balance	+7,475	+6,154	+4,217	+3,475	+3.967	+1,952
Current balance	−2,699	−14,661	−19,623	−15,142	−6,323	−11,819
Direct investment overseas	−19,033	−20,760	−21,521	−9,553	−10,261	..
Portfolio investment overseas	+7,201	−8,600	−31,283	−15.844	−30,908	..
Bank lending abroad	−50,322	−19,267	−27,032	−41,240	+32,231	..
Direct investment in UK	+8,508	+10,236	+17,145	+18,634	+12,045	..
Portfolio investment in UK	+19,210	+14,387	+13,239	+5,276	+16,627	..
UK overseas bank borrowing	+52,814	+34,218	+43,887	+47,612	−24,024	..
Net change in assets/liabilities	−5,810	+9,645	+12,916	+11,091	+5,249	..
Balancing item	−1,651	+5,875	+7,488	+5,938	+636	..
Official reserves, end of year	23,490	28,589	23,966	19,935	23,625	27,494

Overall price index (1985=100)	107·8	114·8	123·7	133·6	142·0	148·5

2B. THE UNITED STATES

27. Population	1987	1988	1989	1990	1991	1992
Population, mid-year est. (mn)	242·8	245·1	247·3	249·9	252·7	..
Crude birth rate (per 1,000 pop.)	15·7	16·0	16·0	16·7	16·3	..
Crude death rate (per 1,000 pop.)	8·7	8·8	8·7	8·7	8·6	..

28. Gross National Product
($000 million current)

Gross national product	4,540	4,900	5,244	5,514	5,677	5,946
Personal consumption	3,052	3,296	3,518	3,743	3,888	4,094
Gross private domestic investment	749	794	838	803	721	770
Net exports, goods and services	−143	−108	−83	−74	−22	−33
Government purchases	881	919	971	1,043	1,091	1,115

29. Government Finance
($000 million, seasonally adjusted)

Federal government receipts	911	972	1,053	1.105	1,121	1,160
from personal taxes(1)	406	413	464	482	473	462
Federal government expenditure	1,074	1,117	1,187	1,270	1,333	1,455
Defence purchases	295	298	301	314	324	315
Grants to state/local govts.	103	111	118	131	153	172
Federal surplus or (−) *deficit*	−161·3	−145·8	−134	−166	−210	−295
State and local govt. receipts	656·1	701·6	750	724	778	836
from indirect business tax(1)	314·0	336·7	356	373	397	423

(1) Includes related non-tax receipts on national income account.

30. Balance of Payments
($ million)

Merchandise trade balance	−159,500	−127,215	−115,917	−108,853	−73,436	..
Balance on current account(1)	−143,700	−126,548	−106,305	−90,428	−3,862	..
Change in US private assets abroad(2)	86,364	81,544	104,637	56,467	71,379	..
Change in foreign private assets in US(2)	172,847	180,417	207,925	65,471	48,573	..

(1) Includes balance on services and remittances and US government grants other than military.
(2) Includes reinvested earnings of incorporated affiliates.

31. Merchandise Trade by Main Areas
($ million)

All countries: *exports* (f.o.b.)	252,866	322,245	360,465	393,893	415,962	..
All countries: *imports* (f.o.b.)	424,082	440,940	475,329	494,903	489,398	..
Western Europe: *exports*	69,718	87,995	98,475	111,375	116,802	..
Western Europe: *imports*	99,934	100,515	102,301	109,254	101,884	..
Canada: *exports*	59,814	70,862	79,746	83,572	85,006	..
Canada: *imports*	71,510	80,921	89,408	93,026	93,008	..
Latin America						
exports	31,574	43,624	48,825	54,272	63,233	..
imports	44,371	51,421	57,438	64,320	62,971	..
Japan: *exports*	28,249	37,732	43,673	47,977	47,213	..
imports	88,074	89,802	93,455	89,667	91,502	..

Dollar purchasing power (1982–84=100)	88·0	84·6	80·7	76·5	73·4	71·3

32. Merchandise Trade by Main Commodity Groups

($ million)	1987	1988	1989	1990	1991	1992
Exports:						
Machinery and transport equipt.	108,596	135,135	148,780	172,522	187,360	..
Motor vehicles and parts	19,952	23,972	23,610	26,656	28,175	..
Electrical machinery	24,359	27,571	32,009	39,807	..	
Food and live animals	19,179	26,415	29,724	29,280	29,555	..
Chemicals and pharmaceuticals	26,381	32,300	36,485	38,983	42,967	..
Imports:						
Machinery and transport equipt.	182,807	201,938	205,761	208,096	210,786	..
Motor vehicles and parts	70,680	71,268	69,340	69,382	67,525	..
Food and live animals	22,224	21,771	20,685	21,932	21,952	..
Petroleum and products	46,724	41,813	52,649	64,561	..	..
Iron and steel	8,493	10,274	9,401	8,915	8,900	..

33. Interest Rates
(per cent per annum, annual averages, unless otherwise stated)

Federal Funds rate(1)	6·66	7·57	9·21	8·10	5·69	..
Treasury bill rate	5·82	6·69	8·11	7·50	5·41	..
Government bond yields: 3–5 years	7·68	8·26	8·55	8·26	6·82	..
Long-term (10 years or more)	8·39	8·98	8·58	8·74	8·16	..
Banks' prime lending rate(2)	8·22	9·32	10·87	10·00	8·46	6.25

(1) Effective rate. (2) Predominant rate charged by commercial banks on short-term loans to large business borrowers with the highest credit rating.

34. Banking, money and credit
($000 million, outstanding at end of year, seasonally adjusted)

Money supply M1(1)	752·3	790·2	783·4	812·0	860·4	966·9
Money supply M2(2)	2,910	3,072	3,130·3	3,298·3	3,402·7	3.477·5
Money supply M3(3)	3,677	3,918	3,990·8	4,093·0	4,160·5	4,180·3
Currency	196·4	211·8	217·6	235·5	259·5	279·6
Deposits of commercial banks	2,009	2,121	2,268	2,563	2,393	..
Advances of commercial banks	1,899	2,021	2,206	2,309	2,288	..
Instalment credit	613·0	667·3	718·9	748·3	742·1	..
Motor vehicle contracts	267·2	290·4	290·8	284·8	263·1	..
Mortgage debt	2,943	3,154	3,556	3,913	4,049	..

(1) Currency plus demand deposits, travellers cheques, other checkable deposits. (2) M1 plus overnight repurchase agreements, eurodollars, money market mutual fund shares, savings and small time deposits. (3) M2 plus large time deposits and term repurchase agreements.

35. Insurance
($ million, unless otherwise stated)

Property-liability, net premiums written	193,246	202,015	207,800	217,800	223,000	230,100
Automobile(1)	81,199	86,379	90,900	95,400	99,400	
Underwriting gain/loss(2)	−7,100	−8,400	−16,500	−18,200	−19,400	..
Net investment income(3)	23,960	27,723	31,200	32,900	34,200	..
Combined net income(3)	+16,860	+19,323	+14,700	+14,700	+14,800	..
Life insurance, total assets, end-year	1,044,459	1,166,870	1,299,800	1,408,208	1,551,200	1,693,400

(1) Physical damage and liability, private and commercial. (2) After stockholder and policy-holder dividends and premium rebates. (3) Property, casualty.

Dollar purchasing power (1982–84=100)	88·0	84·6	80·7	76·5	73·4	71·3

36. Companies(1) ($000 million)	1987	1988	1989	1990	1991	1992
Net profit after taxes	115·6	154·8	136·5	111·3	68·0	..
Cash dividends paid	49·5	57·1	65·2	62·2	60·2	..

(1) Manufacturing corporations, all industries.

37. The Stock Market
($million, unless otherwise stated)

	1987	1988	1989	1990	1991	1992
Turnover (sales), all exchanges	2,284,166	1,584,106	1,844,768	1,611,687	1,776,770	..
New York Stock Exchange	1,983,311	1,377,711	1,576,899	1,389,084	1,532,979	..
Stock prices (end-year):						
Combined index (500 stocks)(1)	247·08	277·7	353·4	330·22	376·18	435·71
Industrials (30 stocks)(2)	1,938·83	2,168·6	2,753·2	2,633·7	3,168·8	3,301·11

(1) Standard and Poor Composite 1941–43=10. (2) Dow-Jones Industrial (Oct. 1928=100).

38. Employment
('000 persons)

	1987	1988	1989	1990	1991	1992
Civilian labour force(1)	119,850	121,666	123,869	124,787	125,303	126,982
in non-agricultural industry	109,229	111,796	114,142	114,728	113,644	114,391
in manufacturing industry	19,112	19,403	19,612	19,063	18,427	18,193
in agriculture	3,210	3,175	3,199	3,186	3,233	3,207
unemployed	7,410	6,695	6,528	6,874	8,426	9,384
Industrial stoppages(2) (number)	46	40	51	44	40	35
Workers involved ('000)	174	118	452	185	392	864

(1) Aged 16 years and over. (2) Beginning in the year. Involving 1,000 workers or more.

39. Earnings and Prices

	1987	1988	1989	1990	1991	1992
Average weekly earnings per worker						
(current dollars): mining	530·85	539·3	569·7	602·0	629·6	638·3
contract construction	479·68	493·1	512·4	526·4	533·0	534·9
manufacturing	406·31	418·4	430·1	442·3	455·0	569·9
Average weekly hours per worker						
in manufacturing	41·0	41·1	41·0	40·8	40·7	41·0
Farm prices received (1977=100)	127·0	138·0	147·0	149·0	146·0	..
Wholesale prices (1982=100)	102·8	106·9	113·6	119·2	121·7	123·2
Fuels and power	70·2	66·7	75·9	85·9	81·2	80·4
Consumer prices (1982–4=100)	113·7	118·4	124·0	130·7	136·2	140·3
Food	113·6	118·3	125·1	132·4	136·3	137·9
Dollar purchasing power (1982–84=100)(1)	88·0	84·6	80·7	76·5	73·4	71·3

(1) Based on changes in retail price indexes.

40. Production

	1987	1988	1989	1990	1991	1992
Farm production (1977=100)	110·0	102·0	114·0	119·0	117·0	..
Industrial production (1977=100)	100·0	105·4	108·1	109·2	107·0	108·7
Manufacturing	100·0	105·8	108·9	109·9	107·4	109·7
Output of main products and manufacturers						
Coal (million tons)	915·8	950·3	979·6	1,029	994·1	1,015·0
Oil, indigenous (000 barrels/day)	8,347	8,140	7,613	7,355	7,417	7,199
Oil refinery throughput (000 barrels/day)	14,626	15,020	15,170	15,260	15,230	15,150
Natural gas ('000 mn. cu. ft.)	16,540	16,990	17,120	17,610	17,930	18,470
Electricity generated ('000 mn. kwh)	2,572	2,704	2,784	2,807	2,826	..
Steel, crude (million tonnes)	89·1	99·9	97·9	96·5	92·0	94·5
Aluminium ('000 tonnes)	3,343	3,944	4,030	4,020	4,000	4,000
Cotton yarn ('000 running bales)	14,359	14,985	11,884	15,064	17,146	..
Man-made fibres (1987$m lbs.)	11,323	11,693	11,979	11,573	11,412	11,660
Plastics/resins (1987$m lbs.)	26,246	26,223	26,551	27,613	27,890	27,900
Motor cars, factory sales ('000)	7,085	7,105	6,639	6,050	5,407	..

2C. INTERNATIONAL COMPARISONS

	Area '000	Population (millions) mid-year estimate		Gross Domestic Product(1) US $ mins(2)	
41. Population and GDP, Selected countries	sq. km.	1989	1990	1990	1991
Argentina	2,767	31·93	32·32	..	..
Australia(3)	7,687	16·83	17·34	295,500	295,400
Belgium	31	9·85	9·84	196,810	201,380
Canada	9,976	26·22	26·6	556,308	588,630
China	9,561	1,122·4		363,773	371,200
Denmark	43	5·13	5·14	130,942	130,250
France	552	56·16	56·73	1,190,403	1,196,400
Germany(4)	357	62·06	64·12	1,487,529	1,574,300
India (incl. India-admin. Kashmir)	3,287	811·3	827·1	302,500	..
Irish Republic	70	3·51	3·50	42,612	43,593
Israel (excl. occupied areas)	22	4·52	4·66	51,220	59,126
Italy	301	57·52	57·66	1,094,825	1,051,805
Japan	378	123·12	123·54	2,983,097	3,346,411
Kuwait(5)	18	2·05	2·14	..	..
Netherlands	34	14·83	15·94	276,896	286,410
New Zealand(5)	270	3·31	3·35	43,786	42,405
Norway	324	4·23	4·24	105,828	105,929
Portugal	92	10·47	9·87	59,837	..
Saudi Arabia	2,200	14·43	14·57	..	..
South Africa	1,220	34·51	35·28	101,554	107,631
Spain	505	38·89	38·96	491,386	527,139
Sweden	450	8·49	8·56	257,781	283,630
Switzerland	41	6·65	6·71	224,878	232,010
Turkey	781	56·74	56·1	108,559	..
USSR	22,403	286·71	288·62		
UK	244	57·24	57·4	981,442	1,017.936
USA	9,372	247·35	249·92	5,423,400	5,677,500

(1) Expenditure basis. (2) Converted from national currencies at average exchange rates. (3) Years beginning 1 July. (4) Combines East and West Germany. (5) Years beginning 1 April.

42. World Production
(Index 1980=100)	1987	1988	1989	1990	1991	1992
Food(1)	117·0	118·0	123	125	123	..
Industrial production(2)	116·3	122·3	126·9	126·9	128·3	..
Crude petroleum, nat. gas	83·1	87·6	92·6	92·7	98·5	..
Manufacturing	120·6	127·1	131·7	131·5	131·8	..
Chemicals	125·2	133·2	138·5	138·7	142·2	..
Paper, printing, publishing	126·6	133·4	138·5	141·9	143·8	..
Textiles	109·2	110·5	111·9	107·3	105·6	..
OECD	113·4	120·1	124·5	124·4	123·7	..
EEC(3)	109·0	113·6	117·5	113·8	113·2	..
Developing market economies(4)	139·7	150·8	159·3	170·5	185·4	..
Caribbean, C. & S. America	117·3	121·6	131·9	142·9	162·5	..
Asia(5)	181·6	197·7	208·1	226·2	243·7	..
France	104·0	108·1	112·0	114·0	114·0	..
Germany, West	107·0	111·2	117·0	123·0	126·0	124·0
Italy	103·0	110·8	114·0	114·0	112·0	..
UK	113·0	118·0	119·0	118·0	115·0	114·0
Japan	122·0	133·5	142·0	149·0	152·0	..
Sweden	114·0	115·1	120·0	116·0	106·0	..
USSR	130·9	134·0	136·0	135·0	124·0	..

(1) Excluding China. (2) Excluding China, N. Korea, Vietnam, Albania. (3) Community of Twelve. (4) Manufacturing. (5) Excluding Japan and Israel.

43. World Trade
$million. Exports f.o.b.,
imports c.i.f.)

	1987	1988	1989	1990	1991	1992
World(1): exports	2,364,800	2,688,500	2,906,300	3,324,600	3,442,200	..
imports	2,424,800	2,767,600	3,005,300	3,447,800	3,555,000	..
Industrial Countries: *exports*	1,712,300	1,987,900	2,126,300	2,452,600	2,502,300	..
imports	1,794,300	2,067,500	2,238,800	2,571,200	2,591,700	..
USA: *exports*	250,405	322,426	363,812	393,592	421,730	..
imports	424,081	459,542	492,922	516,987	508,967	..
Germany, West: *exports*	294,168	323,326	341,231	410,104	402,843	..
imports	228,346	250,473	269,702	346,153	389,908	..
Japan: *exports*	228,631	264,856	273,932	287,581	314,786	..
imports	150,496	187,378	209,715	235,368	236,999	..
France: *exports*	148,534	167,787	179,397	216,588	217,100	..
imports	158,475	178,857	192,986	234,436	231,784	..
UK: *exports*	131,239	145,166	152,344	185,170	184,962	..
imports	154,454	189,339	197,730	222,975	209,946	..
Other Europe: *exports*	599,656	665,620	708,673	855,393	845,800	..
imports	645,564	697,462	767,342	929,431	924,306	..
Australia, NZ, S. Afr: *exports*	55,238	63,401	68,757	72,953	75,672	..
imports	51,923	62,194	71,550	69,005	68,872	..
Less Developed Areas: *exports*	624,644	700,550	764,900	848,422	939,850	..
imports	607,561	700,110	744,750	859,103	963,340	..
Oil exporters: exports	128,840	128,320	154,970	..	..	..
imports	91,370	104,790	102,670	119,700	..	..
Saudi Arabia: *exports*	26,975	23,738	28,382	44,417	..	..
imports	24,345	21,784	21,154	24,069	..	..
Other W. Hemisphere: *exports*	60,491	73,919	79,281	83,296	85,339	..
imports	59,742	59,937	68,719	75,051	86,227	..
Other Middle East(2): *exports*	15,700	..	..	..	..	..
imports	44,588	39,038	..	..	..	..
Other Asia: *exports*	261,002	323,255	358,187	395,760	451,190	..
imports	260,308	337,460	377,212	418,715	477,880	..
Other Africa: *exports*	24,218	25,767	33,069	40,922	..	..
imports	31,316	33,164	42,627	51,145	..	..

(1) Including Egypt. (2) Unweighted average of IMF series for US$ import and export prices in developed countries.

World trade prices (1985=100)(2)	111·6	112·9	111·9	111·6	112·2

44. Volume of World Trade

annual percentage changes	1987	1988	1989	1990	1991
World	6·2	8·5	7·2	4·7	3·4
Developed market economies	5·0	8·6	6·7	5·7	2·8
Developing countries	10·9	10·2	8·5	5·9	10·1
Economies in transition	2·4	4·3	−9·9	−10·7	−21·6
-E. Europe	1·3	3·6	−1·9	−7·9	−16·2
-Former USSR	3·3	4·8	0·0	−13·1	−25·0

45. Prices of Selected Commodities (Index 1985=100)	1987	1988	1989	1990	1991	1992
Aluminium (Canada)	150·4	244·7	187·4	157·5	125·3	120·7
Beef, All origins	110·8	116·9	119·2	119·0	123·7	114·0
Copper, wirebars (London)	125·7	183·4	200·9	187·8	165·0	161·2
Cotton, Egyptian (L'pool)	99·4	133·2	176·4	183·0	169·9	129·8
Gold (London)	140·8	137·8	120·2	120·9	114·2	..
Newsprint New York	106·4	112·7	109·6	106·9	108·1	98·1
Rice, Thai (Bangkok)	105·7	138·7	147·3	131·9	143·8	132·2
Rubber, Malay (Singapore)	129·8	156·2	127·8	114·0	108·8	113·6
Soya Beans, US (R'dam)	96·1	135·2	122·5	110·0	106·8	104·9
Sugar, f.o.b. (Caribbean)	166·7	251·4	315·9	308·6	221·4	223·7
Tin, spot (London)	60·3	63·3	75·5	53·7	48·5	52·9
Wheat (US Gulf Ports)	83·1	106·9	124·6	99·8	94·7	111·3
Wool, greasy (Sydney)	132·9	219·5	201·5	172·8	118·9	..

46. Consumer Prices, Selected Countries (Index 1985=100)	1987	1988	1989	1990	1991	1992
Argentina	440·0	1,948	61,933	1,495	4,062	..
Australia	118·0	127·0	136·6	146·4	151·1	..
France	105·9	108·8	112·6	116·4	120·0	123·3
Germany(2)	100·1	101·2	104·0	107·0	110·7	115·2
India	118·3	129·4	137·4	149·7	170·5	..
Japan	100·7	101·4	103·7	106·9	109·7	..
South Africa	137·7	155·4	178·2	203·8	235·0	267·7
Sweden	108·6	114·9	122·2	135·1	147·8	..
UK	107·8	113·0	121·8	133·4	141·1	146·3
US	105·7	109·9	115·2	121·5	126·6	130·4

(1) From 1990, 1985=0.1
(2) To 1990, West Germany.

World trade prices (1985=100)	111·6	112·9	111·9	111·6	112·2	

47. Industrial Ordinary Share Prices (Index 1985=100) average	1987	1988	1989	1990	1991	1992
Amsterdam	129·2	119·7	151·4	147·6	151·7	159·0
Australia, all exchanges	193·4	164·6	176·6	167·0	168·4	175·3
Canada, all exchanges	131·5	121·8	140·1	126·1	127·9	125·5
Germany, all exchanges(1)	124·5	104·0	133·0	152·8	135·8	131·4
Hong Kong (31 July 1968=100)(2)	2,292	2,687	2,836	3,053	4,297	5,512
Johannesburg	188·0	148·0	207·0	217·0	289·0	324·0
New York	159·2	147·6	178·2	188·1	214·5	..
Paris	177·6	162·1	234·9	226·5	220·8	244·2
Tokyo	196·4	213·9	257·8	218·8	184·9	136·9
UK	163·8	147·6	176·5	172·2	190·2	..

(1) To 1990, West Germany.
(2) Hang Seng index for Hong Kong Stock Exchange only: last trading day of year.

48. Central Bank Discount Rates (per cent per annum, end of year)	1987	1988	1989	1990	1991	1992
Canada	8·75	8·75	12·46	12.82	7·57	7·43
France	9·50	9·50	10·25	10·25	10·25	10·00
Germany(1)	2·50	3·50	6·00	6·00	8·00	8·25
Italy	12·50	12·50	13·50	12·50	12·00	12·00
Japan	2·50	2·50	3·75	6·00	4·50	3·25
Sweden	7·50	8·50	9·50	11·00	10·00	11·50
Switzerland	2·50	3·50	6·00	6·00	7·00	6·00
UK	8·50	13·00	15·00	14·00	10·50	7·00
USA (Federal Reserve Bank of N.Y.)	6·50	6·50	7·00	7·00	3·50	3·00

(1) To 1990, West Germany.

49. Exchange Rates   *Currency units per US dollar*   *per £*
(Middle rates at end of year)

	1988	1989	1990	1991	1992	1991	1992
Australia (Australian dollar)	1·1694	1·2655	1·2965	1·3165	1·4540	2·458	2·2035
Belgium-Luxembourg (franc)	37·26	35·60	30·95	31·36	33·25	58·55	50·30
Canada (Canadian dollar)	1·1907	1·1585	1·1605	1·1593	1·2715	2·1645	1·9335
China (yuan)	3·697	4·7001	5·1974	5·3893	5·7312	10·062	8·7802
France (franc)	6·057	5·7850	5·0855	5·1901	5·5250	9·6900	8·3650
Germany (Deutschmark)	1·773	1·6915	1·4950	1·5198	1·6195	2·8375	2·4525
Italy (lirc)	1,306	1,268·0	1,128·0	1,151·4	1,473·5	2,149·7	2,230·7
Japan (yen)	124·9	143·80	135·65	125·74	124·85	234·75	189·0
Netherlands (guilder)	2·002	1·9116	1·6865	1,7126	1,8190	3,1975	2,7550
Portugal (escudo)	146·2	149·58	134·05	134·76	146·45	251·6	222·25
South Africa (rand)	2·379	2·5480	2·5635	2·7518	3·0525	5·1377	4·6267
Spain (peseta)	113·18	109·40	95·55	96·76	114·55	180·65	173·75..
Sweden (krona)	6·125	6·1925	5·6250	5·5543	7·0725	10·3700	10·7075
Switzerland (franc)	1·5022	1·5425	1·2750	1·3564	1·4655	2·5325	2·2175
CIS (rouble)(1)	0·603	0·6132	0·5655	0·5511	0·5719	1·0290	0·8762
UK (£)(2)	1·8090	1·6125	1·9300	1·8671	1·5140	..	..

(1) Official rate. (2) US$ per £.

50. Defence Expenditure

Expenditure or budget (US$mn.)

					$ per capita	% of GNP
	1988	1989	1990	1991	1991	1990
France	36,105	36,494	36,393	36,403	638	3·6
Germany	35,097	35,008	38,016	34,268	429	2·8
Greece	3,326	3,116	3,041	3,078	307	5·9
Iran	7,353	5,747	5,133	6,125	..	..
Israel	3,811	3,830	3,807	3,909	876	8·4
Japan	28,521	29,491	30,483	31,083	251	1·0
Saudi Arabia	14,887	14,522	15,213	26,227	1,785	..
South Africa	3,468	3,808	3,407	3,081	85	4·7
Sweden	4·442	4,508	4,492	4,250	492	2·4
Turkey	2,664	2,770	3,418	3,870	68	4·9
USSR(1)	20·5	77·3	71·0	96·6	..	..
UK	34,629	34,292	32,470	34,008	566	3·9
USA	295,841	289,149	268,113	264,383	1,046	5·6

(1) Official figures, '000 million roubles. Before 1989, military personnel and operations and maintenance only.

51. Employment and Unemployment

Civilian Employment ('000)	1987	1988	1989	1990	1991	1992
USA	112,440	114,968	117,342	117,914	116,377	..
Japan	59,110	60,110	61,280	62,490	63,690	..
W. Germany	26,626	26,825	27,209	27,997	28,533	..
France	21,018	21,179	21,455	21,684	21,785	..
UK	24,755	25,555	26,376	26,620	25,726	..
Unemployment (%)						
OECD		7·5	6·7	6·2	6·1	6·8	..
EEC		10·8	9·9	9·0	8·4	8·7	..
USA		6·1	5·4	5·2	5·4	6·6	..
Japan		2·8	2·5	2·3	2·1	2·1	..
UK		10·4	8·5	7·1	6·8	8·9	..

XIX DOCUMENTS AND REFERENCE

1. RIO EARTH SUMMIT DECLARATION ON ENVIRONMENT AND DEVELOPMENT

The UN Conference on Environment and Development (UNCED), popularly known as the Earth Summit, was held in Rio de Janeiro (Brazil) on 3–14 June 1992 and was the occasion, reportedly, of the largest-ever gathering of heads of state and government. Published below is the text of the main Rio Declaration on Environment and Development together with an accompanying Statement of Forest Principles. Other texts adopted by the summit included Agenda 21 (setting out in detail the measures required for sustainable development); a Convention on Biological Diversity (requiring signatory states to take certain steps to preserve ecologically valuable areas and species); and a Convention on Climate Change (requiring signatories to limit the emission of 'greenhouse gases').

The United Nations Conference on Environment and Development, Having met at Rio de Janeiro from 3 to 14 June 1992,

Reaffirming the Decalaration of the United Nations Conference on Human Environment, adopted at Stockholm on 16 June 1972 [see AR 1972, pp. 346–7], and seeking to build upon it,

With the goal of establishing a new and equitable global partnership through the creation of new levels of cooperation among states, key sectors of societies and people,

Working towards international agreements which respect the interests of all and protect the integrity of the global environmental and developmental system,

Recognizing the integral and interdependent nature of the Earth, our home,

Proclaims that:

PRINCIPLE 1

Human beings are at the centre of concerns for sustainable development. They are entitled to a healthy and productive life in harmony with nature.

PRINCIPLE 2

States have, in accordance with the Charter of the United Nations and the principles of international law, the sovereign right to exploit their own resources pursuant to their own environmental and developmental policies, and the responsibility to ensure that activities within their jurisdiction or control do not cause damage to the environment of the other states or of areas beyond the limits of national jurisdiction.

PRINCIPLE 3

The right to development must be fulfilled so as to equitably meet developmental and environmental needs of present and future generations.

PRINCIPLE 4

In order to achieve sustainable development, environmental protection shall constitute an integral part of the development process and cannot be considered in isolation from it.

PRINCIPLE 5

All states and all people shall cooperate in the essential task of eradicating poverty as an indispensable requirement for sustainable development, in order to decrease the disparities in standards of living and better meet the needs of the majority of the people of the world.

PRINCIPLE 6

The special situation and needs of developing countries, particularly the least developed and those most environmentally vulnerable, shall be given special priority. International actions in the field of environment and development should also address the interests and needs of all countries.

PRINCIPLE 7

States shall cooperate in a spirit of global partnership to conserve, protect and restore the health and integrity of the Earth's ecosystem. In view of the different contributions to global environmental degradation, states have common but differentiated responsibilities. The developed countries acknowledge the responsibility that they bear in the international pursuit of sustainable development in view of the pressures their societies place on the global environment and of the technologies and financial resources they command.

PRINCIPLE 8

To achieve sustainable development and a higher quality of life for all people, states should reduce and eliminate unsustainable patterns of production and consumption and promote appropriate demographic policies.

PRINCIPLE 9

States should cooperate to strengthen endogenous capacity-building for sustainable development by improving scientific understanding through exchanges of scientific and technological knowledge, and by enhancing the development, adaptation, diffusion and transfer of technologies, including new and innovative technologies.

PRINCIPLE 10

Environmental issues are best handled with the participation of all concerned citizens, at the relevant level. At the national level, each individual shall have appropriate access to information concerning the environment that is held by public authorities, including information on hazardous materials and activities in their communities, and the opportunity to participate in decision-making processes. States shall facilitate and encourage public awareness and participation by making information widely available. Effective access to judicial and administrative proceedings, including redress and remedy, shall be provided.

PRINCIPLE 11

States shall enact effective environmental legislation. Environmental standards, management objectives and priorities should reflect the environmental and developmental context to which they apply. Standards applied by some countries may be inappropriate and of unwarranted economic and social cost to other countries, in particular developing countries.

PRINCIPLE 12

States should cooperate to promote a supportive and open international economic system that would lead to economic growth and sustainable development in all countries, to better address the problems of environmental degradation. Trade policy measures for environmental purposes should not constitute a means of arbitrary or unjustifiable discrimination or a disguised restriction on international trade. Unilateral actions to deal with environmental challenges outside the jurisdiction of the importing country should be avoided. Environmental measures addressing transboundary or global environmental problems should, as far as possible, be based on an international consensus.

PRINCIPLE 13

States shall develop national law regarding liability and compensation for the victims of pollution and other environmental damage. States shall also cooperate in an expeditious and more determined manner to develop further international law regarding liability and compensation for adverse effects of environmental damage caused by activities within their jurisdiction or control to areas beyond their jurisdiction.

PRINCIPLE 14

States should effectively cooperate to discourage or prevent the relocation and transfer to other states of any activities and substances that cause severe environmental degradation or are found to be harmful to human health.

PRINCIPLE 15

In order to protect the environment, the precautionary approach shall be widely applied by states according to their capabilities. Where there are threats of serious or irreversible damage, lack of full scientific certainty shall not be used as a reason for postponing cost-effective measures to prevent environmental degradation.

PRINCIPLE 16

National authorities should endeavour to promote the internalization of environmental costs and the use of economic instruments, taking into account the approach that the polluter should, in principle, bear the cost of pollution, with due regard to the public interest and without distorting international trade and investment.

PRINCIPLE 17

Environmental impact assessment, as a national instrument, shall be undertaken for proposed activities that are likely to have a significant adverse impact on the environment and are subject to a decision of a competent national authority.

PRINCIPLE 18

States shall immediately notify other states of any natural disasters or other emergencies that are likely to produce sudden harmful effects on the environment of those states. Every effort shall be made by the international community to help states so afflicted.

PRINCIPLE 19

States shall provide prior and timely notification and relevant information to potentially affected states on activities that may have a significant adverse transboundary environmental effect and shall consult with those states at an early stage and in good faith.

PRINCIPLE 20

Women have a vital role in environmental management and development. Their full participation is therefore essential to achieve sustainable development.

PRINCIPLE 21

The creativity, ideals and courage of the youth of the world should be mobilized to forge a global partnership in order to achieve sustainable development and ensure a better future for all.

PRINCIPLE 22

Indigenous people and their communities and other local communities have a vital role in environmental management and development because of their knowledge and traditional practices. States should recognize and duly support their identity, culture and interests and enable their effective participation in the achievement of sustainable development.

PRINCIPLE 23

The environment and natural resources of people under oppression, domination and occupation shall be protected.

PRINCIPLE 24

Warfare is inherently destructive of sustainable development. States shall therefore respect international law providing protection for the environment in times of armed conflict and cooperate in its further development, as necessary.

PRINCIPLE 25

Peace, development and environmental protection are interdependent and indivisible.

PRINCIPLE 26

States shall resolve all their environmental disputes peacefully and by appropriate means in accordance with the Charter of the United Nations.

PRINCIPLE 27

States and people shall cooperate in good faith and in a spirit of partnership in the fulfilment of the principles embodied in this Declaration and in the further development of international law in the field of sustainable development.

STATEMENT OF PRINCIPLES FOR A GLOBAL CONSENSUS ON THE MANAGEMENT, CONSERVATION AND SUSTAINABLE DEVELOPMENT OF ALL TYPES OF FORESTS

PREAMBLE

(a) The subject of forests is related to the entire range of environmental and development issues and opportunities, including the right to socio-economic development on a sustainable basis.

(b) The guiding objective of these principles is to contribute to the management, conservation and sustainable development of forests and to provide for their multiple and complementary functions and uses.

(c) Forestry issues and opportunities should be examined in a holistic and balanced manner within the overall context of environment and development, taking into consideration the multiple functions and uses of forests, including traditional uses, and the likely economic and social stress when these uses are constrained or restricted, as well as the potential for development that sustainable forest management can offer.

(d) These principles reflect a first global consensus on forests. In committing themselves to the prompt implementation of these principles, countries also decide to keep them under assessment for their adequacy with regard to further international cooperation on forest issues.

(e) These principles should apply to all types of forests, both natural and planted, in all geographical regions and climatic zones, including austral, boreal, subtemperate, temperate, subtropical and tropical.

(f) All types of forests embody complex and unique ecological processes which are the basis for their present and potential capacity to provide resources to satisfy human needs as well as environmental values, and as such their sound management and conservation is of concern to the Governments of the countries to which they belong and are of value to local communities and to the environment as a whole.

(g) Forests are essential to economic development and the maintenance of all forms of life.

(h) Recognizing that the responsibility for forest management, conservation and sustainable development is in many states allocated among federal/national, state/provincial and local levels of government, each state, in accordance with its constitution and/or national legislation, should pursue these principles at the appropriate level of government.

PRINCIPLES / ELEMENTS

1.(a) States have, in accordance with the Charter of the United Nations and the principles of international law, the sovereign right to exploit their own resources pursuant to their own environmental policies and have the responsibility to ensure that activities within their jurisdiction or control do not cause damage to the environment of other states or of areas beyond the limits of national jurisdiction.

(b) The agreed full incremental cost of achieving benefits associated with forest conservation and sustainable development requires increased international cooperation and should be equitably shared by the international community.

2.(a) States have the sovereign and inalienable right to utilize, manage and develop their forests in accordance with their development needs and level of socio-economic development and on the basis of national policies consistent with sustainable development and legislation, including the conversion of such areas for other uses within the overall socio-economic development plan and based on rational land-use policies.

(b) Forest resources and forest lands should be sustainably managed to meet the social, economic, ecological, cultural and spiritual needs of present and future generations. These needs are for forest products and services, such as wood and wood products, water, food, fodder, medicine, fuel, shelter, employment, recreation, habitats for wildlife, landscape diversity, carbon sinks and reservoirs, and for other forest products. Appropriate measures should be taken to protect forests against harmful effects of pollution, including air-borne pollution, fires, pests and diseases, in order to maintain their full multiple value.

(c) The provision of timely, reliable and accurate information on forests and forest ecosystems is essential for public understanding and informed decision-making and should be ensured.

(d) Governments should promote and provide opportunities for the participation of interested parties, including local communities and indigenous people, industries, labour, non-governmental organizations and individuals, forest dwellers and women, in the development, implementation and planning of national forest policies.

3.(a) National policies and strategies should provide a framework for increased efforts, including the development and strengthening of institutions and programmes for the management, conservation and sustainable development of forests and forest lands.

(b) International institutional arrangements, building on those organizations and mechanisms already in existence, as appropriate, should facilitate international cooperation in the field of forests.

(c) All aspects of environmental protection and social and economic development as they relate to forests and forest lands should be integrated and comprehensive.

4. The vital role of all types of forests in maintaining the ecological processes and balance at the local, national, regional and global levels through, inter alia, their role in protecting fragile ecosystems, watersheds and freshwater resources and as rich storehouses of biodiversity and biological resources and sources of genetic material for biotechnology products, as well as photosynthesis, should be recognized.

5.(a) National forest policies should recognize and duly support the identity, culture and the rights of indigenous people, their communities and other communities and forest dwellers. Appropriate conditions should be promoted for these groups to enable them to have an economic stake in forest use, perform economic activities, and achieve and maintain cultural identity and social organization, as well as adequate levels of livelihood and well-being, through, inter alia, those land tenure arrangements which serve as incentives for the sustainable management of forests.

(b) The full participation of women in all aspects of the management, conservation and sustainable development of forests should be actively promoted.

6.(a) All types of forests play an important role in meeting energy requirements through the provision of a renewable source of bio-energy, particularly in developing countries, and the demands for fuelwood for household and industrial needs should be met through sustainable forest management, afforestation and reforestation. To this end, the potential contribution of plantations of both indigenous and introduced species for the provision of both fuel and industrial wood should be recognized.

(b) National policies and programmes should take into account the relationship, where it exists, between the conservation, management and sustainable development of forests and all aspects related to the production, consumption, recycling and/or final disposal of forest products.

(c) Decisions taken on the management, conservation and sustainable development of forest resources should benefit, to the extent practicable, from a comprehensive assessment of economic and non-economic values of forest goods and services and of the environmental costs and benefits. The development and improvement of methodologies for such evaluations should be promoted.

(d) The role of planted forests and permanent agricultural crops as sustainable and environmentally sound sources of renewable energy and industrial raw material should be recognized, enhanced and promoted. Their contribution to the maintenance of ecological processes, to offsetting pressure on primary/old-growth forest and to providing regional employment and development with the adequate involvement of local inhabitants should be recognized and enhanced.

(e) Natural forests also constitute a source of goods and services, and their conservation, sustainable management and use should be promoted.

7.(a) Efforts should be made to promote a supportive international economic climate conducive to sustained and environmentally sound development of forests in all countries, which include, inter alia, the promotion of sustainable patterns of production and consumption, the eradication of poverty and the promotion of food security.

(b) Specific financial resources should be provided to developing countries with significant forest areas which establish programmes for the conservation of forests including protected natural forest areas. These resources should be directed notably to economic sectors which would stimulate economic and social substitution activities.

8.(a) Efforts should be undertaken towards the greening of the world. All countries, notably developed countries, should take positive and transparent action towards reforestation, afforestation and forest conservation, as appropriate.

(b) Efforts to maintain and increase forest cover and forest productivity should be undertaken in ecologically, economically, and socially sound ways through the rehabilitation, reforestation and re-establishment of trees and forests on unproductive, degraded and deforested lands, as well as through the management of existing forest resources.

(c) The implementation of national policies and programmes aimed at forest management, conservation and sustainable development, particularly in developing countries, should be supported by international financial and technical cooperation, including through the private sector, where appropriate.

(d) Sustainable forest management and use should be carried out in accordance with national development policies and priorities and on the basis of environmentally sound national guidelines. In the formulation of such guidelines, account should be taken, as appropriate and if applicable, of relevant internationally agreed methodologies and criteria.

(e) Forest management should be integrated with management of adjacent areas so as to maintain ecological balance and sustainable productivity.

(f) National policies and/or legislation aimed at management, conservation and sustainable development of forests should include the protection of ecologically viable representative or unique examples of forests, including primary/old-growth forests, cultural, spiritual, historical, religious and other unique and valued forests of national importance.

(g) Access to biological resources, including genetic material, shall be with due regard to the sovereign rights of the countries where the forests are located and to the sharing on mutually agreed terms of technology and profits from biotechnology products that are derived from these resources.

(h) National policies should ensure that environmental impact assessments should be carried out where actions are likely to have significant adverse impacts on important forest resources, and where such actions are subject to a decision of a competent national authority.

9.(a) The efforts of developing countries to strengthen the management, conservation and sustainable development of their forest resources should be supported by the international community, taking into account the importance of redressing external indebtedness, particularly where aggravated by the net transfer of resources to developed countries, as well as the problem of achieving at least the replacement value of forests through improved market access for forest products, especially processed products. In this respect, special attention should also be given to the countries undergoing the process of transition to market economies.

(b) The problems that hinder efforts to attain the conservation and sustainable use of forest resources and that stem from the lack of alternative options available to local communities, in particular the urban poor and poor rural populations who are economically and socially dependent on forests and forest resources, should be addressed by governments and the international community.

(c) National policy formulation with respect to all types of forests should take account of the pressures and demands imposed on forest ecosystems and resources from influencing factors outside the forest sector, and intersectoral means of dealing with these pressures and demands should be sought.

10. New and additional financial resources should be provided to developing countries to enable them to sustainably manage, conserve and develop their forest resources, including through afforestation, reforestation and combating deforestation and forest and land degradation.

11. In order to enable, in particular, developing countries to enhance their endogenous capacity and to better manage, conserve and develop their forest resources, the access to and transfer of environmentally sound technologies and corresponding know-how on favourable terms, including on concessional and preferential terms, as mutually agreed, in accordance with the relevant provisions of Agenda 21, should be promoted, facilitated and financed, as appropriate.

12.(a) Scientific research, forest inventories and assessments carried out by national institutions which take into account, where relevant, biological, physical, social and economic variables, as well as technological development and its application in the field of sustainable forest management, conservation and development, should be strengthened through effective modalities, including international cooperation. In this context, attention should also be given to research and development of sustainably harvested non-wood products.

(b) National and, where appropriate, regional and international institutional capabilities in education, training, science, technology, economics, anthropology and social aspects of forests and forest management are essential to the conservation and sustainable development of forests and should be strengthened.

(c) International exchange of information on the results of forest and forest management research and development should be enhanced and broadened, as appropriate, making full use of education and training institutions, including those in the private sector.

(d) Appropriate indigenous capacity and local knowledge regarding the conservation and sustainable development of forests should, through institutional and financial support and in collaboration with the people in the local communities concerned, be recognized, respected, recorded, developed and, as appropriate, introduced in the implementation of programmes. Benefits arising from the utilization of indigenous knowledge should therefore be equitably shared with such people.

13.(a) Trade in forest products should be based on non-discriminatory and multilaterally agreed rules and procedures consistent with international trade law and practices. In this context, open and free international trade in forest products should be facilitated.

(b) Reduction or removal of tariff barriers and impediments to the provision of better market access and better prices for higher value-added forest products and their local processing should be encouraged to enable producer countries to better conserve and manage their renewable forest resources.

(c) Incorporation of environmental costs and benefits into market forces and mechanisms, in order to achieve conservation and sustainable development, should be encouraged both domestically and internationally.

(d) Forest conservation and sustainable development policies should be integrated with economic, trade and other relevant policies.

(e) Fiscal, trade, industrial, transportation and other policies and practices that may lead to forest degradation should be avoided. Adequate policies, aimed at management, conservation and sustainable development of forests, including, where appropriate, incentives, should be encouraged.

14. Unilateral measures, incompatible with international obligations or agreements, to restrict and/or ban international trade in timber or other forest products should be removed or avoided, in order to attain long-term sustainable forest management.

15. Pollutants, particularly air-borne pollutants, including those responsible for acidic deposition, that are harmful to the health of forest ecosystems at the local, national, regional and global levels should be controlled.

2. AGREEMENT ON THE EUROPEAN ECONOMIC AREA

The 12 states of the European Community (Belgium, Denmark, France, Germany, Greece, Ireland, Italy, Luxembourg, the Netherlands, Portugal, Spain and the United Kingdom) and the seven members of the European Free Trade Association (Austria, Finland, Iceland, Liechtenstein, Norway, Sweden and Switzerland) signed the Agreement on the European Economic Area (EEA) in Oporto, Portugal, on 2 May 1992. The following are the opening articles of what was a vast document of over 1,000 pages. The proposed 19-nation EEA was reduced to 18 members by Switzerland's rejection of participation in a referendum on 6 December 1992. (Treaty supplied by EFTA, Geneva.)

The European Economic Community,
The European Coal and Steel Community,
The Kingdom of Belgium,
The Kingdom of Denmark,
The Federal Republic of Germany,
The Hellenic Republic,
The Kingdom of Spain,
The French Republic,
Ireland,
The Italian Republic,
The Grand Duchy of Luxembourg,
The Kingdom of the Netherlands,
The Portuguese Republic,
The United Kingdom of Great Britain and Northern Ireland

and

The Republic of Austria,
The Republic of Finland,
The Republic of Iceland,
The Principality of Liechtenstein,
The Kingdom of Norway,
The Kingdom of Sweden,
The Swiss Confederation

hereinafter referred to as the contracting parties;

convinced of the contribution that a European Economic Area will bring to the construction of a Europe based on peace, democracy and human rights;

reaffirming the high priority attached to the privileged relationship between the European Community, its member states and the EFTA states, which is based on proximity, long-standing common values and European identity;

determined to contribute, on the basis of market economy, to world-wide trade liberalization and cooperation, in particular in accordance with the provisions of the General Agreement on Tariffs and Trade and the Convention on the Organization for Economic Cooperation and Development;

considering the objective to establish a dynamic and homogeneous European Economic Area, based on common rules and equal conditions of competition and providing for the adequate means of enforcement, including at the judicial level, and achieved on the basis of equality and reciprocity and of an overall balance of benefits, rights and obligations for the contracting parties;

determined to provide for the fullest possible realization of the free movement of goods, persons, services and capital within the whole European Economic Area, as well as for strengthened and broadened cooperation in flanking and horizontal policies;

aiming to promote a harmonious development of the European Economic Area and convinced of the need to contribute through the application of this agreement to the reduction of the economic and social regional disparities;

desirous to contribute to the strengthening of the cooperation between the members of the European Parliament and of the parliaments of the EFTA states, as well as between the social partners in the European Community and in the EFTA states;

convinced of the important role that individuals will play in the European Economic Area through the exercise of the rights conferred on them by this agreement and through the judicial defence of these rights;

determined to preserve, protect and improve the quality of the environment and to ensure a prudent and rational utilization of natural resources on the basis, in particular, of the principle of sustainable development, as well as the principles that precautionary and preventive action should be taken;

determined to take, in the further development of rules, a high level of protection concerning health, safety and the environment as a basis;

noting the importance of the development of the social dimension, including equal treatment of men and women, in the European Economic Area and wishing to ensure economic and social progress and to promote conditions for full employment, an improved standard of living and improved working conditions within the European Economic Area;

determined to promote the interests of the consumers and strengthening their position in the market place, aiming at a high level of consumer protection;

attached to the common objectives of strengthening the scientific and technological basis of European industry and of encouraging it to become more competitive at the international level;

considering that the conclusion of this agreement shall not prejudge in any way the possibility of any EFTA state to accede to the European Communities;

whereas, in full deference to the independence of the courts, the objective of the contracting parties is to arrive at and maintain a uniform interpretation and application of this agreement and those provisions of the Community legislation which are substantially reproduced in this agreement and to arrive at an equal treatment of individuals and economic operators as regards the four freedoms and the conditions of competition;

whereas this agreement does not restrict the decision-making autonomy nor the treaty-making power of the contracting parties, subject to the provisions of this agreement and the limitations set by public international law;

have decided to conclude the following agreement:

PART 1: OBJECTIVES AND PRINCIPLES
Article 1

1. The aim of this agreement of association is to promote a continuous and balanced strengthening of trade and economic relations between the contracting parties with equal conditions of competition, and the respect of the same rules, with a view to creating a homogeneous European Economic Area, hereinafter referred to as the EEA.

2. In order to attain the objectives st out in paragraph 1, the association shall entail in accordance with the provisions of this agreement:

(a) the free movement of goods;
(b) the free movement of persons;
(c) the free movement of services;
(d) the free movement of capital;
(e) the setting up of a system ensuring that competition is not distorted and that the rules thereon are equally respected; as well as
(f) closer cooperation in other fields, such as research and development, the environment, education and social policy . . . .

Article 3

The contracting parties shall take all appropriate measures, whether general or particular, to ensure fulfilment of the obligations arising out of this agreement.

They shall abstain from any measure which could jeopardize the attainment of the objectives of this agreement.

Moreover, they shall facilitate cooperation within the framework of this agreement.

Article 4

Within the scope of application of this agreement, and without prejudice to any special provisions contained therein, any discrimination on grounds of nationality shall be prohibited.

Article 5

A contracting party may at any time raise a matter of concern at the level of the EEA Joint Committee or the EEA Council according to the modalities laid down in articles 92 (2) and 89 (2), respectively.

Article 6

Without prejudice to future developments of case law, the provisions of this agreement, insofar as they are identical in substance to corresponding rules of the treaty establishing the European Economic Community and the treaty establishing the European Coal and Steel Community and to acts adopted in application of these two treaties, shall in their implementation and application be interpreted in conformity with the relevant rulings of the Court of Justice of the European Communities given prior to the date of signature of this Agreement.

Article 7

Acts referred to or contained in the annexes to this agreement or in decisions of the EEA Joint Committee shall be binding upon the contracting parties and be, or be made, part of their internal legal order as follows:

(a) an act corresponding to an EEA regulation shall as such be made part of the internal legal order of the contracting parties;
(b) an act corresponding to an EEA directive shall leave to the authorities of the contracting parties the choice of form and method of implementation . . . .

3.   CONCLUSIONS OF EDINBURGH EUROPEAN COMMUNITY SUMMIT

The European Council (summit) meeting held in Edinburgh (Scotland/UK) on 11–12 December 1992 adopted decisions on a wide range of outstanding European Community issues. Published below are extracts from the official 'conclusions of the presidency' detailing certain of these decisions. (Text supplied by European Commission office, London.)

OVERALL APPROACH TO THE SUBSIDIARITY PRINCIPLE

I. Basic Principles

European Union rests on the principle of subsidiarity, as is made clear in articles A and B of title I of the Treaty on European Union. This principle contributes to the respect for the national identities of member states and safeguards their powers. It aims at decisions within the European Union being taken as closely as possible to the citizen.

1. Article 3b of the EC Treaty covers three main elements: a strict limit on Community action (first paragraph); a rule (second paragraph) to answer the question 'Should the Community act?'. This applies to areas which do not fall within the Community's exclusive competence; a rule (third paragraph) to answer the question: 'What should be the intensity or nature of the Community's action?'. This applies whether or not the action is within the Community's exclusive competence.

2. The three paragraphs cover three distinct legal concepts which have historical antecedents in existing Community treaties or in the case-law of the Court of Justice:
   i) The principle that the Community can only act where given the power to do so—implying that national powers are the rule and the Community's the exception—has always been a basic feature of the Community legal order. (The principle of attribution of power.)
   ii) The principle that the Community should only take action where an objective can better be attained at the level of the Community than at the level of the individual member states is present in embryonic or implicit form in some provisions of the ECSE treaty and the EEC treaty; the Single European Act spelled out the principle in the environment field. (The principle of subsidiarity in the strict legal sense.)
   iii) The principle that the means to be employed by the Community should be proportional to the objective pursued is the subject of a well-established case-law of the Court of Justice which, however, has been limited in scope and developed without the support of a specific article in the treaty. (The principle of proportionality or intensity.)

3. The Treaty on European Union defines these principles in explicit terms and gives them a new legal significance by setting them out in article 3b as general principles of Community law; by setting out the principle of subsidiarity as a basic principle of the European Union; [and] by reflecting the idea of subsidiarity in the drafting of several new treaty articles.

4. The implementation of article 3b should respect the following basic principles:
   - Making the principle of subsidiarity and article 3b work is an obligation for all the Community institutions, without affecting the balance between them.
   An agreement shall be sought to this effect between the European Parliament, the Council and the Commission, in the framework of the inter-institutional dialogue which is taking place among these institutions.
   - The principle of subsidiarity does not relate to and cannot call into question the powers conferred on the European Community by the treaty as interpreted by the Court. It provides a guide as to how those powers are to be exercised at the Community level, including in the application of article 235. The application of the principle shall respect the general provisions of the Maastricht treaty, including the 'maintaining in full of the *acquis communautaire*', and it shall not affect the primacy of Community law nor shall it call into question the principle set out in article F(3) of the Treaty on European Union, according to which the Union shall provide itself with the means necessary to attain its objectives and carry through its policies.
   - Subsidiarity is a dynamic concept and should be applied in the light of the objectives set out in the treaty. It allows Community action to be expanded where circumstances so require, and conversely, to be restricted or discontinued where it is no longer justified.
   - Where the application of the subsidiarity test excludes Community action, member states would still be required in their action to comply with the general rules laid down in article 5 of the treaty, by taking all appropriate measures to ensure fulfilment of their obligations under the treaty and by abstaining from any measure which could jeopardize the attainment of the objectives of the treaty.
   - The principle of subsidiarity cannot be regarded as having direct effect; however, interpretation of this principle, as well as review of compliance with it by the Community institutions, are subject to control by the Court of Justice, as far as matters falling within the treaty establishing the European Community are concerned.

• Paragraphs 2 and 3 of article 3b apply only to the extent that the treaty gives to the institution concerned the choice whether to act and/or a choice as to the nature and extent of the action. The more specific the nature of a treaty requirement, the less scope exists for applying subsidiarity. The treaty imposes a number of specific obligations upon the Community institutions, for example concerning the implementation and enforcement of Community law, competition policy and the protection of Community funds. These obligations are not affected by article 3b: in particular, the principle of subsidiarity cannot reduce the need for Community measures to contain adequate provision for the Commission and the member states to ensure that Community law is properly enforced and to fulfil their obligations to safeguard Community expenditures.

• Where the Community acts in an area falling under shared powers, the type of measures to apply has to be decided on a case by case basis in the light of the relevant provisions of the treaty.

II. Guidelines

In compliance with the basic principles set out above, the following guidelines—specific to each paragraph of article 3b—should be used in examining whether a proposal for a Community measure conforms to the provisions of article 3b.

First paragraph (Limit on Community action)
Compliance with the criteria laid down in this paragraph is a condition for any Community action. In order to apply this paragraph correctly the institutions need to be satisfied that the proposed action is within the limits of the powers conferred by the treaty and is aimed at meeting one or more of its objectives. The examination of the draft measure should establish the objective to be achieved and whether it can be justified in relation to an objective of the treaty and that the necessary legal basis for its adoption exists.

Second paragraph (Should the Community act?)
i) This paragraph does not apply to matters falling within the Community's exclusive competence. For Community action to be justified the Council must be satisfied that both aspects of the subsidiarity criterion are met: the objectives of the proposed action cannot be sufficiently achieved by member states' action and they can therefore be better achieved by action on the part of the Community.

ii) The following guidelines should be used in examining whether the above-mentioned condition is fulfilled: the issue under consideration has transnational aspects which cannot be satisfactorily regulated by action by member states; and/or actions by member states alone or lack of Community action would conflict with the requirements of the treaty (such as the need to correct distortion of competition or avoid disguised restrictions on trade or strengthen economic and social cohesion) or would otherwise significantly damage member states' interests; and/or the Council must be satisfied that action at Community level would produce clear benefits by reason of its scale or effects compared with action at the level of the member states.

iii) The Community should only take action involving harmonisation of national legislation, norms or standards where this is necessary to achieve the objectives of the treaty.

iv) The objective of presenting a single position of the member states vis-à-vis third countries is not in itself a justification for internal Community action in the area concerned.

v) The reasons for concluding that a Community objective cannot be sufficiently achieved by the member states but can be better achieved by the Community must be substantiated by qualitative or, wherever possible, quantitative indicators.

Third paragraph (Nature and extent of Community action)
i) This paragraph applies to all Community action, whether or not within exclusive competence.

ii) Any burdens, whether financial or administrative, falling upon the Community, national governments, local authorities, economic operators and citizens, should be minimized and should be proportionate to the objective to be achieved.

iii) Community measures should leave as much scope for national decision as possible, consistent with securing the aim of the measure and observing the requirements of the treaty. While respecting Community law, care should be taken to respect well-established national arrangements and the organization and working of member states' legal systems. Where appropriate and subject to the need for proper enforcement, Community measures should provide member states with alternative ways to achieve the objectives of the measures.

iv) Where it is necessary to set standards at Community level, consideration should be given to setting minimum standards, with freedom for member states to set higher national standards, not only in the areas where the treaty so requires (118a, 130t) but also in other areas where this would not conflict with the objectives of the proposed measure or with the treaty.

v) The form of action should be as simple as possible, consistent with satisfactory achievement of the objective of the measure and the need for effective enforcement. The Community should legislate only to the extent necessary. Other things being equal, directives should be preferred to regulations and framework directives to detailed measures. Non-binding measures such as recommendations should be preferred where appropriate. Consideration should also be given where appropriate to the use of voluntary codes of conduct.

vi) Where appropriate under the treaty, and provided this is sufficient to achieve its objectives, preference in choosing the type of Community action should be given to encouraging cooperation between member states, coordinating national action or to complementing, supplementing or supporting such action.

vii) Where difficulties are localized and only certain member states are affected, any necessary Community action should not be extended to other member states unless this is necessary to achieve an objective of the treaty.

III. Procedures and Practices

The Treaty on European Union obliges all institutions to consider, when examining a Community measure, whether the provisions of article 3b are observed. For this purpose, the following procedures and practices will be applied in the framework of the basic principles set out under paragraph ii and without prejudice to a future inter-institutional agreement.

a) Commission
The Commission has a crucial rule to play in the effective implementation of article 3b, given its right of initiative under the treaty, which is not called into question by the application of this article.

The Commission has indicated that it will consult more widely before proposing legislation, which could include consultation with all the member states and a more systemtic use of consultation documents (green papers). Consultation could include the subsidiarity aspects of a proposal. The Commission has also made it clear that, from now on and according to the procedure it already established in accordance with the commitment taken at the European Council in Lisbon, it will justify in a recital the relevance of its initiative with regard to the principle of subsidiarity. Whenever necessary, the explanatory memorandum accompanying the proposal will give details on the considerations of the Commission in the context of article 3b.

The overall monitoring by the Commission of the observance of the provisions of article 3b in all its activities is essential and measures have been taken by the Commission in this respect. The Commission will submit an annual report to the European Council and the European Parliament through the General Affairs Council on the application of the treaty in this area. This report will be of value in the debate on the annual report which the European Council has to submit to the European Parliament on progress achieved by the Union. . . .

b) Council
The following procedure will be applied by the Council from the entry into force of the treaty. In the meantime they will guide the work of the Council. The examination of the compliance of a measure with the provisions of article 3b should be undertaken on a regular basis; it should become an integral part of the overall examination of any Commission proposal and be based on the substance of the proposal. The relevant existing Council rules, including those on voting, apply to such examination. This examination includes the Council's own evaluation of whether the Commission proposal is totally or partially in conformity with the provisions of article 3b (taking as a starting-point for the examination the Commission's recital and explanatory memorandum) and whether any change in the proposal envisaged by the Council is in conformity with those provisions. The Council decision on the subsidiarity aspects shall be taken at the same time as the decision on substance and according to the voting requirements set out in the treaty. Care should be taken not to impede decision-making in the Council and to avoid a system of preliminary or parallel decision-making.

The article 3b examination and debate will take place in the Council responsible for dealing with the matter. The General Affairs Council will have responsibility for general questions relating to the application of article 3b. In this context the General Affairs Council will accompany the annual report from the Commission . . . with any appropriate considerations on the application of this article by the Council.

Various practical steps to ensure the effectiveness of the article 3b examination will be put into effect including:

• working group reports and Coreper (Committee of Permanent Representatives] reports on a given proposal will, where appropriate, describe how article 3b has been applied;

• in all cases of implementation of the article 189b and 189c procedure, the European Parliament will be fully informed of the Council's position concerning the observance of article 3b, in the explanatory memorandum which the Council has to produce according to the provisions of the treaty. The Council will likewise inform the Parliament if it partially or totally rejects a Commission proposal on the ground that it does not comply with the principle of article 3b.

DECLARATION ON PROMOTING ECONOMIC RECOVERY IN EUROPE

1. The completion of the European single market at the end of this year, the ratification of the Maastricht treaty, agreement on the future financing of the Community and an early successful GATT settlement are of crucial importance for strengthening the European economy and would give a substantial boost to confidence.

2. The objectives of member states' economic policies should remain as set out in the Maastricht treaty: an open market economy with free competition, sustainable growth respecting the environment, stable prices with sound public finances and monetary conditions and a sustainable balance of payments. These objectives will continue to determine the economic policies of member states. They remain determined to fulfil the convergence criteria established in the Maastricht treaty and to comply fully with the convergence programmes submitted to the Council, including adherence to the medium-term goals of budgetary consolidation.

3. The European Council invited member states to implement in a concerted way economic measures, tailored to national requirements, which would boost confidence and promote economic recovery. The measures should be targeted towards improving the prospects for growth, creating lasting jobs, and consistent with a medium-term framework founded on the principles of convergence established in the Maastricht treaty.

4. Member states should:

• take every opportunity, according to their national circumstances, to exploit the limited margins of manoeuvre available as concerns budgetary policy;

• switch, to the extent possible, their public expenditure priorities towards infrastructure and other capital investment and growth-supporting expenditures which earn a worthwhile return;

• implement measures to encourage private investment, especially by small and medium-sized enterprises (SMEs);

• act to improve further the efficiency of their economies, for example through action to reduce subsidies and measures to enhance competition and market flexibility;

• make efforts to achieve restraint in wage settlements within the public sector. The European Council noted that restraint on wage bills would help to control government current spending, would contribute to much needed improvements in competitiveness and would help reduce unemployment.

Sound government finance coupled with low inflation and wage moderation will help to create the conditions for reductions in interest rates.

5. The European Council will keep economic prospects under close examination and will review the situation further at its next meeting. It invited the Ecofin Council:

• to consider the relevant national actions in the framework of multilateral surveillance;

• to monitor the performance of national economies against their programmes for economic convergence;

• to identify measures to improve the functioning of the labour market.

6. The European Council believes that the effectiveness of these national actions will be strengthened by complementary and supportive action at the level of the Community. To this end the European Council invited:

• the Council and the European Investment Bank (EIB) in full consultation with the Commission to give urgent and sympathetic consideration to the establishment of a new, temporary lending facility of 5,000 million ecu within the EIB. The purpose of the new facility would be to accelerate the financing of capital infrastructure projects notably connected with trans-European networks. These networks may include projects involving the countries of Central and Eastern Europe to the extent that they are of mutual interest and ensure the interoperability of networks with the Community.

For projects financed by this facility the EIB governors would be invited to raise the normal ceiling on the extent of loans from 50 per cent to 75 per cent and the combined (loans and grants) ceiling from 70 per cent to 90 per cent. Other EIB criteria for infrastructure should continue to be met as now.

The European Council recalled that it was reaffirmed in the Maastricht Protocol on Economic and Social Cohesion that the EIB should devote the majority of its resources to the promotion of economic and social cohesion and that its capital needs should be reviewed as soon as this was necessary for that purpose.

• The Ecofin Council and the EIB to give urgent and sympathetic consideration to the establishment as quickly as possible of a European Investment Fund with 2,000 million ecu of capital contributed by the EIB, other financial institutions and the Commission in order to extend guarantees of 5–10,000 million ecu; in total this could support up to 20,000 million ecu of projects;

• the member states and the Commission to establish programmes to utilize the Community funds that the European Council has today agreed. The Cohesion Fund will contribute to projects in the fields of the environment and trans-European networks in the area of transport infrastructure in the Community's less prosperous countries. The structural funds will *inter alia* promote investment projects in infrastructure;

• the Commission to bring forward proposals for improving the management and efficiency of research funded by the Community to achieve better economic effectiveness. To this end the selectivity of actions should be increased, and it should be ensured that Community activities contribute the most value added possible to efforts already under way in the member states.

The above actions could provide Community support for investment in the public and private sectors of the member states amounting to more than 30,000 million ecu over the next few years.

7. The European Council reaffirmed its commitment at Birmingham to an early, comprehensive and balanced GATT agreement. It also welcomed the successful completion in all essential respects of the single market and emphasized the importance of its effective operation, including in the area of state aids, and called upon member states and the Commission to proceed accordingly. The European Council recognized the importance of increasing the level of understanding by business of Community rules, and welcomed the Commission's intention to achieve enhanced consultation with industry and clearer and simpler legislation.

8. Recognizing the importance of SMEs for creating employment and stimulating growth, the European Council called upon the Council and the Commission to ensure that the burdens from Community legislation on small and medium-sized enterprises are reduced (including through the use of simplified schemes and exemption limits in the field of indirect taxation) and that full information about Community support is provided to SMEs. It asked the Commission to accelerate the actions in favour of SMEs which have proven their worth at the Community level.

9. The European Council reiterated its commitment to the European Monetary System as a key factor of economic stability and prosperity in Europe.

10. The European Council is convinced that the full implementation of this declaration will work to boost confidence, reinforce the fundamentals of economic growth and encourage the creation of new jobs. It invited the Commission to report, as appropriate, to the Ecofin Council and other appropriate Councils on their implementation. It also called upon member states to encourage further international cooperation to promote growth with countries outside the Community.

DENMARK AND THE MAASTRICHT TREATY

The heads of state and government, meeting within the European Council, whose governments are signatories of the Treaty on European Union, which involves independent and sovereign states having freely decided, in accordance with the existing treaties, to exercise in common some of their competences,

• desiring to settle, in conformity with the Treaty on European Union, particular problems existing at the present time specifically for Denmark and raised in its memorandum 'Denmark in Europe' of 30 October 1992,

• having regard to the conclusions of the Edinburgh European Council on subsidiarity and transparency,

• noting the declarations of the Edinburgh European Council relating to Denmark,
• taking cognizance of the unilateral declarations of Denmark made on the same occasion which will be associated with its act of ratification,
• noting that Denmark does not intend to make use of the following provisions in such a way as to prevent closer cooperation and action among member states compatible with the treaty and within the framework of the Union and its objectives,
Have agreed on the following decision:

A. Citizenship

The provisions of part two of the treaty establishing the European Community relating to citizenship of the Union gave nationals of the member states additional rights and protection as specified in that part. They do not in any way take the place of national citizenship. The question whether an individual possesses the nationality of a member state will be settled solely by reference to the national law of the member state concerned.

B. Economic and Monetary Union

1. The protocol on certain provisions relating to Denmark attached to the treaty establishing the European Community gives Denmark the right to notify the Council of the European Communities of its position concerning participation in the third stage of economic and monetary union. Denmark has given notification that it will not participate in the third stage. This notification will take effect upon the coming into effect of this decision.

2. As a consequence, Denmark will not participate in the single currency, will not be bound by the rules concerning economic policy which apply only to the member states participating in the third stage of economic and monetary union, and will retain its existing powers in the field of monetary policy according to its national laws and regulations, including powers of the National Bank of Denmark in the field of monetary policy.

3. Denmark will participate fully in the second stage of economic and monetary union and will continue to participate in exchange-rate cooperation within the EMS.

C. Defence Policy

The heads of state and government note that, in response to the invitation from the Western European Union (WEU), Denmark has become an observer to that organization. They also note that nothing in the Treaty on European Union commits Denmark to become a member of the WEU. Accordingly, Denmark does not participate in the elaboration and the implementation of decisions and actions of the Union which have defence implications, but will not prevent the development of closer cooperation between member states in this area.

D. Justice and Home Affairs

Denmark will participate fully in cooperation on justice and home affairs on the basis of the provisions of title VI of the Treaty on European Union.

E. Final Provisions

1. This decision will take effect on the date of entry into force of the Treaty on European Union; its duration shall be governed by articles Q and N(2) of that treaty.

2. At any time Denmark may, in accordance with its constitutional requirements, inform other member states that it no longer wishes to avail itself of all or part of this decision. In that event, Denmark will apply in full all relevant measures then in force taken within the framework of the European Union.

Declaration on Social Policy, Consumers, Environment, Distribution of Income

1. The Treaty on European Union does not prevent any member state from maintaining or introducing more stringent protection measures compatible with the EC treaty:
• in the field of working conditions and in social policy . . . ;
• in order to attain a high level of consumer protection . . . ;
• in order to pursue the objectives of protection of the environment . . . .

2. The provisions introduced by the Treaty on European Union, including the provisions on economic and monetary union, permit each member state to pursue its own policy with regard to distribution of income and maintain or improve social welfare benefits.

Declaration on Defence

The European Council takes note that Denmark will renounce its right to exercise the Presidency of the Union in each case involving the elaboration and the implementation of decisions and actions of the Union which have defence implications. The normal rules for replacing the President, in the case of the President being indisposed, shall apply. These rules will also apply with regard to the representation of the Union in international organizations, international conferences and with third countries.

Unilateral Danish Declaration on Citizenship of the Union

1. Citizenship of the Union is a political and legal concept which is entirely different from the concept of citizenship within the meaning of the constitution of the Kingdom of Denmark and of the Danish legal system. Nothing in the Treaty on European Union implies or foresees an undertaking to create a citizenship of the Union in the sense of citizenship of a nation-state. The question of Denmark participating in any such development does, therefore, not arise.
2. Citizenship of the Union in no way in itself gives a national of another member state the right to obtain Danish citizenship or any of the rights, duties, privileges or advantages that are inherent in Danish citizenship by virtue of Denmark's constitutional, legal and administrative rules. Denmark will fully respect all specific rights expressly provided for in the treaty and applying to nationals of the member states.
3. Nationals of the other member states of the European Community enjoy in Denmark the right to vote and to stand as a candidate at municipal elections, foreseen in article 8b of the European Community treaty. Denmark intends to introduce legislation granting nationals of the other member states the right to vote and to stand as a candidate for elections to the European Parliament in good time before the next elections in 1994. Denmark has no intention of accepting that the detailed arrangements foreseen in paragraphs 1 and 2 of this article could lead to rules detracting from the rights already given in Denmark in that matter.
4. Without prejudice to the other provisions of the treaty establishing the European Community, article 8e requires the unanimity of all the members of the Council of the European Communities, i.e. all member states, for the adoption of any provision to strengthen or to add to the rights laid down in part two of the EC treaty. Moreover, any unanimous decision of the Council before coming into force, will have to be adopted in each member state, in accordance with its constitutional requirements. In Denmark, such adoption will, in the case of a transfer of sovereignty, as defined in the Danish constitution, require either a majority of 5/6ths of members of the Folketing or both a majority of the members of the Folketing and a majority of voters in a referendum.

Unilateral Danish Declaration on Cooperation on Justice and Home Affairs

Article K9 of the Treaty on European Union requires the unanimity of all the members of the Council of the European Union, i.e. all member states, to the adoption of any decision to apply article 100C of the treaty establishing the European Community to action in areas referred to in Article K1(1) to (6). Moreover, any unanimous decision of the Council, before coming into force, will have to be adopted in each member state, in accordance with its constitutional requirements. In Denmark, such adoption will, in the case of a transfer of sovereignty, as defined in the Danish constitution, require either a majority of 5/6th of members of the Folketing or both a majority of the members of the Folketing and a majority of voters in a referendum.

Final Declaration

The decision and declarations above are a response to the result of the Danish referendum of 2 June 1992 on ratification of the Maastricht treaty. As far as Denmark is concerned, the objectives of that treaty in the four areas mentioned in sections A to D of the decision are to be seen in the light of these documents, which are compatible with the treaty and do not call its objectives into question.

SEATS OF EC INSTITUTIONS

Article 1

(a) The European Parliament shall have its seat in Strasbourg, where the 12 periods of monthly plenary sessions, including the budget session, shall be held. The periods of additional plenary sessions shall be held in Brussels. The committees of the European Parliament shall meet in Brussels. The general secretariat of the European Parliament and its departments shall remain in Luxembourg.

(b) The Council shall have its seat in Brussels. During the months of April, June and October, the Council shall hold its meetings in Luxembourg.

(c) The Commission shall have its seat in Brussels. The departments listed in Articles 7, 8 and 9 of the decision of 8 April 1965 shall be established in Luxembourg.

(d) The Court of Justice and the Court of First Instance shall have their seats in Luxembourg.

(e) The Economic and Social Committee shall have its seat in Brussels.

(f) The Court of Auditors shall have its seat in Luxembourg.

(g) The European Investment Bank shall have its seat in Luxembourg.

Article 2

The seat of other bodies and departments set up or to be set up will be decided by common agreement between the representatives of the governments of the member states at a forthcoming European Council, taking account of the advantages of the above provisions to the member states concerned, and giving appropriate priority to member states who do not at present provide the sites for Community institutions.

Article 3

This Decision shall enter into force as of today.

SIZE OF THE EUROPEAN PARLIAMENT

The European Council agreed—based on the proposal of the European Parliament—on the following numbers of members of the European Parliament, from 1994, to reflect German unification and in the perspective of enlargement:

Belgium	25
Denmark	16
Germany	99
Greece	25
Spain	64
France	87
Ireland	15
Italy	87
Luxembourg	6
Netherlands	31
Portugal	25
United Kingdom	87
Total	567

The necessary legal texts will be prepared for adoption in due course.

4. UNITED KINGDOM CONSERVATIVE CABINET

(as at dissolution of Parliament, 16 March 1992)

Prime Minister, First Lord of the Treasury and Minister for the Civil Service	Rt. Hon. John Major, MP
Lord Chancellor	Rt. Hon. The Lord Mackay of Clashfern
Secretary of State for Foreign and Commonwealth Affairs	Rt. Hon. Douglas Hurd, CBE, MP
Lord Privy Seal and Leader of the House of Lords	Rt. Hon. Lord Waddington of Read, QC
Secretary of State for the Home Department	Rt. Hon. Kenneth Baker, MP
Chancellor of the Exchequer	Rt. Hon. Norman Lamont, MP
Secretary of State for the Environment	Rt. Hon. Michael Heseltine, MP
Secretary of State for Defence	Rt. Hon. Tom King, MP
Secretary of State for Education and Science	Rt. Hon. Kenneth Clarke, QC, MP
Lord President of the Council and Leader of the House of Commons	Rt. Hon. John MacGregor, OBE, MP
Secretary of State for Transport	Rt. Hon. Malcolm Rifkind, QC, MP
Secretary of State for Energy	Rt. Hon. John Wakeham, MP
Secretary of State for Social Security	Rt. Hon. Antony Newton, OBE, MP
Chancellor of the Duchy of Lancaster	Rt. Hon. Christopher Patten, MP
Secretary of State for Northern Ireland	Rt. Hon. Peter Brooke, MP
Minister of Agriculture, Fisheries and Food	Rt. Hon. John Selwyn Gummer, MP
Secretary of State for Employment	Rt. Hon. Michael Howard, QC, MP
Secretary of State for Wales	Rt. Hon. David Hunt, MBE, MP
Secretary of State for Trade and Industry	Rt. Hon. Peter Lilley, MP
Secretary of State for Health	Rt. Hon. William Waldegrave, MP
Secretary of State for Scotland	Rt. Hon. Ian Lang, MP
Chief Secretary to the Treasury	Rt. Hon. David Mellor, QC, MP

(as at 31 December 1992)

Prime Minister, First Lord of the Treasury and Minister for the Civil Service	Rt. Hon. John Major, MP
Lord Chancellor	Rt. Hon. The Lord Mackay of Clashfern
Secretary of State for Foreign and Commonwealth Affairs	Rt. Hon. Douglas Hurd, CBE, MP
Chancellor of the Exchequer	Rt. Hon. Norman Lamont, MP
Secretary of State for the Home Department	Rt. Hon. Kenneth Clarke, QC, MP
President of the Board of Trade (Secretary of State for Trade and Industry)	Rt. Hon. Michael Heseltine, MP
Secretary of State for Transport	Rt. Hon. John MacGregor, OBE, MP
Secretary of State for Defence	Rt. Hon. Malcolm Rifkind, QC, MP
Lord Privy Seal and Leader of the House of Lords	Rt. Hon. Lord Wakeham
Lord President of the Council and Leader of the House of Commons	Rt. Hon. Antony Newton, OBE, MP
Minister of Agriculture, Fisheries and Food	Rt. Hon. John Selwyn Gummer, MP
Secretary of State for National Heritage	Rt. Hon. Peter Brooke, CH, MP
Secretary of State for the Environment	Rt. Hon. Michael Howard, QC, MP
Secretary of State for Wales	Rt. Hon. David Hunt, MBE, MP
Secretary of State for Social Security	Rt. Hon. Peter Lilley, MP
Chancellor of the Duchy of Lancaster (Minister of Public Service and Science)	Rt. Hon. William Waldegrave, MP
Secretary of State for Scotland	Rt. Hon. Ian Lang, MP
Secretary of State for Northern Ireland	Rt. Hon. Sir Patrick Mayhew, QC, MP
Secretary of State for Education	Rt. Hon. John Patten, MP
Secretary of State for Health	Rt. Hon. Virginia Bottomley, MP
Secretary of State for Employment	Rt. Hon. Gillian Shephard, MP
Chief Secretary to the Treasury	Rt. Hon. Michael Portillo, MP

5.   UNITED STATES REPUBLICAN CABINET

(as at 31 December 1992)

President	George Bush
Vice-President	J. Danforth Quayle
Secretary of State	Lawrence Eagleburger
Secretary of the Treasury	Nicholas Brady
Secretary of Defence	Richard Cheney
Secretary of the Interior	Manuel Lujan
Attorney-General	William P. Barr
Secretary of Commerce	Barbara Franklin
Secretary of Labour	Lynn Martin
Secretary of Health & Human Resources	Dr Louis Sullivan
Secretary of Transportation	Andrew Card
Secretary of Education	Lamar Alexander
Secretary of Agriculture	Edward R. Madigan
Secretary of Veteran Affairs	Anthony J. Principi
Secretary of Housing and Urban Development	Jack Kemp
Secretary of Energy	James Watkins

CABINET RANK OFFICIALS

Director of the Central Intelligence Agency	Robert Gates
Director of the Office of Management & Budget	Richard Darman
US Permanent Representative at the United Nations	Edward Perkins
US Trade Representative	Carla Hills
White House Chief of Staff	James Baker
Chairman of Council of Economic Advisers	Prof. Michael Boskin
National Security Adviser	General Brent Scowcroft

XX OBITUARY

Amini, Dr Ali (b. 1905), was Prime Minister of Iran 1961–61. A monarchist and a moderate, after the overthrow of the Shah he prudently retreated to Paris, where he led a party in exile. Died 12 December

Anderson, Dame Judith (b. in Australia 1889), stage and film actress, scored her most memorable cinema success as Mrs Danvers in *Rebecca* (1940), but she was basically a tragedy actress in the grand style, playing such roles as Lady Macbeth (first in 1937, with Laurence Olivier) and Medea (with John Gielgud in 1947). While she starred in many films in the 1950s, the stage was the better arena for her over-scale acting talent. Died 3 Jan

Andronikos, Professor Manolis (b. 1919), Greek archaeologist, professor of classical archaeology in the University of Thessalonika 1961–83, led the excavation of an ancient site at Vergina in northern Greece which yielded a stupendous treasure of 4th century BC artefacts and identification of its noblest tomb as that of Philip II of Macedon, father of Alexander the Great. Died 30 March

Arletty, *see* Bethiat, Léonie

Ashby, Lord, FRS (Eric Ashby) (b. 1904), British botanist, was vice-chancellor of Queen's University, Belfast (1950–59), and Master of Clare College, Cambridge (1959–75), after holding the chairs of botany in the universities of Sydney (1938–46) and Manchester (1946–50); but his high repute spread beyond the academic world through his chairmanship of the Royal Commission on Environmental Pollution (1970–73), whose decisive report was largely ignored by the political establishment. A fine administrator and calm counsellor, he exerted great authority in all the walks he trod. Knighted in 1956, he was made a peer in 1973. Died 22 October

Asimov, Isaac (b. in Russia 1920), American professor of medicine (at Boston University 1949–92), ranked behind only Robert Heinlein and John W. Campbell as begetter of contemporary science fiction. At first he wrote mainly short stories, many collected in book form (three volumes of *Foundation Tales* 1951–53); later, full-length novels included *Pebble in the Sky* (1958), *The Gods Themselves* (1972) and *Foundation's Edge* (1982); but his total output was vast, and included works of general science and autobiography. Died 6 April

Atassi, Dr Nureddin (b. 1929), was President of Syria 1966–70. A communist and member of the extreme pan-Arab Baathist party, he reached the headship of state through a bloody coup. Displaced in a bloodless one by General Asad, he spent the rest of his life, bar a few months, in a military prison. Died in Paris 3 December

Aurenche, Jean (b. 1904), French screen-writer, shared with Pierre Bost or Claude Autant-Lara the crafting of many memorable films in the great days of atmospheric French cinema, such as *Le diable au corps* (1947), *Occupe-toi d'Amélie* (1949) and *Les jeux interdits* (1952). After an interval he again teamed with Bost in *L'horloger de Saint Paul* (1973) and *Le juge et l'assassin* (1976). Died 29 September

Babbit, Art (b. 1907), American film cartoonist, worked from 1932 as animator for Walt Disney, creating such characters as Goofy, Geppeto the carpenter in *Pinocchio* and the Evil Queen In *Snow White and the*

Seven Dwarfs. After 1947 his career as freelance animator, particularly of television advertisements, made him the acclaimed doyen of the art. Died 4 March

Bacon, Francis (b. in Ireland 1909), British painter, first became world-famous in art circles with his triptych *Study for Figures at the Base of a Crucifixion* (1944); his extraordinary imagery continued to excite critics; but later he was best-known for his riveting portraits. Intensity of feeling marked all his work. He added something new and strange to representative painting in an age surfeited with abstract art. Died 28 April

Bacon, Dr Francis 'Tom', FRS (b. 1904), British scientist, was known to the world of engineering as 'Fuel Cell Bacon' for his pioneering and devoted promotion of the environmentally clean process of converting fuel into power by chemical electrolysis. The fuel-cell technology he developed was invaluable in space projects, and its use in power generation and transport, though still costly, proceeded in the USA, Japan and Europe. Died 24 May

Begin, Menachem (b. in Poland 1913), as Prime Minister of Israel 1977–83 won the Nobel Peace Prize in 1978 for his part in the Camp David settlement with President Sadat of Egypt. Already a fervent zionist, he reached the Middle East in 1942 as a soldier in General Anders' Polish army. In 1944 he became leader of Irgun Zvai Leumi, the military organization dedicated to the forcible establishment of *Eretz Israel*. Its terrorist atrocities included the blowing-up of the King David Hotel in Jerusalem in 1946, the hanging of two British army sergeants and the massacre of 250 Arabs in Deir Yas in 1948. After the creation of the state of Israel the Irgun was transmuted into a right-wing political party, Herut, which became the main component of the Likud front, in

opposition to Prime Minister Ben Gurion's moderate Labour Party. The 1977 elections swept Likud into power. Camp David seemed to signal a move towards compromise, but Begin frustrated the intended autonomy of the West Bank and Gaza. There followed the Israeli invasion of Lebanon in 1982 and the massacre of Palestinian refugees in Sabra-Chatila. In October 1983 Begin, pathologically depressed, resigned, spending his later years in virtual seclusion. Died 9 March

Bethiat, Léonie (b. 1898), stage-named Arletty, French actress, moved from the music-hall to the cinema in 1931, and starred in a number of films before linking with Marcel Carné in a golden age of French film-making which included *Hotel du Nord* (1938), *Le jour se lève* (1939) and above all *Les enfants du paradis* (1945). Sexy nonchalance was her hallmark. Died 24 July

Black, Eugene (b. 1898), American banker, was president of the World Bank 1949–62, after two years as its first executive director. Highly respected throughout the world, he multiplied the Bank's assets and lending power and successfully mediated conflicts among its members and clients. On retirement he became special financial consultant to the UN and gathered a host of directorships and trusteeships. Died 20 February

Blackwood, Easley (b. 1903), American bridge expert, as an amateur player invented in 1932 the most universally-used bidding convention which forever bears his name. Retiring in 1964 from the life insurance business, he concentrated on bridge—writing, teaching, organizing—and became chief executive of the American Contract Bridge League. Died 27 March

Boudiaf, Muhammad (b. 1919), President of Algeria, had been recalled from exile only in January 1992 to take office in a political crisis.

A leader of the rebel FLN in the war of independence (1954–62), he became deputy premier in the provisional government, but fell out with Ben Bella, who had him arrested in 1963. Released, he chose exile rather than submission to self-perpetuated autocracy, but his democratic principles were no defence against assassination. Died 29 June

Bovet, Daniel (b. 1907), Swiss chemist, won the Nobel Prize for medicine in 1957 for his discovery of antihistamines. They were by no means his only important contribution to preventive, curative and anaesthetic medicine. From 1929 to 1947 he worked at the Institut Pasteur in Paris, later at institutions in Italy. Died 8 April

Brandt, Willy (b. Herbert Frahm 1913), Chancellor of the Federal Republic of Germany 1969–74, in his early life overcame poverty, illegitimacy and exile during the Nazi regime to become leader of the SPD (Social Democrats) in Berlin and in 1957 the city's mayor. He was the SPD's candidate for the federal chancellorship in 1961 and 1965, and became vice-chancellor and foreign minister in an SPD/Christian Democrat coalition in 1966, before heading an SPD/Free Democrat coalition from 1969. In office his persistent *Ostpolitik*, involving reconciliation with the Soviet Union and closer relations with East Germany, achieved the Moscow treaty of 1970, forever renouncing force in Soviet-West German relations, and the Warsaw treaty of the same year pledging the inviolability of the Oder-Neisse border between Germany and Poland. In 1971 he was awarded the Nobel Peace Prize.

Although fortified by a great SPD victory in the federal election of 1972, Brandt resigned less than two years later when it was discovered that one of his closest advisers was an East German spy. He became chairman of an international commission on the North/South divide between advanced and poorer nations of the world: although the two Brandt Reports of 1980 and 1983 were largely ignored by Western governments, they had a lasting effect on public opinion. He continued to play a strong personal role in the German opposition and was president of the Socialist International from 1976 until his death. Died 8 October

Carstens, Karl (b. 1914), professor of law, was President of the Federal Republic of Germany 1979–84. A member of the Nazi party for career reasons in the 1930s, he was cleared of that taint after the war and became a Christian Democrat politician and diplomat. Before election to the presidency he had been state secretary of the Foreign Office 1960–66, deputy minister of defence 1966–67, head of the Federal Chancellor's office 1968–69, member of the Bundestag 1972–79 and its president 1976–79. Died 30 May

Cessna, Eldon (b. 1908), American aircraft designer, in 1930 designed for his father's firm the Air Master plane which thereafter linked his name with a succession of single-engined light aircraft. But he left the Cessna company in 1934, to become design engineer to Douglas Aircraft, North American and Rockwell International, and responsible, wholly or in part, for such planes as the Harvard trainer, the Mustang fighter and the F.86 swept-wing fighter. Died 22 February

Chabukiani, Vakhtang (b. 1910), Georgian ballet master and dancer, was the finest male dancer of his time, recognized as such all over the world although he rarely danced outside the Soviet Union. He joined the Kirov Theatre in 1929 and was soon dancing leading roles. From 1938, the date of his first full-length ballet, *The Heart of the Hills*, he was equally acclaimed as choreographer and ballet producer. In 1934 he danced concert programmes in the US and was ecstatically applauded. Died 5 April

Cheshire, Lord (Group Captain Leonard Cheshire), VC, OM, DSO, DFC (b. 1917), was Britain's supreme bomber ace in World War II, developing and fearlessly applying a dangerous technique of precision bombing against heavily-defended targets, and flying 100 missions. Out of uniform, he set up a foundation providing Cheshire Homes for the Disabled, eventually 270 of them in the UK and abroad, and with his second wife Sue Ryder (already famous for work on behalf of victims of nazism) founded the Ryder Cheshire Mission for the Relief of Suffering, operating all over the world. Died 31 July

Colombo, HE Cardinal Giovanni (b. 1902), was archbishop of Milan 1963–79. While strictly conservative in his ecclesiastical views, he was often a critic of the Italian political and industrial establishment. Died 20 May

Devi, Kanan (b. 1916), Bengali singer and actress, was the glamour queen of Indian cinema in the 1930s, '40s and '50s. Loved by the poor and famous for her voice, her acting and her charity, she was honoured by high awards. Died 17 July

Devlin, Lord (b. 1905), formerly Sir Patrick Devlin, became in 1948 the youngest British high court judge of the 20th century. His most famous case was the trial (and acquittal) of Dr Bodkin Adams in 1957 for euthenasic murder, when he decisively restated the principle of English criminal law that an accused's refusal to testify should never be taken as a sign of guilt. He retired from the bench in 1964 but continued to hold non-judicial public offices. Died 9 August

Dickens, Monica (Mrs. C. O. Stratton) (b. 1915), British author, used her experience as debutante turned hospital nurse and domestic servant to write semi-autobiographical novels, beginning with *One Pair of Feet* (1942); thereafter she never failed as a tragi-comic novelist. Marrying a US naval officer in 1951, she lived in Massachusetts until his death in 1985, when she returned to England and there added service to charity, notably the Samaritans, to her successful career as novelist, children's writer, autobiographer and journalist. Died 25 December

Dietrich, Marlene (b. 1901), German-born actress and singer, became an idol of the Western cinema-going world with her performance as Lola in von Sternberg's *Blue Angel* in 1930. Beautiful in face and figure, already a competent actress on stage and screen, she captivated millions with her throaty voice and sexual allure. The words and music of her song *Falling in Love Again* became common currency everywhere. With von Sternberg she moved to Hollywood, to play in such films as *Morocco* (1930), *Blonde Venus* (1932) and *Destry Rides Again* (1939). In World War II she reverted to her earlier career as a cabaret singer, entertaining US army audiences in overseas theatres of war. Although she starred in some good films in the 1950s, it was as a solo performer, the unique Dietrich, that she was best known to post-war audiences. In 1975 she retired to her home in Paris, repelling publicity and content with worship of her past self. She was awarded the US Medal of Freedom in 1951. Died 6 May

Douglas-Home, William (b. 1912), British playwright, based his first great success, *Now Barabbas*, upon his experiences in prison after being court-martialled for a humanitarian protest when an army officer in World War II. There followed a long catalogue of comedies, varying in commercial success, the best including *The Chiltern Hundreds* (1949), *The Reluctant Debutante* (1955), *The Secretary Bird* (1968) and *The Kingfisher* (1977), all of which had runs abroad. He also wrote three volumes of entertaining autobiography. Died 28 September

Dubček, Alexander (b. 1921), Slovak politician, as first secretary of the Communist Party of Czechoslovakia, was the leader and hero of the Prague Spring in 1968, introducing 'socialism with a human face', which within four months (April–August) was brutally crushed by a Soviet-led invasion ordered by Leonid Brezhnev. Yet he had been a dyed-in-the-wool Communist apparatchik from early youth, advancing to the party's first secretaryship in Slovakia (1963–68), and he never renounced his marxist faith. His personal charm, his modest lifestyle and his patriotism made him a highly popular successor to the hardliner Antoní Novotny. Humiliated by Soviet power and eventually forced from office (1969) he retreated to the shadows of political life until, in 1989, he allied himself with Václav Havel, the President of post-communist Czechoslovakia, and became chairman of the federal parliament. As new leader of the Slovak Social Democrats (1992), he opposed the break-up of the Czechoslovak federation, but the duality of his stance, at once former Communist and democratic reformer, weakened his heroic stature. Died 7 November (of injuries received in a car crash)

Eagle, Dr Harry (b. 1905), American medical scientist, was awarded the National Medal of Science in 1987 for his life's work in biological research, which included advances in the treatment of venereal disease, 'sleeping sickness' and cancer, and most famously the discovery, in 1959, of a way to grow human cells in the laboratory. Died 12 June

Evans, Sir Geraint (b. 1922), Welsh operatic baritone, first sang at Covent Garden in 1948, and at Glyndebourne in 1950. His international career began in 1958, and he was a frequent performer at the San Francisco opera house from the 1960s onwards. His most distinctive roles, which became world-famous, were Mozart's Figaro and Verdi's Falstaff, but for his farewell appearance at Covent Garden in 1984 he chose Dulcamara in Donizetti's *L'elisir d'amore*. Died 19 September

Ferrer, José (b. 1912), American actor and director on stage and screen, reached top rank in both roles and both media in the 1940s, and in 1951 won an Oscar for his film performance as Cyrano de Bergerac—already acclaimed in the theatre. His highly successful career continued to be divided between Hollywood and the New York stage, ranging from *Charlie's Aunt* to Richard III and Toulouse-Lautrec in the film *Moulin Rouge*. His acting was stagey rather than subtle but both as performer and as director he was a formidable figure until the 1960s. Died 26 January

Ffrangcon-Davies, Dame Gwen, DBE (b. 1891), British actress, peaked in lasting fame in 1924 as Juliet to the Romeo of John Gielgud, with whom she also had later successes in *The Importance of Being Earnest* (1940) and *Macbeth* (1942). Her most typical roles were Elizabeth Browning in *The Barretts of Wimpole Street* during the 1930s, Ranevskaya in *The Cherry Orchard* (1954), Mary Tyrone in *Long Day's Journey into Night* (1955) and Miss Madrigal in *The Chalk Garden* (1957). She was a founder member of the English Stage Company and she continued to act into the last decade of her 100 years. Died 27 January

Fieldhouse, Admiral of the Fleet Lord, GCB, GBE (b. 1928), was chief of the UK defence staff 1985–88, having been commander-in-chief of the force which recaptured the Falkland Islands in 1982. Died 17 February

Fischer, Anette (née Klausen, b. 1946), Danish human rights campaigner, was a member of Amnesty's International executive committee from 1984 and its chairman 1991–92. Died 11 July

Franjieh, Suleiman (b. 1910), was President of Lebanon 1970–76. A ruthless warlord, his presidency was marked by nepotism, corrupt favour for his Maronite Christian community, neglect of economic and social needs, and the descent of Lebanon into civil war. Died 23 July

Franks, Lord (Oliver Franks), OM, GCMG, KCB, KCVO, FBA (b. 1905), British academic, administrator and diplomat, was first among the 'wise men' in public affairs of his generation. The major posts he held tell all of his unique abilities: fellow in philosophy at The Queen's College, Oxford (1927–37); professor of moral philosophy, Glasgow University (1937–39); Ministry of Supply, rising to its permanent secretaryship (1939–46); provost of The Queen's College (1946–48); ambassador to the US (1948–53); deputy chairman (1953), chairman (1954–62) of Lloyds Bank; provost of Worcester College, Oxford (1962–76). He had also rendered other high public service, including chairmanship of Oxford's self-inquiry into the structure of the university (1964–66), of a government committee on official secrets (1971–72), and of a committee of privy councillors to review the causes of the Falklands War (1982–83), and work on the governing bodies of great charitable institutions like the Rhodes Trust and the Rockefeller Foundation. To all these duties he brought clarity of thought, political detachment, organizational vigour and warm human relations; during his Washington embassy he formed a particuarly close friendship with Secretary of State Acheson which was of great value to both countries. Franks was knighted in 1946, made a peer in 1976 and awarded the Order of Merit in 1977. Died 15 October

Gailitis, Archbishop Karlis (b. 1936), was elected to the see of the Lutheran Church in Latvia in 1986, whereby the deposed Archbishop Matalis, an arms-length collaborator with Soviet author-ity, was replaced by a fervent apostle of Latvian national revival and independence. Died 22 November

Godfree, Kitty (b. McKane 1896), British tennis player, won the Wimbledon ladies' title in 1924, when she beat the young Helen Wills in the final, and in 1926. She was also successful in the mixed doubles with her husband Leslie Godfree, and in badminton (four times national champion). Died 19 June

Haley, Alex (b. 1921), black American author, entered the big time with his *Autobiography of Malcolm X*, the radical black Muslim publicist, but his greatest work, *Roots*, was the fruit of 12 years' research into the possible history of his family from their origins in Gambia, through the 18th-century slave-trade, to generations of slavery in Maryland. A terrible tale of the suffering of black people, it sold in millions and led to Haley's becoming a powerful public speaker, especially on university campuses. Died 10 February

Harris, (Reg) Reginald H. (b. 1920), British professional cyclist, was world racing champion four times (1949–51 and '54). His British championship titles ran from the amateur in 1947 to the professional in 1974. Died 22 June

Hart, Prof. H. L. A. (b. 1907), professor of jurisprudence at Oxford 1952–68, was mentor of the English-speaking world in the philosophy of law, through his lectures, broadcasts, learned articles and books, including *The Concept of Law* (1961) and *Law, Liberty and Morality* (1963). He resigned his professorial chair to become research fellow of University College, Oxford, 1968–73, and principal of Brasenose College, 1973–78. Died 19 November

Hassouna, Abdel-Khaleh (b. 1898), was secretary-general of the Arab League 1952–72. His pacific diplomacy and negotiating power won him many successes and international honours, including the Légion d'Honneur. Died 21 January

Hayek, Professor Frederick, CH (b. in Vienna 1899), naturalized British economist, Nobel prizewinner 1974, became the world's most influential economist, following Maynard Keynes, of whom he was the converse as theorist and mentor of public policy. His book *The Road to Serfdom* (1944) became a classic of anti-collectivism, but it was in the 1970s that his espousal of the free-market competitive economy, as the generator not only of wealth but also of welfare for the masses, raised him to a prophetic pinnacle reached by no economic predecessor since Adam Smith. In particular, his was the theoretical inspiration behind the reforms of Mrs Thatcher in the UK, and it was his philosophy that filled the vacuum created by the disgrace of communism in Eastern Europe and the Soviet Union. Enticed to England in 1931, after four years as director of the Austrian Institute of Economic Research, he became professor of economic science and statistics at the University of London 1931–50, of science and moral science at the University of Chicago 1950–62, and of economics at the University of Freiburg 1962–69. Thereafter he continued to write books and essays and to inspire seminars and institutions of economics, politics, history and philosophy. His last book, *The Fatal Conceit*, a typically relentless commination against the pretensions of socialism, was published in 1989. Died 13 March

Held, Martin (b. 1908), German actor, was rated as one of the finest actors in Europe, but apart from two short visits to London in the 1960s was little known beyond Germany, where his versatility and brilliant characterization earned him the highest respect and affection. Died 31 January

Howa, Hassan (b. 1922, Indian-race South African, was president (1972–87) of the rigorously anti-apartheid South African Council on Sport, which demanded total international isolation of the country's sport, especially cricket, until full racial integration had been achieved. Died 12 February

Hulme, Denny (b. 1936), was world champion of Formula One motor racing in 1967, driving a Brabham-Repco car. After further grand prix victories he retired to his native New Zealand in 1974. Died 4 October

Jaroszewicz, Piotr (b. 1909), was Prime Minister of Poland in the regime of President Gierek 1970–80. Closely associated with the harsh corrective measures of 1973 that followed over-inflation of the economy, he was deposed and disgraced for his 'mistakes'. Murdered 2 September

Kaysone Phomvihane (b. 1920), was Prime Minister of Laos 1975–91 and thereafter its President. An early recruit to the revolutionary movement, in 1955 he became first secretary-general of the Laos People's Revolutionary Party and commander of the Pathet Lao army. After the Vietnam war he shared power in Laos with Prince Souphanouvong, whom he eventually succeeded as President: they abolished the monarchy, sent the King to his death and established a one-party communist regime, slightly relaxed after the collapse of Soviet communism. Died 21 November

Kelly, Petra (b. Lehman 1947), creator of the German Green Party, learnt her non-violent reformism in the USA in the 1960s; she left the German Social Democratic Party in 1979 to found the Greens, which won 28 seats in the Bundestag in 1983. The party split, and failed in the 1990 all-German elections, and Petra Kelly became a political exile, although still a strong and attractive personal embodiment of minority causes. Died 12 Ocbober

Kemeny, John G. (b. in Hungary 1926), American academic, invented the computer language BASIC which became the basis of much subsequent computer software. He was professor of mathematics at Dartmouth College from 1953 and its president 1970–81. Died 26 December

Khoei, Grand Ayatollah (b. 1899), Shia spiritual leader, though born in Iran spent all his life from early childhood in Iraq. In 1971, after the death of the previous Absolute Object of Emulation of the Shias, a majority acclaimed him as successor, but others, especially in Iran, favoured Ayatollah Khomeini, whose political activism contrasted with Khoei's scholarly and quietist stance, which, however, did not save him from humiliation by Saddam Husain after the Gulf War. Died 8 August

Li Xiannian, (b. 1905), President of China 1983–88, was one of the last of the Chinese Communist 'Old Guard'. Joining the party in 1926, and holding command in the revolutionary army that won victory after World War II, he became a national vice-premier in 1954 and a member of the politburo in 1956. A dedicated follower of Mao Zedong, a stern and ruthless Communist, he rode the storms of the Cultural Revolution and the post-Mao reaction. Although the presidency diluted his political authority he became thereafter chairman of the Chinese People's Consultative Conference and remained a power behind the scene. Died 22 June

Lidiard, Victoria (b. Simmons 1889), English suffragette (agitator for women's franchise), was sentenced to two months' hard labour in 1912 for throwing a stone—one of many in her pockets—through a War Office window. After marrying in 1918 and becoming an opthalmic optometrist, she continued to champion radical and feminist causes. Died 30 October

McClintock, Barbara (b. 1902), American geneticist, won the Nobel Prize for physiology/medicine in 1983 for her discovery of transposable elements in chromosomes, so-called 'jumping genes'. Although she reported her findings in 1951, facing a scientific establishment scornful of her work and hostile to women scientists she retreated to solitary research at the Cold Spring Harbor laboratory: recognition came more than 20 years later. Died 2 September

MacMillan, Sir Kenneth (b. 1929), British choreographer, succeeded Sir Frederick Ashton as director of the Royal Ballet at Covent Garden 1970–77; but his finest work belongs to earlier and later periods. A fruitful decade had begun with *Danses Concertantes* (1955) and concluded with his triumphant *Romeo and Juliet* (1965) and his setting of Mahler's *Das Lied von der Erde* (also 1965) for the Stuttgart Ballet, followed by three years (1966–69) as director of the Staatsoper ballet company in Berlin. Liberated from administration, while remaining chief choreographer for Covent Garden, he produced in 1978 two of his best ballets, *Mayerling* for the Royal Ballet and *My Brother, My Sister* for Stuttgart. There followed many ballets, full length and short, for Covent Garden, Sadler's Wells and the American Ballet Theatre, of which he was for a while associate director. His *The Prince of the Pagodas* (for Covent Garden 1989), to Benjamin Britten's score, had a mixed critical reception, as had some of his earlier works; but his creative power, using classical ballet technique to explore new psychological insights and evoke fresh beauties, was universally acknowledged. Died 30 October

Markus, Mrs Rixi (b. Schaufstein in Austria–Hungary 1910), British bridge-player, was the first woman to be proclaimed international grandmaster of the game. Among the 19 international championships that she won (usually playing with Fritzi

Gordon) was the women's team Olympiad of 1964. Authoress, newspaper columnist, founder of the Lords v. Commons match, and a great promoter of the game for enjoyment and for charity, she was awarded the MBE in 1975 for her many services. Died 4 April

Martin, HE Cardinal Jacques (b. 1908 in France), spent almost all his ecclesiastical career in Rome, for the longest part in the Vatican's Foreign Office, heading its powerful French section and becoming a senior adviser to the Papal Secretary of State before his mentor Pope Paul VI made him Prefect of the Apostolic Household (1969–86). Died 27 September

Maskell, Dan (b. 1908), was respected all over the world as commentator on lawn tennis, including the Wimbledon tournament for 40 years. Starting as a ball-boy at Queen's Club, he became professional coach at Wimbledon in 1929, and was national professional champion 1928–51. He was the Lawn Tennis Association's training manager 1955–73, his unique career as BBC commentator having already begun. Died 10 December

Messiaen, Olivier (b. 1908), French organist and composer, was said by a British obituarist to have changed the nature of European music more than anyone else in the latter half of the 20th century. His music was extraordinarily rich in its sources, from bird-song to African tom-toms, though mostly directed to Christian themes, and its great contribution to contemporary musical culture was its openness to infinitely varied experience and opportunity. A brilliant organist, he composed fine music for that instrument, or using it in orchestral work. He was organist of Sainte Trinité in Paris 1931–92, and professor successively of harmony (1941–47), of analysis, aesthetics and rhythm (1947–92) and of composition (1966–92) at the Paris Conservatoire. Died 28 April

Milchsack, Lilo, Hon. GCMG (b. Lisalotte Duden 1905), founder of the Königswinter conferences, was described as the queen of Anglo-German post-war relations. She was chairman of the Deutsche-Englische Gesellschaft 1977–82 (hon. sec. 1949–77, hon. chairman 1982–92). Died 7 August

Mitchell, Dr Peter, FRS (b. 1920), British biochemist, won the Nobel Prize for chemistry in 1978 for his work on the transformation of food and light into stores of energy for muscles and nerves by living organisms. His theory of this process, at first an inspired idea, was derided by most scientists until its truth was demonstrated by a succession of experiments; thereafter his eminence in his chosen field was recognized the world over. Died 10 April

Morley, Robert (b. 1908), British actor, writer and *bon viveur*, enjoyed a vastly successful career on the stage, in films and television. Among his most memorable roles in the theatre were Sheridan Whiteside in *The Man Who Came to Dinner* (1941), the Prince Regent in *The First Gentleman* (1945), Arnold Holt in *Edward My Son* (1947), lead parts in Roussin's *The Little Hut* (1950) and *Hook, Line and Sinker* (1958), and in the cinema in *The African Queen* (1951), *Around the World in Eighty Days* (1956) and *The Human Factor* (1979). Whatever the medium, he was always his own self, ebullient, humorous, larger than life. He directed a number of plays in the 1950s and '60s, wrote eight plays and six books of reminiscences. His private pleasures were characteristic: food, drink, travel and horse-racing. Died 3 June

Muldoon, Sir Robert, GCMG, CH (b. 1921), was Prime Minister and minister of finance of New Zealand 1975–84. An MP since 1960, he was elected leader of the National Party in 1974 and won three successive general elections. Ostensibly a tough monetarist, he adopted measures of state intervention in the economy which, allied to his personal abrasiveness, divided his party. Died 5 August

Nolan, Sir Sydney, OM, AC (b. 1917), Australian artist, was unsurpassed in the rendering of Australia's landscape and light. He first became well-known in Europe and America for a series of paintings about the famous outlaw Ned Kelly (1945–47, a second series in 1954–55). Travelling the world in the 1950s, he painted another memorable series linking the Gallipoli campaign in World War I with the siege of Troy, followed by one on Leda and the Swan, and yet another of Australian flowers. His vast output included weird portraits and designs for opera and ballet. Now heaped with honours, he retreated to England's West Country. Died 28 November

O'Neill, Professor Gerard (b. 1927), American scientist, was professor of physics at Princeton University 1959–85 and from 1977 founder-president of the Space Studies Institute. His book *The High Frontier: Human Colonies in Space* (1976), though scientifically rigorous, achieved the worldwide sales of high-class science fiction. From 1986 he was founder-chairman of O'Neill Communications Inc., largely to exploit his own radio inventions. Died 27 April

Oort, Professor Jan (b. 1900), Dutch astronomer, gave his name to 'Oort's constants' which regulate galactic rotation relative to the Sun. His studies of the galaxies led to a number of important discoveries. He was professor of astronomy at the University of Leiden 1935–70, general secretary of the International Astronomical Union 1935–48 and its president 1959–61. Died 5 November

O'Reilly, Bill (b. 1905), Australian cricketer, was described by the famous batsman Don Bradman as 'the greatest bowler I ever faced or saw'. His spin bowling, medium-paced by modern standards, was always aggressive and often unplayable. His record in 27 Test matches between 1931 and 1946 was 144 wickets at an average of 22.5 runs. Retiring from the field he became a vitriolic press commentator, hating one-day matches and floodlit cricket just as he had, so he said, formerly hated batsmen. Died 5 October

Pearson, Sir Denning (b. 1908), as chief executive of Rolls Royce Ltd. 1957–70, chairman 1969–70, was largely responsible for the development of its aero-engine business and the manufacture of power units for British and American nuclear submarines. Died 1 August

Perrin, Francis (b. 1901), French scientist (professor of physics, Collège de France 1946–70), though an ardent left-wing pacifist, led the team that produced in 1960 France's first atomic bomb, and as head of the French atomic energy commission was responsible not only for France's nuclear missile programme but also for the great growth of its atomic power stations. His duty of service, for which he received the Grand Cross of the Légion d'Honneur, did not prevent his publicly espousing a total end to nuclear secrecy and opposing France's test programme in the Pacific. Died 17 August

Pierrepoint, Albert (b. 1905), Britain's chief executioner 1946–56, in succession to his father and uncle, hanged altogether 450 condemned persons, including Nazi war criminals. He brought skill and humanity to his craft, and after his retirement openly opposed capital punishment, which, in his view, 'achieved nothing but revenge'. Died 10 July

Pillai, Sir Raghavan, KCIE (b. 1898), Indian civil servant, having reached, by 1942, nearly the highest office open to the ICS under British rule, rendered still greater service to independent India as Cabinet Secretary 1950–53 and secretary-general to the

Ministry of External Affairs 1952–60. Died 31 March

Piper, John, CH (b. 1903), British artist, displayed an extraordinary versatility, achieving peaks of esteem not only in oil painting and water-colour but also in stage and costume design, tapestry, stained glass, ceramics and book illustration. Forsaking abstraction for naturalism in 1937, he was best known to the general public as recorder of Britain's countryside and architectural heritage, but to the cognoscenti as much for his theatrical work (especially for the operas of Benjamin Britten) and his stained glass in Coventry and Liverpool cathedrals, among other sites. Died 28 June

Pucci, Marchese Emilio (b. 1914), Italian couturier, came of a wealthy family and had a career as scholar and wartime bomber pilot before sidling into fashion design in 1948, then swiftly gaining world fame for women's sports and leisure clothes under the label Emilio. Died 10 November

Quadros, Janio da Silva (b. 1917), was President of Brazil for a few months in 1961, resigning, he said 'beaten by reaction', but not before he had radically changed Brazil's internal and international policies, the former to the right, the latter to the left. Re-entering politics 18 years later, he became a reformist mayor of São Paulo 1985–88. Died 16 January

Ray, Satyajit (b. 1921), Indian film-maker, was one of the greatest of the century, to be judged alongside names like Vittorio de Sica and Ingmar Bergman. His first film, *Pather Panchali* (1955), one of three known as the Apu Trilogy, intimate tales of rural life in Bengal inspired by his guru Rabindranath Tagore, was arguably his best, certainly his most famous; neglected in India, sneered at by Hollywood and US critics, it triumphed at the Cannes Festival and was widely shown in Britain and France. Thereafter his many films included *Charulata* (1964), *Kanchenjunga* (1962), *Days and Nights in the Forest* (1969), *The Chess-Players* (1977), *Branches of the Tree* (1990) and *The Stranger* (1991). Nearing death, he received an honorary Oscar for his life's work. Died 23 April.

Reshevsky, Samuel (b. in Poland 1911), American chess grandmaster, after a brilliant phase as a child prodigy, reached a peak in his international career at a British tournament in 1936, when he finished half a point below two of the century's greatest players, Capablanca and Botvinnik. For 20 years thereafter he was the undisputed chess champion of the West, until displaced by Fischer; he won his last US title in 1971. Died 4 April

Rex, Sir Robert, KBE (b. 1909), was Prime Minister of Niue in the South Pacific from 1974, when the island state ceased to be a dependency of New Zealand, until his death. Died 12 December

Riad, Mahmoud (b. 1917), was secretary-general of the Arab League 1972–79, foreign minister of Egypt twice during the 1960s and its permanent representative at the UN 1962–64. He had been opposed to President Sadat's plan of making separate peace with Israel at Camp David, but continued to influence Egyptian foreign policy behind the scenes. Died 25 January

Rice, Peter (b. 1935), British structural engineer, worked with such architects as Richard Rogers and Renzo Piano on a number of highly innovative buildings, including the Sydney Opera House, the Pompidou Centre in Paris, Lloyd's in London and the Pavilion of the Future at Expo '92 in Seville. In 1958 he joined Ove Arup & Partners, of which he was a director from 1978, while running his personal practice in Paris. He was awarded the Royal Gold

Medal for Architecture in 1992. Died 25 October

Roach, Hal (b. 1892), American cinema producer, was in his day the master of the short comic film. In 1917 he made a star of Harold Lloyd; in 1927 he brought together Stan Laurel and Oliver Hardy, whom he directed in countless shorts and several successful longer films until 1940. He was also responsible for several major feature films, including Steinbeck's *Of Mice and Men* (1939), and after World War II went successfully into television. Died 2 October

Romanov, Grand Duke Vladimir Kirillovich (b. 1917), was head of the house of Romanov and claimant to the imperial throne of Russia. Born a few months before the Bolshevik revolution, a great-grandson of Tsar Alexander II and of Queen Victoria, he spent his life in exile, mostly in France but also in England and Spain, returning only for a short visit to St Petersburg in 1991. Died 21 April

Rongzhen, Marshal Nie (b. 1899), Chinese soldier and politician, held key commands in the Long March and the subsequent civil war. He became a member of the central committee of the Chinese Communist Party in 1945 and of the politburo in 1967, but lost his place, and nearly his head, in the Cultural Revolution, returning to the politburo in 1977. From 1955 to 1967 he was in charge of China's nuclear programme, and triumphed with the explosion of an atom bomb in 1964 and a hydrogen bomb in 1967. Died 14 May

Rothenstein, Sir John (b. 1901), was director of the Tate Gallery, London, 1938–64. A son of the painter Sir William Rothenstein, he moved naturally into the world of art and literature, teaching in American universities and directing art galleries in Yorkshire. His tenure at the Tate was marked by its vigorous revival after wartime closure, the

patronage of young British artists and important administrative reforms. Died 27 February

Saraswati, Swami Krishnanand (b. Bhavani Singh 1900), Indian spiritual leader, follower and intimate of Mahatma Gandhi, dedicated the last half-century of his life to service of the poor, especially suffering Indian communities in Africa and Europe, and was revered by people of different faiths all over the world. Died 23 August

Sergeyev, Konstantin (b. 1910), Russian dancer and choreographer, was director of the Kirov ballet 1951–56 and 1960–70. In the 1930s he had been a superb *premier danseur noble*, and his partnership with his wife Natalia Dudinskaya, which continued in ballet direction after he had ceased to dance, was specially acclaimed. His best choreography was in revivals of the Russian classics. Died 1 April

Shawn, William (b. 1907), was editor of *The New Yorker* 1952–87, a period which included both its greatest days, with contributors like J. D. Salinger, John Updike and Truman Capote, and its decline as a business enterprise. Died 8 December

Shuster, Joe (b. 1914), American cartoonist and film animator, created the world-famous character Superman (first published 1938 and still going strong). Died 30 July

Sirica, Judge John (b. 1904), as chief judge of the US federal court for Washington DC, presided over the Watergate trial in 1972 which eventually led to the disgrace of President Nixon. Died 14 August

Stirling, Sir James (b. 1926), British architect, came near to being 'a prophet not without honour save in his own country'. Though awarded the RIBA gold medal (1980) and knighted for his eminent services, he saw many of his buildings or projects in the UK scorned by critics and the public as brutalist and uncomfortable, and his most widely-admired effort was the Stuttgart Staatsgalerie in Germany. His American honours included the Pritzker Prize (1981), the Chicago Architecture Award (1985) and the Thomas Jefferson Medal (1986). Died 25 June

Tal, Mikhail (b. 1936), Latvian chess grandmaster, became world champion in 1960, defeating Botvinnik who nonetheless thrashed him in a return match. Thereafer, dogged by infirmity and illness, he never regained world supremacy, though he won many big championships in the Soviet Union and other countries, equalling Botvinnik's record of six national victories. Died 28 June

Tomasek, HE Cardinal Frantisek (b. 1899), was Archbishop of Prague and Primate of Bohemia 1978–91, but he had been apostolic administrator of the Czech archdiocese since 1965 and had been made a cardinal by Pope Paul VI in 1976. Through the Soviet tyranny of Czechoslovakia— when he was imprisoned for three years—the Dubček interval of 1968 and the Soviet-enforced reaction of the next two decades he had steadfastly upheld the claims of the Church and broader human rights. Died 4 August

Uri, Professor Pierre (b. 1911), French economist and civil servant, was enlisted by Jean Monnet to draft, first, the constitution of the European Iron and Steel Community and then the Common Market text that became the Treaty of Rome, and was therefore among the pioneer creators of the European Community. After a brilliant career in administration and research he moved to socialist politics, but too late in life to achieve his ambition to become French minister of finance. Died 21 July

Van Fleet, General James (b. 1892), was famed in the US as the army general who always won. A captain in World War I, he commanded a battalion in the final 1918 offensive; in World War II, after leading his regiment ashore at Omaha Beach, he commanded the 3rd Army Corps which secured the crossing of the Rhine; and he commanded the 8th Army in the 1951 Korean war. Died 25 September

Viera da Silva, Marie-Hélène (b. 1908), Portuguese-born Parisian artist, was one of the most notable European abstract painters of the century, her highly individual pictures being exhibited all over the world. Died 6 March

Walton, Samuel (b. 1918), American store proprietor, was reckoned the richest man in the US, having risen from the launch of a single shop in 1945 to command of a nationwide retail chain served by 19 huge distribution blocks; but he shared much of the profits with his employees, with whom he worked closely. When near his end he received the supreme US civilian honour, the Presidential Medal of Freedom. Died 5 April

Whitney, Cornelius Vanderbilt (b. 1899), American multi-millionaire and philanthropist, inherited social eminence and a vast family fortune, from which base he created a business empire that included Pan American Airways (founded by him in 1927), and major interests in the film industry. In both world wars he served in the US air force, winning the Legion of Merit and other honours. The Whitney Museum of American Art, founded by his mother, was among the causes that benefited from his wealth. Died 13 December

Woods, Most Rev Frank, KBE (b. 1907), Church of England priest and bishop, was Archbishop of Melbourne 1957–77 and Primate of Australia 1971–77. A devoted ecumenist, he was a central committee member of the World Council of Churches 1968–76 and cultivated mutual understanding with both the Roman Catholic and non-Anglican Protestant churches. Died 29 November

XXI CHRONICLE OF PRINCIPAL EVENTS IN 1992

JANUARY

1 UN envoy Cyrus Vance announced that Serbia and Croatia had agreed to deployment of UN troops.
2 Russia and Ukraine ended state controls on prices, increasing cost of some staples five times.
6 President Zviad Gamsakhurdia of Georgia fled following two-week siege in Tbilisi; 200 had died in unrest.
7 Five EC monitors died when their helicopter was shot down over Croatia.
11 President Bendjedid Chadli of Algeria resigned; second round of elections cancelled following gains by Islamic fundamentalists in Dec. 1991; power assumed by High Security Council.
13 Middle East peace talks resumed in Washington, ending 16 Jan.
    Mongolia adopted new non-communist constitution.
15 EC countries and 12 other nations formally recognized Slovenia and Croatia, marking effective end of Yugoslav federation.
16 Muhammad Boudiaf returned to Algeria after 27 years' exile to become head of state (see 29 June).
    In Gibraltar general election, Socialist Labour Party government of Joe Bossano returned for second term.
17 In Greece, former PM Papandreou acquitted of all charges in connection with Bank of Crete scandal.
19 Zhelyu Zhelev re-elected President of Bulgaria in country's first popular presidential election.
    Israeli coalition, led by PM Yitzhak Shamir, lost its majority following resignation of members opposed to Palestinian self-rule.
20 83 died when French Airbus A-320 crashed near Strasbourg.
21 UN Security Council adopted resolution 731 demanding extradition of Libyans suspected of complicity in Lockerbie bombing in 1988.
24 Opening South African parliament, President de Klerk outlined power-sharing plans; blacks would be able to vote in constitutional referendum but whites would retain veto.
28 In State of Union address, President Bush announced further nuclear arms reductions.
    Third stage of Middle East peace talks, a multilateral round, opened in Moscow, ending 29 Jan.
30 Charles Haughey resigned as PM of Irish Republic.
    Russian President Yeltsin in London for talks with PM Major.
    Ten former Soviet republics admitted to CSCE at ceremony in Prague.
31 UN Security Council, chaired by British PM Major, held historic extraordinary meeting to consider UN role in strengthening global security in post-Cold War era.

FEBRUARY

1 President Bush and President Yeltsin of Russia held weekend talks at Camp David; joint declaration said that Russia and the USA no longer regarded themselves as adversaries.
   President de Klerk of South Africa in London at start of European tour.

4 Irish President Mary Robinson paid historic first visit to Ulster.
6 HM Queen Elizabeth II celebrated 40th anniversary of her accession to the throne.
7 EC's Maastricht treaty, agreed in Dec. 1991, formally signed.
8 Winter Olympic Games opened in Albertville, France.
9 Widespread demonstrations took place in Moscow and other Russian cities against shortages and rising prices.
Military-backed authorities in Algeria declared 12-month state of emergency and banned Islamic Salvation Front.
10 An airlift of emergency Western food aid to former Soviet republics commenced.
11 PM Major held talks with Ulster leaders to discuss mounting violence in province.
Albert Reynolds appointed PM of Irish Republic.
In USA, former world heavyweight boxing champion Mike Tyson convicted of rape; he was gaoled for six years on 26 March.
14 Following talks at Minsk, Russia agreed to allow Ukraine, Moldavia and Azerbaijan to opt out of CIS plan for unified command of armed forces.
In UK, private member's bill to outlaw foxhunting defeated by 12 votes.
16 Sheikh Abbas Musawi, Hizbullah's secretary-general, died in Israeli helicopter gunship attack on his car in southern Lebanon.
17 HM Queen Elizabeth II began week's visit to Australia.
20 Fighting intensified in southern Lebanon as Israeli forces fired on Shia villages suspected of harbouring Hizbullah guerrillas.
21 UN Security Council authorized deployment of 14,000-strong peacekeeping force in Croatia.
22 Ruling Nationalist Party, led by PM E. Fenech Adami, returned at general election in Malta.
23 In Russia, 10,000 involved in violent protests against government of President Yeltsin.
24 At resumed Middle East peace talks in Washington, US Secretary of State said Israel must halt building of Jewish settlements in occupied territories if it was to obtain $10,000 million loan guarantees (see 11 Aug.).
26 Irish Supreme Court overturned High Court ruling which had sought to prevent 14-year-old rape victim seeking abortion in Britain.
Canada announced withdrawal of its 7,000 troops from Europe by 1994.
Armenian forces reported to have massacred some 200 Azerbaijani citizens in disputed enclave of Nagorno-Karabakh.
28 UN Security Council voted to approve creation of UN Transitional Authority in Cambodia (UNTAC).
29 Bosnia-Hercegovina voted for independence from Yugoslav federation; Serbs boycotted referendum.

MARCH

1 Montenegro voted overwhelmingly in favour of remaining part of Yugoslavia.
2 Eight former Soviet republics and San Marino admitted to UN.
3 250 miners died in colliery disaster in northern Turkey.
6 President Mutalibov of Azerbaijan resigned amid mounting violence over Nagorno-Karabakh between Azerbaijan and Armenia.
British government announced plans for introduction of a national lottery.
7 A new four-party coalition government, led by Jean-Luc Deheane, formed in Belgium.
10 In UK, budget day: Chancellor introduced a new 20p tax rate and forecast PSBR of £28,000 million (4.5 per cent of GDP); White Paper set out proposals to merge budget and autumn statement from 1993.

Former Soviet Foreign Minister Eduard Shevardnadze named head of state of Georgia (see 11 Oct.).

13 Some 500 people died in earthquake in eastern Turkey.

16 In UK, dissolution of parliament.

17 At a referendum in South Africa, white voters overwhelmingly endorsed President de Klerk's proposals for constitutional reform.

28 people died in car-bomb attack by Islamic Jihad against Israeli embassy in Buenos Aires.

20 CIS leaders, meeting in Kiev, agreed to send peacekeeping force to Nagorno-Karabakh and to set up joint commission to study division of military property of former USSR.

21 Voters in Tatarstan overwhelmingly supported proposals for independence from Russia.

22 In Albanian parliamentary elections, Democratic Party gained overwhelming majority of parliamentary seats, ending nearly 50 years of communist rule.

23 27 died in air crash at New York's La Guardia airport.

24 CSCE conference opened in Helsinki; admission of Georgia, Croatia and Slovenia brought membership to 51.

25 In World Cup cricket final in Melbourne, Pakistan beat England by 11 runs.

30 President Walesa on official visit to Germany, the first by a Polish president since 1918.

31 At meeting in Moscow, representatives of 18 of the 20 autonomous republics within Russian Federation signed a federation treaty.

UN Security Council resolution 748 imposed mandatory arms and air travel sanctions on Libya because of its refusal to hand over two Lockerbie suspects; sanctions came into force on 15 April.

P.J. Patterson sworn in as PM of Jamaica following resignation of Michael Manley.

APRIL

2 Edith Cresson resigned as PM of France and was succeeded by Pierre Bérégovoy.

In Libya, demonstrators burned down Venezuelan embassy and attacked several other embassies.

3 President Alia of Albania resigned and was succeeded by Sali Berisha; Alexander Meksi appointed PM on 13 April.

4 In UK, Grand National won by Party Politics at 14–1; Oxford won Boat Race by one-and-a-half lengths.

5 President Fujimori of Peru staged military-backed coup, suspended constitution and arrested opposition politicians (see 22 Nov.).

In Italy, an inconclusive general election resulted in losses for the centre-left coalition parties and gains for anti-Rome regionalists (see 28 June).

6 EC countries and USA agreed to recognize independence of Bosnia-Hercegovina amid mounting civil conflict there.

7 Gen. Suchinda Kraprayoon, leader of military junta, appointed PM of Thailand (see 24 May).

8 PLO leader Yassir Arafat injured in plane crash in Libyan desert.

9 In UK general election, Conservatives, led by PM John Major, returned with greatly reduced majority.

In Miami, former Panamanian dictator Gen. Noriega convicted of drug-trafficking.

10 Three dead, 91 injured in IRA bomb explosion in City of London, biggest bomb in mainland Britain since World War II.

In parliamentary elections in Iran, moderate supporters of President Rafsanjani gained control of Majlis.

11   In UK cabinet reshuffle Kenneth Clarke became Home Secretary, Malcolm Rifkind Defence Secretary and Michael Heseltine President of the Board of Trade/Trade and Industry Secretary; Virginia Bottomley and Gillian Shephard became first two women in Major cabinet.

12   In UK, London Marathon won by Antonio Pinto of Portugal.

16   President Najibullah of Afghanistan overthrown as mujahideen closed on Kabul.
     In Italy, Carlo de Benedetti and Licio Gelli gaoled for their roles in collapse of Banco Ambrosiano in 1982.

20   King Juan Carlos of Spain opened Expo '92 world fair in Seville, described as biggest exhibition in history.

21   In Bosnia-Hercegovina, full-scale fighting erupted in Sarajevo as Serb forces fired on city centre held by Muslims and Croats.

22   In Mexico, more than 200 died in series of gas explosions in sewers of Guadalajara.

23   EC peace mission, led by Lord Carrington, held talks at Sarajevo airport with warring Bosnian factions.

26   Alpha Oumar Konaré elected President of Mali.
     In UK, Lord Justice Taylor succeeded Lord Lane as Lord Chief Justice.

27   In Germany, public sector workers began strikes, causing biggest postwar disruption to transport, postal services and refuse collection; dispute settled on 7 May.
     Serbia and Montenegro proclaimed foundation of new Yugoslav state.
     In UK, Betty Boothroyd elected Speaker of House of Commons, first woman to hold 700-year-old office.

28   President Cossiga of Italy resigned (see 25 May).
     In Ghana, draft constitution, to end 11 years of military rule, overwhelmingly approved in a referendum (see 3 Nov.).
     President Momoh of Sierra Leone overthrown in military coup.
     Islamic Jihad Council assumed power in Afghanistan following entry of mujahideen forces into Kabul on 25 April; Seghbatullah Mujjaddedi appointed head of state (see 28 June).

29   Violent riots and looting broke out in Los Angeles following acquittal of four white policemen accused of beating up a black motorist; five days of disorder left nearly 60 dead and damage estimated at $1,000 million.

MAY

2   European Economic Area agreement between EC and EFTA states signed in Oporto, Portugal.

6   In UK, state opening of parliament; Queen's Speech foreshadowed 16 bills including measures for privatization of British Coal and elements of British Rail.
     In Lebanon, government of Omar Karami resigned following street riots over collapsing economy; Rashid al-Solh formed new government on 16 May (see 31 Oct.).

7   In UK local elections, Conservatives made net gain of 308 seats.

8   Some 40 died in days of rioting in Malawi, the worst since independence in 1964.

11   Presidential elections in the Philippines; results declared on 17 June gave Gen. Fidel Ramos a narrow margin over his nearest rival; he was sworn in as successor to President Aquino on 30 June.

12   HM Queen Elizabeth II, addressing European Parliament in Strasbourg, emphasized EC's role in sustaining peace in postwar Europe but stressed need to preserve diversity of member states.

EC monitors withdrew from Sarajevo where intensified Serbian shelling made their task impossible; UN peace-keeping troops withdrew on 15 May.

15   In speech at The Hague, Mrs Thatcher attacked European federalism and warned against attempts to create a European super-state.

18   UNHCR official reported that more than one milion refugees had been created by collapse of Yugoslavia.

Hans-Dietrich Genscher retired after 18 years as German Foreign Minister and was succeeded by Herr Klaus Kinkel.

21   EC agriculture ministers reached agreement on plans for reform of common agricultural policy (CAP).

23   In Sicily, leading anti-Mafia judge Giovanni Spadolini died in terrorist car bomb explosion.

24   Gen. Suchinda Kraprayoon resigned as PM of Thailand after week of pro-democracy riots in Bangkok in which many had died (see 13 Sept.).

25   Oscar Luigi Scalfaro elected President of Italy.

UK PM Major on four-day visit to Poland, Czechoslovakia and Hungary.

26   16 died in Serbian mortar bomb attack on bread queue in Sarajevo.

28   In UK, administrators took control of London's Canary Wharf, the largest property development in Europe: the developers were unable to finance its continuation.

29   In Croatia, Dubrovnik came under fire for first time in six months; residents of Sarajevo suffered worst shelling of siege so far.

In first elections in Fiji since 1987 coup, Sitiveni Rabuka endorsed as PM and would lead new coalition.

30   UN Security Council adopted resolution 757 imposing sweeping sanctions against Serbia/Montenegro in response to its aggression against Bosnia-Hercegovina.

JUNE

2   In Denmark, referendum voters rejected EC's Maastricht treaty on political and economic union.

3   Delegates from more than 100 nations attended opening of UN Earth Summit (UNCED) in Rio de Janeiro; conference ended on 14 June with declaration on environmentally-sound development and adoption of conventions on biological diversity and climate change.

In UK, Derby won by Dr Devious at 8–1.

6   President Bush and UK PM Major held weekend talks at Camp David.

At elections in Czechoslovakia, separatist parties headed poll in Czech Lands and Slovakia.

7   Azerbaijan held presidential elections; Abulfaz Elchibey, leader of Azerbaijani Popular Front, sworn in as republic's first non-communist president for 70 years on 16 June.

9   HM Queen Elizabeth II on four-day state visit to France.

In Thailand, King Bhumibol appointed Anand Panyarachun PM.

10   British PM Major on official visit to Colombia.

15   Eight-year Middle East hostage crisis ended with release of two Germans in Beirut, last Westerners to be freed.

16   President Bush and Russian President Yeltsin held summit talks in Washington; they announced major reductions in strategic nuclear weapons, exceeding those contained in 1991 START treaty.

18   In referendum in Ireland, voters overwhelmingly endorsed EC Maastricht treaty.

In South Africa, 45 died in massacre by armed Zulu supporters of Inkatha at Boipatong township, south of Johannesburg.

21   Czech and Slovak delegations, meeting in Prague, agreed to end Czechoslovak federation, founded in 1918 (see 31 Dec.).

23   In South Africa, ANC announced withdrawal from constitutional negotiations, demanding international inquiry into Boipatong massacre.
     In Israeli general election, Labour Party gained decisive victory; Yitzhak Rabin's new coalition was approved by Knesset on 13 July.

26   Two-day EC heads of government meeting opened in Lisbon; agenda included emergency plan for relief supplies to Sarajevo and progress of Maastricht treaty ratification.
     Denmark defeated Germany 2–0 in European football championship final in Gothenburg, Sweden.

28   President Mitterrand of France visited besieged city of Sarajevo.
     Burhanuddin Rabbani appointed interim President of Afghanistan (see 30 Dec.).
     Italy's 51st postwar government, led by Giuliano Amato (Socialist), sworn in.

29   President Muhammad Boudiaf of Algeria assassinated; Ali Kafi succeeded him on 2 July.
     Control of Sarajevo airport handed over to UN forces by Serbs to enable commencement of humanitarian flights.
     OAU summit conference opened in Dakar, Senegal.

30   French lorry drivers and farmers began a week-long blockade of motorways and main highways, causing chaos throughout France.

JULY

2   UN peace-keeping forces arrived in Sarajevo as first humanitarian flights began to arrive to relieve population on verge of starvation.
     In Czechoslovakia, caretaker government, headed by Jan Strasky, sworn in.

5   In UK, André Agassi (USA) won men's championship at Wimbledon; Steffi Graf (Germany) was ladies' champion.

6   18th summit of major industrial nations (G7) opened in Munich; Russian President Yeltsin addressed conference on 8 July and was promised backing for his reform programme.
     In Nigeria, Social Democratic Party gained majority in parliament in first federal elections for a decade.

7   In Canada, federal government and nine English-speaking provinces, meeting at Charlottetown, agreed constitutional changes including special status for French-speaking Quebec (see 26 Oct.).

8   Thomas Klestil succeeded Kurt Waldheim as President of Austria.
     Hanna Suchocka appointed PM of Poland.
     In UK, White Paper The Health of the Nation (Cmnd. 1986) outlined strategy to give Britons longer, healthier lives.

9   Chris Patten sworn in as Britain's last governor of Hong Kong.
     Two-day CSCE summit conference opened in Helsinki, the largest ever held in Europe; political declaration (10 July) affirmed CSCE as authority to consider all threats to European security and as forum for East-West arms talks.

10   WEU and NATO established naval presence in Adriatic to enforce UN sanctions against Serbia.
     Former Panamanian leader Manuel Noriega gaoled for 40 years for drug-trafficking by Miami court.

13   In Israel, inaugural session of Knesset approved new Labour-led coalition under Yitzhak Rabin.
     Shankar Dayal Sharma elected President of India; he was sworn in on 26 July.

14 In UK, White Paper *New Opportunities for Railways* (Cmnd. 2012) outlined plans for privatization of British Rail.
Milan Panic elected PM of rump Yugoslavia (Serbia and Montenegro) (see 29 Dec.).

17 Three days of talks in London between Bosnia's warring factions ended; a ceasefire agreement was not effective; UK Foreign Secretary Douglas Hurd visited Sarajevo.
Slovakia's regional parliament issued a declaration of sovereignty.

18 In UK, John Smith elected leader of Labour Party in succession to Neil Kinnock.

19 Italy's top anti-Mafia judge, Paolo Borsellino, assassinated in Palermo, Sicily.

20 Václav Havel resigned as President of Czechoslovakia following Slovakia's declaration of sovereignty.

21 Israeli PM Yitzhak Rabin in Cairo for talks with President Mubarak.
Puntsagiyn Jasray elected PM of Mongolia.

23 A two-day summit conference of 21 Ibero-American nations opened in Madrid; declaration rejected all forms of authoritarianism, thus isolating President Castro of Cuba.

24 Thousands of Muslims began fleeing northern Bosnian town Bosanski Novi to escape alleged 'ethnic cleansing' atrocities.

25 XXV Olympic Games opened in Barcelona, ending 9 Aug.

27 In Seychelles, President René gained overwhelming victory in first multi-party elections for 16 years.

29 Former communist leader of East Germany Erich Honecker returned to Berlin to face trial: he had sought refuge in Chilean embassy in Moscow in 1991 (see 22 Nov.).

AUGUST

2 In Bosnia–Hercegovina, two children died in sniper attack on bus evacuating orphans from Sarajevo.
Croatia held first elections since achieving independence; ruling Croatian Democratic Community of President Tudjman gained overwhelming victory.

3 In South Africa, a two-day strike, called by ANC in support of demands for constitutional reform, brought much of country to a halt.

4 UN Security Council adopted resolution condemning Serbian-run detention camps in Bosnia-Hercegovina.

10 Northern Ireland Secretary banned Ulster Defence Association loyalist paramilitary group.
Sixto Ballén sworn in as President of Ecuador in succession to Borja Cevallo.

11 Israeli PM Rabin in Washington for talks with President Bush; $10,000 million loan guarantees for Israel were announced, following partial freezing of settlement-building in Israeli-occupied territories.

14 UN Security Council adopted resolutions authorizing military action in support of relief operation in Bosnia and denouncing war crimes there.

15 Etienne Tshisekedi elected PM of Zaïre.

19 In elections in Bahamas, 25-year-old government of Sir Lynden Pindling defeated by Hubert Ingraham's Free National Movement.

23 Bosnian Muslims launched fierce counter-attack against Serb forces in Sarajevo.
Hizbullah made significant gains in first parliamentary elections in Lebanon for 20 years.
Southern Florida devastated by hurricane Andrew; 200,000 made homeless.

24 Middle East peace talks resumed in Washington.

26 Britain hosted two-day London conference on conflict in former Yugoslavia; declaration condemned human rights violations and outlined terms for political settlement.

President Bush announced aerial exclusion zone below 32nd parallel in southern Iraq to protect Shia Muslim rebels from attacks by forces of Saddam Husain.

27 Lord Owen succeeded Lord Carrington as EC's peace negotiator for former Yugoslavia.

Czech and Slovak leaders agreed that Czechoslovakia would split into two independent states on 1 Jan. 1993.

30 16 died in Serb artillery attack on Sarajevo market-place.

31 UN officials reported that 2,000 people were dying of starvation in Somalia daily.

Pascal Lissouba, leader of Pan-African Union for Social Democracy, sworn in as President of Congo following his election victory on 16 Aug.

SEPTEMBER

1 Tenth summit conference of Non-Aligned Movement opened in Jakarta, ending 6 Sept.

3 Peace conference on former Yugoslavia opened in Geneva, co-chaired by Lord Owen for EC and Cyrus Vance for UN.

In Bosnia-Hercegovina, four crew members died when Muslim forces shot down Italian relief plan near Sarajevo.

4 In Bulgaria, former communist leader Todor Zhivkov gaoled for seven years for embezzlement of state funds.

7 In South Africa, 28 killed and 200 injured when Ciskei armed forces fired on ANC protest rally in Bisho.

President Nabiyev of Tajikistan forced out of office amid mounting political confrontation.

13 In general election in Thailand, Democrat Party emerged as single largest party; its leader, Chuan Leekpai, appointed PM on 23 Sept.

In Peru, Abimael Guzman, leader of Sendero Luminoso guerrilla movement, arrested in Lima; a military tribunal gaoled him for life on 7 Oct.

15 UK Defence Secretary Rifkind announced deployment of British troops in Bosnia to assist in protecting humanitarian convoys.

More than 2,000 reported dead in flooding in northern Pakistan, NW Frontier Province and Punjab.

16 Britain suspended its membership of European exchange rate mechanism (ERM) after a tumultuous day on world currency markets.

Talks on future of N. Ireland resumed at Stormont.

20 In a referendum in France, voters approved ratification of Maastricht treaty by very narrow majority.

Estonia held first post-independence elections; no candidate gained overall majority in presidential poll (see 5 Oct.).

21 James Molyneaux, leader of Ulster Unionists, attended talks in Dublin with Irish ministers: he was the first Ulster leader for 70 years to discuss future of province in Irish capital.

22 Some 80 people died in severe flooding in Vaucluse and Ardèche regions of France.

23 UN General Assembly voted to suspend rump Yugoslavia's membership of UN.

Le Duc Anh elected President of Vietnam under new constitution adopted in April 1992.

24 In UK, David Mellor resigned from government following newspaper revelations about his private life; Peter Brooke succeeded him as Heritage Secretary.

27 At general elections in Romania, Democratic National Salvation Front became largest party in parliament; its leader President Iliescu was re-elected President in further poll on 11 Oct.

28 In Nepal 167 died when PIA Airbus A-300 crashed at Kathmandu.

29   In Brazil, Congress voted for impeachment of President Collor for alleged corruption and suspended him from office; Collor formally resigned on 29 December; Itamar Franco was sworn in as President.
     In Angola's first democratic elections, President dos Santos defeated Jonas Savimbi in presidential contest; the latter rejected result (see 3 Nov.).

OCTOBER

4   At ceremony in Rome, President Chissano and Renamo leader Afonso Dhlakama signed peace agreement to end 16-year civil war in Mozambique.
     About 70 died when El Al cargo Boeing 747 crashed on high-rise flats in Amsterdam.
5   In Guyana, People's Progressive Party gained narrow election victory; its leader Cheddi Jagan sworn in as President on 9 Oct. in succession to Desmond Hoyte.
     In Kuwait, anti-government candidates won nearly 70 per cent of seats in elections to reconstituted National Assembly.
     Estonian parliament elected Lennart Meri as President.
     17th Franco-African conference opened in Libreville, Gabon, ending 7 Oct.
9   UN Security Council adopted resolution banning all military flights over Bosnia.
11   At elections in Georgia, Eduard Shevardnadze confirmed as head of state with 90 per cent of vote.
     President Biya won narrow majority at Cameroon's first multi-party presidential election, amid allegations of ballot-rigging.
12   500 died in an earthquake in Cairo.
     14th congress of Chinese Communist Party opened in Beijing, ending 18 Oct.
     In UK, British Coal announced plans to close 31 pits with loss of 30,000 jobs; on 19 Oct., following widespread public protest, Trade Secretary Heseltine announced moratorium on closure of 21 pits until 1993 and £165 million aid for affected areas (see 21 Dec.).
15   First of 2,400 British troops, who would join UN humanitarian mission, left for Bosnia.
16   EC held special summit in Birmingham to discuss progress on Maastricht treaty and European currency crisis.
17   World leaders attended state funeral in Berlin for former German Chancellor Willy Brandt (see XX:OBITUARY).
19   HM Queen Elizabeth II on five-day state visit to Germany.
25   British and German delegations and veterans attended ceremonies in Egyptian desert to commemorate 50th anniversary of battle of El Alamein.
     In Lithuanian parliamentary elections, ex-communist Democratic Labour Party (DLP), led by Algirdas Brazauskas, defeated ruling Sajudis; in second poll on 15 Nov. DLP gained absolute majority of seats.
     Emperor Akihito on first visit to China by a Japanese monarch.
26   In referendum in Canada, voters overwhelmingly rejected Charlottetown accord (see 7 July).
28   In Bulgaria, Union of Democratic Forces government, led by PM Filip Dimitrov, resigned.
31   In Lebanon, a new government, led by Rafiq Hariri, was appointed.

NOVEMBER

3   In USA, Governor Bill Clinton of Arkansas (Democrat) defeated President George Bush (Republican) in presidential election; he would be sworn in on 20 Jan. 1993.

In Angola, more than 1,000 reported dead in fighting between government troops and Unita guerrillas (see 29 Sept.).

In Ghana's first multi-party election since 1981, Jerry Rawlings elected President with 58.5 per cent of vote.

4   In Romania, President Iliescu named Nicolae Văcăriou as PM; new government formed on 19 Nov.

9   President Yeltsin of Russia on two-day official visit to Britain; an historic bilateral treaty of friendship, the first since 1766, was signed by him and PM Major.

In UK, trial of three executives of Matrix-Churchill collapsed, amid allegations of government complicity in illegal arms dealing with Iraq in late 1980s; on 10 Nov. PM announced judicial inquiry into affair.

11 In UK, Church of England Synod voted in favour of ordination of women to priesthood.

12 In Germany, trial opened in Berlin of former E. German leader Erich Honecker and four colleagues, accused of killing people seeking to escape to West.

In UK, Chancellor of Exchequer, in autumn statement, outlined £4,000 million package aimed at promoting economic recovery.

18 In Pakistan, thousands participated in anti-government demonstrations in Islamabad.

19 In UK, High Court ruled that doctors could disconnect feeding tube from victim of 1989 Hillsborough disaster to allow him to die with dignity.

20 In UK, fire caused an estimated £60 million damage at Windsor Castle.

GATT negotiators reached outline agreement on US-EC differences on EC farm subsidies, ending US threat to impose 200 per cent import tax on certain European farm products; but French objections to agreement made speedy conclusion of GATT negotiations unlikely.

NATO agreed to enforce UN trade embargo on rump Yugoslavia; WEU defence group ordered full naval blockade in Adriatic.

22 Peru held elections to replace parliament abolished in April (see 5 April); an alliance loyal to President Fujimori gained 38.6 per cent of vote.

24 In China, 141 died when Boeing 737 crashed at Guilin.

25 At general election in Ireland, Labour Party made substantial gains, although Fianna Fáil remained largest party in parliament; agreement on formation of new government had not been reached at year end.

26 In UK, PM Major announced that HM The Queen had decided to pay tax on her personal fortune.

27 Germany banned neo-nazi Nationalist Front following weeks of mounting violence, against immigrants.

Venezuelan government put down attempted coup by rebel soldiers.

DECEMBER

1   Congress of People's Deputies of Russia opened in Moscow; on 14 Dec. conservative deputies chose Viktor Chernomyrdin as PM, having rejected President Yeltsin's candidate, Yegor Gaidar, architect of radical reform programme.

3   UN Security Council adopted resolution authorizing military intervention in Somalia to protect humanitarian supplies to that war-torn and drought-stricken country.

4   President Bush ordered 28,000 troops to Somalia in 'Operation Restore Hope' to bring relief to starving Somalis; first marines landed on 9 Dec.

6   In referendum in Switzerland, voters rejected participation in planned European Economic Area to come into effect on 1 Jan. 1993.

In India, Hindu zealots destroyed historic mosque in holy city of Ayodhya; some 400 died in ensuing sectarian violence across northern India.

9   In UK, it was announced that Prince and Princess of Wales had agreed to separate after 11 years of marriage; PM Major said decision had no constitutional implications.

11 Two-day summit of EC heads of government opened in Edinburgh; agreements were reached to exempt Denmark from certain conditions of Maastricht treaty and on budget arrangements.

12 1,200 people died in earthquake and tidal waves in eastern Indonesia.

17 Israel expelled 415 alleged Palestinian terrorists in wake of murder of Israeli policeman by Muslim fundamentalist gunmen; at year end deportees remained stranded in southern Lebanon.

18 At election in South Korea, Kim Young Sam elected first genuinely civilian President after 30 years' military influence.

19 President Bush and PM Major held weekend summit talks at Camp David; they agreed to work together to press for UN resolution to enforce 'no-fly' zone over Bosnia.

    Taiwan held first free parliamentary elections for 40 years; although ruling Kuomintang gained majority, government of Hau Pei-tsun resigned on 22 Dec. because of party's poor performance.

20 Serbia and Montenegro held elections for Yugoslav presidency; Serbian leader Slobodan Milosevic defeated PM Milan Panic amid allegations of fraud.

21 In Portugal, 54 died in plane crash at Faro airport.

    In UK, High Court ruled that government and British Coal had acted unlawfully in deciding to close 31 pits without consultation.

22 In Libya, 150 died when Libyan Boeing 727 crashed near Tripoli.

24 In USA, President Bush announced pardons for former Defence Secretary Caspar Weinberger and five other former officials over alleged involvement in Iran-Contra affair.

27 US war plane shot down Iraqi MiG south of 32nd parallel, the 'no-fly' zone, in southern Iraq.

29 In Kenya's first free elections for 26 years, President Daniel Arap Moi returned to office amid opposition allegations of ballot-rigging.

    USA and Russia agreed text of START-II treaty, reducing nuclear stockpiles by two-thirds; treaty scheduled for signature at Bush-Yeltsin summit early Jan. 1993.

    Radoje Kontic replaced the deposed Milan Panic as PM of rump Yugoslavia.

30 In Afghanistan, interim President Burhanuddin Rabbani elected head of state.

31 Federation of Czechoslovakia ended after 74 years, to be replaced by separate Czech and Slovak republics.

    President Bush visited US troops in Somalia.

    UN Secretary-General Boutros-Ghali visited UN forces in Sarajevo, also meeting Bosnian and Serb leaders.

INDEX

Page references in bold indicate location of main coverage.